New Financial Instruments

Wiley Frontiers in Finance

Series Editor: Edward I. Altman, New York University

New Financial Instruments

Second Edition

Julian Walmsley

John Wiley & Sons, Inc.

New York • Chichester • Weinheim • Brisbane • Singapore • Toronto

To Jane

This text is printed on acid-free paper.

Library of Congress Cataloging in Publication Data:

Walmsley, Julian.
      New financial instruments / Julian Walmsley. — 2nd ed.
         p.   cm. — (Wiley series in financial engineering)
      Includes bibliographical references and index.
      ISBN 0-471-12136-3 (cloth : alk. paper)
      1. Financial instruments. I. Title. II. Series.
    HG4521.W184   1997
    332.63'2—dc21   97-22590

Printed in the United States of America

10 9 8 7 6 5 4 3 2 1

Preface

This book is an entirely revised and expanded edition of the book that was published in 1988. Since then, there has been a continuing flood of new financial instruments and I have again tried to set them out in a systematic way. The aim has been to give the reader a survey of the major innovations of the last decade.

There are bound to be omissions, for which I apologize in advance, but I hope that the broad canvas will be helpful. Inevitably, depth has been sacrificed for breadth. My goal has been to set out a clear and simple explanation of the instruments. Specialists may feel that I have oversimplified, but I have tried to remedy this by providing further sources in the bibliography.

Part I provides the foundations, describing basic traditional instruments and covering some analytical tools that help understand the more complex new instruments. It also explains the building blocks used behind many of the new instruments: futures, swaps, and options. Part II describes the new instruments themselves. We begin with a chapter on the newer options instruments, covering both exotic options and the various interest rate option instruments such as swaptions, caps, and captions. The next three chapters cover various aspects of securitization (CMOs, PACs, VADMs, asset-backed securities, etc.), and new types of bonds (including medium-term notes). These are followed by a chapter on structured notes, a controversial and complex section of the market. Chapter 13 considers credit derivatives, an important and rapidly developing area, while the remaining four chapters look at preferred stock, convertibles, warrants (including the warrant equivalents of exotic options), equity derivatives, and new types of equity.

The reader who compares this edition with the last one will notice that about 80 percent of the text is new, with notable growth in the sections on options instruments (including warrants) and structured notes. The globalization of markets has meant that a far wider range of markets—such as Brazil, China, Colombia, and Russia—is touched on.

Another difference is that many more of the instruments, particularly the American products, are either trademarked or service marked. Any firm is entitled to do this to protect its intellectual investment in developing a new product. But this is by no means always to the benefit of the investor. Investment banks rarely make a market in a product that another firm has trademarked. I would go so far as to suggest that any product that has been trademarked or service marked by an investment bank is inevitably less liquid than one that has not been. The trend is deplorable from the investor's viewpoint and ought to be resisted. This leads on to the wider point—developed more fully in Chapter 1—regarding the benefits of these new instruments. In many cases, these products have definite advantages, but very often at the price of illiquidity. This critical point is too often overlooked. No matter how attractive the payoff structure, the investor should always consider first whether or not the product is likely to be liquid. But this does not mean, as some have suggested, that all these new instruments are pernicious in themselves. The balance of advantage is discussed further in Chapter 1.

It would not have been possible to write this book without a great deal of help from others. I owe a particular debt to my former colleagues, too numerous to mention individually, at Barclays Bank, NationsBank, and Mitsubishi Finance. While working at Oil Insurance Ltd. in Bermuda I benefited also from extensive discussions with, amongst others, Paul Abberley at Lombard Odier Investment Services and Richard Foulkes at Schroder Capital Management International. I must also thank those who read and commented on various parts of the manuscript: Nick Webber at the Financial Options Research Centre at the University of Warwick, Mike Smith at the ISMA Centre at the University of Reading, and Catherine Heard at Linklaters. It goes without saying that responsibility for any remaining errors is mine alone. Finally, I must once again thank my wife Jane for tolerating many lost weekends and evenings.

JULIAN WALMSLEY

London, England
November 1997

TRADEMARKS AND SERVICE MARKS

CAC-40 is a registered trademark of the Société des Bourses Françaises SA.

CHIPS and Common-Linked Higher Income Participation Securities are service marks of The Bear Stearn's Companies, Inc.

Datastream is a registered trade name, trademark, and service mark of Datastream International Limited.

DAX is a registered trademark of the Deutsche Borse, AG.

Dow Jones Industrial Average is a registered trademark of Dow Jones & Co., Inc.

EAFE is a service mark of Morgan Stanley Capital International Perspective.

ELKS, Equity Linked Securities, DECS, and Debt Exchangeable for Common Stock are service marks of Salomon Brothers, Inc.

Eurotop 100 Index® is a registered trademark of the European Options Exchange.

FT-Actuaries Word Indices, FT-Actuaries World Index, and FTAWI are trademarks and service marks of The Financial Times Limited.

FT-SE is a joint trademark and service mark of The London Stock Exchange and The Financial Times Limited.

GLOBEX® is a registered trademark of the GLOBEX Joint Venture, L.P.

GROI and Guaranteed Return On Investment Certificates are service marks of the Swiss Bank Corporation.

LEAPS®, Long-term Equity AnticiPation Securities®, and OEX® are registered trademarks, and FLEX, FLexible EXchange, and SPX are trademarks of the Chicago Board Options Exchange, Inc.

LYONs® is a registered service mark of Merrill Lynch & Co., Inc.

Major Market Index is a service mark of the American Stock Exchange, Inc.

MIPS, ACES, and Pharmaceutical Exchange Notes are service marks of Goldman, Sachs & Co.

MITTs, Market Index Target-Term Securities, SMART Notes, Stock Market Annual Reset Term, PRIDES, and Preferred Redeemable Increased Dividend Equity Securities are service marks of Merrill Lynch & Co., Inc.

Nikkei Stock Average is a trademark and service mark of Nihon Keizai Shimbun Inc.

PERCS, Preferred Equity Redemption Cumulative Stock, and PEPS are trademarks of Morgan Stanley & Co., Inc.

PRIMES and SCORES are trademarks of the Americus Shareowner Service Corp.

Protected Equity Note is a service mark of the Banker's Trust & Co., Inc.

Russell 2000® is a registered trademark and service mark of Frank Russell Company.

Standard & Poor's ®, S&P®, S&P 500®, Standard & Poor's 500, 500, SPDRs®, and Standard and Poor's Depository Receipts® are trademarks of Standard and Poor's.

SUNS and Stock Upside Note Securities are service marks of Lehman Brothers, Inc.

SuperTrust, SuperUnit, and SuperShare are trademarks of Leland O'Brien Rubinstein Associates Incorporated.

Toronto 35 Index, TIPs, and Toronto 35 Index Participation Units are registered trademarks of The Toronto Stock Exchange.

YEELDS and Yield Enhanced Equity Linked Debt Securities are service marks of Lehman Brothers, Inc.

Contents

ix

PART **I**

FOUNDATIONS

Chapter 1

Financial Innovation

Some time in our childhood, many of us have seen a chart of the history of travel. It shows how the speed of travel has risen over the centuries. The first part of the chart is a long, low curve, sloping slightly upward. It runs from when man first started walking, through the taming of the horse, the invention of the boat, the wheel, the chariot, the carriage, and the first train. After that, the slope of the line picks up sharply, with the coming of the automobile, the first airplane, the jet engine, the supersonic jet, and finally the arrival of space travel. The explosive upward sweep is the more impressive when you look at the long struggle of the previous centuries. One is tempted to feel the same when looking at the pace of financial innovation today.

In the beginning, there were four instruments: (1) a bank deposit, (2) a bill of exchange (banker's acceptance), (3) a bond, and (4) equity. Bank deposits go back to the thirteenth century. One of the earliest names known to us is Ricciardi of Luca, who, during 1272–1310, lent £400,000 to English kings, and failed when they defaulted. An early example of sovereign risk! The bill of exchange dates back to the same period. It was probably the first interest-bearing instrument, though early usury laws meant that the interest was charged in commissions or exchange rates. Bonds of different types can be traced far back in history; the French developed the *rente* in the sixteenth century. It was regarded not as a borrowing but as the sale of a stream of income. This let the investor get around the Church's usury rules. Perhaps the first true government bond was the Grand Parti of Francis I in 1555. It was open to all lenders, large and small, rather than a few bankers.

Equity had its origins in syndicates of merchant adventurers: the Muscovy Company was chartered in 1553, the East India Company in 1600. The first permanent joint-stock company was the Dutch East India Company, formed in 1602.

To these four instruments, preference shares were added in the nineteenth century. They came to prominence first in the British railway mania of 1845. The ratio of preference shares to total railway issues rose from 4 percent in 1845 to 66 percent in 1849. During the nineteenth century also, the United States saw the beginnings of commercial paper.

In 1966 came the certificate of deposit (CD), a bank deposit that was a bit like a bond. The first floating rate note, a bond that was a bit like a bank deposit, appeared in 1970. In 1972, the first financial futures contracts were written, and, in 1975, the first interest rate futures contract. In the 1980s, the curve of innovation took a steep upward path. Table 1.1 shows the pace of change. [Because some innovations, e.g., exotic options, appeared first in the over-the-counter (OTC) market, it is not always possible to be exact about the date of introduction.]

TYPES OF INNOVATION

In this chapter, we look at financial innovation in its own right: its nature, causes, and consequences. Probably the two main questions asked by an investor, or another observer of the current financial scene, would be: (1) How has the recent stream of innovations affected me, as an investor or participant in financial markets? (2) What risks do the innovations entail?

There are various ways of looking at innovation. Some have split it into process innovation and product innovation. Process innovation is change in the process of financial markets. For example, the development of SWIFT (Society for Worldwide International Financial Telecommunications) for international payments; the deregulation of commissions on the New York Stock Exchange and the subsequent changes in U.S. securities trading; and the development of the "grey market" in the Eurobond market. All of these are changes in the process of financial activity. By contrast, product innovation is the development of new products: zero coupons, currency options, and the like. Mostly, in this book, we will focus on product innovation, but occasionally we will need to touch on process innovation. Another way to classify innovation is as aggressive or defensive. Aggressive innovation is the introduction of a new product, or process, in response to a perceived demand. A very large part of innovation since at least the late 1970s is aggressive innovation, in the sense that many securities firms and banks have been scrambling to secure market share by showing an ability to innovate.

But there are also examples of defensive innovation, in response to changed environment or transactions costs. For example, much of the transformation of the London system in 1983–1985 could be seen as defensive innovation. It was caused by the change in legal environment brought on by the government's challenge to the existing stock exchange system.

The effects of innovation can usefully be split into four categories: (1) risk transfer, (2) liquidity enhancement, (3) credit generation, and (4) equity generation. Risk-transferring innovations are new instruments or techniques that allow investors or traders to transfer the price or credit risks in financial positions. These have been among the most important innovations in recent years. They include interest rate and foreign exchange futures and options, currency and interest rate swaps, and a host of other futures and options contracts enabling the hedging of various price risks. Probably the two biggest factors in

Table 1.1   Financial Innovations after World War II

1957	Creation of European Economic Community (EEC) leads to introduction of EEC unit of account—the first artificial currency unit of modern times
1950s	Start of Eurodollar market
1961	Introduction of private European Unit of Account for bond issue by Portuguese company SACOR—the first Eurobond
1963	Issue of $15 million Eurobond for Autostrade—generally considered the start of the Eurobond market
	Introduction of U.S. Interest Equalization Tax (IET) sparks growth of Euromarkets
1966	Introduction of certificate of deposit in United States
1968	Creation of U.S. Government National Mortgage Association (GNMA; "Ginnie Mae")
1969	Introduction of GNMA pass-through
1970	First floating rate note (FRN) in Euromarket
	Creation of U.S. Federal Home Loan Mortgage Corporation (FHLMC; "Freddie Mac")
	Creation of International Monetary Fund (IMF) Special Drawing Right (SDR)
	Introduction of European Currency Unit (ECU; private unit of account for a Eurobond issue)
1971	Creation of NASDAQ (National Association of Securities Dealers Automated Quotations) in United States
1972	Chicago International Money Market (IMM) introduces first financial futures (currency futures)
1973	Creation of Chicago Board of Options Exchange (CBOE)
	Introduction of Eurco (European Composite Unit) in Euromarket
1974	First domestic U.S. FRN. IET abolished; U.S. citizens permitted to buy gold
1975	Introduction of first interest rate futures (on GNMAs)
1976	Australian traded options market established
1977	Chicago Board of Trade (CBOT) introduces Treasury bond futures
1979	U.S. "New Economic Policy" triggers massive interest rate instability
	Creation of European Monetary System; introduction of official European Union (ECU)
	First revolving underwriting facility in Euromarket
1980	Introduction of seven-day put U.S. municipal bonds ("lower floaters")
	First partly paid Eurobond (Alcoa)
	First Eurobond issued with debt warrants (Kingdom of Sweden)
1981	First original issue discount/zero coupon bonds
	New simplified SDR introduced
	First dual-currency bond in Euromarkets
	IBM/World Bank currency swap
	First interest rate swap
1982	First CATs (Certificates of Accrual on Treasury Securities) and TIGRs (Treasury Investment Growth Receipts)
	First options on Treasury bond futures
	Introduction of stock index futures

(continued)

Table 1.1 *(Continued)*

	Traded currency options market begins in Philadelphia
	First adjustable-rate preferred stock
	Foundation of London International Financial Futures Exchange (LIFFE)
	Rule 415 brings bought deal to U.S. bond markets
1983	Creation of collateralized mortgage obligations (CMOs)
	Introduction of options on S&P index
1984	Creation of Certificates for Automobile Receivables (CARS)
	Introduction of STRIPS (Separate Trading of Registered Interest and Principal of Securities) on Treasury bonds
	First Money Market Preferred Stock
	Options on Eurodollar futures begin trading on Chicago Mercantile Exchange (CME)
	First Eurobond with credit enhancement from an insurance company (Rockefeller, guaranteed by Aetna)
	British Telecom issue: perhaps first global initial public offering (IPO)
1985	Introduction of capped FRN; stripped caps
	First mismatch, mini-max, and partly paid FRNs in Euromarkets
	Creation of Shogun bonds (US$ bonds in Japan)
	Creation of Tokyo futures exchange
	First variable-duration notes (interest payable in bonds)
	First zero-coupon convertible bonds
	"Heaven and Hell" bonds
	US$ harmless warrants ("wedding warrants")
	First synthetic fixed-rate bond Bearer Eurodollar Collateralised Securities, Market Eurodollar Collateralised Securities (BECS, MECS)
1986	US$ biannual interest payment bond
	Hybrid FRN/Euronote
	Capped FRN with income warrants
	Participating mortgage bonds
	Stepped coupon bonds and First Euro-medium term note (FRNs)
	Step-down floaters
	Deferred coupon bonds and FRNs
	Treasury-indexed US$ bonds
	Bear/bull bonds on stock indexes, gold
	S&P-indexed bonds
	US$ oil-indexed bonds
	Reverse floater
	FRN with warrants
	Foundation of MATIF (French futures exchange)
	First stripped U.S. mortgage-backed securities
	Creation of Real Estate Mortgage Investment Conduit (REMICs) in United States
	First stripped U.S. municipal bonds

Table 1.1 *(Continued)*

	Australian mortgage-backed bond market begins
	Compound options
1987	Americus Trust issues Prescribed Right to Income and Maximum Equity (PRIMES) and Special Claim on Residual Equity (SCORES)
	Principal Exchange-Rate-Linked Securities (PERLS) issued
	First U.K. mortgage securitization
	First Planned Amortization Class (PAC) bond in U.S. mortgage-backed market
	First use of conduits for U.S. commercial mortgage securitization
	Super-floater CMOs
	Establishment of yen commercial paper market
1988	American Depository Receipts (ADRs) on Obligations Assimilables du Trésor (OATs)
	Preferred Equity Redemption Cumulative stock (PERCs) issued
	Stock Warrant Off-Balance Sheet Research and Development (SWORDS) issued in United States
	Money-back equity warrants
	Share-Adjusted Broker Remarketed Equity Securities (SABRES) in United States
	Variable-rate notes (VRNs) introduced
	Introduction of Bund futures on LIFFE
	French legislation permits Fonds Commun de Créances
1989	Legal & General Guaranteed Equity Fund
	First issue of Contingent Value Rights
	First collateralized bond obligations (CBOs)
	DEM Medium Term Note (MTN) market permitted
	Lookback options
	Asian options
	Barrier, digital options
	Basket options
1990	Foundation of Deutsche Termin Börse (DTB) in Germany
	CBOE introduces Long-Term Equity Anticipation Securities (LEAPS)
	Toronto Index Participation Securities (TIPS) introduced
	Deutsche Action Index (DAX) participations launched
	Bond spread warrants
	Outperformance warrants
	Nikkei warrants listed on American Stock Exchange
	Fixed-floating hybrid notes
	Fixed/reverse floaters hybrids
	Nikkei-linked "rescue" bonds
1991	First Guaranteed Return on Investment (GROI) issue in Switzerland
	Stock Index Growth Notes (SIGNS) issue in United States
	First conduit issuance of multifamily-pool mortgage-backed bond in United States

(continued)

Table 1.1 *(Continued)*

	Fed funds Forward Rate Agreements (FRAs)
	"At issuer's option" bonds (repayable in third-party shares at issuer's option)
	Diff swaps
	Leveraged diff notes
	REX warrants issued on German fixed-income market index
	German commercial paper market established
	Buoni Poliennali Tesori (BTP) futures introduced on LIFFE
	Formal Australian warrant market established
1992	Leland O'Brien introduces SuperUnits
	Preferred Purchase Units (PPUs)
	Yield Decrease Warrants issued in United States
	CBOT catastrophe insurance futures and options
	Corridor/range notes [CMT-linked, LIBOR (London Interbank Offered Rate)-linked]
	Further liberalization of German domestic bond market issuance
1993	First Asian currency note program in Thai baht
	American Stock Exchange introduces S&P Depositary Receipts (SPIDERS)
	CMT floaters
	CMT-LIBOR spread notes
	Cross-country inverse floaters (e.g., the lower of 26% −3x Swedish swap rate or 22% − 3x French swap rate)
	First Equity-Linked Securities (ELKS), Market Index Target-Term Securities (MITTS), Preferred Event-Triggered Adjustable Ratio Liquid Securities (PEARLS) issues in United States
	First U.S. issue of Automatically Convertible Equity Shares (ACES) and Monthly Income Preferred Stock (MIPS), Debt Exchangeable for Common Stock (DECS)
	First credit derivative trades
	First French Auction Rate Coupon—Titres Subordonnés à Durée Indéterminée (ARC-TSDI)
	Securitization of derivatives positions of Goldman Sachs
	Securitization of consumer loans in United Kingdom
	"Going public bonds" in Hong Kong (Henderson Capital International)
	Eurobond + knockout equity warrants (Benetton, Roche)
	Resettable equity warrants in United States
	Large variety of "structured medium-term notes"
1994	Canadian Structured Derivative Products Corp. founded
	Performance Equity-Linked Redemption Quarterly-Pay Securities (PERQs) issued
	CMT Yield Increase Warrants in United States
	Notes embedding covered call on Telmex
	New York City securitizes unpaid back taxes
	Share ratios introduced in Australia
	United States convertible with interest rate ratchet

Table 1.1 *(Continued)*

	Third-party LYONS
	MegaDeal bonds introduced to U.S. commercial mortgage-backed market
	Airline Portfolio Securities (ALPS)—securitization of aircraft leases
	Silver-Denominated Preferred
	Resetting collar FRN
	Capped chooser warrants on DAX
	Cross-currency corridor notes
	Banking on Overall Stability Options (BOOSTS)
	First dual-currency securitization (FULMAR)
1995	First "synthetic PERC" in United States
	Securities Tied to Equity Performance (STEPs) (synthetic DECS)
	TARGETS issued in United States
	Quarterly Income Preferred Securities (QIPS) (variant of MIPS)
	Trust Originated Preferred Securities (TOPRS) in United States
	First "jumbo" Pfandbrief
	Finland launches first government securitization of rental housing in Europe
	Controversial use of contracts for differences by Swiss Bank Corporation (SBC) in Trafalgar House bid
	Convertible with annual reset price
	Power warrants on Vnesheconombank and Argentine Brady debt
	Flip bonds (embedded Bermuda swaptions)
1996	Repeat Offering Securitisation Entity (ROSE) funding: corporate loan securitization in United Kingdom
	First Pfandbrief in Czech koruna
	Federal Reserve Bank of New York assists "future flow" Mexican securitization
	TEC-10 floaters in France
	Catastrophe preferred equity puts
	Puttable And Redeemable Convertible Knockouts (PARCKs)
	"Sleepy" and "onion" warrants
	First use of securitization in United Kingdom to fund acquisition (Stagecoach/Porterbrook)
	First mortgage-backed securitization in Netherlands
1997	Shared appreciation mortgage introduced in United Kingdom
	Emerging market CBOs
	U.S. Treasury issues inflation-linked Treasury bonds
	Convertible with hailstorm insurance risk
	Parallel bonds (redenominable into Euro)

developing these markets were the breakdown of fixed exchange rates, and the emergence of floating currencies in the mid-1970s, coupled with the adoption by the Federal Reserve of its New Economic Policy in October 1979, which led to unprecedented instability of interest rates.

Also in this risk-transfer category come innovations concerned with transferring credit risk. These include the trend toward tradable loans, securitization and credit enhancement the provision of letters of credit or insurance to guarantee weaker credits. The most recent developments in this area are so-called "credit derivatives," discussed in Chapter 13.

Liquidity-enhancing innovations improve the "moneyness" or the negotiability of financial instruments. These include note issuance facilities, securities sold with put options, and the creation of secondary markets for trading securitized instruments. Mortgage-backed securities are a classic example. Mortgages are now, effectively, liquid assets.

Credit-generating innovations broaden the supply of credit, either by mobilizing dormant assets to back borrowings, or by tapping previously untouched pockets of credit. An example of the former is securities backed by specific buildings. An example of the latter is the use of interest rate or currency swaps to issue securities in markets that the issuer would not normally wish to tap directly, because it would have no use for the currency or kind of funding provided.

Equity-generating innovations have been more limited than other types, but they include, for example, variable rate preferred stock, which tapped an entire new market of investors, and equity contract notes. The growth of global depository receipts (Chapter 17) falls into this class.

SOURCES OF INNOVATION

The demand for these innovations has been spurred by the increasing instability of the international financial environment; the supply has been spurred by four main factors.

1. *The intensifying competition among financial institutions, particularly between securities houses and banks.* A reputation for innovativeness is seen as a key competitive advantage in acquiring market share.

2. *Regulation.* The development of the Euromarket since the early 1960s, in an atmosphere almost completely free from regulation, has meant that it has always been innovative. On the other hand, the relatively conservative nature of its existing clientele has held back this tendency somewhat. By contrast, in the United States, more adventurous investors tended to be faced with a much more strictly regulated industry. But a tendency to deregulation emerged in the late 1970s. It followed the abolition of fixed commissions in 1975 and the move toward deregulating the banking system in the latter part of the 1970s. This, together with the introduction of Rule 415 in 1982, intensified competition.

Similarly, the London market, the traditional center of the Eurobond market, applied a further twist to deregulation. Major international banks were allowed to buy into stockbrokerage firms and to become market makers in equities, in addition to their traditional ability to deal in corporate bonds in London. With some banks—notably J.P. Morgan, which set up J.P. Morgan Securities in London in 1979, specifically to develop a securities capability—there was "positive feedback" to New York. Having demonstrated their capacity in London, they were permitted by the Federal Reserve, under its so-called Section 20 exemptions, to increase their activities in the United States. Deregulation in New York and London triggered a wave of deregulation elsewhere—in Tokyo, Paris, and Frankfurt, for example—during the 1980s.

   3. *The impact of technology.* Without the advent of the personal computer, much recent innovation would have been impossible. The author can testify from personal experience that the complex calculations that are routine today in the interest rate and currency swap market were, for practical purposes, out of the question before the advent of the Apple II and the IBM PC. Another technological thrust has been the impact of Reuters, Telerate, Quotron, and other electronic providers of price information. The investor and borrower have become much more quickly aware of prices in the market. This, in turn, has contributed to an explosion in trading volume around the globe. And the new technologies allow analysts and traders to make complex calculations quickly and to act promptly when prices are out of line. The arrival of the Internet will almost certainly hasten this process.

   4. *The impact of derivatives on the underlying cash markets.* Many firms, after initially setting up separate derivatives groups, merged them with the teams trading the underlying instruments. Thus, instead of having a bond group and a bond derivatives group, the two were merged, often resulting in a "technology transfer." Techniques that had been developed for derivatives— notably, value-at-risk and simulation technology—could be applied across the trading book as a whole. Improving risk management across the whole business led to other efficiencies, although, as Barings proved, high-technology risk management systems are only as good as the information they are given.

THE EFFECTS AND THE RISKS

The firms that were early exploiters of these innovations started a trend. Trading volumes began to balloon. The derivatives market now is huge, as shown in Table 1.2. From the growth of the Eurodollar market (widely viewed at the time as a likely source of global financial disaster) until today, each wave of financial innovation has caused fear in some quarters. And each wave has produced disasters. From the failure of the Herstatt Bank in 1974, to the collapse of Barings in 1995 (shortly after the announcement of heavy losses at Orange County and derivative-based lawsuits involving Procter & Gamble and Gibson Greetings),

Table 1.2   Estimates of Derivatives Market Activity (Notional Amounts, Daily Averages in $billion)

Reporting Country	OTC Contracts		Exchange-Traded Contracts	
	Foreign Exchange	Interest Rate	Foreign Exchange	Interest Rate
United Kingdom	292	59	9	238
United States	132	32	5	191
Japan	112	26	0	451
Singapore	63	16	0	24
France	36	19	1	90
Germany	45	11	0	36
Hong Kong	56	4	0	14
Total	953	209	15	1,121

Source of Data: BIS Survey of Derivative Markets Activity, Spring 1995.

there have been problems. There will be disasters in the future, caused by unwise use of instruments yet to be invented. Yet this situation must be seen in perspective. Most impartial studies have concluded that the majority of the financial innovations discussed in this book have been beneficial. They have made risk transfer more efficient, and often have enhanced liquidity in the underlying instrument.

One important effect of the innovations has been the dispersion of risk across the financial system as a whole. This has two possible effects. First, risks might be transmitted through the system until they reach "fault-lines." The impact of the risk position may fall on an institution far removed from the initial apparent risk. A classic example is the "earthquake bond" issued by SEK, the Swedish export credit company. It was largely placed with Japanese insurance companies and included a clause providing that it could be redeemed early by the investors if an earthquake occurred in Tokyo. So it might be that a movement in the SEK/JPY exchange rate might be triggered by an earthquake in Tokyo, as the associated financial flows moved the market. (The development of contingent surplus notes is touched on in Chapter 9.) More generally, as the Orange County and similar affairs illustrated, risks may often be transferred to institutions not really capable of analyzing them well. (On the other hand, it could be argued that this is not a feature unique to new financial instruments or the derivative markets. During the South Sea Bubble of the 1720s, investors were induced to buy shares in a company whose purpose was "So Secret, None to Know What it Is." P.T. Barnum's remark that "There's one born every minute" remains true; the mere fact of having computers and sophisticated derivatives does not mean that common sense can be abandoned.)

A second, more controversial feature of the new shape of the financial system is that the bulk of its participants now have a vested interest in instability. This is because the advent of high-technology dealing rooms has raised the level of fixed costs. High fixed costs imply that a high turnover is required for profitability to be achieved. High turnover tends to occur only when markets are volatile. A telling example of this can be found in the 1993 paper in which the Group of Thirty discuss best practice in derivatives trading. Firms should estimate the damage that could be caused not merely by violent swings in the markets but also by "prolonged periods of stability."

Innovation and volatility, therefore, have become intertwined. Innovations have been made in response to volatility, but they have also created an environment where, unless volatility continues, the number of players in the system as a whole may have to contract. Trading growth and position-taking among professionals have also become important features of the market, because speculative position-taking on secondary markets has become a standard source of profits at a time when competitive pressures weigh heavily on profit margins. A subsidiary point is that risk-transferring innovations have allowed traders to build much larger positions. In the past, risk was limited by cutting down positions. Now, the positions are held, but they are hedged with derivative instruments; gross exposures do not shrink in the same way. Large basis risk positions can build up unnoticed.

However, there is much that is positive about these trends. The benefits to the investor are many. He or she can choose from a far wider range of instruments. Many are tailored to meet specific investor requirements. Others give the ability to hedge risks that previously could not be guarded against. Old instruments have become more liquid and flexible.

Against this, the investor has the problem of choosing the right instrument. In the days of the Model-T Ford, when purchasers could have any color as long as it was black, choosing an automobile was simple. Now, it is more time-consuming. Even gaining an understanding of some of the instruments is difficult, although this book aims to help solve that problem. Also, some of the more exotic new instruments are not at all liquid. The investor must accept being effectively locked in.

On balance, however, the innovations that have been made are almost certainly beneficial for the system as a whole. The different types of risk involved in the various instruments have been unbundled. This should increase the efficiency of the financial system, because each element of a deal can be provided—and the associated risk taken—by the financial entity that can do so most efficiently. The increase in the number of separate risks should not, of itself, increase the total risk for the system as a whole. Much ink has been spilled, particularly after the crash of 1987 and following the collapse of Barings, about the degree of "systemic risk" posed by new financial instruments, particularly derivatives. On the other hand, the world's financial system remains more or less intact, and many lessons have been learned during the past decade about the effects of interlinking financial markets. Complacency is a continuing danger and we must guard against it, but it is also right to balance the systemic benefits of the new instruments against their systemic risk.

Chapter **2**

Basic Instruments

This chapter briefly outlines the traditional capital market instruments and their features, so as to give a framework for analysis. The instruments are:

Bonds.

Preferred stock.

Convertibles.

Equities.

Warrants.

It may help to begin with some basic analysis. Some of the key features of each instrument are laid out roughly in Figure 2.1. Many of the finer points will be covered in later chapters. A partially shaded block shows that the instrument has, in part or optionally, the feature described in the vertical list on the left side of the figure. The blank blocks show where the feature is absent.

Figure 2.1 also includes the features of bank deposits. Their key differentiating feature, compared to fixed-rate bonds, is that, at all times, we are certain of their principal value. If for any reason we have to break the deposit before maturity, the principal amount will be returned to us (although there might be a penalty charge). The principal value of a bond, however, varies from day to day, in line with interest rates (see below). In addition, by virtue of government backing for the banking system in most countries, we are effectively guaranteed the principal amount of our bank deposits. This does not apply to bonds. Another key distinction (not shown) is that bank deposits are not tradable.

Another crucial distinction is whether the owner of the security benefits from any of the profits of the firm or takes any part in controlling its management. As Figure 2.1 shows, equities have the right to profit participation and to management control. Convertibles and warrants have an indirect right to profit participation (their value rises in line with that of the equity) but not to management control.

Figure 2.2 (p. 16) extends Figure 2.1 to allow for some of the features that we will be discussing later in the book. Again, the partially shaded blocks show where a feature is present optionally or in part. The CDs line has been added because, although usually thought of as a money market instrument,

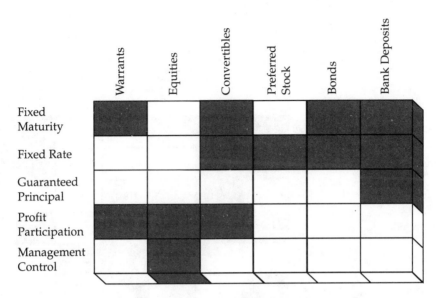

Figure 2.1　Key features of traditional capital market instruments.

medium-term CDs are commonly issued for up to 5 years, which, these days, is considered a capital markets maturity. As Figure 2.2 shows, CD prices do move in line with interest rates, unlike those of bank deposits, so the "Guaranteed principal" box is blank.

Still, as with bank deposits, bonds, and convertibles (if not converted), the cash value of CDs at final maturity is known; hence, the "Final maturity" box is filled in. This column was introduced mainly to apply to the indexed bonds line. As we shall see in Chapter 12, many of the newer varieties of bonds whose redemption values are linked to a currency, a stock market index, or some other index, have no known final value.

Convertible preferred stock (preferred stock convertible into equity) does have, like a convertible, an indirect right to profit participation. Recent issues of convertible preferred have had floating rates; hence the partially shaded box in the "Fixed rate" column.

These classifications are a very blunt instrument; later in the book, we will meet with instruments that blur across two or more of our distinctions. But these may help in initiating our task of classifying the new hybrids that the gardeners in the investment banking world have been breeding.

BONDS

A classical bond bears a fixed rate of interest and matures on a date fixed at the time of issue. So, from the time of issue, all of the cash flows on the bond—except the reinvestment income—are known in advance. This relative certainty

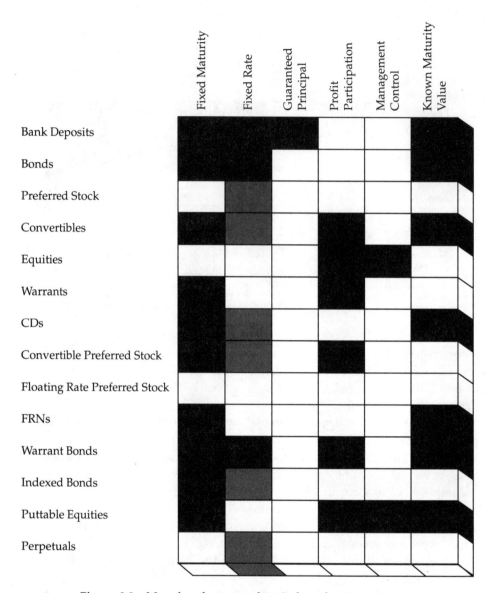

Figure 2.2   More key features of capital market instruments.

has made the bond an attractive investment instrument for those who need funds on hand at some future date, such as pension funds or life assurance companies.

In later chapters, we will look at several bond features in more detail. Here, we will only sketch in some basic elements. The classical fixed-rate bond consists of a fixed set of cash flows: the initial purchase price, in exchange for which the investor is paid a series of fixed interest amounts (the "coupon"), followed, finally, by repayment of the face amount of the bond at its maturity. The cash flows (excluding the initial purchase price) are illustrated in Figure 2.3.

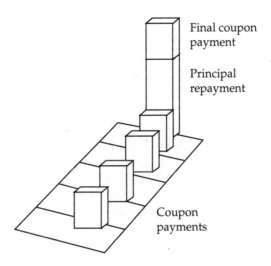

Final coupon
payment

Principal
repayment

Coupon
payments

Figure 2.3   16 Bond cash flows.

The price of a bond at any given time is the present value of the future cash flows of the bond. (Present value calculations are laid out in Chapter 3.) We take the prevailing rate of interest applicable to the maturity date of the bond and use this interest rate to discount, back to today, each cash flow. The sum total of the present values of each cash flow is the amount that a rational investor today would pay for the bond. (As we shall see when we consider swaps, it is possible to value streams of cash flows by applying to each cash flow the "zero coupon" rate applicable to that maturity. But market convention in the bond market is to calculate the price using the yield to maturity.)

If, however, we have the price of the bond but not the yield to maturity, we find the yield by a process called *iteration*. We make a guess at the yield. From this, we calculate what the price would be. If the price is too high, we raise our guess at the yield, and vice versa. Then we repeat the process until we find the yield that implies today's price.

Another important feature of a bond is its relative price volatility. This is commonly measured by its "duration," defined in Chapter 3, which also discusses a related measure called "convexity."

Equities and preferred stock tend to be of a fairly standard legal form, but bonds have been issued in a wide variety of types, some of which will be discussed in more detail later. One variable is the type of security they offer. Government bonds are unsecured; they are backed only by the government's promise to pay. In the United States, such unsecured bonds issued by corporations are called debentures (in the United Kingdom, a debenture is a secured bond). Mortgage bonds are backed by a mortgage on all or part of the issuer's assets. Other special types of bonds include collateral trust bonds and equipment trust certificates. Collateral trust bonds are bonds that have extra security from other securities placed with the trustee. The collateral deposited with the trustee is sometimes the stock or bonds of a subsidiary or of other companies. Or, it may be marketable securities, as in the case of mortgage-backed securities, which are often secured by GNMAs as collateral.

Much recent "securitization" (discussed in Chapter 8) has used variants of collateral trust bonds. The mortgage-backed securities industry, credit-card-backed issues, and the like, have depended on structuring issues with adequate security so that the investor need not be primarily concerned with the quality of the issuer. Two major structures have been used: (1) pass-through, which applies when the underlying cash flows are passed directly through to the investor, (2) and pay-through, which applies when the investor is paid by the issuer out of the cash flows of the underlying assets.

Apart from the underlying security, we shall see later that the classical bond has had a host of other variations. They have included, for example:

1. Altering the interest component:
    a. Floating rate notes (FRNs).
    b. Zero coupons.
    c. Step-up/down coupons.
    d. "Range notes".

2. Altering the principal value:
    a. Dual-currency bonds.
    b. Equity-linked notes.
    c. "Power" notes.
    d. Index-linked bonds.

3. Altering the maturity:
    a. Extendables/Retractables.
    b. Perpetuals.
    c. Put/Call options.

A range of other devices are implemented. Most are covered in Chapters 9 and 12.

Convertible Bonds

Later in this book, we will look at various hybrid securities. Convertibles and preferred stock are the oldest hybrid securities. Preferred stock is debt-like equity; a convertible is equity-like debt. The holder of a convertible bond can exchange the security, at his or her option, for the common stock of the issuer, in accordance with the terms of the bond indenture.

Usually, the indenture will say that the bond is convertible into common stock at a specified price. For example, a $1,000 bond might be convertible into common at $50 per share; that is, it is worth 20 shares. If the price of the stock went to $75, the convertible would be worth $1,500. The actual fixing of the conversion price—normally, 15 to 20 percent above the price of the outstanding shares—is set by the issuer.

For the issuer, the convertible has several advantages. The issuer can sell convertible bonds at a lower coupon than it could sell straight debt or even mortgage bonds. The attraction of possible equity profits for the investor allows a lower coupon. Further, on conversion, its interest charges are reduced. Also, the company can often get a higher price for its stock by selling convertible bonds that will be converted in the future to equity, at a higher price than today's price. Similarly, selling convertible bonds does not necessarily depress the price of outstanding shares today, because there is no immediate dilution of the equity. Disadvantages are: the possibility of dilution on conversion, and the tax impact of the reduction in interest payments after conversion.

From the point of view of the investor, the convertible is also attractive. If the affairs of the company go badly and the stock price does not rise, the investor is, as a bondholder, a creditor. This protects his or her position. On the other hand, if all goes well, the stock can be bought at what may prove to be a favorable price.

Another way of describing a convertible is to say that the value of a convertible bond consists of two parts: (1) the value as a fixed-rate bond and (2) the potential value as equity. The value as a fixed-rate bond can easily be found by comparing the coupon on a convertible with a yield on a similar straight. If the borrower must offer a yield of 10 percent on a straight fixed-rate bond with a final maturity of 10 years, and on a convertible the proposed coupon is 7 percent, the bond value would be 81.6 percent of the issue price (yield to redemption of 10 percent). The minimum potential value as equity is the conversion value. This equals the number of shares that each bond converts into, multiplied by the market price of the shares.

Analysis of the conversion premium and other data needs to be adjusted in the case of issues convertible across currencies. Take, for example, an XYZ (U.K.) Ltd. 9 percent convertible US\$ bond issued at 100 percent with a fixed exchange rate of US\$2 = £1 and a share conversion price fixed at issue of £2.50. Assuming that the current exchange rate is US\$1.50 = £1, the current bond price is 90 percent, and the current share price is £2.25, the conversion premium is found from the formula:

$$P = \left(\frac{MV \times CP \times FR - 1}{NV \times SP \times CR} \right) \times 100$$

where P = premium (discount);
      MV = current market value of bond expressed as a percentage;
      NV = issue value of bond expressed as a percentage;
      CP = conversion price fixed at time of issue;
      SP = current share price;
      FR = fixed exchange rate;
      CR = current exchange rate.

Applying this formula to our example, we see that:

$$P = \left(\frac{90 \times 2.50 \times 2.00 - 1}{100 \times 2.25 \times 1.50} \right) \times 100 = 33.33 \text{ percent.}$$

Convertibles are a rather specialized market because (1) they are relatively complex to value, at least compared with other traditional instruments; and (2) they are generally used in only a few countries. Convertible bonds have not been given much innovation in recent years, apart from zero-coupon convertibles (see Chapter 15).

PREFERRED STOCK

The next major type of traditional security is preferred stock. Like common stock, preferred stock is an equity or share in the earnings and assets of the corporation. But there are several differences:

1. The preferred stockholder has priority over the common stockholder for dividends. In general, when liquidation occurs, preferred stock ranks ahead of common stock.

2. The dividends paid to the preferred stockholder are predetermined. Those paid to the common stockholder can rise with the performance of a company. No matter how much money the corporation makes, the preferred stockholder will receive the stated rate of dividend.

3. Most, but not all, classical preferred stocks have cumulative features. They usually provide that, if the full dividend is not paid, it accrues to the benefit of the preferred stockholders. The company cannot pay dividends on common stock until all dividend accumulations are paid to preferred stockholders.

4. Unlike common stock, almost all preferred stocks are callable at the option of the corporation at a specified price. Usually, the price is at par or higher; an example is the 4.5 percent preferred stock of Du Pont, which is callable at $120 per share.

5. A preferred stockholder does not usually have the right to vote for the directors. He or she has no voice in the management of the company.

Preferred stock has been subject to a good deal of innovation in recent years. In many ways, it has become much more "debtlike." The major innovation in the U.S. market has been floating-rate preferred stock, but preferred has been combined with other instruments and made convertible into equity or exchangeable into debt. These developments are noted in Chapter 14.

EQUITIES

In some ways, equities are perhaps the simplest form of security. The common stock of a company is detailed in its certificate of incorporation, which states the number and type of equal units (shares) into which the stock is divided. The owner of a share is part owner of the assets and earnings of the corporation. A share has no maturity date, nor does it have any fixed claim on the assets or earnings. A share is a claim on the assets of the company after all other creditors have been paid off.

Still, owning stock gives certain rights. Chief among these—and in theory, most basic—is that stockholders have the right to name the board of directors. Also, they must vote on any major changes in the corporation, such as dissolution, consolidation, or amendments to the charter or bylaws. The next basic right is to a dividend, if one is declared. This right (along with the voting right, which can be of great value during a takeover) forms the basis for pricing stock.

One way of finding the theoretical value of a stock is to use the present value formula to discount the future stream of dividends expected from the company. The stock today should, in principle, be priced at the present value of that stream. But many stocks pay low (or no) dividends, yet their price rises. This occurs because investors believe that the funds that would have been paid out as dividends by the firm are being reinvested at a rate above the market capitalization rate. That is, the firm is investing the funds at a rate above that required by the investor.

The valuation of a firm's investment success and management quality is fundamental to valuing equities, but these factors lie beyond the scope of this book. Investors' primary concern is to arrive at an estimate of a company's prospective earnings per share. In the absence of such an accurate forecast, they must rely on historical data. Two ratios are then generally taken as most significant: price/earnings ratio, and yield.

Equities are the sector of the capital markets that (so far) have been least affected by innovations. The main developments have been: a tendency toward a global market in certain key stocks; the use of "puttable" equity; the development of equity contract/commitment notes; and variants such as "stapled" and "targeted" shares. All these are discussed in Chapter 17. Various equity derivatives, which are covered in Chapter 16, have also been introduced in recent years.

WARRANTS

Another "classical" instrument we have to consider is the warrant, which is a kind of option. (Its pricing and valuation will be affected by option pricing factors, discussed in Chapters 6 and 7.) A warrant gives the holder the privilege of buying a specified number of shares of the underlying common stock at a specified exercise price. The purchase can be made at any time on or before an expiration date. A "classical" warrant is typically an instrument issued by an entity—often as an accompaniment to a bond or equity issue—granting the investor the right to undertake a certain transaction with that issuing entity. Thus, a bank might issue a warrant allowing the investor to buy a currency from the bank at a prefixed rate. Similarly, a classical equity warrant is a transaction whereby the company issuing equities grants the buyer of the warrant the right to buy further equity from the company at some preset price. In contrast, the "covered" warrant issue (an issue by a third party, which is backed by a holding of shares, discussed below) will not normally lead to the issuance of fresh equity. On exercise, it will be extinguished by the delivery of already existing securities.

Warrants are important in a number of domestic markets (as discussed further in Chapter 15) and also in the international markets. The first Eurobond with a warrant attached was made in 1963, but, until 1981, this section of the Euromarkets was something of a backwater. Thereafter, fueled mainly by Japanese issuance, the "Eurobond + warrant" segment of the market became a substantial market in its own right. Warrant issues in the Eurobond markets have usually had maturities of between 5 and 15 years; most Japanese issues carry maturity of 4 or 5 years. Generally, the warrant exercise period starts soon after the issue date, and warrants are exercisable up to a specified final date. With shorter maturities, the final date will normally be about the same as the final redemption date of the bond, but with longer bond maturities the exercise period may be restricted to perhaps the first 5 or 10 years. Warrants are generally detachable shortly after issue.

Bonds with equity warrants resemble convertibles except that the warrant can be traded separately. There is one other difference: When the warrants are exercised, new money is normally used to subscribe for the shares, and the total capitalization of the borrower increases. This is unlike the conversion of a convertible bond, which merely shifts debt capital into equity capital. Until the warrant is exercised, the holder has no right to vote at shareholders' meetings or to participate in dividend distributions. Apart from these differences, convertibles and bonds with equity warrants are very close economic substitutes. Japanese issuance of warrant bonds was driven by Ministry of Finance regulations, but otherwise there is little to choose between them. Occasionally, a specific consideration drives the choice between the two; for example, in April 1993, Pilkington, a British glass company, issued the first domestic U.K. sterling warrant bond since 1987 rather than a convertible, because of the high yield on its shares. The shares yielded 6.4 percent at the time, and investors had generally required a margin of 3 percent over the share yield to be attracted into a convertible bond. Pilkington felt this was unattractive and went for the bond + warrant alternative.

The price of a warrant in the market depends on a number of factors. The primary attraction of a warrant is the leverage, or gearing, that it offers.

Consider a stock with a share price of $35. Suppose there is a warrant to subscribe at $35 for the shares in any year for the next 5 years, and the price of the warrant itself is $5.

The $5 premium exists because the warrant has a time value (this is discussed further in Chapter 6). During the time the owner holds the warrant, there is a chance that the share price will rise further. If it rises to, say, $45, the owner could exercise the warrant for an immediate profit. This potential immediate profit is called the intrinsic value. At a share market price of $35, the warrant has no intrinsic value. If the share is trading at $45, the warrant has an intrinsic value of $10 ($45 – $35). If the share price rises to $55, the intrinsic value would be $20. (See Figure 2.4.)

The interest to the speculator is that the premium tends to be set by longer-term factors (described in more detail in Chapters 6 and 7, on options; the warrant is a kind of option). The premium tends to be stable in the short run. So, in our example, the price of the warrant would be $5 when the share is trading at $35, and would move to $15 ($5 premium + $10 intrinsic) if the share rises to $45, and to $25 ($5 premium + $20 intrinsic) if the share rises to $55.

Look again at Figure 2.4. If the share is trading at $45; the warrant is at $15. In this case, the share price is about three times that of the warrant: this is known as the leverage (or *gearing,* in U.K. terminology) of the warrant. The higher the leverage, the greater the profit/loss potential. Suppose that the premium remains stable. Then a rise of $10 in the stock (to $55, or 22 percent,) would imply a rise of $10 in the price of the warrant, or 66 percent ($10 on $15). The warrant's gain is the underlying gain multiplied by the leverage. It is this which makes the warrant attractive to the speculator (and, of course, dangerous also, because the reverse effect can also occur).

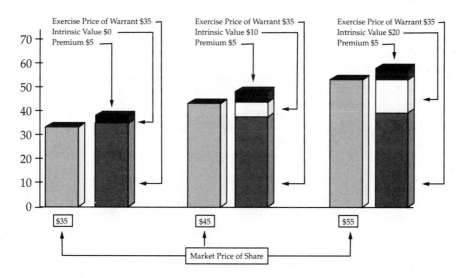

Figure 2.4 Warrant leverage.

The premium implies a break-even rate of rise of the stock. The break-even point is:

$$\left(\frac{\text{Warrant premium}}{\text{Share price}}\right) \times 100$$

So, in our example, over the 5 years of the warrant, the stock's price must rise by at least $5/$45, or 11 percent—an annual appreciation of 2.2 percent. One should also allow for the dividends lost by buying the warrant rather than the stock (though against this should be set the lower interest costs of the lower capital outlay).

A number of other calculations are relevant to equity warrants. For a bond + equity warrant issue, one would want to know the equity content: the percentage value of the equity entitlement at the exercise price, expressed as a percentage of the face value of the bond. The equation is:

$$\text{Equity content} = \frac{\begin{array}{c}\text{Number of shares warrent} \\ \text{holder is entitled to}\end{array} \times \text{Exercise price}}{\text{Face value of bond}}.$$

Among the other indicators to be considered is the capital fulcrum point, which is

$$\left(\frac{\text{Exercise price}}{\text{Current share price} - \text{Warrant price}} - 1\right) \times 100.$$

This formula aims to measure how fast the share price must rise before investment in the warrant is more profitable than direct investment in the underlying shares. (The dividend yield on the shares is ignored.) The gross fulcrum point allows for this:

$$\text{Gross fulcrum point} = \left(\frac{\text{Exercise price}}{\text{Current share price} - \text{Warrant price}\,(1+y)^n} - 1\right) \times 100.$$

Valuation of a warrant is a bit more complex in the international markets because of currency questions. But this only increases their trading attraction because they can provide a double play on equity and currency. Let's take a typical example.

A US$ bond issued by Nippon Widget Corporation will mature on March 15, 2002, with a coupon of 2.875 percent. With it, on issue, is a warrant with a face amount of $5,000, expiring March 3, 2002, to buy 1,000 shares of Nippon Widget at ¥1,135 per share. Thus, the exercise cost of the warrant is 1,000 × 1,135 = ¥1,135,000. The yen conversion rate for the warrants is fixed at the time of issue at US$1 = ¥167.75. Today's exchange rate is US$1 = ¥155, and today's share price is ¥1,620.

The dollar cost of exercising the warrants is ¥1,135,000/167.75= US$6,766.02. The cost in yen of buying the shares directly in the market today would be $1,000 \times 1,620 = ¥1,620,000$, and the dollar equivalent at today's rate would be ¥1,620,000/155 = US$10,451.61.

Thus, the intrinsic value of the warrant is the market cost of the shares less their cost via the warrant, or $10,451.61 - $6,766.02 = $3,685.59. Suppose the price in the market for the warrant is quoted as 82—that is, $4,100 per $5,000 nominal. Then the premium on the warrant is the purchase price less the intrinsic value: $4,100 - $3,685.59 = $414.41.

Is this premium worth paying? There are two approaches. The crude one is to take the premium paid, calculate the break-even share price that is implied, and then decide whether the share price will get there or not. The alternative, is a more scientific approach. A warrant is a type of option, and its theoretical price, or fair value, can be found according to options theory. The way in which this is done is explained in Chapters 6 and 7.

Warrants on Bonds, Currencies, and Interest Rates

A more recent development has been the introduction of warrants on fixed-interest instruments and currencies. Developments here have taken two main forms. First, warrants have been attached to bonds, allowing the investor to buy another bond at some prefixed level. The investor can then gamble on the possibility of a further decline in interest rates. Second, a number of "naked" warrant issues—warrants unaccompanied by other funding—have been issued, mostly by banks or investment banks, which are able to hedge the risks entailed.

The first kind of warrant was sold by the Kingdom of Sweden in a Yankee issue in December 1980. It sold a 5-year note with a warrant attached that allowed the holder to buy another 5-year note with an identical coupon at par. The warrant expired after 6 months (it turned out to be worthless). During 1981, more than a dozen issues were made in the European and U.S. markets. How often the technique is used will clearly be influenced by expectations about the immediate course of rates: if rates are expected to drop in the short term, investors are more likely to be attracted by the warrants.

Warrants have proved a very fertile source of innovation in the international markets, and a number of warrant applications have been devised. They are discussed in more depth in Chapter 15.

Chapter 3

Some Analytical Tools

This chapter sets out some of the tools that we will need in the rest of the book. We cover the basics of the present value calculations that will be needed, together with a simple explanation of the zero-coupon curve, risk measures such as duration, and convexity. We also discuss the basic statistical approaches that underlie modern portfolio theory and value-at-risk approaches.

PRESENT VALUE CALCULATIONS

Because present value is fundamental to many of the financial instruments we will consider, a brief explanation is included here to refresh readers' familiarity with the concept. The present value of a sum of money due at some future date (D) is that amount of money which, if it were invested at the interest rate prevailing for deposits from today to D, would accumulate to $X.

Let us work through an example. You offer to buy my car for $10,000, but you do not have enough money to pay me today. You offer to pay me the $10,000 in one week's time. I need the car to go to work, so I will have to replace the car today. If you do not pay me today, I will have to put up my own money to pay for the replacement car today. I have implicit faith in your ability to pay and in your trustworthiness. The only question in my mind is whether the present value of what you will pay me is more or less than what I will have to pay today for the replacement car.

Suppose I know that I can invest my money for one week at 8 percent. I also know that if I invest $9,984.47 for 7 days on a 360-day basis I will have 9,984.47 × (1 + [8/100 × 7/360]) = $10,000. Expressed another way, I know that the present value of $10,000 in 7 days' time is $9,984.47, using a discount rate of 8 percent. In fact, $9,984.47 = $10,000/(1 + [8/100 × 7/360]).

Present Value over Several Periods

The formula we just defined is fine for discounting a single sum of money for a period of less than a year. To get the more general formula, it helps to start at the other end: a sum of money invested today. A sum with a present value of

100, invested today at an annual interest rate of r percent, will yield $100(1 + r)$ at the end of year 1. (Note that r is a decimal: 10 percent = 0.10). At the end of year 2, the yield will be $100(1 + r)^2$, and at the end of year n, it will be $100(1 + r)^n$. The formula is: Future value in year n = Present value $\times (1 + r)^n$.

Turning the formula round, we state:

$$\text{Present value} = \frac{\text{Future value}}{(1 + r)^n}.$$

Another way of saying this is: The present value is the future value discounted back to today at a rate of r. It is very important to realize that once we have discounted a sum of money back to today, it is valued in today's money. A sum of money, say $150, due in one year's time—discounted back to today, to produce, say, $135—is valued in today's money. Another sum, say $2,000, due in 5 years' time—discounted back to today, to produce, say, $1,750—is also valued in today's money. Because the two sums are valued in the same money, we can add them together.

Therefore, provided we discount each cash flow properly, we can discount every single cash flow in a stream of multiple cash flows back into a single sum of money. This is what happens when a bond dealer works out the price of a bond. Each coupon payment on the bond is discounted back to today. The present value of each coupon, together with the present value of the bond's repayment amount, are added together. The total is the present value of all the cash flows of the bond. That total is what the stream of cash flows is worth today. Therefore, it will be the price that the dealer will be willing to bid for the bond.

Consider a stream of cash due at the end of each of the next 5 years:

Year 1: $110.00.

Year 2: $121.00.

Year 3: $133.10.

Year 4: $146.41.

Year 5: $161.05.

Suppose we want to find the present value of this stream of cash flows. We can invest money for the 5 years at 10 percent, so that is the rate of discount we consider appropriate. What is the present value of the stream of flows?

The formula we apply is:

$$\text{Present value} = \frac{\text{Future value in year n}}{(1 + r)^n}.$$

The sum due at the end of Year 1 is to be discounted by $(1 + r)^1$—that is, 1.10— so $110 in a year's time is worth $100 today. Similarly, the sum due at the end of Year 2 is to be discounted by $(1 + r)^2$—that is, we work out $121/(1.10)^2$, which also turns out to be $100. Likewise, $133.1/(1.10)^3$ is worth $100; and each of the others proves to be also worth $100 today. So, although the cash total of that stream of cash is $671.56, its total net present value is $500. We can write:

Present value of a future stream of cash flows =

$$\frac{\text{Future value in year 1}}{(1+r)} + \frac{\text{Future value in year 2}}{(1+r)^2} + \ldots + \frac{\text{Future value in year n}}{(1+r)^n}.$$

Yield Curves, Zero-Coupon Curves, and Forward Rates

A basic tool in fixed income markets is the yield curve, a series of observations of the interest rates available to investors either directly through the bond market, or through the swap market and related markets. A typical yield curve might allow us to invest for 1 year at 8 percent, 2 years at 9 percent, and so on.

Many of the instruments we will consider later are built around single cash flows at future dates. To value these cash flows, the conventional yield curve is not adequate. We need to use the zero-coupon curve. The zero-coupon rate for any given maturity is the amount the market would be prepared to pay on a deposit or bond that pays no interim interest payments, but only a lump sum at maturity. (These bonds are discussed in Chapter 9.) (Some people refer to the zero-coupon curve as the spot rate curve.) The zero-coupon curve is important to interest rate swap dealers (see Chapter 5) because they can, if they choose, treat their interest rate positions as individual cash flows, which should be valued at the zero-coupon rate for that maturity. More generally, it is important because it gives us the value today of a given cash flow at some future date, independent of reinvestment risk. It is an important element in constructing a number of the instruments we will look at later.

Sometimes, we cannot observe the implied zero-coupon curve directly; it has to be worked out step by step. A convenient way to do this is as follows. Look at the 1- to 5-year yield curve for Eurodollar deposits. Interest payments, in line with Euromarket practice, are on an annual basis, so the 1-year deposit rate is in fact a zero-coupon rate; there are no interim interest payments. The 2-year deposit rate is not, because there would normally be a payment of interest at the end of Year 1.

Suppose we are contemplating investing $1,000 and have the following interest rates:

Investment Period	Interest Rate
1 year	8%
2	9
3	10
4	11
5	12

Suppose we are interested in finding out what 2-year zero-coupon rate is implied by these rates. Suppose we deposit $1,000 for 2 years at 9 percent. We know we will get two cash flows: a payment of $90 at the end of Year 1, and a payment of $1,090 at the end of Year 2. We will also receive a year's interest on the $90 coupon payment, but we do not know what that will be worth.

One way around this uncertainty is to take the following approach. I know the 1-year zero-coupon rate is 8 percent, so I know that the present value of $90 today is $83.33 (i.e., $90/1.08, ignoring day-count questions and discounting on an annual basis). I am indifferent as to receiving $90 in a year's time or receiving $83.33 today by, say, selling my right to the coupon to someone else. I decide to sell it. I now have a 2-year zero-coupon deposit. I place $1,000 − $83.33 = $916.67 today, and in 2 years I will receive $1,090.

Now it is quite simple to work out the 2-year zero-coupon rate: it is 9.045 percent. This technique can be applied step by step. The 3-year deposit gives me cash flows of $100, $100, and $1,100. I sell off the first two cash flows for $92.59 and $84.10, respectively. That makes my net investment today $823.31, which returns $1,100 in 3 years' time, for an implied zero-coupon rate of 10.14 percent.

At the end of this process, I have the following yield curves:

Year	Deposit Yield Curve	Zero-Coupon Yield Curve
1	8%	8.00%
2	9	9.05
3	10	10.14
4	11	11.30
5	12	12.56

The next step, which may be required for some of the instruments we will consider later, is to find out the implied forward rates that underlie this zero-coupon curve. Assuming I have a zero-coupon rate for 2 years and a zero-coupon rate for 3 years, there will be a given forward rate for an investment starting in 2 years' time and maturing in 3 years. This forward rate will be such as to make me indifferent between investing in the 2-year zero-coupon bond, reinvesting at the forward rate for the last year, or investing now in the 3-year zero-coupon bond. I proceed as follows.

I know that, on a zero-coupon basis, I can earn 8 percent for 1 year and 9.05 percent for 2 years. The forward rate is the rate that will make me indifferent between the two. If I continue to ignore day-count issues and treat this as purely annual investing, I know that I will earn over 2 years, from an investment of $1.00, $(1.09)^2$, and, over 1 year, will earn $1.08. Therefore, the forward rate that makes me indifferent between these two alternatives is:

$$F = \frac{(1.0905)^2 - (1.08)}{1.08} = 10.112 \text{ percent.}$$

Looking at that result another way, if I earn $1.08 after Year 1 and reinvest it at 10.112 percent, I earn a cumulative total of $1.18919, which is the same as $(1.09)^2$.

Generalizing, I can write:

$$r_{n-1,n} = \frac{(1+r_n)^n - (1+r_{n-1})^{n-1}}{(1+r_{n-1})^{n-1}}.$$

In other words, the forward rate from period $n - 1$ to period n is the amount earned by investing for n periods at the rate for period $n(r_n)$, less the alternative amount earned for investing at the rate for period $n - 1(r_{n-1})$, expressed as a percentage of the principal accumulated up to period $n - 1$.

Forward-Forward Deposit Agreements

We should add one slight extension of the above discussion of forward rates: The money market practice is slightly different. In the past, banks often traded among themselves in a market for forward deposits. That is, Citibank would agree to lend Morgan $10 million for 3 months, starting 3 months from now. Although this practice is now less common, it remains the underpinning for calculating short-term forward money rates (specifically, forward rate agreements, discussed in the next chapter) when no financial futures are available, because it is always open to us, in theory, to go into the deposit market instead. In the London market, this type of trading has usually been referred to as "forward-forward" trading.

The formula to be used is the forward rate formula (up to 1 year):

$$Rf = \frac{R2 \times N2 - R1 \times N1}{(N2 - N1)(1 + R1 \times N1/(100 \times B))}$$

where Rf = forward rate;
     R2 = long period rate;
     R1 = short period rate;
     N2 = days in long rate;
     N1 = days in short rate;
     B = interest basis (360 or 365 days).

It may help to understand this formula if we realize that the top line represents the net difference between, say, lending long and borrowing short. (The first term is our earnings from lending long; the second term is the cost of the shorter-period funding.) The second item on the bottom line is the principal and interest due at the end of the first period.

The difference between this formula and that of the previous section is that this formula is applicable for periods of up to 1 year; whereas the approach of the previous section was concerned with forward rates over 1 year in maturity.

Example: A bank is lending for 60 days at 20 percent, against a deposit for which it has paid 10 percent for 30 days. What is the break-even rate on the second period—that is, how much can it afford to pay for a deposit starting on day 31 and maturing on day 60? We assume the deposit and loan are for US$1 million and interest is paid on a 360-day basis. Then, in the first period, the bank pays interest of:

$$\frac{10}{100} \times \frac{30}{360} \times \$1,000,000 = \$8,333.33.$$

Over the lifetime of the loan, the bank earns interest of:

$$\frac{20}{100} \times \frac{60}{360} \times \$1,000,000 = \$33,333.33.$$

However, in accordance with Euromarket convention, interest earned on the 2-month loan is not paid to the bank until the end of the 2 months, whereas the bank must pay interest on the 1-month deposit at maturity. So, for the second period, it has to fund not only its $1 million principal amount but also the $8,333.33 it has paid in interest. The amount to be funded in the second period is then $1,008,333.33.

We know that the bank has earnings of $33,333.33 over the 2 months and costs (so far) of $8,333.33. A net amount of $25,000 is therefore available to pay the interest on the new principal amount of $1,008,333.33. To calculate the forward-forward interest rate, we work the $25,000 as a percentage of the principal and annualize up from the 30-day period to a 360-day period:

$$\text{Forward rate} = 100 \times \frac{360}{30} \times \frac{\$25,000}{\$1,008,333.33} = \$1,200 \times 0.0247933$$
$$= 29.75196 \text{ percent.}$$

This formula is simply an adaptation of the general forward rate calculation set out above, to make it conform to money market conventions.

Continuous Compounding

We should make one further extension to the concept of discounting: the notion of continuous time. In our calculations, we have implicitly assumed that time was divided into distinct periods—3 months, 1 year, and so on. In some markets, notably options, it is customary to assume that interest or dividends are paid continuously.

Consider an amount of $1 invested for t years at a rate of r (where r is expressed as a decimal) per annum. If interest is compounded annually, the final amount is $(1 + r)^t$. If the interest is compounded semiannually, the final amount will be $(1 + r/2)^{2t}$, and if it is compounded m times per year, the final amount will be $(1 + r/m)^{mt}$. If we let m grow in size, to the point where interest is being paid infinitely often (i.e., continuously), it can be shown that the final amount is e^{rt}, where e is the exponential constant, approximately 2.71828.

This is valid because one way of defining e is:

$$e = {}_{\lim m \to \infty}(1 + 1/m)^m.$$

Restated in financial market terms, e is the amount of money we get if we invest \$1 for 1 year at a rate of 100 percent compounded continuously. We will end up with \$2.71828 approximately.

As a result, in the options context, it is often necessary for us to discount continuously, using the discount factor e^{-rt} (i.e., $1/e^{rt}$).

Negative Interest Rates

Many people raise their eyebrows at the idea of negative interest rates. But they do occur, and they can be highly profitable. It is very pleasant to be paid to borrow money. Negative rates generally happen in one of two ways: (1) there is intense upward pressure on a currency, or (2) there is intense downward pressure that is expected to be only temporary. These conditions can be seen in the forward markets, which is why they are mentioned here.

Negative interest rates can be thrown up in the forward rate markets if a currency is under sufficiently intense pressure. During the spring of 1981, the French franc was extraordinarily weak, and the Banque de France was determined to support it by squeezing money market rates in the then thinly traded Euro-French franc deposit market. Overnight Euro-French francs at one point were lent out at over 5,000 percent, and one-week money was running at over 300 percent. If we apply the forward-forward formula, we can see the implication that money for the rest of the week was worth –400 percent. Although this kind of situation can fairly be called an extreme case, fluctuations on this scale do occur in narrow money markets and can be very profitable. More recently, during 1996, when Japanese interest rates were at extremely low levels (the central bank discount rate was 0.5 percent), trades were done in the market that contemplated the possibility of negative interest rates. [Indeed, where transactions were taking place at a spread below LIBOR (London Interbank Offered Rate) arguments arose as to whether the documentation of the applicable swaps had envisaged negative interest rates, and there were some disputes over the matter.]

We will need these zero-coupon and forward rate calculations at various points in the future; they play an important role in the construction of a number of the instruments we will consider. We turn now to another important set of concepts, the measurement of risk in some of these instruments. We begin with duration, the most basic measure of interest risk sensitivity.

DURATION

We can define duration as the weighted average time until the receipt of cash flows from an instrument, where the weights are present values of cash flows.
    More formally, we can write:

$$D = \frac{\sum_{t=1}^{n} \dfrac{t C_t}{(1+y)^t}}{P},$$

where D = duration;
       P = price of bond;
       C_t = cash flow at time t;
       y = yield.

    In the case of a zero-coupon bond, there is only one cash flow: the payment at maturity. Therefore, for zero coupons, the duration is always equal to the maturity of the bond. Consider now a 10 percent 2-year bond yielding 10 percent today.

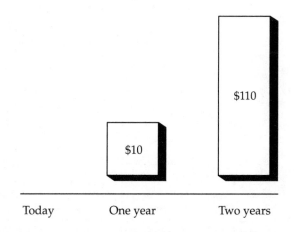

| Today | One year | Two years |

    Suppose we treat it as two zero-coupon bonds: a 1-year bond of $10 and a 2-year bond of $110, as shown above. The duration of the combined package will be the average duration of the two bonds, weighted by the size of the bond. Because we are measuring the duration today, it makes sense to weight the two bonds in terms of today's money—that is, in present value terms.
    The duration of this bond consists of "the sum of time to receipt of cash flow × present value of cash flow, all divided by the price." Because the bond is a 10 percent bond and we are valuing it at a yield of 10 percent, its price is par, or 100. The calculation is:

$$(1 \times 9.0909 + 2 \times 90.909) \div 100 = 1.909.$$

This incidentally illustrates the point that, for a coupon-bearing bond, duration is always less than for the corresponding zero-coupon bond. The 2-year coupon-bearing bond has a duration of 1.91 years; the zero-coupon bond would have a duration of 2 years.

Some people may find it easier to think about duration in more visual terms. A helpful representation was given by R. W. Kopprasch in "Understanding Duration and Volatility" (Salomon Brothers, September 1985). Figure 3.1 shows the cash flows and present values of a 5-year bond. The shaded area of each cash flow represents its present value. We can imagine that Figure 3.1 is a series of tins resting on a seesaw. The size of each tin is the cash flow due; the water (shading) in the tin is the present value of the cash flow. The distance between the centers of each cash flow container represents the amount of time between the cash flows. That is, each tin is one period apart.

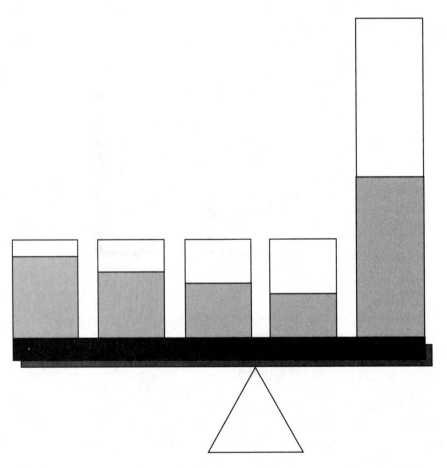

Figure 3.1 Duration: The weighted average of the time to receipt of cash flow.

If an investor were looking at this 5-year bond on a coupon date, the first (left most) tin would be one period away from the start, the second would be two periods away, and so on. The duration would be the distance from the investor to where we could put a fulcrum and balance the whole system (see Figure 3.1). This point would be the bond's "center of gravity."

Looking at duration in this way makes it clear that the duration of a zero-coupon bond equals its maturity. Because there is only one cash flow, the fulcrum must be positioned at that cash flow. For all other bonds, the duration is less than the maturity. (If there are intervening cash flows, the fulcrum cannot be at the end of the seesaw and still balance it.)

Duration is important because modified duration [defined as Duration/(1 + y) where y is the current yield on the bond] measures the sensitivity of the bond's price to changes in the yield curve. (A short proof of this statement is given in the Appendix to this chapter.) This can be seen by drawing a chart of the bond's price at different levels of yield (Figure 3.2). The slope of that line is the bond's modified duration.

The definition of duration that we have been using is sometimes called Macaulay duration, after the man who invented it. As we have said, there is a related concept called modified duration, which is the Macaulay duration

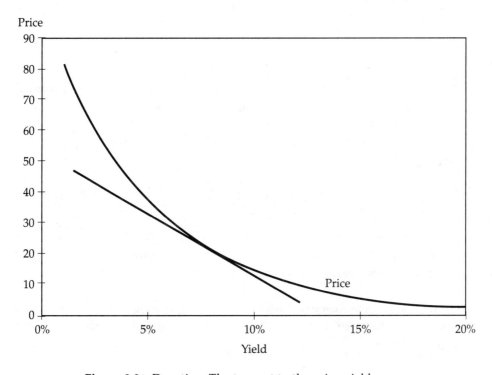

Figure 3.2 Duration: The tangent to the price-yield curve.

divided by $(1 + r)$. (We need to be sure that r is correctly defined as the periodic yield. If r is 10 percent per annum, we would write 1.10; if it were a semiannual yield, we would write 1.05.)

Let's look at a 4-year zero-coupon bond, yielding 10 percent. Its current price will be $68.30 per $100 face value, due in 4 years' time. That price is found via the standard present value calculation, which here is fairly simple: $PV = \$100/(1 + r)^4$.

What would the price of the bond be at a yield of 10.01 percent? From the same formula, we can find that the price is $68.28. What is the percentage change in price for a one-basis-point rise in yield? If we work out the prices of the bonds very precisely, we will find that, at 10 percent, the price is $68.30135; at 10.01 percent, the price is $68.27651, and the percentage difference, expressed as a percentage of the original price of $68.30135, is –0.036 percent. The percentage change in price is 3.6 times as large as the change in yield. In other words, for a change in yield of 0.01 percent, the value of the bond changes by 0.01 percent × MD, where MD is the modified duration, the U.S. term for a measure of the volatility of the bond. (In the U.K. bond market, it is usually referred to as volatility.)

Thus, one of the chief practical uses of duration is as a measure of the volatility of a bond. To be precise, modified duration is a measure of the percentage volatility of the full price (that is, including accrued interest) of a bond, given small changes in interest rates.

Convexity

Modified duration as a measure of percentage volatility is only valid for small changes in yield. For larger changes, one must consider the security's convexity. (The term comes from the price-yield curve for a normal bond, which is convex.) Mathematically speaking, the convexity is the second derivative of the price-yield curve:

$$C = \frac{10,000}{P} \times \frac{\delta^2 P}{\delta Y^2}$$

where C = convexity,
     P = dirty price of bond (i.e., including accrued interest), and
     Y = periodic yield (e.g., semiannual).

A less formidable formula, which is a practical approximation, is to define Pp and Pm as the price of the bond if yields rise and fall respectively by one basis point. Then

$$C = \frac{10^3 \times (Pp + Pm - 2P)}{P}.$$

KEY RATE DURATION (KRD)

A refinement of the concept of duration was introduced recently by T. S. Y. Ho ("Key Rate Durations: Measures of Interest Rate Risks," *Journal of Fixed Income*, 1992), among others. This concept focuses on the idea of analyzing interest rate risk with respect to sectors of the yield curve. The duration of a bond is measured with respect to one key portion of the yield curve. Thus, one might consider duration in relation to the 10-year zero rate. A variant of this is to consider duration in relation to on-the-run Treasury bond yields, sometimes called "key Treasury rate duration." The concept is relevant to the analysis of structured notes that carry embedded in them risks derived from changes in the shape of the yield curve.

COMPOSITE DURATION (STRUCTURED NOTES)

The analysis of the duration of a structured note is not as simple as the same type of analysis of a Treasury bond or any "normal" straight bond. The exact calculation will vary enormously, depending on the structure of the bond. What follows is an attempt to explain a possible line of approach [drawing on the treatment given by S. Y. Peng and R. E. Dattatreya, *The Structured Note Market*, Probus Publishing, Chicago (1995), which should be consulted for a fuller discussion of the issues involved].

The duration of a Treasury bond is dependent on the yield used to discount the cash flows involved. We may therefore call it the "discounting rate duration." But the performance of a structured note may be dependent on some other interest rate. We may have, for example, a $10 million bond whose redemption value or coupons may be set by, say, the 5-year Swiss franc swap rate. The bond value is then linked not just to U.S. interest rates but also to Swiss franc rates. Following Peng and Dattatreya, we will call this second duration the "index rate duration." This is the sensitivity of the bond's price to changes in the underlying index (in this case, the Swiss franc rate). We could also define the concept of "composite duration" or "net duration." This is the composite of the two underlying durations.

As an example of risk measurement on a structured note, we will consider a 3-year Euromedium-term note issued by the Federal National Mortgage Association (FNMA). It pays an annual coupon defined as the 10-year Constant Maturity Treasury (CMT) rate, less 12-month LIBOR plus 2 percent. (The CMT rate is a rate for 10-year Treasury bonds. It is constantly updated to reflect the current yield on new 10-year Treasury bonds.)

The first step is to see that, as is typical with the recent wave of structured notes, we have two durations to look at. The first is the conventional or *discounting duration*. This is the impact on the price of the bond of a change in the yield of the instrument whose yield we use to value the cash flows of the bond.

With a conventional bond, the cash flow valuation yield is the yield on the bond. That yield reflects the rate at which money can be invested or reinvested during the life of the bond. But with this bond, the yield definition is exotic. We can't be sure that at any time in the 3-year life of the bond we can invest money at (10-year CMT – 12-month LIBOR) + 2 percent. We therefore will use the 3-year Treasury bond yield to value the cash flows. A change in the 3-year Treasury yield will change the value of the FNMA note, and the impact of that change will be reflected in the discounting rate duration.

The second duration we have to think of is the impact on the bond price of changes in the index rate(s) that defines the coupon of the bond. We'll call this the *index rate duration*. With a conventional bond, the coupon is the coupon, and this sensitivity does not arise. But with this bond, we have two variable items: (1) the CMT coupon is refixed annually as the then-current 10-year Treasury bond yield, and (2) LIBOR will also vary each year.

Let us deal with the LIBOR component first. It is possible to convert from a stream of LIBOR coupons to a fixed swap rate. (This is explained in Chapter 5.) Normally, the LIBOR is a 6-month LIBOR. But we can often construct the swap against a 12-month LIBOR for no additional cost. Thus, the stream of 12-month LIBOR coupons embedded in the FNMA note can be treated as being equal, for interest risk purposes, to the 3-year swap rate (because 3 years is the underlying maturity of the note). This in turn is equal to the 3-year Treasury yield plus or minus some spread (which, over a 3-year period can be assumed not to vary very much). In this case, the LIBOR flows are being deducted from our coupon. It is as if we were paying LIBOR to receive a 3-year Treasury rate; the value of the LIBOR stream is equivalent to being long a 3-year Treasury bond. If we assume, for the purposes of this example, an interest rate level of 5 percent, then the duration of the position is about –2.75 (negative, because rising yields imply falling prices).

Next, we consider the CMT component. At this point, we need to look at the key rate duration of the various parts of the CMT component.

The present value (PV) of the coupon income represented by the CMT component is calculated as follows. It is the sum of the current 10-year Treasury coupon plus the 10-year Treasury coupon fixed a year from now, plus the 10-year coupon fixed 2 years from now. Each of these must be discounted at the appropriate rate for that cash flow. We can then write:

$$\text{PV of CMT coupons} = \frac{T_{10,0}}{(1+r_1)} + \frac{T_{10,1}}{(1+r_2)^2} + \frac{T_{10,2}}{(1+r_3)^3}$$

where we define $T_{10,1}$ as the 10-year rate fixed a year from now, and $T_{10,2}$ as the rate fixed 2 years from now. Similarly, we define $(1 + r_2)$ as the discount factor applicable to a cash flow to be received 2 years from now.

We have no way of knowing what the 10-year Treasury rate will be 1 year from now. But because we know the forward 10-year rates built into the current

Treasury bond yield curve, we know what the current market forecast of those rates is. We can find the market's forecast of what the 10-year Treasury rate will be by looking at today's 1-year rate and today's 11-year rate. Similarly, we can find from the 2-year rate and the 12-year rate what the implicit forecast is for 10-year yields starting 2 years from now.

This calculation is laborious, though of course it can be done via software. For the purposes of this example, let us note that, in the present case, the length of time until the forward starts (1 and 2 years) is small in relation to the maturity of the bond (10 years). In this case, it is more or less fair to assume that the forward rate is close to the rate on the final-maturity bond. That is, the 10-year rate for 1 year forward is close to the yield on the 11-year bond, and the 10-year rate 2 years forward is proportional to the yield on the 12-year bond. This simplifying assumption is made only for the purpose of exposition.

Now we can argue that the CMT component of this bond consists of three sets of yields. They are roughly equivalent to the 10-, 11-, and 12-year Treasury bonds. The effect of a change in the 10-year bond will be slightly greater than that of the 11-year bond, because the yield is received a year from now, whereas the yield of the 11-year bond (i.e., the CMT 10-year due to be fixed next year and paid the following year) is received in 2 years.

We have now worked out how to find the three key rate durations (KRDs) of the 10-, 11-, and 12-year bonds. The KRD of the 10-year bond is the impact of a 1-basis-point change in the 10-year bond yield. The effect of this change will last for 1 year (in the following year, the coupon will be refixed). So the total effect is 1 basis point, which will be received in 1 year's time. Discounting it at our previously assumed rate of 5 percent, we find that the present value of this change is 0.96. Because a rise in the yield will benefit us (remember that we have separated out, into the discount rate duration, the effect of changing the discount rate), the sign of the KRD is positive, making it +0.96. Similarly, for the 11-year KRD, we need the impact of a 1-basis-point change for 1 year, received in 2 years' time. The present value of this at 5 percent is +0.91. For the 12-year KRD, we need the present value of a 1-basis-point yield for 1 year, received 3 years from now. This comes to +0.85.

We can summarize the position as follows:

Component	Index	Key Rate for Index	Key Rate Duration (KRD)
Index rate	10-year CMT	T_{10}	.96
		T_{11}	.91
		T_{12}	.85
	12-month LIBOR	T_3	−2.75
Discounting	Treasury rate to maturity	T_3	−2.75

In aggregate, therefore, we can say that this note has a duration of −5.5 with respect to any change in the 3-year Treasury bond. Roughly speaking, a 1

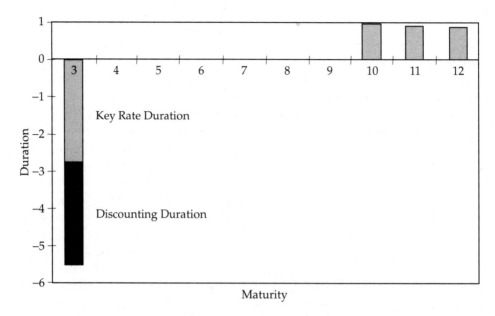

Figure 3.3 Key rate duration and discount duration.

percent rise in 3-year bond yields will cost us 5.5 percent. But a rise in the 10-, 11-, or 12-year yields would help us. Therefore, the note is a bet on the yield curve steepening (we want the 3-year rate to fall and the 10-, 11-, and 12-year rates to rise).

We have a depiction of the situation in Figure 3.3. If we assume a parallel shift across the whole curve, the duration is $-2.75 - 2.75 + .96 + .91 + .85 = -2.78$ (i.e., about the same as the straight 3-year note).

LIMITATIONS OF DURATION AND THE CONCEPT OF CONVEXITY

Convexity can be used to correct one major limitation of duration, but there are other subtler but more severe limitations of both duration and convexity. Duration and convexity work well for single-bond portfolios, but most actual situations involve multiple-bond portfolios. Consider a simple portfolio consisting of equal amounts invested in one bond with duration of 5 years and another with duration of 10 years. The overall duration is 7.5 years. If the yields on both bonds change by an equal number of basis points (and letting the yield change be small, to ignore the convexity problem), duration will accurately give us the change in value of the portfolio and enable us to immunize. But parallel shifts in the yield curve are not particularly common.

Also, in global bond portfolios, a basis-point change is more probable in some currencies (e.g., the Italian lira) than in others (e.g., the Swiss franc). Duration says nothing of the probability of a change; it only measures the effect of a change. To handle these problems, people have begun to consider more complex measures of risk, of which the most prominent is value at risk (VAR). Before approaching this concept, we will start with some introductory statistics that underlie the VAR approach.

STATISTICAL CONCEPTS

Mean and Standard Deviation

Two important concepts are the mean and standard deviation of a series of numbers. Consider five firms that ship goods by road from New York to Boston. The firms' losses due to accidents, theft, and so on, are: $10, $20, $30, $50, and $90 respectively. The mean, or average, is ($10 + $20 + $30 + $50 + $90)/5 = $40.

In many cases, however, we must know how much variation in experience has taken place. We therefore need a measure of the variability of the data. The most common measure is the variance, or its square root, the standard deviation. We calculate the deviation of each case from the mean (designated $\overline{X}$). Because the deviations may be positive or negative, and hence would cancel if added up, we first square the deviations before adding them:

X	$(X - \overline{X})$	$(X - \overline{X})^2$
10	−30	900
20	−20	400
30	−10	100
50	10	100
90	50	2,500
		4,000

For technical reasons involving the sample size, we divide the total of 4,000 by (n − 1), where n is the number of observations. Thus, we arrive at a figure for the variance of 4,000/4 = 1,000. But this is in units of dollar-squared, which is not very meaningful. The standard deviation is the square root of the variance, and so is measured in more understandable units. In this case, $\sqrt{1,000}$ = $31.62. Thus, we can say the average (or mean) loss is $40, and the standard deviation is $31.62. This gives an idea of how variable the underlying data are.

The formal definitions are as follows:

$$\text{Mean } \bar{x} = \frac{\sum_{i=1}^{n} x_i}{n}$$

$$\text{Variance } \sigma^2 = \frac{\sum_{i=1}^{n} (x_i - \bar{x})^2}{n-1}$$ (if the variance is for a population rather than a sample of the population, we divide by n).

Covariance and Correlation

It is often necessary to consider how two sets of data are related. A common measure of relationship is the covariance of the two sets of data. Suppose that two stock markets, A and B, show the following pattern of percentage return, measured over 100 periods:

		A			
B	10	20	30	40	Total
10	20	4	1		25
20	10	36	9		55
30		5	10		15
40				5	5
Total	30	45	20	5	100

In other words, if B produces a 10 percent return, A also produces 10 percent during 20 percent of the time; but during 4 percent of the time, A produces 20 percent when B produces 10 percent, and, during 1 percent of the time, if B produces 10 percent, A produces 30 percent. We could calculate from these data that the variance of A's returns is 70, and the variance of B's is 60.

But we are interested in how well correlated the two markets' returns are. If the two returns are perfectly correlated, there is nothing to choose between them, and their results are probably explained by general world economic conditions. However, there might be a significant difference between them.

For this information, we need the covariance, which is defined as:

$$\sigma_{A,B} = \frac{\sum_{i=1}^{n} (A_i - \mu_A)(B_i - \mu_B)}{n}$$

where A_i and B_i are the returns earned by A and B, μ is defined as the mean of the variable in question, and we have n observations. If we do the calculations, we find that the covariance is 49; but, like the variance, its units of measure are confusing. In this example, because both items are measured in percentages, the covariance is measured in percentage squared, which is not very meaningful. A more useful measure is the correlation, which we define as follows:

$$\rho = \frac{\sigma_{AB}}{\sigma_A \sigma_B}$$

The advantage of this definition is that it is independent of scale. Correlation is always between −1 and +1 (or −100 percent to +100 percent). A correlation of −1 indicates a perfect negative correlation: a rise in one variable is associated with a matching fall in the other. Conversely, a correlation of +1 implies that a rise in one is always associated with a matching rise in the other. And a correlation of zero means that the two are independent.

In our example, we have $49/\sqrt{60} * \sqrt{70} = 0.76$. In other words, about three-fourths of the time, the two markets are producing similar returns.

PROBABILITY DISTRIBUTIONS

A probability distribution is a model for an actual or empirical distribution. Consider an experiment in which three coins are tossed simultaneously and the number of heads that show is recorded. The number of heads, X, can take any one of the values 0, 1, 2, or 3. Thus, X is called a discrete random variable. There are eight possible heads (H)/tails (T) outcomes to the experiment: TTT, TTH, THT, HTT, THH, HTH, HHT, HHH. Assuming the coins to be fair, each outcome is equally likely. In repeated trials, therefore, we would expect X to take the value 0 in one out of eight, the value 1 in three out of eight, and so on. Therefore, the probability distribution for the experiment, denoted by P(X) is:

n	0	1	2	3
P(X = n)	1/8	3/8	3/8	1/8

Actually performing the experiment would produce an empirical distribution that should grow closer to the theoretical distribution as the number of tosses increases.

The cumulative distribution function gives the probability that an observation X is less than or equal to the value n; it is usually denoted by F(x). For the example above, we have:

n	0	1	2	3
F(n)	1/8	4/8	7/8	1

It is certain that n will be less than or equal to 3; the chances are 7 out of 8 that it will be less than or equal to 2, and so on.

In this example, we are considering a discrete set of outcomes (0, 1, 2, 3) and hence a discrete probability distribution. It is equally possible to have a continuous probability distribution—for example, the probability that the return on a portfolio lies between 5 percent and 10 percent is associated with a continuous probability distribution.

Some Important Probability Distributions

In this section, three important probability distributions will be discussed: (1) the binomial distribution for discrete variables (those where events can be classed as happening at specific points in time rather than in continuous time), and (2) the normal and (3) log normal distributions for continuous variables.

The binomial distribution is a discrete probability distribution and is defined as follows. Suppose there are n independent trials of an experiment with only the same two possible outcomes at each trial, usually denoted "success" and "failure," and p is the probability of success in a single trial. Then the probability, p(x), of obtaining x successes from the n trials is given by the binomial distribution. This is:

$$p(x) = \frac{n!}{x!(n-x)!} p^x (1-p)^{n-x}$$

where n! means "n factorial," i.e., $n \times (n-1) \times (n-2) \times (n-3) \times \ldots \times [n - (n-1)]$.

As is well known (and illustrated below), the binomial distribution can be approximated by the normal distribution.

The Normal Distribution. The Central Limit Theorem (often loosely described as the law of large numbers) is the reason for the central role of the normal distribution in statistical theory. Very many distributions tend toward the normal, given a sufficient number of observations.

Consider the following simple example. A conventional six-sided die is tossed n times, and the total score T is noted. If n = 1, T may take the values 1, 2, 3, 4, 5, 6 with probability 1/6 in each case. The binomial formula has been simplified to p(x) = p. This gives a uniform distribution, which has a mean of 3.5 and a variance of 2.916, and is plotted in Figure 3.4. The normal distribution, with the same mean and variance, is also shown. The two probability distributions are clearly quite different.

Suppose now we toss the die twice: n = 2. Now T may take the values 2, 3, . . . , 12 with probabilities 1/36, 2/36, 3/36, 4/36, 5/36, 6/36, . . . 1/36. That is, the probability of throwing a total of 2 is the probability of throwing 1 each time: which we know is (1/6)*(1/6) = 1/36. But we can throw a total of 3 in two ways: by throwing 2 and 1, or 1 and 2. Hence, the probability that T = 3 is 2/36. We can throw a total of 4 in three ways: 1 + 3, 3 + 1, or 2 + 2; hence, its probability

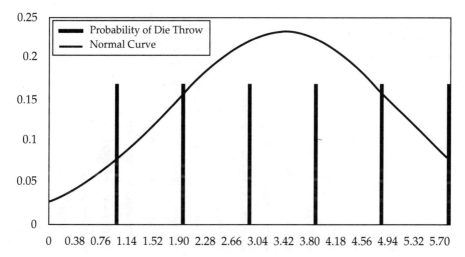

Figure 3.4   The uniform and the normal distribution.

is 3/36, and so on. This distribution, with mean 7 and variance 5.83, is plotted in Figure 3.5, together with a normal distribution having the same mean and variance. They resemble one another rather more closely than before.

Similarly, when n = 3, we get a probability distribution with a mean of 10.5 and a variance of 8.75. In Figure 3.6, we plot the normal distribution having the same mean and variance. Here, the resemblance between the two distributions is quite noticeable.

This example was chosen because the two distributions converge quickly. But the same process holds good, even if it happens more slowly, for many statistical distributions. Hence the great importance of the normal distribution in statistics. If we have large numbers of observations—for example, of percentage

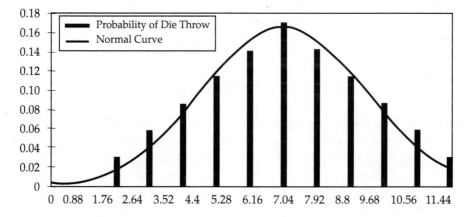

Figure 3.5   Throwing the die twice.

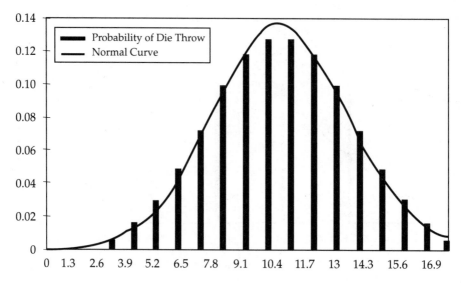

Figure 3.6   Three throws of the die.

changes in exchange rates, or claims under motor insurance policies—it is often practical to assume that they are normally distributed.

The Log-Normal Distribution.   A random variable X has a log-normal distribution with mean μ and variance σ if Y = ln(X) (where ln denotes natural logarithm) has the normal distribution with mean μ and variance σ. Often, as we shall see in the discussion of value at risk below, it is convenient to assume that the returns from holding an asset are normally distributed. It is often convenient to define the return in logarithmic form as $\ln(P_t/P_{t-1})$, where P_t is the price today and P_{t-1} is the previous price. If this is assumed to be normally distributed, then the underlying price will have a log-normal distribution. The log-normal distribution never goes to a negative value, unlike the normal distribution, and hence is intuitively more suitable for asset prices. The distribution is shown in Figure 3.7.

CONFIDENCE INTERVALS

Suppose that we have an estimate, $\bar{x}$, of the average of a given statistical population, where the true mean of the population is μ. Suppose also that we believe that, on average, $\bar{x}$ is an unbiased estimator of μ. Although this means that, on average, $\bar{x}$ is accurate, the specific sample mean that we observe will almost certainly be above or below the true level. Accordingly, if we want to be reasonably confident that our inference is correct, we cannot claim that μ is precisely

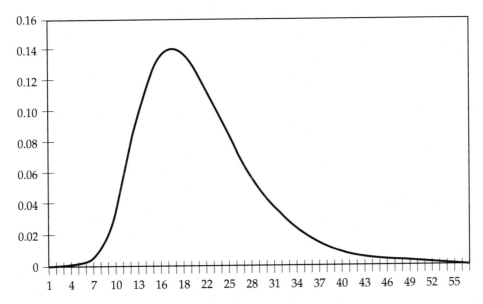

Figure 3.7 The log-normal distribution.

equal to the observed $\bar{x}$. Instead, we must construct an interval estimate or confidence interval of the form: $\mu = \bar{x} \pm$ sampling error.

The crucial question is: How wide must this confidence interval be? The answer, of course, will depend on how much $\bar{x}$ fluctuates. The first step is to establish how stringent our requirements are. Suppose that we decide that we want to be 95 percent confident that our estimate is accurate. Suppose also that we believe that the elements of the population are normally distributed. In that case, we would expect that the population would be distributed along the lines portrayed in Figure 3.8.

A well-known feature of the normal distribution is that 2.5 percent of the outcomes of a normally distributed process can be expected to fall more than 1.96 standard deviations from the mean. Therefore, 95 percent of the outcomes can be expected to fall within ±1.96 standard deviations; that is, there is a 95 percent chance that the random variable $\bar{x}$ will fall between μ −1.96 standard deviations and μ + 1.96 standard deviations. This would be referred to as a "two-sided" confidence interval. It measures the probability of a move upward or downward by the random variable outside the limits we would normally expect.

A case can be made, however, that we should consider a one-sided test only if we are concerned with the risk of loss; a move upward into profit is of less concern. It is well known that 5 percent of the outcomes of a normally distributed process can be expected to fall more than 1.65 standard deviations from the mean. This would be referred to as a one-sided confidence interval.

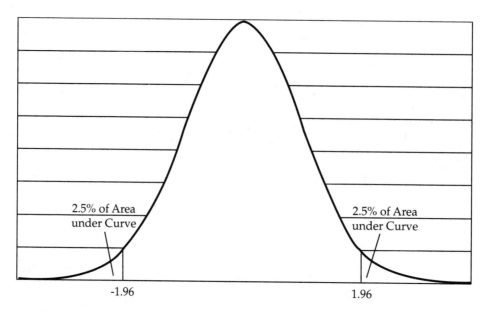

Figure 3.8 95 percent of the outcomes can be expected to fail within ±1.96.

In less scientific language, suppose we have a position in sterling: We are long of sterling at $1.70. We believe that (1) $1.70 represents the mean of sterling's distribution, and (2) the sterling exchange rate has an annual standard deviation of 17 cents (10 percent volatility). In that case, if we wish to have a 95 percent confidence interval for sterling, we will set the interval at 1.65 times 17 cents (assuming a one-sided confidence interval)—that is, an interval of 28.05 cents. In other words, we are 95 percent confident that sterling will remain above $1.4195 during the next year.

Alternatively, if we were to set a two-sided confidence interval, we would use an interval of 1.96 times 17 cents, or 33.32 cents. In this case, we would expect, with 95 percent confidence, that sterling would remain in the range of $1.3668 to $2.0332.

An annual standard deviation of 17 cents will translate into a smaller daily movement. In fact, to convert from annual to daily, we must divide the annual rate by $1/\sqrt{250}$. (The denominator of 250 arises from the assumed number of 250 working days in the year. We use the square root to conform with the definition of the normal distribution.) Thus, the daily standard deviation is $17/15.811 = 1.07517$ cents.

Hence, on a daily basis, using a one-sided confidence interval, we would be 95 percent confident that sterling would not fall by more than $1.65 \times 1.07517 = 1.77404$ cents. That is, we would be 95 percent confident that sterling would remain above $1.6822. Using a two-sided confidence interval, we would be 95 percent confident that sterling would remain within the range $1.70 ± (1.96 × 1.07517) = $1.6789 – 1.7211.

MODERN PORTFOLIO THEORY

Studying the correlation between markets led Harry Markowitz, in 1952, to develop the so-called "mean–variance" framework for analyzing investment risk and performance. These ideas led to the development of so-called modern portfolio theory. This, in turn, lies behind risk measurement techniques such as RiskMetrics™—discussed below—and the current debate over the implementation of the BIS rules for measuring market risk.

The point of modern portfolio theory is that *risk falls as one includes different types of assets, as long as their returns are not perfectly correlated. Diversification pays.* Suppose you hold both equities and bonds. Normally, *both* won't perform badly in the same year, so a weak performance of one will be offset by the other. The portfolio as a whole will be more stable than either asset individually. Diversifying has reduced your risk.

Let's look at a practical example. Suppose you think, after studying history and making your forecasts, that the following asset classes will produce a certain pattern of risks (defined as standard deviation of return) and returns. Let's say, over the next 5 years, you expect these performances:

	U.S. Bonds	Non-U.S. Bonds
Return	8%	9.5%
Risk	9	12

You believe the returns will have a correlation of 0.4; that is, U.S. bond returns will vary in line with non-U.S. bond returns 40 percent of the time.

To work out the risk of the combined portfolio, we need the covariance between the two assets—that is, the standard deviation of each asset (or pair of assets) multiplied together and weighted by the correlation between the assets. The covariance is then $.09 \times .12 \times .4 = .00432$. We'll also need the variances of the two assets, or the square of the standard deviation (.0081 and .0144, respectively).

Combining Assets

We can find the risk and return of a portfolio by combining these elements. Suppose we start by holding everything in U.S. bonds. Then we gradually push up the share of non-U.S. bonds to 100 percent. Finding the return requires only an easy calculation: a weighted average. The risk is a little more tricky.

Let's start with the risk when we have 30 percent in non-U.S. bonds. The calculation is $.0081 \times .49 + .0144 \times .09 + 2 \times .7 \times .3 \times .00432 = .0070794$. In words: (U.S. bonds variance × square of 70 percent weight) + (non-U.S. bonds' variance × square of 30 percent weight) + 2 × (70 percent U.S. weight × 30 percent non-U.S. weight × covariance).

The result is the variance of the combined portfolio. To find the standard deviation, we take the square root, which comes out at .084139 or 8.41 percent. Now we do the sums for all the different weights:

U.S. Fixed	Non-U.S.	Risk	Return
100%	0%	9.00%	8.0%
90	10	8.65	8.1
80	20	8.45	8.2
70	30	8.41	8.3
60	40	8.54	8.4
50	50	8.82	8.5
etc.			

Combined Portfolio

As you push up the share of non-U.S. bonds to 30 percent, the risk of the combined portfolio falls from 9.00 percent to 8.41 percent. *While the risk is falling, though, the return is rising.* You can get 30 basis points more return for less risk, if you push the share of non-U.S. bonds from 0 percent to 30 percent.

Value at Risk

These concepts underlie one of the basic ideas in modern financial risk management, value at risk (VAR). This measures the potential loss in market value of a portfolio using estimated volatility (which defines an adverse rate or price move) and correlations (which indicate how rates and/or prices move in relation to one another). Portfolio optimization techniques on the basis of the Markowitz mean-variance approach have been applied in investment management since the 1950s. But only recently have the methods for estimating portfolio risk been extended to measure short-term trading risks taken by banks or other market participants. Risk is measured within a given confidence interval, typically 95 percent or 99 percent. The longer the time horizon over which we are measuring, the greater the possible dispersion of outcomes, as illustrated in Figure 3.9, which shows a series of normal curves whose standard deviation increases over time. Today, the curve is fairly tightly bunched around zero; in a short time interval, we expect mostly small changes. As time passes, the curves flatten (the frequency of any given change becomes less) and become broader (there is a wider range of possible outcomes). The width of the area included within the confidence interval—our value at risk—will increase, as will the size of the best case/worst case changes.

The VAR concept seeks to measure the possible losses from a position or portfolio under "normal" circumstances. The definition of "normal" is critical. The answer to this question is, in essence, a statistical one.

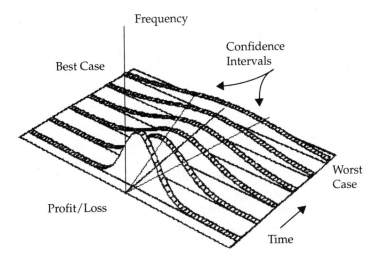

Figure 3.9   The longer the time horizon the greater the dispersion of outcomes.

RiskMetrics

In 1994. J.P. Morgan introduced RiskMetrics™, a model for risk measurement issuing VAR. Here, we simply assume that changes in prices and yields of financial instruments are normally distributed. Given this assumption, volatility can be expressed in terms of the distribution of changes' standard deviation from the mean. The RiskMetrics approach has been to use 1.65 standard deviations as its measure of risk, which encompasses 95 percent of occurrences (because risk measures only a negative outcome, one side of the distribution is excluded). That is, the RiskMetrics approach uses a one-sided 95 percent confidence interval as its measure.

The RiskMetrics approach's assumptions imply two key results:

1. By setting a confidence level of 95 percent, we say that we accept a 5 percent chance that the market will move beyond our parameters. That is, on 1 day in 20, sterling will fall by more than 1.77404 cents (using a one-sided confidence interval).

2. We accept the risk that, in reality, the exchange rate moves in a nonnormal manner. Many rates evidence "fat tails": the number and size of large changes are higher than forecast by a normal distribution. On the other hand, J.P. Morgan argues that there is not yet sufficient evidence to suggest that this discrepancy is large enough to justify abandoning the assumption of normal distribution.

The RiskMetrics approach defines market risk, first, in terms of *absolute market risk:* the estimate of total loss expressed in currency terms (e.g., dollars at risk). Alternatively, we may define risk in terms of *relative market risk.* This concept, more relevant to the investment management community, measures the risk of underperformance against a benchmark index.

Second, RiskMetrics defines risk in terms of a time horizon, "Daily Earnings at Risk," which measures the potential loss. Value at risk measures the potential loss in a position that one assumes can be hedged or closed out over a given period. It will be applicable for positions that take longer than 24 hours to neutralize, or for investment portfolios that have a longer performance measurement cycle. RiskMetrics bases its estimates of volatility and correlations on historical data. This is J.P. Morgan's choice. There are various alternative approaches to estimating future volatility—for example, subjective forecasts or, alternatively, implied volatilities from exchange-traded instruments can be used. On the other hand, many instruments are not exchange-traded. Nor is the forecasting power of implied volatility necessarily greater than that of historical volatility. The RiskMetrics approach therefore has been to use exponentially weighted moving averages of historical rate movements. This ensures that the volatility estimates will not only respond quickly to market shocks, but will also gradually revert back to more "normal" levels.

In essence, RiskMetrics consists of two things: (1) a publicly available process to map positions into their risk components and estimate their market risk, and (2) the RiskMetrics data set of market volatilities and correlations which is reestimated daily. These are published in computer-readable form via Reuters, Telerate, the Internet, and a number of other systems. In 1996, J.P. Morgan came to an agreement with Reuters that the latter would take over the data maintenance for RiskMetrics.

APPENDIX

Proof that modified duration gives the sensitivity of a bond to interest rate changes.

$$\text{Formal definitions: price of bond: } P = \sum_{t=1}^{n} \frac{C_t}{(1+y)^t}$$

$$\text{Duration: } D = \frac{\sum_{t=1}^{n} \frac{tC_t}{(1+y)^t}}{P}$$

Where D = duration
       P = price of bond
       C_t = cash flow at time t
       y = yield

Now we differentiate P with respect to y:

$$dP/dY = -\sum_{t=1}^{n} tC_t(1+y)^{-t-1}$$

Multiply by $(1+y)$: $(1+y)\, dP/dY = -\sum_{i=1}^{n} tC_t(1+y)^{-t}$

Finally divide by P: $\dfrac{dP}{dY}\dfrac{1+y}{P} = -\sum_{t=1}^{n}\dfrac{tC_t}{(1+y)^t P} = -D$

If we define modified duration (MD) as $D/(1+y)$ then

$$-\frac{dP}{dY}\frac{1}{P} = MD$$

Thus modified duration measures the proportionate impact on the price of the bond of a change in yield; the sign is negative because, of course, rising yields depress bond prices. For example, if modified duration is 5.1 years, if yield rises by 1 percent the bond price falls by 5.1 percent.

Chapter **4**

Forwards and Futures

FORWARDS

In many financial markets, participants will agree with one another to buy or sell an instrument for delivery at a fixed future date. There are two possible ways of doing this: through a forward contract or through a futures contract. The key difference between these two is that the forward contract is normally a bilateral contract between the two parties. No one else is involved. The two parties rely on each other to complete the bargain. Hence, they may have credit risk on each other if one of the parties fails to complete (the market may have moved adversely in the interim, causing them loss from the counterparty's failure).

A futures contract resembles a forward in that it is a contract for future delivery. But the differences are:

1. The futures contract will be traded on an organized exchange, such as the Chicago Board of Trade (CBOT) or the London International Financial Futures Exchange (LIFFE).

2. The contract will be for a standardized amount.

3. The counterparty to the contract will normally be the clearing division of the exchange or an independent clearinghouse, cutting out the two parties' credit risk on each other.

4. To protect itself, the clearinghouse will require each party to the contract to deposit margin with it.

The differences between the two contracts are evident from the cash flows (Figures 4.1 and 4.2).

Figure 4.1 illustrates a normal forward contract: an agreement today to exchange, at some later date, a financial instrument against cash. No cash flows take place between now and the delivery date. (Margined forward contracts are an exception, but, because these are generally not as common as standard forwards, we will ignore them here.)

By contrast, Figure 4.2 illustrates that when we enter into a futures contract (in this example, for the future delivery of a bond), there will usually be interim

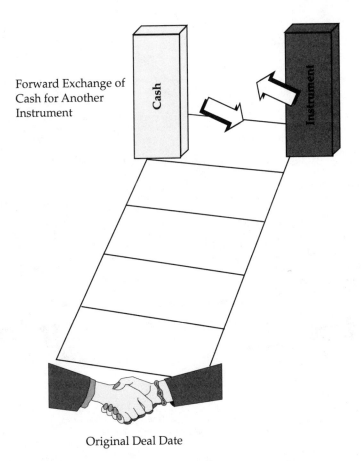

Cash

Instrument

Forward Exchange of
Cash for Another
Instrument

Original Deal Date

Figure 4.1 Forward contract.

cash flows between now and the delivery date as we make or receive margin payments to and from the futures clearinghouse.

Forward Contracts

Because they are generally the simpler instrument to analyze, we will begin with forward contracts. Suppose I contract today to deliver a Ford car to you, at a price of $10,000, payable today. Then you propose a variation: because you will be out of the country, you request a postponement of the payment, and of the delivery of the car, for one year. What is now a fair price for the car, given that I have to wait a year for my money? Suppose the rate of interest is 10 percent annually. If I had $10,000 today, I could invest it and have $11,000 a year from now. I decide to charge you $11,000 for the forward delivery of the car.

The asset being sold forward here (the car) paid no interest. But most instruments in financial markets bear interest or pay dividends. So the forward price of such an instrument needs to be adjusted. The final price takes account

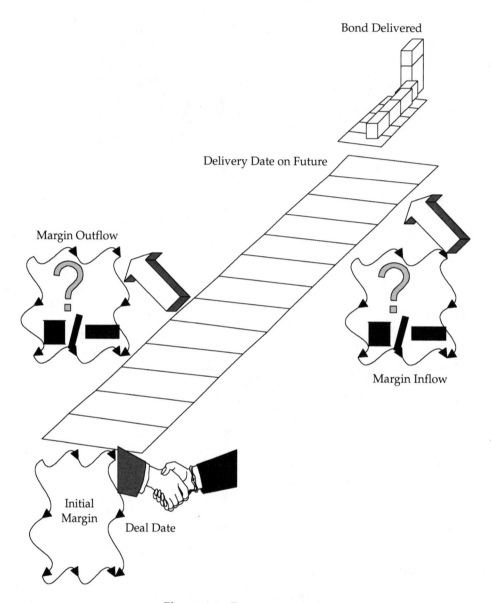

Figure 4.2 Futures contract.

of the interest or dividends forgone by the buyers when they accept delayed delivery, as against the interest the buyers earn on the cash to be used in payment for the instrument.

Consider a 30-year U.S. Treasury bond paying an annual rate of interest of 6 percent. (For simplicity, we will assume that the interest is paid in a lump sum at the end of the year.) Suppose that: (1) the market value today of this bond is 100; (2) we contract to sell forward $10,000 (face value) of this bond for delivery in 1 year; and (3) the rate of interest for 1 year is 10 percent. At the end of the year, we will have a $10,000 face value bond (with a market price of 100, assuming no change in rates) plus the coupon of $600. But the buyer will have $11,000 from the proceeds of investing cash for 1 year. If we sold today to someone else, we too could be in that favorable position. To induce us to sell the bond forward, the price of the bond cannot be a par amount of 100. It must be more. In fact, it must be:

$$100 \times \frac{\$11,000}{\$10,600} = 103.77$$

Only at this price is the present value of the asset receivable (bond plus 1 year's coupon) equal to the present value of the asset payable in exchange (today's $10,000 invested for a year).

From this example, we can construct a general rule: The forward price of an asset is found from its accumulated value from today to the forward delivery date. We compare the forward price with the accumulated value of the asset that will be exchanged for it. In our example, we exchanged a bond for cash, but the exchange could well be one currency for another, or a bond being exchanged for equity. We can write:

$$F = S \times \left(\frac{1 + r1}{1 + r2} \right)$$

where F = the forward price for asset 2 in terms of asset 1;
  S = the price today (the "spot" price);
  r1 = the return on asset 1;
  r2 = the return on asset 2.

In our example, we have F = 100 × (1.10/1.06) = 103.77. We can state a further general rule: The asset with the lower return must trade at a premium in the forward market. This compensates the seller for delaying delivery. As we saw above, the bond had a lower return than cash, and therefore it had to be sold at a premium forward—103.77 compared with its price of 100 today. Similarly, in forward foreign exchange markets, the low-coupon currency always trades at a forward premium. This relationship is critical to forward foreign exchange markets, forward rate agreements, bond and equity futures, and the instruments that are constructed from these underlying markets.

The "Carrusel."   This interesting variant of the forward contract has developed in the Colombian market. A "carrusel" is a contract whereby two or more investors agree to own, in turn, a single security for periods of time that add up to its entire maturity. The parties to the contract are identified as head, body, and tail. The head is the party that buys the security from a broker, registers the transaction, and commits to the sale of the security at a future date and price. The body is made up of one or more investors. They commit themselves to buying and selling the same security, at prices and future dates specified at the beginning of the contract. The tail is the last buyer of the security, who holds it until maturity.

The carrusel was developed by stockbrokers as a marketing tool to entice investors to buy securities with maturities that extended beyond their planned investment horizons. It offered some assurance that the security could be sold even if the market went through a temporary phase of illiquidity—a common situation in Colombia. Brokers also realized very quickly that with an upward-sloping yield curve, returns to investors could be made to appear attractive, because they were forward rates. Investors unfamiliar with this analysis could be persuaded of the attraction.

The instrument is not a very efficient derivative; it implies a chain of forward credit risks. On the other hand, it represents an interesting extension of the repo market to the forward market.

Currencies

Although by no means a new instrument, we should mention here that there has existed, for years, a very large market for forward contracts on foreign currencies. (This is discussed in more depth in my earlier book, *Foreign Exchange and Money Markets Guide,* John Wiley & Sons, Inc., 1992.) We will return to this market later, in the context of currency options, but it may be helpful to outline the basic mechanics briefly here.

A forward foreign exchange contract is an agreement between a bank and another party to exchange one currency for another at some future date. The rate at which the exchange is to be made, the delivery date, and the amounts involved are fixed at the time of agreement.

The following terms are common in discussion of currencies:

- **Spot:** A foreign exchange contract for exchange of currencies in two working days.

- **Outright forward:** A foreign exchange contract for the exchange of currencies at some specified future date.

- **Swap:** A contract that consists of two simultaneous contracts; (1) a sale/purchase of a currency for one date (normally, spot) and (2) the *contra* purchase/sale at a later date. Effectively, the swap is a trade in the forward margin between the two currencies.

A related instrument traded in the foreign exchange markets is the swap. Swaps of this type are covered briefly in Chapter 5, where they are compared with the more recent "currency swap." The prime difference between the two is that the traditional forward foreign exchange swap involves only a spot purchase coupled with a forward sale (or vice versa). There are only two movements of cash, whereas the currency swap normally entails a number of cash flows over several years.

Another instrument that should be mentioned here is the *nondeliverable forward contract.* Although this is hardly a new instrument in the sense applied elsewhere in this book, it has been included because of its growth in importance in a number of emerging markets, particularly in Asia. It is, in some ways, the equivalent of a cash-settled OTC futures contract; alternatively, it can be thought of simply as a traditional forward foreign exchange contract. The difference, compared to the traditional forward foreign exchange contract discussed above, is that, instead of having each party deliver currency to settle the contract, a cash settlement is made of the profit or loss.

Suppose a U.S. multinational wants to hedge its exposure to the Philippines peso. It might wish to sell pesos forward, but this activity might be against regulations in Manila. Instead, it might sell forward in New York to an American bank, using a nondeliverable forward contract. The American bank can (1) seek a counterpart with the opposite need, (2) find a way to hedge in Manila, or (3) accept the open exchange risk. When the contract comes to settle, the profit or loss is paid in New York.

The primary reason for using such an approach is to circumvent exchange control regulations—or, possibly, for tax reasons. Deals of this kind were done for years in the Irish punt market, for example, when Irish regulations required that a deal done in Dublin had to be supported by documentary evidence of an export/import transaction. However, there have also been recent suggestions that the instrument could be used to cut down counterparty exposure on forward foreign exchange (since the settlement risk is only the cash difference—compare SAFEs below).

FRAs

Forward-forward rates are dealt through an active market in London and in certain other centers for forward rate agreements (FRAs). These are contracts between banks and their customers, or other banks, that allow for the forward hedging of interest rate movements; they are the money market equivalent of forward foreign exchange contracts. Another way of describing them is to say they are single-period interest rate swaps.

Forward rate agreements provide a very useful way to hedge against future movements in interest rates. Their prime advantage is that they allow this to be done without tying up large parts of the balance sheet. Until the FRA market was developed in the early 1980s, banks would trade their view of interest rates through the forward-forward market (see above). But this meant taking and placing deposits for the periods in question, which meant inflating both the asset and liability sides of the balance sheet. FRAs are a much more efficient method of handling the interest rate hedging required.

■ **A Forward rate agreement** is one where a notional borrower agrees with a notional lender on the rate of interest that will be applied to a notional loan for some period in the future. (Note the use of the word *notional*; there is no actual borrowing or lending involved. When the time comes to settle, all that happens is an exchange of cash equal to the difference between the actual rate on the day of settlement and the rate agreed on in the FRA.)

- **The buyer of the FRA** is the notional borrower—the party seeking protection against a rise in rates.

- **The seller** is the notional lender—the party seeking protection against a fall in rates.

- **The contract amount (CA)** is the notional sum on which the FRA is based.

- **The contract rate (CR)** is the rate of interest being hedged, usually LIBOR.

- **The contract period (CP)** is the term from settlement date to maturity date—that is, the term of the notional deposit/loan.

- **The settlement date** is the date on which the settlement sum is payable.

- **The maturity date** is the date on which the notional loan/deposit matures.

- **The settlement rate (SR)** is the rate fixed on the fixing date as being that applicable to the settlement on the FRA.

- **The fixing date** is the date on which the settlement rate is fixed; for LIBOR, that would normally be 2 business days ahead.

- **The settlement sum** is the sum paid in settlement of the FRA.

The settlement sum, if paid at maturity, would be $(SR - CR) \times CP/360 \times CA/100$, assuming the currency in question is dealt on a 360-day-year basis. However, the custom in the FRA market is to pay the settlement sum on the settlement date. (The practical benefit is that this clears the deal off the books and cuts down the credit exposure that would arise if one had to wait until the notional maturity date to be paid.)

Thus, the settlement sum has to be discounted back from the amount that would be payable at maturity to its present value today. For this, we use the present value formula developed in Chapter 3. Thus, for a sum paid on the settlement date, the value would be discounted back at the LIBOR agreed on for the settlement date:

$$\frac{(SR - CR) \times \dfrac{CP}{360} \times \dfrac{CA}{100}}{1 + SR \times \dfrac{CP}{36,000}}$$

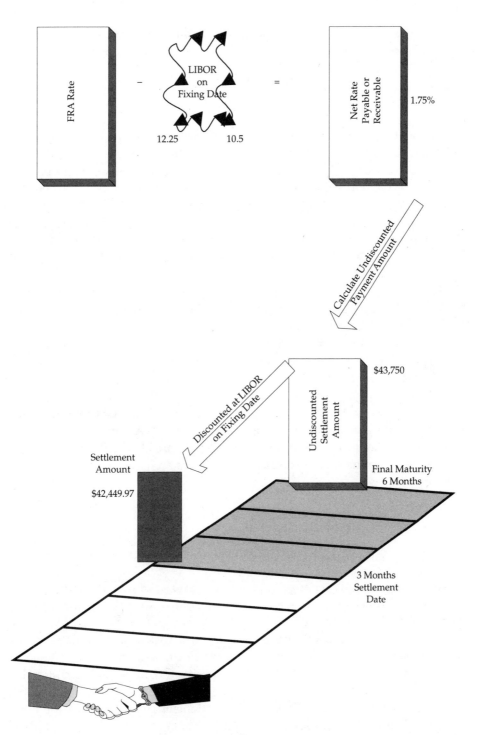

Figure 4.3 FRA Calculations.

Note that the numerator is the same as before; the denominator is the discount factor to bring the value back to today. The formula can be simplified to

$$\frac{(SR - CR) \times CP \times CA}{36,000 + (SR \times CP)}.$$

Let's look at an example. I buy a 3×6 FRA for a contract amount (CA) of $10 million. The rate (CR) is 10.5 percent. The contract period (CP) is 90 days. When the contract comes to settle, the settlement rate (SR) is 12.25 percent. Then the settlement value of the FRA is $(12.25 - 10.5) \times 90/360 \times 10,000,000/100/[1 + (12.25 \times 90/36,000)]$. This gives us $43,750/1.030625 = $42,449.97. Had we been prepared to wait for settlement until the end of the contract period, the sum payable would have been $43,750; the discount factor we apply to find the present value on the settlement date is 1.030625. Figure 4.3 on page 61 illustrates the trade.

The way in which FRAs are priced is simple. If there is a financial futures market for a comparable instrument, pricing is taken from the futures market. If not, it is taken from the cash deposit yield curve. Forward forward rates for the period in question are worked out (using the formula set out in Chapter 3) and applied to FRAs. Thus, if I wanted to find the correct price for the 3×6 sterling FRA, I could look at either the LIFFE 3-month sterling deposit future contract, or the yield curve for 3-month and 6-month sterling deposits. From these I would work out the forward deposit rate for 3 months versus 6 months and this would give me the rate applicable for the FRA. Because the forward deposit market and the FRA and futures markets are all closely integrated, arbitrage will keep the three markets in line. FRAs are now traded widely in all major currencies.

SYNTHETIC AGREEMENTS FOR FORWARD EXCHANGE (SAFE)

A SAFE is the foreign exchange equivalent of a forward rate agreement: a contract for differences that acts as a substitute for a forward-forward foreign exchange deal. It originated in proprietary products developed by certain commercial banks, and was developed into an instrument available to the London market as a whole under the aegis of the British Bankers' Association. It is not very widely used, but its ability to reduce settlement risk is attractive.

In essence, the SAFE cuts down the settlement risk—and thus the credit exposure—on a forward-forward foreign exchange contract. Suppose today 1 month against 4-month forward-forward dollar sterling swaps were trading at 55/51. Today is May 6, 1999 with spot May 10 and the 1-month date June 10, the 4-months date September 12.

Suppose I buy sterling forward-forward at 51 (that is, I contract to sell it on June 10 and buy it back on September 12). Suppose on June 10 when the deal then comes to settle, the forward margin for that period is 60. Then I can close out at a profit of 9 points. But that profit would in theory only be due in September. To cut down the settlement risk, we can settle the difference today, just like we did in the forward rate agreement. As with the FRA, we will use the relevant BBA interest settlement rate to discount the sums involved.

So far we have ignored any movements in the spot rate during the life of the deal. Suppose now we allow for this; say the spot rate in May is $1.8600 and it has moved to $1.9000 when the deal comes to settle. Suppose I deal a SAFE of £10 million. Then, bearing in mind there will be 93 days from June 10 to September 12 and assuming a BBA interest settlement rate of 7.5 percent, the settlement amount would be:

$$\$10,000,000 \times \left[(1.9000 - 1.8600) + \frac{(1.8600 - .0051) - (1.9000 - .0060)}{\left(1 + \frac{93}{360} \times \frac{7.5}{100}\right)} \right] = \$16,431.64.$$

This SAFE exactly corresponds to a matched pair of swaps. Under the first, forward-forward sap done on May 6, I buy £10 million at $1.8600 value June 10 and sell £10 million at $1.8549 value September 12; this is closed off with a second swap on June 8 where I sell £10 million at $1.9000 value June 10 and buy back £10 million at $1.8940 value September 12. The key difference is that under the SAFE I am not contractually obliged to make or take payments in the amount of £10 million: I am only obliged to settle the difference amount, which as we see is a very small sum compared with the principal amounts. Thus, like a forward rate agreement and an interest rate swap, and for the same reasons (it is driven by interest differentials) the SAFE incurs a credit exposure which is only a fraction of the amount of the notional underlying principal. Compare the nondeliverable forwards discussed earlier. (The background to SAFE is discussed more fully in my *Foreign Exchange and Money Markets Guide*, John Wiley & Sons, Inc., 1992.)

FUTURES

Futures contracts are standardized agreements to buy or sell a specific commodity at a specific time and place in the future, at a price established through open outcry in a central, regulated marketplace. The two key components of a futures contract are: (1) the agreement is standardized and (2) price is the only variable. The origins of such contracts go back to Chicago in the nineteenth century, when futures contracts on grain were first developed. (Some would argue that they go back to the Dutch tulip mania of 1634.)

A financial futures contract is a contract to deliver, or take delivery of, a financial instrument at a future date. For example, a U.S. Treasury bill futures contract is a contract to deliver, or take delivery of, a Treasury bill on a specified date. In some cases (e.g., Eurodollar futures contracts), the contract may be settled by a cash payment.

Let us work through a simple example. I want to invest in a U.S. Treasury bond, with a face value of $100,000, for delivery in June. I can wait until June—taking the risk that the price might move against me—or I can buy a futures contract. I go to the futures market and see that the price for June 15 delivery is 92; if I were to settle today, I would have to pay $92,000. I buy one contract. I do not pay for the bonds today. Instead, I put up a margin deposit.

Suppose the amount of this margin is fixed by the Exchange at $4,000 per contract. I deposit $4,000 with my futures broker. The deposit is evidence of my good faith that I will fulfill my obligation to take delivery of the bonds in June. As bond prices vary, the value of my futures contract varies. I have a profit or loss on my purchase. If losses erode the value of my margin, my broker will call on me to put up extra margin. Conversely, if I earn profits, I will get back some margin. The aim is to keep the margin stable (in line with the value of my obligation).

When the contract comes to settlement, suppose I decide to take delivery of the bonds. A settlement price for the bonds is fixed; say that price is 105. Then I must pay $105,000 for my bonds; but on that settlement day, my futures contract is also worth $105,000. So I have a $13,000 profit on the futures contract, which offsets the rise in price of the bonds. The futures contract has served to fix my bond purchase price.

The main attraction of futures in risk management is their leverage (gearing, in U.K. terminology). Suppose a trader deliberately takes a position, either as a straightforward speculation or as an arbitrage. The simplest case is a trader who wants to back his or her judgment on the outlook for interest rates or currencies. The essential difference between doing this in the futures market and doing it in the "cash market" is that, in the futures market, one can trade on margin. This gives a high degree of leverage, allowing a speculator to make large profits compared to the amount of margin money committed.

Suppose that, on December 1, 2001, a trader thinks interest rates will rise in the next few months, causing bond prices to fall. The trader deposits the required margin (say, $4,000 per contract) with a broker. He sells two Treasury bond futures contracts at 67-00. Two weeks later, interest rates have risen. Prices for Treasury bond futures contracts have dropped to 66-08. The trader closes the position by buying two bond futures contracts and makes a profit of $750 on each contract. The $1,500 profit on the $8,000 margin is a return of over 18 percent during the 2 weeks, before deducting commission and exchange fees. Leverage has increased the trader's returns.

This leverage works both ways; it is possible to lose more money than originally invested. Because of this, prices are marked to market on a daily basis by the exchanges, and settlement is made daily through the clearing corporation. Thus, if prices move against an investor, his or her account is debited.

If the debits reduce the money in the margin account below the prescribed "maintenance" level, additional margin must be posted to bring it back up to the required amount. Hence, through margin calls, investors quickly feel the effect of any weakening in their position. This margin call system has generally protected the exchanges and their member firms from losses via investor default. Although investors are highly leveraged, the margin maintenance system quickly brings to light any potential problems.

Another attractive feature for those who wish to trade in the major futures markets is that they are very liquid. For example, volume on the Chicago Board of Trade Treasury long bond futures contract on March 27, 1997, was over 490,000 contracts for a face value of $49 billion. One could shift a significant volume in this market without making a major impact. In other instruments, this is less true. Many futures contracts have not proved successful, and daily volume is negligible. In this case, someone wishing to trade in a particular instrument that is not readily available is reduced to trading in a proxy instrument and making allowances by means of appropriate weighting factors.

Development of the Market

Table 4.1 (p. 66) gives the year of introduction of major contracts, Table 4.2 (p. 67) shows the main activity in the first half of 1997.

The first financial futures contracts were created when the International Monetary Market (IMM) in Chicago opened futures trading in seven foreign currencies in May 1972. The first interest rate futures contract was introduced in October 1975, but the first really successful interest rate futures contract was the 91-day Treasury bill contract introduced by the Chicago Mercantile Exchange (CME) in January 1976. The Chicago Board of Trade (CBOT) began to issue futures contracts on U.S. Treasury bonds in August 1977.

In September 1982, the London International Financial Futures Exchange (LIFFE) opened for business. It started with Eurodollars; the pound sterling; short sterling interest rates; long gilt-edged government securities; Swiss franc, Japanese yen, and deutsche mark futures. In 1988, it introduced a successful futures contract based on German government bonds (Bunds), and followed this in 1989 with a future based on DEM LIBOR and an option on the Bund future. Next, it issued contracts on the Japanese and Italian government bonds. By 1993, 63 percent of LIFFE's turnover was non-sterling-based, showing just how internationally oriented LIFFE is. Of a total turnover of $135 billion equivalent, the Euromark contract accounted for $45 billion; the short sterling deposit contract, for $36 billion; and the Bund contract, for $12 billion. The rest was spread more or less evenly across the product range.

At the time of writing, the impact on LIFFE's business of the projected replacement of the DEM by the new European economy, the Euro, in 1999 is not

Table 4.1   Year of Introduction of Some of the Major Futures Contracts

1972	IMM	Foreign exchange
1974	IMM, Comex	Gold
1975	CBOT	GNMA
1976	IMM	Treasury bill
1977	CBOT	Treasury bond
		90-day commercial paper
1978	Sydney	Gold futures
1979	Sydney	Bank bill futures
	CBOT	U.S. Treasury 10-year notes
1980	IMM	CD
	Sydney	AUS$ futures
1981	IMM	Eurodollar
1982	LIFFE	£, DEM, CHF, yen
		Euro$, long gilt, 3-month sterling deposits
	CME	S&P 500
1983	Sydney	All Ordinaries Share Price Index
1984	LIFFE	FTSE 100, U.S. Treasury bonds
	Sydney	Australian Treasury bonds
1985	Tokyo SE	JGB futures
1986	MATIF	French government bonds
	SIMEX	Nikkei–DJ futures
1988	Tokyo SE	TOPIX futures
	Osaka SE	Nikkei 225 futures
	LIFFE	Bund future
	MATIF	CAC-40
	CBOT	5-year Treasury note futures
1989	TIFFE	Euroyen, yen/$
	LIFFE	Euro-DEM LIBOR future
1990	DTB	Bund future, DAX future
	CBOT	2-year Treasury note futures
1991	LIFFE	Italian government bond futures
	DTB	BOBL future
1992	MEFF	Spanish government bond future
1993	MEFF-RV	Spanish IBEX-35 future
1994	Osaka	Nikkei 300 futures
1995	IDEM (Italy)	MIB30 equity futures index
1996	MATIF	Notionnel contract altered to match ECU/Euro contract
		MEFF rebases IBEX to IBEX-35+

Table 4.2 Futures Activity, First Half 1997

Million Contracts		Jan–Jun 1997
Chicago Board of Trade	CBOT	116.7
London International Financial Futures Exchange	LIFFE	101.0
Chicago Mercantile Exchange	CME	99.5
Deutsche TerminBorse	DTB	51.4
Marche a Terme International de France	MATIF	37.4
Swiss Options and Financial Futures Exchange	SOFFEX	18.1
Mercado Espanol de Futuros Financieros (Renta Fija)	MEFF RF	14.9
Sydney Futures Exchange	SFE	14.3
Tokyo International Financial Futures Exchange	TIFFE	12.8
Singapore International Monetary Exchange	SIMEX	11.7

Source of Data: Risk, August 1997.

yet clear. But because LIFFE has also established business in Italian BTP bond futures, Swiss LIBOR, and Japanese government bonds (JGBs), it seems likely that it will survive the impact of the European Monetary Union, albeit perhaps with some difficulty, given that the Euro government bond contract and money market contracts will be the subject of fierce competition with MATIF and DTB (see below).

The Tokyo futures market was established in October 1985. In September 1988, the Tokyo Stock Exchange introduced futures based on its TOPIX equity index, and its Osaka counterpart introduced a contract on the Nikkei 225 equity index. In June 1989, the Tokyo International Financial Futures Exchange (TIFFE) opened for business, trading Euroyen and Eurodollar deposit contracts as well as a yen/dollar contract. The former has been successful but the yen/dollar future's volume has been negligible.

After TIFFE, the next important financial futures exchange to open was in France. The Marché à Terme Internationale de France (MATIF) was opened in February 1986 as a center for derivatives trading. The MATIF has established itself as a serious challenger to LIFFE, as has the Deutsche Termin Börse (DTB), which opened in 1990. The latter has been particularly successful in equity options (by 1993, the DAX option was the second most widely traded option contract in the world, after the S&P100), but has had more of a struggle in fixed income, given that LIFFE already had DEM interest rate contracts. However, the DTB BOBL contract (on 5-year German government bonds) defeated the LIFFE BOBL contract in 1993. A key feature of the DTB is that it was the first fully electronic futures exchange (partly because regional jealousies in Germany militated against establishing a single floor in Frankfurt). Its technology has allowed it to install screens overseas, but has also created difficulties for a closer working relationship with Paris. Mutual cooperation was attempted in 1995–1996 in a bid to take over LIFFE's role as the leading European exchange, but broke down because of resistance from the French floor-trading community. In August 1997 DTB announced a merger with SOFFEX, the Swiss exchange.

Organization of the Markets

In most exchanges, with the exception of DTB, which was electronic from the start, trading takes place in the pits during specific hours. However, most exchanges increasingly also have electronic systems for out-of-hours trading (Globex for MATIF until January 1997, when MATIF announced plans to link with the French Stock Exchange's Nouveau Système de Cotation), the APT system for LIFFE, Project A for the CBOT, and so on. The following description focuses on the CME as a typical example. There is a separate trading area for each contract, so there is a bond pit, a Eurodollar pit, and so on. Orders are received on the trading floor by telephone or telex, and passed to the broker in the pit. Traders shout out the quantity and the price at which they want to buy or sell. They also use standard hand signals, especially when trading is noisy.

At the close of each day's trading, every member submits a trade confirmation record for every deal done on behalf of the firm or its customers. Every one of these trades must be "cleared," that is, verified and guaranteed, by the clearinghouse. The clearinghouse settles the account of each member firm at the end of the trading day by matching each of the day's purchases and sales. It collects all losses and pays all profits. Its contribution to the safety of the market is to be the buyer from every seller and the seller to every buyer. A sale of Eurodollar contracts by A to B becomes a sale (by A) to the clearinghouse and a purchase (by B) from the clearinghouse.

This is a key safeguard for users of the exchanges. There is no need to worry who has taken the other side of the trade. The exchange clearinghouse itself guarantees the performance of every trade because the exchange is the other party to every contract. However, the exchange will deal directly only with its clearing members, not with public customers.

In effect, the exchange does business only with its clearing members, and the clearing members do business with all others. For example, the exchange sets margins for its clearing members, and they in turn set margins for their customers. Thus, customer margins flow directly to the clearing member, who, in turn, must settle with the exchange at the close of business each day. The exchange requires a daily cash settlement from the clearing member, based on the day's market positions and activity and regardless of the status of the member's customer margin money. A clearing member might let a customer be short of margin for a period of time, but the short position would have to be funded at the member's own expense. The clearinghouse would not allow a clearing member to be undermargined overnight. The exchange also supervises the financial status of its clearing members. So far, these arrangements appear to have been successful in preventing major problems; both the CBOT and the CME state that there has never been a financial loss due to default on a futures contract on their exchanges. Even the collapse of Drexel Burnham Lambert in the early 1990s was handled in an orderly fashion without loss to market participants.

A wide range of instruments is now traded in the financial futures markets, from the simplest (a Eurodollar or Treasury bill contract) to the more complex (Treasury bonds, stock index futures) and the exotic (yield curve spread futures in Chicago). An exhaustive survey would probably also exhaust the reader's patience, because the differences among many of these—for example, a contract on 3-month U.S.$ deposits and a contract on 3-month sterling deposits—are relatively minor and are confined to clearing and settlement issues rather than any major differences in concept. Therefore, this chapter focuses on four types of contract:

1. Money market future. We discuss the Eurodollar contract.
2. Bond future. We discuss the U.S. Treasury bond future contract in some detail and touch on JGB, Bund, and BOBL futures. We also touch on yield curve spread contracts.
3. Foreign exchange future. We consider the CME sterling contract.
4. Equity index future. We work at the S&P 500 contract and also at the FTSE 100, DAX-30, CAC-40, and Nikkei 225.

While some variations may occur in different countries, the principles set out for the contracts should apply worldwide.

Money Market Futures

Eurodollar Future Contracts. Perhaps the simplest futures contract is the Eurodollar future. It is also probably the most important short-term interest rate futures contract worldwide. To give an idea of the scale of the CME's liquidity in this contract, in normal times 500 lots and often 1,000 lots can change hands without changing the price. That is, up to $1 billion can be done in a single trade without affecting the market.

The Eurodollar contract is traded in substantially similar form in Chicago (on the CME) and in Singapore (on SIMEX). SIMEX and the CME have a "mutual offset" arrangement whereby positions taken in Singapore can be closed in Chicago, and vice versa.

The CME contract is for a $1 million face value Eurodollar time deposit with 3-months' maturity. Last trading day is the second London business day before the third Wednesday of the delivery month. The traditional delivery months had been March, June, September, December, and the spot (current) month, but recently the CME introduced "serial" Eurodollar futures. These fill in the gaps, and two are listed at any one time. Thus, in September, there are two serial contracts for October and November, as well as the normal December contract. After the October contract expires, a January contract is added.

A specific feature of this contract is that it is cash-settled. Unlike the Treasury bill or Treasury bond contracts, physical delivery of the underlying instrument does not take place. The primary reason is that there would be an implied credit risk on the bank whose Eurodollar deposit was delivered. Because the Eurodollar futures market now stretches out almost to four years' maturity, predicting the credit quality risk would be difficult.

The cash settlement has been an important element in the success of the contract. The domestic U.S. CD contract (settled by actual delivery of CDs) was introduced in 1981. The Mexican crisis of 1982 and Continental Illinois's collapse in 1984 quickly meant that the traditional CD "run" (whereby the top ten U.S. banks' paper was traded interchangeably) disintegrated. Traders delivered the weakest CDs into the futures contract; buyers of CD futures found themselves "wearing" weak paper. This process destroyed the contract. Cash settlement means there is no risk of this happening.

The CME Eurodollar specifications are as follows:

Eurodollar Time Deposit

Size: $1,000,000.

Hours: Regular Trading Hours (RTH): 7:20 A.M.–2:00 P.M.
    GLOBEX: 2:45 P.M.–7:05 A.M. Mon.–Thurs.; 5:30 P.M.–7:05 A.M.

Months: March, June, September, December, two serial months, and spot month.

Minimum Price Fluctuation: .01 (1 basis point at $25/pt) ($25).

Limit: RTH: No limit.
    GLOBEX: 200 points.

Source: CME.

The price is quoted in terms of the CME index, that is, the difference between the deposit rate and 100. Thus, a Eurodollar deposit rate of 9 percent is quoted in index form as 91.00. Prices are quoted in multiples of 0.01 (thus, the minimum possible change in the value of the contract—the tick value—is U.S.$25: $0.01/100 \times 90/360 \times \$1,000,000$).

The settlement mechanics are that, on the last trading day, the CME clearinghouse uses the British Bankers Association (BBA) quoted LIBOR rate, which is obtained as follows:

BBA Survey Procedure

- At 11:00 A.M. London time, sixteen BBA-designated banks provide quotes that reflect their perception of the rate at which U.S. dollar deposits are generally available to the marketplace.
- The four highest and four lowest rates are eliminated.
- The average of the remaining eight quotes is calculated.
- The average, rounded out to the fifth decimal place, is the fixing for the day.

This use of the BBA rate rather than the previous practice (until January 1997, the CME's own settlement rate was calculated) was decided on to help convergence of CME interest rate contracts with OTC interest rate markets, which typically fix to BBA rates.

Using the BBA fixing results, the final settlement price is rounded to the fourth decimal place (the previous practice rounded to the second decimal place). At expiration, the final settlement price will be rounded to the nearest $0.25 per contract, rather than the previous $25. These rates are currently displayed daily on Telerate page 3750.

Suppose the result of this calculation works out at 8.5 percent. The "settlement price," which is used to work out the payments due to and due from holders of outstanding futures contracts, will then be $100 - 8.5 = 91.5$. On the settlement date, the interest rate implied by the futures contract must be equal to the cash 3-month deposit rate prevailing at that time. Futures prices therefore give a quick forecast of where the market sees the 3-month Eurodollar rate going.

Suppose today is June 13, 2001. The September Eurodollar futures contract is trading at 93.5. The market is saying that, in September, Eurodollar rates will be at 6.5 percent. (Remember the contract prices as 100 − the Eurodollar rate.) My own belief is that, by the time we get to September 15, the rate will have risen to 9 percent so that, on its settlement date, the Eurodollar future will trade at 91. The market expects rates to fall, I expect rates to rise. I sell 50 September Eurodollar contracts at 93.5. If I am right, the futures contract will settle at 91 in September. I sold at 93.5; I close out the position by buying back at 91. I will make a profit of 2.5, or 250 ticks. With the value of a tick at $25, my profit will be $6,250 per contract, or $312,500 in total.

Here, I simply traded on my view of rates. But I might have argued that, by dealing today at 93.5, I have effectively "locked in" a deposit rate of 6.5 percent in September. That ability to lock in future rates is what makes the Eurodollar futures market so attractive to banks. It allows them not only to trade speculative interest rate views but also to offer hedges to their corporate customers who are borrowing and to arbitrage against other markets, notably the rate for forward rate agreements (see Chapter 3) and interest rate swaps (see Chapter 5).

Treasury Bill Futures. The CME Treasury bill future was the first successful interest rate futures contract and, though it has lost ground to the Eurodollar contract, it remains an important instrument in its own right. The main reasons for its decline are, first, the Euro contract, introduced in 1982, was soon traded on other exchanges worldwide, but a position in the CME Treasury bills contract can be traded only during Chicago hours. Second, trading in the secondary Treasury bill market can be affected by the amount of paper that is locked away. In the spring of 1989, for example, of $7 billion of 3-month bills auctioned, $4.4 billion were bought by "noncompetitive" buyers intending to hold the bills as investments to maturity. With only $2.6 billion available; an aggressive investment bank, working perhaps with one or two other institutions, could easily establish a sizable enough position in the cash market to squeeze the futures market. A few squeezes of this type were enough to discourage some trading in the futures market, which in turn made the market easier to squeeze.

The standard contract is for 13-week U.S. Treasury bills having a face value at maturity of U.S.$1 million. The delivery unit on the CME is Treasury bills maturing 90 days hence. As an option, the seller can deliver 91- or 92-day maturity bills. (The vast majority of deliveries are made in 91-day bills.) The price is quoted in terms of the CME index, that is, the difference between the actual yield and 100. Prices are quoted in multiples of 0.01 (the tick value is U.S.$25, as for the Eurodollar contract).

Contracts for the 90-day Treasury bill are traded for March, June, September, and December. Trading in the contract normally ends on the second business day after the 13-week Treasury bill auction of the third week of the delivery month (usually, the Wednesday following the third Monday of the month). Delivery takes place the following day (Thursday).

Unlike the Eurodollar contract, the Treasury bill contract settles by delivery of a Treasury bill. So the pricing of the Treasury bill future is primarily driven by its relationship to the cash market for Treasury bills. The link between the two markets is called the implied repo rate. The basic idea behind the implied repo rate can be set out as follows. Suppose I buy a Treasury bill that is deliverable into the futures contract. At the same time, I sell a Treasury bill future, with the aim of delivering the cash bill as settlement of my futures position. This position will have a revenue and a cost. The revenue will be the profit (if any) on the sale price of the future in excess of the cost of the cash bill. The cost will be the financing of my holding of the cash bill until I deliver it in the futures settlement. The implied repo rate is the rate that I can afford to pay as a cost of financing and still break even.

The implied repo rate measures the time value of money for the time period between cash and futures settlement dates. If the implied repo rate is above the actual financing rate for the period, futures are expensive relative to the underlying instrument. The best strategy would be to buy cash and sell futures. Conversely, if the implied repo rate is below the actual rate, futures are cheap relative to the instrument. The best strategy would then be to buy futures and sell cash.

In practice, these rules cannot be automatically followed. For one thing, the trader will be uncertain about the amount of variation margin that will have to be paid or received in the interval from now to maturity. Also, it may not be possible to arrange financing for the period from now to maturity at a single fixed rate.

Calculating the Implied Repo Rate. Suppose today is August 3, 1998. I can sell September bill futures at 89.14 (that is, a rate of 10.86 percent). Delivery will be due on Thursday, September 22, so the December 22 bill is the deliverable bill to the September contract. Assume that today I can buy the cash Treasury bill that will mature on December 22 at a discount of 10.52 percent. Is it profitable to buy the cash bill and sell it into the September future?

The purchase price of the cash bill is found as follows:

$$P = \frac{100 - R \times N}{360}$$

where P = bill price;
   R = discount rate;
   N = days to bill maturity.

In this case, R = 10.52 percent and N = 140 (delivery date is August 4). Therefore, P = 100 − (10.52 × 140/360) = 95.909. The selling price in September, via the futures contract, is found from the same formula, with R = 10.86 percent and N = 91. Therefore, P = 100 − (10.86 × 91/360) = 97.225.

From these two prices, we can now find out the implied repo rate. It is the annualized rate of return that is earned by buying the bill at 95.909 and selling it 49 days later at 97.255. We can afford to pay a financing cost that is no higher than that return. The calculation is the same as for any other annualized return:

$$\text{Implied repo} = \left(\frac{97.255}{95.909} - 1 \right) \times \frac{360}{49} = .1031 \text{ or } 10.31 \text{ percent.}$$

If we do this trade, we will earn a return of 10.31 percent. If we can finance our Treasury bill holding for less than that, we will make a profit. However, we would be unlikely to lock up our financing for the whole period in advance. A more common use of this trade, if there is an arbitrage opportunity, is to put the trade on hold until the arbitrage disappears. At that point, we would unwind our financing and sell the position. Thus, our financing would normally be the overnight repo rate (hence the origin of the term). The position would then be subject to financing risk. If overnight repo rates jumped sharply, we would have to cut the position, probably at a loss.

Generalizing from the above, the general formula for the implied repo rate is as follows:

$$\text{Implied repo rate} = 100 \times \frac{(Pf - 1)}{Pc} \times \frac{360}{N}$$

where Pf = futures price;
Pc = cash price;
N = days in the trade.

For the Treasury bill calculation, if we want to express the formula in terms of interest rates, it is:

$$IRP = \left[\frac{\left(100 - \dfrac{Rf \times 91}{360}\right)}{\left(100 - \dfrac{Rc \times Dc}{360}\right)} - 1 \right] \times \frac{360}{Dc}$$

where Rf = futures bill discount rate;
Rc = cash deliverable bill discount rate;
Dc = number of days to cash bill maturity.

Other Short-Term Contracts

Fed Funds Contract. In 1989, the Chicago Board of Trade introduced a 30-day interest rate futures contract. Initially, it was not widely used, but the interest rate volatility of 1994 boosted volume significantly; it is now commonly called the Fed funds futures contract. The contract calls for delivery of the interest paid on a principal amount of $5 million overnight Fed funds held for 30 days. The contract is cash-settled against the monthly average of daily Fed funds effective rates calculated and reported daily by the Federal Reserve Bank of New York.

Note that the Fed funds contracts listed for later months track the 1-month forward rate implied by an *uncompounded* average of expected overnight Fed funds rates. For this reason, the forward rates implied by 30-day futures prices tend to be lower than comparable term rates, which are typically based on compounded averages.

Brazilian DI Futures. This future, trading on the Brazilian Bolsa de Mercadorias & Futuros (BM&F), is based on the overnight interbank deposit (DI) rate published by the central clearinghouse (CETIP). It is included here because of an unusual feature. Unlike the Eurodollar futures contract, the DI contract is traded monthly, and its price reflects not the forward-forward interest rate but the implied discount factor to the settlement date of the contract. Each contract is traded with a face value of 100, 000 Reales for one month. The last trade date is the business day preceding the expiration day. Because the price reflects the discount factor, forward rates have to be calculated by compounding the present value of the first future—the reverse of the normal procedure. (See the discussion of forward rate calculations, in Chapter 3.)

Extensions along the Curve

Bundles, Packs, and Stubs. In September 1994, the Chicago Mercantile Exchange (CME) introduced "bundles" of Eurodollar contracts. A Eurodollar bundle is the simultaneous sale or purchase of one each of a series of consecutive Eurodollar futures contracts. The first contract in any bundle is usually the first quarterly contract in the Eurodollar "strip" (a consecutive set of contracts, usually covering 1 year). The exception to this convention is the 5-year "forward" bundle. This covers years 5 through 10 of the Eurodollar futures strip. For example, on May 20, 1996, the first contract in the 5-year "forward" bundle would be June 2001 (the 21st contract in the strip) and the last would be March 2006 (the 40th contract).

For any bundle, the price will be quoted in terms of net change from the previous trading day's settlement price. Specifically, the bundle's price quotation will reflect the simple average of the net price changes of each of the bundle's constituent contracts.

For example, suppose that all of the nearest 21 contracts (e.g., the June 1996 to the June 2001) have risen by three ticks since yesterday's settlement. The prices of the next seven (September 2001 to March 2003) have risen by four ticks. Under these conditions, the quotation for the seven-year bundle would be:

$$\frac{(21 \times 3) + (7 \times 4)}{28} = 3.25 \text{ ticks.}$$

This example highlights the fact that bundles are quoted in increments of a quarter of a basis point, unlike the underlying futures contract, which is quoted in increments of full basis points.

After a buyer and a seller have agreed on the price and quantity of a bundle, they must assign mutually agreed-on prices to each of the constituents. In principle, any set of prices may be used, provided that at least one constituent contract lies within that contract's trading range for the day. (This prevents bundle prices from moving too far out of line from the current market.) In practice, most traders use a computerized system provided by the CME. The system calculates the average price of the bundle from the components, and then adjusts for any discrepancy between the result and the agreed-on price at which the bundle was traded. In adjusting the component contract prices, the adjustment is applied to the most distant contract first.

A second innovation introduced by the CME is the Eurodollar "pack," the simultaneous purchase or sale of an equally weighted, consecutive series of four Eurodollar futures. Generally, nine different packs are trading at any given time: Red, Green, Blue, Gold, Purple, Orange, Pink, Silver, and Copper, representing years 2 through 10.

A bundle consists of several packs. For example, a 3-year bundle consists of 12 futures contracts. Another way of constructing a similar position would be to buy the four Eurodollar contracts comprising Year 1, together with the packs for Years 2 and 3. Packs are quoted in the same way as bundles—as a net change from the previous settlement price. They are quoted in minimum increments of one-half ticks (e.g., +2.5 bid/+3 ask).

A "LIBOR stub" contract consists of three equally weighted, consecutive 1-month LIBOR contracts. All three contracts are executed simultaneously, at an average net price change from yesterday's settlement price. This creates a synthetic Eurodollar futures contract, but the advantage is that it can be constructed for nonstandard dates. (The Eurodollar future contract is March/June/September/December; we could construct a LIBOR stub from February to May.) This is convenient for over-the-counter swaps traders.

The Strip Yield Curve. A very important application of Eurodollar futures lies in their use to create synthetic Eurodollar deposits for either a hedge or an arbitrage. To understand this application, we begin with the idea of the strip.

For any financial instrument for which there is a futures market, we can create a synthetic longer-term instrument by using the underlying cash instrument plus a series, or strip, of futures contracts. For example, suppose it is March 15, and I buy a 3-month Treasury bill maturing June 15. I could also buy June, September, December, and March Treasury bill futures so that I can fix the rate at which I roll over the cash 3-month bill when it expires. In fact, I have created a synthetic 15-month Treasury bill.

We can take the same approach with Eurodollar futures. The combination of a 3-month deposit with three subsequent Eurodollar futures contracts can create a synthetic 1-year deposit that can be arbitraged against the actual 1-year deposit. But in terms of balance sheet usage, it is more effective to arbitrage against the 1-year interest rate swap market (see Chapter 5). To do this trade, we need to know how to work out the 1-year rate from the futures strip.

We want to find the long period deposit rate from the short period rate and the forward-forward rate. This is the reverse of the approach set out in the forward-forward rate formula of Chapter 3. So we have:

$$\text{Long period rate} = \frac{360}{\text{Long period days}} \times \left[\frac{\begin{array}{c}\text{Futures rate} \times \text{(difference between}\\ \text{long and short period days)}\end{array}}{360} + 1\right] \times \left[\frac{(1 + \text{Short rate} \times \text{Short days})}{360} - 1\right]$$

or

$$R2 = \frac{360}{N2}\left(\frac{R'(N2 - N1)}{360} + 1\right)\left(\frac{1 + R1 \times N1}{360} - 1\right)$$

where R1 = short period deposit rate;

R' = rate implied by futures contract;

N1 = short period days;

N2 = long period days;

R2 = long period rate.

To work out the strip, we start by working out the 6-month rate from the 3-month rate and the nearby futures contract. Then we find the 9-month rate from the resulting 6-month rate and the next futures contract. Then the 12-month rate from the resulting 9-month rate and the next futures contract.

Let's take an example. Today is March 15. We know what the 90-day Eurodollar rate is in the ordinary, or "cash," market. We know the 90-day Eurodollar prices on the CME for June, September, and December. What we want to know is: In the ordinary Eurodollar market, what would the rates for 180-day, 270-day, and 360-day Eurodollars have to be to match the prices implied by the futures market? Suppose we have:

> 90-day Eurodollar: 14.40 percent.
>
> CME June Eurodollar: 84.88 = 15.12 percent.
>
> September: 84.96 = 15.04 percent.
>
> December: 85.16 = 14.84 percent.

We take the cash Eurodollar rate and the June futures Eurodollar rates for 90 and 180 days, respectively. Putting them into the formula, we get:

$$R2 = \frac{360}{180}\left[\frac{0.1512\,(180 - 90)}{360} + 1\right]\left[\frac{1 + 0.1440 \times 90}{360} - 1\right]$$

$$= 2[(0.0378 + 1)(1 + 0.036) - 1$$

$$= 0.1503216$$

$$= 15.03 \text{ percent.}$$

A 180-day Eurodollar should fetch 15.03 percent to match the combined 90-day Eurodollar plus June futures contract. The next step is to work out a 270-day Eurodollar, using the 180-day rate we have just calculated as the cash rate, R1, in our formula. The result of combining the 15.03 percent "synthetic"

180-day Eurodollar with the 15.04 percent on the September futures contract comes out at 15.4 percent. We then take this synthetic 270-day rate and combine it with the December futures contract rate to produce a synthetic 360-day Eurodollar at 15.696 percent.

These successive steps have produced a strip yield curve that looks like this, compared with the actual (or cash market) yield curve:

	Strip Yield Curve	Cash Market Yield Curve
90-day "cash" Eurodollar	14.40 percent	14.40
Synthetic 180-day Eurodollar	15.03 percent	14.40
Synthetic 270-day Eurodollar	15.41 percent	14.30
Synthetic 360-day Eurodollar	15.696 percent	14.30

The strip yield curve calculated from these formulas sometimes differs from the implied forward rates in the "cash" markets, for two reasons. First, the participants in the futures markets may not entirely share the view of participants in the cash markets. Second, the two markets may be imperfectly linked. The Eurodollar cash and futures markets are very tightly bound together, but, at times, they can move out of line, if only briefly. In addition, there are credit exposure considerations in the cash markets that do not affect futures trading.

Futures and FRAs. Eurodollar futures are closely linked to the market for forward rate agreements (FRAs) and to the interest rate swap market for "swaps against the strip" (see Chapter 5). Suppose today is March 13, 2002, and the 3- and 6-month Eurodollar deposits, value March 15, are trading at 8.25 percent and 8.5 percent, respectively. Suppose the days in each period are 90 and 180, respectively. We know from our forward-forward formula (see Chapter 3) that the FRA rate should be $(8.5 \times 180 - 8.25 \times 90)/[(180 - 90) \times (1 + \{8.25 \times 90/36000\})] = (1{,}530 - 742.50)/(90 \times 1.020625) = 787.5/91.85625 = 8.57$ percent.

That would imply a futures price for June (the price for a 90-day Eurodollar deposit running from June 15 to September 15) of 91.43. Suppose that the future were trading at 91.25, implying a forward rate of 8.75. Then it would be possible to buy the future (hedging against a fall in rates) and also to buy the FRA (hedging against a rise in rates). The future would lock in a lending rate of 8.75 percent and the FRA would lock in a borrowing rate of 8.57 percent, for a spread of 18 basis points. In other words, if the FRA rate is below the rate given by the future, buy the future and buy the FRA. Conversely, if the FRA rate is above the future, sell the FRA and sell the future.

The hedge will not be as perfect as it looks, because of the time value of money on the variation margin. Consider a company with a $10 million floating rate loan linked to 6-month LIBOR. Fearing that rates will rise, it buys a 6 ×

12 FRA from its bank. Suppose, for the value on March 19, 2001, we have the following conditions:

LIBOR	Future
3 months	8.50 percent Jun 91.28
6 months	8.70 percent Sep 91.17
9 months	8.88 percent Dec 91.02
1 year	9.05 percent

For convenience we take 1 year as having 360 days and 6 months as having 180 days. Thus, the forward rate is $(9.05 \times 360 - 8.7 \times 180)/[180 \times (1 + \{8.7 \times 180/36000\})] = 9.01$ percent. Suppose the bank loads its quote to 9.10 percent. Having done the deal, it wants to hedge using the futures market. It sells 10 September contracts (at an implied rate of 8.83 percent) and 10 December contracts at an implied rate of 8.98 percent.

The implied total cost over the 6-month period that is locked in by the futures contracts is worked out by compounding the near contract (at 8.83 percent) up over the second period at the second rate of 8.98 percent: $(1 + 8.83 \times 90/3600) \times (1 + 8.98 \times 90/36000) = 1.022075 \times 1.02245 = 1.045020584 = 4.502$ percent per 6 months, which equates to just over 9 percent annually.

It looks as if the bank has locked a 10-basis-point profit over 6 months on $10 million—say, $5,000. But now suppose, on the day after the deal is done, the cash Eurodollar rates fall 1 percent and stay fixed at that level until the September futures date. We would have the following rates:

LIBOR	Future
3 months	7.50 percent
6 months	7.70 percent Sep 92.07
9 months	7.88 percent Dec 91.92
1 year	8.05 percent

Both the September futures contract that we sold, and the December contract, have risen by 90 ticks. Bearing in mind that the tick on this contract (see above) is worth $25 and we did 10 contracts in each maturity, our loss totals $2 \times 10 \times 90 \times 25 = \$45,000$. Because we have assumed that rates now remain rigidly fixed to the September delivery date, there are no further changes in our position and no variation in margin movements. We have to fund this loss till the delivery date. Say we do this at the 6-month rate of 7.7 percent. Our funding cost is then $1,732.50 ($45,000 at 7.7 percent for half a year). One-third of our apparent profit disappears.

The problem is that the value of a future settlement amount under the FRA is being hedged with an instrument that throws up changes in value today. One way around this would be to hedge not the settlement amount but the present value of the settlement amount (this is called "tailing the hedge"). With the passage of time, that present value rises. The size of the hedge gradually increases as we get closer to the settlement date, if we want to be perfectly hedged. (But by that time, we might be more confident about the trend in rates and happy to leave the balance of the position open.)

Brazilian Swap Futures.   Before leaving the money market futures section, it may be worth mentioning a Brazilian contract that includes an overnight swap contract. The BM&F swap futures contract is quite widely drawn in its terms. It defines its basis as:

> 1. Underlying asset
> The difference between the following values:
> a) the initial value indexed by parameter "1," defined as follows: variable "1," or a percentage of variable "1," or variable "1" increased by an interest rate;
> b) the initial value indexed by parameter "2," defined as follows: variable "2," or a percentage of variable "2," or variable "2" increased by an interest rate. Variables "1" and "2" are necessarily distinct from each other.
>   For the purposes of this contract, a variable is defined as any index, interest rate, exchange rate, price variation rate, among others, disclosed in Annex I of this contract.

In practice, there are only four contracts of any importance: an overnight interest rate swap, a term rate interest rate swap, and two currency swap contracts. Contracts can be traded on the basis that the exchange will or will not guarantee the contract. On the expiration date, the BM&F will calculate the settlement value of the contract. If positive, the settlement value will be credited to the buyer of the contract; if negative, it will be credited to the seller of the contract. The settlement value will be settled in cash on the expiration date. If one or another of the parties has chosen to trade with the guarantee option, margins will be calculated by the Exchange and required to be held. The positions assumed on this contract are nontransferable. Exceptions will be made only at the Exchange's discretion, so this contract is not really comparable to some of the other contracts discussed.

Bond Futures

Treasury Bond Future.   In the arena of bond contracts, the U.S. Treasury bond contract probably remains the most important on a worldwide basis, although the JGB contract (in Tokyo), the notionnel (on MATIF), and the Bund (on DTB and LIFFE), are also important internationally. The U.S. Treasury bond contract is traded on the Chicago Board of Trade. The chief U.S. Treasury bond contract is the long bond contract, so that is the one we will discuss. Its specifications are as follows:

Trading Unit: One U.S. Treasury bond having a face value at maturity of $100,000 or a multiple thereof.

Deliverable Grades: U.S. Treasury bonds that, if callable, are not callable for at least 15 years from the first day of the delivery month or, if not callable, have a maturity of at least 15 years from the first day of the delivery month. The invoice price equals the futures settlement price times a conversion factor plus accrued interest. The conversion factor is the price of the delivered bond ($1 par value) to yield 8 percent.

Price Quote: Points ($1,000) and thirty-seconds of a point; for example, 80-16 equals $80^{16}\!/_{32}$.

Tick Size: $\frac{1}{32}$ of a point ($31.25/contract); par is on the basis of 100 points.

Daily Price Limit: 3 points ($3,000/contract) above or below the previous day's settlement price (expandable to $4\frac{1}{2}$ points). Limits are lifted on the second business day preceding the first day of the delivery month.

Contract Months: March, June, September, December.

Delivery Method: Federal Reserve book-entry wire-transfer system.

Last Trading Day: Seventh business day preceding the last business day of the delivery month.

Last Delivery Day: Last business day of the delivery month.

Trading Hours: 7:20 A.M.–2:00 P.M. Chicago time, Mon.–Fri. Evening trading hours are 5:20–8:05 P.M. (CST) or 6:20–9:05 P.M. (CDST), Sun.–Thurs. Project A Afternoon session hours are 2:30–4:30 P.M. Chicago time, Mon.–Thurs. Project A Overnight session hours are from 10:30 P.M.–6:00 A.M., Sun.–Thurs. Trading in expiring contracts closes at noon on the last trading day.

Source of Data: CBOT.

Quotations on the bond contracts, to make them comparable with the cash market, are in terms of the price of the notional underlying Treasury bond. They are quoted not in decimals but in thirty-seconds. Thus, a price of 98-16 means 98 and $^{16}\!/_{32}$ or 98.50 in decimal terms. (In this book, when referring to bond contracts, I shall write 98-16 to show a price in thirty-seconds and 98.50 if the price is converted to decimals.) The notional face amount of the bond is $100,000. Delivery may be made on any day during the last month of the contract's life. The party who is short the contract may decide when to deliver. When the decision is made, the CBOT notifies the holder of a long position that delivery must be taken. The long position chosen is the one put on at the earliest date of all the long positions still outstanding. The following day, the short delivers to the long, against cash payment in Fed funds.

The bond delivered must be of "deliverable grade"; that is, it must be a standard coupon-bearing U.S. Treasury bond maturing at least 15 years from the first day of the delivery month. The price of the cash bond that is implied by the futures contract is converted, by means of a "conversion factor" supplied by the Exchange, to an equivalent price comparable to that of the deliverable bond. Suppose the future is trading at 101.50 in decimal terms, and there is a deliverable, 18-year bond with a coupon of 11.25 percent. Suppose the Exchange's conversion factor for this bond is 0.954. The adjusted futures price for this bond is then $101.50 \times 0.954 = 96.831$.

From another viewpoint, suppose I own this 11.25 percent bond. I know I can sell it into the futures market for 96.831. Suppose the actual cash price in the market is 96.55. (In both cases, for simplicity, we ignore accrued interest.) Suppose the first delivery date for the futures contract is in 10 days' time. I can borrow 10-day money for 8 percent, and there is no coupon due on the cash bond between now and the futures delivery date. If I borrow the price of the bond, buy the cash bond, sell it into the futures market, and hold it until the time comes for delivery into the futures settlement process, I can make a profit.

I work this out as follows. Work out the discount factor, which gives the present value today of 96.831 in 10 days' time at 8 percent. The result, using a 360-day year, is $(1 + 8/100 \times 10/360) = 1.002222$. Discounting the adjusted futures price back to today gives $96.831/1.002222 = 96.616$. So the present value today of the adjusted futures price of this bond—the price at which I can sell it—is 96.616; but I can buy the bond for 96.55. So I can buy the cash bond today, sell it for future delivery, and finance it until the delivery date at 8 percent, to show a profit overall. Such a trade is called a cash-and-carry. This type of arbitrage means that the fair value of the future is determined by the price of cash Treasury bonds and by short-term financing costs.

In this example, we have ignored the coupon payable on the cash bond. While I hold the bond, the coupon is accruing in my favor. Suppose we are looking at the 8.75 percent bonds of November 2008, and they are currently trading in the market at 68-26, or 68.8125 in decimal terms. If the accrued interest outstanding on that bond today is 2.12 in decimal terms, then the total price of the cash bond today is 70.9325—say 70.93. Today is August 11, and the September contract price is 64-03 or 64.09375. Assume I deliver on the first possible date, September 1. Thus, I will hold the bond for 20 days, financing it at 8 percent. My total cost, therefore, will be $70.93 \times (1 + 8/100 \times 20/360) = 70.93 \times 1.004444 = 71.25$.

On September 1, the accrued interest on the cash bond, for which I will be paid by the buyer, will be 2.60. Suppose the conversion factor for this particular cash bond is 1.0757. Then the adjusted futures price is $64.09375 \times 1.0757 = 68.95$. Including the accrued interest, the total price will be 71.55. There is a difference of 0.30 between the all-in adjusted futures price (71.55) and the all-in cash price allowing for financing cost to delivery (71.25). That difference would be my profit on the trade.

A comparison of the yield on the bond we buy and the financing cost shows us the cost of carry. Suppose we buy a bond yielding 12 percent and finance it at 8 percent. Carrying this position earns us 4 percent per annum—a positive carry. Conversely, if short rates are above long rates, financing cost is more than the yield on the bond.

A related concept is that of "basis," which is defined as the difference between the cash price and the futures price. As the delivery month on the futures contract approaches, the cash and futures prices tend to converge. The basis approaches zero because the influences on the price of both the cash commodity and the expiring futures contract are identical at the time of delivery. If there were a difference between the two prices, there would be an opportunity for arbitrage. If the Treasury bond futures contract sold at a higher price than cash Treasury bonds, traders could sell the futures contract, buy Treasury bonds in the cash market, and make delivery on the futures contract to cover their futures sale, realizing an arbitrage profit.

There is a similarity to the forward foreign exchange margin. The forward margin also tends to get smaller as the period of the forward contract shortens. It reaches zero when the forward price is for spot. And just as the forward margin is influenced by the relative interest rates of the two currencies involved, so the basis is influenced by interest rates, although in a different way. Basis is positive or negative, depending on whether the cash price is higher or lower than the futures price.

If short-term interest rates are below long-term rates, dealers who hold bonds are earning coupon income, which is more than the cost of financing. The dealers can afford to quote lower prices on deferred sales, which leads to discounts on distant contracts. In this situation, basis is positive (basis = cash − futures = +). The dealer is earning "positive carry"—coupon income exceeds financing costs. Positive carry means a positive basis and a positive yield curve. If the yield curve has a negative slope, so that long-term rates are below short-term rates, dealers face financing costs that exceed their coupon income. They must then charge higher prices on deferred sales to compensate for holding the bonds. They face negative carry, and the futures market will show a negative basis. A negative yield curve, therefore, means negative carry and negative basis.

One final point on cash and carry: The calculations depend on whether carry is positive or negative. As the short, in the example above, I have the choice of delivery date. Normally, for a cash and carry, one would calculate carry to the last rational delivery date. Thus, if carry is positive, I will deliver on the last possible day; if negative, on the first possible day.

Cheapest to Deliver. How do we know which bond will be delivered into the futures contract? The answer is: The bond that is cheapest to deliver for the trader who is short. Let's take an example. Suppose the futures contract is at a price of 79-05. Suppose also that the cash market has just three issues available for delivery against that contract: (1) the 8¾ percent 2015 at 85-28 (10.30 percent); (2) the 9⅛ percent 2016 at 88-29 (10.34 percent); and (3) the 10⅜ percent 2017 at 99-27 (10.39 percent).

Comparing yields, the 10⅜ percent is the highest; in terms of price, the 8¾ percent is the lowest. Intuitively, it would seem that one of these two bonds is the "cheapest" in the futures market.

However, if the T-bond futures conversion factors are 1.0790, 1.1194, and 1.254 respectively (these were the actual factors on the day in question), then the price of the 8¼ percent bond would have to be 85.41 (in decimal terms) while it is actually 85.88 in the market. The 9⅛ percent would have to be 88.61 (against an actual 88.91) and the 10⅜ percent 99.26 (actual 99.84).

Comparing the theoretical and actual prices, we can see that if the short is buying in the market, he or she will have a loss of 0.47 point on the 8¾ percent, and 0.58375 on the 10⅜ percent, and will have a loss of only 0.30 on the 9⅛ percent. Therefore, of these three issues, the 9⅛ percent is the "cheapest" for the short to buy. The 10⅜ percent, which, in yield-to-maturity terms was "cheapest" or best value, represents the greatest loss in terms of delivery to the futures market.

The comparison above was done on the day of delivery. If we are considering, before delivery, which bond is the cheapest to deliver, we take the adjusted futures price and compare it with the cash prices of the different bonds in the market—the reverse of the cash and carry we did earlier. There, we started with the cash price, worked out the all-in cost (allowing for financing), and compared it with the futures price to see whether we could make a profit. Here, we are finding the financing rate, the implied repo rate. The bond that is the cheapest to deliver is the one that has the highest implied repo rate. The long pays the financing cost; the short earns it. So the short looks for the highest implied repo rate.

In general, if bond yields are above 8 percent, then the lower the coupon and the longer the maturity, the cheaper it will be to deliver. If bond yields are below 8 percent, then the shorter the maturity and the higher the coupon, the cheaper the bond is to deliver.

Japanese Government Bonds.   In Japan, the government bond future contract is, unusually, traded on the Tokyo Stock Exchange. [The Euroyen contract is traded on the Tokyo International Financial Futures Exchange (TIFFE) and the Nikkei 225 stock index is traded on the Osaka exchange.] The Japanese government bond market has a number of special features—most notably, the heavy concentration on a single, 10-year benchmark issue. Attempts to generate a futures market yield curve of the type available on U.S. Treasury bonds have never been successful. The contract specifications are shown at the top of page 85.

Bund.   After the JGB and the U.S. Treasury bond, the German government bond is probably the third most important bond contract in the world. This

---

10-year JGB Futures

Trading Hours: 9:00–11:00A.M.; 12:30–3:00 P.M.

Contract: Standardized 6 percent, 10-year JGB.

Deliverable Grade: Listed JGBs having maturity of 7 years or more, but less than 11 years.

Contract Months: March, June, September, December cycle (five contract months traded at any one time).

Delivery Date: The 20th calendar day of each contract month.

Last Day of Trading: The 9th business day prior to each delivery date. The trading day in a new contract month begins on the next business day following the last trading day of the previous month.

Trading Unit: JGBs ¥100 million face value.

Minimum Fluctuation: $\frac{1}{100}$ point per 100 points (¥10,000 per contract).

Daily Price Limit: 2 points upward or downward (¥2 million per contract).

Payment or Receipt as the Result of Offsetting: The 3rd business day following the offsetting (T + 3).

Delivery of Bonds: Sellers of futures contracts are granted options regarding deliverable issues.

Source of Data: TSE.

---

contract is unique in that it is traded competitively on two exchanges: LIFFE and the DTB. LIFFE had the advantage of starting 2 years before the DTB, and established an unassailable lead in the 10-year Bund contract, but the DTB continues to trade the Bund and has succeeded in establishing itself as the prime location for trading the 5-year Bund, generally known as the BOBL. In the next few years, with the arrival of the new European currency, the Euro, there is likely to be a renewed struggle between LIFFE and DTB over these contracts.

The specifications for the LIFFE contract are shown on the top of page 86.

LIFFE Basis Trading Facility. During 1995, in an effort to encourage the trading of the relationship between cash bonds and their futures counterparts, LIFFE introduced the Basis Trading Facility (BTF). As those who have been actively involved with basis trading between futures and cash bonds will know, a key problem is to get both sides, or "legs," of the trade done at specific prices. Cash bond market makers can be held to a specific number of bonds at an agreed-on price, but trades entering the futures pits can be: (1) not filled, leaving the trader holding a large cash position, with no futures match; (2) partially filled, leaving the trader with a similar but smaller problem; (3) filled at

---

German Government Bond (Bund) Future

Unit of Trading: DM 250,000 nominal value notional German government bond with 6 percent coupon.

Delivery Months: March, June, September, December.

Delivery Day: The 10th calendar day of the delivery month. If that day is not a working day in Frankfurt, then the delivery day will be the next Frankfurt working day.

Last Trading Day: 11.00 A.M. Frankfurt time, three Frankfurt working days prior to the delivery day.

Quotation: Per DM 100 nominal value.

Minimum Price Movement (Tick Size and Value): DM 0.01–DM 25.

Trading Hours: 7.30 A.M.–4:15 P.M.

APT Trading Hours: 4:20 P.M.–5:55 P.M.

Contract Standard: Delivery may be made of any Bundesanleihen with 8½ to 10 years remaining maturity as of the 10th calendar day of the delivery month, on a free-of-reallowance basis, as listed by LIFFE. Delivery may be made via accounts at (1) Deutscher Kassenverein AG; (2) Euroclear; or (3) Cedel S.A.

Exchange Delivery Settlement Price (EDSP): The LIFFE market price at 11.00 A.M. Frankfurt time on the last trading day. The invoicing amount in respect of each deliverable Bund is to be calculated by the price factor system. A final List of Deliverable Bunds and their price factors will be announced by the Exchange 10 market days prior to the last trading day of the delivery month. Adjustments will be made for full coupon interest accruing as of the delivery day.

Source of Data: LIFFE.

---

the expected price, which is fine; or (4) filled at a variety of prices, which is a headache for position keeping.

Therefore, LIFFE officials sought a device that would facilitate basis trading. The LIFFE BTF operates on a set of rules that permits the necessary number of trades to be effected at the required single price, thereby removing execution risk from the futures leg. The contracts themselves are traded at a special post staffed by a LIFFE official on the exchange floor, separate from the actual trading pit in question.

The counterparties will agree on the terms of the basis trade in its entirety, including the size and price of the futures leg. The LIFFE member then instructs a BTF floor member to present the trade details, noted on a registration slip, to an Exchange official at the designated post on the LIFFE floor. The official then executes the trade.

The trade details are logged onto a dedicated computer system, which carries out a number of checks. The exchange official then signs off the registration slip and time-stamps it. At this point, the trade is deemed to have been executed. The BTF member has 30 minutes from the organization of the trade to register the details with the Exchange official. This enables LIFFE to check that the basis trade encompassed a futures level compatible with the market prices at the time of organization.

To establish an audit trail and verify the integrity of the basis trade, the party organizing the trade [or his or her client(s)] is required to enter details of the related cash bond component onto the International Securities Market Association (ISMA) TRAX reporting system. (ISMA, based in Zurich, is the self-regulatory body for international securities trading; TRAX is run from its offices in London.) LIFFE later receives from ISMA confidential verification of the cash bond element of the transaction. TRAX is used for trade confirmation and matching purposes and not clearing purposes, leaving BTF counterparties free to clear their trades on the system of their choice.

DTB BOBL

As mentioned earlier, the DTB has succeeded in establishing itself as the location for trading the 5-year Bund. The DTB Bundesobligation contract (or BOBL, as it is commonly known) specifications are shown on page 88.

Other Government Bond Futures Markets.   A number of other countries—France, the U.K. gilt market, Italy, Spain, South Africa, Canada, Australia, Austria, Belgium, and the Netherlands—have established government bond futures markets. Among the other emerging markets that have developed government bond futures markets is China, although the financial futures industry has had a rather rocky history there. The general problems of futures markets, which multiplied in an uncontrolled fashion, are partly to blame. The problems led, in May 1994, to a "rectification program" that reduced the number of exchanges from 40 to 15. Government bond futures had been introduced in early 1994 on the Shanghai Securities Exchange and, by early 1995, helped by the very low margin of 1 percent, had become the most actively traded financial instrument in China. On February 23, 1995, trading volume surged to $100 billion. This included $37 billion in orders for the July contract received in the last eight minutes of trading. Trading in government bond futures on the Exchange was suspended for eight days after the price manipulation scandal came to light. After a second scandal in May 1995, government bond futures trading was suspended indefinitely. Since the Exchange had never been registered as a futures exchange, it was not in fact regulated by the authorities.

Medium-term notional debt security issued by the German Federal Government or the Treuhandanstalt, with a term of 3½ to 5 years and an interest rate of 6 percent.

Settlement: A delivery obligation arising out of a short position in a BOBL futures contract may only be performed by the delivery of debt securities designated by DTB— specifically, Federal Debt Obligations (Bundesobligationen) or Federal Treasury Bills (Bundesschatzanweisungen) with an original term of no more than 5¼ years and a remaining term of at least 3½ years. In addition, debt securities that were deliverable into the Bund future contract with a remaining term of 3½ to 5 years, as of the delivery day, are also deliverable. A minimum issue amount of DM 4 billion for each issue is required.

Contract Size: DM 250,000.

Quotation: In a percentage of the par value, with two decimal places.

Minimum Price Movement: 0.01 percent, representing a value of DM 25.

Delivery Months: The three nearest quarter-end months in the cycle March, June, September, December.

Notification: Clearing Members with open short positions must notify DTB, by the end of the Post-Trading Period on the last trading day of the delivery month of the futures contract, which debt securities they will deliver.

Last Trading Day: Two Exchange trading days prior to the delivery day of the relevant quarter-end month. Trading in the contract for this delivery month ends at 12:30 P.M.

Daily Settlement Price: The average of the prices of the five last trades, or, if more than five trades have occurred during the final minute of trading, the average of the prices of all trades that occurred during this period. If it is not possible to determine a price under these conditions, or if the price so determined does not reflect the true market conditions, DTB will set the settlement price.

Delivery Day: The delivery day is the 10th calendar day of the respective quarter-end month if this day is an Exchange trading day; otherwise, the delivery day is the next succeeding Exchange trading day. Delivery is made by Clearing Members through DKV (Deutscher Kassenverein AG).

Source of Data: DTB.

Treasury Yield Curve Spread Futures. A new development in government bond futures-related markets is worth mentioning: futures on the relationship between markets. In October 1996, the Chicago Board of Trade introduced futures and options on a range of yield curve spread (YCS) contracts. Although previous attempts to introduce futures based on combinations of existing instruments had generally failed, the CBOT argued that it was difficult for many to trade yield curve spreads through existing futures because of changes in the cheapest-to-deliver bonds.

To date, the products have not yet been very successful. However, some details are included here because the concept does seem useful and may in due course be applied in other markets.

Listed U.S. Treasury Yield Curve Spread Contracts:

2-year/3-year	3-year/10-year
2-year/5-year	3-year/30-year
2-year/10-year	5-year/10-year
2-year/30-year	5-year/30-year
3-year/5-year	10-year/30-year

The YCS futures contract is defined as $25,000 times the sum of 100.00000 plus the spread difference in annualized percentage yields between the on-the-run (OTR) longer maturity U.S. Treasury instrument and the OTR shorter maturity U.S. Treasury instrument. The contract is stated:

$$\$25,000 * [100.0000 + (\text{Yield, OTR Longer Maturity} - \text{Yield, OTR Short Maturity})].$$

Component spread legs are based on current active (i.e., OTR) 2-year, 3-year, 5-year, 10-year, and 30-year U.S. Treasuries, not the cheapest-to-deliver instrument. The OTR Treasury is defined as the most recently auctioned security beginning on the day following its auction.

Expiring futures contracts will be cash-settled, based on the spread difference in annualized percentage yields between two OTR Treasuries of varying maturity at contract expiration. The CBOT will determine final contract settlement values based on a survey of ten randomly selected firms from the official list of designated primary dealers in U.S. Government securities, as identified by the Federal Reserve Bank of New York.

The spread contracts do not roll down the curve with the passage of time. For example, a 2-year/30-year spread in 6 months is still a 2-year/30-year spread, not a 1½-year/29½-year spread.

The futures payoff will move exactly with changes in the slope of the yield curve and will not be affected by changes in market levels. Contract duration and convexity equal zero.

The contract is designed to measure the impact of upward sloping, flat, or inverted yield curves. More upward sloping curves mean higher contract values (i.e., above 100); inverted curves mean the opposite (i.e., below 100). A price of par (100) indicates a flat curve.

Foreign Exchange Futures

Foreign exchange futures are not as important in their own right as interest rate futures contracts, because the liquid interbank forward foreign exchange market has always provided tough competition for the futures. But there is an important market for arbitraging between the futures and forward markets, and it is important to understand the mechanics.

We will take as an example the Chicago Mercantile Exchange contract for sterling. This is for an amount of £62,500. Delivery date is the third Wednesday of the contract month, and delivery is made by payment of sterling against dollars paid by the buyer of the contract.

The operation of the market is very simple. Say today is January 11, 1998. The March futures contract settles on the third Wednesday, March 17, 1998. The future is trading at $1.7217. Knowing that in the interbank forward market the $/£ rate for that date is $1.7212, I buy interbank forward £625,000 and sell 10 futures contracts to make a 5-point profit.

Because this type of arbitrage is so easy, many banks specialize in "trading the CME dates." Therefore, the futures market price is, in practice, fixed by the cash market price for that day.

Equities

Indexes.   The most common form of equity future is the future on an index. Of these, the first to be introduced was the U.S. contract on the S&P 500 equity index, which remains the most important equity futures contract worldwide. Before giving details, it may be relevant to point out that the same underlying economics applies to equity futures as to bond futures. That is, the calculation of the forward price of the underlying instrument so as to achieve a cash and carry trade is the same. However, there is one difficulty in practical terms. With a bond, we know exactly the underlying rate of interest being earned. With an equity index, we cannot predict with certainty what dividends will be received—at least, not after the dates of those dividends already announced by companies.

Traders deal with this problem either by making arbitrary assumptions about dividend payment patterns or by making a detailed analysis of upcoming dividends and forecasting the likely payment. Another complication is that, in at least one case (Germany's DAX index), the underlying price of the index is expressed as including dividends paid. The S&P 500 and the FTSE 100 are pure price indexes and do not include dividends.

Equity index futures have been used for a wide range of activities. The best known, perhaps, is "index arbitrage," which involves buying or selling the futures contract when its calculated fair value is perceived to be out of line with the underlying cash stock market. Arbitrage of this type was blamed for the crash of 1987, but in fact this was largely due to a second technique, called "portfolio insurance"—investors used futures to create a dynamic hedge for their portfolios. (Dynamic hedging is discussed in Chapter 7.) The most important day-to-day use of equity futures is by large institutional investors, who often use futures markets to make tactical allocation switches between stock markets or between the stock and bond markets. The very low transaction costs in the futures markets make this the most efficient place for making these switches.

U.S.: S&P 500. The most important contract in the United States is the S&P 500 futures contract, although there are several other smaller contracts. The contract was introduced in 1982. The specifications of the contract are:

Standard & Poor's 500

Size: $500 × S&P's 500 Stock Index.

Hours: RTH: 8:30 A.M.–3:15 P.M.
  GLOBEX: 3:45 P.M.–8:15 A.M. Mon.–Thurs.; 5:30 P.M.–8:15 A.M.

Months: March, June, September, December.
  GLOBEX: Lead Month.

Minimum Price Fluctuation: .05 (5 pt) ($5/pt) ($25).

Limits in Place: See CME Rulebook.
  GLOBEX: 1,200 points.

Source of Data: CME.

U.K.: FTSE 100. After the S&P 500, the FTSE 100 equity futures contract is the second in the world. It started trading in May 1984. Its contract details are shown in the box at the top of page 92.

Germany: DAX-30. As mentioned above, the DAX index is a total-return index; that is, it includes the value of dividends paid during its life, unlike the FTSE 100 or the S&P 500. The contract specifications are shown in the box on the bottom of page 92.

FTSE 100 Index Future

Unit of Trading: Valued at £25 per index point (e.g., value £100,000 at 4,000.0).

Delivery Months: March, June, September, December (nearest three available for trading).

Delivery Day: First business day after the last trading day.

Last Trading Day: 10:30 A.M. on the 3rd Friday in delivery month.

Quotation: Index points.

Minimum Price Movement (tick size and value): 0.5–£12.50.

Trading Hours: 8:35 A.M.–4:10 P.M.

APT Trading Hours: 4:32–5:30 P.M.

Contract Standard: Cash settlement based on the Exchange delivery settlement price.

Source of Data: LIFFE.

DAX Contract Specifications

Contract Size: DM 100 per DAX index point.

Quotation: In points, with one decimal place.

Minimum Price Movement: 0.5 point, representing a value of DM 50.

Settlement Months: The three nearest months of the cycle March, June, September, December.

Last Trading Day: The exchange trading day prior to the respective settlement calculation day.

Settlement Calculation Day: The third Friday of the respective settlement month if that is an exchange trading day; otherwise, the exchange trading day immediately preceding this Friday.

Final Settlement Price: The value of the DAX index calculated on the basis of the opening prices determined on the FWB for the DAX-listed shares on the settlement calculation day.

Cash Settlement Day: Cash settlement based on the final settlement price; due on the second Exchange trading day following the last trading day.

Margin: DTB determines the daily margin requirement, using its risk-based margining method.

Trading Hours: 9:00 A.M. to 5:00 P.M. (Frankfurt time).

Source of Data: DTB.

France: CAC-40.   The French market index covers 40 major French stocks. The specifications are:

MATIF CAC-40 Index Futures Specifications

Symbol: CAC.

Underlying: CAC-40 stock index.

Trading Unit: French francs (FRF) 200 × futures quoted index.

Price Quotation: Index, 1 decimal.

Tick Size: 0.5 index point; i.e., FRF 100.

Delivery Months: Three spot months, three quarterly: March, June, September, December. Two six-monthly: March, September.

Delivery Mode: Cash settlement.

Daily Price Limit: ± 120 index points.

Regular Initial Margin: FRF 30,000.

Open Outcry Hours: 10:00 A.M.–5:00 P.M.

First Trading Day: First business day following the last trading day.

Last Trading Day: Last business day of the maturity month at 4:00 P.M.

Source of Data: MATIF.

Japan: Nikkei 225.   The Japanese market is unique in several ways. First, the Nikkei 225 contract is traded not just in Tokyo but also in Singapore. SIMEX, the Singapore exchange, took advantage of the restrictions imposed by the Japanese authorities on domestic equity futures trading and has had an active business in Nikkei 225 contracts, in addition to the activity on the Osaka exchange, where the contract is traded in Japan. (The supposedly risk-free arbitrage between Singapore and Osaka being conducted by Nick Leeson was the cause of the collapse of Barings in 1995.)

Second, the Nikkei 225 has a number of disadvantages as an index. Specifically, statisticians would call it a "price-weighted index" rather than a "capitalization-weighted index." In other words, an obscure firm carries weight equal to the mighty Mitsubishi-Tokyo Bank. As a result, the index is easy to manipulate, and a number of derivative trading firms have been suspected of doing this. The authorities introduced a new index in 1994, the Nikkei 300, which is capitalization-weighted. However, the new contract has never really taken off.

Specifications for the Nikkei 225 are shown on page 94.

Nikkei 225 Index Futures

Contract Size: Index × ¥1,000.

Contract Cycle: March, June, September, December.

Expiry: Based on opening level of index constituents on day after last trading day: Thursday before second Friday of the month.

Trading Hours: 9:00–11:00 A.M.; 1:00–3:10 P.M.

Settlement: Cash.

Minimum Fluctuations: 10 points (¥10,000).

Source of Data: OSE.

Other Markets. Italian equity derivatives are traded on the Italian Derivatives Market (IDEM), which was set up in November 1994. The first contract was the successful MIB30 equity index contract, which traded a volume of 1 million contracts during its first full year of operation. During 1995–1996, the MIB30 option contract was introduced followed by options on major Italian equities. Trading is electronic, on a system provided by the Swedish OM exchange and managed by a separate company called Ced Borsa. Clearing is handled by the Cassa di Compensazione e Garanzia, the clearinghouse.

Spain has been trading actively since 1991 on the MEFF (Mercado Español de Futuros Financeiros); in the latter part of 1996, it was announced that the successful IBEX-35 contracts would be increased in size to allow more convenient trading for large institutions.

Equity index futures have been introduced in a number of countries such as Korea, Malaysia, and elsewhere. Indeed, as a symbol of the rapid integration of former Communist countries into the world's financial markets, March 1997 marked the start of futures contracts on equity indexes in the Hungarian, Polish, Czech, and Slovak markets. The contracts, priced in dollars, are traded on the Austrian futures and options exchange, OTOB.

Individual Shares

Sydney. Futures contracts on individual shares were introduced by the Sydney Futures Exchange (SFE) in May 1994. Initially, three contracts were listed, based on the shares of BHP, National Australia Bank, and News Corporation. In addition to the normal advantages of futures—leverage and forward delivery—other benefits of using share futures for Australian investors included absence of stamp duty charges and reduced margining requirements for spread transactions.

Share futures are quoted in terms of cents per share. Every one-cent movement in the contract has a value of $10. Contracts are traded in quarter-months and are identical to those used for share options traded on the Australian Options Market. Settlement of all outstanding positions at expiry is effected through a cash settlement process. All profits and losses are either credited or debited to the investor by the Sydney Futures Exchange Clearing House, in cash.

Each share futures contract is based on 1,000 shares of the underlying stock. Therefore, if an investor buys a BHP share futures contract at a price of $20, this effectively represents the same exposure as holding $20,000 of physical BHP shares.

The product encountered regulatory problems, triggering a battle between the Australian Stock Exchange and the SFE. (Similar regulatory problems have held back the introduction of the concept in the United States.) When the SFE persisted, the Stock Exchange retaliated by introducing Low Exercise Price Options (LEPOs) on individual shares—which, for practical purposes, operate like futures on individual shares (see Chapter 16). This was followed by the introduction of Flex options.

Neither, however, was a tremendous success: the SFE traded 36,190 share futures in the first half of 1996, a 49 percent decline from 1995 levels, and the combined volume of LEPOs and Flex options on the Stock Exchange totaled only 55,000 during the same period.

Hong Kong.   Share futures were introduced in Hong Kong in March 1995. But the contracts were hastily introduced—reportedly to head off a threat of other exchanges' listing similar contracts—and met with opposition from some of the Hong Kong authorities. In any event, trading volume has proven to be very limited.

Property.   Property futures are difficult to classify; they could conceivably be considered as equity, but have been placed here because they are rather specialized. Various attempts have been made in the United Kingdom to develop a property futures market. The first attempt, by the Futures and Options Exchange (FOX) failed; BZW, the British investment bank, introduced in November 1996 an over-the-counter property futures contract offering investors a 1- or 2-year return linked to movements in commercial property values, according to the Investment Property Databank annual index, which is widely used in U.K. practice. BZW offered contracts at 101 and 101.5, respectively, for December 1997 and December 1998, using December 31, 1995 as a base of 100. If the index is above the fixed level at expiry, BZW will pay the investor; if it has fallen below that level, then the investor must pay BZW.

Chapter **5**

Swaps

THE SWAP MARKET

We need to be clear about what we mean by swaps in this chapter. Interest rate, currency, and equity swaps are covered, but not traditional forward foreign exchange swaps. The latter instruments have been around a long time and are not dealt with here. (They are discussed at length in my *Foreign Exchange and Money Markets Guide,* John Wiley & Sons, Inc., 1992.)

To prevent confusion, the difference between traditional forward foreign exchange swaps and currency swaps is illustrated in Figure 5.1.

In this chapter, we can use a general definition:

■ A **swap** is a contract to exchange a series of cash flows that are calculated by reference either to a rate fixed in advance or to some known price or index.

Thus, I could swap a fixed rate of 6 percent on $100 million against the right to receive 6-month LIBOR on the same amount; or, 7 percent on DEM200 million versus 8 percent on the FRF equivalent amount.

Swaps, as defined above, took off during the 1980s. From perhaps $2 billion in notional value outstanding in 1980, the interest rate and currency swap market has now grown to the point where an estimated $20 *trillion* (i.e., $20,000 billion) of contracts are now outstanding. This represents an 84 percent per annum compound growth rate over 15 years, and makes the swap market the fastest growing of any financial markets in recent years. The first swaps to emerge were currency swaps, which began in the mid-1960s. But the market remained fairly small during the 1970s. The emergence of the interest rate swap, in 1980–1981, together with the decision by the World Bank to start an ambitious currency swap program, transformed the situation.

The market now has a huge range of counterparties that use swaps for a range of different reasons. Banks use swaps for asset and liability management. Companies and government bodies use them for similar purposes and also to raise finance through the bond market—notably, the Eurobond market—at rates that are better than those their bankers can offer. This flexibility has underpinned the huge growth in the market.

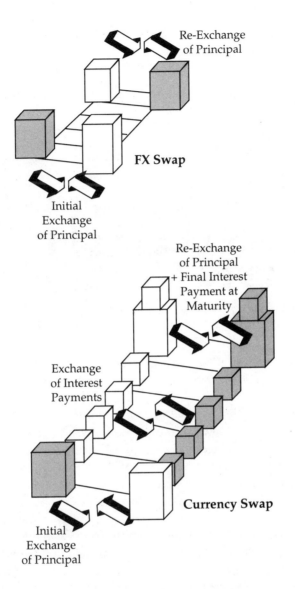

Figure 5.1 Comparison of the traditional foreign exchange swap and the currency swap.

Figure 5.2 illustrates the relative growth of interest rate swaps, currency swaps, and interest rate options (which are discussed in the next two chapters). Although the currency swaps market started before the market for interest rate options, it has been overtaken by the latter.[1] The primary reason is the

---

[1] The International Swaps Dealers Association (ISDA) statistics do not signal the start of the interest rate options market, but rather the point at which the ISDA Board felt it worth gathering the statistics. On the other hand, the general point remains true: interest rate options markets are much larger and have grown faster than the currency swap market.

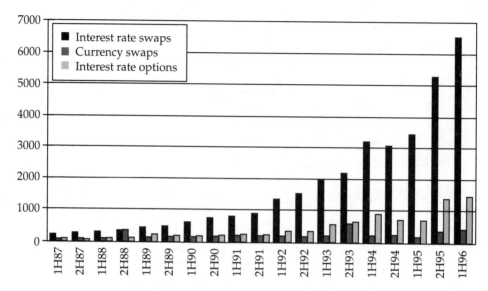

Figure 5.2   Swap market growth rate, 1987–1996.

impact on banks' capital adequacy ratios of the currency swap structure: it involves (normally) a re-exchange of principal at maturity. This is discussed further below.

Swaps have had a great impact on bond markets. Earlier issuers of new bonds were relatively tied down. If they issued, say, a deutsche mark bond, the extent to which they could hedge the long-term exchange risk of the bond was rather limited. The growth of the currency swap market meant that, for the first time, issuers could tap the currency market where they could raise the cheapest funds. A company such as BMW could issue a bond denominated in New Zealand dollars and then do a currency swap to transform its liability into deutsche marks. The growth of the interest rate swap market meant a similar liberation in the choice between fixed and floating rate bonds.

Once the swap technique had been invented, people found many other ways of using it. Interest rate swaps have been used to switch from floating to fixed rate, from fixed to floating rate, from fixed rate to zero coupon, from zero coupon to floating rate, from zero coupon to semiannual fixed rate, and so on. Essentially, the combination of interest rate and currency swaps now means that any stream of cash flows can be transformed into virtually any other stream: annual International Securities Market Association (ISMA) basis Japanese yen payments can be transformed into quarterly U.S. dollar, amortizing lease type payments, if desired, at a price. Swaps have been applied to a range of other markets including equities (see below), commodities, and even market volatility (see below).

Despite early worries about the credit risk implied in swaps, an ISDA survey in the early 1990s showed total write-offs of US$33 million on portfolios aggregating over $250 billion, a default rate of 0.01 percent—considerably better than traditional banking default rates. (However, a U.K. government veto on swap payments due from the London borough of Hammersmith and Fulham caused problems. Partly for political reasons, the municipality had used swaps and options to generate revenue from speculative transactions. The legality of the municipality's undertaking such activity was later overturned by the House of Lords, on the grounds that it was outside the legal framework governing municipalities. This then overturned swaps with a number of other municipalities.)

Interest Rate Swaps

The cash flows of an interest rate swap are illustrated in Figure 5.3, which shows an exchange of a fixed rate of interest (the unshaded blocks, all of the

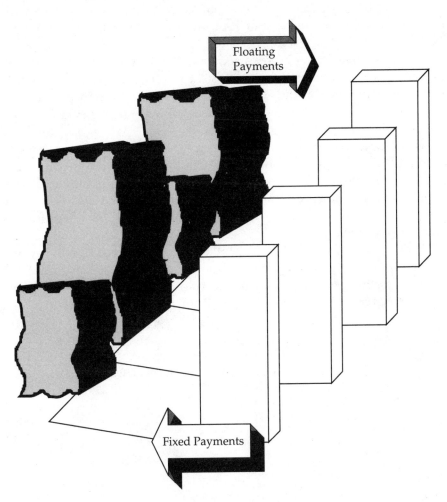

Two-year swap with semiannual payments of fixed against floating LIBOR

Figure 5.3   Fixed and floating swap cash flows.

same size) against a floating rate (the shaded blocks with various squiggles). In this example, the swap is a 2-year swap with semiannual payments of interest. (Although, for purposes of exposition, the payments are shown in the diagram as being made in full, market practice would normally be to net the two amounts into a single sum, positive or negative.)

As Figure 5.3 shows, in the swap there is no actual borrowing or lending. A swap is purely a contract to exchange interest flows. An example may help.

Suppose it is December 1, 1998, and you are the corporate treasurer of XYZ Ltd. You have borrowed floating-rate money from a syndicate of banks, for 5 years at 6-month US$ LIBOR + ½ percent. The amount borrowed is $10 million. Your company does not have the financial strength to access the public bond markets, so it is hard for you to raise 5-year money at a fixed rate. However, you fear that interest rates will rise. You decide to enter into a swap with a bank to fix, for 5 years, the cost of your interest rate liabilities, which would otherwise rise as LIBOR rises.

Suppose the bank quotes you a fixed rate, against 6-month LIBOR, of 9.5 percent, payable semiannually on a 30/360 basis (i.e., assuming 12 months of 30 days, as is common in the U.S. corporate bond market and the Eurobond market). Payment on both sides is in arrears. You are then committed to the cash flows shown in Table 5.1.

On the other side will be the floating rate income. The bank pays you 6-month LIBOR. Consider two outcomes: (1) LIBOR rises by ¼ percent every 6 months over the period, from a starting level of 8 percent; and LIBOR falls by ¼ percent. Let us assume, for simplicity, that LIBOR is paid also on a 30/360 basis—(normally, it is actual/360 for US$ swaps). We will then have the swap flows shown in Table 5.2.

The payments by the bank to you will exactly match your LIBOR payments to your banking syndicate, except for the latter's ½ percent margin. So the LIBOR payments always net to zero, and your cost is fixed at the 9½ percent swap rate plus the ½ percent syndicate margin, for an all-in cost of 10 percent.

Table 5.1 Interest Rate Swap Cash Flows

1 Jun 1999	$475,000
1 Dec	475,000
1 Jun 2000	475,000
1 Dec	475,000
1 Jun 2001	475,000
1 Dec	475,000
1 Jun 2002	475,000
1 Dec	475,000
1 Jun 2003	475,000
1 Dec	475,000

Table 5.2 Swap Flows if Rates Rise/Fall

	Fixed Payment	Income	
		Case I: LIBOR Rises	Case II: LIBOR Falls
1 Jun 1999	$475,000	$400,000	$400,000
1 Dec	475,000	412,500	387,500
1 Jun 2000	475,000	425,000	375,000
1 Dec	475,000	437,500	362,500
1 Jun 2001	475,000	450,000	350,000
1 Dec	475,000	462,500	337,500
1 Jun 2002	475,000	475,000	325,000
1 Dec	475,000	487,500	312,500
1 Jun 2003	475,000	500,000	300,000
1 Dec	475,000	512,500	287,500

Origins of IRS

The origins of the interest rate swap (IRS) technique were in the Eurobond market, where fixed rate issuers wished to raise floating rate money. A typical example in the early days would have been a Japanese bank. Because most banks typically lend money on a floating rate basis, Japanese banks were not in the habit of issuing fixed rate Eurobonds. They did not need fixed rate funds. Therefore, their paper was relatively scarce in the fixed rate bond market, and it commanded attractive premiums. Thus, they were able to issue cheaply and then to swap into floating rate funds.

An example would be as follows: a strong borrower, AAA, would pay LIBOR + ⅛ percent for a 7-year revolving credit from its banks, if it chose to arrange one. For a 7-year bond issue, it would pay 11 percent. Conversely, a weaker borrower, BBB, must pay 12 percent for a 7-year bond issue or LIBOR + ½ percent for 7-year money from a bank.

The difference between the two borrowers in the bank credit market is only ⅜ percent. But in the bond market it is 1 percent: a "credit differential" of ⅝ percent. The first swaps used this differential to arbitrage. AAA issued a bond and entered into a swap with BBB—let us assume, at 11.25 percent. Both borrowers were able to save money. Here, the ⅝ percent is split to assign ⅜ percent for AAA and ¼ percent for BBB.

There has been a tendency in the academic literature to explain swaps in terms of relative comparative advantage. This explains why the technique was created, but I think it is better to think of the interest rate swap market as an arena where we trade LIBOR for forward delivery. Just as there is a market for the forward delivery of DEM against US$, so there is a market for the forward

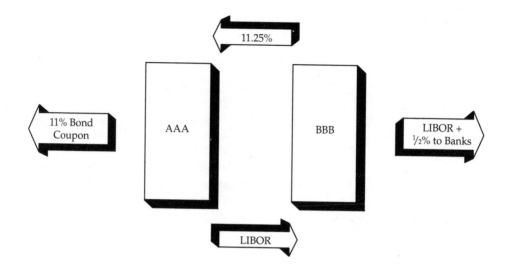

Net cost for AAA:	$11\% - 11.25\% + \text{LIBOR} = \text{LIBOR} - \frac{1}{4}\%$
Net cost for BBB:	$11.25\% - \text{LIBOR} + \text{Libor} + \frac{1}{2}\% = 11.75\%$
Net saving for AAA:	$\frac{3}{8}\%$
Net saving for BBB:	$\frac{1}{4}\%$

Figure 5.4 AAA swaps with BBB.

sale or purchase of LIBOR. A firm doing a swap where it pays 10 percent per annum on $100 million against 6-month US$ LIBOR for 5 years is contracting to buy forward deliveries of 6-month US$ LIBOR on $100 million. We can say that 10 percent per annum is the price of forward deliveries of 6-month US$ LIBOR for 5 years.

Hence, the interest rate swap market has become an arena for transferring interest rate risk that sits alongside the interest rate futures market and the FRA market. In all these markets, those who anticipate rising rates trade with those who either expect a fall in rates or else have a requirement to switch their exposure to a floating-rate basis (e.g., banks that have borrowed fixed rate funds, which they now plan to lend on a floating rate basis).

Quoting an Interest Rate Swap

Suppose today is March 3, 2001. You are pricing a swap for your company, which is interested in swapping out of 6-month US$ LIBOR and paying a fixed US$ rate. Upon consulting a Reuters swap screen, you see the data shown in Table 5.3.

Table 5.3 Swap Quotes

Treasury Bond	Swap Spread	Swap Cost
2-year	7.64 T + 47/54	8.11/18
3-year	7.75 T + 65/70	8.40/45
4-year	7.78 T + 68/76	8.46/54
5-year	7.90 T + 70/78	8.60/68

To use these data, you need to know that swap rates are priced off the corresponding U.S. Treasury bond. Thus, if the company were to pay a fixed rate for 2 years, the swap cost would be the 2-year Treasury rate, 7.64 percent, plus the swap spread of 54 basis points, for a total of 8.18 percent, plus the credit spread (if any) being charged by the intermediary bank for providing the swap. If the company wanted to deal in the opposite direction (i.e., receive a fixed rate), the spread would be 47 basis points for a total cost of 8.11 percent, which is what it would be paid by the market, less any credit spread charged by the bank.

It is important to be aware that the rate is quoted on a "Treasury bond basis," that is, a semiannual actual/365 rate. To convert this to a 360-day rate, we multiply by 360/365 to convert 8.18 percent to 8.07 percent (note the 11-basis-point difference). To convert this to an annual rate (to make it comparable to, say, a Eurodollar money market rate), we need to use the following formula:

$$r = \left(1 + \frac{i}{n}\right)^n$$

where r = annual rate;
    i = semiannual rate;
    n = number of periods per annum (2 in this case).

We then have:

$$r = \left(1 + \frac{.0807}{2}\right)^2$$
$$r = 8.23 \text{ percent.}$$

In summary, to convert a Treasury bond rate to an annual money market rate: (1) multiply by 360/365, reducing the nominal rate (by 11 points, in this case) and (2) compound up to annual, raising the nominal rate (by 16 points, in this case). If the company borrows on a Eurodollar money market basis but is charged interest semiannually rather than annually, then the current swap rate for comparison purposes would be 8.07 percent.

Table 5.4 Cash, Zero, and Forward Rates

Year	Cash Market Rate (%)	Zero Coupon Rate (%)	Forward Rate (%)
1	5	5	5
2	6	6.0302987	7.0707071
3	7	7.0969352	9.2625064

The Pricing of Interest Rate Swaps (IRS)

IRS Pricing.   A number of practical issues must be looked at in swap pricing, but it may help to start with a simple framework. Suppose we are pricing a 3-year swap. For simplicity, suppose it is priced against annual LIBOR, and we have the annual rates shown in Table 5.4 (worked out as explained in Chapter 3).

We know that a rational way to price the 3-year swap is to proceed as follows. The 3-year swap rate must equal the "present value" average of the forward rates. That is, the rate will be set so that the present value of the fixed cash flows on the swap equals the present value of the cash flows of the forward rates. If this were not so, it would be possible to set up a series of long-dated forward rate agreements whose value would be greater/less than the swap's. We could create an arbitrage, at least in theory. (In practice, this would depend on the availability of such agreements in the market.)

We can put this another way. The present value average is the rate that would make the present value of sums placed at the forward rate (discounted at the zero-coupon rate for the given final maturity) equal to the present value of sums produced by the swap.

We have a situation where the present value of sums placed at the forward amount is (assuming a principal amount of $100):

$$\frac{5\%}{(1.05)^1} + \frac{7.0707\%}{(1.060303)^2} + \frac{9.2625\%}{(1.07069)^3}$$

and we want to find the swap rate that makes the above units equal to:

$$\frac{\text{Swap rate}}{(1.05)^1} + \frac{\text{Swap rate}}{(1.060303)^2} + \frac{\text{Swap rate}}{(1.07069)^3}$$

In this case, the applicable rate is 7 percent, the same as the cash rate for Year 3. This seems a trivial result for all that hard work, but this is because, in our example, we used (1) equal principal amounts in each period; (2) a spot (i.e., nondeferred) start for the swap. But this simple method can be applied where one or both of these conditions does not apply, which makes the method much more interesting and useful. We now turn to these variants.

IRS Variants

Amortizing Swaps. Suppose we want to price a 3-year amortizing swap, where the principal amount outstanding on the swap is Year 1, $100 million; Year 2, $75 million; and Year 3, $50 million. We proceed exactly as in the previous discussion, except that each term is weighted according to the amount involved. The present value of the forward flows is:

$$\frac{100 \times 5\%}{(1.05)^1} + \frac{75 \times 7.0707\%}{(1.060303)^2} + \frac{50 \times 9.2625\%}{(1.07069)^3}$$

and we want to find the swap rate that makes the above units equal to:

$$\frac{100 \times \text{Swap rate}}{(1.05)^1} + \frac{75 \times \text{Swap rate}}{(1.060303)^2} + \frac{50 \times \text{Swap rate}}{(1.07069)^3}$$

The answer comes out to be 6.5378 percent. It is lower than the previous result because the higher amounts of principal in the early years, when rates are lower, have pulled it down.

Deferred-Start (Forward) Swap. Applying the same technique to a deferred-start swap is equally simple; we just set the outstanding principal amount to zero for each year until the swap starts. Suppose we have the same conditions as before, but now we want to quote a 2-year swap for $100 million, starting 1 year from now. We simply plug in principal amounts of 0, 100, and 100, as before. Once again, we have the value of the forward flows as:

$$\frac{0 \times 5\%}{(1.05)^1} + \frac{100 \times 7.0707\%}{(1.060303)^2} + \frac{100 \times 9.2625\%}{(1.07069)^3}$$

and we want to find the swap rate that makes the above units equal to:

$$\frac{0 \times \text{Swap rate}}{(1.05)^1} + \frac{100 \times \text{Swap rate}}{(1.060303)^2} + \frac{100 \times \text{Swap rate}}{(1.07069)^3}$$

This answer turns out to be 8.1181 percent. By delaying the swap until the higher rates start to apply, we have pulled up the average.

This technique could also be applied to an amortizing swap with a forward start date. One simply sets to zero the principal amounts until the start date of the amortizing swap. Similarly, it can be applied to an accreting swap—one whose principal value grows over the time period (i.e., the reverse of an amortizing swap). It can also be applied to a so-called "roller-coaster" (one whose principal value rises and falls).

Forward swaps have had a wide range of uses. They allow hedging of exposures that have not yet begun. Sometimes they can be used to achieve arbitrage; for example, there was a period when U.S. municipalities could achieve attractive funding by entering forward-start swaps to lock up attractive rate levels. The municipal bond curve was very cheap compared to the Treasury curve, and the swap curve was unaffected.

Index Amortizing.   Up to now, we have implicitly assumed that when we set up the swap, we knew its amortization pattern. There is a class of swaps for which we do not know the pattern in advance: index amortizing swaps. Sometimes referred to as sinking fund swaps, this class of swaps was originally created in the United States as an off-balance-sheet alternative to more traditional investments such as collateralized mortgage obligations. Usually, in these swaps, the investor receives a fixed rate and pays a floating rate (generally LIBOR) on a notional principal. This principal amortizes down according to the level of a chosen index. The index was originally tied to prepayments on outstanding mortgage-backed securities. Since 1990, in a number of swaps, the amortization has been tied to the pattern of interest rates, in an effort to mimic the behavior of the mortgage market. Table 5.5 shows an example.

In this example, we have a 5-year amortizing swap for an initial notional amount of $100 million. The fixed rate is at 5.25 percent, payable semiannually on a 365-day basis, versus LIBOR on a 360-day basis. The terms of the swap provide for a 2-year "lockout" period, during which no amortization takes place. Thereafter, the swap amortizes provided LIBOR is fixed between 3 percent and 6.75 percent. (If LIBOR is below the floor, the amortization rate is 100 percent, or full immediate prepayment; if above, no prepayment takes place.) The speed of amortization is determined by a multiplier of 0.25 percent of the notional amount per basis point. Table 5.6 on page 107 gives an example.

In this example, we have no amortization in periods 1 through 4 (the first 2 years) because of the lockout. In period 5, LIBOR is within the amortization

Table 5.5   Index Amortizing Swap Transaction

Term (years)	5
Notional	$100 million
Fixed rate	5.25%
Basis	365 days
Floating rate index	6-month LIBOR
Basis	360 days
Lockout period (years)	2
Payment frequency (per annum)	2
Amortization frequency (per annum)	2
Amortization schedule:	
LIBOR floor	3
LIBOR ceiling	6.75%
Multiplier	0.25% of notional per basis point below ceiling
Clean-up level (% of principal)	10%

Table 5.6   Index Amortizing Swap Example

Period	Observed LIBOR	Reduction	Outstanding Principal
1	6 %	0 %	$100,000,000
2	6.75	0	100,000,000
3	6.25	0	100,000,000
4	5.5	0	100,000,000
5	5.25	37.5	62,500,000
6	6	18.75	50,781,250
7	6.5	6.25	47,607,422
8	6.75	0	47,607,422
9	6	18.75	38,681,030
10	6	0	—

range, so the principal is reduced as follows: $[1 - [675 - 525] \times (0.0025)]$. Thereafter, LIBOR starts to rise, and the amortization rate slows down. In the last period, total amortization is achieved. If, at any time, the notional principal outstanding falls to less than 10 percent of the original, there is a "clean-up" provision under which the remainder of the swap is immediately terminated. Figure 5.5 shows the above payment pattern, together with what happens if LIBOR is always below or always above the limits.

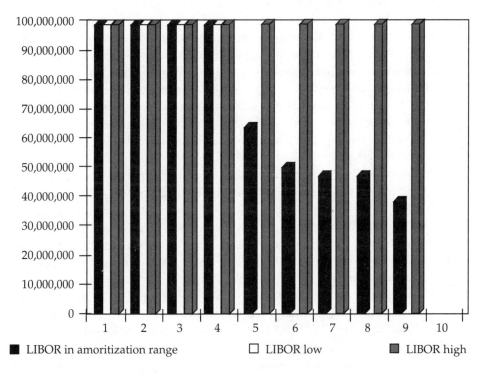

Figure 5.5   Index amoritizing swap.

Blended Rate Swaps.   Another application of the technique discussed above is in creating a blended rate swap. Consider a borrower who has just raised 5-year fixed rate money at 6.35 percent. Suppose this could be swapped to LIBOR flat. Alternatively, the borrower might consider a 5-year blended rate swap under which he or she receives 6.35 percent and pays a blended rate of 5.85 percent and 6-month US$ LIBOR – 0.25 percent. At the start of the swap and during a two-year lockout period, the blend is 100 percent fixed rate at 5.85 percent. Thereafter, the blend can shift proportionately into LIBOR – 0.25 percent according to movements in LIBOR. If LIBOR rises above a given level, the proportion of floating rate rises. In essence, this swap uses the same technique as the index amortizing swap: but here the notional amount of the swap remains constant throughout. Instead of the notional amount being "repaid," the total notional amount is partially unswapped.

The swap could offer an attractive opportunity. On the other hand, there is a potential opportunity cost if rates rise or fall dramatically. If rates fall sharply, it would have been better not to do the swap at all, or to have done a conventional swap. Likewise, if rates rise sharply, it would be better not to swap out of the fixed rate debt. The main attraction would be to a borrower who is not entirely certain about future rate movements but believes they will be cyclical.

Premium/Discount Structure (Off-Market).   We often need to set up a swap to match cash flows that are at a rate different from the current market level. A common example arises in the case of an asset swap, where we are doing a swap against a bond that was issued some time ago. The coupon on the bond is well away from the market price, which is often why the bond is "swappable" in the first place. The bond may be either at a substantial premium or a discount; in either case, the typical investor may have tax considerations. Another situation might occur where a client has an existing borrowing and wants to swap out, while ensuring that the future cash flows of the swap and the borrowing are matched.

In essence, we need to find the present value of the net income or loss that will accrue over the life of the swap from the off-market flows. Depending on our valuation approach, we might calculate this either by using the zero-coupon curve or by valuing the flows at the swap rate. Table 5.7 illustrates an example. We have a $50 million notional principal; the current annual swap rate is 6.657 percent, but we have to match a stream at 8 percent. This will give us a net income per period of $671,371.87. Discounted at the swap rate, for the first period, that would have a present value of $629,466.67; discounted at the zero-coupon rate for that maturity, it is worth $634,867.02. The entire stream is worth $2,778,205.04, or $2,751,153.16 if valued at the zero-coupon curve. This would be the fee that we would have to pay if we were contracting to receive the 8 percent; likewise, the fee we would charge (neglecting the question of bid-offer spreads) if we had to pay the 8 percent.

Table 5.7 Off-Market Swap Structure

Principal	$50,000.00		Year	Zero-Coupon Yields
Term in years	5		1	5.75%
Swap rate (annual)	6.657%		2	6.25
Off-market rate	8%		3	6.75
			4	7.25
			5	7.75

				Net Present Value (NPV) of Income	
Period	We Pay	We Receive	Income	NPV@Swap Rate	NPV@Zero Coupon-Rate
1	$3,328,628.13	$4,000,000.00	$671,371.87	$ 629,466.67	$ 634,867.02
2	3,328,628.13	4,000,000.00	671,371.87	590,177.07	594,710.03
3	3,328,628.13	4,000,000.00	671,371.87	553,339.82	551,898.85
4	3,328,628.13	4,000,000.00	671,371.87	518,801.85	507,427.43
5	3,328,628.13	4,000,000.00	671,371.87	486,419.65	462,249.82
				$2,778,205.04	$2,751,153.16

Zero-Coupon Swaps

Zero-coupon swaps are contracts in which one of the counterparties, instead of paying a series of cash flows, chooses to pay a lump sum amount of cash at maturity. Zero-coupon swaps might be useful to firms that will not have ready access to cash during a set time period but expect the cash to be available later. The swaps entail more credit risk to the counterparty, who is thus likely to seek more attractive rates, making the swap more expensive to the firm. Alternatively, we can roll up the LIBOR payments that would be due under the swap, compounding them at the next period's LIBOR, and settling a final net amount at the end of the swap.

To calculate the zero-coupon rate, we can proceed in various ways, depending on our view of the credit risk and other matters. A simple way to proceed would be to take the equivalent conventional swap rate and compound up the swap flows at the forward rate for each period, derived from the cash market rates and the implicit zero-coupon curve. Suppose we have the situation shown in Table 5.8.

If we consider a bond purchased at 100 whose cumulative value at maturity is 127.6671, we find that the implied zero swap rate is 8.3098 or 8.31 percent. However, our pricing will be influenced by how the deal is structured, because if the LIBOR flows are paid out, the potential credit risk will be considerable.

Table 5.8 Zero-Coupon Data

Conventional swap rate for maturity: 8.2500 percent

Year	Cash Market Rate	Zero-Coupon Rate	Forward Rate	Swap Flow	Cumulated Value
0.5	6.5 %	6.6056%		$4.1250	$ 4.1250
1	7.25	7.3935	8.1873%	4.1250	8.4155
1.5	7.5	7.6555	8.1813	4.1250	12.8780
2	7.75	7.9230	8.7295	4.1250	17.5534
2.5	8.125	8.3374	10.0111	4.1250	22.5360
3	8.25	8.4687	9.1272	4.1250	27.6671

Spreadlock Swap

The "spreadlock" or "deferred rate setting" swap is used when we want to lock in the swap spread but not the interest rate. We think the swap spread is at a good level, but we do not want to lock in the absolute interest rate level. Either we expect rates to rise or fall in our favor, or we have not yet put in place the underlying finance to which the swap will be linked.

In brief, the technique consists of a contract wherein the two parties agree to trade a swap at a specific spread, with the underlying interest rate to be fixed later. For example, Borrower A contracts with Bank B that it will receive T + 125 for 5 years. (Perhaps because it expects to issue a bond at, say, T + 100 at some time during that period, and by means of the spreadlock, it ensures that it will receive sub-LIBOR funding.) The contract provides that, during the next 3 months, A can fix the swap level at any time. When A fixes the deal, the level of T is agreed, usually by some means laid down in the contract. At that point, the swap becomes a normal swap.

Here is how this is hedged. As soon as the deal is done, Bank B sells short the 5-year Treasury bond. At the same time, it does a swap under which it receives, say, T + 130 for 5 years, 3 months. Bank B's total costs, therefore, are determined by this matching swap, together with the cost of running the hedge. Suppose that, at the time the deal is done, T is standing at 6.5 percent. Bank B is selling short the Treasury bonds; when it buys them back, it will buy them back *plus* accrued interest. The coupon, T, of 6.5 percent is therefore accruing against Bank B.

Against this, Bank B will be doing reverse repos in the market (see Figure 5.6). It will be borrowing bonds and placing cash (received from the short sale of the bonds initially) in the market. Suppose it receives 4.5 percent on the cash in the reverse repo. It is then incurring a hedging cost of 2 percent while the hedge is in place (6.5 percent T-bond coupon accruing against it, less the 4.5 percent received on the reverse repo cash amount).

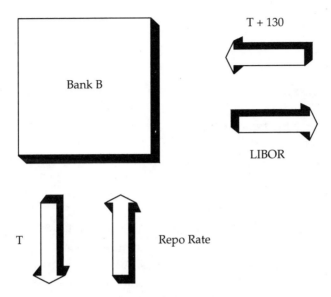

Figure 5.6 Spreadlock hedge structure.

If the hedge is run for 3 months, the cost is approximately ½ percent (2 percent for a quarter of a year). Bank B, in its initial pricing of the deal, would allow for the cost of running the hedge for all or part of this period, and would amortize the up-front cost over the remaining 5 years of the swap. The day-to-day practicalities of managing the hedge mean that the longer the permitted spreadlock period (3 months, in our example), the higher the operating costs and the greater the risks of managing the hedge; hence, a larger premium is likely to be charged.

Overnight Rate Swaps

Overnight Index Swaps (OIS) began to develop in 1995. Such swaps are normally against a published index of a daily benchmark funding rate, paid on a compounded basis. Their attraction is the ability to switch a longer-term rate to an overnight rate, thereby allowing a match against, for example, repo positions. By early 1996, the daily average turnover in the French market, the first to develop, was around FRF100 billion. In April 1996, the Bank for International Settlements announced that it would publish an official settlement rate for overnight ECU deposits, to permit trading in OIS ECU swaps.

In Frankfurt, after an initial failure with the monthly overnight average, a successful overnight index swap structure was developed using the Frankfurt interbank overnight average (Fiona). The rates involved are published by the Zentraler Kreditausschuss (German Banking Association). The swap terms vary from 2 days to 12 months; value date is normally 2 working days after the trade. The overnight rate is compounded up, using the following formula:

$$r_t = \frac{360 \times \left\{ \prod_{t=t_0}^{t_{n-1}} \left(1 + \frac{r_t d_t}{360} \right) - 1 \right\}}{n}$$

where r_f = interest rate to be determined for the floating leg of the Fiona swap;

t_0 = value date of swap start;

t_n = value date of maturity;

r_t = rate fixed for day t;

d_t = number of days for which r_t is valid (generally, 1, except at weekends or holidays);

n = number of days in swap.

The most recent recruit to the ranks of overnight indexed swaps is the sterling market, which began in March 1997. The market uses as its overnight rate reference the Sterling OverNight Interbank Average (SONIA). SONIA is the daily weighted average of all overnight interbank deposits of more than £5 million made before 3 P.M. through the seven largest money brokers—about 70 percent of the market.

Swaps against overnight rates have developed in a number of other markets. In Brazil, for example, there is a market in floating DI (the overnight rate published daily by the central clearinghouse, CETIP). This swap, floating DI versus fixed R\$, would typically work as follows. Party A would pay party B a previously negotiated fixed rate (e.g., 66 percent per annum). Party B will pay party A a floating amount, which is linked to the DI rate at the maturity date. The term is normally short—30, 60, or 90 days—and there is only a single payment at maturity. Unusually, market convention is that the fixed side of the swap is calculated with daily compounding.[2] During the first half of 1995, approximately \$80 billion worth of such swaps were traded through the BM&F. Swaps are cleared through CETIP. Even larger quantities of swaps are registered directly with CETIP; a recent report stated that \$4 billion of swaps were being registered direct each day, compared with \$1.2 billion at the futures exchange.

Basis Swaps

In contrast to simple fixed to floating rate swaps, basis swaps involve two floating rates—for instance, U.S. dollar LIBOR and the U.S. Treasury bill rate. A borrower such as the World Bank, wishing to raise money against a borrowing target measured against U.S. Treasury bills, might do a Eurobond issue that is swapped by the bank, leading the issue into LIBOR. That bank might have quoted a swap rate into Treasury bills that the World Bank felt was

---

[2] Discussed in detail by H. Shefi, *Risk* (December 1996), Latin America Supplement.

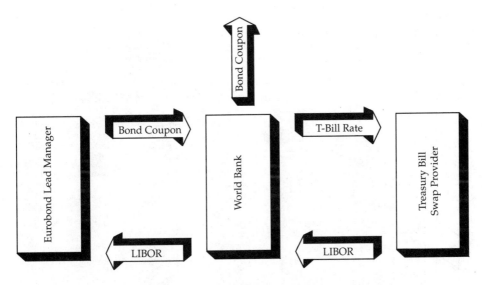

Figure 5.7 Treasury bill/LIBOR basis swap.

uncompetitive. The World Bank might prefer to take the swap into LIBOR and arrange a separate swap into the Treasury bill rate. The structure would then be as shown in Figure 5.7.

LIBOR in Arrears

At certain times, depending on the shape of the short-term yield curve, a swap may be done where LIBOR is fixed in arrears; that is, the floating rate is set at the end of the interest rate accrual period rather than at the beginning, as would normally be the case. End users who believe that short-term rates will not rise as much as forward rates predict might seek to receive a fixed rate while paying LIBOR in arrears. (Equally, and perhaps more common, one might do a basis swap of conventional LIBOR vs. LIBOR-in-arrears.)

Suppose we have the situation given in Table 5.9.

Table 5.9 Arrears Reset Data

Year	Cash Market Rate	Zero-Coupon Rate	Implied Forward Rate
0.5	3.5 %	3.5 %	
1	3.875	3.9162	4.3342%
1.5	4.375	4.4364	5.4845
2	4.75	4.8306	6.0222
2.5	5.25	5.3672	7.5412
3	5.5	5.6349	6.9836

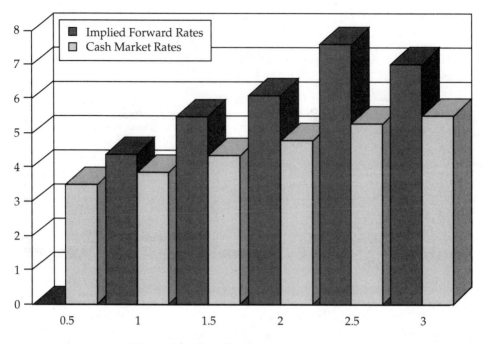

Figure 5.8 Benefit of arrears reset swap.

In this situation, as can be seen from Figure 5.8, the payer of the 3-year fixed rate stands potentially to benefit from an arrears reset swap. Instead of receiving the initial LIBOR of 3.5 percent, the payer expects to receive 4.3342 percent. This is the current market expectation for 6-month LIBOR 6 months from now, as implied by the forward rate. The payer expects to receive, in the final period, 6.9836 percent. A crude estimate of the benefit from the arrears reset structure therefore is $(6.9836 - 3.5) = 3.4836$ percent. This would be spread out over the life of the swap and built into the price. (In practice, we would work out the two sets of cash flows implied by the swaps, and discount the difference using the appropriate zero-coupon rates. We would need to allow for the fact that if the swap were long term, the arrears structure has more convexity than the conventional structure; it has been shown[3] that, on a 10-year swap, the adjustment might be of the order of 2 to 3 basis points.)

Swaps Against Different Notional Amounts

The swaps discussed in this section are perfectly normal interest rate swaps, but, for various reasons, they are carried out in an amount different from the underlying amount of the associated asset. Two examples may be relevant:

---

[3] A. Li and V. R. Raghavan, "LIBOR-in-Arrears Swaps," *Journal of Derivatives* (Spring 1996).

(1) a domestic U.S. municipal bond issue paying 50 percent of the 6-month LIBOR rate (where the coupon is low because of the tax exemptions available in the past to investors in municipal bonds), and (2) an inverse floater.

First, we will consider the municipal bond. Suppose we have a $100 million issue on which the coupon is fixed at 50 percent of 6-month LIBOR. Thus, for example, if the LIBOR level is 8 percent, the coupon is 4 percent (or 2 percent per 6-month period, roughly speaking), as illustrated in Table 5.10. The issuer, however, wishes to pay a fixed rate. The way to fix the rate is to do a swap, not for $100 million, but for $50 million. (If the coupon were 60 percent of LIBOR, the swap should be for $60 million.) Suppose the swap rate is 10 percent. The coupon flows on the swap will match those on the bond.

A similar application (i.e., to match the swap perfectly to the underlying asset, we do the swap in a ratio to the asset rather than the same amount) occurs if we wish to swap an inverse FRN (see Chapter 9) into a fixed rate. Suppose we have an inverse FRN that pays interest at 14.5 percent − 0.5 × LIBOR. The issuer intends to swap this into a fixed rate.

The construction method is as follows. We have an underlying factor, say 2. Suppose today's swap rate is 8 percent. We construct the floater to pay a maximum coupon of [Swap rate (1 + Factor) − Spread]. So we might have (8*3 − 1) = 23 (i.e., the FRN coupon is 23 − 2 × LIBOR. We then do the swap amount on the FRN issue size × factor (e.g., if the FRN were $100 million, we would do a $200 million swap). We would then have the cash flows shown in Table 5.11. As we can see, the issuer has fixed at an attractive rate (swap rate − 1 percent).

Table 5.10 Municipal Swap Cash Flows

LIBOR	Coupon: Income Bond	Swap	Combined
5%	2.5%	−2.5%	5%
6	3	−2	5
7	3.5	−1.5	5
8	4	−1	5
9	4.5	−0.5	5
10	5	0	5
11	5.5	0.5	5
12	6	1	5
13	6.5	1.5	5
14	7	2	5
15	7.5	2.5	5
16	8	3	5
17	8.5	3.5	5
18	9	4	5
19	9.5	4.5	5

Table 5.11   Swapping Out an Inverse Floater

| LIBOR | Coupon: Income | | |
	Inverse Floater	Swap	Combined
5%	13%	6%	7%
6	11	4	7
7	9	2	7
8	7	0	7
9	5	-2	7
10	3	-4	7
11	1	-6	7

ASSET SWAPS

An important investment application for swaps is in the so-called "asset swap" market. Asset swaps are a way to shift paper from one market to another. Bonds have been issued consisting of floating rate notes swapped into fixed rates. An example would be the BECS issue in 1985, in which $100 million of U.K. government U.S. dollar floating rate notes were swapped into fixed rate dollar bonds, producing "synthetic U.S. dollar gilt-edged bonds." More often, a fixed rate bond coupled with an interest rate (and perhaps a currency) swap is used to produce a synthetic floating rate note.

It was not long before investment banks realized the value of the asset swap technique. Put bluntly, a failed fixed rate bond could be transformed into a floating rate note and placed with banks, who are well accustomed to buying floating rate instruments. The technique has been particularly widespread in the Japanese equity warrant bond market.

At its height, bonds in this market were being issued with coupons as low as 1 percent or 2 percent. The attractions of the warrant were so great that the bond to which the warrant was attached could have a relatively low coupon. Thus, immediately after the bond was issued and the warrants were stripped away from it, the straight bond would fall to a sharp discount: a price of $70 or even $60 per $100 nominal. Traditionally, many investors are not interested in buying deep discount, low-coupon bonds, for accounting (and other) reasons. Thus, while the warrant was a roaring success, the bonds would languish.

It was not long before the asset swappers perceived the opportunity. They would move in to buy the unwanted bonds, couple them with an interest rate swap, and sell them to the banks. These bonds, however, were operationally a great deal more complex to swap, because of the deep discount nature of the cash flows.

Asset swap activity has had both positive and negative effects. On the positive side, for every new issue, there is now generally a floor point below which the bond cannot fall. At some point, it becomes "swappable": the bond's spread over Treasuries is above the spread that the swap market requires to swap into floating rate. At that point, the bond can be redistributed into the floating rate market, a tactic that provides a natural floor price for the bond in the fixed rate market. On the negative side, the asset-swapped bonds tend to be firmly held to maturity, which somewhat reduces liquidity for the remaining bonds (by reducing the total "float"—tradable bonds—down to a level where it is not worth market makers' time to quote prices on the bond).

The mechanics of a typical deal are as follows. In January 1999, an investing institution is offered US$5 million of XYZ Corporation notes. They are senior unsecured obligations of XYZ, which at the time is rated BBB by Standard & Poor's. Maturity of the notes is March 15, 2003, and they pay a coupon of 10 percent semiannually in arrears; the bond is a domestic U.S. corporate bond. They are optionally redeemable on or after March 15, 2002, at the option of XYZ, at 100 percent of the principal amount plus accrued interest.

But the investor is a bank; it has no interest in a fixed rate instrument, because this will expose it to interest rate mismatch. It funds at floating rates. Accordingly, the institution selling the bond arranges an interest rate swap. The amount of the swap is US$5 million, the same notional principal as the amount of the notes purchased. It matures on March 15, 2003, to coincide with the notes' maturity date. Under the swap, the investor effectively hands the coupon over to the seller; that is, it makes fixed payments semiannually in arrears of 10 percent of the principal amount, on March 15 and September 15, to the selling institution. The fixed rate payments are calculated on a 30/360-day basis. The first fixed rate payment is for the full half-year's coupon from September 15, 1998, to March 15, 1999—that is US$ 250,000. (Because the bonds are sold to the investor flat, excluding accrued interest, the investor hands the accrued interest over to the selling institution.) In exchange for receiving the fixed rate coupon, the seller makes floating rate payments to the investor semiannually in arrears at a rate of 6-month $ LIBOR plus 112.5 basis points (say) on the principal amount of $5 million. In the event that XYZ calls the bonds early, the seller grants the investor the right to terminate the swap early, without penalty.

From the investor's point of view, he or she has bought senior unsecured notes of XYZ, yielding LIBOR + 1⅛ percent. The cash flows are as shown in Figure 5.9.

The transaction is not quite so straightforward from the point of view of the seller. Two main issues arise: (1) the handling of the premium or discount on the bond, and (2) the swap termination. Given that market rates at the time of doing the deal were well below 10 percent for the period to maturity on the bond, the bond itself would trade at a premium. Thus, the seller paid a premium for the bond, which it did not receive from the investor. This loss has to be funded and then factored into the price of the swap the seller gives to the investor. The cost of funding the accrued interest also has to be factored in. The

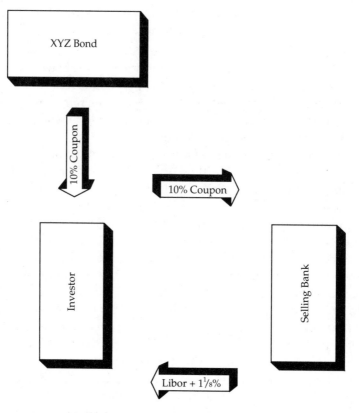

Figure 5.9 XYZ asset swap cash flows.

second complication is the swap termination in the event that the bond is called early: the selling institution has effectively written an interest rate option to the buyer, which has to be properly priced (see Chapters 6 and 7, on options).

The asset swap business today is typically dependent on imbalances between the supply and demand for a particular bond or market. Substantial profits were available during the first Japanese bank crisis of 1992, the ERM crisis of the same year, and the bond market collapse of 1994. In other cases, banks take proprietary positions in bonds where they believe the improving quality of the credit has not yet been recognized by the market. They swap the bonds into floating rate and then sell the paper to syndicated loan departments when the market has recognized the improved credit.

CURRENCY SWAPS

The currency swap market is thought to have begun in the United Kingdom during the 1960s. Exchange controls existing at that time prevented U.K. firms that wished to invest abroad from simply selling sterling to buy foreign currency. The Bank of England, wanting to prevent outflows of sterling, required British firms to borrow overseas to finance overseas investments. This had a drawback in that overseas subsidiaries were often quite weak credits compared with the U.K. parent. Yet, because of the exchange controls, the U.K. parent often could not guarantee the overseas subsidiary. Bankers came up with the idea of a swap between the U.K. parent and an overseas counterparty. The use of the swap meant that the Bank of England could be sure that an outflow of sterling today would be offset by an inflow at a later date, when the swap unwound.

It may be helpful to start with a brief outline of how a currency swap works. Suppose that ICI needs US$ for its operations in the United States, and DuPont needs sterling for its U.K. operations. A solution to their needs is for ICI to sell its sterling to DuPont for dollars. To cut out the risk of exchange rate movements, they contract to reverse the deal in, say, 5 years. ICI sells £10 million to DuPont in exchange for $18 million.

Effectively, ICI is lending sterling to DuPont, and DuPont is lending dollars to ICI (Table 5.12). (The legal structure does not involve any assets on the balance sheet, nor is the deal documented as a loan; it is an exchange of currencies.) During the life of the deal, ICI pays the rate for 5-year dollar loans—say, 7 percent—and DuPont pays the rate for 5-year sterling loans—say, 9 percent. At the end of the deal, ICI and DuPont re-exchange. (In some countries, such as the United Kingdom, it is desirable to interpose a bank between the two parties, because tax law would otherwise require the interest payments to be made net of tax. Interposing a bank also has the advantage of insulating the two parties from the credit risk of the other.)

The cash flows are set out in Table 5.12 from ICI's point of view, assuming that ICI borrowed the £10 million to lend to DuPont, also at 9 percent. At the start of the deal, an inflow of £10 million from the original funding is paid across to DuPont. In exchange, there is an inflow of $18 million from DuPont. The net effect is an inflow of $18 million.

Table 5.12   Currency Swap Cash Flows

	Swap Cash Flows		Original	
Year	$	£	Funding (£)	Net ($)
0	18m.	(10m.)	10 m.	18m.
1	(1.3m.)	0.9m.	(0.9m.)	(1.3m.)
2	(1.3m.)	0.9m.	(0.9m.)	(1.3m.)
3	(1.3m.)	0.9m.	(0.9m.)	(1.3m.)
4	(1.3m.)	0.9m.	(0.9m.)	(1.3m.)
5	(19.3m.)	10.9m.	(10.9m.)	(19.3m.)

In each of the next 5 years, ICI pays its lending bankers £0.9 million in interest on the original funding, receives a corresponding payment of £0.9 million, from DuPont and pays out $1.3 million to DuPont. (Where practical, these payments are netted off.) The last payment includes redemption of the principal amounts. The net result is that a sterling stream of cash flows is transformed into a dollar stream.

Let us look at an issuer who wants to raise 5-year money in U.S. dollars. His advisers tell him that the cheapest course would be to raise 5-year deutsche marks and swap them into U.S. dollars. How will this work?

Suppose the rate (ignoring fees) for 5-year DEM Eurobonds is 7 percent, and the bond is issued at par for DEM200 million. Today's spot US$/DEM rate is $1 = DEM2.00. An American company wants 5-year DEM financing at a rate of 8 percent, in exchange for being paid 10 percent on the US$ equivalent financing it will provide. We assume that the deal can be structured so that all interim flows, and the principal being re-exchanged at maturity, can be exchanged at a rate of $1 = DEM2.00.

Here, the issuer's bond cost is 7 percent, but he earns 8 percent on the swap, so there is a net additional 1 percent saving, making a total US$ cost of 9 percent per annum. What has happened is that the issuer, perhaps because it is a better known credit in the Euromarket, is able to raise 5-year money cheaper than its swap counterpart; in exchange for passing on the cheap DEM, it is able to borrow cheap dollars.

Notice that the final cash flow includes exchange of principal amounts, unlike the interest rate swap deal; thus, the credit exposure (see below) on a currency swap will usually be much larger than under an interest rate swap. (In fact, in a currency swap, it is theoretically possible to lose more than 100 percent of the principal amount.)

The IBM/World Bank Swap

A more detailed real-life example may be of interest. In 1981, IBM and the World Bank entered into a currency swap: the World Bank, which had issued comparatively little US$ paper, could raise funds at an attractive rate in the U.S. market. It wanted CHF and DEM, but had issued a lot of bonds in Switzerland and Germany. IBM wanted to crystallize its foreign exchange gains on some existing CHF and DEM bonds outstanding. The solution benefiting both was for the World Bank to issue a US$ bond and swap the proceeds with IBM. Details of the transaction have never been published in full; the following outline draws on D. R. Bock's description (*Swap Finance*, B. Antl, ed., Euromoney Publications, London, 1986, pp. 218–223).

The bond issue was launched on August 11, 1981, settling August 25, which became the settlement date for the swap. The first annual exchange under the swap, however, was to be on March 30, 1982, the next coupon date on IBM's bonds—215 days (rather than 360 days) from the start date.

Table 5.13 IBM/World Bank Swap Cash Flows

	CHF		DEM	
Exchange Date	CHF Flows	Discount Factor	DEM Flows	Discount Factor
3/30/82	12,375,000	0.95507746	30,000,000	0.93957644
3/30/83	12,375,000	0.88433099	30,000,000	0.84646526
3/30/84	12,375,000	0.81882499	30,000,000	0.76258132
3/30/85	12,375,000	0.75818128	30,000,000	0.68701020
3/30/86	212,375,000	0.70201045	330,000,000	0.61892811
NPV	CHF191,367,478		DEM301,315,273	

The first step was to calculate the value of the CHF and DEM flows, which were valued, say, at 8 percent and 11 percent per annum, respectively. The initial 215-day period meant that the discount factors were $215/360 = 0.597222$, 1.597222, 2.597222, and so on. Applying the Swiss franc rate of 8 percent, then, the discount factors were

$$1/1.08^{0.597222} = 0.95507746; \; 1/1.08^{1.597222} = 0.88433099; \text{ and so on.}$$

Agreement on the final terms of the swap was reached on August 11, two weeks before the settlement date. So the World Bank bought the CHF and DEM net present value (NPV) amounts worked out as above, using two-week forward foreign exchange contracts. Supposing that these contracts were at CHF2.18 and DEM2.56 per US$, the dollar amounts needed by the World Bank were $87,783,247 to buy the CHF and $117,701,753 for the DEM, totaling $205,485,000.

It was then necessary to work out the dollar amount of the bond to be issued. Supposing the issue to be at a coupon of 16 percent with fees of 2.15 percent (i.e., net proceeds of 97.85 percent), the dollar amount of the bond issue had to be $205,485,000/0.9785 = $210,000,000. The final results of the deal were as shown in Table 5.13.

Cross-Currency Basis Swap without Re-Exchange at Maturity. Suppose companies ABC and XYZ enter a cross-currency floating rate (basis) swap, trading deutsche mark LIBOR for dollar LIBOR for 3 years. The normal method is as follows. Suppose the spot rate today is US$1 = DEM1.65 and the 3-year outright forward rate is US$1 = DEM1.50. Then ABC and XYZ would agree to exchange, say, US$100 million against DEM165 million today, reversing the exchange in 3 years. That is, the forward exchange is done at today's spot rate, rather than the outright forward market rate currently quoted, because the two interest rates are different. Hence, one side will benefit from a higher rate of interest. The profit/loss generated by re-exchanging at today's spot will offset that.

To make this concrete, suppose we have the following set of interest and exchange rates today:

US$/DEM spot rate: 1.65

Year	DEM Rate	Zero-Coupon Rate	Forward Rate	Forward US$/DEM
1	8%	8%	8%	1.7301
2	7	6.9653	5.9406	1.7448
3	6	5.9204	3.8611	1.6904

Year	US$ Rate	Zero-Coupon Rate	Forward Rate
1	3%	3%	3%
2	4	4.0202	5.0505
3	5	5.0689	7.1981

Given these interest rate levels, it is likely that DEM LIBOR will be above US$ LIBOR. So, whoever, in this swap, is paying the US$ rates is likely to benefit at the expense of the other party. But this is compensated for by re-exchanging at the spot rate. If I lend DEM165 million, and borrow US$100 million (which is what the basis swap amounts to, although it is not in legal terms a loan/borrowing), then, at maturity, I would like to be able to pay back US$100 million and receive DEM169.04 million at the implied forward market rate. But that way I would benefit twice. By re-exchanging at DEM1.65, I give up the exchange rate profit in exchange for earning the higher DEM interest rates.

But suppose the goal is to structure this swap *without* a re-exchange at maturity, and without the initial exchange. We just contract that I will earn DEM LIBOR from you and I will pay you US$ LIBOR. You will want some incentive to enter into this trade: I will have to pay you something for giving up the re-exchange at maturity. The way in which we work this out is as follows.

The value of the re-exchange, measured in US$, is [(1.6904 – 1.65)/1.6904] = 2.39 percent. The present value, discounting using the 3-year US$ zero-coupon rate, is 2.0605 percent. You will be willing to enter into the transaction only if I pay you that amount *today*. Alternatively, we can convert it back into a sum of basis points per annum, using the Payment (PMT) function in a spreadsheet or calculator. We find that an annual payment, over 3 years, will extinguish an amount of 2.0605 percent. The answer turns out to be 0.7566 percent. So you would be willing—subject to credit risk—to accept an equivalent structure under which I pay you US$ LIBOR + 0.7566 percent in exchange for your paying me DEM LIBOR.

Differential (Quanto)

The differential ("diff") swap, sometimes called a quanto swap, allows users to take a view on the interest rate differential between two markets. A differential swap is somewhat like the swap discussed in the previous section. One party pays the floating rate of one currency and receives the floating rate of another currency, plus or minus a spread. The difference is that payments are denominated in one currency. A typical example might be a 3-year diff swap whereby a DEM borrower wishes to pay the lower US$ LIBOR rates on a borrowing totaling DEM175 million. Unlike the swap discussed previously, the US$ LIBOR is paid here on a DEM amount. The spot rate is DEM1.75. The counterparty, Bank X, is willing to do this trade, provided it receives US$ LIBOR + 136 basis points. This margin compensates it for the hedging costs in the transaction, discussed below.

The borrower, Company A, contracts that it will pay Bank X US$ LIBOR + 136 basis points on a principal amount of DEM175 million, and will receive from Bank X DEM LIBOR on the same amount. All payments are to be made in DEM. The cash flows involved in the swap are shown in Table 5.14, from the point of view of Company A, on the assumption that the LIBOR movements are as set out below.

Company A, in the first period, is paying Bank X 6-month US$ LIBOR plus the margin of 136 basis points (i.e., 4.86 percent), and receives from Bank X the DEM LIBOR of 6.25 percent for a net receipt of DEM1,243,277.78. Thereafter, assuming the LIBOR adjustments are as set out in Table 5.14, Company A receives a stream of future payments that vary with the relationship between the two LIBORs. Had the LIBORs moved differently, Company A might have ended up making payments on the swap rather than always receiving from Bank X.

The pricing of the swap will be driven by the way in which Bank X manages its exposure. In the marketplace, there are a number of ways to hedge diff swaps. One possible route would be to fix the interest payment cash flows by entering into 3-year fixed–floating swaps in US$ and DEM. This could be done in two ways: (1) as a pair of straight swaps, or (2) by aligning the nominal coupon on the two swaps (i.e., one swap becomes an off-market swap with an up-front payment to balance it).

Suppose that the latter alternative is taken: the two swaps are aligned by setting the US$ swap rate equal to the DEM rate. Suppose that the market rates for interest rate swaps in the two currencies are 7.375 percent for DEM

Table 5.14 Diff Swap Cash Flows

Date	Days	6-Month US$ LIBOR	6-Month DEM LIBOR	Margin	Total	Counterparty Payments (DEM)	Counterparty Receipts (DEM)	Net (DEM)
01/03/98								
01/09/98	184	3.5 %	6.25%	136	4.86	4,347,000.00	5,590,277.78	1,243,277
01/03/99	181	3.75	6.5	136	5.11	4,496,090.28	5,719,097.22	1,223,006
01/09/99	184	4	6.75	136	5.36	4,794,222.22	6,037,500.00	1,243,277
01/03/00	182	4.25	7	136	5.61	4,963,291.67	6,193,055.56	1,229,763
01/09/00	184	4.5	7.25	136	5.86	5,241,444.44	6,484,722.22	1,243,277
01/03/01	181	4.75	7.5	136	6.11	5,375,951.39	6,598,958.33	1,223,006

and 4.875 percent for US$. We know from the earlier discussion of swaps at off-market rates that this will require an up-front adjustment. In this case, the present value of the incremental swap flows is US$ 6,612,064.87. (For simplicity, the discounting is done here at the swap rate rather than the zero-coupon rates.) This would result in the cash flow structure shown in Figure 5.10.

If we strip out from this the matching cash flows, we are left with the situation shown in Figure 5.11.

The critical problem is that Bank X is receiving from Company A US$ 6-month LIBOR on DEM175 million, but is paying away 6-month US$ LIBOR on US$100 million. These two amounts are equivalent only if the exchange rate remains at US$1 = DEM1.75. Depending on which way exchange rates have moved, we will have a net receipt or a net payment from this pair of cash flows.

An alternative way of looking at the problem is to focus on the US$ interest rate swap and argue that, provided US$ LIBOR is below 7.375 percent, we will have a positive US$ cash flow from the swap in the swap warehouse; if it is above 7.375 percent, our cash flow will be negative. Institutions manage their exposures under the diff swap in various ways. They use options or some

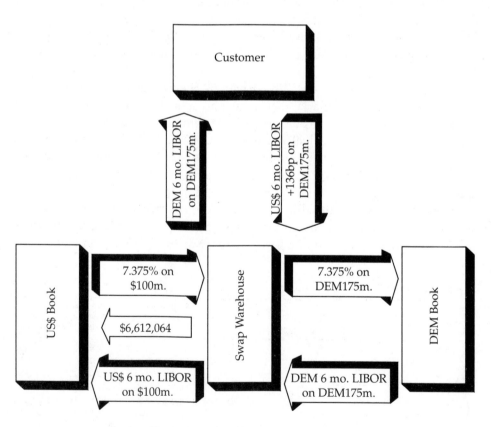

Figure 5.10 Diff swap cash flows.

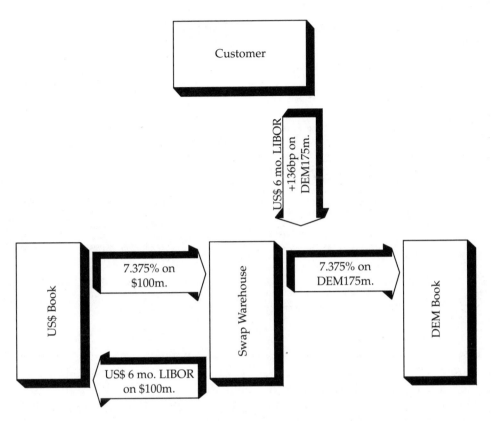

Figure 5.11 Net diff swap flows.

version of dynamic hedging, or they seek to offset the trade with matching components elsewhere in their book.

Swapping Out of a Dual Currency Bond

A dual currency bond involves an issue in which the coupon is denominated in a currency different from the principal. Chapter 12 gives a fuller discussion; here, we discuss an approach to swapping out the exposure implicit in the bond.[4] There has been substantial activity in this market, but the most common use has been by Japanese investors (as noted in Chapter 12). More often than not, the Australian dollar has been the currency chosen to enhance yield on Japanese investments. In the Japanese retail market, the dual currency bond, paying a yen-denominated coupon and redeemed in Australian dollars, has been a very popular structure. The reverse dual, with yen principal and an Australian dollar coupon, has tended to be more popular in the professional

---

[4] This section draws on the discussion by S. Das, *Swaps and Financial Derivatives*, 2nd ed. (London: IFR Publishing, 1994).

Table 5.15   Returns to Investor, Assuming Different Exchange Rates

Principal	50,000,000,000 in JPYm.
Coupon	3.55%
Redemption	50,000,000,000 JPY
Initial exchange rate (AUS$/JPY)	99.05%
AUS$/US$	0.7869%
US$/JPY	125.8736815

			Case 1: No Change in Exchange Rates		Case 2: Forward Currency Rates		Case 3: A 5 Percent per Annum Depreciation	
Period	Principal	Interest AUS$	JPY/AUS$ Rate (%)	Bond Cash Flows (JPY)	JPY/AUS$ Rate (%)	Bond Cash Flows (JPY)	JPY/AUS$ Rate (%)	Bond Cash Flows (JPY)
0	−50,000,000,000		99.05	−50,000,000,000	99.05	−50,000,000,000	99.05	−50,000,000,000
1		17,920,242	99.05	1,775,000,000	91.10815	1,632,680,180	94.0975	1,686,250,000
2		17,920,242	99.05	1,775,000,000	84.26433	1,510,037,142	89.39263	1,601,937,500
3		17,920,242	99.05	1,775,000,000	78.36467	1,404,313,952	84.92299	1,521,840,625
4		17,920,242	99.05	1,775,000,000	73.28133	1,313,219,224	80.67684	1,445,748,594
5		17,920,242	99.05	1,775,000,000	68.90793	1,234,846,856	76.643	1,373,461,164
6		17,920,242	99.05	1,775,000,000	65.156	1,167,611,237	72.81085	1,304,788,106
7		17,920,242	99.05	1,775,000,000	61.952	1,110,194,879	69.17031	1,239,548,701
8		17,920,242	99.05	1,775,000,000	59.23503	1,061,506,100	65.71179	1,177,571,266
9		17,920,242	99.05	1,775,000,000	56.95486	1,020,644,887	62.4262	1,118,692,702
10	50,000,000,000	17,920,242	99.05	51,775,000,000	55.07043	50,986,875,456	59.30489	51,062,758,067
Realized JPY Yield				3.55%		2.5174%		2.7373%

institutional market; given that the principal is currency-protected, this is the more conservative structure. A recent report from the Australian bank, Westpac, stated that the total volume of public dual currency bonds and reverse dual currency bonds for the period from August 1995 to July 1996 was ¥2.1 trillion (US$21 billion), of which ¥1.3 trillion were dual currency and the rest were mainly longer-term reverse dual floating rate notes.

Suppose that we have the situation outlined in Table 5.15. We have a client who is issuing ¥50 billion of a 10-year reverse dual currency bond, which will pay a coupon of 3.55 percent. The coupon is payable in Australian dollars on the AUS$ equivalent of the JP¥ principal amount at the time of issue, but the bond is redeemed in Japanese yen. Table 5.15 illustrates the return to the investor with different exchange rate assumptions: (1) no change in exchange rates; (2) exchange rate outcome is as implied by the forward exchange market; (3) there is a steady 5 percent depreciation in the Australian dollar against the Japanese yen.

The issuer does not wish to take any currency exposure, being an American entity. We enter into a structure whereby the issuer, on the launch date of the bond, pays the ¥50 billion proceeds to us in return for the US$ equivalent, $397,223,624 (based on a spot exchange rate of ¥125.87). Over the life of the transaction, the issuer pays us US$ 6-month LIBOR minus some margin semi-annually in return for receiving the exact Australian dollar coupon of AUS$17,920,242 . This eliminates any currency exposure for the issuer on the coupons. At maturity, the initial exchange is reversed. (See Table 5.16.)

To cover ourselves, we enter into two sets of transactions illustrated in Figure 5.12 and Table 5.17: (1) a currency swap of JP¥ against US$ floating LIBOR,

Table 5.16   Bond Swap from Issuer's Viewpoint

In = +, Out = −

		Bond Swap			
				Interest	
Period	Principal	JPY	AUD$	AUD$	US$
0	50,000,000,000	−50,000,000,000			397,223,624
1			−17,920,242	+17,920,242	USD LIBOR −X
2			−17,920,242	+17,920,242	USD LIBOR −X
3			−17,920,242	+17,920,242	USD LIBOR −X
4			−17,920,242	+17,920,242	USD LIBOR −X
5			−17,920,242	+17,920,242	USD LIBOR −X
6			−17,920,242	+17,920,242	USD LIBOR −X
7			−17,920,242	+17,920,242	USD LIBOR −X
8			−17,920,242	+17,920,242	USD LIBOR −X
9			−17,920,242	+17,920,242	USD LIBOR −X
10			−17,920,242	+17,920,242	USD LIBOR −X
	−50,00,000,000	+50,000,000,000			−397,223,624

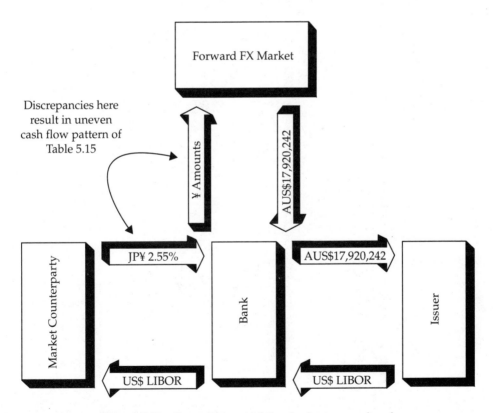

Figure 5.12   Swapping out of the dual currency bond.

Table 5.17 Hedges: Currency Swap and Forward Foreign Exchange Contracts

Our hedges: In = +, Out = −

Period	Swap Against Dual Bond JPY	Swap Against Dual Bond USD	Hedge Transactions JPY into USD LIBOR JPY	Hedge Transactions JPY into USD LIBOR USD	Net Flows JPY	Net Flows AUD	Zero Coupon Interest Rates JPY	Zero Coupon Interest Rates AUD	LTFX Rates A$	Net Cash Flow	PV A$
0	50,000,000,000	−397,223,624	−50,000,000,000	397,223,624					99.05		
1	−17,920,242	X	1,275,000,000	−X	1,275,000,000	−17,920,242	2.1	11	91.10815	−3,925,886	−3,536,834
2	−17,920,242	X	1,275,000,000	−X	1,275,000,000	−17,920,242	2.15	10.75	84.26433	−2,789,284	−2,274,078
3	−17,920,242	X	1,275,000,000	−X	1,275,000,000	−17,920,242	2.2	10.5	78.36467	−1,650,156	−1,223,033
4	−17,920,242	X	1,275,000,000	−X	1,275,000,000	−17,920,242	2.25	10.25	73.28133	−521,541	−353,000
5	−17,920,242	X	1,275,000,000	−X	1,275,000,000	−17,920,242	2.3	10	68.90793	582,707	361,815
6	−17,920,242	X	1,275,000,000	−X	1,275,000,000	−17,920,242	2.35	9.75	65.156	1,648,179	943,142
7	−17,920,242	X	1,275,000,000	−X	1,275,000,000	−17,920,242	2.4	9.5	61.952	2,660,207	1,409,342
8	−17,920,242	X	1,275,000,000	−X	1,275,000,000	−17,920,242	2.45	9.25	59.23503	3,604,183	1,775,969
9	−17,920,242	X	1,275,000,000	−X	1,275,000,000	−17,920,242	2.5	9	56.95486	4,465,907	2,056,228
10	−17,920,242	X	1,275,000,000	−X	1,275,000,000	−17,920,242	2.55	8.75	55.07043	5,231,928	2,261,357
	−50,000,000,000	397,223,624	50,000,000,000	−397,223,624						Profit	1,420,909

X = USD LIBOR-margin.

at the current market rate of 2.55 percent, and (2) a series of forward foreign exchange contracts selling JP¥ and buying AUS$. This results in a pattern of cash flows where we are short of funds in the early years and develop a surplus later. Present valuing the cash flows at the relevant zero-coupon rates results in an overall profit on the transaction of $1,420,90.

Forex Ratio Swap

In Brazil, a version of the currency swap is traded in the form of a fixed US$ rate against a fixed R$ rate, with the unknown being the exchange rate at maturity. For mark-to-market purposes, the US$ leg of the swap is adjusted by the foreign exchange (forex) ratio (current exchange rate/original exchange rate), and the final exchange of cash flow is based on the original interest rates and the final forex adjustment. The unusual feature of the arrangement is that the swap is traded and paid in local currency. This technique is generally applicable to any country that operates exchange controls and wishes to allow its citizens to hedge against exchange risk while not threatening an outflow of foreign exchange reserves.

EQUITY SWAPS

Swaps can be done against equity indices and, indeed, against individual equities also. A common structure might be one where an investor pays 6-month LIBOR and receives the total return on the Nikkei-225 or FTSE-100 index. The technique has a number of applications. For example, an investor might be holding a solid portfolio of floating rate notes paying a return of LIBOR + ½. She might be unwilling to dispose of the paper on the grounds that comparable-quality paper is not readily available in the amounts that might be required if she wanted to buy back into the FRN market. But, at the same time, she believes that, over the next 12 months, the S&P500 index will perform very well. The solution might be an equity swap to pay LIBOR and receive the S&P500 total return. This allows her to switch into the equity markets without disturbing the underlying assets.

A ruling by the Internal Revenue Service, in May 1995, that an equity swap against an underlying stock position was a "straddle" for tax purposes, had some negative effects on the U.S. equity swap business. The characterization as a straddle meant that losses realized on the swap could not be deducted until the gains on the stock leg of the position were realized.

Offshore Equity Swap

An example of the use of equity swaps to circumvent restrictions on foreign investors is provided by the introduction of the Korean stock index futures in May 1996, the Kospi 200 contract. Foreigners were restricted to holding 15 percent of the 3-month daily average of open interest, and individual foreign investors were restricted to 3 percent. Recognizing the problem, Korean securities houses such as Hyundai Securities responded by offering foreigners equity swaps linked to the index. A master swap agreement was established between the foreign client and an offshore subsidiary or special-purpose vehicle of the Korean securities company. Under the master agreement, foreigners executed equity swaps with the offshore entity replicating the futures contract. Because the swap transactions involved two nonresident parties and were booked overseas, the foreign investment limits did not apply. The Korean securities house was able, without restriction, to hedge its exposure in the domestic market. Another application of the equity swap technique was by Jardine Fleming Unit Trusts, which launched its Thailand Capital Fund in October 1996. The fund guarantees return of principal to investors, and so investors' money is invested in fixed-income assets to ensure a guaranteed return. The coupons are passed to the swap counterparty, who in exchange pays the return on the Stock Exchange of Thailand (SET) index to the fund.

Volatility Swaps

In August 1996, an interesting swap was done by National Westminster with Foreign & Colonial, an investment trust. The investment management firm took the view that the implied volatility of the S&P 500 futures contract was overstated. At the time of the deal, the implied volatility was about 13 percent. The deal was structured in the form of a 1-month put warrant, which was listed in Luxembourg—a necessity to meet the fund's regulatory needs. But economically, the deal was in fact a swap.

The series of 385,000 warrants were sold to the investor at an issue price of US$1.41115 per warrant. The warrants were exercisable only on September 19, 1996, when National Westminster made a payout per warrant based on the following formula:

$$\$20 \times [0.09 - (A \times 253)].$$

In this formula, 0.09 is the strike price, representing an annualized volatility of 30 percent (squared; i.e., the variance). The notional contract value per warrant is $20. The A represents the average of the squares of the natural logarithms calculated in respect of the daily return for each valuation date (i.e., the actual volatility variance). This is then annualized by multiplying by 253, the number of business days in the year. The strike price was set so high (30 percent) because the deal was intended to be effectively a swap, rather than an option. The strike was chosen at a level that was very unlikely to be hit.

COMMODITY SWAPS

An important extension of the swap technique has been to the commodity markets—an interesting example of history moving full circle, since it was the commodity markets that developed futures, without which swaps would not have grown to the scale they presently have. Although nonfinancial and commodity swaps will not be discussed in any depth in this book, it is worth noting that the technique has been applied in a very large range of markets. Chase Manhattan, for example, has for years been an active market maker in energy swaps; in the United Kingdom, there is an active market for electricity swaps; in November 1996, Citibank announced a joint venture to market tanker freight swaps with Mallory Jones, an established U.S.-based tanker broker. There is an active market in Forward Freight Agreements linked to the U.S. Gulf-to-Japan route.

An example of how the commodity swap technique can fit into the wider framework of international finance was a deal done in the mid-1980s with a Mexican copper firm. This deal opened the way to voluntary new bank lending to a Mexican borrower at a time when the country was not seen as a good risk. The Mexican firm borrowed about $200 million from a banking syndicate, with repayments coming from the sale of copper to a Belgian company. The sale price was fixed at the average market price at time of delivery, so the Mexican firm would clearly be exposed to a fall in the copper price over the 3-year term of the loan. The solution was a 3-year copper swap with a French bank, under which the bank contracted to pay a fixed price for the Mexican firm's copper, in exchange for receiving the floating, market price. To eliminate its risk, it is understood, the French bank entered into a matching, opposite swap with a copper user that wished to hedge against a rise in copper prices.

HYBRID SWAPS

There are many possible variants of the basic swap technique. In some cases, interest rate swaps have included links to commodity markets. This type of integrated hedging structure aims to link interest expense to profitability. Using such a composite hedge, an oil refiner, for example, is able to index its floating interest rate charges to the company's gross profit margin. This "crack spread" tends to determine the cash flow of the refiner and thus its ability to service interest rate payments. It is possible to develop a custom-made interest rate swap where the interest rate charged is linked to the crack spread. If the refiner's profits fall, squeezing cash flow, its interest costs decline at the same time. In essence, a crack spread option is embedded in the interest rate swap. The customer may be able to handle the separate components, in which case it is clearly better off handling each transaction individually. However, for many clients, having the transaction "bundled" together can be administratively more convenient.

These applications are part of a wider trend of integrating commodity and financial markets. For example, the gold market has developed significant activity in gold borrowing and lending; gold loans have been made to gold producers, and the banks involved in the loans are active borrowers of gold from gold holders, so that there is now a gold LIBOR just as there is a dollar LIBOR or a yen LIBOR. The whole financial markets technology—swaps, options, caps, floors, collars, and so on—can, in principle, be applied to any commodity. However, the practical restrictions are that there has to be a sufficiently widely traded benchmark and, preferably, a decent futures market for hedging.

Swaps have also been developed with "triggers," whereby a client pays a given interest rate unless a foreign exchange rate or commodity price moves through a trigger level. Accrual swaps pay out only if LIBOR remains within a certain range. These and other hybrid variants are discussed in Chapter 7, after we have introduced in Chapter 6 the options that underlie them.

Chapter 6

Option Basics

Since 1973, there has been rapid growth in the use of options. Options lie behind many of the instruments we will consider in this book. Options are also important because they bring an extra dimension to financial instruments. The development of options markets has meant it is possible to trade volatility; that is, one can take a view not on the direction of a price change, but on how volatile it will be. In many cases, such as the "straddle" strategy discussed later, the trader takes no view on the direction of the market but bets that it will be more volatile than today.

Because of their importance, and the many "exotic" option varieties that have developed, we will devote this chapter and the next to these instruments. This chapter deals with the basic structure of options. We will also look briefly at some of the major valuation models currently in use. In the next chapter, we will set out the main kinds of options presently available.

People think options are complex. This is true in part. Arriving at the exact theoretical value of many options is a difficult matter. But the basic fact about an option is that it is a one-way bet. You pay a price for the privilege of a one-way bet. Deciding on whether that price is worth it to you is very simple. It has very little to do with the market's calculation of fair value—where all the complexity lies. The golden rule is to use your common sense and assess the value to *you*.

Either the option meets your business or investment needs at a price that you think is worth it, or not. If you are buying an option, the value to you may be much more—or much less—than the market is charging. Conversely, if you are selling (or writing) an option, no matter what you think the fair value of the option is, its price will be what the market will pay for it. All those elaborate computer models mean nothing if no one wants to buy the option at the price that you have chosen to believe is fair. This distinction between "marking-to-model" and "marking-to-market" was brought home sharply to NatWest Markets, the capital markets subsidiary of National Westminster Bank in London, in March 1997. The bank announced a £50 million loss arising from mispricing of interest rate options (specifically, by pricing caps using average volatilities rather than a separate volatility for each caplet; see Chapter 7).

Given all that, we still need to know how the market arrives at the price, if for no other reason than to make sure we are not somehow being robbed.

Before discussing the major pricing models, we will start by setting out briefly the background.

THE OPTIONS MARKET

Though their growth is recent, options have been around a long time. Some point to the Dutch tulip mania as the first appearance of options; others have gone further back, although these early contracts containing option elements can hardly be considered as options in themselves. "Traditional" options on equities (effectively, an over-the-counter option written by a market maker) developed on the London stock market in the 19th century. But, until 1973, it was possible to buy an option but it was not really possible to trade it. Exchange-traded options were introduced in 1973 by the Chicago Board of Options Exchange (CBOE). The single most important CBOE innovation was to set up standard option prices and expiry dates. This allowed development of a secondary market, which brought liquidity into options trading.

The growth of exchange-listed options has been rapid.The CBOE was followed by the American Stock Exchange, the Philadelphia Stock Exchange, the Midwest Stock Exchange, and the Pacific Stock Exchange. Early entrants into the market elsewhere were the European Options Exchange (in Amsterdam), the London Stock Exchange, and the London International Financial Futures Exchange (LIFFE, set up in 1982, merged with the Stock Exchange's London Traded Options Market in 1990). In Sweden, the Optionsmaklarna (OM) has become an international player, with operations in London and other centers. In France, the Monep is active and the Deutsche Terminborse has options on equities. Table 6.1 shows selected contracts worldwide.

The debate on over-the-counter versus exchange-traded options has lasted a long time. The merits of exchange trading are *transparency*—the last price at which the contract traded is always known—and (usually) *liquidity*—a traded option that has been bought can be sold again. Resale is not so easy for an over-the-counter option. Proponents of over-the-counter options point to their flexibility—an option can be tailored to suit the user's needs; in particular, it can be written for a longer term. Most exchange-traded options have a maximum maturity of 1 year, and the vast bulk are for 3 or 6 months. Liquidity in certain options markets—notably, currency and some interest rate options—is also sometimes better in the over-the-counter market than on the exchanges. In stock market options, the reverse is often true, at least for options on individual stocks.

Another issue that arises in comparing OTC versus exchange-traded options is the legal and tax position. In many cases, the tax treatment of an option varies, depending on whether it is traded on a recognized exchange. Likewise, the legal position regarding OTC options can be tricky (in the United Kingdom, the municipality, Hammersmith & Fulham, was found not to have the

Table 6.1 Options Contracts

	Contract Name	Exchange	Currency
Options on Futures			
Flexible Options on 5-Year U.S. Treasury Note Futures	CBOT	US$	
Flexible Options on 10-Year U.S. Treasury Note Futures		CBOT	US$
Flexible Options on 2-Year U.S. Treasury Note Futures	CBOT	US$	
Flexible Options on U.S. Treasury Bond Futures		CBOT	US$
Options on 10-Year U.S. Treasury Note Futures		CBOT	US$
Options on 2-Year U.S. Treasury Note Futures		CBOT	US$
Options on 5-Year U.S. Treasury Note Futures		CBOT	US$
Options on Catastrophe Insurance Futures	CBOT	US$	
Options on Long-Term Municipal Bond Index Futures		CBOT	US$
Options on U.S. Treasury Bond Futures		CBOT	US$
Options on Deutsche Mark Futures	CME	US$	
Options on Eurodollar Futures		CME	US$
Options on Japanese Yen Futures	CME	US$	
Options on S&P 500 Futures		CME	US$
Options on Swiss Franc Futures	CME	US$	
Options on DAX Futures	DTB	DM	
Options on Long-Term Bund Futures		DTB	DM
Options on the BOBL Future		DTB	DM
Option on 3-Month Eurodollar Interest Rate Future	LIFFE	US$	
Option on 3-Month Eurolira Interest Rate Future	LIFFE	ITL	
Option on 3-Month Euromark Interest Rate Future	LIFFE	DM	
Option on 3-Month Sterling Interest Rate Future		LIFFE	GBP
Option on Bund Futures Contract	LIFFE	DM	
Option on Italian Government Bond Future	LIFFE	ITL	
Option on Long Gilt Future		LIFFE	GBP
Option on ECU Bond Futures		MATIF	ECU
Option on PIBOR 3-Month Future	MATIF	FRF	
Option on the Notional Bond Futures		MATIF	FRF
MIBOR 90 Plus Option		MEFF	ESP
Monthly 10-Year Option		MEFF	ESP
Option on 10-Year Notional Bond Future	MEFF	ESP	
Option on 3-Year Notional Bond Futures	MEFF	ESP	
Option on MIBOR 90 'Futures		MEFF	ESP

(continued)

Table 6.1 *(Continued)*

	Contract Name	Exchange	Currency
Options on 10-Year Commonwealth Bond Futures	SFE	AUD	
Options on 3-Year Commonwealth Treasury Bond Futures	SFE	AUD	
Options on 90-Day Bank Accepted Bill Futures		SFE	AUD
Options on All Ordinaries Share Price Index Futures	SFE	AUD	
Overnight Options on 10-Year Commonwealth T- Bond Futures		SFE	AUD
Overnight Options on 3-Year Commonwealth T- Bond Futures		SFE	AUD
Options on Eurodollar Futures		SIMEX	US$
Options on Futures on Swiss Government Bonds	SOFFEX	CHF	
Three-Month Yen Futures	TIFFE	JPY	
Options on Cash Markets			
Stock Options		AMEX	US$
Stock Options		CBOE	US$
Options on S&P and Other Indices	CBOE	US$	
LEAPS		CBOE	US$
DAX Options		DTB	DM
Stock Options		DTB	DM
Equity Options		LIFFE	GBP
FTSE-100 Index Option (American Style Exercise)	LIFFE	GBP	
FTSE-100 Index Option (European Style Exercise)	LIFFE	GBP	
Currency Option US$/DM	MATIF	DM	
Currency Option US$/FRF		MATIF	FRF
Option US$/DM		MATIF	DM
US$/DM Currency Options		MATIF	US$
US$/FRF Currency Options		MATIF	US$
Currency Options	PHLX	US$	
Stock Options		PHLX	US$
Euroyen	SIMEX	JPY	
JGB		SIMEX	JPY
Nikkei 225		SIMEX	JPY
Nikkei 300		SIMEX	JPY
Taiwan Index		SIMEX	US$
LEPO—Low Exercise Price Options		SOFFEX	CHF
SMI Options—Long Term		SOFFEX	CHF
SMI Options—Short Term		SOFFEX	CHF
Stock Options—Short Term		SOFFEX	CHF
Stock Options—Long Term		SOFFEX	CHF

legal power to write OTC option contracts). By contrast, when dealing on an exchange, one's counterparty is the clearinghouse. For practical purposes, in normal circumstances, the question of credit risk does not arise.

Options are now traded on many different kinds of underlying instrument. Most firms break down their book into foreign exchange, interest rates, equity, and commodities, and I shall broadly follow this approach. Included in these are options on futures. Although an option on a future might seem more complex than an ordinary option, in fact it is often simpler. The future consists of a single instrument with a fixed expiry date, rather than, in some cases, a bundle of cash flows.

Finally we should mention warrants, a kind of sister market to the options market. A warrant is an option; the basic difference is that a warrant is usually listed on a stock exchange rather than traded on an options exchange. Also, a warrant usually has a longer life—warrants exist with maturities of 10 or 15 years. These are dealt with separately in Chapter 15.

BASICS OF AN OPTION CONTRACT

An option is an agreement between two parties. One party grants the other the right to buy or sell an instrument under certain conditions. The instrument may be a stock, bond, futures contract, interest rate, or foreign currency. The counterparty pays a "premium" for the right to buy or sell the instrument at a future time, without committing to do so. There are two basic types of options: puts and calls. A call option gives the buyer the right to buy, or "call away," a specified amount of the underlying instrument at the specified price, during a specified period. The price at which the instrument may be bought is the exercise price or the strike price. The last date on which the option may be exercised is called the expiry date, or the maturity date. A put option gives the buyer the right to sell, or put to the writer, a specified amount of the underlying instrument at the strike price until the expiry date.

The period during which the option can be exercised depends on its type—American or European. (These terms are relics of history, not geographical. American options are traded in Europe and vice versa.) Under an American option, the holder of the option has the right to exercise at any time before maturity. Under a European option, the holder may only exercise at the time of expiration.

A call option is best described by a simple example. Suppose Bank A sells us a 3-month European call option on the DEM at a strike of DEM2.00, in an amount of DEM10,000,000. This means that we have the right, in 3 months, to pay $5,000,000 to buy DEM10,000,000. If the DEM strengthens to, say, DEM1.90 per dollar (so that it would cost us $5,263,157 to buy DEM10,000,000 in the market) the option will have substantial value to us. Conversely, if, at the maturity of the option, the spot rate is DEM2.20, the option will have no value.

To put together some basic building blocks for analyzing options, let's look at an option on sterling at $2.00 per £1—a call option, American style. How would the option behave on the last day of its life? When spot sterling is trading in the market at, say, $2.20, it would be possible to buy the option, exercise it at $2.00, and sell at $2.20. The option will be worth at least $0.20—the difference between $2.00 and $2.20. If the option costs less, one could buy, exercise, and sell for a net profit. And it will be worth no more than $0.20. If it were worth more, anyone buying the option would take a loss (assuming we are trading in the final few minutes of the option's life). Conversely, if sterling were trading at $2.10 at this time, the option would be worth $0.10. If the pound were below $2.00, the option would be worthless—sterling would be cheaper if bought directly in the market rather than by exercising the right to buy at $2.00.

We said that if sterling were trading at $2.10 at the maturity of the option, it would be worth $0.10. This difference between the currency price and the exercise price of the call option is often called its intrinsic value. Thus, when sterling is at $2.10, the option has an intrinsic value of $0.10; with sterling at $2.30, the option's intrinsic value is $0.30. The only thing that affects intrinsic value is the gap between the price of the underlying instrument (in this case, sterling) and the strike price. Any excess premium over the intrinsic value of the option is called the time value, which is discussed more fully below.

If sterling is above the strike price, then the option has intrinsic value and is said to be "in the money." If the sterling's value equals the strike price, then the intrinsic value is zero and the option is said to be "at the money." If sterling is trading below the strike price, then the option is said to be "out of the money."

OPTION PAY-OFF DIAGRAMS

It is possible to draw an *option pay-off diagram* showing the outcomes for different exchange rates at maturity. Table 6.2 and Figure 6.1 show the results. This

Table 6.2   Intrinsic Value of Sterling Call

Call Option Payoff Profile
Strike   2.00

Market Rate at Maturity	Intrinsic Value of the Option
1.6	0
1.8	0
2	0
2.2	0.2
2.4	0.4

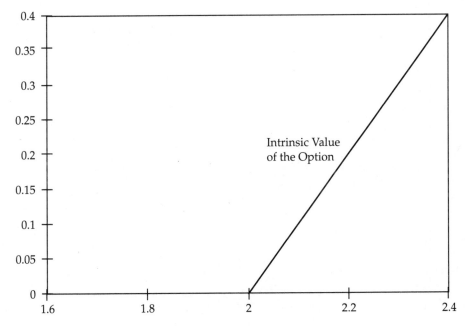

Figure 6.1   Intrinsic value of sterling call at expiration.

is the basic payoff profile of a call option, to which we will often return. At this stage, the key point to note is that there is unlimited profit potential as sterling rises, and limited loss as it falls. (There will be a loss, not shown in Table 6.2. The loss is the amount of premium spent in buying an option that turned out to be worthless at expiry.)

We can do the same exercise for a put on sterling at $2.00 (see Table 6.3). Again, we can draw the profile of the put in the last few minutes of its life

Table 6.3   Intrinsic Value of Sterling Put

Put Option Payoff Profile

Strike   2.00

Market Rate at Maturity	Intrinsic Value of the Option
1.4	0.6
1.6	0.4
1.8	0.2
2	0
2.2	0
2.4	0
2.6	0
2.8	0

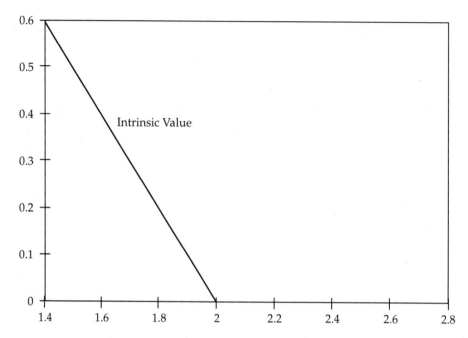

Figure 6.2 Intrinsic value of sterling put at expiration.

(Figure 6.2). There is unlimited profit potential, this time as sterling falls, and limited risk of loss—the maximum loss will be the premium paid out.

Let's look at the position that would arise if, instead of buying a call, we had sold (or written) a call. When we bought a call, we had the right, but not the obligation, to buy sterling at $2.00. But now we have sold the call. We have the obligation to sell the pound at $2.00. If sterling rises above $2.00, we must sell it to the party who bought the option, instead of selling in the market-place, and we will have a loss. The loss is unlimited; for example, if sterling rises to $3.00, our loss will be $1.00 per pound. If sterling, at the expiry of the option, closes below $2.00, we will make a profit. Our profit will be the pre-mium we charged for selling the option, but is limited to the premium. The writer of a call has unlimited risk, with a limited profit potential, as shown in Figure 6.3.

The same applies if we were to write a put (Figure 6.4), so why would any-one be crazy enough to write options? Writing an open (or "naked") options position can be very risky, but it can be well rewarded, in the shape of a sub-stantial premium. After all, that is how insurance companies make money. They take risks in exchange for premium income. Also, there are hedging tech-niques that can reduce the risk.

Finally, because we will need to combine positions later, it will be helpful to show a similar payoff diagram for the straightforward long and short positions.

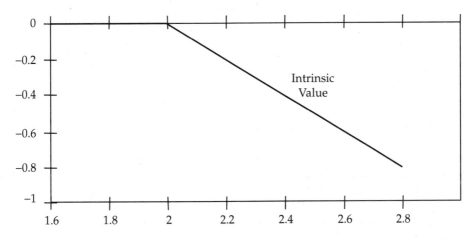

Figure 6.3 Profile of a short call position.

Figure 6.5 shows the payoff if we are long sterling at, say, $2.00. Our profit rises as sterling rises. As sterling falls, we start to have a loss. Likewise, we can draw the payoff from being short.

These profiles—long the underlying asset, long the put or call, and short the put or call—are the basic building blocks of all options strategies. They can be combined in many different ways, some of which are discussed later in the chapter.

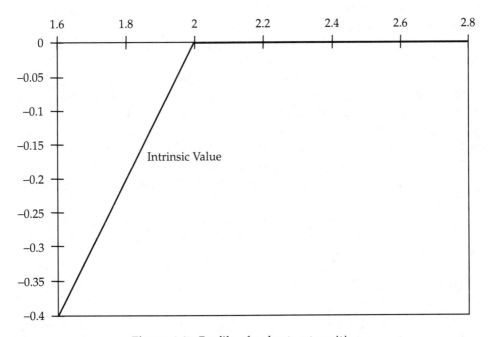

Figure 6.4 Profile of a short put position.

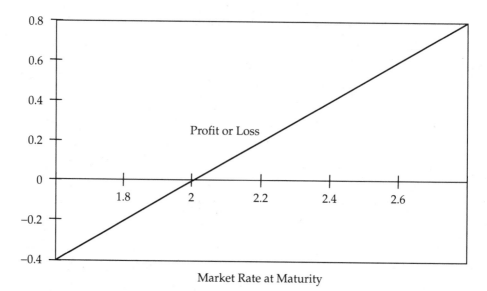

Figure 6.5 Payoff profile of long asset position.

OPTION VALUATION

We come now to the theory of how to value options. Once again, it should be stressed that this is a black art. It is not a science. We mentioned earlier the case of NatWest Markets; the fact is that, in pricing options, there will almost always be room for disagreement about the assumptions being made in the option pricing model. In the NatWest case, there was a clear difference between the prices being used internally and those quoted in the market, and the latter were widely available. Thus, it was reasonable to say that NatWest's prices were "wrong." In other cases, the market will be limited or illiquid, or market traders may not have fully understood an instrument that is highly specialized. There will always be some doubt about the value of an individual option, because its value depends on an estimate of the future volatility of the underlying instrument. There will be a general market view of the appropriate level of volatility to be used, but if your estimate differs, then the option will be worth more (or less) to you.

The first, and most important, model used in options pricing was developed by Fisher Black and Myron Scholes in 1973. The Black–Scholes model made several critical assumptions:

1. Prices may change rapidly but cannot "jump." One can trade continuously in the market.

2. There is a risk-free rate of interest for borrowing and lending from the current period until the expiration of the option.

3. Transactions costs and taxes are ignored.
4. The continuously compounded rate of return of the asset has a normal distribution—that is, the asset price is log-normally distributed.

Given these assumptions, Black and Scholes showed that the price of the option would be determined by:

1. The current price of the underlying instrument.
2. The exercise price of the option.
3. The remaining life of the option.
4. The level of interest rates.
5. The projected volatility of the underlying instrument.

Of these, all but the last are known at the time the option is priced; thus, volatility is the key to options pricing.

In looking at the option's value, the first two factors are primary. This is clear if we look at the option on the day that it expires. Recall our earlier example of a $2.00 call on sterling. (We will assume for the moment that interest rates in sterling and dollars are identical.) On the day that the option expires, only the currency price and the striking price of the option determine the option's value. Other factors have no bearing. We said that if sterling were trading at $2.10 at the maturity date, the option would be worth $0.10. When sterling is at $2.10, the option has an intrinsic value of $0.10: at $2.30, the intrinsic value is $0.30. The only thing that affects intrinsic value is the gap between the price of the underlying instrument (in this case, sterling) and the strike price.

But in the period before the expiry of the option, there is another element in its price, in addition to its intrinsic value. This is referred to as the time value premium. In general, the time value premium is found by the following formula for an in-the-money call option on an asset (sterling, in our example above):

Call time value premium = Call option price + Strike price − Asset price

For example, sterling is trading at $2.05, and the sterling October $2.00 call is priced at $0.08. The in-the-money amount (the intrinsic value) is $0.05 ($2.05 − $2.00) and so the time value (price less intrinsic value) is $0.03 ($0.08 − $0.05).

The intrinsic value of the option is easy to calculate. The "fair value" of the time value premium is not so simple. It depends only partly on the time to maturity. It also depends on the volatility of the underlying asset and on interest rates. It will vary, too, according to how far in the money or out of the money the call option is.

If the call is out of the money, then the premium and the time value premium are the same. Let's say sterling is at $2.05 and a sterling October $2.10 call sells at $0.04. The call has no intrinsic value by itself when the currency (at $2.05) is below the striking price ($2.10). So both the premium and the time value premium of the call are 4 points.

The option's time value premium decays much more rapidly in the last few weeks of its life than it does in the first few weeks. In fact, for reasons we will see later, the rate of decay is related to the square root of the time remaining. To illustrate this, we can draw a graph of the effect of time on an option's premium (the effect of "time decay," as it is often called). Figure 6.6 shows the effect of holding everything else constant. As the option comes closer to expiry, it loses value more and more quickly.

Another important point about time value is that it is always greatest for an option that is at the money. If the option is deep in or out of the money, its time value is very low. We can see the reason if we think of the deal from the point of view of the option writer. Suppose we are quoting to write an option to sell sterling at $2.10. Once the option is written, then, as we get closer to the expiry, if sterling is near $2.10, we will need to be thinking about buying some sterling to cover our commitment to deliver sterling at $2.10. Suppose, with 30 days to go on this option, sterling is at $1.80. The risk of our having to deliver on this option is quite small—sterling is not very likely to rise 30 cents in 30

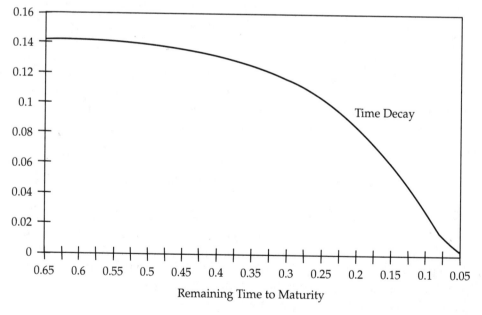

Figure 6.6 Time decay.

days. As one day passes and there are now 29 days to run, our risk will decline, but not by very much because the risk was already small. So the fall in the premium we will charge will not be large. The effect of time value on the premium is small in these circumstances.

Conversely, suppose we are quoting the same option and sterling is trading today at $2.40. The option is virtually certain to be exercised. We will buy sterling now to cover our position, because we will almost certainly have to deliver. Again, if the maturity of the option that we are quoting were to be shortened by a day, our risk would not be much less, so the premium we would charge would not fall much. The time value of a deep in-the-money option is low.

It is when the option is at the money that our uncertainty is greatest. If we are quoting a $2.10 option for sterling, and sterling is trading at $2.10, then the market could go either way from now till maturity. In these circumstances, an extra day's life on the option really does have an effect on our risk. Time value is at its greatest when the option is at the money.

Figure 6.7 shows the value of the option premium at maturity and 30 days before maturity. The shaded area between the two lines is the time value of the option and, as can be seen, the gap between the two lines is at its widest when the option is at the money.

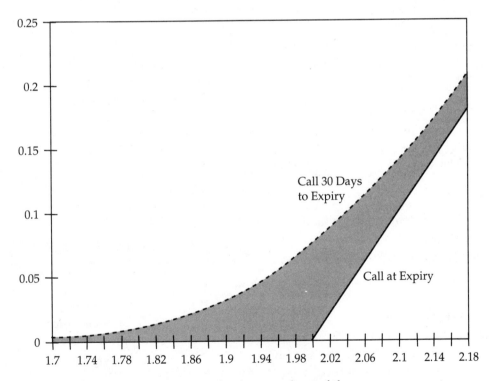

Figure 6.7 Time value in, at, and out of the money.

THE BINOMIAL MODEL

Writers of options in the market will price their options differently because they do not have shared views on future volatility. These differences make option pricing a bit of a black art. To add to the confusion, there are a number of different options pricing models. The most widely known is that of Black and Scholes. The Black model is a variant of Black–Scholes that is suitable for options on futures. Other popular models are the Garman–Kohlhagen modification of Black–Scholes (widely used for currency options) and the Cox–Ross–Rubinstein model, or binomial model, which overcomes the problems the Black–Scholes model has in handling dividend payments on underlying equities. The binomial and Black–Scholes models converge when trading is assumed to be continuous. In practice, bigger errors are likely to result from wrong forecasts of volatility than from minor variations in the underlying theoretical models. Of the models mentioned, the binomial is among those most commonly used. It is also rather easier to explain intuitively, so we will start with it before moving on to the Black–Scholes model.

Let's assume an American call on sterling at $2.00. Spot sterling today is trading at $2.05. We'll call the exercise price of $2.00 E, and the spot price S. Then $S - E = \$0.05$. That is, if we buy the option and exercise today, the option will pay us $0.05. So the call will be worth at least $0.05, and probably more if there is any time to expiry. If we write the value of the call as C, we know we must have $C \geq S - E$. Also, because we know we can choose to walk away from the option, its value can never be negative; we can never be harmed by owning it. So we know the value of a call will always be $C \geq 0$. In fact, we can write $C \geq$ (maximum of 0, $S - E$).

Can we make this more exact? One way to proceed is to start with the concept of a riskless hedge—a hedge that eliminates all risk.

The assumptions behind most riskless hedge valuation models are as follows:

1. Prices may change rapidly but cannot "jump."
2. There is a risk-free rate of interest for borrowing and lending from the current period until the expiration of the option.
3. Transactions costs and taxes are ignored.

What we will do is set out a "binomial tree" showing the possible outcomes of the movement in sterling over time. At any point, sterling can move up or down. At each point along the branches of the tree, we will work out the fair price of an option on sterling, working back from the future to today. This approach was initiated by William Sharpe and developed further by Cox, Ross, and Rubinstein.

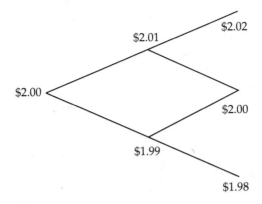

Figure 6.8 Sterling binomial tree.

We assume a starting price for sterling of $2.00. Then we assume the price of sterling in each period can rise or fall by $0.01; it is equally likely to rise or fall. A two-period example is shown in Figure 6.8. At the start of the first period, we want to value a European call option. It has a strike of $1.99. It expires after two periods (at the start of the third period). How do we set about this?

We begin by assuming, for simplicity, that interest rates in both currencies are equal. (This assumption is relaxed explicitly in the Garman–Kohlhagen model, which is widely used for pricing currency options; see below.) The next step is to consider the value of the option at expiry.

At expiry, sterling can be $1.98, $2.00, or $2.02. The option will be worth $0.03 if sterling's price is $2.02, $0.01 if it is $2.00, and nothing if it is $1.98. Next, to get back from period 3 to period 2, we use the concept of a riskless hedge. We set up a hedge, giving us no exposure to the market price of sterling.

Let us assume sterling's price is $2.01 at the start of period 2. We want to find the option price. We do this by imagining a portfolio. It is long one pound sterling, and short one call option on sterling with a strike of $1.99.

At the start of the next period (period 3), the price of sterling could rise from $2.01 to $2.02 or fall to $2.00. The option writer must deliver sterling at the strike price of $1.99. So, at $2.02, a loss of $0.03 will occur. If sterling falls

Portfolio Value Once Sterling Has Risen to $2.01

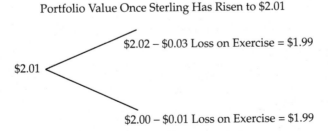

Figure 6.9 Portfolio value if sterling is at $2.01.

to $2.00, the loss will be $0.01. So, at the start of period 3, whether the price moves up or down, the value of the portfolio will be $1.99 ($2.02 – $0.03 or $2.00 – $0.01).

So there is no risk in this portfolio. It can earn no more than the risk-free rate. (If it did, arbitragers would borrow to invest in it and would drive down the return.) Likewise, it cannot earn less (there would be arbitrage in the opposite direction). So the rate of return on the risk-free portfolio must equal the risk-free rate. Let us assume that the risk-free rate is 0.02 percent per period. The return on the portfolio will also be 0.02 percent per period.

We can now find a price for the option at the start of the second period, given the price of $2.01 we assumed above. We know the portfolio earns the risk-free rate. And we know it ends up worth $1.99. So the starting value, or cost, of the portfolio must be $1.99 discounted back over one period. That is, $1.99/1.0002 or $1.9896.

But we know also that the cost of the portfolio is $2.01 (the price of the sterling) less the premium on the option sold. Therefore, the option must earn $2.01 – $1.9896 = $0.0204. If it did not, the portfolio would not be worth exactly $1.9801. Any other option cost would mean the risk-free portfolio does not earn the risk-free rate. *So, if the price of sterling at the start of period 2 is $2.01, then the value of the option must be $0.0204.*

We can now use the same method to solve for a different price. What is the option price, if the price of sterling at the start of period 2 is $1.99? In this case, we set up another portfolio. It has one pound sterling, plus, now, two short calls.

We chose the number of calls to be two as follows. We ask: How many calls are needed to make the portfolio riskless? That is, how many calls will make the portfolio worth the same value whatever happens to sterling's price (whether it rises from $1.99 to $2.00 or falls to $1.98)?

To find this, say K is the number of $1.99 calls written. We know that if the price rises to $2.00, we must deliver at $1.99, and each call will lose $0.01. And if the price falls to $1.98, there is no loss. So we want K such that

$$\$2.00 - K \times \$0.01 = \$1.98 - K \times \$0.$$

Therefore,

$$\$2.00 - \$1.98 = K \times \$0.01 - K \times \$0 = K \times \$0.01$$

and so

$$\$0.02 = \$K \times \$0.01.$$

Solving for K shows that we need two short calls to make the portfolio riskless. (Before, we had $2.02 – K × $0.03 = $2.00 – K × $0.01, so $0.02 = $0.02 × K, and hence K = 1.)

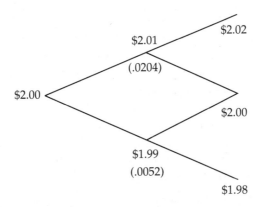

Figure 6.10 Sterling binomial tree: Period 2 prices.

The price at the start of period 3 can go from our assumed $1.99 to either $2.00 or $1.98. At $2.00, the option has a $0.01 loss, for a total loss of $0.02 on the two options. At $1.98, the option expires worthless. Thus, the portfolio next period will be worth $1.98, regardless of whether the price goes up to $2.00 or down to $1.98 ($2.00 − $0.02 or $1.98 − $0). So its initial cost must be $1.98/ 1.0002; that is, $1.9796.

On our assumption, sterling costs $1.99. By the same reasoning as before, the two options must earn $1.99 − 1.9796 = $0.0104. So, each option must be worth $0.0052. We now know the option's value for the two possible prices of period 2 (Figure 6.10).

There is one last step. We must work back to today. Suppose we set up a portfolio that is long one pound sterling, and short 1.32 call options. To find that number (1.32), we use the same approach as before. We say we must have $2.01 − $0.0204K = $1.99 − $0.0052K, so $0.02 = ($0.0204 − $0.0052)K and K = $0.02/$0.0152 = 1.32.

In Table 6.4, we see that if the price of sterling goes up to $2.01, the value of the portfolio will be $1.9831. It will still be worth that amount if the price of sterling falls to $1.99. Therefore, the cost of the portfolio today must be its future value discounted back to today: $1.9831/1.0002, or $1.9827. But that cost must also equal $2.00, the value of our holding of sterling today, minus the revenue from selling 1.32 calls. *So each call must sell for ($2.00 − 1.9827)/1.32 = $0.0131.*

Table 6.4 Portfolio Values (Long £1 Short 1.32 calls)

Price of £	Short Call Position Value	Portfolio Value
$2.01	1.32 × $0.0204	$2.01 − $0.0269 = $1.9831
$1.99	1.32 × $0.0052	$1.99 − $0.0069 = $1.9831

We have at last worked back to answer our question. We have found the fair price for the option today if sterling is selling for $2.00. Given the risk-free rate of interest and the set of possible future prices, $0.0131 is the only possible answer. In principle, to solve for the fair value of longer-term options, all we need is a bigger set of possible prices. Then we can use the same method to find the current fair price of the option.

Notice all the assumptions *not* made in what we have done. We have made no assumptions about:

1. The probability of an upward or a downward move in the market.
2. The investor's degree of risk-aversion.

In other words this model is applicable across all investors, regardless of market conditions. This attribute has given it generality, which makes it useful. We will explore the binomial a little further, because various kinds of binomial tree are fundamental to pricing options in situations where the Black–Scholes model will not work. The binomial is, in fact, a very powerful tool.

Risk-Neutral Transition Probabilities

A little earlier, we glossed over the meaning of the term p in the formula in Table 6.5. For most normal conditions, we have 0<p<1 and so it rather resembles a probability. It is common to speak of it as the up-transition probability, or the risk-neutral transition probabilities. When using binomial trees, we create a risk-neutral world by choosing the transition probabilities to ensure that the expected value is equal to growth at the risk-free rate. (A European binomial option is detailed in Table 6.6.)

Assume that, in our world, the rate of interest is positive. We can see intuitively that if we are looking at an option on a risky instrument that pays no interest or dividend, then, unless we expect the instrument to rise in value over time, we would never hold it. It would always be better to hold a risk-free bank deposit or bond. Hence the requirement that the expected value of the instrument is equal to growth at the risk-free rate.

Although p is not, strictly speaking, a probability (we started by saying we would make no forecast about the probability of a rise or fall in the instrument), it must be set in such a way that it is consistent with a rise in the asset at a rate equal to the risk-free rate (often called the drift). This is consistent with making no forecast, because p is not set subjectively. It is set in an objective manner to meet the condition that the asset must rise in line with the risk-free rate.

The approach adopted by Cox, Ross, and Rubinstein[1] was to set the up "probability" at $u = e^{\sigma\sqrt{t}}$ and the down probability $d = 1/u$. The transition

---

[1] Cox, Ross, and Rubinstein. "Option Pricing: A Simplified Approach," *Journal of Financial Economics*, 1979.

Table 6.5   Summary

It may be helpful to summarize this process, as follows:

Suppose the price of sterling today is S. If the price rises, it will go up to Su. If it goes down, it will go down to Sd. Consider a call option on sterling whose value today is C. The value will go up to Cu if sterling rises, and it will fall to Cd if sterling falls.

We can draw the situation like this:

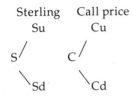

We can think of the up and down movements as the branches of a tree. The time between steps in our tree is taken as one year. Our tree will look like Figure 6.8. Suppose we are at the first step in the process we went through earlier; we are at the start of the last period of the option's life (period 3), and sterling has risen to $2.01. We now set up our hedged portfolio by saying that the portfolio value (V0) today is:

$$V0 = S + hC$$

where h is the "hedge ratio." We want to find h such that:

$$V1 = Su + hCu = Sd + hCd$$

i.e., the portfolio value after one step, V1, is the same if the price goes up or down. The previous equation implies that

$$H = -\frac{(Su - Sd)}{(Cu - Cd)} \text{ or } -\frac{(\$2.02 - \$2.00)}{(\$0.03 - \$0.01)}$$

in our earlier example. (Remember, the option strike is $1.99 and so its value at expiration will be $0.03 if sterling is $2.02 and $0.01 if sterling closes at $2.00.) In this case, h = −1: We would be short one call option and long one pound sterling to be risk-neutral. But if we set up this portfolio, we know that it is risk-free. We know that V1 will always be the same. That in turn implies that

$$V1 = V0(1 + rt)$$

where r = the risk-free rate of interest and t = the length of the step in terms of time. Earlier, we defined our rate of interest as 0.02 percent per period, so here we set t = 1 because we have defined the rate of interest as a periodic rate.

Then V1 = 1.0002 × V0 = 1.0002 × ($2.01 − C)

We can combine the two equations and rewrite them so that:

$$C = \frac{pCu + (1-p)Cd}{(1+rt)}$$

where we have simplified the result above by writing:

$$p = \frac{S(1+rt) - Sd}{(Su - Sd)}$$

In our example, p = $2.01 × 1.0002 − $2.00\($2.02 − $2.00) = $0.010402/$0.02 = $0.5201

So we can find C:

$$C = \frac{\$0.5201 \times \$0.03 + \$0.4799 \times \$0.01}{1.0002} = \frac{\$0.020402}{1.0002} = \$0.0204 \text{ as we saw before.}$$

Then, as the chefs say, repeat as necessary, to get back to the starting value.

Table 6.6   European Binomial Option: A Worked Example

Suppose we have a foreign currency trading at 100 (S = 100) and paying a rate of interest of 3 percent (r_f = 0.03), and, in our world, the risk-free interest rate is 10 percent (r_d = 0.10). We have estimated the volatility of the currency as 30 percent per annum (σ = 0.3) and we are interested in a 3-month option (t = 0.25 year) with a strike of 100 (E = 100).

We want to construct a binomial tree of price outcomes. We believe that the returns on the currency are normally distributed, and we want to construct the tree so that if its branches were expanded to infinity, we would get a normal distribution. The returns on the currency are, we believe, normally distributed (i.e., symmetrically distributed). We have to define return properly.

If the currency starts at 100, goes to 110, and falls to 100, we get: +10 percent; −9.0909 percent (nonsymmetrical returns) because in the second period the base is 110, not 100. We can get round this by defining the return as a logarithm: ln(110/100) = 0.0953 = 9.53 percent, and ln(100/110) = −0.0953 = −9.53 percent (using the natural logarithm).

For a normal distribution with a variance of σ^2 measured over a period t, the variance is $\sigma^2 t$. If we divide the period into n steps, the variance at each step is $\sigma^2 t/n$; in other words, the standard deviation (volatility) is $\sigma\sqrt{(t/n)}$. So if we divide our 3-month period into, say, 5 subperiods, we have an applicable volatility of $0.30\sqrt{(.25/5)}$ = 0.3 × 0.223607 = 0.067082.

So we define the return in each period on this asset as log(0.067082) or (if it falls in value) log(−0.067082). So the price change in each period is the antilogarithm of ±0.067082, i.e., 1.0693838 or 0.935118 (say, up = 1.0693838 and down = 0.935118).

There is a probability p that the price of the asset will rise. Hence, the probability of a fall is 1 − p. Let us define INT = $r_d^{t/n}$, where r_d = 1 + the domestic rate of interest, and INT can be thought of as the "periodic interest rate." We also define FGN = $r_f^{t/n}$ where r_f = 1 + foreign rate of interest, and so FGN is the "periodic foreign interest rate."

Suppose, today, r_d = 1.10 and r_f = 1.03. Then INT = 1.00478 and FGN = 1.00148.

Then we can define p = [INT/FGN − down]/[up − down] = 0.50776 in our example, and 1 − p = [up − INT/FGN]/[up − down] = 0.49224.

Effectively, p is the probability of an upward move, and 1 − p is the probability of a downward move, which would be consistent with the interest rate environment that we have. Using all these assumptions, let us look now at what happens to the currency over the five steps we are considering.

Table 6.6 *(Continued)*

Tree of currency price movements:

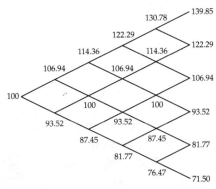

In this tree, in the first period, the price can move to 106.94 or 93.52; in the second, it can move from 106.94 to 114.36 or back to 100; and so on.

The next step is to consider the value of a call option on an asset that behaves like this. Suppose the call has a strike of 100. If the asset has reached 139.85, the call payoff is 39.85. If it has reached 122.29, the payoff is 22.29. Suppose we are now in period 4; the asset price has reached 130.78. We know it can go up to 139.85 or down to 122.29. What is the value of the call at that point?

It must be the present value of the expected outcome, that is, the present value of each payoff, weighted by the probability of the payoff. We have defined the probability of an up move as 0.50776; and the probability of a down move as 0.49224. We know that the payoffs are 39.85 and 22.29.

Therefore, the value of the call at this point must be $(0.50776 \times 39.85 + 0.49224 \times 22.29)/1.00478 = 31.06$.

We can repeat this process for each node of the tree, bearing in mind that the call is worthless for payoffs below the strike:

Payoff

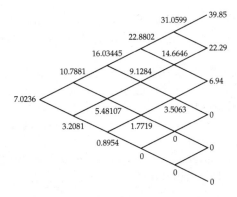

On these assumptions, the option is worth 7.0236. We have considered only the first five steps in the tree; in practice, we would consider much larger trees.

probability $p = \frac{e^{\mu t} - d}{u - d}$ where μ is defined as the expected annual rate of return of the asset. Up to a very good approximation, these assumptions make the local volatility at each node of the tree equal to σ and the expected rate of return equal to μ.

Standard Trees and Flexible Trees

So far, implicitly, we have assumed that the volatility at each node of the tree is equal. This is a common assumption, and the binomial tree constructed from fixed volatility assumptions is the standard approach. In a standard binomial tree, the up and down ratios and the transition probabilities are the same at every node. The length of each time period is also the same. Flexible trees are so-called because very few restrictions are placed on the up and down ratios and the transition probabilities of the tree. We only require that the tree be re-combining: that is, at any time, an up move followed by a down move must be exactly the same as a down move followed by an up move. In other words, the branches of the tree do not wander all over the place but rejoin. We will see later that flexible trees are becoming important tools in the pricing of options.

All this may seem far from the real world. After all, prices move all the time, not just once per period. Even worse, they can move to any one of many new values, not just two, as we have assumed. But if the reader is willing to accept our basic assumptions, any objections can be overcome by suitably changing the binomial model. Our model worked over three periods. If we divide these into infinitely short segments, we move toward continuous price changes. Now we have a very large number of observations. In these circumstances, we can generalize the model to become the Black–Scholes model, which we will do in a moment.

NORMAL DISTRIBUTION

Before we turn to the Black–Scholes model, we will look at the normal distribution. The normal or bell-shaped distribution is well known in statistical theory (see Figure 6.11).

The normal distribution is important because it is a quite realistic picture of the distribution of a number of common occurrences. The reason for this is the Central Limit Theorem, once described as "one of the most remarkable in all mathematics." The theorem says that no matter what the type of the underlying distribution, provided it has a finite variance, it will approximate the normal distribution for large samples. (We saw in Chapter 3 how the binomial tends to approximate the normal distribution reasonably quickly.)

Most statistical distributions that are likely to apply in the real world have finite variances. So that means that we can argue that, for sufficiently large samples, we are often justified in assuming that the underlying distribution

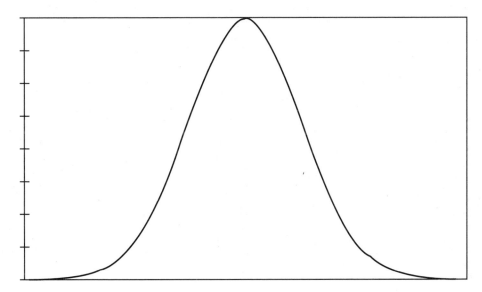

Figure 6.11   The normal distribution.

of changes in the exchange rate (or whatever else we are writing an option on) is normal. More exactly, the standardized, continuously compounded rate of return of the asset (sterling, in our example) tends to approximate a normal distribution. Hence, the relative change in price (S*/S) has a normal distribution, where S* is the new price and S is the old. (The exchange rate itself will have what is called a "log-normal" distribution; its logarithm is normally distributed.)

Suppose we write an option on a currency whose price is 100. We know the price movements of the exchange rate over the past 6 months. They suggest that its probability distribution is quite like a normal distribution. Over the past 6 months the currency price's mean, or average, is 100. Its standard deviation, or variability, is 12.

How do we find the probability that the currency's price on maturity of the option is a given distance from the mean? We use the area underneath the curve, between the mean and the price at maturity. How do we measure this area? The easiest way is by looking up a table for the "standardized normal" distribution (the distribution of a normal variable with mean 0 and standard deviation of 1).

Next, the standardized normal distribution has to be applied to our currency. We do this by taking all the possible exchange rates. We subtract from them the mean of 100, and then divide the result by 12, the standard deviation. We have now "standardized" our exchange rate distribution. In mathematicians' terms, we apply the transformation (x minus mean/standard deviation). An example will illustrate this.

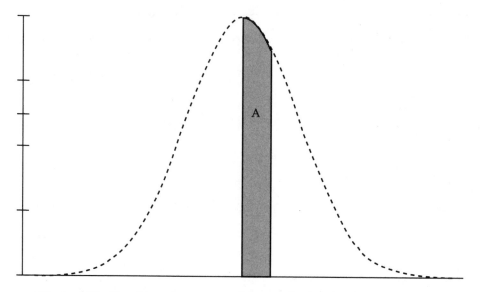

Figure 6.12   Possible prices at maturity: standardized normal distribution.

Let's take the probability of the exchange rate as being, say, 0 to 3 percent higher than the original price—that is, between 100 and 103. We take x = 100 and x = 103 and write (x − mean)/standard deviation, or (100 − 100)/12 = 0 and (103 − 100)/12 = 0.25. To find the probability that x is between 0 and 0.25 in the standard normal distribution, we look it up in the statistical tables for the normal distribution. In Figure 6.12, it is shown by the area under the curve, marked with the letter A. The area A is roughly 10 percent of the total area under the distribution curve. The chance of the price being between 100 and 103 at maturity is therefore 10 percent. The cost of this event to the option seller will average 1.5 percent (the average difference between 100 and 103).

Suppose we repeat this for each slice of 3 percentage points above the strike price. We get a whole series of probabilities for each event, and each event has a cost, halfway between the percentage points. We can weight each of these costs by the probability and get a total—say 4.8 percent. In fact, what we have done here is add up the cumulative area under the normal curve. The technical term for this is the cumulative normal density. Given this cost, the option seller will decide the uncertainty surrounding this estimated cost, and if necessary, will add some protective loading, and will then price the option accordingly.

BLACK–SCHOLES FORMULA

We have seen, in a general way, how the binomial model works, and how it can be argued that, for large numbers of independent observations over time, the logarithm of changes in price, log(S*/S), has a normal distribution (that is, the price has a "log-normal distribution"). The assumption of normality does agree with common sense; it says that small relative changes, either up or down, are very common, but large changes become proportionately less common. The normal distribution has a mean, μ, and a variance, $\sigma\sqrt{T}$. If we consider the behavior of log(S*/S) over T periods, we will find that, over that time, it has a mean of μ and a variance of $\sigma\sqrt{T}$.

Now we can move on from the binomial model to the Black–Scholes model. Black–Scholes assumes that the price is log-normal, which, as we have seen, is usually reasonable—though not for interest rates, which we discuss later—and this assumption gets us away from specifying a binomial-type path for prices. Instead, we can set up a (fairly) simple formula. We can write the Black–Scholes formula like this:

$$C = N(d1)S - e^{-rT}N(d2)E$$

where N(.) refers to the cumulative normal density. [We saw how to use N(.) earlier, when we explained the normal density.]

This formula says that the value of the call is equal to the expected value of what we will get from the call, minus the expected cost. We can say that N(d1)S is the expected value of the asset we will acquire under the call; we will get an asset with a value of S. That asset is weighted by a probability; N(d1) is the probability we will exercise. [We will see later that N(d1) is also the "delta" of the option.] And $e^{-rT}N(d2)E$ is the expected cost, in present value terms, of having to exercise the option. The call is worth the net difference between what we expect to get and what we expect to have to pay for it.

What are d1 and d2? We define d1 as $[\ln(S/E) + (r + \sigma^2/2)T]/\sigma\sqrt{T}$. What does this unwieldy beast mean? In a certain sense, d1 reflects the value of being able to exercise the option. Let's start by thinking about it in the case of an at-the-money option. Here, S = E, hence S/E = 1. Now, ln(1) = 0 (recall that ln is the *natural* logarithm not to the base 10). So now, d1 = 1 + (r + $\sigma^2/2$)T/$\sigma\sqrt{T}$. It may help to rewrite this as two components: $rT/\sigma\sqrt{T} + \sigma^2 T/2/\sigma\sqrt{T}$.

Let's suppose that our option is in the amount of $1. Then rT is the value we get by not buying $1 of stock today, since we can keep the money in cash and earn interest. If we divide our period of time into units of $\sigma\sqrt{T}$, then we can say that $rT/\sigma\sqrt{T}$ is approximately the interest that is earned in that period ("approximately" because we are neglecting compounding). That is the first part of d1. The second part arises from the volatility of the share. It can be simplified by dividing through by $\sigma\sqrt{T}$ to arrive at $\sigma\sqrt{T}/2$. Over the period T, a share with a volatility of σ is likely to make an up or down move of $\sigma\sqrt{T}$. It is equally likely to go up or down. We are only interested in the payoff if it goes up, since we can walk away from it if it goes down. Because a 50/50 chance is involved, the expected profit, over our chosen subinterval of $\sigma\sqrt{T}$, is $\sigma\sqrt{T}/2$. We can interpret d1 as the cash value of the interest earned by buying the option rather than the share, plus the payoff if the share goes up, over a specific interval of $\sigma\sqrt{T}$ in length.

All of this was on the assumption that we are at the money. If we are out of the money, the probability of achieving d1 is less. If we are in the money, it is greater, and this adjustment is made by including the $\ln(S/E)$ component. To find the resulting probability, we then use the cumulative normal, $N(.)$, function.

Another way of looking at the Black–Scholes formula is to realize that its creators adapted it from another source: an equation for heat transfer in physics. To illustrate this similarity, assume you have a block of metal in a room in which the temperature is 20 degrees Celsius. If the block is heated until its temperature reaches 200 degrees, and then allowed to cool, the center of the block will stay hot for some time but will then begin to cool rapidly. (You can think of the market volatility today as the "heat" level.) If you plot this, you will see a pattern resembling the curve in Figure 6.6, showing how time decay affects the price of an option.[2]

It may help to make this formula a bit more concrete. Suppose we have a 1-year option (i.e., $T = 1$). The rate of interest is 10 percent (i.e., 0.10), the annualized volatility is 15 percent (0.15), and the option is at the money so that $S = E$. Let us assume that the option is on a share with a current price of $100. Then $rT = 0.10$ and $\sigma^2 T/2 = 0.0225/2 = 0.01125$. $\sigma\sqrt{T} = 0.15$ and so we have d1 = $(0.10 + 0.01125)/0.15 = 0.741667$. We can use the Excel™ function NORMDIST (setting the function to have a mean of 0 and a variance of 1) or its equivalent in other spreadsheets, or look it up in a statistics book, to find that $N(0.741667) = 0.770855$. That is, there is a 77 percent chance that we will exercise a 1-year at-the-money option on these assumptions if volatility is 15 percent. So the first term of the Black–Scholes value is 77.0855.

The second term is the discounted value of the exercise price multiplied by $N(d2)$. We know that d2 = d1 − $\sigma\sqrt{T}$ = $0.741667 - 0.15 = 0.591667$. Again, we use Excel or our statistics book to find $N(d2) = 0.722963$. We know that $e^{-rT} = \exp(-0.10)$ which again we can find from Excel or elsewhere to be 0.904837. So we know the discounted value of the exercise price ($E.e^{-rT}$) is 90.4837 and the second component of the Black–Scholes formula is $0.722963 \times 90.4837 = 65.41641$. This is the expected cost of exercising the option if it expires in the money.

The value of the call, then, is the difference between the expected payoff from exercising, less the expected cost of exercise: $77.0855 - 65.41641 = 11.66913$.

---

[2] This example is borrowed from Robert Tompkins, *Options Analysis*, 2nd ed. (New York: Macmillan, 1994).

AMERICAN VERSUS EUROPEAN OPTIONS

We have said that an American option is one that can be exercised at any time until maturity, and a European option is one that can be exercised only at maturity. Common sense tells us that the American option must always be worth at least as much as the European; it conveys more rights and so must be worth more.

The question is: How much more? The answer depends on the nature of the underlying asset. For instance, if the asset underlying the option is an equity that pays dividends, there can be circumstances in which it is optimal to exercise early. Likewise, for a currency option on a high interest rate currency (e.g., sterling), if the option is deep in the money, it may be worth exercising in order to get the high yield.

Early exercise will normally carry an advantage only if the option's price does not itself reflect the value of the dividend due on the equity or the interest rate payable on the currency; that is, if the market is not pricing efficiently. It can be shown that the right of early exercise is not in itself normally worth a great deal. It will almost always be better to sell an American option in the marketplace than to exercise it. The reason is that, until it expires, the American option will have some time value. In an efficient market, someone will always be willing to pay something for that time value.

There are three exceptions to this rule. Under the following conditions, early exercise may be worthwhile: (1) when an American option on an instrument is about to pay a cash flow; (2) when dealing costs in the options market are high; (3) when the option is so deep in the money that time value is negligible; and (4) when cross-margining considerations apply.

When dealing costs in the options market are high, it may be cheaper to exercise the option than to incur the dealing cost by selling the option. Likewise, we saw earlier that when an option is deep in the money, it will have almost no time value, and exercise may then be the best choice. Suppose spot sterling is $1.50. We own a 3-month $1.40 call worth $0.10; that is, the call has no time value. Suppose 3-month forward sterling is trading at $1.45. We can exercise the option at $1.40, sell in the spot market at $1.50, and realize a profit of $0.10. If we still need sterling, we can buy forward at $1.45. Alternatively, we can sell the option for $0.10 and buy forward at $1.45. In either case, the net cost of forward sterling to us is $1.35.

Finally, the holder of an in-the-money option on a futures position who is hedging a futures position may find it optimal to exercise, because of the difference between the margining procedures. The futures position is tying up variation margin, but the option position is not giving the benefit. This exception does not apply on the CME or LIFFE, where the two positions can be linked together. It is relevant, though, when we are considering two exchanges where we cannot offset.

VOLATILITY

The more volatile an instrument, the higher the associated option price. Volatility is a measure of how the price of the underlying instrument varies. The word *volatility* covers a multitude of possibilities: (1) the volatility that we have deduced from other traded options (implied volatility); (2) our forecast of volatility; or (3) an estimate of volatility as derived from recent history. Unless otherwise stated in this book, volatility will be taken to refer to historic volatility, defined as the standard deviation (see Chapter 3) in price returns of the instrument underlying the option.

To be precise, the definition of annual historic volatility normally used in the options markets is:

$$\text{Volatility} = \sqrt{\text{Variance}\left[\log\left(\frac{P_t}{Pt-1}\right)\right] \times 250}$$

where $t = 1/n$, and n is the number of trading days over which volatility is measured (we assume 250 trading days per annum). An alternative measure is to do the same calculation assuming 365 calendar days rather than 250 trading days.

Measuring the volatility of an instrument in terms of its standard deviation gives us an idea of its likely trading range, all other things being equal. For example, if a currency priced at $1.00 has an annualized volatility of 20 percent, then the most likely range of prices (i.e., within one standard deviation) by the end of the year is between $0.83 and $1.20 ($1.00 divided by 1.2 and multiplied by 1.2, respectively).

Let's take a call option on sterling with a strike price of $2.10, when the currency is at $2.00. If the expected volatility of sterling is 20 percent, there is a greater chance that the price will be above $2.10 at the expiry of the option than if expected volatility is only 10 percent. The fact that there is a higher probability of large price falls is of no concern to the holder of a call option because the loss is limited to the premium paid. The holder will be prepared to pay more for an option on a currency that has an expected volatility of 20 percent, than for an option on a currency with an expected volatility of 10 percent. The writer of the call option faces a greater risk on the more volatile currency, and therefore will charge a higher premium to write it.

Estimating the future volatility of the underlying instrument is one of the hardest tasks in pricing an option. It is the only variable affecting the option premium that is not directly observable in the market when the option is priced. All we know at that point is what its volatility has been in the past. Conversely, once the option is priced (for example, an exchange-traded option, where we can see the price at which the option last traded) we can work out what volatility is implied in the price, assuming we know the options pricing formula that was used.

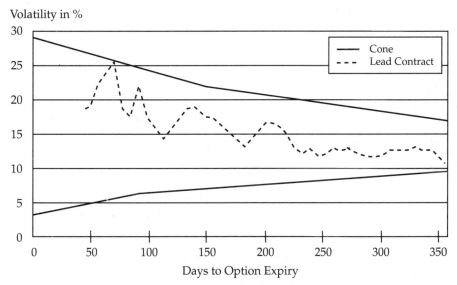

Volatility in %

Source: J. K. Walmsley. *Foreign Exchange & Money Markets Guide.* John Wiley, NY, 1992.

Figure 6.13 A volatility cone.

Finally, one key assumption of the Black–Scholes model is that volatility is known and constant during the life of the option. This is, of course, not possible in reality. Nor, in practice, do we find the market (apparently) using a consistent volatility across the whole range of strike prices. Rather, we find the market has a range of volatilities, higher for out-of-the-money options and lower for at-the-money ones. This is called the "volatility smile" and we turn now to some problems in the concept of volatility.

Volatility Cones

Given the critical importance of the volatility estimate in pricing an option, it may be worth spending some time thinking about how we should make that estimate. Often, traders use gut feel, or pricing in line with implied volatilities seen in the market. This may be satisfactory. The evidence in other markets indicates that spending huge sums of money or large amounts of time in building sophisticated forecasting models does not necessarily achieve performance improvements in proportion to the effort. One study concluded: "on a time-varying ex ante basis, the simpler the model, the better it performs . . . evidence from this study strongly supports the 'keep it simple' approach to forecasting."[3] The same study recommended exponential smoothing or regression analysis as likely techniques for volatility forecasting.

---

[3] E. Dimson and P. Marsh. "Volatility Forecasting without Data-Snooping," *Journal of Banking & Finance* (1990).

For many, looking at volatility via the volatility cone (Figure 6.13) is helpful. This starts by considering the term structure of volatility. The smoothly curved lines represent upper and lower bounds of historical volatilities for trading horizons ranging from 1 month to 1 year. The data are drawn from the two previous years.

The resulting volatility cones show that short-term historical volatilities are substantially more variable than longer-term historical volatilities. This can be seen in the greater distance between the maximum and minimum 50-day historical volatilities (shown toward the left of the figure) and the maximum and minimum 350-day historical volatilities (shown at the right).

Volatility Smiles

A key problem in volatility estimation is that it is very common to find a skewed distribution of volatility when we observe the implied volatilities available in the market. This phenomenon became more obvious after the crash of 1987. Typically, out-of-the-money options are generally priced with higher volatilities. This is often called the "volatility smile." The effect usually is somewhat symmetrical, but, particularly in equity markets, the smile is more often what has been described as "a lopsided leer." This phenomenon can be seen in Figure 6.14,[4] which shows the leer for the U.K. equity market (FTSE options, August 1991).

Figure 6.15 shows the volatility smile for the March 1997 Euromark option contract on LIFFE,[5] and its evolution over time:

Implied Binomial Trees

In 1994, three researchers from both sides of the Atlantic published research describing the development of an options pricing model that automatically incorporated the smile and term structure effect seen in options markets.[6] Two approaches were involved: (1) the implied volatility tree and (2) the implied binomial tree. The former, in essence, takes observed option volatilities for future dates and uses them to construct the binomial tree. We can depict the outcome visually if the tree is twisted to allow for differing volatilities at different nodes (Figure 6.16).

---

[4] Data from R. G. Tompkins, *Options Analysis* (Probus, 1994).

[5] Many thanks to Bryan Eddery of LIFFE for supplying the data.

[6] B. Dupire, "Pricing with a Smile," *Risk Magazine* (January 1994); E. Derman & I. Kani, "Riding on a Smile," *Risk Magazine* (February 1994); M. Rubinstein, "Implied Binomial Trees," *Journal of Finance* (July 1994).

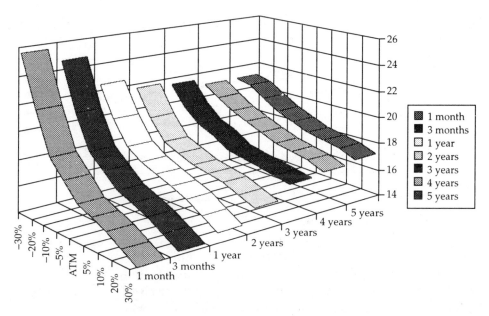

Figure 6.14 Volatility smile for FTSE options.

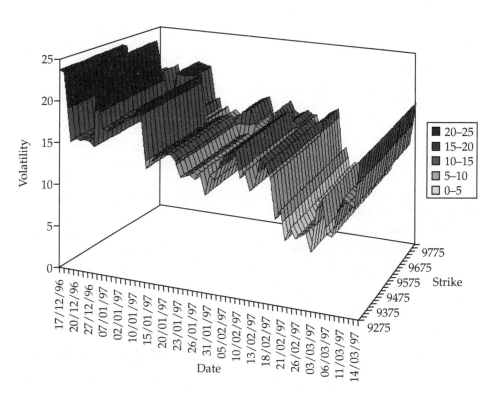

Figure 6.15 Volatility surface for Euromarks, March 1997.

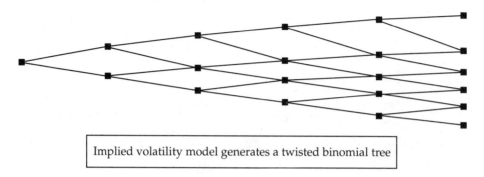

Implied volatility model generates a twisted binomial tree

Figure 6.16   Implied volatility tree.

The latter, the implied binomial model, starts with a given asset price distribution for a particular future date and then builds a binomial distribution whose terminal distribution is equal to the given distribution. Where do we get this distribution from? Two possibilities suggest themselves: (1) deduce it from existing options prices; (2) take a specific set of market views. (In a sense, we are coming full circle here to the approach to options pricing before the risk-neutral Black–Scholes model was accepted; but this time we are imposing it onto a much more sophisticated framework.)

The implied binomial tree model has three steps:

1. For a given future date, set up a risk-neutral probability distribution for the asset.
2. Build a binomial tree whose last nodes end on the given future date, and whose last nodes coincide with the distribution set up in step 1.
3. Use this tree to value options.

The third step is the same process as the one we did earlier. The first step can be done, as mentioned, by working from a complete set of European option prices for some given forward date (obtained, if necessary, by interpolation/extrapolation from existing market data).

The implied volatility and implied binomial tree approaches are potentially very powerful and flexible options pricing tools. It seems likely we will see considerable development in this area.

VOLATILITY INDEXES

At some point, it seems likely that there will be a market in pure volatility; but it is some time in developing. In 1993, the Chicago Board of Options Exchange introduced the CBOE Market Volatility Index (ticker symbol: VIX) to measure the volatility of the U.S. equity market. It provides investors with up-to-the-minute market estimates of expected volatility by using real-time OEX index option bid/ask quotes. The VIX is calculated by averaging the S&P 100 Stock Index at-the-money put and call implied volatilities. As yet, there has been little interest in trading a future or option on the VIX. Similarly, the DTB has a volatility index, but no derivative on that index.

Measures of Option Risk and Sensitivity

In managing an options book, dealers pay attention to a number of risk measures. The most important measures are referred to as delta, gamma, vega (or kappa), and theta. Other measures sometimes referred to are rho and lambda. In this section, we will consider how they apply to our old favorite, the $2.00 sterling call. We will calculate them for a 3-month option in an environment where the volatility is estimated at 20 percent, the domestic currency interest rate is 8 percent, and the foreign currency rate is 6 percent.

The delta of an option is the change in the price of the option that results from a change of $1 in the price of the underlying asset. Delta varies between 0 and 1 (or 0 percent and 100 percent, depending on how you want to express it). Figure 6.17 shows how delta rises from very low values when the option is out of the money to 1 when the option is deep in the money. At that point, the option is certain to be exercised, has no time value, and behaves like the asset itself.

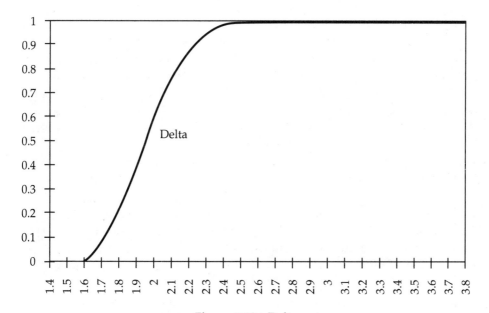

Figure 6.17 Delta.

We defined delta as the change in the option price for a change in asset price. That means that delta can be defined as the slope of the tangent to the option's price curve. It measures the sensitivity of the option's price to the underlying asset. The more in the money the option is, the more sensitive its price is to that of the asset. Conversely, for a deep out-of-the-money option, even quite a large change in the asset price will have no effect. The question is sometimes asked: Why does delta change if volatility changes? The answer is: Because a change in volatility changes the shape of the premium/asset price curve; hence, the slope of the curve (delta) changes.

Another way of looking at delta is to say that it measures the probability that the option will be exercised. When the option is deep out of the money, there is little chance that it will be exercised, and delta is 0. When the option is deep in the money, the option is almost 100 percent certain to be exercised, and delta will be 1. When the option is at the money, the chances are 50/50 and delta will be around 0.5. The implication here is that delta can be used as a measure of the exposure implied by an option position. Suppose we have written a call on $100 million Eurodollar futures at 90.5 (an implied interest rate of 9.5 percent). Suppose the delta of the position is currently 0.25, which indicates a 25 percent chance that the option can be exercised against us. On a probability-weighted basis, our exposure is equivalent to being short $25 million worth of Eurodollar futures at 90.5. Therefore, to hedge our position, we could buy $25 million of futures. This is the concept of delta-weighted hedging, which is widely used by many market makers in options.[7]

The next important measure of option sensitivity is gamma, which measures the sensitivity of delta to changes in the asset price. Thus, gamma is a measure of the stability of delta. The higher gamma is, the more rapidly delta changes as the price of the asset changes. If we look again at Figure 6.17, we can see that delta does not change much as the asset price changes, if the option is deep out of the money. Thus, gamma is low. Nor does delta respond much to changes in asset price when the option is deep in the money. Again, gamma is low. Gamma is highest when the option is at the money. It is then that delta is moving most quickly. For the delta-weighted hedger, it is important to measure gamma. A high gamma means the hedge must be adjusted much more often; delta hedging a high-gamma position tends to be much more expensive. Gamma is highest when the option is at the money and when it is short-dated. It is lowest for long-dated out-of-the-money options.

Another way of looking at gamma is to say that it measures the curviness of the option premium curve. Just as delta measures the slope of the tangent to the curve at today's price, so gamma measures the curviness of the curve at that point. (In the language of calculus, delta is the first derivative and gamma is the second derivative.) We might say that delta is the speed of change, and

---

[7] See J. K. Walmsley, *Foreign Exchange & Money Markets Guide* (New York: John Wiley & Sons, Inc., 1992); R. G. Tompkins, *Options Analysis*, 2nd ed. (New York: Macmillan, 1994).

gamma is the acceleration. Figure 6.18 shows the effect of gamma for different asset price levels. (The curve ought to be smooth but the spreadsheet used had only 10 different spot points in it.)

Offsets to gamma—ways of hedging our gamma exposure—would be to sell short-dated at-the-money options if we are long, and buy if we are short. We can avoid building up exposure to gamma by dealing in out-of-the-money far-dated options.

The next measure we must look at is called vega (or kappa or zeta or epsilon). This measures the impact on the option's premium of a 1 percent change in volatility. We said earlier that the more volatile the underlying asset, the more valuable the option on the asset will be. There will be a greater chance that the option could move in our favor during its lifetime. Vega particularly affects longer-dated options pricing.

Vega is at its largest for at-the-money long-dated options. If an option is deep in or out of the money, a change in volatility will not mean very much, whereas it could have a significant effect if the option is at the money. Likewise, vega is more important for a long-dated option because the longer time allows a greater chance for the option to move in the buyer's favor. Figure 6.19 shows the effect of vega for different asset price levels. Offsets to vega are to write options if we are long of vega, and buy options if we are short. If we do not want to build up vega, we should tend to deal in out-of-the-money options.

The fourth important measure of options' sensitivity is theta, which measures the impact of time on an option's fair value. More exactly, it measures the effect of shortening, by 1 day, the option's life to maturity on the

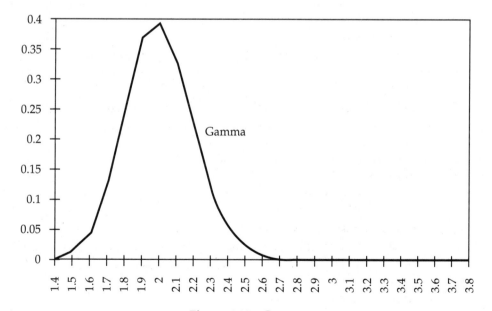

Figure 6.18 Gamma.

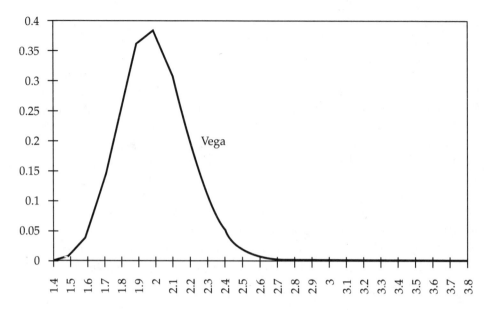

Figure 6.19 Vega.

option premium. We have said that, early in an option's life, the effect of time decay is not very large. It increases as the option's life shortens, and the reason for this is fairly clear. The percentage impact on the option's value of a 1-day shortening of its life is small if the option has 90 days to run, but much larger if it has only 1 day left. Also, theta has a bigger impact on at-the-money options. We saw earlier that time value for deep in- and out-of-the-money options is small. Figure 6.20 shows how theta behaves for different price levels.

It may be of interest to consider the above measures in three dimensions, that is, to plot them not only against changes in the spot but also over time from now until the maturity of the option. Figures 6.21 through 6.24 illustrate the situation.

Delta (Figure 6.21) starts off with the S-shaped curve described earlier, but then it sharpens to an almost vertical shape at expiry, reflecting the fact that, at that point, the option is either in or out of the money.

To allow the delta shape to be more easily seen, the delta diagram was turned around, compared with the gamma diagram (Figure 6.22) and its successors. We can see from the gamma chart that gamma presents the biggest problems when we are very close to expiry and the option is at the money (a reflection of the vertical delta line seen in Figure 6.21).

For volatility to have an impact, the market must have time to be volatile. As we get closer to expiry, therefore, vega has less influence (Figure 6.23). Likewise, if we are deep in or out of the money, a 1 percent change in volatility levels will not make much difference.

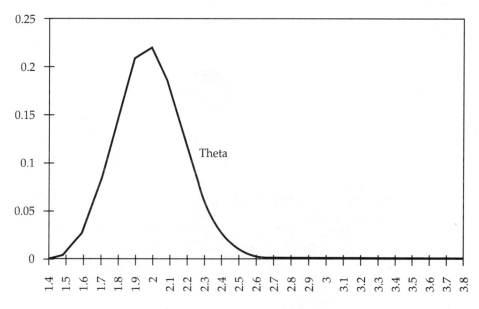

Figure 6.20 Theta.

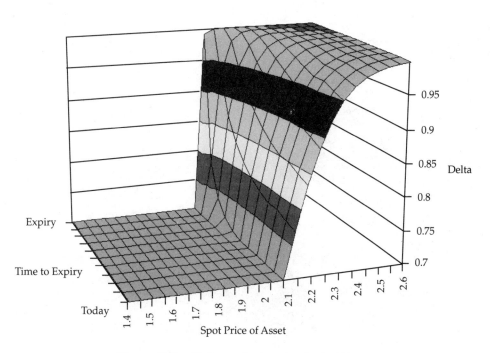

Figure 6.21 Delta against spot rate and time.

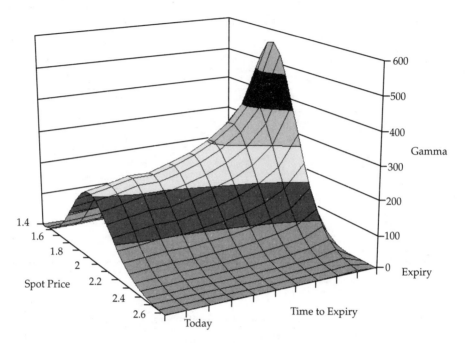

Figure 6.22   Gamma against spot rate and time.

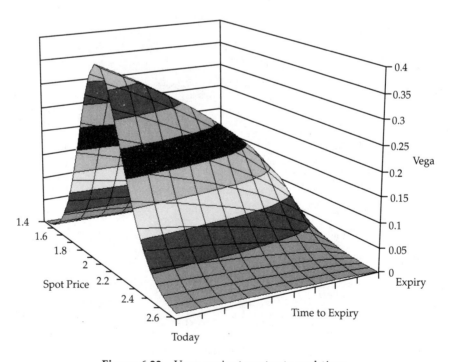

Figure 6.23   Vega against spot rate and time.

Figure 6.24 shows that, for a given change in the time to expiry, theta has its largest effect on the option price as we are close to maturity.

Two other measures are sometimes used: rho and lambda. Rho measures the sensitivity of the option's price to interest rates and can be defined as the dollar change in the option's price for a 1 percent change in the rate of interest. Rho can be divided into two effects: (1) the effect of interest rate changes on the price of the asset, which will be important if the option is on a bond or on a currency for forward delivery, and (2) the effect of the fact that an option is a geared, or leveraged, instrument. The option gives the holder a claim on the asset, without having to finance its purchase. For example, I could buy an option on 1,000 IBM shares, whose worth is $100,000; if the option costs me $2,500, I have obtained effective control of $100,000 of assets for $2,500. My alternative would have been to borrow the remaining $97,500 to finance outright purchase of the underlying shares. Rho is not often important in assessing options, but can be so, for example, in the case of long-dated currency options (see below) because, in this case, the forward exchange rates themselves are influenced directly by interest-rate movements.

Lambda is the percentage change in option price for a percentage change in stock price; effectively, it is the delta restated in percentage terms. (Economists would say that lambda is the elasticity of the option price with respect to the asset price.)

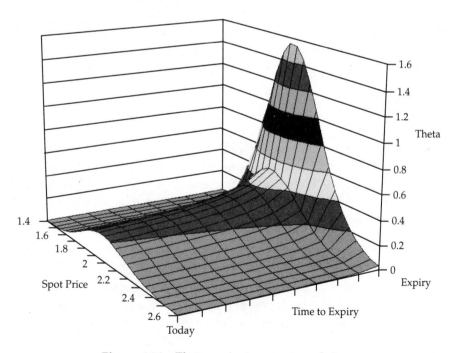

Figure 6.24 Theta against spot rate and time.

COMBINED POSITIONS

In this section, we discuss some of the different combinations of puts and calls that options traders use. We will display the profit payoff diagram for each strategy and will look at some of the basic risk–reward issues. Throughout this section, we will, for brevity, use the following symbols:

Symbol	Meaning
+	Long
–	Short
C	Call
P	Put
@E1, @E2	At exercise price 1, at exercise price 2; E1 is the lowest, E2 is a higher price, E3 is the next higher, and so on.
T1, T2	Nearest maturity date, next maturity date, and so on.

The first strategy we will introduce is a very important one because it shows the relationship of puts and calls to the underlying asset. If you look at the diagram for being long an asset (Figure 6.5), you will see a line sloping up from left to right. If you look at the diagram for being long a call (Figure 6.1), you will see a line sloping up from left to right in the top right corner of the diagram. If you look at the diagram for being short a put (Figure 6.4), you will see a line sloping up from left to right again, but this time in the bottom left corner. This suggests that being short a put and long a call, at the same strike, will produce the same payoff profile as being long an asset. This is, in fact, right; it will always be true that, for any given strike level for a put and call, we can write:

$$+\text{asset} = +C - P.$$

Thus, being long a call and short a put (at the same strike price) on a given asset is equivalent in profit terms to being long an asset. Conversely, to be short the asset is the same as being long a put and short the call. More formally, using C for the price of the call, P for the price of the put, A for the price of the asset, and E for the strike price, we could write:

$$A - E = C - P.$$

The intrinsic value of the option (the difference between the asset price and the strike of the option) will be equal to the difference between the price of the call and the price of the put (at the same strike). This is known in the trading jargon as "put–call parity."

Note that the above statement of put–call parity is strictly true only for American options—those allowing exercise at any time. If the two options involved were European options, which can only be exercised at maturity, we would have to allow for the time value of money:

$$PV(A - E) = C - P$$

where PV means the present value. Also, we can rearrange the original equation. We can write, for example:

$$+asset + put = +call \quad or \quad +asset - call = -put.$$

If we owned the asset and a put on the asset, it would be the same as owning a call on the asset; if we owned the asset and had sold a call on it, it would be the same as being short a put on the asset. This put–call parity is often useful when we want to construct a synthetic position—either to create a put (for example, if we cannot buy a put directly in the market) or even to create a synthetic asset from the put and the call.

We start with the two simplest cases: purchase of a call option or a put option.

Long a call option: +C @E1

Outlook: Bullish.

Profit Potential: Unlimited.

Loss Potential: Limited.

Time Decay: Against the buyer. Worst at the money.

The buyer of a call option on sterling at $2.00 thinks sterling will rise above that level. As it does, the buyer's profit is unlimited [as we saw from the payoff diagram (Figure 6.1)].The risk is that sterling is below $2.00 at maturity. If so, the option buyer's loss is limited to the premium paid. Because the seller charges a time value element in the price of the option, the buyer of a call option suffers the effects of time decay. The time premium is largest for an at-the-money option, so time decay is worst for the buyer of such an option.

Long a put option: +P @E1

Outlook: Bearish.

Profit Potential: Unlimited.

Loss Potential: Limited.

Time Decay: Against the buyer. Worst at the money.

The buyer of a put option on sterling at $2.00 believes sterling will fall below that level. As it does, the buyer's profit is unlimited (compare Figure 6.2). The risk of loss is that sterling settles above $2.00 at maturity. In that case, the option buyer's loss is limited to the premium paid. The buyer of the option pays time value to the seller and so time decay works against the buyer. Time value is highest for an at-the-money option, and time decay is most negative for an at-the-money put.

As we consider various combinations of options, we will see a range of different combinations, but they can usually be broken down into three types:

1. Vertical spreads: Options with the same expiry date, but a different strike price.
2. Horizontal spreads (sometimes referred to as calendar spreads): Options at the same strike price, but a different expiry date.
3. Diagonal spreads: Combinations of vertical and horizontal spreads.

Depending on where the strike prices of the options composing them are fixed, spreads can cost a net premium or earn a net premium. In the former case, they are referred to as debit spreads; in the latter, as credit spreads. We begin with vertical spreads, which do not have the complications of time built in. The first of these is the bull spread.

Bull spread: +C @−C @E2; or: +P @E1 −P @E2

Outlook: Bullish, but not overwhelmingly.

Profit Potential: Limited.

Loss Potential: Limited.

Time Decay: Fairly neutral (depending on where the option strikes are set).

The buyer of a bull spread on sterling between, say $2.00 and $2.10 buys a call on sterling at $2.00 and sells a call at $2.10 (Figure 6.25). The sale of the call at the higher exercise price brings in premium that helps offset the cost of the $2.00 call. This is cheaper than buying a $2.00 call outright. But the saving is at the cost of giving up any profit beyond $2.10. So this deal would be done if one were bullish on sterling but unconvinced it would go to $2.10.

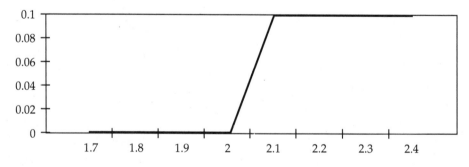

Figure 6.25 Bull call spread.

The strategy can be exercised by doing puts at the same level. Here, the $2.00 put pays off below $2.00; its cost is paid for by selling a put at $2.10. This cuts the total premium paid, but costs money if sterling goes above $2.20. The basic view is that sterling will trade between $2.00 and $2.10.

In both cases, time decay on the option sold helps offset the time decay on the option bought. The net effect depends on how close the two strike prices are.

Cylinder: +P @E1 −C @E2; or +C @E1 −P @E2

Outlook: Bearish, but wanting cheap protection.

Profit Potential: Limited.

Loss Potential: Limited.

Time Decay: Neutral, depending on strikes.

A popular strategy, particularly for corporations hedging their exchange risk, is the cylinder (or the fence, or the tunnel—the strategy has been given many different names by the marketing teams of different banks anxious to convince their customers that they invented the idea).

Here, protection is bought below a certain level, at the risk of giving away profit if the rate goes above a certain level (or vice versa, if the strategy is dealt in the opposite direction). By adjusting the strike prices, cylinders can be structured so that they are net debit spreads or net credit spreads, or so that the net premium is zero. The fact that a zero cost is charged does not mean the customer is getting a free ride. The strikes may have been set so that, on the other side, the bank can sell off the two component positions at a handsome profit.

The zero up-front cost is the feature that has traditionally made the cylinder attractive to corporate customers. Corporate treasurers do not want to have to explain to their boards of directors why they are paying out good money to get protection against an exchange rate move that may never happen. (A number of companies, for some reason, do not accept the analogy with insurance on physical property. A fire insurance premium is good money paid out to protect against something that may never happen.)

Figure 6.26 illustrates a hedging application: the payoff of a cylinder strategy hedging a position that is long sterling at $1.70, has bought the put at $1.50, and has sold a call at $1.80.

Straddle: +C @E1 +P @E1

Outlook: Market volatility will rise. Neutral on market direction.

Profit Potential: Unlimited.

Loss Potential: Limited to premium.

Time Decay: Doubly negative (both legs of the trade decay are against you).

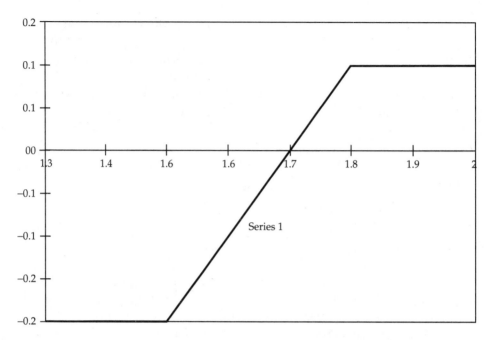

Figure 6.26 Cylinder.

The next strategy, the straddle, is unique to the options market. Until now, all the strategies we have looked at have involved a view on the direction of the market. Such a view could be traded in the cash market without difficulty. But the straddle allows taking a position on the volatility of the market without committing to a view on its direction. If we think the volatility of the market will rise, we can buy a straddle; if we think it will fall, we can sell a straddle.

Above the strike, the call pays off; below the strike, the put pays off. Whichever way the market moves, you make money. But it has to move enough to cover the double premium paid out to get into the deal, and it has to move fairly quickly because time decay is working against you twice as hard.

Strangle: +C @E1 +P @E2

Outlook: Market volatility will rise. Neutral on market direction.

Profit Potential: Unlimited.

Loss Potential: Limited.

Time Decay: Doubly negative.

The strangle is a similar strategy, but the put and call have different exercise prices. Normally, one or both of the options bought are out of the money, so that the cost of the strangle is less than the straddle. A drawback is that, to pay off, the strangle needs a larger market move than the straddle. Suppose we do the same as before but with a call strike price of $2.10 (Figure 6.28).

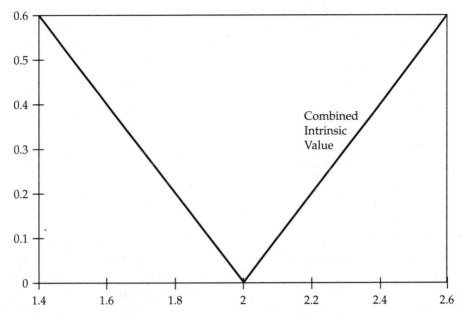

Figure 6.27 Payoff profile from a straddle.

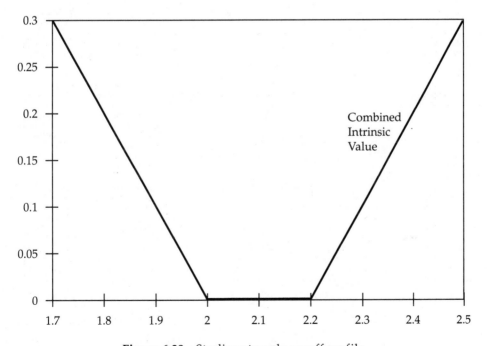

Figure 6.28 Sterling strangle payoff profile.

The buyer of a strangle has the same volatility view as the buyer of a straddle, but looks for a different payoff pattern. The strangle loses money over a wider range than the straddle, but loses less if the market does not move at all. Thus, it is essentially a less aggressive bet than the straddle. The short seller of the strangle takes the opposite view: he or she is a seller of volatility.

Butterfly: +C @E1 −2C @E2 +C @E3

Outlook: Market will stay stable.

Profit Potential: Limited.

Loss Potential: Limited.

Time Decay: Fairly neutral (depending on strikes).

The butterfly consists of sale of a straddle combined with purchase of call options below and above the straddle's strike. It is a straddle with stop-loss protection. It is a position loved by options brokers (sometimes known as "the Cadillac spread") because it involves four separate contracts and thus four sets of commission. Options traders need to consider the transactions costs involved. But it can be a good, limited-risk method of profiting from the sale of volatility. The short butterfly position is sometimes called a sandwich spread—the dealer hopes to sandwich the price movement within the spread.

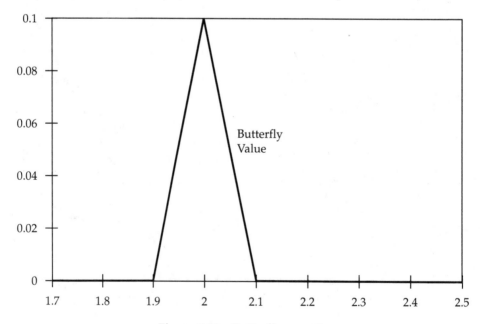

Figure 6.29 Butterfly spread.

Condor: +C E1 −C E2 −C E3 +C E4

Outlook: Market will stay stable.

Profit Potential: Limited (but over wider range than butterfly).

Loss Potential: Limited (but more than butterfly).

Time Decay: Fairly neutral (depending on strike levels).

The condor is to the strangle what the butterfly is to the straddle. That is, the condor is a strangle with stop-loss. The dealer buys calls outside the range of the strangle to cut down the risk of a large countermovement.

Up to now, all the positions we have looked at have been balanced, in the sense that options sold and bought have generally matched. Ratio spreads are spread trades where the puts and calls bought or sold are in a ratio to each other. Thus, the call ratio spread consists of buying a call at one strike and selling several calls at another.

Call ratio spread: +C @E1 −nC @E2 (where n is usually from 2 to 5)

Outlook: Bearish, but not aggressively so.

Profit Potential: Limited.

Loss Potential: Unlimited.

Time Decay: In our favor (how much depends on how many calls are sold).

The same approach can be taken with a put ratio spread.

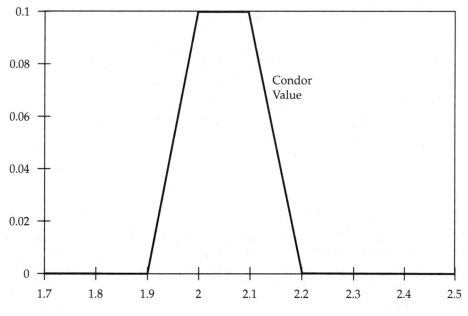

Figure 6.30 Condor.

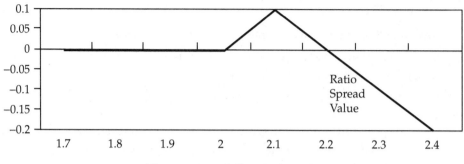

Figure 6.31 Call ratio spread.

So far, all the strategies we have considered are option combinations that expire on the same day. Collectively, these spreads are called vertical spreads. Now we come to consider the effect of time; we allow the options to mature on different dates. Options strategies involving different maturities are often called horizontal or calendar spreads. One could, in principle, have many of the above spreads with different maturity dates for different components of the spread, but this would reduce the risk protection given and, in most cases, break up the logic of the spreads. The most widely used calendar spread is the simple sale of a call for one maturity coupled with the purchase of a call for a further maturity.

Calendar spread: −C @T1 +C @T2

Outlook: Neutral on market direction, long volatility, short time decay.

Profit Potential: Limited. Maximum potential if the asset price is near the strike when the first option matures. At that point, we would close out the far option.

Loss Potential: Limited. Losses on the near short should in part be offset by the long position for the far date; though this may not always happen.

Time Decay: Works in our favor (the near option decays faster than the further option).

Finally, we look at an option trade where everything is known from the start; the entire position is locked up from day 1. This is called a box spread. It relies on the put–call parity (see above) to buy and sell two artificial assets established at different effective prices. We buy a call and sell a put at E1 and sell a call and buy a put at E2. In effect, it is a bet on the funding cost/interest earned between doing the trade and its maturity. In another context, it has often been used in markets where there is a difference in tax treatment between interest income/expense and capital gains/losses from options.

Box spread: +C E1 −P E1 −C E2 +P E2

Outlook: Neutral on market. Aims to lock up an interest rate.

Profit Potential: Limited.

Loss Potential: Limited.

Strategies Combining Options and Assets

Up to now, we have looked only at options positions where the options are traded on their own, or in combination with other options. Now we look at combining options positions with underlying assets.

The first such application would arise in the simple case where we hold a position and would like to protect it through options. Imagine we have bought £1,000,000 at $1.80, and sterling is now trading at $1.95. We have a profit, but we feel sterling will move up further. On the other hand, we would like some protection in case it falls unexpectedly. Suppose the $1.90 put is trading at $0.03. We decide to cover ourselves on the Philadelphia Exchange by buying 32 contracts (of £31,250 each). This costs us $0.03 × 31,250 × 32 = $30,000. At the worst, where sterling falls sharply, we will sell at $1.90 − $0.03 = $1.87. So our minimum profit is $(1.87 − 1.80) × 1,000,000 = $70,000. The payoff profile is shown in Figure 6.32.

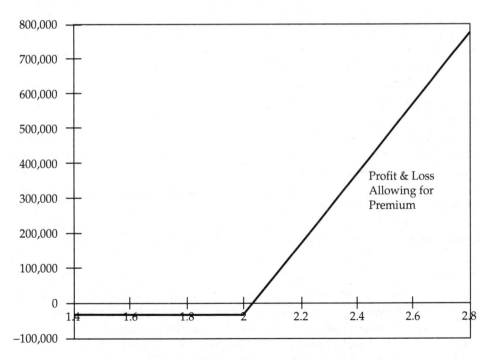

Figure 6.32 Synthetic call on sterling (asset + put).

As we mentioned earlier, in the discussion of put–call parity, this position can be looked at as a synthetic call on sterling because an alternate way to trade here would have been to sell out the existing position to lock in profits, and then buy a call on sterling. Which of these two routes we take will depend on the relative pricing of the puts and calls. If no puts are available, it would be possible to create a put by selling the underlying asset short and buying a call.

Another trade combining the underlying asset with options is a conversion (and its opposite, a reversal). A conversion is a sale of an artificial asset covered by the purchase of the asset. The sale of the artificial asset is done by selling a call and buying a put, which is equivalent to a short sale of the asset.

An example would be options on the December Eurodollar futures. Suppose the future is trading at 92.00. Let the December 91.00 call on the future be trading at 1.50 and the put at 0.20. We buy the put for 0.20 and sell the call for 1.50 for a net credit of 1.30. Effectively, we are short the future. To close our position, we buy the future at 92.00. What will happen at expiry? Suppose the future settles at 90.00 when the December expiry arrives. Then the 91.00 put will be worth 1.00 and the call will have no value. Our options positions give a profit of 1 point.

But we are long the future at 92.00, which we now close out at 90.00 for a loss of 2 points. Thus, our net position is a loss of 1 point at expiration. We made 1.50 on the initial position so the net profit on the deal as a whole is 50 basis points (slightly more, if we allow for the interest we could earn on the initial profit). There is a similar outcome if the future settles at maturity at, say, 94.00. Now, the 91.00 call loses us 3 points, the put expires worthless, and the future makes a profit of 2 points, for a net loss once again of 1 point.

A reversal is an opposite trade: Buy the artificial asset and sell short the actual asset; that is, buy a call and sell a put, covering with a short sale of the asset.

An important trading strategy involving the underlying asset and the related options is the covered write. Here, we own the underlying asset and write a call option against it. Our risk is covered by our ownership of the underlying asset—that is, if the call is exercised against us, we already own the asset that must be delivered. Our risk is thus limited to the fact that we will sell the asset at a price that may be less than we could otherwise get for it if the market really improves. On the other hand, we will have earned option premium income to compensate us for this risk.

Suppose we have bought $10 million worth of Eurodollar March futures at 89.5. We think that rates will not improve that much; we expect rates at that date to be trading at 10 percent. We might write a call option for $10 million at 91.00 for a premium of, say, 0.50. That means that the net cost of our position is effectively the 89.5 we paid for the futures, less the 0.5 of premium earned, or

89.00. Suppose we are right, and rates are at 10 percent when the delivery date comes. Then no one will exercise the call against us, since traders can buy in the market at 90 rather than the 91 they would pay via the call option. We have earned 1 point profit. Now suppose that we were wrong. Rates collapsed. The future traded at 93 on the settlement date. The call is exercised against us and we must sell at 91. But our net cost was 89, so we have earned 2 points profit. If we had not written the call, we would have made a 4-point profit. We have limited our gain, but if the market remains stable, the call option premium is an enhancement to income (see Figure 6.33).

Covered call writing is a very popular strategy in the stock market. Investors use it to earn a supplementary income. Applied consistently over time, it can be a money-spinner. One is effectively writing insurance policies—and insurance companies, over time, tend to prosper if they are prudently managed. It is common to write shorter-dated options, to take advantage of the fact that time value works more rapidly in the writer's favor.

Simple covered call writing has some weaknesses. If the market falls sharply, the option written loses value very quickly and its time value disappears. Conversely, a sharp rise in the market will have a similar effect on time value. Dynamic covered call writing is an attempt to get around this problem by making sure that the option written always has large time decay. As the market rises, we "roll up" the strike (buy back the outstanding option and sell a new one with a higher strike). Conversely, we roll down if the market falls. This approach itself has two problems: (1) higher transactions costs, and (2) increased risk of being "whipsawed." The market rises sharply: We buy back the old option and write a new one at a higher strike, incurring a dealing spread. The market now falls sharply: We reverse the process, incurring more dealing costs, and so on.

Another problem for an equity fund manager is that writing calls in a bull market is a certain recipe for underperforming competitors who do nothing but sit there holding the stock.

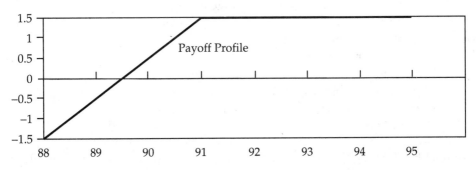

Figure 6.33 Covered call write: payoff profile.

BLACK–SCHOLES VARIANTS AND OTHER MODELS

Everybody agrees that the Black–Scholes model is incredibly useful. Everybody also agrees that it doesn't actually quite work in practice. Adjustments have to be made. Extensions have been developed to deal with specific technical problems with the Black–Scholes model: Interest rate options have to be looked at separately because it will not always be true that the price of the asset is independent of the risk-free rate of interest. The model needs to be modified to handle assets deliverable in the future (for example, for options on futures contracts), and this variation gives the Black model. The Black–Scholes model is not well adapted for situations where dividends or other cash flows are earned on the underlying asset; there is a possibility of early exercise in certain circumstances. In these situations, the binomial model discussed earlier would normally be used. Equity options models have to reflect the fact that dividends are normally paid in "lumpy" amounts. The Garman–Kohlhagen variant of the Black–Scholes model is used in the foreign exchange markets to allow for the impact of two different currencies' interest rates. We now discuss some of these modifications.

BLACK FUTURES OPTION MODEL

In 1976, Fischer Black introduced a variant of the Black–Scholes model to deal with futures prices. In this model, the underlying asset price is replaced with the futures price, and both the future and the strike price are discounted to present value, as follows:

$$C = e^{-rt}[F.N(d1) - E.N(d2)]$$

where $d1 = \dfrac{\ln(F / E) + (\sigma^2 / 2)t}{\sigma\sqrt{t}}$;

$d2 = d1 - \sigma\sqrt{t}$;

t = time to expiry (as a percentage of a year);
F = price of future;
E = exercise price of option;
r = risk-free interest rate for period t;
N = cumulative normal density;
$\ln$ = natural logarithm;
σ^2 = variance of the rate of return;
e = exponential function.

The Black model has a number of attractions; among them: it is simple to use and it handles assets due at a forward date. It is widely used in practice in the financial industry, particularly for options on futures but also for interest rate caps, as we will see in the next chapter.

Currency Options

We come now to consider currency options in more detail. One simple point should be made at the outset. Up to now, when we have talked about an option, it has been quite clear what the option was on. But now we have scope for confusion. Is a DEM/US$ call a call on the DEM and a put on the US$, or a call on the US$ and a put on the DEM? For exchange-traded options, this is not generally a real problem; but when quoting OTC options, it is very important for all parties to be clear precisely what is meant.

Consider the following example:

1. Buy a June 15 DEM call struck at DEM1.50 for 2 percent.
2. Buy a June 15 DEM call struck at DEM1.50 for $0.0133.
3. Buy a June 15 DEM call struck at $0.67 for $0.0133.
4. Buy a June 15 US$ put struck at DEM1.50 for DEM 0.026.

All of these are quotations for precisely the same deal! The method used in statement 1 or 2 might be used in the OTC market in London or New York; the method in statement 4 might be used by a Continental bank in the OTC market; the method in statement 3 is used in the exchange-traded market. The questions are: Which is the base currency and which is the quoted? Is the currency quoted in indirect or direct terms (that is, DEM1.50 per dollar or $0.67 per DEM)? Is the premium quoted as an amount of currency or, as is common in the wholesale interbank market, as a percentage? Clearly, we need to know the convention prevailing in our market.

Options pricing for currency options follows the same basic principle as for other options pricing. But there are several differences, of which the most important arise from the fact that we now have two sets of interest rates to consider, one in each currency. We know, therefore, that the forward exchange rate will be different from the spot rate, so there are two sets of effects to consider:

1. The effect of the interest differential.
2. The effect of changes in the interest differential.

Let us look first at a situation where spot sterling is trading at $2.00, and 3-month forward sterling is trading at $1.95. Let us then look at a 3-month American call on sterling with a strike of $1.95. The option is in the money, because we can exercise at $1.95 and sell at $2.00. So the American call is worth at least its intrinsic value of $0.05. But suppose the option were a European option; we

Table 6.7   Foreign Exchange Option Conventions

Higher interest rate currency (e.g., ITL, GBP):
At-the-money calls struck at spot rate.
At-the-money puts struck at forward rate.

Low interest rate currency (e.g., JPY, CHF):
At-the-money calls struck at forward rate.
At-the-money puts struck at spot rate.

can exercise only at expiry. The value, S, of the optioned asset is not the spot price but the forward price. In other words, the American call includes the forward points; the European call does not.

To allow for this, the conventions listed in Table 6.7 tend to be used.

Garman–Kohlhagen Currency Options Model

In 1983, Garman and Kohlhagen modified the Black–Scholes model to handle foreign currency options by allowing for the mixture of domestic and foreign interest rates. Using the same notation that we had before, the Garman–Kohlhagen model for a European call is:

$$C = e^{-r_f T} SN(d1) - Ee^{-r_d T} N(D2)$$

where r_f is the foreign interest rate and r_d is the domestic interest rate to the expiry date of the option. The first term reflects the fact that the spot rate is not the true price of the asset because we are dealing with a European call; the spot has to be converted into the equivalent of a forward rate. The definitions of the other terms are as before, except that d1 is rewritten:

$$d1 = \frac{\ln(S/E) + \left(r_d - r_f + \dfrac{\sigma^2}{2} \right) T}{\sigma^2 \sqrt{T}}.$$

By comparison, the original Black–Scholes formula was:

$$C = N(d1)S - e^{-rT}N(d2)E.$$

We can, if we choose, rewrite the Garman–Kohlhagen formula in terms of forwards:

$$C = [FN(D1) - EN(D2)]e^{-r_d T}$$

where

$$D1 = \frac{\ln\left(\frac{F}{E}\right) + \left(\frac{\sigma^2}{2}\right)T}{\sigma\sqrt{T}}$$

and

$$D2 = D1 - \sigma\sqrt{T}.$$

Using this rather simpler notation, we can also write the formula for a European put as follows:

$$P = [F\{N(D1) - 1\} - E\{N(D2) - 1\}]e^{-r_dT}$$

Currency options also differ from other options in that, in the foreign exchange market, unlike most interest rate markets, there is a widely traded and liquid forward market. This means that the buyer or seller of an option always has the choice of comparing the option with the price available in the forward market, and there is the possibility of combining the two. These are the so-called "third generation" products, which are discussed in Chapter 7.

Equity Options

If we are prepared to say that an equity pays a constant and continuous dividend, expressed as a percentage of the share price, rather like an interest rate, then it is easy to treat equity options as another extension of Black–Scholes—similar to the Garman–Kohlhagen model, but replacing the foreign currency interest rate with the dividend rate. The same applies to options on equity indexes.

But reality is not quite like that. Firms pay dividends in lumps. Furthermore, they do so according to a pattern that is often seasonal. There are two possible approaches: (1) modify the Black–Scholes model to allow for this, or (2) try to construct a binomial tree that allows for dividend payments. Depending on the need for which we want the model (e.g., to price a short-term option when the dividends are already known, or a longer-term option when we do not know the future pattern), either approach may be suitable.[8]

---

[8] The issue is thoroughly discussed in N. A.Chriss, *Black–Scholes and Beyond* (Burr Ridge, IL: Irwin, 1997); see also, e.g., R. Jarrow and S. Turnbull, *Derivative Securities* (Cincinnati, OH: South-Western College Publishing, 1996).

Interest Rate Option Models

In many respects, by far the most difficult work in options is in the interest rate area. It is here that much current research is being done and a number of different models have emerged. The critical issue is that the basic assumption in Black–Scholes is that the underlying rate of interest is constant. This is useless when we are trying to price an option on a variable rate of interest. A further problem is that, in most cases, such as bond options, the underlying instruments are influenced not just by a single rate of interest but by the whole yield curve. In addition, if we are looking at a bond option, we have to face the fact that, as the bond approaches maturity and its life shortens, its volatility decreases. So the Black–Scholes assumption of a constant volatility is also broken.

Most approaches are some form of the binomial model; we make some assumptions about the term structure of interest rates and then use them to generate a "lattice" of forward interest rate levels. The main differences between the models lie in the way the interest rate process is specified, and these are set out in Table 6.8 for some of the better-known models.

In addition to the models cited in Table 6.8, there are a number of others: Cox, Ingersoll, and Ross; Vasicek, Longstaff, and Schwartz; Brennan and Schwartz, for example—which have been developed and used by practitioners in particular circumstances.

There is no space here to discuss these in detail, so, at the risk of grossly oversimplifying, the issues at stake are: (1) the underlying number of factors allowed to influence the term structure model; (2) the specification of the underlying volatility; and (3) the presence or absence of restrictions imposed to ensure that the resulting lattice is recombining.

Broadly, in a one-factor model, the process for the short-term, risk-free interest rate involves only one source of uncertainty. The drift and volatility are assumed to be functions of the interest rate but stable over time. These models include the Vasicek and Cox–Ingersoll–Ross models. Two-factor models usually involve a process where a short rate and a long rate are modeled; for example, the Brennan and Schwartz model assumes the short rate tends to revert to a long rate, which in turn follows a stochastic process. The Longstaff–Schwartz model is another example of this kind. The Heath–Jarrow–Morton (HJM) model can be thought of as a two-factor model but is capable of generalization to a multifactor approach.

The HJM model, however, produces trees that do not recombine. This presents practical difficulties, particularly if we are pricing path-dependent options. For a standard tree with n steps, we will have $n + 1$ terminal values. But when we have to consider all the possible paths through the tree, we have to deal with the fact that in an n-period tree, there are 2^n paths. This means that, in a 100-step tree, there are about 1.27 million trillion trillion paths! Put another way, if each human being on earth (say, 5 billion people) represented a path, we

Table 6.8 Various Interest-Rate Process Models

Ho-Lee Model

dR = θt dt + σdz

where dR = absolute change in interest rate;
        θt = mean of interest rate process as a function of time;
        dt = change in time;
        σ = volatility of absolute interest rate change;
        dz = standard random walk (Wiener process) with z a function of $\sqrt{t}$.

Black–Derman–Toy Model

dR/R = θt dt + σdz

where dR/R = proportional change in interest rate.
(Other components are as in Ho-Lee.)

Hull and White Model

dR = [(θt + a(t).(b − r)]dt + σdz

where a(t).(b − r) is an adjustment constant bringing the rate back to a long-term constant level r ("mean reversion").
(Other components are as in Ho-Lee.)

Heath, Jarrow, and Morton Model

dR(t,T) = a(t,T) +Σσ(t,T)F(t,T)dz(t)

where dR = absolute change in interest rates, which is a function of the time t of the
           option and of the maturity T of the underlying asset (typically, a bond);
  a(t,T) = mean of interest rate dispersion process as a function of time;
  F(t,T) = forward rate seen at time t for a period maturing at time T;
  dz(t) = Wiener process driving term structure movements.

would need 254 million trillion planets to represent the total. That's a lot of heads to count, and much of the practical work on path-dependent options pricing is concerned with speeding it up. Now we add to it the fact that, in the HJM model, such a tree does not recombine. That means, essentially, that, for each pair of nodes, we do not go back to a single node; each node has two new nodes. We can see that the number of nodes starts to grow exponentially.

In practice, ways around this problem are found either by using techniques to speed the computation: control variate techniques, finite differences, and so on.[9] Alternatively, we may make assumptions that lead to recombining trees and that limit the full generality of the HJM model.

---

[9] These are discussed in J. C. Hull, *Options, Futures and Other Derivatives*, 3rd ed. (Englewood Cliffs, NJ: Prentice-Hall, 1997); P. Wilmott, J. Dewynn, and S. Howison, *Option Pricing: Mathematical Models and Computation* (Oxford, England: Oxford Financial Press, 1993), among others.

PART *II*

NEW FINANCIAL INSTRUMENTS

Chapter 7

Options Instruments

In Chapter 6, we looked at some of the concepts underlying options, their pricing, and the risks associated with them. In this chapter, we set out a review of the main option instruments that have been developed.

INTEREST RATE OPTIONS

Interest Rate Guarantee

We begin the discussion by explaining the interest rate guarantee (IRG). As the name suggests, an IRG gives an investor or borrower a guaranteed interest rate. It is, in essence, an option to buy or sell an interest rate forward rate agreement (FRA) on a specified date at a specified rate, for a given price today. It is for one period only (multiperiod guarantees are called caps, discussed below; hence, an alternative name for the IRG is sometimes the "caplet"). The pricing calculation is also discussed below, in the section on caps. The timing of the IRG interest rate payment as described here differs from the FRA in only one point: under an IRG, the interest payment is in arrears, whereas under the FRA it is paid in discounted form on the settlement date (see Chapter 4).

A typical example of an IRG would be a contract on 3-month LIBOR for $10,000,000 expiring on January 16, 2001, at a strike of 6.75 percent. Suppose that on January 16, 2001, the level of LIBOR is 9 percent. Then a client who had purchased the IRG would receive $(9 - 6.75)/100 * \$10,000,000 * 91/360 = \$56,875$. The pricing of the IRG is based on the Black model for futures (see below).

CAPS AND FLOORS

The market for caps and floors is an extension of the market for interest rate guarantees, and also of that for fixed-income options. The interest rate cap sets a maximum level, or cap, on a short-term rate index. The buyer of the cap is compensated if the index goes above a certain level (the strike level). Similarly, a floor provides a minimum rate on some index. Because most cap and floor agreements are private, it is difficult to estimate the size of the market. But the volume is certainly large. Individual trades of $1 billion or more are by no means unknown.

A cap or floor contract is specified by the following:

1. **Underlying index.** Caps and floors can be created on many indexes. For example, caps can be bought on 1-, 3-, or 6-month LIBOR. Caps and floors have been set on LIBOR, commercial paper, prime, Treasury bills, certificates of deposit, and certain tax-exempt rates in the U.S. market, and on equivalent rates in many other currencies.

2. **Maturity.** Time to expiry has ranged from 3 months to 12 years.

3. **Frequency.** This covers primarily the reset dates, on which the level of rates is compared with the strike level to determine what payment needs to be made. Monthly, quarterly, and semiannual reset dates are most common. The cap will specify the frequency of payment dates (usually but not always the same as the reset frequency).

4. **Strike level.** Usually, one fixed level applies to the entire program, although the level can change over time in a predetermined way.

5. **Notional principal amount.** Like the strike level, the amount underlying the contract can be constant or it can change over time.

A typical cap agreement could have the following terms:

Underlying index	3-month LIBOR (as per Reuters LIBO screen)
Term of cap	3 years
Rate fixing	Quarterly
Strike level	8%
Payment	Quarterly, in arrears (actual/360 calculation basis)
Notional amount	$30 million
Up-front fee	1.12% of par ($336,000)

In this agreement, the writer of the cap would pay the owner of the cap in any quarter when 3-month LIBOR was over the 8 percent cap level on the fixing date. As an example, if LIBOR were quoted at 9 percent on the fixing date, the payment would be, for a 92-day period:

$$\frac{9}{100} \times \frac{92}{360} \times \$30,000,000 - \frac{8}{100} \times \frac{92}{360} \times \$30,000,000 = \$76,666.67.$$

In this case, the writer would pay the holder of the interest rate cap $76,666.67. If LIBOR were at or below 8 percent, no payment would be made.

The pricing of the cap is based on the Black model for futures (see Chapter 6). We said in Chapter 6 that the model was as shown in Figure 7.1. Let us

$$C = e^{-rt}[F.N(d1) - E.N(d2)]$$

where $d1 = \dfrac{\ln\left(\dfrac{F}{E}\right) + \left(\dfrac{\sigma^2}{2}\right)t}{\sigma\sqrt{t}}$;

$d2 = d1 - \sigma\sqrt{t}$;

   t = time to expiry (as a percentage of a year);

   F = price of future;

   E = exercise price of option;

   r = risk - free interest rate for period t.

Figure 7.1   The Black model.

now consider the interest rate cap shown in Table 7.1, which we will look at as a sequence of interest rate guarantees, or caplets.

   We are considering a cap dealt on May 25, 1997, on £10,000,000. It has a strike rate of 8.5 percent on 6-month sterling LIBOR; that is, if LIBOR rises above 8.5 percent, we are paid the difference between LIBOR and 8.5 percent on £10,000,000. The first fixing will be on November 25, 1997, and our estimate of volatility of LIBOR for the 6 months to May 25, 1998, is 12 percent per annum. We have zero coupon rates for the various periods, and estimates of the volatility for those periods. We now proceed to apply the Black model.

   Let us look at the first-period caplet (the term often applied to the components that, when added together, produce the value of the cap). We are interested in the forward rate for the period (i.e., the rate from November 1997 to May 1998), because that is the rate to which the cap will apply. Using the usual formula, we can calculate the forward rate for that period: it is 7.9861 percent. If we owned an asset that paid the forward rate on £10,000,000 for the period in question, it would produce 7.9861 percent × £10,000,000 × 181/365 = £396,022.59. This is the value of F in Figure 7.1. If the asset paid the strike rate of 8.5 percent, it

Table 7.1   Sample Cap

Date	May 25, 1997
Cap strike rate	8.50%
Principal amount	£10,000,000.00

Zero Rates To:		Volatility (% p.a.)
November 25, 1997	6.375	
May 25, 1998	7.25	12
November 25, 1998	7.75	11
May 26, 1999	8	10

would produce 8.5 × £10,000,000 × 181/365 = £ 421,506.85. This is the value of E in Figure 7.1.

Now we can write ln(F/E) = −0.062365 (remembering that we use natural logarithms). Because we are concerned with the time to the rate fixing, not the maturity of the caplet, t = 184/365 years = 0.50411 year. We can then find $\sigma\sqrt{t} = 0.12 \times \sqrt{0.50411} = 0.085201$.

Using the Black formula above, we find that d1 = −0.689373 and hence d2 = −0.774574. Hence, consulting our normal distribution tables or using the Excel function for this calculation, we can find that N(d1) = 0.245294 and N(d2) = 0.219296. The main body of the Black formula, [F.N(d1) − E.N(d2)], then comes to £4,707.41. This is the future value of the caplet; we need to discount it back, to complete the Black formula.

For the period in question, the value of the discount factor to the maturity of the caplet (1 year) e^{-rt} is $e^{-.0725} = 0.932401$. So the present value today of this caplet is £4,389.19. An alternative approach would be to discount, not using the continuous time factor e^{-rt} but the bond market discount factor of $1/(1 + r)^t$, in which case the discount factor works out to 0.93007 and the caplet value to £4,378.20.

To find the value of the cap as a whole, we repeat this process for the other two caplets for the 6-month periods ending November 25, 1998, and May 26, 1999, to arrive at a final value for the cap as a whole of £42,046.04 (using continuous time discount factors) or £42,254.00 (using period discount factors). Before worrying too much about the discrepancy between these two prices, it may be helpful to realize that plugging in a volatility of 10.1 percent instead of 10 percent for the most distant caplet produces a continuous-time cap value of £42,222.70. In other words, any discrepancy caused by the choice of discount method is very likely to be swamped by errors in estimating volatility.

This point, indeed, recurs in different guises throughout any discussion of options. Arcane differences between pricing models are more than likely to be swamped by (a) difficulty in getting the right volatility and (b) market gapping and other structural hedge management problems, which are likely to mean that the ex post cost of the option is radically different from the ex ante premium charged. "When an option trader sells a structure that is worth $5 on his theoretical value sheets, he can expect, barring transaction costs, to manufacture it for somewhere between $4 and $6."[1]

One final point should be made on caps, because it often trips up the unwary. If I buy a cap with a strike price of 8.5 percent and today's LIBOR is 7 percent, then I might expect the value of the cap to increase if LIBOR jumps to 7.5 percent. The probability of LIBOR's rising through the strike is greater, so the price of the cap should rise. But, provided that the *only* move is in the current 6-month LIBOR, this is not in fact true. The reason is that the cap is an

---

[1] N. Taleb, *Dynamic Hedging: Managing Vanilla and Exotic Options* (New York: John Wiley & Sons, Inc., 1997), p. 2.

Table 7.2   Impact of a Rise in LIBOR on the Cap Value

Date	May 25, 1997	
Cap		
Strike rate	8.50%	
Principal amount	£10,000,000.00	

Zero Rates To:		Volatility (% p.a.)
November 25, 1997	7	12
May 25, 1998	7.25	11
November 25, 1998	7.75	10
May 26, 1999	8	

	Discrete Time	Continuous Time
Cap value	£38,466.36	£38,267.88
As % of principal	0.38%	0.38%

option, not on the cash market rates, but on forward rates. If 6-month LIBOR rises but 1-year LIBOR remains the same, then the forward rate (LIBOR for 6 months, starting 6 months from now) will *fall.*

Referring to our previous cap, suppose that 6-month LIBOR rises to 7 percent; we will then have the results shown in Table 7.2. The value of the cap has actually fallen by about 10 percent, despite the rise in cash LIBOR. (On the other hand, if the forward rates had risen, the value of the cap would, of course, have increased.)

APPLICATIONS OF CAPS AND FLOORS

Probably the most widespread use of caps is by borrowers who for some reason—either because it suits their cash flows or because they have no access to the swap markets (perhaps because they are highly leveraged)—prefer to pay an up-front premium in order to receive rate protection.

Another common application has been the issue of a capped liability. This technique was developed in June 1985, with a floating rate note issue for Banque Indosuez. To assess the mechanics, assume that an issuer seeks to issue $100 million of FRNs with a 12-year maturity. Without a cap, it would have to pay perhaps 3-month LIBOR plus ¹⁄₁₆ percent. It might pay an up-front fee of ½ percent, producing net proceeds of $99.5 million. To calculate the present value of the notes, we assume a constant rate of 8 percent over the life of the notes. In this case, the effective cost to the issuer is LIBOR plus 12.8 basis points. As an alternative, it might have issued a capped FRN, paying a higher coupon rate of LIBOR plus ⁵⁄₁₆ percent, in exchange for investors' assuming the cap risk. It could sell the cap to the lead manager of the issue for, say, $3 million or 3 percent. In this case, its net proceeds from the issue are $102.5 million, and assuming the same 8 percent, its effective cost is LIBOR minus 1.4 basis points.

After being applied to FRNs, the technique was applied to bank CDs, and subsequently to medium-term notes in an issue for Clark Equipment Credit, in September 1985. In March 1986, the technique was reversed, with a floating rate note issue for Banque Batif, the banking subsidiary of Thomson, the French electronics company. Here, the FRN was issued together with "floor" certificates that entitled the holder to the difference between 8 percent and 6-month LIBOR, if LIBOR dropped below the strike rate. (The issue was subsequently reopened with a further issue of FRNs, this time carrying floor warrants at 6¾ percent.)Thereafter, a flood of issues emerged, some of which are discussed further in Chapter 12.

The issue of capped liabilities—or collared liabilities—tends to proceed in cycles. When interest rates are low, investors become desperate for incremental yield and will buy capped or collared floating-rate notes enthusiastically. As interest rates rise, however, capped floating-rate notes become less attractive. At the same time, however, these instruments become less liquid for the same reason. As investors try to sell out, the price collapses. At some time, the instruments then become sufficiently cheap that professional traders can buy them, strip out the cap, and asset-swap them as an attractive proposition. This cycle has already been gone through twice (1985–1988 and 1993–1995) and seems likely to return as each generation of investors is replaced by a new generation unwilling to learn from history.

Cap Analysis

As mentioned, caps are widely used by borrowers wishing to control their interest rate risk. In some cases, a useful way for a borrower to analyze the value of a cap—apart from pricing it using the Black–Scholes model, or some similar option pricing model—is to consider its total cost over the life of the cap deal, given a particular interest rate outlook. Table 7.3 shows an analysis of a quarterly cap on 3-month LIBOR.

We have a $100 million borrowing at LIBOR repaid after 3 years, plus a cap with a strike rate of 8.50 percent, costing 1.12 percent, for 3 years, on an amount of $100 million. The alternative is fixed-rate funding for 3 years at 8 percent. Our first step is to amortize the cost of the cap over the deal's life. At 8 percent, this amortized cap cost comes to 0.11 percent per quarter.

Suppose that, for the first quarter, 3-month LIBOR is fixed at 6 percent. Then our borrowing cost is $1.52 million, and there is no payment under the cap. Hence our total cost for the period is $1.63 million. Now suppose that LIBOR jumps to 10 percent and remains there for the life of the deal. Our borrowing cost jumps to $2.53 million per quarter, and we receive a payoff from the writer of the cap of $0.38 million, making our net cost $2.15 million plus the amortized cost of the cap ($2.26 million).

Table 7.3 Cap Payoff Value

Cap strike rate	8.50%	Payments p.a.	4
Cap fee	1.12%	Amortized cap cost	0.11
Fixed funding	8.00%	IRR (semiannual	
Term in years	3	bond equivalent)	8.90%

Quarter	LIBOR Rate	Liability Cash Flow (in millions)	Cap Payoff (in millions)	Capped Cash Flow (in millions)	Cap Cost Amortized at 8%	Net Cash Flow (in millions)
0		−$100				−$100
1	6.00%	1.52	$0.00	$1.52	0.11%	1.63
2	10.00	2.53	0.38	2.15	0.11	2.26
3	10.00	2.53	0.38	2.15	0.11	2.26
4	10.00	2.53	0.38	2.15	0.11	2.26
5	10.00	2.53	0.38	2.15	0.11	2.26
6	10.00	2.53	0.38	2.15	0.11	2.26
7	10.00	2.53	0.38	2.15	0.11	2.26
8	10.00	2.53	0.38	2.15	0.11	2.26
9	10.00	2.53	0.38	2.15	0.11	2.26
10	10.00	2.53	0.38	2.15	0.11	2.26
11	10.00	2.53	0.38	2.15	0.11	2.26
12	10.00	102.53	0.38	102.15	0.11	102.26

We can price the true cost of funds under this outlook as the internal rate of return (IRR) of the column headed "Net Cash Flow." This comes to 8.9 percent on a semiannual bond basis. In this case, therefore, we would have been better off to have fixed in the first place at 8 percent rather than to pay the cap premium. Rates did not remain low for long enough to allow us to pay off the cost of the cap.

Table 7.4 shows that, in this situation, LIBOR would have to remain at 6 percent for 5 quarters (15 months) for the cap to be a better alternative. Table 7.5 highlights a point that may not be immediately obvious. As far as the borrower is concerned, it does not matter how high rates go, once they go through the cap strike level. If, instead of going to 10 percent, they go to only 8.75 percent, the smaller payoff is balanced by a smaller borrowing cost, so that the IRR of the entire deal is still 7.99 percent. All that matters is that LIBOR should go through the strike level; after that, it does not matter how high rates go. This is due to the cap's being an option, and thus a one-way bet. The converse, of course, is true for the writer of the cap.

Another way of looking at the break-even is to ask: Given that the LIBOR for the first period is fixed at 6 percent, what rate can be reached in period 2 and remain thereafter, so that we break even? As Table 7.6 shows, the answer is 7.53 percent. If rates go above 7.53 percent and remain there, then we would have been better off taking fixed rate funding. Incidentally, a quick and dirty

Table 7.4   Cap: Time to Breakeven

Cap strike rate	8.50%	Payments per annum	4
Cap fee	1.12%	Amortized cap cost	0.11%
Fixed funding	8.00%	Internal rate of return	
Term in years	3	(IRR) (semiannual bond equivalent)	7.99%

Quarter	LIBOR Rate	Liability Cash Flow (in millions)	Cap Payoff (in millions)	Capped Cash Flow (in millions)	Cap Cost Amortized at 8%	Net Cash Flow (in millions)
0		−$100				−$100
1	6.00%	1.52	$0.00	$1.52	0.11%	1.63
2	6.00	1.52	0.00	1.52	0.11	1.63
3	6.00	1.52	0.00	1.52	0.11	1.63
4	6.00	1.52	0.00	1.52	0.11	1.63
5	6.00	1.52	0.00	1.52	0.11	1.63
6	10.00	2.53	0.38	2.15	0.11	2.26
7	10.00	2.53	0.38	2.15	0.11	2.26
8	10.00	2.53	0.38	2.15	0.11	2.26
9	10.00	2.53	0.38	2.15	0.11	2.26
10	10.00	2.53	0.38	2.15	0.11	2.26
11	10.00	2.53	0.38	2.15	0.11	2.26
12	10.00	102.53	0.38	102.15	0.11	102.26

Table 7.5   Cap Payoffs: Effect of Small Rise in LIBOR

Cap strike rate	8.50%	Payments per annum	4
Cap fee	1.12%	Amortized cap cost	0.11%
Fixed funding	8.00%	Internal rate of return	
Term in years	3	(IRR) (semiannual bond equivalent)	7.99%

Quarter	LIBOR Rate	Liability Cash Flow (in millions)	Cap Payoff (in millions)	Capped Cash Flow (in millions)	Cap Cost Amortized at 8%	Net Cash Flow (in millions)
0		−$100				−$100
1	6.00%	1.52	0.00	$ 1.52	0.11%	1.63
2	6.00	1.52	0.00	1.52	0.11	1.63
3	6.00	1.52	0.00	1.52	0.11	1.63
4	6.00	1.52	0.00	1.52	0.11	1.63
5	6.00	1.52	0.00	1.52	0.11	1.63
6	8.75	2.22	0.06	2.15	0.11	2.26
7	8.75	2.22	0.06	2.15	0.11	2.26
8	8.75	2.22	0.06	2.15	0.11	2.26
9	8.75	2.22	0.06	2.15	0.11	2.26
10	8.75	2.22	0.06	2.15	0.11	2.26
11	8.75	2.22	0.06	2.15	0.11	2.26
12	8.75	102.22	0.06	102.15	0.11	102.26

Table 7.6   Cap: Break-Even LIBOR

Cap strike rate	8.50%		Payments per annum		4	
Cap fee	1.12%		Amortized cap cost		0.11%	
Fixed funding	8.00%		Internal rate of return			
Term in years	3		(IRR) (semiannual			
			bond equivalent)		7.99%	

Quarter	LIBOR Rate	Liability Cash Flow (in millions)	Cap Payoff (in millions)	Capped Cash Flow (in millions)	Cap Cost Amortized at 8%	Net Cash Flow (in millions)
0		−$100				−$100
1	6.00%	1.52	$0.00	$ 1.52	0.11%	1.63
2	7.53	1.91	0.00	1.91	0.11	2.01
3	7.53	1.91	0.00	1.91	0.11	2.01
4	7.53	1.91	0.00	1.91	0.11	2.01
5	7.53	1.91	0.00	1.91	0.11	2.01
6	7.53	1.91	0.00	1.91	0.11	2.01
7	7.53	1.91	0.00	1.91	0.11	2.01
8	7.53	1.91	0.00	1.91	0.11	2.01
9	7.53	1.91	0.00	1.91	0.11	2.01
10	7.53	1.91	0.00	1.91	0.11	2.01
11	7.53	1.91	0.00	1.91	0.11	2.01
12	7.53	101.91	0.00	101.91	0.11	102.01

approximation to this break-even rate can be found by taking the annual cap cost (0.44 percent) and deducting it from the fixed funding rate of 8 percent. The resulting figure is 7.56 percent—not far from the true rate.

As we saw in Chapter 6, puts and calls are related to each other through the price of the underlying security. In the case of caps and floors, the common denominator is the interest rate swap. Let us assume a flat yield curve. Three-month LIBOR and a 5-year interest rate swap are both at 8 percent. In this case, a 5-year cap is equivalent to a 5-year floor plus a commitment to pay the 5-year swap rate of 8 percent. This holds true when both the cap and the floor are struck at the swap rate. If the fixed rate is paid on the same basis, this is the floating rate. It can be shown that these positions will produce the same cash flows under any interest rate movement.

For a rate above the cap level—say, 10 percent—the holder of the cap will be paid the difference between LIBOR and 8 percent (i.e., 2 percent). The floor and swap combination produces the same cash flow. Because rates are above 8 percent, the floor by itself produces no income, but the swap entitles the holder to the difference between the 8 percent fixed outflow and the 10 percent LIBOR (2 percent again). For rates below the cap level—say, 6 percent—the cap holder receives no payment. The holder of the floor plus the swap also has no net cash flow. The floor generates a positive cash flow equal to the difference between 8 percent and LIBOR (2 percent), which is just enough to cover the shortfall on the interest rate swap between the fixed payment outflow of 8 percent and the floating payment received, 6 percent. At exactly 8 percent, none of the instruments produces cash flows.

SWAPTIONS

The swaption is an option on an interest rate swap. The most common type of swaption is a European option on a bullet swap (that is, a swap with a fixed notional amount and a fixed term to maturity). If you buy an option on which the underlying asset is a swap on which you will receive fixed, then you are said to buy the right to receive, or to buy a receiver's swaption; conversely, if you want to pay fixed, you are said to buy the right to pay or to buy a payer's swaption.

An example of an option to pay fixed would be the right to enter into a 2-year swap where you receive 6-month LIBOR and pay 9 percent annually on £10,000,000, where both the swap value date and the exercise date are in 12 months' time. What is the underlying asset of this option, and what is the strike price? We can argue that the person entering into the swap will be paying a series of fixed cash payments—the fixed rate—in order to obtain an underlying notional asset whose income stream will be 6-month LIBOR. Hence, the strike price is the fixed payments due on the swap, and the underlying asset is the floating receipts on the swap. Because this is an option on an instrument for forward delivery, it is necessary to use the Black model, rather than the Black–Scholes model.

In order to use the Black formula—or, indeed, any similar option model—to value the asset, we have to assume that its value will be normally distributed; this assumption is, of course, not always true in practice. Interest rates tend to display "mean reversion," so that the calculated option price will usually be an approximation. The market usually handles this by adjusting the volatility used to price the option.

Let us work out the price at which a market maker would write this swaption. The option period is 1 year and the option is on a 2-year swap with a notional principal amount of £10,000,000, with the market maker receiving fixed annually at 9 percent and paying LIBOR semiannually. Volatility for a 2-year swap starting in 1 year's time is estimated to be 11 percent. The sterling yield curve is as follows (using the 1-year LIBOR rate and the swap rates for 2 and 3 years):

January 12, 1996	7.75%
January 12, 1997	8.25
January 12, 1998	8.5

The first step is to construct the implied zero coupon-curve and the annual "par yield curve." Bearing in mind that LIBOR rates are calculated on the basis of annual interest at maturity, while the swap rates are semiannual rates, we get:

True Annual Rates	Implied Zero-Coupon Curve (Annual) Rates
7.75 %	7.75 %
8.42016	8.4486
8.6806	8.7253

The next step is to calculate the swap rate on which the swaption will apply. This is a 2-year swap, but it will not start until the exercise date of the swaption, 1 year from now. Hence, we need the market rate for a 2-year swap deferred for 1 year.

The underlying calculation principle is that the market maker, in order to hedge this transaction, would have to enter into a 3-year swap starting from today, with a 1-year swap in the opposite direction to lay off the risk for the first year, until the deferred swap comes into operation. For simplicity, we will assume the 1-year swap is quoted on the basis of the true 1-year rate above versus 6-month LIBOR. For simplicity, we will discount cash flows using the 3-year rate rather than the appropriate zero coupon rate.

To calculate the deferred swap, we proceed as follows. We assume that the 3-year swap, the 1-year swap in the opposite direction, and the 2-year deferred swap are all set up for the same dates and thus use the same LIBOR for the floating side. Thus, all of the floating-rate flows will net off against each other, and we will be concerned only with the fixed-rate flows. If we neglect bid-offer spreads for simplicity, we see that the present value (PV) of the deferred swap's cash flows must equal the PV of the 3-year swap's flows minus the PV of the 1-year swap's cash flows. That is, the cash flows on both sides of the deal must be equal, in present value terms.

One approach is to calculate the present value of a basis point (PVBP) for the 3-year swap. This is the PV of 0.01 percent paid semiannually for 3 years, valued at the 3-year zero-coupon rate. Similarly, we find the present value of a basis point for the 1-year swap (PV of .01 percent paid semiannually for 1 year, valued at the 1-year zero-coupon rate). Therefore, we can derive the PVBP of the deferred swap by subtraction (since present value is additive).

Because the present value of the cash flows of the deferred swap must equal the present value of the longer swap less the present value of the shorter swap, the next step is to calculate the deferred swap rate from the formula:

$$\begin{array}{l} \text{Deferred swap rate} \\ \times \text{PVBP deferred swap} \end{array} = \begin{array}{l} \text{Long swap rate} \times \text{PVBP long swap} \\ - \text{short swap rate} \times \text{PVBP short swap} \end{array}$$

Rearranging and inserting the appropriate rates we find:

$$\text{Deferred swap rate} = 9.2812 = \frac{8.7253 \times 2.5564 - 7.75 \times 0.9281}{1.6283}.$$

We now have the value of the underlying asset to which we should apply the Black model. This contract gives us the right to pay 9 percent for 2 years in exchange for 6-month LIBOR, starting 1 year from now, when the current implied forward swap rate for that period is 9.2812 percent. Applying the Black model gives us a valuation of £90,710.11 for this option—approximately 0.91 percent of the principal amount.

Shifts in the yield curve will affect the swaption's value. In practice, the yield curve will usually shift in a nonparallel fashion. The effect on the swaption's value will depend on the exact shape of this shift and may not be intuitively obvious. In particular, if short-term rates rise faster than longer term rates—as would be quite normal—the forward swap rate, and hence the swaption value, will *fall* rather than rise. This effect parallels that mentioned earlier for the cap. Conversely, a fall in short rates relative to long rates will increase the forward swap rate and hence the value of the swaption.

Finally, we should note the comparison with an interest rate cap. The interest rate cap confers the right to receive LIBOR minus the strike, or to pay nothing. The swaption, if exercised, may lead us at some point to pay out sums under the swap. Thus, the swaption must always be worth less than an interest rate cap for a corresponding period.

Swaptions became popular in the mid-1980s, when bonds with embedded put and call options began to be issued in significant numbers. (See Chapter 9 and Chapter 12.) Swaptions are commonly used to strip the options out of callable and puttable bonds.

CAPS VERSUS SWAPTIONS

Finally, it may be instructive to look at an example[2] comparing (a) a standard cap to a swaption to (b) a constant maturity treasury (CMT) cap. (CMT structures are discussed in Chapter 12, on structured notes.) Suppose a firm wishes to hedge exposures to interest rates for four 6-month periods: 12–18 months, 18–24 months, 24–30 months, and 30–36 months. The firm could hedge in various ways, including the purchase of a 2-year cap starting 12 months from now, a 2-year CMT cap starting 12 months from now, or a 12-month option on a 2-year swap (a swaption).

To compare the premiums for the swaption with those for the standard cap and the CMT cap, one would need to specify exercise prices for the different structures so that the structures would be "equivalent." One might seek to structure the relationship between the exercise price and the current

---

[2] C. Smithson, "ABC of CMT," *Risk Magazine* (September 1995).

or forward rate to achieve an approximately equivalent approach. Suppose we are given the following market rates:

	Current	One Year Forward
Six-month LIBOR	5.88 percent	6.09 percent
Two-year swap rate	6.09	6.41
Two-year CMT rate	5.95	6.28

Then premiums could be calculated for various exercise prices as follows:

	6%	6.5%	7%	7.5%
1-year swaption on 2-year swap	132	87	55	33
2-year cap starting 1 year hence:				
on 6-month LIBOR	174	133	101	76
on 2-year CMT	174	131	97	71

The swaption is cheaper (because it is worth less, as already pointed out); the differences between the two caps arise primarily from the different forward shapes of the LIBOR and CMT volatility surfaces, with LIBOR likely to be somewhat more volatile.

LOW EXERCISE PRICE OPTIONS (LEPOs)

The reader may have wondered about the implications of setting the strike price on an option very low. The result of doing this is that the option itself will be deep in the money. It will have very little time value. In fact, it will behave rather like the underlying instrument.

On a number of occasions, low exercise price options (LEPOs) have been created, with a strike of very close to zero. A notable example occurred during the early days of the Swiss Options and Financial Futures Exchange (SOFFEX). As is not uncommon when an options exchange is first brought into existence, there was some animosity between the stock market operators and the options traders. It was not always easy for the options traders to get a stock that they needed. In desperation, SOFFEX resorted to creating LEPOs. In effect, synthetic equity was created. This allowed options traders to buy the equity they needed to close out their positions. Similarly, LEPOs were used by the Australian Stock Exchange to combat the Sydney Futures Exchange when the latter created futures on individual shares.

Another application has been to allow the creation of synthetic equity when restrictions made the underlying equity difficult to obtain: for example, when foreigners are restricted from buying shares, one possible alternative would be to create LEPOs (or the equivalent warrants—see Chapter 15).

Exotics

We come now to a large class of options that are generically referred to as "exotic" options. An exotic option can be broadly defined as an option that redefines one or more of the conditions of the "standard" options discussed above. For ease of reference, exotic options in this chapter will be grouped into two main classes, with subgroups:

1. *Path-independent options.* It does not matter how the underlying option has moved during the course of its life. We can subdivide these options into:

    a. Those that vary the standard terms of an option in terms of payoff, time of premium payment, and so on.

    b. Compound options—options on options.

    c. Multifactor options—options whose value depends not on just one asset but on two or more.

2. *Path-dependent options.* The value of these options is influenced not just by the condition of the market on the expiry date, but on how it behaved during the life of the option. In some cases (such as binary barriers), this class includes variants of the path-independent class).

This is a rapidly developing field, so the following treatment is not guaranteed to be comprehensive. Many adaptations of instruments to specific markets may make them appear different, and of course it is in the interests of investment bankers to proclaim the novelty of any instrument they are marketing. A Bermudan rainbow option on Brent crude, DAX-30, and Eurodollar futures, cash-settled in Vietnamese dong, would undoubtedly be a novel instrument that is not discussed here. But I believe the following sections cover the currently important underlying exotic options. The reader will see, however, that it is possible to create an almost infinite variety of specific instruments using these tools, as the Vietnamese example illustrates. To keep the discussion in this chapter within reasonable bounds, I have confined myself here to a brief description of the major instruments.

Path-Independent Options

We begin with options that consist of a variation of the standard terms of the option instrument in regard to exercise date, premium payment, and payoff style, but the path traversed by the underlying asset during the life of the option makes no difference to the payoff.

Bermudan. A Bermudan option, as the name implies, lies between a European and an American option. Unlike an American option, it does not permit a continuous right to exercise the option. But it does permit the option to be exercised on specific dates before expiry, unlike a European option. A typical application of the Bermudan option would be in the fixed-income markets. A 10-year bond may be callable in the September of the last 5 years of its life. An investor owning the bond might be interested in an option that allows replacing the bond if it is in fact called during these periods; but the investor might be unwilling to pay the full cost of an American option because this gives unnecessary "extra" cover. The pricing of the option will normally be found by using a binomial approach. We evaluate the option at those nodes in the binomial tree where the possibility of exercise could occur. Having found all those nodes at which exercise is possible, we discount back to today's probability-weighted value for the option.

Forward Start (Delayed) Option.[3]   Among the simplest of these options is the forward start option, an option that is paid for now but will start some time in the future. Consider an option that starts at time t_1 and matures at time t_2. Suppose it is on a non-dividend-paying equity whose current price is S and whose price at time t_1 is S_1. We can see from the Black–Scholes formula that the value of an at-the-money call option is proportional to the stock price. The value of the option at time t_1 is therefore cS_1/S, where c is the value today of an at-the-money option with a life of $t_2 - t_1$. Using risk-neutral valuation, the value of the forward start option today (time t) is

$$e^{-r(t_1-t)} \, \hat{E}\left[\frac{cS_1}{S}\right]$$

where $\hat{E}$ means the expected value. We already know c and S, and in a risk-neutral world $\hat{E}[S_1] = Se^{rt_1}$, so it follows that the value of the forward start option is c. It is the value of a normal at-the-money option whose life is $t_2 - t_1$. If the underlying asset pays interest or dividends at a rate d, then the value of the forward start option becomes ce^{-dt_1}.

Practical applications of the delayed option might include situations where a compound option might be used, and they have been built into employee compensation option structures (where the option is made available to employees only if they are still at the firm). They have also been used by fund managers creating guaranteed return funds or using so-called "90/10" structures. In the latter case, the fund manager invests 90 percent of the fund in cash or a low-risk instrument and 10 percent in options or warrants. At the expiry of the operation, if clients are satisfied, they may wish to roll over into a new 90/10 fund. (The option pricing levels at that later time are of course unknown today.) If today's volatility levels are low and the fund manager believes that the bulk of the 90/10 fund will be rolled over, it might make sense to buy forward options to cover the rollover. Delayed options are also used in so-called cliquet structures (see below).

---

[3] See J. C. Hull, *Options, Futures and Other Derivatives* (Englewood Cliffs, NJ: Prentice-Hall, 1997), Ch. 18.

Digital/Binary.   Binary (or digital) options are among the simplest kinds of exotic options, at least as far as pricing is concerned. Hedging is a different matter. These options are a straight bet that an underlying market will finish above or below the strike price at expiration. The payoff of this event is a fixed amount, regardless of the level of the underlying asset. Binary or digital options come in two basic varieties: (1) all-or-nothing, and (2) one-touch. (I shall use the terms digital or binary interchangeably throughout.)

The all-or-nothing option pays out only if the underlying asset finishes in the money at the expiry of the option. The one-touch call option pays out as long as, at some time during the life of the option, the underlying price rose above the strike price.

Such options permit the construction of a number of interesting investor instruments (see, for example, "range notes," discussed in Chapter 12). Aside from their use in the construction of range notes, binaries are often used by foreign exchange traders either in situations where they see a rate jump, or, conversely, in quiet markets. As an example of the former, in early 1997, a number of Indonesian firms were reported buying European-style out-of-the-money double binary options on the rupiah; a typical trade might have involved an option that paid off 2.5 percent on the notional amount of the trade if the rupiah depreciated to between IDR2490.8 and 2538.7 against the dollar (a depreciation of 4 to 6 percent compared with the then spot of IDR2395) within the following 12 months. If the rate did not jump sharply, then the option did not pay off. Conversely, many trades have been done on the basis that, provided the exchange rate remains within a given range, the option pays off. (Parallel examples can be seen in the warrant market—for instance, the "EARN" warrants issued by Bankers Trust; see Chapter 15.)

Thus, these options have many uses. For the writer of the option, however, they pose a tough hedging challenge, because of the all-or-nothing payout. As they come close to expiry, and the option swings above and below the trigger level, the payout switches from zero to positive, triggering huge swings in delta. A delta of 1,000 percent would not be uncommon. (For a normal call option, delta ranges between 0 and 100 percent, or 0 to 1.) A large digital option transaction presents a very large risk to the writer. Hedging these instruments is the option trader's equivalent of Russian roulette. One possible approach is to take the "actuarial" view: build up a book consisting of many trades with as wide a spread of strikes as possible. Around each strike, there will be huge swings in the delta; but across the book as a whole, the risk is averaged down to manageable levels.

We now consider the simplest form of digital options that are path-independent, that is, they pay out at expiry according to whether the asset is above or below the strike, and they pay out a fixed amount.

All-or-Nothing.   Of these types of binary option, the easier to price by far is the all-or-nothing digital. What we are interested in pricing with the all-or-nothing digital is the expected value of the asset (for the asset-or-nothing call) or the cash value of the strike price (for the cash-or-nothing call). We already know these from the Black–Scholes model:

$$\text{Asset-or-nothing call} = S.N(d1).e^{-dT}, \text{ and}$$

$$\text{Cash-or-nothing call} = E.N(d1).e^{-rT},$$

where S, N(d1), and T are as defined in the Black–Scholes model in Chapter 6; d is the dividend earned on the asset in continuous time; and r is the rate of interest.

The Binary Family Tree.[4] It is possible to construct a "family tree" of binary options, according to (1) whether they are path-independent or path-dependent, or (2) whether they pay out at expiry or when a barrier is hit, provided they are above or below a given strike level (the latter two categories sometimes are referred to as binary barriers). Barrier options are discussed separately below, in the path-dependent section. We give here, for background, the family tree for path-independent binary options.

We can see from the family tree in Figure 7.2 that path-independent digitals are the building blocks for two specific types of exotic option. The first, the so-called "supershare," was proposed by N. Hakansson[5] in 1976. A firm would buy a portfolio of shares and issue against it supershares that would pay off at expiry as follows. Provided the portfolio value lies between a lower bound, V_d, and an upper bound, V_u, the investor receives a given share of the portfolio; otherwise, the investor receives nothing. In other words, the investor buys an asset-or-nothing call struck at V_d and sells an asset-or-nothing call struck at V_u.

The second exotics built from these binaries are the so-called "gap" options. The payoff is of the form: 0 if $S < = E$ (i.e., if the asset finishes below the strike, we receive nothing), or $S - X$ if $S > = E$ (i.e., if it finishes above the strike, we do not get the normal call payout of $S - E$; instead, we get $S - X$, where X is the "height" of the gap, $X - E$). If we set $X = E$, the gap options revert to standard calls and puts. Other types of binary/barrier binary options are discussed below.

More recently, there has been a further extension of this concept[6] to the bivariate cash-or-nothing. This option pays out a fixed amount when the prices of two assets are between predetermined limits at expiry. The concept could be extended to multivariate (rainbow) cash-or-nothing options and barrier binary options.

The digital option has been extended to the interest rate market in a number of ways. Perhaps the best known is the range note, also known as an accrual

---

[4] The discussion in this section follows M. Rubinstein and E. Reiner, "Unscrambling the Binary Code," *Risk* (October 1991).

[5] N. Hakansson, "The Purchasing Power Fund: A New Kind of Financial Intermediary," *Financial Analysts Journal* (November–December 1976).

[6] R. Heynen and H. Kat, "Brick by Brick," *Risk* (June 1996).

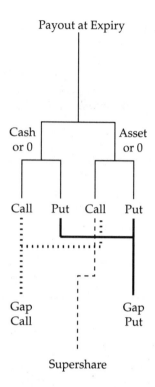

Figure 7.2 Path-independent binary options (payout at expiry).

note, corridor note, or fairway bond. The latter term comes from a golf-course analogy: these bonds usually pay off provided interest rates remain within a given range (i.e., they remain on the golf fairway). As soon as interest rates go outside the range, the coupon stops being paid.

A variant is an accrual note with a "trigger" from another market. Suppose a customer places ITL100 million on deposit for 1 year at 10 percent but wants to enhance the yield by betting that DEM/ITL will not be above 1050 every month. Spot is currently 1007.95. The customer can sell twelve digital options to a bank, with a payout of ITL1 million each, at a strike of 1050.

Suppose the bank pays the customer ITL3,703,788 total premium for the digitals, and the payment is added to the original principal and placed on deposit. At the end of the year, assuming the currency has behaved well, the customer receives principal plus interest totaling ITL114,074,166; the total return has been 14.07 percent. But if wrong, the customer pays out ITL1,000,000 for each month the currency is out of the range. If, after entering the trade, the currency immediately rises through 1050, the net return is reduced by ITL12,000,000 and by the interest on that, for a return that is closer to 2 percent. Some examples of these are discussed in Chapter 12.

Pay Later (Contingent Premium). For pay later options, no premium must be paid unless the option is exercised. But the option must be exercised if the underlying asset is equal to or greater than the strike price of the option. This is true even if the intrinsic value received will be less than the premium payable.

The key advantage of the pay later option to the option buyer is that no premium is ever payable if the option expires out of the money. The pricing of the option is actually quite simple. Suppose we are looking at a pay later call. The buyer gets a standard call option but has also sold to the option writer a digital all-or-nothing option, where the digital premium is set equal to the premium of the standard call, so the net cost is zero. We adjust the size of the digital call to achieve this. As a result, the formula is:

$$\text{Pay later call} = [S.N(d1).e^{-dT} - E.N(d1).e^{-rT}] - (R[S.N(d1).e^{-dT}])$$

where R = the quantity of the asset-or-nothing option that is sold, such that the premiums of the ordinary call and the asset-or-nothing option are identical.

Installment options are another variation of pay-later options. The premium for an installment option is split into a series of payments, payable according to a schedule established at the outset. As each installment becomes due for payment, the buyer of the option has the choice to make the payment, and so retain ownership of the option, or to simply not pay and allow the option to be canceled along with the obligation to pay any remaining installments. The sum of the installments, if held to maturity, is greater than the price of a standard option because: (1) the value of the buyer's right to cancel must be included, and (2) the seller must be compensated for interest forgone because of the delays in payment.

The most common application of installment options is the installment put as a cost-reducing hedging tool. For a fund manager hedging a longer-term exposure, buying standard puts to hedge can become expensive if the market requires the purchase of further puts at the new level. The installment put allows the fund manager to hedge the position for a smaller up-front cost.

Compound.   A compound option is an option on an option. Its most common use is in the foreign exchange markets, in the so-called "tender-to-contract" situation, a scheme designed to help corporations bidding for contracts overseas. They know that if they win a contract, they will have foreign currency exposure that they will need to hedge; on the other hand, if the contract is not won, they will have no exposure.

Schemes have been devised to meet this kind of situation. One choice is to write a compound option—an option contract giving the right to buy an option at some future date on certain terms. Another choice is to charge the full premium for the underlying option on day one, subject to a partial refund of the premium if the tender fails to win the contract. In exchange for the right to obtain the partial refund, the option buyer gives up the right to exercise the option independently of any success in the underlying tender; that is, if the tender fails, then the option cannot be exercised.

The value of a compound call-on-call option was first formally defined by R. Geske[7] and later extended by M. Rubinstein.[8] If we consider a currency compound option, we can write the value of a call on a call as:

$$CaCa = S.e^{-R_f T}N_2(x;y;p) - E_2 e^{-R_d T}N_2(x - \sigma\sqrt{t};y - \sigma\sqrt{t};p) - E_1 e^{-R_d T}N(-x + \sigma\sqrt{t})$$

where CaCa denotes the premium for the call on the call;

E_1 = exercise price for "mother" option;
E_2 = exercise price for "daughter" option;
S = spot exchange rate;
R_f = foreign interest rate;
R_d = domestic interest rate;
σ = volatility of underlying currency;
t = expiry date of compound option (the "mother" option);
T = expiry date of underlying ordinary option (the "daughter" option);
N_2 = bivariate normal density;
$N()$ = cumulative normal (univariate) density;

$$p = \sqrt{\frac{t}{T}};\ x = \frac{\ln\left(\frac{S}{S*}\right) + \left(R_d - R_f + \frac{\sigma^2}{2}\right)t}{\sigma\sqrt{t}};\ y = \frac{\ln\left(\frac{S}{E_2}\right) + \left(R_d - R_f + \frac{\sigma^2}{2}\right)T}{\sigma\sqrt{t}}.$$

To put this rather formidable piece of algebra in context, one can compare the simpler binomial pricing approach for a call on a call.

In Chapter 6, we devised the pricing tree for a standard European call using a five-step underlying asset tree where s = 0.3, t = 0.25, r = 1.10, d = 1.03, S = 100, X = 100, UP = 1.06938, DOWN = 0.935118, DOMINT=1.00478, and FORINT=1.00148. Given these variables, the asset tree produces payoffs of 39.85, 22.29, and so on, and given these payoffs, we can find the following call values:

Standard call values					Asset Payoff
					39.85
				31.0599	
			22.8802		22.29
		16.03445		14.66457	
	10.78814		9.128422		6.94
7.023606		5.48107		3.506265	
	3.20851		1.771883		0
		0.895417		0	
			0		0
				0	
					0
t=0	t=1	t=2	t=3	t=4	t=5

[7] R.Geske, "The Valuation of Compound Options," *Journal of Financial Economics*, 7 (1979).
[8] M. Rubinstein, "Double Trouble," *Risk Magazine* (September 1995).

Now let us consider a call on this call. Say the strike level of the call on the call is 8.00, and its maturity, t(c), is 0.15. We know that the underlying call is valued over five steps and has a total maturity of 0.25, so that each step is 0.05 apart. The call on the call has a maturity of 0.15, which is equivalent to three steps. The payoffs on this call will then be the values of the underlying call after three steps. These values are 22.88, 9.13, 1.77, or zero. Because the strike of our call on the call is 8.00, its payoffs will be 14.88, 1.13, or zero.

To value the call on a call at the previous step, we proceed as we would for a normal call. The value is the present value of the expected payoffs of the call. The only difference here is that, instead of payoffs on the underlying asset, we are looking at payoffs on a call on the asset.

Because the volatility and other parameters are unchanged, we know that the probability of an UP move is 0.50776, and the probability of a DOWN move is 0.49224.

Now we can value the call on the call, using the same procedures as we would for a normal call: C = [0.50776 × 14.88 + 0.49224 × 1.13]/1.00478 = 8.07.

What is the value today of this call on a call? We can work back through the nodes to arrive at the following tree:

```
                              14.88
                     8.072487
            4.358776                1.13
   2.343873              0.570245
            0.288172                0
                     0
                                    0
```

Notice that we are paying 2.34 to buy a call on another call with a strike of 8; that is, our total cost if we exercise the right to buy the second call will be 10.34, which compares with the standard call of 7.02, quoted above.

The purchase of an option on a cap (sometimes called a caption) or an option on a floor (floption or floortion) is an example of the compound option concept applied to the interest rate arena.

Chooser ("As-You-Like-It") Options.   You buy a chooser when you buy an option that allows you to choose later whether it is a put or a call—truly, as Mark Rubinstein has observed, these are "options for the undecided!" The most typical application would be where a trader anticipates an extreme market move but is uncertain of the direction. The reliance on extreme volatility is illustrated by the fact that these options first came into prominence at the time of the Gulf War, during extreme volatility in oil markets. In fact, a chooser is very similar to a straddle. The difference is that, at some point, the buyer must choose between the put and the call. Therefore, the chooser will be worth less than the straddle. Putting that another way, compared to a straddle, a chooser is a cheaper way to buy volatility.

The key features of chooser options are:

1. The buyer of the chooser decides, on the first maturity date (the choice date), whether the option is to be a put or a call.
2. The selected option expires on the second maturity date.
3. In a typical structure, the choice feature can be canceled at any time until the choice date.
4. Standard chooser options have the same strike and expiry dates for the two options.
5. Complex choosers allow the call and the put to have different expiry dates and strike prices.

The payoff of the chooser option at the choice date is the greater of the call option or the put option values on that day. The payee receives the best of the call or the put. Another way of looking at this is to argue that buying the chooser offers the best of:

1. A call on the asset at strike price S and exercise price E for the whole period of the option (i.e., to final maturity), or
2. A put on the asset when the asset price is $Se^{-d(T-t)}$ and the put strike is $Ee^{-r(T-t)}$, where d is the dividend earned on the asset, t is the time to the choice date, and T is the time to final maturity, and r=the risk-free rate.

In that case, the chooser call value is:

$$\text{Chooser} = S.N(x)e^{-dT} - E.N(x - \sigma\sqrt{T})e^{-rT} - S.N(-y)e^{-dT} + E.N(-y + \sigma\sqrt{T})e^{-rT}$$

where T is the time to final maturity; t is the time to choice;

$$x = \frac{\ln\left(\frac{Se^{-dT}}{Ee^{-rT}}\right)}{\sigma\sqrt{T}} + \frac{\sigma\sqrt{T}}{2};$$

and y is almost the same, but substituting $\sigma\sqrt{t}$ for $\sigma\sqrt{T}$:

$$y = \frac{\ln\left(\frac{Se^{-dT}}{Ee^{-rT}}\right)}{\sigma\sqrt{t}} + \frac{\sigma\sqrt{t}}{2}.$$

A moment's thought will suggest that the value of the chooser must increase with the length of time in which to choose. Consider five Black–Scholes standard chooser options[9] on foreign currency, all with current underlying asset price S = 100, strike price E = 100, time to expiry T = 1 year, domestic interest rate = 10 percent, foreign currency interest rate = 5 percent, and underlying volatility = 30 percent. We can then find the following chooser values:

t	Value
0	13.39
0.1	15.17
0.2	16.5
0.5	19.28
1	22.46

Where t = 0 (we have no time to choose), the chooser's value is the same as the call option. Where t = T = 1 (we have a complete choice throughout the life), the chooser is equivalent to a straddle and its cost will equal the straddle's. In between, as we can see, the value rises with the length of time available to make a choice.

Power.   The power option allows the holder the payoff of a standard option, but with the value of the underlying asset raised to some power, e.g., LIBOR squared. The power option is of most interest to the gambler looking for action; however, the pricing is actually not too strange.

If the underlying asset S is log-normally distributed (i.e., returns from S are normally distributed), then S^n will have a similar distribution. If we consider the Black–Scholes world, we assume that the asset follows the normal geometric Brownian motion which is described by

$$\frac{ds}{S} = \mu dt + \sigma dz$$

So:

$$dS = \mu S dt + \sigma S dz.$$

We can then set out the implied stochastic process for the general case S^n, which gives us:

$$d(S^n) = \left[\frac{n\mu + 1}{2\sigma^2 n(n-1)}\right] S^n dt + [n\sigma] S^n dz.$$

Where the payoff is squared—for example, so n = 2—we have:

$$d(S^2) = [2\mu + \sigma^2] S^2 dt + [2\sigma] S^2 dz.$$

---

[9] This example originated in M. Rubinstein, "Options for the Undecided," *Risk* (April 1991).

Therefore, we have to replace the standard drift term in the Black–Scholes world (μ) by ($2\mu + \sigma^2$) and the volatility (σ) by 2σ. Substituting these values into Black–Scholes will give us the pricing for the power option.

Note that the impact of the power option on the payoff comes not just from the power factor but also from the impact on volatility. In the case of a squared payoff, the impact of volatility is doubled.

Option to Exchange One Asset for Another (Margrabe Option). The formula for the value of an option to exchange one asset for another was originally developed by William Margrabe in 1977. The formula is:

$$C = X_1 N(d_1) - X_2 N(d_2)$$

where C = value of the call option;

$$d1 = \frac{\ln \dfrac{X_1}{X_2} + \dfrac{\sigma^2}{2} t}{\sigma \sqrt{t}};$$

$d_2 = d_1 - \sigma \sqrt{t}$;

$\sigma^2 = \sigma^2_{x1} + \sigma^2_{x2} - 2\rho_{x1, x2}\sigma_{x1}\sigma_{x2}$;

σ_{X1} = volatility of first asset;

σ_{X2} = volatility of second asset;

$\rho_{X1.X2}$ = correlation between first and second assets;

   t = time to expiry as a percentage of a year;

X_1 = price of first asset;

X_2 = price of second asset.

Although this might seem complex, it is in fact simply Black–Scholes with two changes:

1. The fixed exercise price has been replaced by the price of the second asset, X_2.
2. The volatility is the combined volatility of the two assets, which is calculated by allowing for the correlation between them.

This option pricing model is relevant in a number of cases, notably where we consider the "best of two," or rainbow options, to which we now turn.

Rainbow. The so-called rainbow option allows the investor to receive the best performing asset among a set of assets. For example, the investor might buy an option giving the best of the S&P 500, the FTSE 100, and the DAX. Where there is a two-factor option (e.g., the better of the FTSE 100 and the DAX), we have a simple option to exchange one asset (the underperforming asset) for another (the better performing asset). This is, of course, the Margrabe option just discussed.

When more than two assets are involved, the pricing cannot readily be calculated by means of a closed-form solution, and pricing is normally done by means of a Monte Carlo simulation or a similar technique.

Spread. A moment's thought suggests that holding an option on the best of two assets is also equivalent to holding one of the assets and holding an option on the spread between the two assets. Thus, where the Margrabe option can be used, it can be applied to the spread option also.

Alternatively—and particularly in situations where Margrabe/Black–Scholes is not applicable, such as interest rate yield spreads—one could seek to model the spread itself as an asset. This approach would need to contend with the fact that, unlike a normal asset, a spread could quite possibly go negative. Closed form formulas for spread options (apart from the Margrabe applications) are not generally available, and we have to resort to numerical methods.

Quanto. A quanto option is one where the payoff depends both on an underlying price and on the size of the exposure as a function of the underlying price. The term comes from the phrase "quantity-adjusted option." The most typical application is for a fund manager. Suppose a U.S.-based investor purchases 100,000 French shares at a price of FRF8 per share. The initial cost is FRF800,000. The investor then sells forward FRF800,000 against dollars for one year, to protect against currency risk. After a year, a look at the position reveals that the shares have gone up to FRF12. The value of the position is now FRF1,200,000. But the hedge was for only FRF800,000. The investor is under-hedged. The quanto option aims to solve this problem.

There are four basic versions of the quanto (we consider a call quanto):

1. A foreign equity call struck in the foreign currency. This is the simplest case. The payoff is simply the standard call option value converted at the current exchange rate.

2. A foreign equity call struck in the domestic currency. The holder of this option can exchange a domestic strike price for the foreign equity. This is a variant of the Margrabe option to exchange one asset for another.

3. A fixed exchange rate foreign equity call. This version of the quanto is a little trickier. It helps to think of the French stock[10] as behaving like a dollar-denominated stock that pays a dividend yield (which we will assume to be continuous) of $r_d - r_f + q - \rho \sigma_s \sigma_x$ where:

---

[10] See, e.g., J. C. Hull, *op. cit.*, pp. 299–301, for a more formal discussion.

r_d = U.S. domestic interest rate;

r_f = foreign (French) interest rate;

q = dividend yield on French stock;

ρ = correlation between the French stock price and the French franc exchange rate;

σ_S = volatility of the French stock price;

σ_x = volatility of the French franc exchange rate.

We can then plug this into our standard option valuation models and proceed accordingly.

4. An equity-linked foreign exchange call. This type of quanto is, in effect, a fixed exchange rate foreign equity put, with the roles of the equity and the exchange rate reversed; hence, we can apply the technique just used for the fixed exchange rate foreign equity call.

Basket.   The basket option consists of an option on a set of underlying assets. Typical uses might be by a portfolio manager who holds, say, Shell, Citibank, and Toyota. The manager could buy put options on each, or an option on a basket holding the three. Typically, the basket will be cheaper as long as the underlying assets are not perfectly correlated. Their volatilities will tend to offset each other, and the volatility of the basket will be less than that of its parts. Another common use of the basket option is to hedge a group of currencies (e.g., a portfolio manager might hedge an exposure to all European currencies by buying a basket option on those currencies).

Various approaches to valuing basket options have been taken. One approach is to argue that the value of the portfolio, rather than that of the underlying assets, is likely to behave log-normally, and then to apply the standard formulas. Alternatively, we can calculate the weights of the components of the basket, determine their correlations, derive a composite volatility for the portfolio, and then apply Black–Scholes to the portfolio. Another approach is to argue that, with an Asian option, we monitor one asset n times, whereas with the European basket option, we monitor n assets one time (at expiry). If we fudge the correlations, we could apply modifications of Asian option pricing models (discussed below).

The most common approach seems to be to assume arbitrarily that the basket will follow a log-normal distribution whose volatility is defined by the volatilities of its component parts.

Path-Dependent Options

We turn now to options whose value is determined in part by the path that the asset price has taken during the life of the option. In general, these options are much more difficult to value, and some form of numerical method is generally needed, though in some cases closed-form formulas have been developed.

Asian (Average) Options.   The Asian option is an average rate option. There are two kinds of average rate option: (1) fixed strike and (2) floating strike. The former is by far the most common: A cash settlement is made on the expiry date, according to the difference between the strike rate and the average exchange rate over the option's life. Average rate options are valuable hedging tools for many corporate investors whose risk is not on large cash flows on particular dates, but on smaller cash flows on a regular basis. Also, the premium will normally be substantially less than for a European or an American option, because the volatility of the average is much less than the volatility of the asset. Corporate hedgers regard this as another attraction.

If the underlying asset price S is assumed to be log-normally distributed, the geometric average of S is also log-normally distributed, and an analytical formula for the Asian option can then be calculated. Unfortunately, in the real world, most client applications revolve around arithmetic, not geometric, averages. The arithmetic average of the log-normal does not produce tractable results. Various pricing methods are used, most of which attempt to track the bias between the log-normal distribution and that of the arithmetic average. One well-known approach[11] seeks to calculate the mean and variance of the probability distribution of the arithmetic average exactly; we then assume that the distribution of the average is the log-normal distribution with the same mean and variance.

The average strike (floating strike) variant of the Asian option sets the strike price of the option to the average price of the asset during the option's life. The payout is the difference between this strike and the asset price on the expiry date. Another variant is the "flexible Asian" option. For this option, the observations that count for the average do not all get the same weight. This might be of interest, for example, to a firm whose DEM cash flows to be hedged back into dollars are heavily concentrated in, say, months 1, 7, 9, and 11 of any given year.[12]

Another variant can be seen in the interest-rate cap market, where the cap payout is not based on the normal quarterly payout against 3-month LIBOR but is taken over the year as a whole. A payment is made only if LIBOR is above the strike during the year as a whole on a cumulative basis. Suppose that we have a 6 percent cap and the LIBOR fixings are 5 percent, 7 percent, 8 percent, and 5 percent over the year. On a normal cap, we would receive 0 percent, 1 percent, 2 percent, and 0 percent, or a total of 3 percent. On this variant, we would receive 1 percent. It thus provides cheaper cover for a firm that is aiming to meet an annual budgeted interest cost without being unduly concerned whether any given quarter is above or below the set level.

---

[11] A. Kemna and A. Vorst, "A Pricing Method for Options Based on Average Asset Values," *Journal of Banking and Finance* (March 1990).

[12] See P. G. Zhang, "Flexible Arithmetic Asian Options," *Journal of Derivatives* (Spring, 1995).

Barrier.   An important and popular class of path-dependent options is the barrier option. There is no doubt that the barrier option market has grown substantially, but no hard figures are available. One recent estimate is that the market has grown from $123 billion in 1992 to over $2,000 billion in 1996.[13]

As an example, a down-and-out barrier option expires prematurely if the exchange rate falls below a certain level during the life of the option. Thus, a $1.9500 call on sterling with a down-and-out feature at $1.8500 (the "outstrike") will become valueless if the rate at any time falls below $1.8500. Down-and-out call options may be attractive to option sellers; and, because conventional options involve no risk of premature expiry for the buyer, down-and-out options are always cheaper than the corresponding European option. Up-and-out options are the converse; they expire prematurely if rates ever exceed a specified level. Range options expire prematurely if rates ever move outside a specified range. A $1.9500 call with a trading range of $1.85/2.05 will expire valueless if sterling falls below $1.8500 or rises above $2.0500. Conversely, outside trading range options expire valueless unless rates have been both sides of a specified range. A $1.9500 call with an outside trading range of $1.85/2.05 is valueless at maturity unless rates have been both below $1.8500 and above $2.0500 during the life of the option.

It is possible to construct a closed-form valuation model for barrier options, but the mathematics is nontrivial. In practice, a binomial approach is often a reasonable substitute.

As an illustration of the barrier concept, we present the following simplified example. It builds on the same example as was used in Chapter 6. We consider a down-and-out option on a currency using the same underlying variables as before, so we have $\sigma = 0.3$, $t = 0.25$, $Rd = 1.10$, $Rf = 1.03$, $S = 100$, $X = 100$, $UP = 1.06938$, $DOWN = 0.935118$, $DOMINT = 1.00478$, and $FORINT = 1.00148$. We have the same underlying asset (currency) tree as before:

Currency tree

```
                                        139.85
                               130.78
                    122.29               122.29
             114.36              114.367
      106.94          106.94             106.94
 100          100              100
        93.51              93.51             93.51
             87.44              87.44
                    81.77             81.77
                          76.47
                                        71.50
```

---

[13] H. Hsu, "Surprised Parties," *Risk* (April 1997).

Now we want to price a down-and-out call on this currency. This is a call option that is canceled if, at any point, the underlying currency touches 95. We can apply the same principles as before. The value of the option is the present value of the probability-weighted average of the payoffs. Hence, in period 4, when the currency's value is at 130.78, so that we know that the payoffs will be either 139.85 or 122.29, the value of the down-and-out is 31.06—the same as the value of an ordinary call, because we have not gone below the 95 threshold, nor can we in the next period. But if the currency's value is at 100, so that the next step down into period 5 would be to 93.51, then the value of the barrier would be breached. The option would expire worthless. So we allow for those points where the option would disappear. Then we can construct a tree of option prices by discounting back the probability-weighted average of each pair of outcomes (just as we did in Chapter 6, except some of these outcomes are zero). We will produce the following tree:

```
                                        39.85
                               31.06
                      22.88               22.29
              16.03              14.66
      10.36             9.13               6.94
5.24              4.61             3.51
      0                  0                  0
              0                  0
                      0                  0
              0
                                 0
```

As this example shows, the pricing of a barrier option is quite simple in concept (though the practicalities of devising realistic trees are not quite so simple).

A variant of the standard barrier option (indeed, one could say, a constituent part of the standard barrier option) is the binary barrier option. Figure 7.3 shows a "family tree" of path-dependent binary barrier options, drawn from the same source as the family tree of path-independent binaries exhibited earlier.

As can be seen in Figure 7.3, there are at least 28 different variants of the binary barrier option. (Some are given different names in the market; e.g., up-and-out and up-and-in calls are sometimes called reverse knockout options.) Space does not permit a full discussion, but the interested reader is referred to the original article.[14] In this section, we will simply pick out some key items.

Consider, for example, the option labeled (13) in the diagram, which is a down-and-in cash-or-nothing call that pays out a sum X at expiry if the asset price S has fallen below the barrier level H at some time, but, at expiry, S > E

---

[14] M. Rubinstein and E. Reiner, *op cit.*

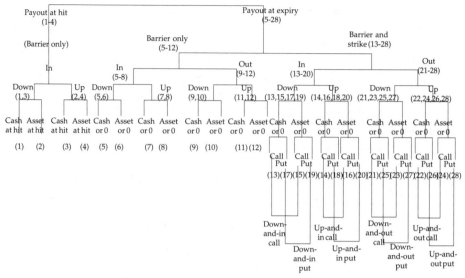

Source of Data: M. Rubinstein & E. Reiner, "Unscrambling the Binary Code," *Risk Magazine* (October 1991).

Figure 7.3 Path-dependent binary options.

where E is the strike level. Otherwise, it pays nothing. The option labeled (15) in the diagram is a down-and-in asset-or-nothing call that pays off S if, at expiry, S > E, provided that S has fallen below H at some time. Otherwise, it pays nothing.

Suppose we go short (13), where X is set equal to E. In other words, we sell an option where we must pay E, if at expiry S > E, provided S has fallen below H at some time. At the same time, we buy (15). Suppose that during the life of the option the barrier is breached—S falls below H—so that the two options "knock in." Now, if at expiry S > E, we will receive S but must pay E. A moment's thought will convince us that by selling (13) and buying (15) we have in fact created a down-and-in call option. Figure 7.3 shows how the other barrier options can be created by using binary barriers as building blocks.

Throughout, we have talked rather glibly about the barrier without addressing the question of how it is measured. A particular problem with barrier options, notably in the currency markets but also elsewhere, has been that if the option is close to the barrier as it comes to expiry, market makers will often try to push the market through the barrier level. A related point is the period during which we monitor the barrier. Standard documentation in the foreign exchange markets often specifies that trading hours run from 6 A.M. Sydney time Monday morning to 5 P.M. Friday in New York.

Another issue is whether the documentation specifies that the barrier is hit if a price is traded, or a price is quoted on a screen. The latter situation, obviously, lends itself to manipulation. Recent standard documentation developed by the British Bankers' Association and the New York Federal Reserve's

Foreign Exchange Committee requires actual transactions to be the basis of a barrier event.

A related point is the frequency with which we check whether the barrier is hit. In currency markets where there is continuous worldwide trading (e.g., dollar–mark, dollar–yen), it is fairly easy to check continuously; not so for a DEM/ITL barrier, or for a barrier on a swaption. In the latter case, it has been shown[15] that the price of a daily observed barrier might well be 10 percent higher than for a continuously observed swaption—a contract that is theoretically available but not in fact practicable.

These binary options have played an important role in certain markets, notably in the "range" instruments traded in interest rate and foreign exchange markets. "Range trading" became very fashionable when the market seemed directionless and volatilities were high.

In the most straightforward version, the range binary option, investors receive a payout of several times the premium paid, but only if the underlying exchange or interest rate remains within a preset range. More exotic variants were often embedded in bonds (discussed in Chapter 12) and warrants (Chapter 15). These create products that allow daily accrual of interest on days when the range conditions are satisfied. In some cases, accrual is stopped once the range is broken. In other cases, accrual is restarted after a range breach if the underlying exchange or interest rate subsequently trades back inside the range.

To give an idea of the scope for leverage in range trades, in mid-1996, foreign exchange products were being structured that gave 8:1, 10:1, and even 15:1 payoffs on a straightforward double knock-out structure. There were more complex versions: Bankers Trust's Quattro product gave four ranges. If an investor was correct on all four ranges, the payoff was eight times the premium. Even if only one range remained unbroken, the Quattro holder received double the premium. (See Chapter 15 on the Quattro warrants.) Although these instruments are highly leveraged, they limit losses to the premium paid. This differentiates them from more conventional bets on low volatility, such as the sale of straddles, which expose the holder of the position to unlimited risk. Holders of notes in which these options are embedded can lose significant amounts of their principal if the bonds are not accruing and are sold before maturity.

Foreign exchange dealers learned this the hard way in 1995–1996. Deals were struck when volatilities on European cross-rates were close to or at all-time highs. This pushed the price of binary range products down dramatically because it seemed likely that the ranges would be broken. Subsequent sharp falls in volatility—for example, deutsche mark/lira volatility fell from around 15 percent in early 1995 to nearer 5 percent by the end of 1996—meant that the ranges were not breached. In addition, the popularity of the product with both institutional investors and corporate hedgers, who used the range option in

---

[15] T. Cheuk and T. Vorst, "Breaking Down Barriers," *Risk Magazine* (April 1996).

place of vanilla options to reduce hedging costs, exacerbated dealers' problems. Prices fell below the levels at which they covered hedging costs as dealers competed for business. Moreover, the scramble to hedge positions, once it became clear that the downward trend in volatilities was permanent, itself forced down volatility. Option holders made huge profits and underhedged option dealers took significant losses. At least three major banks cut their exotic foreign exchange teams after the event, though no confirmation was forthcoming that these moves were linked to the range trading debacle.

Demand for range binary options was also driven by demand from corporate treasurers who saw them as a cost-effective hedging instrument. In combination with vanilla options or forwards, range binaries can be used to create cheap and even self-financing hedges. If we take a company that is long dollars and wants insurance, it can buy a dollar put and a range option on the relevant exchange rate. If volatility falls, then the value of the put will fall but the value of the range option will rise. The put may expire worthless but the range may pay out, funding, or partly funding, the put premium.

Range options can also be used as a substitute for forwards to create what some banks call the range bonus forward (inaccurately; no forward contract exists, only an option contract). Instead of buying an outright forward, a treasurer can decide to take some of the forward points and use them to buy a range option. Suppose the forward dollar/deutsche mark outright is 1.67 and spot is 1.68. The hedger could take one pfennig of premium to buy a range position that produces, say, four pfennigs of windfall profit if the view is correct.

In the interest rate markets, path-dependent caps and floors such as knock-ins and knock-outs have been quite widely used, again because of the premium reduction. A borrower might look at, say, a knock-in LIBOR cap with a strike of 7 percent and a trigger of 6 percent. As long as rates are below 6 percent, no cap exists. Once rates rise above 6 percent, the seller's liability begins: a cap is created, with a strike of 7 percent.

Buyers of such a cap might think they are not much at risk to rising interest rates when LIBOR is below 6 percent. They might believe, however, that an interest rate rise past 6 percent suggests a strong rising trend. The cap buyers make no up-front payment. But they pay the seller if LIBOR rises past the trigger of 6 percent. As with all contingent premium options (see above), the premium paid, if paid, is a good deal more than the premium for a conventional cap. Once the cap is knocked-in, however, the cap purchaser is protected if interest rates rise past 7 percent.

Another variant that has been offered in the market is the up-and-out cap with a refundable premium. This is a cap with a predetermined range. The lower limit is the cap's strike, and the upper limit is the level above which the protection disappears. If the cap disappears, the buyer is refunded the premium payable for that period.

At each fixing, the floating reference rate is compared to the established limits. There are three possible outcomes:

1. The market rate is below the strike: no payment is made.
2. The rate is in the predetermined range: the seller pays the buyer the interest differential between the market rate and the strike rate.
3. The rate is above the knockout level: the cap is deactivated. No interest differential is paid, but the seller reimburses the part of the premium that applies to the period.

The product thus represents an intermediate solution between a standard cap and a standard up-and-out cap.

Finally, we should note that a problem experienced with barrier options—and even more so with double barrier options, where there is a barrier above and below the strike—is the impact of the "volatility smile." The strike will be at a different volatility level than the barrier(s). One possible approach is to use the "skewed" tree models of Dupire, Derman, and Kani or, alternatively, Monte Carlo simulation with a full 3D surface of volatility between today and the option expiry. Both these approaches are computationally intensive. An alternative rough-and-ready approach is to build a model that specifies a separate volatility for the strike and for the barrier(s). This can be reasonably workable as a quick-and-dirty approximation in, for example, short-dated foreign exchange options where skews are less extreme and the volatility curve is fairly flat.

Look-Back. The look-back option gives the buyer the right to "look back" over the period of the option and deal at the best possible rate during that period—for which, of course, a sizable premium is charged. Consider a 3-month sterling look-back call, traded with spot initially at $1.7500. If sterling falls continuously over the 3 months to, say, $1.7000, the option will be at the money on expiry. If sterling rises continuously, the option will behave as a $1.7500 call. If sterling is volatile—falling to, say, $1.6500 before returning to $1.7500 at expiry—the option behaves as a $1.6500 call. Because the look-back option will always expire in or at the money, the premium will always be greater than for the at-the-money spot European option.

Two types of look-back are available: (1) the "standard" look-back and (2) the "extrema" look-back. The valuation of a standard European look-back can be done by means of a closed-form formula:[16]

---

[16] See, e.g., Hull, *op. cit.*, and the references cited there.

$$\text{Look-back} = Se^{-r_f T}N(a1) - Se^{-r_f T}\frac{\sigma^2}{2(r-r_f)}N(-a_1) - S_{min}e^{-rT}\left[N(a_2) - \frac{\sigma^2}{2(r-r_f)}e^{Y_1}N(-a_3)\right]$$

where $a_1 = \dfrac{\ln\left(\dfrac{S}{S_{min}}\right) + \left(r - r_f + \dfrac{\sigma^2}{2}\right)T}{\sigma\sqrt{T}}$;

$a_2 = a1 - \sigma\sqrt{T}$;

$a_3 = \dfrac{\ln\left(\dfrac{S}{S_{min}}\right) + \left(-r + r_f + \dfrac{\sigma^2}{2}\right)T}{\sigma\sqrt{T}}$;

$Y_1 = \dfrac{-2\left(-r - r_f + \dfrac{\sigma^2}{2}\right)\ln\left(\dfrac{S}{S_{min}}\right)}{\sigma^2}$;

r_f = the foreign interest rate (in the case of a currency look-back, or continuously payable dividend in the case of an equity);

S_{min} = the minimum level reached by S during the life of the option.

S = underlying asset price

r = domestic interest rate

Although the look-back formula looks formidable, and at first blush it might seem difficult to hedge an instrument that guarantees to pay out the best possible price, in fact the hedging is (in principle) not too difficult. At the start of the transaction, we buy a call option—assuming we have sold a look-back call to the client—struck at-the-money. If the market falls, we sell that call and buy a new at-the-money call. In this way, we always own a call that we have bought at the bottom of the market. The costs of this hedging are high because we lose money every time we sell a hedging call that is now out of the money, and the bid-offer spreads are higher if we hedge in this way. So, the look-back option will be expensive—as one would expect, anyway, for an instrument that is guaranteed to pay out at maturity (unless the minimum falls on the last day of the option). A common rule of thumb is: Estimate the look-back as costing double the standard call option.

An alternative, less common formulation of the look-back is the extrema look-back. Suppose we have an extrema look-back call with a strike level of E and a previously observed maximum value of the underlying of V. Let M be the maximum value observed from now, the date of trading the option, to its expiry. Then, if E was fixed below V, the extrema payoff is the better of V − E or M − E. If E was fixed above V, and M is below E, the payoff is zero. In other words, the look-back payoff here considers the extreme value not just during the life of the option but also during some earlier period; and it pays off the better of the already observed maximum or any new maximum (less the strike).

Another variant is the partial look-back, where the buyer is allowed to select a subperiod of the option's life to look back over.

Cliquet/Ratchet Option. The cliquet option was first popularized in France, hence the name. The option was introduced in the form of bonds with payoffs linked to the CAC-40 stock market index, and was widely marketed to retail customers as well as professional investors. The cliquet allows the option's strike price to be reset at a set number of dates (usually annually) to the current asset price. Any positive intrinsic value is locked in at that point. From the investor's viewpoint, this is a very attractive structure. In effect, the option gives us the right to lock in any profits at regular intervals, before we buy back into the market at the new market level. One could think of it as the equivalent of a tax-driven "bed-and-breakfast" deal where we automatically crystallize any capital gains.

An example would be the FRF300 million Crédit Lyonnais Guernsey issue, issued in June 1992 and maturing on July 17, 1996. The bond coupon was set at a minimum of 0 percent and maximum of 18 percent linked to the performance of CAC-40 index—the initial level set at FRF1,913 on June 17, 1992. The cliquet options allow the CAC strike to be reset every year, which is attractive to investors. Gains accrued to date can be locked in. If the index falls, the investor can buy a call at a lower strike. Even if the index has not risen above the initial strike of FRF1,913 by the bonds' maturity, the investor will have received income every year that the index rises. If the index fell in any one year, the investor would receive no coupon and the next year's strike would be reset at the lower level. In this structure, the rise in the index is paid out in the form of bond coupons during the life of the deal; in other structures, the payment is made at maturity.

Pricing and hedging of the cliquet structure are surprisingly straightforward. If we consider the bond just mentioned, we have four successive coupons to be paid out. Their value is fixed by the cliquet. After the first year's call option, at a price that is, of course, already known, we have, in fact, three successive 1-year call options that will be struck at-the-money when they come into existence. These are none other than forward, or delayed-start options, whose value we found earlier in this chapter to be the same as a call struck at-the-money today for a 1-year maturity.

Ladder. A variant of the cliquet says, "Instead of refixing the strike every year, we fix it when the market has risen a given percentage." This is called a ladder option—a special case of the look-back call. We can look back only at certain points: the "rungs" of the ladder. As the number of rungs increases toward infinity, the ladder starts to resemble a look-back. Many ladder options have been combined with zero-coupon bonds to achieve the combination of a guaranteed minimum return plus the locking-in of a rise in the market.

An example might be a bond that guarantees the investor the return of the assets at maturity plus the ability to lock in to a rise of 50 percent and 75 percent from today's levels. If the market rises only 49 percent, a look-back option would have been a better bet. In return for taking this risk, the ladder option can be bought more cheaply.

An example of the application of the ladder was the issue by ABN Amro Bank, in 1993, of 4,000 ladder call warrants on 100 units of the European Options Exchange (EOE) Index, exercisable on December 17, 1993, at Netherlands Guilders (NLG) 280. These warrants had barriers every 10 points from 290 to 320, which guaranteed cash settlement in NLG at the higher of the maximum barrier reached or the final EOE index level.

Pricing of the ladder option is not as easy as pricing of the cliquet option, because a closed-form solution is not yet available. However, we can replicate the behavior of a ladder by a suitable combination of barrier and conventional options, as the following example demonstrates.

We wish to issue a ladder option bond whose redemption value gives the investor a payout like that of a ladder call option on the NLG, with one rung set at 115 percent of the current NLG level. That is, if at maturity the NLG were to be below today's level, the investor simply receives the original principal back. If at maturity the NLG is between 100 percent and 115 percent of today's level—say, 108 percent of today's level—and has never been above 115 percent, the payout is the increase. The investor would receive 108 percent.

However, if at any time the NLG traded above 115 percent of today's level, the investor is guaranteed a payout of 115 percent—even if the NLG has subsequently collapsed to, say, 90 percent of today's level. If the NLG settles above 115 percent—e.g., at 125 percent—then the investor gets 125 percent of the principal amount back.

We could hedge our position as follows:

1. Buy a call option on the NLG at a strike of 100 percent of today.

2. Buy a long put spread, that is, sell a put with a strike of 100 percent of the NLG and buy a put with a strike of 115 percent.

3. Sell an up-and-out put spread; that is, buy an up-and-out with a strike of 100 percent and an out of 115 percent, and sell an up-and-out put with a strike of 115 percent and an out of 115 percent.

We consider the payoff of this package on the following assumptions:

- NLG settles at 80, never having touched 115 percent.
- NLG settles at 80, having touched 115 percent.
- NLG settles at 125.

	Rung (115)		Rung (115)		Rung (115)
	Not Touched	Touched	Not Touched	Touched	Touched
Outcome	80	80	100	100	125
Call	0	0	0	0	25
Put spread:					
−Put	−20	−20	0	0	0
+Put	35	35	15	15	0
Short knockout put:					
+Up-and-out					
@spot	20	0	0	0	0
−Up-and-out					
@rung	−35	0	−15	0	0
Total payoff	0	15	0	15	25

The above package of options has provided an exact hedge of the ladder structure required.

Shout. The "shout" option is another twist on the cliquet/ladder concepts. In this case, the strikes on the option are set, not at fixed dates as with the cliquet, nor at fixed market levels as with the ladder, but at the option of the buyer. When the buyer wants to fix the strike, the buyer "shouts" to the writer.

The pricing of the shout option assumes rationality on the part of the shouter. It will be rational to shout only if the intrinsic value of the option obtained thereby is greater than zero. More precisely, it is rational for the buyer to shout if the expected value of the option obtained is greater than the expected value of the option obtained without shouting (i.e., if a buyer of a shout call option does not expect the market to fall further). This decision is very closely similar to the decision on whether to exercise an American call option, and rather similar valuation methods are required—i.e., we set up a binomial tree and "prune" it in line with the "rational shout" behavior.

The shout is cheaper than the look-back, because the shout requires the buyer to take the risk of possibly shouting at the wrong moment. But if we call the market well, we get the same payoff as a look-back.

Comparisons

It may be helpful to pause at this point, in order to draw some comparisons. Figures 7.4 through 7.7 compare various exotic options on sterling at a strike price of $1.75 when the current spot rate is also $1.75—i.e., they are at-the-money. Each option is for 1 year, and the assumed sterling interest rate is 6.375 percent. The dollar interest rate is taken as 5.75 percent. Where barriers apply, they are taken, for down-and-out/in and up-and-out/in, as $1.70 and $1.80, respectively. For "touch" options, the same levels are used. The fixed payoff used

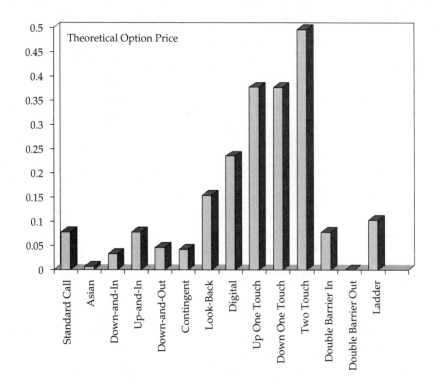

Figure 7.4 Premiums for various exotics.

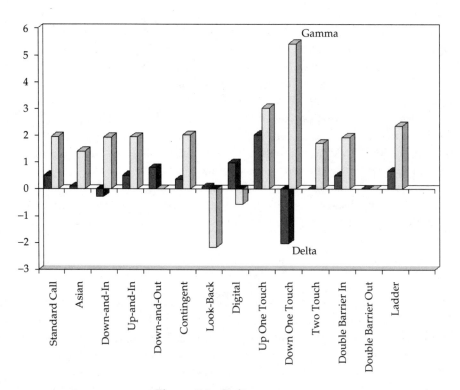

Figure 7.5 Delta, gamma.

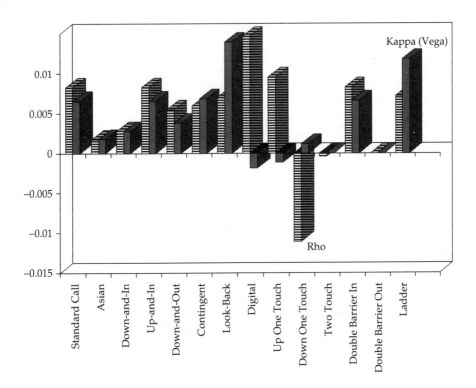

Figure 7.6 Rho, theta, vega.

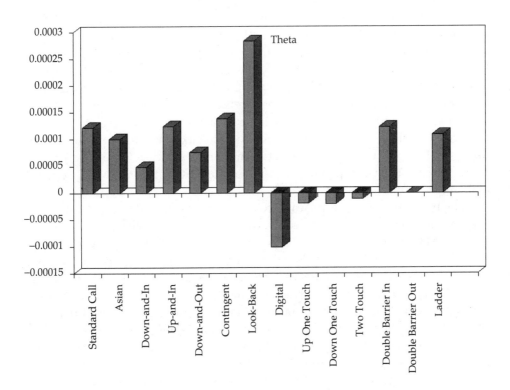

Figure 7.7 Theta.

for digital and touch options is 0.5. The size of this payoff explains the relatively higher price for these options. The ladder option is assumed to have rungs at $1.80 and $1.85.

It should be very firmly stressed that these comparisons are extremely rough. Inevitably, they are snapshots of dynamic instruments. This applies particularly to the digital and barrier options, where delta and gamma are extremely volatile around the strike and the barrier.

OPTION HYBRIDS

Forward Contracts with Embedded Options

In many cases, forward contracts have been combined with options, particularly in the foreign exchange market. In practice, most of these products were developed to allow corporate treasurers or fund managers to use options without appearing to do so. This avoided the need for lengthy explanations to a board or to trustees whose grasp of the advantages of options might be rather limited. Some banks also used these products to conceal from their customers the true costs of the product they were buying. In most cases, it is cheapest for the customer to buy the component parts separately. However, where there are regulatory or tax advantages, these products may be useful. For example, in the United Kingdom, until a few years ago, the Inland Revenue took the view that an option was a wasting asset, therefore losses on options purchased were not tax-deductible. A loss on a forward exchange contract, however, was allowable. Thus, combining the forward and the option allowed for better tax treatment.

We will look at three kinds of hybrid product: (1) the break forward, (2) the range forward, and (3) the participating contract. (Unfortunately, the marketing departments of many banks, in an effort to make the bank's product seem different, have dreamed up many different names for these products. Thus, a break forward has been called a Boston option, a FOX [forward with optional exit], and so on.)

The break forward is a forward contract combined with a call or put. For example, a corporate customer requires to buy forward sterling value June 15. Today is March 15; the interest rate to June 15 is 10 percent. The forward rate is $1.65 for June 15, and the $1.60 June 15 put costs $0.036. The bank will offer to sell forward to the customer at a certain rate, with a "free" put at $1.60. How is that forward rate determined? The bank will protect itself by buying forward sterling to sell to the customer and by buying the $1.60 puts. It will fund the cost of the premium paid today on those puts at 10 percent. The funded put then costs $0.036 \times (1 + 10 \text{ percent} \times 91/265) = \$0.0009 + \$0.036 = \$0.0369$. The bank offers to sell forward at $1.65 + \$0.0369 = \$1.6869$ (instead of the $1.6500 available in the market) with a "free" put at $1.60. The corporate customer buys forward at $1.6869. If sterling is below $1.60 at maturity, the customer exercises the put. Say sterling were at $1.55; then the customer will exercise the put (crystallizing a loss of $1.6869 – $1.6000 of $0.0869) and will buy in the market at $1.55. The next total cost to the customer will be $1.6369 ($1.5500 + $0.0869). But that will still be less than the $1.6500 that the customer would have paid if it had simply covered forward.

The range forward is an extension of the break forward to give an upper and a lower limit. Outside the range of those limits, the customer is protected. Inside the range, the customer is exposed. Suppose again our corporate customer wants to buy forward sterling value June 15. As before, today is March 15; the interest rate to June 15 is 10 percent, and the forward rate is $1.65 for June 15. As before, the $1.60 June 15 put costs $0.036; the $1.90 June 15 call costs $0.042. The bank offers to sell to its customer at whatever the June 15 spot rate turns out to be. The offer is subject to a maximum of $1.90 and a minimum of $1.60, and the trade will be adjusted by a set amount representing the bank's fee for the deal. The customer knows it will not have to pay more than $1.90 (plus fee). In exchange, it gives up the hope of profiting below $1.60.

What is happening is that the bank effectively sells a call to the customer and buys a put from the customer. It sells the call for $0.042, buying the put for $0.036, for a net cost to the customer of $0.006. This cost is funded for 91 days at 10 percent for a total cost at maturity of $0.0062. So the final deal includes a fee of $0.0062 added to whatever rate the contract is traded at. A variant of this approach is to adjust the strike prices of the upper and lower limits so that the net premium payable is zero.

Participating contracts are an interesting variation. In the two previous deals, the cost to the customer is varied by changing the strike levels of the option. Another way to do this is to set a particular strike and then vary the cost by varying the proportion of the deal's size. Once again, our corporate customer requires to buy forward sterling value June 15; today is March 15; the interest rate to June 15 is 10 percent, and the forward rate is $1.65 for June 15. The $1.70 June 15 put costs $0.08, and the $1.70 June 15 call costs $0.05. The bank offers to sell forward to the customer at $1.70—an above-market rate—but will share 37.5 percent of its profits on the deal with its customer.

How is that share arrived at? In fact, it's fixed by the ratio of the costs of the call to that of the put: 37.5 percent is given back because the call costs 62.5 percent of the put (0.05 versus 0.08). Suppose the deal is for £62,500,000 and the exchange-traded puts and calls that the bank uses to hedge its position are for £62,500 each. The bank will hedge its upside risk by buying 1,000 calls, and will fund this by selling 625 puts, for no net outlay of premium. If sterling falls, the bank has sold at $1.70 to the customer, but will profit from the fact that it has sold only 625 puts; this profit is available to be passed on to the customer. (In real life, the percentage will be adjusted to allow the bank a profit.)

The range forward uses puts and calls with different strikes to arrive at a premium of zero, or close to it; the participating contract uses the same strikes but adjusts the amount of the deal on one side to achieve the same result.

Embedded Option Swaps

Along with forward contracts, hybrids of swaps and options have been created; an enormous variety of possible swaps can be created by embedding in the swap some type of option—for example, a swap where the client pays 6-month LIBOR and receives 6-month LIBOR plus a spread of, say, 110 basis points. In exchange, the client accepts that if LIBOR touches a certain level, then the coupon for the period is forfeited. These "one-touch swaps" were popular for a period in 1994.

Another alternative might be the look-back basis swap. With this structure, the client pays the highest LIBOR fixing in the reset and receives LIBOR set at the start of the period plus a spread. In a 2-year deal with 6-month resets, for example, the client might receive 6-month LIBOR + 120 and pay the highest daily 6-month LIBOR rate in each 6-month period.

One investment bank, in November 1996, was offering the following swap, which essentially was designed to act as a "play" on convergence within the European currencies that were expected to enter the European Monetary Union. The swap consisted of the following 2-year trade: the client would pay FRF 3-month PIBOR and would receive (FRF 3-month PIBOR + 0.64 percent)*n/Q where:

n = number of days where FRF 3-month PIBOR > DEM 3-month LIBOR;

Q = exact number of days in the quarter.

The risk in this swap is that the German interest rate level may rise above the French. If this were to occur, then the client would pay 3-month PIBOR and receive nothing. The underlying option is a cross-currency binary interest rate option.

Participating Swaps

One variant of the swap is the participating swap. (This is the swap analogy of the participating forward discussed earlier.) Designed for floating rate borrowers who wish to hedge against an increase in money market rates, and who think rates are unlikely to drop below a certain level, the swap fixes a borrowing rate, but allows a benefit from any decline in rates within a range determined at the start of the transaction. For example, the swap might be for 5 years at a fixed rate of 7 percent, with a range of 4–7 percent. If rates fall below 4 percent, the borrower pays the fixed swap rate of 7 percent. But if they are between 4 percent and 7 percent, the borrower pays a floating rate. If rates are above 7 percent, the borrower pays the fixed swap rate of 7 percent.

This product is an interesting alternative to the standard swap for a floating rate borrower who is willing to pay a fixed rate slightly higher than that of a standard swap, in return for the chance to benefit from a fall in rates within the given range.

OTHER OPTIONS MARKETS

FLEX Options

As has been mentioned previously, options are traded both on exchanges and in the form of over-the-counter transactions. Because the various options exchanges feared a loss of business to the over-the-counter market, they sought methods of adapting, to attract business that otherwise would be traded in over-the-counter markets. One result was the so-called "FLEX" option.

In 1993, the Chicago Board Options Exchange (CBOE) introduced FLexible EXchange (FLEX) Options. Designed for initial transactions of at least $10 million of notional principal, FLEX options allow users to select option contract terms. Initially the options were based on the S&P 100 and S&P 500 indexes. For these markets, users may specify any of the following terms:

1. Underlying: S&P 100 or S&P 500.
2. Type: call or put.
3. Expiry: up to 5 years.
4. Strike price: may be specified as an index level, as a percentage, as a numerical deviation from a closing index level or an intraday value level, or as any other readily understood method for dividing an index level.
5. Exercise style: American, European, or capped.
6. Settlement values: opening; closing; average of opening and closing; average of high and low levels; average of opening, closing, high, and low levels of the index spot.

For example, a FLEX option user could create an S&P 500 call option expiring December 31, 2001, struck 6 percent out-of-the-money (i.e., 636 if the index level is 600) with American-style exercise and an exercise settlement value based on an average of opening and closing index values.

The first step in the process occurs when a member of the CBOE makes a "Request for Quote" (RFQ). The market is informed of the RFQ and a period of 20 minutes is allowed. After that time, the appointed market makers in the option concerned must respond verbally with bids and offers in the minimum size. At the same time, qualified market makers, dealers, and floor brokers, acting on behalf of customers, may submit their best bids and offers, in a minimum of $1 million underlying value. The member who requested the price can then trade at the best bid or offer, or can request an improvement in the price. If the best bid or offer is not promptly accepted, the quotes are no longer valid. If a trade is done, the result is published to the market just like other trades.

In 1994, the Chicago Board of Trade introduced flexible Treasury options, adapting many of the features of the FLEX option structure to the bond futures market. A Request for Quote procedure was adopted; traders can choose the strike price, expiration date, and exercise style. The options can be on futures in the long Treasury bond, or 2-, 5-, or 10-year Treasury notes.

In June 1995, the FLEX concept was adopted by LIFFE, with an FTSE 100 FLEX-style option (European style exercise). The contract offers cash settlement based on the exchange delivery settlement price, which is based on the average level of the FTSE 100 index between 10:10 A.M. and 10:30 A.M. on the last trading day.

FLEX options on LIFFE have a maximum maturity of 2 years. For institutional investors, one attraction of the FLEX option, compared with OTC options, is that the counterparty to the trade is the London Clearing House. In addition, FLEX options with the same exercise price and expiry day as European FTSE option contracts will automatically convert into such options when they are listed. Institutional investors have also appreciated the advantages of being able to choose nonstandard expiry dates. A feature of early trading was the volume of trades with expiries at the end of December and of June, suggesting asset allocation trades designed to protect half-yearly reporting results. Another benefit was observed: the limited range strike prices and expiry dates in the listed index option market had made the execution of zero cost collars (see Chapter 6) very difficult indeed. The new FLEX options permitted efficient execution of zero cost collars.

In October 1996, a further step forward was taken when the Chicago Board Options Exchange and the American Stock Exchange introduced FLEX options on 26 of the most actively traded stocks. The FLEX options targeted institutional investors for their new offerings; all FLEX transactions represent at least 25,000 shares. Companies included The Walt Disney Company, Intel, Merrill Lynch, General Motors, and ADRs issued by Telefonos de Mexico, Telebras, and Grupo Televisa.

UCOM

In 1982, the Philadelphia Stock Exchange (PHLX) pioneered listed options on currencies (standardized contracts). More recently, it has developed a marketplace known as the United Currency Option Market® (UCOM®), which trades three types of option:

1. Standardized currency options on eight major currencies and two cross-rate pairs, with American or European style exercise. Maturities include a range of 2 weeks to as long as 2 years, with a choice of mid-month or month-end expiration.

2. Virtual Currency Options ("3-D" or Dollar-Denominated Delivery) contracts. 3-D deutsche mark options, for example, are cash-settled DEM options that automatically settle in U.S. dollars. 3-Ds were designed to allow investors to trade currency options without the need to establish foreign currency accounts or international bank lines. The

investor merely pays or receives the difference between the strike price and the settlement value. 3-Ds are European-style options with maturities ranging from 1 week to 9 months.

3. Customized currency options. The trading mechanics are very similar to those for FLEX options on the CBOE and elsewhere: Request for Quotes (RFQ), quotes, and trades are published as text messages over the Options Price Reporting Authority (OPRA). The issuer and guarantor of all these options is the Options Clearing Corporation (OCC).

Any two currently approved currencies, including the U.S. dollar, may be matched for trading. Either may represent the base or underlying currency; for example, US$/JPY (strike prices expressed in US$ per JPY) or JPY/US$ (strike prices expressed in JPY per US$); DEM/FRF (strike prices expressed in DEM per FRF) or FRF/DEM (strike prices expressed in FRF per DEM). In all, 110 possible currency pairs are available for trading. Contract size for the currency pairs is determined by the underlying currency. Exercise style is European.

A participant may trade a customized currency option with either a standard expiration date (termed a "Standard-Expiry Option") or with a customized date (termed a "Custom-Dated Option"). Standard-Expiry Options and Custom-Dated Options have distinct exercise and assignment processes. Standard-Expiry Options conform to existing exercise and assignment practices for all standardized contracts.

Custom-Dated Options follow a unique exercise and assignment process upon expiration (all time notations are for the U.S. Eastern time zone):

8:00 A.M. (Eastern Time)   Trading ceases in expiring Custom-Dated Options.

10:00 A.M.(Eastern Time)   Window closes for exercise instructions in expiring Custom-Dated Options. The OCC will then disseminate a preliminary indication of the percentage of open interest exercised in each series.

10:15 A.M. (Eastern Time)   Custom-Dated Options expire, and final assignment notification, based on a pro rata assignment process, begins.

Catastrophe Insurance Options

The Chicago Board of Trade has attempted to introduce derivatives for property/casualty (PC) catastrophe insurance. In 1995, PCS Catastrophe Insurance Options were introduced. These options track catastrophe loss indexes aggregating insured losses nationally, regionally, and in select catastrophe-prone states. Daily indexes are provided by Property Claim Services, a nationally recognized industry authority for catastrophic property damage estimates. Each PCS index has both a small-cap and a large-cap option contract listed. The small-cap contracts track aggregate estimated catastrophic losses from $0 billion to $20 billion. The large cap contracts track aggregate estimated catastrophic losses from $20 billion to $50 billion. Each contract has a loss period and a development period. The loss period is the time during which a catastrophic event must occur to be included in a particular index. The development period is the time after the loss period during which PCS estimates and re-estimates for catastrophes that occurred during the loss period continue to affect the PCS indexes. Option users can choose either a 6- or a 12-month period. The PCS index value at the end of the chosen development period will be used for settlement purposes, even though PCS loss estimates may continue to change thereafter.

These contracts represent an interesting development in the use of options—true insurance. However, the actual volume of trading activity has been rather limited, partly because of the fact that each insurance company has very specific exposures that may not easily be laid off by hedging with an aggregate index. Furthermore, the contracts' use is permitted by a limited number of U.S. insurance regulators as investment instruments only. Therefore, they do not reduce statutory liabilities in the way that traditional reassurance does.

A second approach to insurance derivatives is being developed by the New York Catastrophe Exchange (CATEX). The aim is to create a real-time electronic market to which the money at risk from specific catastrophe exposures can be traded between participants, enabling risks to be diversified directly.

Chapter **8**

Securitization

LOAN TRADING AND SECURITIZATION; LOAN TRADING AND COMMERCIAL PAPER

Securitization is the transformation of an illiquid asset into a security that is tradable, and therefore liquid. The technique is, in one sense, a part of the mortgage-backed securities market, which we discuss later; in another sense, it could be described as an extension of the commercial paper and FRN markets. The first edition of this book devoted one chapter to securitization. The phenomenon is now of such importance that two separate chapters, on mortgage-backed and asset-backed securities (Chapters 10 and 11), are included in this book in addition to this chapter. Securitization has also applied to short-term financing. Bank loans have been transformed into tradable assets, and commercial paper has been used as a substitute.

Loan Sales

Faced with competition from the commercial paper market, and the growth of securitization in general, commercial banks have turned to selling loans. For decades, banks have sold, participated in, placed, or syndicated their loans—usually only with other banks. The "new" loan selling started to develop in the early 1980s. Loan sales are now a stand-alone business in numerous money-center banks. In the Euromarkets, loan sales have also taken place for many years. As in the United States, recent market trends have encouraged much faster growth in loan sales.

In this context, loan sales are generally defined as assignment of, or sales of, subparticipations in loans, where loans on one bank's books are sold to maturity, and on a nonrecourse basis, to another investor—not necessarily a bank. The loans are generally short-term; they may be sold with or without the knowledge of the borrower (usually with). They are serviced by the seller and are not generally salable in the secondary market. A further refinement is "strip sales," the process whereby drawings under, say, a 5-year revolving facility might be sold as individual shorter maturities on a repeated basis.

There are four major reasons for the interest of commercial banks in selling loans:

1. Narrow spreads on loans kept on the books, and increasing pressure on capital ratios.
2. To increase liquidity of the bank's balance sheet.
3. Off-balance-sheet "skim earnings," which are particularly attractive when capital ratios are under pressure.
4. The ability to continue servicing customers, even though the bank could not afford to lend to them. or, alternatively, to reduce exposure to a customer.

The common methods of selling loans are: (1) assignment, (2) participation or subparticipation, and (3) novation. Assignment, completed by notice to the borrower, is the basic conventional manner of selling a loan. In an assignment, the buyer becomes a direct lender to the borrower under the credit agreement, and is entitled to all voting privileges granted to the banks under the agreement. Assignments are transferred directly between the two parties and are recorded on the books of the agent. Usually, the borrower's and/or the agent's approval is required, but some credit agreements provide a definition of an "eligible assignee." (A disadvantage in the United Kingdom is that, to be fully effective, under U.K. law, the obligor must be notified of the assignment.)

The words *participation* and *subparticipation* are often used interchangeably. Here, subparticipation is used to describe a portion of, or an interest in, a loan. Subparticipations can be either funded or by way of risk. In broad terms, a funded subparticipation is an agreement whereby the buyer (or subparticipant) will put the seller in funds for an agreed participation in a loan. In return, the seller pays to the buyer a pro rata share of the payments of principal and interest received from the borrower. The buyer, therefore, takes a credit risk on the seller. Most subparticipation agreements do not transfer full voting rights. But they do transfer at least the right to vote on questions concerning "money terms" (maturity, amortization, coupon and fees, release of collateral, or forgiveness of debt). Subparticipations are easier to create than assignments because they are usually not subject to the assignment definitions in the credit agreement. In general, the funded subparticipation is the most common participation technique.

A risk subparticipation would provide that, instead of the buyer's funding the seller, the buyer guarantees, in return for a fee, a proportion of any failure of the borrower to pay. The buyer, in effect, funds its subparticipation only if a default occurs. The advantages of this structure are that restrictions on assignment in loan documentation are fairly common; effective restraints on this type of subparticipation are rare. Subparticipation is a contractual arrangement between the buyer and seller. It is not usually appropriate or necessary to give notice of it to the borrower. It is, in a sense, a type of credit derivative (see Chapter 13).

A disadvantage to the buyer is that, generally, no direct claim can be brought against the seller. Hence, the buyer is exposed to the credit risk of both the borrower and the seller. In a risk subparticipation, the seller is also exposed to a double credit risk: the borrower may fail to pay, and the buyer may fail to indemnify.

Novation involves amending the loan documentation so that the seller is replaced by the buyer as to rights and obligations. This is more expensive because the other parties to the documentation will be involved. But it is desirable in cases where the loan perhaps has not been fully drawn, so that the seller would otherwise be obligated to put up funds for any further draw-down. An assignment can transfer only rights, not the obligation to provide further funds.

Bank Loan Trading

Estimates of the early growth of the U.S. loan sale market are that the volume in 1982 was negligible, but it rose to $5 billion in 1983, $15 billion in 1984, and $20 to 40 billion in 1985. After these early beginnings, the market for bank loan trading began to develop quite quickly. A particular stimulus was the growth of so-called Highly Leveraged Transactions (HLT; also known in some quarters as Hope and Luck Transactions) where the syndication process often involved a substantial sell-down to other participants outside the original syndicate.

In the Euromarkets, the transferable loan instrument (TLI) was introduced in 1984. In its most basic form, a transferable loan was an enhancement of the traditional syndicated loan, transferability simply being the ability of lenders to transfer participants in the loan in a simple, legally sound, and standardized form. The TLI structure incorporated transferable loan certificates, a transfer agent, a register of holders, and an off-shore registrar. The first transaction was a £25 million facility for Irish Telecommunications Investments, increased by the end of syndication to £50 million. Market acceptance was enthusiastic. Before the year end, some 15 different facilities, all incorporating transferability, had been arranged; by the end of the following year, more than £5 billion of transferable loan facilities had been arranged.

Transferability soon became standard practice in syndicated loans. By 1987, transferability was, wherever possible, being incorporated into most new loan facilities, and the mechanism for doing so had been greatly simplified. At the back of virtually every loan agreement there was a transfer certificate; this remains common practice.

The introduction of transferability led to an increase in activity in the secondary market. In 1987, the Bank of England published the consultative paper "Loans Transfers and Securitization," which was followed 18 months later by the Notice to Authorized Banks, using the same title.

Broadly speaking, the market both in the United States and in Europe can be subdivided into three parts: (1) trading of loans to "emerging markets" borrowers; (2) trading of distressed loans in the domestic market; and (3) selling off of normal loans to domestic borrowers, often as part of the syndication process.

Loans to Emerging Markets Borrowers

This market may be said to have begun in 1984, in the wake of the LDC debt crisis that began when Mexico defaulted in 1982. In 1987, the process accelerated when major U.S. money center banks took increased reserves against their LDC loans. Having written them down, they were less inhibited about selling them. Estimated secondary market loan trading volume in 1988 was $40 billion, up from $5 billion in 1985. In 1989, the Brady initiative for Mexico launched the market for Brady bonds (discussed in Chapter 9). Growth in trading of bank loans and the need to harmonize trading practices led to the foundation of the Emerging Markets Traders Association (EMTA). By 1992, figures from the EMTA showed total trading volume for debt instruments (including Brady bonds) at $734 billion. Over time, trading in Brady bonds came increasingly to dominate LDC loan trading. By 1994, Brady trading was seven times loan trading, whereas in 1992 they had been roughly equal.

Loan trading in this market is generally conducted in accordance with EMTA Market Practices and standard documentation; settlement of loan trades normally occurs on T + 21 calendar days. EMTA has developed multilateral netting arrangements for loan trading, and a facility called Match-EM for automated trade confirmation and matching.

Loans to Distressed Borrowers

There is also a market for the trading of "distressed loans." In the United States, this began during the early 1980s, not long after the development of the trading of emerging markets loans. (There had been transactions of this type before, but not really a systematic market.) The market then began to take off after the leveraged buyout boom of the late 1980s, which inevitably resulted in a series of disasters. Names such as Allied Department Stores, Federated Department Stores, and Southland Corporation all collapsed after highly leveraged financings. This in turn led to a specialized subsector of distressed lendings—the so-called "debtor-in-possession" lendings. Under the U.S. Bankruptcy Code, a company that files for Chapter 11 protection is a "debtor-in-possession" (DIP) of its assets. It is essentially a new entity that can operate unencumbered by its preexisting debt burdens until the company and its creditors agree on a viable reorganization plan. The bankruptcy court may give DIP creditors a "superpriority" claim on an insolvent company's cash flow as well as unencumbered assets that are not pledged to senior, secured creditors. DIP loans are due in full, once a company adopts a reorganization plan and emerges from Chapter 11. Therefore, in order to leave Chapter 11 as a solvent entity, the company must first pay off its DIP creditors under the superpriority clause. Hence, this type of loan became very popular during the early 1990s, and there was substantial market activity in this area.

The growth of such markets depends a great deal on the legal and accounting framework and on the attitude of the central bank concerned. In the United

Kingdom, the Bank of England expressed concern that secondary market trading of distressed loans might hinder the process of corporate reconstruction. The United Kingdom does not possess the equivalent of Chapter 11 bankruptcy, though, in 1986, the concept of a voluntary arrangement with creditors was introduced. Hence, the Bank has pressed for the adoption of the so-called London Approach to the problem. Under the London Approach, the Bank of England discourages commercial banks from appointing receivers too quickly, urges them to share information, and wants all creditors to try to reach a common agreement.

The Bank of England accepts, of course, that banks and other original lenders should have the option of selling distressed debt. However, there is an inherent conflict between the philosophy of traders, who tend to thrive on instability, and of lenders involved in a workout, who are trying to create stability.

These difficulties are magnified where a troubled corporation may have borrowed from up to 100 or more banks based in various countries. Much of the problem arises from differences in insolvency legislation among countries. Efforts to resolve that issue are being made, particularly through the United Nations Commission on International Trade Law (UNCITRAL). Work is also being done under the auspices of INSOL International, the worldwide federation of insolvency specialists.

Trading in Conventional Domestic Bank Loans

In addition to the above markets, there is, of course, a well-established market for trading loans of companies. Very often, the syndication of a bank loan for a company will be accompanied by a selling process whereby banks will "sell down" their initial loan commitment to other banks.

In the London market, attempts have been made to develop a formal secondary market by the formation of a Loan Market Association whose objective is to draw up common legal guidelines and settlement methods for the London market. The inaugural meeting of the Association was held in March 1997, with 29 banks as full members and a group of 43 banks, law firms, and rating agencies as associate members. In addition, the Bank of England, British Bankers Association, and Bank of Japan have joined as courtesy members.

A basic problem lies at the heart of any major expansion of loan trading: the ultimate implication is that loans, like bonds, would need to be marked to market if there were a continuous market for loan trading. This is a development many banks are unwilling to contemplate.

DEVELOPMENT OF SECURITIZATION

Bills of Exchange and Commercial Paper

The first form of securitized loan was the bill of exchange, or banker's acceptance. This is a bill drawn by a borrower and "accepted" by a bank, signifying that if the borrower defaults, the bank will meet the liability. Nowadays, apart from the United Kingdom, where bills of exchange play an important role because they are used by the Bank of England in its monetary policy operations, the bill of exchange is less important than commercial paper.

One interesting development has been the creation by the Kingdom of Belgium of a multicurrency Treasury Bill program. In many respects, the program resembles a multicurrency Euro-commercial paper program, but it is documented under Belgian law and the National Bank of Belgium serves as issuing and paying agent. There is, in principle, no reason why any country should not follow this example (though it would be necessary to obtain clearance from the country whose currency was being used). A number of European countries, including the United Kingdom, have issued Treasury bills already in ECU, but this had a more specifically political objective of encouraging the development of the ECU market.

Commercial paper has existed since the 19th century, but, from the 1920s through the 1960s, the market was dominated by finance company paper. In 1966, nonfinancial paper outstanding was $0.8 billion. By 1978, nonfinancial paper was $17.4 billion, or 51 percent of New York City banks' commercial and industrial loans. By the end of 1985, nonfinancial commercial paper outstanding was around $88.5 billion, or about 149 percent of New York banks' commercial and industrial loans. Thereafter, due in part to pressure on commercial banks' capital ratios, commercial paper markets grew rapidly.

Commercial paper outstanding in the United States in November 1996 stood at a level of $760 billion: $576 billion was financial company paper (much of this, however, is issued by finance subsidiaries of industrial companies—e.g., GMAC) and $183 billion was nonfinancial company paper. Of these totals, foreign organizations accounted for $65 billion, or 8.5 percent of total unadjusted commercial paper.

Internationally, the 1980s and 1990s have brought development of domestic commercial paper markets in a number of countries. There is a substantial market in France, where the money market SICAV funds have been active investors, and to a lesser extent in the United Kingdom (where the commercial bill of exchange has traditionally been used actively by the Bank of England in its money market operations, and so has provided a competitive funding alternative). In recent years, Germany's Bundesbank has finally conceded the development of DEM commercial paper, and this market has also become fairly large. There is also a Euro-commercial paper market, discussed below.

Along the way, the commercial paper market has had to endure ups and downs. The collapse of Penn Central in 1970 severely hit the U.S. commercial paper market, and the international commercial paper market was equally shaken in 1989 by the collapse of DFC, a New Zealand semistate entity. This disaster was followed rapidly by others, including the collapse of Polly Peck and Drexel Burnham, both of which had substantial commercial paper outstanding at the time of default. It should be added, also, that there is a large market from time to time in "structured" commercial paper—commercial paper whose redemption characteristics reflect the impact of some option or swap transaction. This market is essentially a submarket of the "structured note" market and is accordingly discussed in Chapter 12.

Commercial Paper Special-Purpose Vehicles and Conduits

In a number of cases, special-purpose vehicles have been set up in order to facilitate the securitization of assets by issuing commercial paper against the assets of the special-purpose vehicle. This may be done for a number of reasons; for example, in the U.S. market, it would be common for a foreign issuer that had no other presence in the U.S. market to adopt this alternative. A special-purpose vehicle might be set up, say, in Delaware, and structured so that it is insulated from the foreign borrower; it would be given a separate rating by Moody's or Standard & Poor's.

A typical example of this type of transaction was the issue of $178 million of commercial paper, in December 1991, by Bishopsgate Funding Inc. The issuer was a limited-purpose Delaware corporation formed specifically to issue commercial paper. The proceeds from the initial issuance of the notes were swapped via a currency and interest rate swap with UBS Securities (Swaps) Inc., whose obligation under the swaps is guaranteed by UBS. The proceeds were swapped into sterling and lent to Rosehaugh Stanhope (Broadgate Phase 6) PLC. Phase 6 is the vehicle company used to build 135 Bishopsgate in London. The property is let to National Westminster Bank, which pays rent quarterly in sterling. Payments are made to the swap counterparty, which makes monthly U.S. dollar payments to the issuer. Notes are issued at maturities coinciding with the monthly swap payment dates, and the issuer uses the swap payments to pay the notes. If new notes cannot be issued, the issuer can draw under a liquidity facility. If payment is not forthcoming, maturing notes will be repaid by payments under a surety bond issued by FGIC, a monoline insurer.

Another alternative is for a financial institution to set up a conduit to handle the issuance of commercial paper for a number of borrowers. An example was BZW's creation, in 1993, of a special-purpose securitization vehicle, Sceptre International, to fund corporate trade receivables in the international commercial paper markets. The object of the securitization vehicle is to buy diversified pools of trade receivables from European companies and European subsidiaries of multinationals. Other, related structures are discussed at more length in Chapter 11.

Euro-Commercial Paper

The international market for commercial paper is commonly called Euro-commercial paper. Attempts were made in the early 1970s to develop a Euro-commercial paper market, which actually reached a peak of $2 billion in outstandings. But, in 1974, the lifting of U.S. balance of payments controls cut back the market; U.S. corporations found it cheaper to fund domestically. The growth of today's market began with underwritten facilities. Underwritten note facilities began in 1978, with an issue by the New Zealand Shipping Corporation. But the instrument attracted little attention. None was issued in 1979, and the period from 1978 to 1983 saw a total of only 86 facilities representing U.S.$9 billion. In 1984, approximately $18 billion were issued, and, in the first 9 months of 1985, a total of $32 billion.

The revolving underwriting facility (RUF) and its siblings—the Note Issuance Facility (NIF), SNIF (Short-term NIF), and the like—typically consist of a medium-term commitment by the underwriting banks to buy notes issued by the borrower. The mechanism by which the paper is sold is typically the tender panel. A group of underwriting banks agrees to bid for the paper, or the borrower employs the services of a single bank or investment bank, as the sole placing agent, to place paper at a certain price.

There was then a tendency to develop facilities that gave the borrower several options in raising funds. These facilities were known as MOFFS (Multiple Option Funding Facilities) or GNFs (Global Note Facilities). Typically, they allowed the borrower to access the Euronote market, U.S. commercial paper, or bank lines, including a swing line, which is required by the U.S. rating agencies for any facility being used as a standby for U.S. commercial paper. (Part of the line must be available in the form of same-day funds.)

Another development was the TRUF (Transferable Revolving Underwriting Facility). An extension of RUF, TRUF contains documentation to allow underwriters to transfer their commitment to another bank, providing the borrower is satisfied that the quality of its backup does not suffer in the process. Thus, not merely is the lending transferable, but also the commitment to lend.

During the early development of the market, the emphasis was mainly on underwritten facilities. More recently, however, the emphasis has tended to shift toward issues that are not underwritten—true Euro-commercial paper. The reasons for this are partly the emphasis of central banks on capital ratios, and partly structural. Early underwritten facilities used the rather cumbersome device of the tender panel. (A number of the issues were for Australian entities, and, for Australian tax reasons, a tender panel was desirable.) However, many tender panel banks were not specialists in the placement of short-term securities, and the paper traded weakly as a result.

During the latter part of the 1980s, therefore, many borrowers switched to Euro-commercial paper programs. By 1990, an estimate by Moody's put the total outstanding at U.S.$70 billion (compared with U.S.$557 billion for the domestic U.S. commercial paper market at that time). During the early 1990s, however, the volumes outstanding in the Euro-commercial paper market tended to stagnate, mainly due to competition from domestic commercial paper markets and the rapidly growing medium-term notes market. The total reached only U.S.$87 billion by December 1995, although growth picked up again during 1996, according to BIS figures, and reached a total of $107 billion

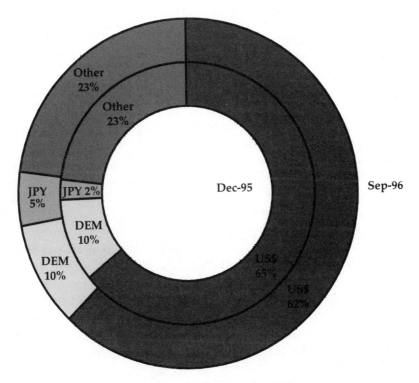

Figure 8.1 ECP currency breakdown.

by September 1996. Figure 8.1 shows the change in currency composition during 1996. Note the growth in the role of Japanese yen during the course of the year.

CREDIT ENHANCEMENT

An important aspect of securitization is credit enhancement. Many of the new securities have attractive features, yet they are unfamiliar to investors. To make them attractive, credit enhancement has been used to ensure that investors accept the paper. The first major wave of credit enhancement was in U.S. municipal markets. In 1980, the volume of new insured municipal issues was about $1.4 billion. By 1983, it had topped $12 billion and amounted to 15 percent of the market. The suppliers of credit enhancement have been: (1) the banks, which have provided letters of credit to support new issues, and liquidity lines for those issues; and (2) the insurance industry. A number of special-purpose insurance companies, such as American Bond Assurance Corporation (AMBAC) and Mortgage Bond Insurance Association (MBIA), were established in the early 1970s. Financial Guaranty Insurance Company (FGIC) was founded in 1982, and Bond Investors Guaranty in 1983. Financial

Security Assurance was formed in 1985 with the specific objective of writing "security insurance" on corporate financial instruments.

The major benefit of credit enhancement for the issuer is that it makes what is, perhaps, a complex transaction much simpler to sell. The investor has the comfort that, if for some reason the transaction falls apart, the investment can still be paid out by the insurance. The investor needs to be satisfied that (1) the guarantor has the financial ability to give protection, and (2) the guarantor's obligation in such an event is unconditional. Suppose these conditions are satisfied, and we had paper backed by an unconditional surety bond from an unquestioned insurance company with tough underwriting standards, or a letter of credit from a top-class bank with a good reputation for credit analysis. This creates an insured or guaranteed debt instrument that can be sold to other investors without their requiring updated financials or complex analysis of the underlying issue. This enhances liquidity of the issue and gives the investor comfort about being able to sell the paper if the need arises.

Other forms of external enhancements are: (1) corporate guarantee; (2) letter of credit; and (3) pool insurance. A guarantee from another party, or a letter of credit from another party, may provide AAA backing at the time of issue. The danger is that the guarantor, or the issuer of the letter of credit, may later be downgraded. For example, in the early 1990s, mortgage-backed securities issued by Citibank Mortgage Securities Inc. were downgraded when Citibank, the guarantor, was downgraded.

Pool insurance policies cover losses resulting from defaults and foreclosures. Additional insurance must be purchased to cover losses resulting from bankruptcy, fraud, and various other hazards. Like the guarantee, any downgrading of the insurer would cause a problem.

Internal Credit Enhancement

The alternative to the above structures is internal credit enhancement, of which the most common forms are senior/subordinate structures and reserve funds. The senior/subordinated structure is by far the most widely used. The subordinate tranche acts as a cushion for the senior tranche, absorbing initial losses. As an example, if we had a $300 million issue, of which $275 million was senior and $25 million was subordinated, any losses would be absorbed by the owners of the subordinated tranche, up to the amount of $25 million.

Reserve funds come in two forms: (1) cash reserve funds and (2) excess servicing spread accounts. The former are deposits of cash arising from issue proceeds. When the issue is paid, some of the cash is set aside. These funds are often used alongside letters of credit or other external enhancements. A security might have 7 percent credit support, of which 6 percent is from a letter of credit and 1 percent from a cash reserve fund. Excess servicing spread accounts are used to accumulate any surplus left each month after all expenses have been paid. The amount in the reserve account will, therefore, gradually increase if all goes well.

Cash Flow versus Market Value Structures

Generally speaking, structured finance securitizations may be of two kinds: (1) cash flow structures or (2) market-value structures. In a cash flow structure, some or all of the cash flows from the assets supporting the structure are dedicated to repayment of principal and interest. Figure 8.2 illustrates the process of creating a cash flow structure. In Step 1, the originator creates the underlying assets. In Step 2, the originator creates the transaction structure by setting up a separate legal entity that will be the issuer. The issuer may be a special-purpose vehicle that issues debt, or a trust that represents investors' interests in the assets, or another entity. The cash flow from the loans (i.e., the collateral) will be used to make interest and principal payments to investors. Credit enhancements, either internal or external, may also be included.

In Step 3, shown in Figure 8.3, investors buy the securities by making a one-time payment to the issuer, who transfers the proceeds to the originator as a one-time payment for the assets. In Step 4, payments on the underlying collateral are the main source of cash to pay principal and interest. Borrowers continue to make periodic payments to the servicer, and those payments are passed through to investors. If the cash flow from the collateral is insufficient, then the credit supports may be drawn on.

By contrast, in market value structures, the liquidation value of the assets is used to support the security. To make this protection work, the structure requires that if investors are not paid on schedule, or if some other "trigger event" occurs (for example, if the market value of the collateral falls below a specified level), then the collateral is sold in the secondary markets. Investors receive repayment from the proceeds.

There are three basic types of market value structures. In one structure, debt is backed by assets that are pledged to a trustee for the benefit of investors. In another structure, the assets are sold to a special-purpose vehicle and then pledged as collateral for debt or preferred stock. In a third structure, debt or preferred stock is issued by an income (mutual) fund and the investors have a claim on all the assets of the fund.

Future-Flow Structures and Other Variants

In July 1996, the Mexican Province of Mendoza issued a $150 million fixed rate note collateralized by oil royalty payments made by six oil companies to the province. The final maturity of the bonds was 6 years, but, with quarterly amortization of principal and interest, the average life was 3 years. The royalty payments are diverted to a trust that will pay out the note holders. The trust is overcollateralized to the tune of 1.2 times the note issue.

This structure was one of a class sometimes referred to as "future flow" financings. Asset-backed transactions involve repackaging existing portfolios of assets. Future flow deals involved the payment, over a fixed period, of income flows into a trust. The future receivables are generally sold to the trust, which

Step 1: Loan Origination & Servicing

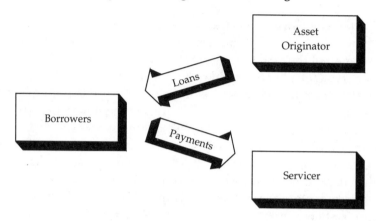

An asset originator makes loans to borrowers, who make payments to a servicer (which may be part of the same organization).

Step 2: Adding the Transaction Structure

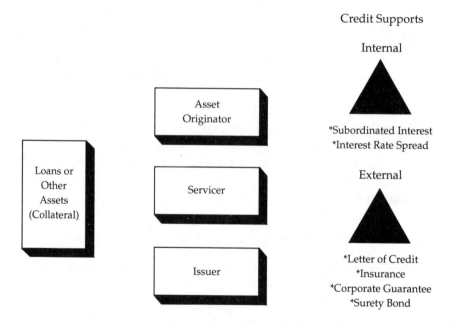

The originator sets up a separate legal entity, the issuer. It may use internal or external sources of credit enhancement in structuring the deal.

Source: Credit Analysis of Structured Securities, Moody's Investor Services, 1991.

Figure 8.2   Creating the securitization.

Step 3: The Securities Are Sold

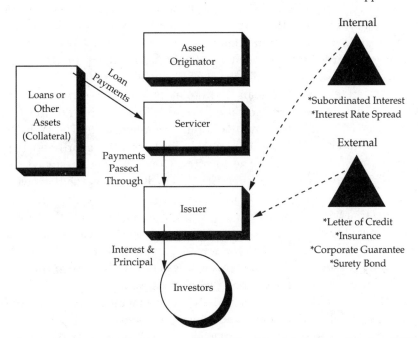

Step 4: The Transaction's Cash Flows over Time

Source: Credit Analysis of Structured Securities, Moody's Investor Services, 1991.

Figure 8.3   The life of the securitization.

issues the bonds or notes and repays principal and interest. Any surplus is returned to the issuer. By having the trust offshore, the structure allows investors to circumvent some of the sovereign risks (convertibility or transfer risk) typically attached to emerging markets investment.The first such structure was developed by Telmex in 1987, when it sold telephone receivables via an offshore trust.

An interesting and unusual credit support mechanism was put in place by the Federal Reserve Bank of New York, in July 1996, for the issue of a floating rate note by Mexico. The rating granted to Mexico by Moody's was Ba2. Normally, no issuer can be granted a credit rating higher than the one granted to the country itself. Moody's rating takes account of the transfer risk of foreign currency: the risk that Mexico might not have available sufficient foreign exchange to redeem the issue. In this example, the transfer risk was reduced by the diversion, on a daily basis, of payments owed to Mexico directly to the Federal Reserve Bank of New York. Specifically, purchasers of Pemex oil exports were obliged to pay directly to Swiss Bank Corporation in New York, and SBC remitted the funds daily to the Federal Reserve Bank of New York. As a result, the Mexican floating rate note achieved a Moody's rating of Baa3, higher than the rating accorded to the sovereign issuer itself.

A not dissimilar structure used by Calvin Klein Inc., in 1993, involved a securitization that also entailed business risk. The borrower was in financial difficulty, and a bridge loan was needed. The solution was to create a special-purpose vehicle, Ivory Trust. The special-purpose vehicle borrowed $58 million from Citibank. It invested the proceeds in $58 million of senior secured notes issued by Calvin Klein. Calvin Klein assigned to the trust royalties arising from a license agreement between itself and a subsidiary of Unilever. The lender takes the business risk that the flow of royalties might dry up.

An interesting hybrid of loan trading, asset-backed finance, and capital market-style auctions was the so-called Dated Widely Active Royalty Financing Structure (DWARFS) totaling JPY73 billion launched for The Walt Disney Company in March 1997. This transferable loan facility securitized the revenues from Tokyo Disneyland. The royalties from this were assigned to TDL Funding (Cayman), a special purpose trust, which acted as the borrower. The loan margin on the transaction was 30 basis points for the first three years, stepping up to a back-stop margin of 60 bp for years 4–7 and 90 bp for years 8–11. However, these are back-stop margins because in year 4 and again in year 8 the loans are auctioned to the lowest bidder (in terms of margin). The structure was chosen because the borrower was not willing to go through the extra disclosure required for the bond market rating agencies, but the 11-year tenor would not readily have been available in the Japanese loan market. It remains to be seen whether investors purchasing the loans acquire the nickname of Dopey or Grumpy, but no doubt Disney would argue that the credit was Snow White.

Chapter **9**

New Types of Bonds

As an instrument, the classic bond can hardly be described as new. Its origin can be traced back to at least the 16th century. But in the global bond markets in recent years we have seen a wide variety of changes to the classic form. Typically these are intended to create hybrids, and as such inevitably cause problems for a book author seeking to put them into neat categories. Many of these are discussed later in Chapter 12, "Structured Notes." Others, notably equity-linked bonds, are covered in Chapter 15, "Convertibles and Warrants," and Chapter 16, "Equity Derivatives." In this chapter, we look at developments in floating rate notes, at zero coupons, and at perpetual bonds. We also cover coupon variants.

FLOATING RATE NOTES

The growth of floating rate securities has been one of the main features of the debt markets in the past two decades. During the early part of this period, the growth was partly due to the high level of prevailing rates. Issuers were reluctant to contemplate locking into high rates for the lifetime of their issue. In addition, investors have become more familiar with the instruments.

The oldest instrument of this class is the floating rate note (FRN). Floaters have traditionally been in heavy demand among investors in times of volatile interest rates. Their principal value is stable compared to bonds. The first FRN was issued in the Euromarket in 1970; the first domestic U.S. FRN was issued by Citibank in 1974.

The Eurodollar FRN market has been sizable for many years, but its most rapid growth took place in the late 1970s and early 1980s, when the liquidity of the FRN market attracted banks to lend via FRNs rather than through syndicated credits. If they had to lend at unrealistic spreads, the reasoning was, it might as well be on a tradable asset. By the mid-1980s, though, the FRN market had come under pressure from two competing sources of funds: (1) the Euro-commercial paper (discussed in Chapter 8) and (2) swap-driven bond issuance (discussed in Chapter 5), which often raised funds at 50 to 60 basis points below LIBOR, while the FRN market provided funds at a spread over LIBOR.

The logical response was for the FRN market to move away from LIBOR toward LIMEAN (the average of LIBOR and the bid rate, LIBID) and even toward LIBID. By 1986, a prime sovereign credit such as the United Kingdom could offer its FRNs at LIBID – 10 basis points and still be eagerly sought after.

A corollary point is that the FRN market has proved itself capable of handling huge issues. The U.K. issue of $4 billion, which was easily absorbed despite the pricing, showed this capability. Such FRNs have great liquidity, and the trading attractions of the instrument have compensated for its intrinsically low yield. However, other issues, which were never likely to be so tradable, were also brought to the market at low spreads, leading to considerable indigestion. The climax came with a bloodbath in the perpetuals market (see below).

For investors, the most attractive feature of the FRN (at least, the FRN with a fixed maturity) is the fact that an FRN normally reprices to par every 6 months (or whenever the coupon is set). Hence, there is reasonable certainty of principal, coupled with protection against rising rates. Each FRN has distinctive trading characteristics. They can be attributed to factors such as: differences in coupon spread versus LIBOR; maturity dates; and frequency of coupon refix dates. Longer-term FRNs are a relatively less liquid market (because banks, which are major traders and investors in FRNs, tend to concentrate on shorter maturities for reasons of prudence). Hence, these FRNs, as a class, tend to be more volatile. The coupon refixing effect means that FRNs that refix quarterly tend to be more akin to true money market instruments, with little price volatility; semiannual coupon FRNs tend to be more volatile.

A number of valuation methods are in use; the formulas involved are set out in, among other books listed in the Bibliography, P. J. Brown, "Formulae for Yield and Other Calculations" (London: ISMA, 1992).

DIFFERENT FRN INDEXES

Table 9.1 shows some of the floating rate indexes that have been used for Eurodollar FRNs. The "plain-vanilla" FRN has given rise to innumerable variations. In the Euromarkets, LIBOR (London Interbank Offered Rate) has generally been the preferred index. In the U.S. domestic market before 1984, many FRNs were issued at a spread over 3- or 6-month Treasury bills, generally with a weekly reset of the rate. In 1984, there was a swing toward LIBOR as the basis index. As a trade-off, issuers tended to remove put options. These had allowed holders of the early Treasury-based floaters to put the notes back to their issuers at 6-month intervals. The put cushioned the risk of principal loss. More recently, as discussed in Chapter 12, there has been a wide range of indexes, in both the domestic and the European markets. But the classic FRN, in the international markets at least, still uses 6-month LIBOR as its basis.

Table 9.1   Some Types of Floating Rate Index

LIBOR (London Interbank Offered Rate): 1-, 3-, or 6-month LIBOR.

LIMEAN (average of LIBOR and LIBID).

LIBID (London Interbank Bid Rate).

6-month LIBOR reset monthly ("mismatch formula").

Lower of .xxx percent of 1-month LIBOR or .yyy percent over 6-month LIBOR.

.xxx percent over 3-month LIBID; maximum Z% ("capped").

91-day Treasury bill rate.

Step-up/step-down structures.

Rate fixed every 49 days by Dutch auction.

TMP, FIBOR, and other domestic rates in various countries + a wide range of "exotic" structures discussed in Chapter 12.

In addition to the choice of rate—LIBOR or U.S. Treasury bills are the most common—there have been many variations on the rate-setting method. LIBOR floaters originally reset every 3 months if paying 3-month LIBOR, and every 6 months if paying 6-month LIBOR.

Another index formula that has been adopted is the variable-spread formula. The variable spread FRN was first introduced in December 1984, for the Nordic Investment Bank (NIB), which aimed to diversify its funding sources by borrowing in New York at a rate linked to the U.S. Treasury bill rate. But if Treasury bill rates fall relative to LIBOR, a T-bill-based FRN is liable to weaken in price relative to other FRNs. Hence, under the formula adopted, the rate was to be fixed quarterly at a spread over the Treasury bill. The spread is itself fixed by taking 55 percent of the differential between LIBOR and Treasury bills, with a minimum of 35 basis points. This was combined with a 3-month put option for the investor, to attract traditional buyers of short-term paper in the U.S. market.

Perpetuals

In March 1980, Citicorp introduced the "puttable perpetual" FRN, an issue that had no set redemption date. But it could be redeemed at the option of the noteholder on interest fixing dates semiannually, after a period of 2½ years. Because the IRS regards perpetual debt as equity from the point of view of disallowing interest deductions on perpetuals, U.S. entities have issued only puttable perpetuals and related variants, not true perpetuals. Fixed-rate perpetuals are discussed separately below.

The first true perpetual FRN was introduced by National Westminster Bank with a $300 million issue in April 1984. The notes are not redeemable by the noteholders but bear an attractive ⅜ percent margin over LIBOR. The notes are junior subordinated debt, rated after outstanding debt but before common or preferred stock. Because of Bank of England requirements, subsequent issues of perpetuals by U.K. clearing banks had to be convertible into equity under certain circumstances in order to qualify for primary capital. They represent, however, an attractive method of raising primary capital without diluting the banks' equity base, and so all the major U.K. banks have made one or more issues of perpetual FRNs.

The arrival of the perpetual was followed by the introduction of the "flip-flop," a note that allowed the investor to "flip" out of the perpetual into a shorter-term note and then "flop" back in again. The concept was introduced in June 1984, for the Kingdom of Sweden FRN. A subsequent issue was the $500 million World Bank issue in February 1985, which was the first flip-flop Treasury-bill-based perpetual FRN. It pays the 3-month U.S. Treasury bill rate + 50 basis points. Every 3 months, the investor has the option of converting into a 3-month note with a flat 3-month Treasury bill yield. At maturity of the note, the investor can switch back into the perpetual if desired.

This technique has been used on several occasions, particularly after the 1986 panic in the perpetual market (see below). For example, in March 1989, the R&I Bank of Western Australia issued US$300 million of exchangeable floating rate notes. On any coupon date from 1994 onward, these were exchangeable into an equal amount of 5-year floating rate notes. Conversely, the investor could switch back into the perpetual during the first 4 years of the dated floating rate note's life.

Most perpetual issuers have been banks, which used the funds as a source of primary capital. As mentioned earlier, U.S. banks have been restrained by tax considerations except when the perpetual incorporates an investor put option, but for U.K., Australian, and Canadian banks, perpetuals have been an important source of capital. Nonbank issuers have been rare, in view of the credit quality consideration implicit in a perpetual issue.

One nonbank issuer has been Hydro Quebec, for the interesting reasons that: (1) a perpetual allows it to strengthen its balance sheet without recourse to its state shareholder, and (2) because a perpetual carries no repayment obligation, a foreign currency issue entails no foreign exchange risk on the borrowing (apart from interest payments). (Compare the FIPS issue discussed below.) Similar thinking probably lay behind the ECU125 million issue by Saint-Gobain, the nationalized French company, in April 1985.

Puttable perpetuals and flip-flops offer a major advantage: They have a possible maturity date. The importance of this became vividly apparent during the course of a crisis in the perpetual FRN market in late 1986. At that time, the appearance of some richly priced collateralized FRNs (see below) yielding LIBOR + 50 basis points or more led investors to question why they were holding perpetuals at LIBOR + ⅛ percent. The resulting panic saw at least one U.K. clearing bank perpetual drop to 86, an enormous fall for an FRN. There was no question regarding the quality of the issuer, but trading in the whole perpetual market effectively closed down for a period. The initial excess paper was gradually absorbed over time by a number of ingenious repackagings (see Chapter 11).

Another crisis hit the perpetual market in 1990–1991, during the period when serious pressure was placed on American bank balance sheets. For example, in December 1986, Citibank issued $500 million of subordinated perpetual floating rate notes. By January 1991, these had traded down to 62.5 bid, 65.5 offered. By January 1997, they had returned to more reasonable levels: 96.25 bid, 97.13 offered.

Variable Rate Notes

The first attempt to reopen the perpetual market after the debacle in 1986 was the introduction of variable rate notes (VRNs) in 1988. Whereas traditional FRNs paid a coupon in the form of a fixed spread over LIBOR, the VRN reset both the LIBOR and the spread regularly. When the note is first issued, the initial margin over LIBOR for the first interest payment period is set by the remarketing underwriter after consultation with the issuer. The remarketing underwriter is then responsible for marketing and placing these notes with investors. Seven business days prior to each interest payment date, the remarketing underwriter sets a new agreed-on margin over LIBOR for the next interest period. The issuer's agreement is obtained before the margin is reset.

If the remarketing underwriter and the issuer fail to reach agreement on the appropriate refix margin, then the margin will be automatically set at the maximum margin previously agreed to by the issuer and the remarketing underwriter. Failure to reach an agreement can be potentially costly to the issuer because the maximum margin is usually punitive. From the investor's viewpoint, however, this situation is the most problematic, because, under those circumstances, the VRN structure requires the investor to continue holding the paper. In other words, the ability to sell the paper back to the remarketing agent disappears just when it is most likely to be required. This feature has tended to make the growth of the VRN market rather limited.

Step-Up/Step-Down

The perpetual market reopened gradually, in a rather restricted form. No one was prepared to go for the pure perpetual concept, and some form of protection was typically needed. The general solution was to incorporate rising margins over LIBOR. For example, in September 1993, KOP, a Finnish bank, issued $150 million of perpetual FRNs, with a coupon that increased by 150 basis points (bp) after 5 years, giving the bank an economic incentive to call the issue and refinance.

A recent issue of perpetual floating rate notes is typical of the current structure generally used. Banque Nationale de Paris (BNP) issued, in October

1996, $150 million of undated floating rate notes bearing a coupon of LIBOR + 62.5 bp to November 2006. Thereafter, the coupon rises to LIBOR + 2.125 percent. The issuer has every incentive to call the issue for early redemption in 2006. Hence, investors assessed the paper as having a 10-year maturity. But, because the issue is undated, it qualifies as upper tier 2 capital under the Basle committee rules for banking capital, and so is useful to the issuer. In the sterling market, the first issue of this type was the £150 million subordinated perpetual step-up note issued by the Royal Bank of Scotland in March 1997. This pays 3-month LIBOR + 50 bp up to year 10, and LIBOR + 150 bp thereafter.

The Royal Bank of Scotland deal, in comparison with the BNP deal, illustrates that the size of the step-up permitted by regulators varies from country to country. The maximum step-up in the United Kingdom is 100 bp; in France, it is 150 bp. The Spanish rules allow a step-up of only 50 bp, and the Norwegian rules, 75 bp. Clearly there is a trade-off between the size of the step-up and the likelihood that the issue will be a genuine perpetual. If the BNP step-up had been, say, 700 bp, the deal would unambiguously have been a disguised 10-year issue; if it had been 7 bp, it would unambiguously have been a true perpetual.

Other FRN Structures: Partly Paids; Income Rights

In June 1985, the first partly paid FRN was issued, with a $600 million issue for Banque Nationale de Paris. Of the total, only $100 million was drawn. These notes were offered through a conventional FRN syndication to an authorized list of 250 participating banks. The notes were registered and tradable, but only among the 250 banks authorized to underwrite the issue.

The underwriters were committed to subscribe to any amount of the remaining $500 million that the borrower might issue, in bearer form, during the 10-year life of the deal.

But that obligation stands only if the participating bank holds any of the original $100 million issue. Because the FRNs are registered, BNP can identify who is holding them. The structure created for BNP a committed back-up issue facility that is, at the same time, tradable. The underwriting commitment is therefore liquid.

A related concept was the cleverly named Securitized Note Commitment Facility (SNCF) for Société Nationale des Chemins de Fer (SNCF) in February 1986. This consisted of a $600 million facility. It had an initial 10 percent tranche of $60 million of FRNs with a 10-year maturity, yielding LIBOR + ¼ percent. Investors taking on the FRN also took on a commitment to the remaining 90 percent of the facility. That consisted of up to $540 million of 3-month Euronotes at LIBOR + ⅛ percent in tranches of $60 million. That is, the investors committed to buy, during the facility's lifetime, on one week's notice, 3-month Euronotes up to their maximum commitment (nine times their

FRN holding). Like the whole area of underwritten facilities, structures of this type have increasingly been hit by capital adequacy requirements.

Another innovation in the FRN market was the income rights package of November 1984, for the Kingdom of Sweden FRN. The Swedish debt office wanted to attract a broad range of investors, but found Japanese buyers deterred by its LIBID pricing. Thus, a sweetener was added: income rights. A total of 70,000 income rights were offered, at $70 each. Applications for them had to be related to bids for the FRN. The rights entitled the holder to receive a payment of a $3/16$ percent annual income on a notional principal sum of $10,000. Adding this to the LIBID earned on the FRN produced an apparent income of LIBOR + $1/16$ percent, and investors were attracted.

A related concept, floor certificates, is discussed in Chapter 15.

Collateralized FRNs became a feature of the FRN market from mid-1984 to January 1986. Fourteen thrift institutions brought sixteen deals to the Eurodollar market for a total of over $2 billion. In general, these issues were rated AAA by the rating agencies, because of the degree of collateralization. An example of this type of issue is the $500 million issue by Prudential Insurance Company of America in November 1986. It paid 0.45 percent over 1-month LIBOR, with an 11½ percent cap. It was collateralized by a GNMA CMO. Its stated maturity was 29 years, based on the longest GNMA mortgage, but its expected average life was 3.5 years, assuming a constant prepayment rate of 25 percent. Many collateralized FRNs have been issued as part of the asset-backed securities market. They are discussed further in Chapters 10 and 11.

Non-Dollar FRNs

Floating rate notes have been issued in a wide range of currencies: sterling, yen, French francs, Swiss francs, deutsche marks, ECU, Dutch guilders, and Hong Kong dollars are the more notable. Most of these have been Euro issues, or else they were placed domestically in the country of the currency. But there have been some non-dollar FRN issues in the United States. For example, in September 1985, Banque Nationale de Paris (BNP) issued an ECU 150 million 10-year LIBOR-based FRN in the domestic U.S. market. A feature of this deal was that the coupon is determined from US$ LIBOR, hedged into ECU using the spot and 3-month forward exchange rates, thereby circumventing the relatively illiquid ECU deposit market.

Currency-Convertible FRNs

FRNs have been issued that are convertible into other currencies. An example was the issue by Credit National of a 10-year US$150 million FRN in the New York market in November 1985. The floating rate was linked to the 91-day U.S. Treasury bill rate, but the holder could convert the FRN, on any interest payment date during the first 2 years, into ECU FRNs with the same coupon, payment dates, and maturity, at a fixed conversion rate. The issue was callable after 2 years at par, with no put options. The attraction to the investor was the currency gamble for the first 2 years; to Credit National, it was 10-year money with no put options and a call after 2 years.

Variable Rate Municipal Issues in the United States

A market that has produced some interesting features is the U.S. municipal variable rate market. Many of these instruments are merely structured notes repackaged for the tax-exempt market and given a proprietary acronym in a futile effort to distinguish them from competing products. They are discussed in Chapter 12 under structured notes. A more interesting area has been the rapid growth in variable rate financings. Typically, these have been achieved by the issue of long-term bonds yielding short-term rates, coupled with short-term puts for the investor. These are often referred to as variable rate demand notes (VRDNs).

The original reason for the development of the market was the sharply inverted yield curve of 1979–1981. Banks holding tax-exempt municipal securities were funding long-term low-yielding assets at very high short-term rates, so they were reluctant to continue buying municipal bonds. With the banks no longer being keen buyers, investment banks had to find a new market for the issues. The solution was to place the bonds with a new group of investors: the tax-exempt money market funds, which had just begun operations in 1979. These funds were under strict guidelines from the SEC to buy tax-exempt obligations with maturities of 1 year or less, and to keep the dollar-weighted maturities at under 120 days. The funds' problem was that not much paper was issued in the very short-term area. The solution was to devise a tax-exempt bond that allowed the investor to demand his or her money back within 7 days. The SEC was persuaded to accept that, in this case, the demand period could be considered the maturity of the security. Accordingly, a 30-year note could be considered as maturing in 7 days. The interest on the bond was thus a 7-day rate (usually expressed as, say, 50 percent of prime, or linked to a short-term index such as the J. J. Kenny index; others are linked to the Treasury bill rate).

The normal structure for such a deal might have a nominal maturity of 30 years, but with the interest rate payable fixed for, say, 7 days. From the issuer's point of view, the bonds are attractive: 30-year money at 7-day rates. The technique also ensures that any tax exemption that has been granted on the issue remains in place, because it is a 30-year issue. (Tax-exempt commercial paper issues, for example, run the danger that the tax exemption might disappear and leave the issuer unable to roll over the paper.)

The investor, on the other hand, has a liquid short-term investment that can be held for 30 years if so desired. The investor's position is normally protected by ensuring that a liquidity facility is in place. If so, a bank will provide a letter of credit stating that it will lend the issuer sufficient funds to buy back any bonds that are put. A remarketing agent (usually an investment bank) then re-sells the bonds at the going market rate. A second back-up arrangement is that a bank can provide a "liquidity line" on which the borrower can draw if the re-marketing agent is having difficulty placing the bonds.

Again, the interest on the bond is a 7-day rate (usually expressed as, say, 50 percent of prime, or linked to a short-term index such as the J. J. Kenny index; others are linked to the Treasury bill rate). In late 1983, the concept was refined further to a daily put—an example being the Salomon Brothers product, DATES (daily adjustable tax-exempt securities).

A further variant on this approach was developed in the early 1980s: the "mandatory tender." This allows the issuer of municipal bonds to require cur-rent bondholders to put back or tender bonds to the bond trustees and allow the bonds to be remarketed. This is in contrast to a call for redemption, which involves the repayment of the debt. The mandatory tender was used in situa-tions where the security on a bond issue was about to change, or the interest rate was about to be reset. For example, when a letter of credit backing the issue expired and was replaced by another letter of credit, the rating agencies required the mandatory tender.

A popular feature resembling mandatory tenders, introduced in 1992, is called detachable call rights. Under this type of program, an issuer may sell separate call rights. These give an investor the right, on or after a certain date, to require mandatory tender of a certain bond for purchase at a specific price (e.g., 102 after 10 years, declining to par after 12 years). (On the basis that "if it walks like a duck and quacks like a duck it usually is a duck," these are actu-ally put options.)

A recent extension of the variable rate demand note (VRDN) market has been the growth of secondary derivatives aiming at creating VRDN-like struc-tures. The background has been a growth in demand for the underlying asset—tax-exempt U.S. money market funds' assets grew by 40 percent be-tween 1993–1996—while the supply of the assets has remained constant or di-minishing. To fill the gap, several investment banks have developed synthetic floating rate receipt programs. The maturity of a long-term bond is syntheti-cally shortened by adding a put feature. Adding the put feature allows the bond to be sold to a money market fund while meeting the requirements of the Investment Company Act Rule 2a-7 (which limits the overall maturity of the assets in the fund to 397 days or less).

Two of the most popular of these secondary market derivatives (estimated by Standard & Poor's to account for 78 percent of the secondary market deriva-tives rated by them) are tender option bonds (TOBs) and putable floating rate receipts. TOBs are variable-rate trust receipts created from fixed-rate bonds that have been deposited in a trust structure. They have many of the same characteristics as primary-market variable-rate bonds with put features.

Putable floating rate receipts combine the variable interest rate-setting mechanism and put feature of TOBs with the two-class structure of Dutch auction/inverse floater programs. The two classes of holders of these instruments are the floating rate holder and the inverse or residual holder. Only the floating rate receipts have put options and, therefore, are money market fund eligible. Although the inverse or Dutch auction floater receipts are not eligible for investment by money market funds, they appeal to corporations, insurance companies, and other institutional investors.

Forward Issuance of Municipal Securities

In 1989, a hybrid municipal security was introduced: Refunding Escrow Deposits (REDs). This product involved a municipal entity issuing a taxable security and entering a forward agreement to issue tax-exempt bonds. The tax-exempt bonds have specified coupon, maturity, and interest payment dates, and call provisions, and are to be delivered on the forward delivery date. The taxable security pays interest at a predetermined rate until it matures on the forward delivery date. At that time, the investor in the REDs receives the tax-exempt bonds. The product was designed to achieve advance refunding for certain bonds that could not otherwise be refunded in advance on a tax-exempt basis.

An alternative approach was adopted with municipal forwards. These are long-term contracts committing an investor to buy a tax-exempt bond for future delivery on the forward delivery date. The coupon, maturity, and interest payment dates, and the redemption provisions, are included in the contract. The main difference between this product and the previous one is that here we have no interim taxable investment. However, many of these transactions require the investor to enter into an escrow agreement and deposit with a custodian cash or securities as collateral, to ensure that the investor will carry out the commitment to buy the tax-exempt notes on the forward delivery date.

ZERO-COUPON BONDS

Zero-coupon bonds were treated as a curiosity by Homer and Leibowitz in their classic *Inside the Yield Book* (Prentice-Hall, New Jersey, 1972). In fact, one or two issues were made on a zero-coupon basis in the 1960s in the U.S. municipal bond market, for small issues by Michigan, Minnesota, and certain other states; and in the Euromarket for BP Tanker-Eriksberg in June 1966. But, for all practical purposes, the zero-coupon market began in 1980 with some private placements, followed by the first public issue in April 1981, by J. C. Penney (it had been preceded, in March 1981, by Martin Marietta with the first deep discount bond). Like interest rate swaps, zero-coupon bonds were treated at first as a curiosity that would soon disappear. If not, why had they not been used before?

The answer as far as zero coupons is concerned probably lies in a combination of two factors: (1) the historically high levels of interest rates in 1980–1981, and (2) the realization of certain tax advantages for zero-coupon issuers. The high rates of 1980–1981 meant that zero-coupon bonds were attractive to the investor. For the investor, the zero coupon has two key attractions. First, it locks in the reinvestment rate on the investment. As is well known, the conventional yield-to-maturity measure on a bond is not strictly accurate. It assumes that interim coupon payments can be reinvested at that same yield to maturity. Because a zero coupon has only one cash flow, at maturity, reinvestment risk does not arise. This is particularly so because, for all practical purposes, a zero-coupon bond is fully protected against early call.

Second, because the zero coupon has only one cash flow, at maturity, its duration is equal to its maturity (see Chapter 3 for a discussion of duration). Its duration is always longer than that of a conventional bond of comparable maturity. Therefore, a zero coupon is much more volatile. When rates fall, this makes it a very attractive investment. Indeed, in the first 12 months after the start of the zero-coupon market, gains of up to 40 percent were seen at the long end. An investor in long-term zeros would have earned a total compound rate of return in 1983–1986 of nearly 200 percent.

These factors made zero coupons attractive to investors. Issuers were able to make pretax savings ranging from 50 to 150 basis points. Another inducement to the growth of the zero-coupon market was a temporary tax benefit. Until July 1982, the U.S. tax authorities permitted straight-line amortization of the original issue discounts. This acceleration of the tax deductions of the issuer made zero coupons attractive financing instruments.

Probably the major influence in getting the zero-coupon market off the ground, however, was the very high level of interest rates during 1980–1981. The saving to the issuer is very small with a 5 percent coupon, but grows exponentially, becoming sizable above 10 percent. In the 15–16 percent environment of 1981, the savings were quite large.

The original reason for the development of the zero-coupon market lay in special tax advantages. These still persist in a number of cases, but there is a more basic advantage to zero coupons. They add investment value. First, they cut out reinvestment risk. Second, they give investors direct access to the zero curve, discussed in Chapter 3.

Extensions of the Zero Concept

The next major step in the development of the zero-coupon market was the introduction by several investment banks of "receipts" products. These include the TIGR (Treasury Investment Growth Receipt) and CATS (Certificates of Accrual on Treasury Securities). Several such securities were introduced in

August 1982. Probably the most widely traded were the CATS. From a par amount of $2.51 billion at the end of December 1982, the market grew to $10.54 billion at the end of 1983, and to $44.6 billion at the end of 1984.

The method by which these receipt securities are created is that the investment bank involved will purchase an amount—say, $100 million—of, say, 10-year Treasury bonds. The securities are held by a custodian bank. The investment bank then issues a receipt, such as the CATS, which evidences ownership of the serially maturing interest payments and principal payments on the Treasury bonds. Suppose, for example, that the coupon on the bonds is 10 percent. Then an amount of $5 million is payable semiannually on the bonds. Thus, the investment bank would sell a total of 20 sets of certificates for $5 million each, maturing in 6 months, 1 year, 18 months, 2 years, and so on. In addition, $100 million of receipts would be sold evidencing ownership of the principal. By this means, the ownership of principal and interest could be separated.

These were followed by the introduction of Separate Trading of Registered Interest and Principal of Securities (STRIPS) in February 1985. Under this system, selected Treasury securities are held in the book entry system operated by the Federal Reserve in a way that allows separate trading and ownership of the interest and principal payments.

The amount of coupon-bearing bonds necessary to obtain $1,000 units of STRIPS depends on a coupon on the bond; a bond whose coupon is quoted in eighths of a percentage point needs much larger amounts, because one has to pay the 8 percent in round thousands also. Thus, at a 10 percent coupon rate, bonds must be stripped in multiples of $20,000; bonds with a coupon of 11.25 percent must be stripped in multiples of $160,000, and those with an 11.625 percent coupon must be stripped in multiples of $1.6 million.

The rationale behind STRIPS was that, in 1984, the Treasury noted that the zero-coupon "receipt" securities were becoming so popular that the demand for Treasury bonds had increased. It was decided that if the Treasury officially sponsored its own product, debt service costs might be reduced even further. The innovation proved successful, and has been adapted to the French, the U.K., and now even the German government bond market.

Variants on the Zero Coupon

In March 1985, Utah Associated Municipal Power Systems issued GAINS (Growth and Income Securities). This was a hybrid zero coupon, convertible to a conventional coupon. For an initial price of $1,668.50, the GAINS investor bought a zero that appreciated to a par of $5,000 in 11 years—an implicit internal rate of 10 percent compounded semiannually. At that point, the zero converted to a straight bond, paying a 10 percent cash coupon on the full face amount until maturity in 2007. The issuer saved, compared with a typical level debt-service bond issue, by deferring interest payments on a significant portion of the whole issue. The issuer pays more principal back in the early years, when the interest rates are lower, and less principal later, when interest rates are higher.

In April 1985, the zero-coupon concept was taken a step further by LYONS (Liquid Yield Options Notes), with a $840 million issue by Waste Management of zero-coupon convertibles. The notes had an effective yield of 9 percent over their 16-year life, and an issue price of $250 per face value of $1,000. They were convertible into 4.3 shares of Waste Management common. The issue came shortly after a ruling by the Financial Accounting Standards Board (FASB) that zero-coupon convertibles should not be considered common stock equivalents unless their effective yields are less than two-thirds of yields on AA-rated bonds at the time of pricing. Prior to the ruling, all zero convertibles were considered common stock equivalents.

In May 1985, the zero-coupon technique was used ingeniously by BP, which borrowed $160 million through a dual issue of zero-coupon bonds and annuity notes, combining the cash flows to produce a synthetic current coupon bond. The zero-coupon component had an issue price of 38.55, which itself was partly paid—12.05 percent due in June, and 26.50 percent due in December 1985. The maturity date was June 20, 1995, and the issue amount was US$182.46 million. The annuity notes matured a year earlier, on June 20, 1994. The issue amount was $100 million, with a coupon of 10.5 percent (compared with 10.75 percent yield on the zero-coupon portion). The annuity notes were also partly paid so that the total payment in the first year was slightly lower.

The cash payments per $10,000 bond were as shown in Table 9.2.

By combining the zero coupon—and its rising outstanding liability—with the declining liability created by the sinking fund on the annuity bond, BP achieved a combined structure equivalent to a current coupon bond, which it then swapped into a floating rate of interest. But the attraction of structuring the deal in this way was to tap a perceived pool of demand at that time for zero-coupon notes. The total cost to BP is estimated at 20 basis points below

Table 9.2   BP Annuity + Zero

Year	US$ Interest	Sinking Fund	Total Annual Cash Flow
1	$630	$ 721	$1,351
2	974	797	1,771
3	891	880	1,771
4	798	973	1,771
5	696	1,075	1,771
6	583	1,188	1,771
7	458	1,313	1,771
8	320	1,451	1,771
9	168	1,603	1,771

Treasuries on the fixed total coupon. A large part of this saving was from the part payment feature. BP did not have to pay interest to investors on the portion not initially paid. It could fund the first 6 months more cheaply through the short-term market than the bond coupons, thus saving around 20 basis points per annum.

In December 1985, a similar technique was used by the World Bank. This was a three-part deal. It consisted of a $200 million 15-year Eurobond maturing in 2000, together with a 30-year serial zero-coupon bond. The serial zero repaid in annual tranches starting in 2001. The third part was the purchase by the World Bank of stripped U.S. Treasury bonds with a face value of $200 million, to be used to repay the Eurobond at maturity. The arrangement resulted in a steady annual flow of payments to the investor, mimicking the interest payments on a conventional bond. After the Eurobond matures, the serial zero redemption amounts produce about $20 million per annum for the remaining 15 years. The use of the $200 million stripped Treasuries eliminated the need for the World Bank to provide for a large interim redemption amount; and the combined structure produced a 40-basis-point saving for the bank.

Zero-Coupon Issues in Other Currencies

It was inevitable that the zero-coupon concept, once it had been proved viable in the United States, would spread to other countries. But the extent to which the concept was able to travel was much affected by tax questions. Different countries treated the discount element of a zero-coupon issue in different ways. As mentioned earlier, the Japanese investor benefited from a very favorable treatment. Another aspect, perhaps not widely touched upon, is that the zero-coupon bond presents certain advantages to those who do not wish to draw attention to their income. Unlike the normal bearer Eurobond, with its coupon-clipping, the investor makes a single payment and receives back a single payment, without having to handle intervening income.

Zero coupons have now been offered in a range of currencies: sterling, deutsche marks, Australian dollars, Luxembourg francs, and Danish Krona, among others. The sterling zero coupons were christened ZEBRAS—Zero-coupon Euro sterling Bearer or Registered Accruing Securities—and were backed by gilt-edged stocks maturing between 1992 and 1996. The gilt-edged stocks were held by a Dutch company (for tax reasons), which issues the zero-coupon bonds. The issue proceeds totaled £94.295 million, and the redemption amounts totaled £193.24 million. However, U.K. tax treatment for investors in zero coupons was not favorable, until a change of heart by the authorities in the mid-1990s. As of the time of writing, an officially sponsored gilt strips market is expected to develop in the last quarter of 1997.

In February 1986, a DM1.4 billion, 30-year issue was brought for the Bundespost. A trust formed in the Channel Islands, Euro DM Securities Limited, issued a zero coupon and then bought DM1.4 billion of Schuldschein from the

Bundespost to match its liabilities under the issue. The structure enabled the German government agency to do a zero-coupon issue without encountering the political resistance in the domestic markets that a direct zero-coupon issue would have entailed at that time.

A similar deal was the March 1986 issue by Euro-DM Securities Limited. It issued DM1,056.2 million face amount of bonds, to raise proceeds of DM230.09 million of 15-, 20-, and 30-year zero coupons. The offering was collateralized by Schuldschein Loans of the Bundesbahn with payment exactly matching the maturities of the bonds. This reduced the total costs for the Bundesbahn to well below those on standard "Schuldschein."

In March 1987, Deutsche Bank brought to the Euromarket an annuity bond for BMW Finanz NV. It consisted of five separate issues, A through E. They carry no coupons but have effective yields ranging from $6\frac{1}{4}$ to $7\frac{1}{4}$ percent. The A tranche matured in 1992 and was repaid in five equal installments over the next 5 years; the B tranche matures in 1997 with five repayments, the C tranche in 2002, and so on. This is the first German deal to combine the zero-coupon structure with the sinking fund effect of an annuity bond.

Finally, another use of the zero-coupon markets should be noted: they have often been used to provide collateral with an exact match of maturity dates for some other security. For example, in March 1986, Continental (Bermuda) Limited—a subsidiary of Continental Industries, a Vienna company specializing in East–West trade—issued $250 million of floating rate notes backed by $250 million face value of U.S. Treasury zero-coupon obligations, together with a reserve fund invested in short-term US$ securities, and backed further by a guarantee from the Hungarian Foreign Trade Bank Limited. The technique is also at the foundation of the Brady bond market (discussed below).

MEDIUM-TERM NOTES

Medium-term notes (MTNs), in themselves, are not particularly innovative. They are perfectly ordinary, classical fixed-rate corporate bonds. The major innovation lies in their relatively short maturity, and, more importantly, in the fact that they are generally offered on a continuous basis. Using a continuously offered medium-term note program, a corporation can sell individual notes on a continuous basis in relatively small amounts, typically $2 million to $5 million. In effect, MTN programs resemble commercial paper programs. They extend commercial paper issuing techniques from the maximum CP maturity of 270 days; they run from 9 months to 10 years. One difference is that MTN issuers do not usually have lines of credit or other outside backing for their issues—a common occurrence in the commercial paper market.

Traditionally, the issuing process was that MTNs were generally sold on a best-efforts basis through dealers acting as agents on the issuer's behalf. The major issuers posted rates and offered notes over a range of established maturities—typically, 9 months to 1 year, 1 year to 18 months, 18 months to 2 years, and so on. Within any maturity range, however, the investor has the option of choosing the final maturity of each note. The rate scale is set at a spread over comparable-maturity Treasuries, and is adjusted in response to the issuer's needs and general market conditions.

In recent years, particularly in the Euromarket, there has been a trend toward underwritten issuance of MTNs. Increasingly, the MTN market is beginning to look like the traditional bond market, and indeed many participants see them as blending together.

The market was effectively created by GMAC in 1972. In its early years, it was dominated by the finance subsidiaries of the automobile makers, but in the late 1980s and early 1990s, huge programs were set up by FNMA and FHLMC. In the early years, a major problem was the insistence of the SEC that it approve any amendment to all corporate bond registration statements. This resulted in GMAC having to "put someone on a plane every time we changed our rates." The arrival of Rule 415 in 1982 provided a substantial help to the market. A second major catalyst was the appointment of Merrill Lynch and Salomon Brothers as agents for GMAC's MTN program in 1983. Their commitment to developing secondary market liquidity encouraged investors, which in turn encouraged new issuers. In 1985, GMAC made two huge deals, one for $3 billion in April, and one for $5 billion in December. A second sign of the growing importance of the market was the entry of the World Bank, with a $500 million program, in April 1986, of Continuously Offered Longer-Term Securities (COLTS), which were made available in maturities of 3 to 30 years or longer. Thereafter, the market has developed steadily in the United States, and also in the Euromarkets, discussed next.

The Euro-MTN Market

In April 1986, the MTN market in Europe opened, with an issue by First Interstate of $150 million, and a program of $200 million for the Nordic Investment Bank. Initially, the chief concern of investors in the Euromarkets was liquidity. One approach to this problem was taken by Merrill Lynch in respect of a program for Electrolux. This structure, called multitranche tap notes, demanded that, for any one tranche, the borrower must issue at least $50 million of paper, after which a tap is operated up to a set amount. This means that there is always a core of paper to provide liquidity. The Electrolux bond was quoted live all day on a Reuters screen.

As investors became more convinced of the potential liquidity of MTNs, the market grew. By 1987, the first multicurrency program was launched by the Kingdom of Spain, issuing in US$ and ECU. Very quickly, the market saw as much interest in the ECU notes as in the US$ issuance, and this really triggered the growth of the Euro-MTN market. In 1990, the Bank of England allowed issuers who did not possess a banking license to issue sterling MTNs. In

July 1992, the Bundesbank deregulated the requirements for the issue of Euro-MTNs, and in 1993, the Japanese Ministry of Finance allowed Japanese companies to issue directly under MTN programs. This was swiftly followed by similar actions by the Swiss and the French authorities.

During the period from 1989 to 1993, an average of 60 programs per year were put in place, and documentation of the programs became so standardized that economies of scale began to be possible. The charts in Figures 9.1 through 9.3 illustrate the huge variety of structures (many of which are discussed in Chapters 12, 13, 15, and 16) that have been issued in the Euromarket, and their relative importance compared with "plain vanilla" issuance. They also illustrate the Japanese market's enthusiasm for weird and wonderful structures.

We can see from these figures that, despite the emphasis in market discussions (and, indeed, in this book) on specially structured MTNs, the vast majority continue to be "plain vanilla," without any special structural features.

In the charts, we can see that, among the less common variants, the Japanese market was most attracted to the range FRN, while the sterling market preferred the FX/structured category. (These categories were used by *Euromoney* in compiling the data, but will not always overlap with mine.)

In March 1996, the Euro-MTN market overtook in volume the domestic U.S. MTN market. In the 10 years from 1986 to 1996, one source *(Euromoney)* recorded 10,000 deals in 32 currencies from 500 issuers. By the same date, Euro-MTNs had grown to represent 45 percent of the international market in terms of new issuance.

One obstacle to the globalization of the market remains: the SEC. Global MTN programs do exist, but their cost and complexity are significant. SEC registration fees and disclosure requirements, and the associated legal costs, are enough to dissuade all but the most active issuers, such as the main U.S. agencies. As of the time of writing, active Euromarket issuers such as Abbey National still have separate programs for the United States and the Euromarkets.

To give a flavor of how international issuers use the MTN market, it may be helpful to discuss the tactics of one or two issuers. ASEA Brown Boveri (ABB) is a major and highly respected international borrower. In 1993, it launched an MTN program that was, in fact, specifically designed to broaden its issuing capability beyond the MTN market. Its "Programme for the Issuance of Debt Instruments" (PIDI) permits ABB to offer either conventional bonds or MTNs within a single framework. During 1993, it issued almost $500 million under the program; issues included a $100 million FRN, an ITL250 billion ($162 million) 10-year bond, and a C$150 million 10-year bond. In addition, it issued a range of small tranches in different currencies, such as a DEM30 million 2-year FRN and a JPY1 billion 6-year note.

Another issuer in the MTN market is Kaufhof, the German retailer. It launched, in 1993, a DEM500 million program, notable for meshing German and Euromarket practices. To accommodate the preferences of both domestic and international investors, its notes may be listed in London or Frankfurt and

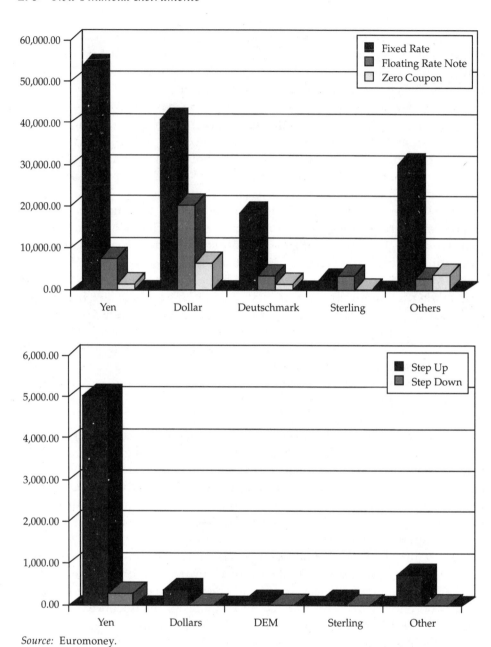

Source: Euromoney.

Figure 9.1 The "plain vanilla" EMTN market.

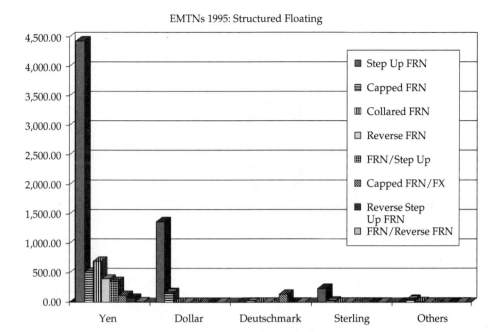

EMTNs 1995: Structured Floating

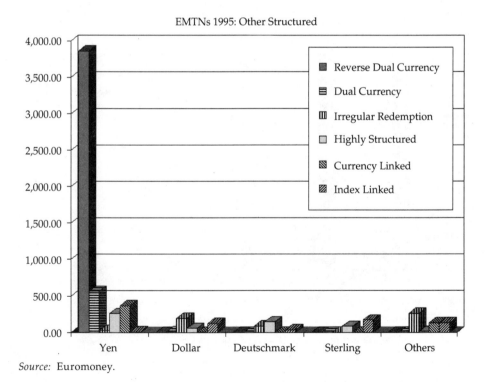

EMTNs 1995: Other Structured

Source: Euromoney.

Figure 9.2 Structured EMTNs 1.

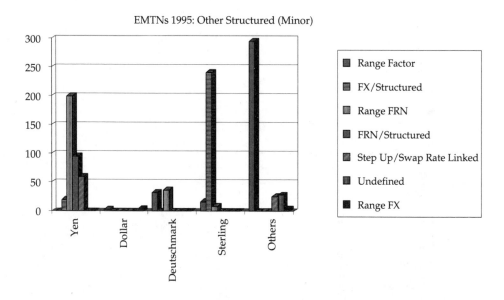

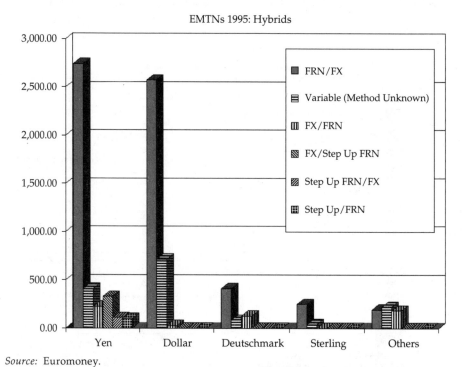

Source: Euromoney.

Figure 9.3   Structured EMTNs 2.

clear through either the Kassenverein or through Cedel and Euroclear. More-over, the program was the first multicurrency MTN program to use German law as its governing law.

Its flexibility means that the MTN market has become a major interna-tional source of funds. Indeed, the MTN market has increasingly begun to be seen as a substitute for the traditional bond markets. It is not unknown for an issuer to make an issue of MTNs in the amount of $100 million; similarly, it is not unknown for an issue of this size to be underwritten by an investment bank. Syndication of such issues also takes place from time to time. Indeed, the only true distinction between an MTN issue and a traditional bond issue is that the former will be done under MTN documentation, and the latter will take place using traditional bond-style documentation. A huge variety of issue structures have been developed in the market, many of which are discussed in Chapter 12.

Bank Deposit Notes

In the late 1980s, Bank Deposit Notes became a common feature of the domes-tic U.S. market. Essentially, these are equivalent to MTNs issued by banks. In practice, deposit notes are quite similar to certificates of deposit. Both are se-nior unsecured obligations of a bank and rank pari passu with deposits. The distinctions between the two are primarily technical, related to interest calcu-lations. The CD works on a money market basis; the deposit note, on a bond market convention. Certificates of deposit settle next day and calculate interest on an actual/360 basis. Deposit notes settle 3 business days later and calculate interest on a 30/360 basis. Typically, deposit notes have longer maturities—normally, 3 years or more.

PERPETUALS (FIXED RATE)

Like zero coupons, perpetuals were treated by Homer and Liebowitz as cu-riosities. They have a much longer history than zeros, however. Sir Henry Pelham arranged the first consolidation of British Government debt into irre-deemable bonds ("consols") in 1749. The subscribers to the foundation of the Bank of England in 1694 contributed £1.2 million of capital in exchange for a payment of £100,000 in perpetuity. But the use of undated debt (i.e., debt hav-ing no final maturity) in private finance is much more recent. As mentioned above, Citicorp introduced a "puttable" perpetual FRN in 1980; National West-minster created the first true perpetual FRN in April 1984.

The first undated fixed-rate bond issue by a nongovernment and nonbank entity was in January 1985, for KLM, the Dutch airline (majority owned by the Dutch Government). The issue, in Switzerland, was for CHF200 million ($75 million equivalent). It was subordinated, repriced every 10 years, and redeemable at KLM's option at any repricing date. The coupon is readjusted every 10 years on the basis of the arithmetical mean of Swiss Bank Corporation's index of the overall yield to maturity of foreign bonds on the Swiss Stock Exchange, and the new-issue foreign bond index (excluding States and Provinces) of Pictet and Cie, plus a margin of ⅛ percent, rounded if necessary to the nearest ⅛ percent. The rate for the first 10 years was 6⅛ percent, representing a premium of perhaps ¾ percent over the rate KLM might have paid for 10-year subordinated debt. The issue was oversubscribed and quickly traded up to a price of 102, largely because of KLM's excellent reputation in the Swiss market.

In January 1986, New Zealand Railways Corporation issued CHF150 million of undated bonds, with a coupon of 5¾ percent for the first 10 years. The maturity of the bond is described as "up to the liquidation of the company" or until the Government of New Zealand ceases to hold beneficially at least 51 percent of the capital of the company. The debt is senior debt. The issue is callable at the end of each 10-year period. The coupon resets like that on the KLM deal. Scandinavian Airlines issued CHF200 million on the same terms a few days later.

Also in January 1986, Air Canada issued a CHF300 million perpetual at 6¼ percent without 10-year repricing, thereby creating the first true fixed rate perpetual Eurobond. The coupon was ½ percent higher than the earlier undated issues from SAS and New Zealand Railways. In May, Austrian Airlines issued on similar terms.

EMBEDDED CALL AND PUT OPTIONS

Embedded options refers to the existence, within the structure of a security, of certain implied options. Of these, by far the most widespread, because they have been in existence for many years, are call options. Other structures that embed options are discussed in Chapter 12.

A callable bond can be thought of as a combination of a long position in a noncallable bond and a short position in a call option that the investor has written to the issuer. Analyzing a callable bond, therefore, boils down to analyzing the value of the call option. Anything that increases the likelihood of call also increases the value of the option. So, the higher the coupon and the lower the yield on the underlying bond, the more valuable is the option. Likewise, the lower the initial call price and the longer the period over which the issuer can call the bond, the more valuable the option.

Call options are also more valuable, the shorter the period of call protection. This is because the shorter the period of call protection, the greater the present value of the cash flows that the issuer can call away from the investor. Also, as in all options, the more volatile the underlying interest rates, the more valuable the call.

Perhaps the least obvious factor affecting the call option's value is the shape of the yield curve. The higher short-term rates are, relative to long-term rates, the more valuable is the call. This implies that, as the yield curve steepens, callable bonds will be worth more. Conversely, the flatter the yield curve, the less a callable bond is worth. This relationship makes sense when one thinks that investors often buy callable bonds on a yield-to-call basis. If callable bond yields did not fall with short-term rates, high-coupon callable bonds would be very attractive relative to noncallable short-term bonds on a yield-to-call basis.

Call options are often not valued systematically. Investors, for example, pay great attention to the coupon but give less attention to call protection, which can be extremely valuable. The issue is of critical importance to the U.S. mortgage-backed securities market, because mortgage borrowers effectively have a call option in the ability to refinance their mortgage. Much work has been done on "option-adjusted-spreads" in that market; some of this is discussed in the next chapter.

Callable bonds are less convex than noncallable ones. The call feature tends to reduce duration as rates fall. It makes it likely that the cash flows will stop after the first call date. Because a callable bond is a combination of a short call option and a noncallable bond, these two components tend to offset each other. The duration of a callable bond may move in either direction as rates move. In any event, it will move less favorably than a noncallable one.

Puttable Bonds

A use of embedded options that developed in the early 1980s was put bonds. Many issues have allowed the investor to "put" the bond back to the issuer at certain dates. Perhaps the biggest single market developed along these lines has been in the U.S. municipal bond market. In this market, it is now common to see 30-year bonds issued bearing an overnight or 7-day interest rate, by means of the incorporation of a put option, as discussed earlier (see the section on "Variable Rate Demand Notes").

Aside from their use in perpetuals, mentioned earlier, puttable bonds have become common in the Euromarkets. In Canada, bonds known as extendables and retractables have long been common. A 30-year bond "retractable" to a 10-year maturity has, in essence, a put attached with an effective exercise date 10 years after issue. An extendable technically incorporates a call option, but a 10-year bond extendable to 30 years is, practically speaking, indistinguishable from a 30-year bond retractable to 10 years. Either can be redeemed after 10 years, or after 30 years. Thus, both extendables and retractables may be included under the broad category of puts, provided the option is in favor of the investor in both cases.

A typical example of such a retractable would be the C$100 million 1986–1996/2001 bonds issued by the Province of Newfoundland. This carried a coupon of 10 percent until July 25, 1996. Investors had the option to require early repayment on that date; similarly, the issuer had the right to reset the coupon on that date. The new rate was actually fixed at 7.5 percent, and the bond was kept in existence.

An example of an early puttable bond was the US$50 million 8½ percent issue by the National Bank of Hungary, in 1972. The high coupons and volatile conditions of 1980–1981 led to a spate of such puttable issues. An example was the issue by the Municipal Finance Authority of British Columbia, in October 1981, for US$54 million at an initial coupon of 17 percent. Its final maturity was 16 years (October 1997), but interest reset and put option dates were fixed for October 1985, 1989, and 1993. The issue was callable on the same dates as the put option. A similar structure was used for AB Svensk Exportkredit; this US$75 million issue in November 1981, at 16½ percent, had a final maturity of 12 years, with puts and calls in 1984, 1987, and 1990.

An extension of the puttable bond technique may be seen in the February 1986 issue by American Express Credit Corporation. The $100 million 10-year issue starts with an 8.45 percent coupon. The investor can put the paper back to the issuer after 5 years; if the put is not exercised, the coupon is stepped up to 9.45 percent. The benefit to the issuer is that it lowers the cost of the coupon for the first 5 years by perhaps 30 basis points; the investor has the choice of keeping the paper or putting it back to the issuer if rates have risen sharply.

Another variation of the concept was an issue, in January 1987, by Transcontinental Gas Pipeline Corporation in the U.S. domestic market. The $100 million 10-year noncallable debt had a 2-year put, allowing investors at that point—and that point only—to sell the debt back to the issuer at 132.5 basis points over the U.S. Treasury bond level. The launch price was Treasuries + 110 basis points; it was estimated that the issuer would have had to pay Treasuries + 155 basis points if the put feature was excluded.

In recent years, there has also been a tendency to promote the use of put bonds as a natural hedge for callable bonds in a portfolio. For example, an investor holding CMOs (discussed in the next chapter)—with the underlying prepayment risk, which increases when interest rates fall—might want to hold a put bond as a natural hedge.

In the past, the lower yields associated with puttable bonds have been unattractive for many investors, such as insurance companies. However, in early 1995, Standard & Poor's began calculating a capital charge when assessing the creditworthiness of life insurance companies. S&P's methodology tried to extract the option risk in the mortgage-backed securities. They did this by stressing interest rates and comparing them to single-A noncallable corporates under the same conditions. This convexity test helped create demand for puttable bonds as an offset for CMOs.

A surge in investment-grade corporate puttable bonds issued in the U.S. market occurred in 1996. Securities Data estimated the total as nearly $15 billion in the first 11 months, up from $8.9 billion in 1995. Recent developments in this area also include "step-ups," in which the coupon is increased if not put, and multiple-year puttable bonds. In 1996, the Province of Quebec issued a 30-year bond that is puttable every year after 10 years; similarly, the Tennessee Valley Authority issued a bond that matures in 2036 but is puttable at years 2 and 10—the so-called "put-put" bond.

In the United Kingdom, there have been one or two notorious examples of puttable convertible bonds that were issued by firms which were perceived as having glamorous growth prospects (hence the convertible aspect) but not necessarily very solid financing (hence the put). The advertising firm of Saatchi & Saatchi, just before the crash of 1987, issued a puttable convertible that never looked anywhere like being converted. When the time came to meet the put, the firm's finances had to be restructured to get around the problem.

Indexed Sinking Fund Debentures

In July 1988, the Federal National Mortgage Association (FNMA) issued $500 million of 8.70 percent indexed sinking fund debentures. Five additional issues totaling $3.2 billion followed over the next 15 months. The key feature of these bonds is that they use a sinking fund that depends on interest rate levels. Principal repayments vary inversely with market interest rates, rising (falling) when interest rates fall (rise) in relation to a set base rate. As will be seen in Chapter 10, mortgage repayments in the United States show a similar pattern, and these bonds attempted to match the payment pattern of FNMA's liabilities with its assets. (Compare also the index market amortizing swap structures of Chapter 5.)

Take as an example the 8.70 percent debentures. The base annual sinking fund percentage is 40 percent. Provided interest rates are unchanged, on each semiannual sinking fund date, FNMA redeems half of the base percentage (i.e., 20 percent of the outstanding balance of the bonds). Suppose the initial amount outstanding were $100 million. Then, on the first sinking fund date, FNMA would redeem $20 million; on the second, $16 million (20 percent of $80 million outstanding).

But if interest rates change, the percentage of the outstanding balance that is redeemed will vary. It varies with the relationship between the 10-year constant-maturity-Treasury (CMT) yield and 8.85 percent (which is the base interest rate for the debenture). The pattern is shown in Table 9.3.

If the average 10-year CMT rate falls to 5.10 percent (the 8.85 percent base rate minus 375 basis points), then the maximum sinking fund repayment (50 percent) would be made. But if the CMT rate rises to 10.61 percent (8.85 percent plus 176 basis points), then no sinking fund payment is made.

To the FNMA, one of the main benefits of this type of issue structure was that it helped FNMA match the repayment pattern of its assets with the repayment pattern of its liabilities. However, after 1989, FNMA moved away from these indexed sinking fund debentures. First, it issued medium-term notes with only 1 year of call protection. Second, it began issuing, in 1992, medium-term notes with similar interest-rate-contingent sinking funds. But

Table 9.3 Impact of Sinking Fund Adjustment

Change from Base Rate (Basis Points)	Sinking Fund Adjustment	Annual Sinking Fund	Semiannual Sinking Fund
−375 & below	+60%	100%	50%
−374 to −325	+55	95	47.5
−324 to −275	+50	90	45
−274 to −225	+45	85	42.5
−224 to −175	+40	80	40
−24 to +25	0	40	20
+26 to +75	−10	30	15
+76 to +125	−20	20	10
+126 to +175	−30	10	5
+176 & above	−40	0	0

Source of Data: J. D. Finnerty, "Indexed Sinking Fund Debentures: Valuation and Analysis," *Financial Management* (Summer 1993).

the sinking fund in these notes adjusts continuously. This contrasts with the step function changes in the debenture sinking fund (where, if the CMT falls 274 basis points, we have a sinking fund percentage of 42.5 percent, but it increases to 45 percent if the CMT falls one more basis point to the 275 level). This was because of investors' worries that, as a sinking fund date approached, valuing the debenture was difficult if the CMT was close to one of the trigger levels.

Index-Linked Bonds

Index-linked bonds are not, in themselves, a new feature of the investment scene. For many years, they have been issued as part of government and of private finance. But governments have been ambivalent about them. Traditionally, they have been associated with countries suffering from hyperinflation: Israel, Brazil, Argentina, and Iceland have all used index linking, as have France, Sweden, and Finland. More recently, the United Kingdom, Australia, and, most recently of all, the U.S. Treasury have all issued index-linked bonds. (In this chapter, the term index-linked is taken to refer to inflation-linked. Bonds whose redemption values are linked to equity or other indexes are discussed in Chapters 12 and 16.)

Such bonds have generally been indexed to some measure of inflation, but there have also been others, particularly in France. Of the latter, the best known are perhaps the Pinay, the Giscard, and the Barre (named after the respective Finance Ministers who launched them). The Rente Pinay had a redemption value linked to the gold Napoleon coin. The 1973 Giscard offered 7 percent with capital and interest linked to the gold value of the ECU, and the 1977 Barre offered 8.8 percent and reimbursement linked to the ECU.

In the United Kingdom, index-linking of National Savings was introduced in 1975, but in a very restricted form. In 1981, index-linked government bonds were introduced, again with restrictions, which were lifted in March 1982. The U.K. market is now quite substantial: about 15 percent of the total U.K. market. In 1983, the Australian government followed suit. From relatively small beginnings, the index-linked market in Australia has now grown to approximately AUS\$10 billion in issue.

The U.S. Treasury inflation-linked inaugural issue (Treasury Inflation Protected Securities, or TIPS) came to market in January 1997 with \$7 billion of 10-year bonds. The principal value of the securities will be adjusted for inflation daily, and the semiannual coupon payments will represent a fixed percentage of the inflation-adjusted value of the principal. The coupon is fixed at 3.375 percent. The issue triggered five immediate successors in the shape of issues by Tennessee Valley Authority, the Federal Home Loan Board (FHLB), J.P. Morgan, Toyota Motor Credit Corporation, and Korea Development Bank. (The latter came via the Yankee market.)

Two types of structure have been used in this market: (1) the accrual structure (chosen by the Treasury) and (2) the current-pay structure. In the former, semiannual payments represent a fixed percentage of the inflation-adjusted principal. With the current-pay structure, which was adopted by a number of corporate issuers in February 1997, the inflation accrual is paid out with each coupon.

In both these markets, and in a number of other centers, the existence of inflation-proof bonds has permitted the development, albeit limited, of an inflation swap market (see Chapter 5). Following the introduction of the U.S. inflation-linked bonds, a number of swaps were done between LIBOR and the consumer price index.

One or two U.K. deals have been index-linked. An example is the £30 million issue by the Nationwide Building Society in July 1986. It is a 35-year loan stock whose interest and capital will be upgraded every 6 months to keep pace with inflation. Its real rate of return was set at 3.89 percent—a margin of 60 basis points over the gross real rate of return on the U.K. 2½ percent Index-Linked Treasury Stock 2020 at the time of launch. The funds are used to provide index-linked mortgage loans at 4½ percent.

Severn River Crossing PLC listed, in April 1993, an issue of £131 million of index-linked debenture stock on the London Stock Exchange. The issue matures on June 30, 2012, and carries an initial coupon of 6 percent. It was completed, in February 1991, on a private placement basis. The stock was listed in 1993, when the company granted permission for the stock to be publicly listed after 18 months of trading. The issue was the largest U.K. corporate index-linked stock and also the largest U.K. infrastructure project to include a public offering of debt securities as part of the financing. The deal made up the final stage in a £531 million financing required for the project. The issuer is a special-purpose vehicle that has the concession to operate and maintain the existing Severn bridge crossing as well as to design, construct, operate, and maintain the second estuarial crossing.

SUBORDINATED BONDS

Profit and Loss Certificates

An issue from Deutsche Schiffsbank AG, Bremen, in 1992, consisted of DEM75 million of profit and loss sharing certificates, with a maturity of 12 years and 3 months (due December 2004). The certificates paid a coupon of 10 percent annually. The payments will be suspended if the fiscal year ends with a loss or if the interest payments lead to a loss. The borrower must make up for the suspended payments if the annual results return to profit. Should Deutsche Schiffsbank's core capital be reduced to cover losses, the redemption value of the certificates will be lowered. An obligation to increase the redemption value exists until maturity of the bond but only if the bank's legal reserves are at or above the required minimum. The certificates rank pari passu with all other subordinated debt. They do not confer voting rights. They are, in effect, the debt equivalent of Genussschein (see Chapter 17); another recent variant is the Tier III capital bonds (see below).

QUIDS

In April 1995, the Tennessee Valley Authority offered $600 million of Quarterly Income Debt Securities (QUIDS). These were 50-year bonds that were deeply subordinated and allowed the issuer to defer payment of interest for up to 5 years. From the point of view of the rating agencies, they have features resembling equity but are still tax-deductible. Shortly thereafter, McDonald's offered $450 million of 30-year subordinated deferrable interest debentures paying 8.35 percent, in exchange for its outstanding 7.72 percent perpetual preferred. Although bearing a higher coupon, the QUIDS were more attractive to McDonald's because the coupons were tax-deductible. However, for corporate investors receiving the 70 percent corporate-dividends-received deduction available under U.S. tax law, the exchange offer was not well received; only 26 percent of investors converted. (See Chapter 14 for a discussion of the related MIPS.)

QUICS

AMR Corporation, in November 1994, issued QUICS (Quarterly Income Capital Securities). Like QUIDS, these bonds are a version of the MIPS product (see Chapter 14) but in debt form. They are convertible bonds with a 5-year interest deferral. Thus, from the point of view of credit rating agencies, they would be treated almost the same as preferred convertibles.

Brady Bonds

Brady bonds, a specialized segment of the bond market, may be said to have begun in 1984, in the wake of the LDC debt crisis that began when Mexico defaulted in 1982. In 1987, the process accelerated when major U.S. money center banks took increased reserves against their LDC loans. Having written them down, they were less inhibited about selling them. The next step came in February 1988, when J.P. Morgan launched Mexico's Aztec bonds, consisting of $3.7 billion of Mexican sovereign loan debt restructured into $2.6 billion worth of 20-year securities, at a floating coupon of LIBOR plus 1.625 percent, with the principal fully collateralized by U.S. Treasury zero-coupon bonds. The disappointing outcome, combined with a lack of progress in Argentina and Brazil, led to a change in the official strategy and to the 1989 Brady Plan for Mexico, which suggested that the world's major banks grant debt relief in exchange for financial instruments.

In February 1990, Mexico became the first country to issue Bradys, converting $48.1 billion of its eligible foreign debt to commercial banks, and offering banks two options for the exchange of their loans into tradable securities.

Types of Brady Bonds. The Mexican Discount Bonds gave a 35 percent discount in the face value of the debt, but offered a market-based coupon of LIBOR plus 0.8125 percent. The par bonds were issued at face value, but had a below-market coupon of 6.25 percent. Banks also had a third option: They could carry the full principal amount of the loans on their books while making new lending of at least 25 percent of their existing exposure over 3 years. The principal on both types of bonds was fully collateralized by U.S. Treasury zero-coupon bonds. Also, there was a rolling interest guarantee covering 18 months' worth of interest payments.

Although structures have become more complex over time, the basic principles of each new Brady rescheduling have been based on the Mexican deal. One major option added in later issues was the buy-back option, which allows a country to repurchase part of its debt at an agreed discount, enabling it to participate in a debt reduction program.

Debt Conversion Bonds or New Money Bonds are short-term floating rate bonds (as issued by Venezuela, Uruguay, and the Philippines without collateral). Creditors exchanged loans for bonds at par. They then made additional loans to the Brady-issuing nation, at a floating rate of interest.

Front Loaded Interest Reduction Bonds (FLIRB's) arise from loans exchanged for medium-term step-up bonds at below-market interest rates for the initial 5 to 7 years. After that, they pay a floating rate for the remainder of the term. They provide partial interest collateral in the form of cash, with collateral rolled over for subsequent periods upon timely interest payments. These variations are generally less liquid than the par/discounts, but they have a much shorter average life because amortization payments begin ordinarily after 5 to 7 years.

Commercial banks have rescheduled interest in arrears of Brazilian, Argentine, and Ecuadorian debt, capitalizing the interest into new short-term floating rate bonds (Interest Due and Unpaid Bonds, as in Brazil's IDU and Ecuador's PDI). These bonds have been issued prior to the rescheduling of principal into the Brady format.

The Bolivian rescheduling of 1992 offered a further twist: an environmental option. Creditors could opt to tender base debt and past interest in exchange for Short-Term Exchange Program Bonds (STEP Bonds), which could be issued only to a nongovernmental, nonprofit organization. These bonds had a face value of 16 cents on the dollar plus a 50 percent premium, making them worth 24 cents. They were zero-coupon bonds maturing 9 months after issue, and the proceeds were used for approved Bolivian social or environmental projects.

Analyzing Brady Bonds. Despite their esoteric features, Brady bonds lend themselves to the same valuation techniques applied to more conventional fixed-income securities. The basic notion is that the price of a given bond represents the present value of its stream of payments.

Each Brady bond has three distinct features: (1) principal collateral, (2) interest collateral, and (3) the sovereign portion. When evaluating a Brady bond, we must strip out the enhancements attached to understand the risk and valuation. Removing the present value of the U.S. Treasury strip and the present value of the guaranteed interest stream will produce the stripped yield—the yield-to-maturity of the unenhanced interest stream. This stripped yield is based on the credit quality of the issuing nation.

Further analysis of collateralized Brady bonds includes assessing the present value of the collateral as a percentage of the Brady's market price. The value of the U.S. Treasury component acts as a floor, in that the bond would not trade below the value of the collateral.

Bonds include, in several cases, detachable warrants or recovery rights predicated on economic/industry performance. Probably the most high-profile of these are Mexico's Value Recover Rights (VRRs), based on numerous variables such as oil price, GDP, and oil production levels.

Performance of a particular country's Bradys can vary widely. During 1996, fixed rate par bonds, which are typically longer-dated instruments carrying collateral on the principal as well as a rolling guarantee on the interest, significantly underperformed uncollateralized floating rate instruments, particularly those at the shorter end of the yield curve. The main reason for this was a decline in the value of the underlying collateral as U.S. Treasury rates rose, and the relative unattractiveness of a fixed rate coupon in a rising interest rate environment.

Brady Repo and the Growth of the Market. Although the repo, as an instrument, is hardly new, the repo market in Brady bonds—and, indeed, in emerging markets instruments—has played a key role in the development of the market. Whereas in 1994 the average daily repo volume of Brady bonds in New York was reported at $75 million, by mid-1996 it was estimated to be closer to $500 million. The origin of the market was the Mexican banks that started to repo their bonds with a dollar-based dealer in the international market, benefiting from receiving dollar financing at a cheaper rate compared with other sources such as interbank borrowing. The international repo dealer then matched the trade with an international cash investor. The ability to finance Brady holdings via the repo market has been a considerable factor in allowing trading volumes to build up in the market.

Since the first Brady bond was issued for Mexico in 1990, the market has grown fast and now comprises the largest and most liquid market for Latin America. Overall, there is around US$190 billion of eligible loan debt from 13 countries in Asia, Africa, and Eastern Europe, as well as Latin America. Secondary market turnover for Brady bonds alone amounted to US$1.58 trillion in 1995, according to statistics from EMTA (the Emerging Markets Traders' Association), and represent 57 percent of all trading in emerging markets products, including options, local markets, Eurobonds, and short-term paper. The corresponding 1996 figures were a staggering $5.3 trillion turnover for the market as a whole, with Brady bonds accounting for 51 percent ($2.7 trillion). However, the market as a whole continues to be very focused on Argentina, Brazil, and Mexico, which, among them, accounted for 77 percent of total emerging markets' trading. In Eastern Europe, the most traded paper was bank loans to Vneshekonombank, the former Soviet Union foreign trade bank, at $181 billion, with GKO (Russian government bills) turnover totaling $31 billion.

Other Instruments

In August 1996, International Asset Transactions launched a Brazil B-strips program that essentially consists of stripping the coupons from the Brady bonds. Bondholders submit their bonds to the depository bank and, in exchange, receive tranche A or B receipts. The A receipts are the principal amount and the B receipts are the coupon amounts.

Nonrecourse Project Finance Bonds

In January 1995, Europe's first nonrecourse public bond issue in the power sector was brought to market. The 9.5 percent, £200 million issue is amortized from 2006 to 2010 in five equal installments. The issue replaced a bank syndicate's nonrecourse debt financing arranged for AES and Tractebel to purchase the Kilroot Electric plant in Northern Ireland.

Part of the reason the deal was possible was that the Kilroot plant was up and running, so the market was refinancing an existing power plant. The power purchase agreement was such that, by going the bond route, the final maturity of the financing could be extended beyond that which had been available in the bank market at the time of the original sale.

OTHER SPECIALIST BOND TYPES

Dragon Bonds

This term has been used to describe bonds issued for placement in Asia. However, it has not really evolved into a separate market; on the whole, dragon bonds are traded as part of the Eurobond market rather than constituting a separate market.

Tier Three Capital Bonds

Under the Basle Committee rules, banks were permitted in 1996 to issue a new kind of security, the so-called "Tier Three capital." This consists of unsecured, subordinated capital with a maturity of at least 2 years. Interest and principal payments on Tier Three capital must be deferred if payment would mean that the bank fell below its minimal regulatory capital requirement. In June 1996, ING Bank issued $250 million of floating rate notes in the form of Tier Three capital. In October 1996, ABN Amro Bank's Chicago branch issued Tier Three capital in the form of global subordinated 5-year bonds yielding 40 basis points over Treasuries.

Contingent-Surplus Notes

A somewhat similar concept, though a different structure, lies behind the contingent-surplus note. Arkwright Mutual Insurance Company and Nationwide Insurance Enterprise both used this structure in 1996. A trust is created and it then borrows funds ($100 million in the Arkwright case, and $400 million in the Nationwide case), which are invested in Treasury bonds. The insurance companies have the right, during the 20-year life of the trusts, to require the trusts to sell the Treasury bonds and invest the proceeds in surplus notes. (These are issued by the insurance companies, and pay the Treasury rate plus the annual fee.) In exchange for this right, the companies pay an annual fee (2.75 percent and 2.2 percent, respectively). This structure does not transfer the catastrophe risk directly to the investor. Instead, the insurance company retains the risk. But the investor is committed to buying the surplus notes. It could be thought of as a long-term forward underwriting of the issuance of surplus notes.

This is not dissimilar to the issue, by Swedish Export Credit (SEK), of a bond whose redemption was linked to the occurrence of an earthquake in Tokyo. The Japanese insurers with whom the bonds were placed required the ability to retrieve their cash if there were an earthquake in Tokyo.

A related transaction was the private placement of securitization of the property catastrophe reinsurance risk of St. Paul Re, a large U.S. reinsurance firm. Under the terms of the deal, a special-purpose vehicle was created (George Town Re), which was ceded a proportion of St. Paul's risk. George Town then issued two classes of securities whose payments are linked to the performance of the ceded business: $44.5 million of 10-year principal-guaranteed notes, and $24 million of 3-year preference shares in George Town.

The most recent innovation in this area has been the hurricane bond. In June 1997, Residential Reinsurance issued $477 million of bonds to fund $400 million in catastrophe reinsurance for United Services Automobile Association (USAA). The issue was divided into two tranches, with the less risky paying 2.73 percent, and the more risky 5.76 percent over LIBOR. The reinsurance is triggered if a category 3, 4, or 5 hurricane hits one of 20 U.S. states within 12 months from the date of the issue and causes more than $1 billion of claims against USAA. The issue took well over a year to launch; a public offering led by Merrill Lynch was aborted in November 1996, whereas the successful issue was a private placement led by Merrill, Goldman Sachs, and Lehman Brothers. The 1997 issue also offered more attractive pricing.

In a series of not-unrelated moves, the French insurance giant AXA announced a new joint venture with Banque Paribas, Alternative Risk Finance, to offer alternative insurance solutions; Swiss Re grouped all its nontraditional insurance operations together under the name of Swiss Re New Markets in July 1997; and Crédit Suisse purchased the old-established Swiss insurance company, Winterthur. All three transactions offer further examples of the increasing linkage between banks and insurance businesses—a trend which is only rational, considering that both industries are closely involved in risk protection and risk management.

Deferred Annuity

In March 1996, the U.K. market saw the issue of £165 million of bonds for Road Management Consolidated, yielding 80 basis points over gilts at the time of launch. It was the first large sterling bond to be structured as a "deferred annuity": principal is to be repaid, along with interest, from December 2000 to final maturity in 2021. The issue is guaranteed by AMBAC, a U.S. monoline insurer.

Junk Bond Structures

A number of structures have been developed specifically for the U.S. junk bond market. These include so-called "extendable reset bonds," which typically provide that the issuer must reset the coupon on specified dates so that the bond will trade at a predetermined price. The coupon rate will generally be the average of rates suggested by two investment banks. An example might be the issue of $200 million of 11.5 percent 10-year bonds by Viacom, which required that, after 3 years, the bond coupon must be reset so that the bond has a market value of $100. Other bonds required annual resets; in some cases, the reset feature was limited by the operation of an interest rate cap.

Another feature developed in the junk bond market was the so-called "pay in kind" (PIK) bond. In a PIK bond, the coupon is fixed and the issuer has the right to choose whether to make the coupon payments in cash or kind. Borrowers will pay the coupon in kind when rates have risen. Consider, for example, a 13 percent PIK bond. If the credit quality of this issuer has declined and its cost of funds has risen to 15 percent, the issuer is essentially able to put more of the bonds to investors at the 13 percent rate. It will readily be appreciated that such instruments are potentially very unattractive for investors and would generally only be issued by firms with potentially high risks. Accordingly, of course, they would normally carry a high coupon to compensate the investor for the risks.

Parallel Bonds

This is a very new category of bond. The term applies to bonds that contain specific provisions regarding conversion to the Euro (the new European currency planned to be created in 1999). The first issue of this type, from the Republic of Austria, in January 1997, was an issue of FRF5 billion with a coupon of 5.5 percent and final maturity in 2004. Its terms were identical to existing Austrian government bonds denominated in Austrian schillings. During the transition to the single currency, investors have the option of exchange into their domestic counterparts. Conversely, the issuer retains the right to consolidate bonds that are not exchanged into a large-size issue of similar instruments.

The European Investment Bank issued a Euro/ECU 1 billion 5.25 percent 7-year parallel bond at the end of January 1997. Siemens, the German industrial conglomerate, also issued a variation of this type of bond in February 1997. The transaction consisted of three 10-year bonds with identical coupons and structure, denominated in deutsche marks, French francs, and Dutch guilders. Siemens will redenominate the component tranches into Euro once the relevant currency is part of EMU. When the three components are redenominated, the three bonds will be consolidated into a single issue. This will achieve a combined single bond of very large size, which will be attractive to investors because of its liquidity.

SPECIALIST ISSUING STRUCTURES

Bonds have been issued by a huge variety of different entities in many different issuing processes. The following sections merely comment on some interesting recent techniques that may be more generally applicable.

Of these, by far the most important is the technique underlying a global bond issue. Global bond issuance was launched in 1989 by the World Bank, which wanted to create a liquid, marketable debt security attractive to investors around the world. The global bond format has proven popular. By 1995, more than 100 different borrowers around the world had used global bonds to raise the equivalent of almost US$200 billion in a total of twelve different currencies.

Many different issues claim to be global; some are not as global as they might claim. A fair definition of a true global can be taken from a brochure by the World Bank:

> The bonds are legally eligible for primary market sale into each of the world's major bond markets, without the imposition of lock-up provisions. As a result, the bonds are available for distribution to a wide range of investors. The bonds can be settled and cleared on any one of several systems, and they can flow back and forth between the systems with minimal transaction costs. This means not only that investors in a variety of locations can take advantage of home-market settlement and clearance of World Bank global bonds, but also that cross-border trading in the bonds is easier.

Another important group of users of the technique have been the U.S. Federal National Mortgage Association, Federal Home Loan Mortgage Corporation, and Federal Home Loan Bank System. The first such issue—$1.5 billion of 10-year bonds—was launched by the Federal National Mortgage Association in June 1994. FNMA has now launched globals in US$, DEM, and JPY, and, most recently, in sterling, with a £1 billion issue in February 1997. The global concept was launched in the Czech koruna in September 1996, with a World Bank issue for Kc2 billion.

Global bond issuance has had to overcome many technical hurdles, but as the concept has become more important, local jurisdictions have, to some extent, sought to accommodate it. For example, until 1993, it was assumed that global issues had to be registered with the SEC in their entirety. Given that the SEC charged approximately $\frac{1}{32}$ percent to register a financing, on a $10 billion issue, registration with the SEC alone would cost $3.5 million. In 1993, the SEC's stance was changed to allow registration of that portion of the issue expected to be sold in the United States, plus some portion to allow for "flowback" from other markets into the U.S. market.

Following in the wake of the World Bank and the sovereign or semisovereign issuers have been a few corporate names; The Walt Disney Company, for example, did a $2.6 billion global issue in March 1996. The number of companies that can issue in such size is relatively limited.

The other major innovation in recent years in the United States has been the development of the private placement market through the so-called Rule 144A market. This rule was introduced by the SEC in April 1990, in part to stimulate capital raising in the United States by non-U.S. issuers. Some of the former restrictions (under Rule 144) governing resale of privately placed securities (or "restricted securities") have been lifted under Rule 144(a), where the sale is made to "qualified institutional buyers" (QIBs). Rule 144(a) aims to add liquidity to the private placement market. A QIB is currently defined as an institution that owns and invests, on a discretionary basis, at least US$100 million (or, in the case of registered broker-dealers, US$10 million) in securities of an unaffiliated entity.

Other techniques used in recent years include the $50 million of Multi-Mode Remarketed Secured Notes issued in 1993 by Detroit Edison. The bonds are secured by a first mortgage on the utility's operating facilities. These were 35-year instruments in that their final maturity was 2028. However, the initial issue paid an interest rate of 3.32 percent for a 30-day period. At the end of the period, Detroit Edison had the ability to reset the interest rate to a new period. The bonds were remarketed by Citibank, the sole underwriter of the issue, charging fees appropriate to the new reset maturity. This structure means that Detroit Edison has much of the flexibility that might be found with a medium-term note program, but circumvents the need for utility regulators' approval of new issues of securities, and also the need to reinstate the mortgage.

Tap Bonds/Fungible Issues

Another specialist type of issue technique is the tap bond. Further amounts of an issue are made available "on tap." This is a technique well known to government bond markets; the U.K. government has issued tap stocks for many years, and so have a number of other countries. The technique was introduced to the Euromarkets in 1977 with an issue for Osterreichische Kontrollbank AG (OKB). OKB issued US$50 million (US$25 million initial tranche) in September 1977. It was followed by issuers that included Export Development Corporation of Canada, Citicorp, the Kingdom of Sweden, European Investment Bank, and numerous others. One of the main advantages in the tap issue technique is that it saves commissions for the borrower. Although commissions are paid on the initial tranche, they are not generally payable on subsequent tranches. A second major advantage is that tap issues allow the issuer to respond quickly to a "window" in the market. A third plus is that subsequent issues of the tap stock, which are fungible with the original issue, enhance trading liquidity in the original issue.

A related technique is, of course, to "reopen" an existing issue and increase its size—a technique used regularly by the U.S. Treasury and imitated abroad. The concept of a bond that is "reopened" in this manner lies at the heart, for example, of the French Treasury's approach to the OAT market. The difference, at least in theory, is that, with the tap stock, we know from Day 1 the total amount of the bond that will be issued; with the reopening technique, we do not.

Chapter **10**

Mortgage-Backed Securities

MARKET DEVELOPMENT

Mortgage securitization began to grow explosively in the United States in the 1970s. It was fueled by two major developments: (1) the interest rate instability of the period, and (2) the growth of support for the market by GNMA, FNMA, and FHLMC—respectively, Government National Mortgage Association ("Ginnie Mae"), Federal National Mortgage Association ("Fannie Mae"), and Federal Home Loan Mortgage Corporation ("Freddie Mac").

The interest rate volatility of the period badly hurt many thrift institutions and drove them to find new ways of managing their balance sheets. The techniques used at first were pass-through securities and mortgage-backed bonds. Then, in the early 1980s, the collateralized mortgage obligation (CMO) was introduced. CMOs and a number of later variations on that theme are discussed in this chapter.

To put this market segment in perspective, as of June 30, 1996, total outstanding U.S. bond market debt was as shown in Table 10.1.

As can be seen, mortgage-backed securities account for an important part of the U.S. market, and their importance continues to grow. At the time of writing, the major issuer of pass-throughs is FNMA, with $118 billion of issuance in the first three quarters of 1996, compared with $93 billion for FHLMC and GNMA's total of $77 billion.

Originally, pass-throughs were backed by a pool of single-family mortgages. In 1984, FNMA created the first pass-through security collateralized by

Table 10.1   U.S. Marketable Debt ($ trillion), June 30, 1996

U.S. Treasury	$3.3 trillion
Corporate bonds	2.0
Agency mortgage-backed securities	1.6
Municipal	1.3
Money market	1.3
Federal agency	0.9
Asset-backed	0.3

Source of Data: Public Securities Association.

multifamily mortgages through swap programs, a pool of adjustable rate mortgage loans. FHLMC also participated in this market for a while, but then dropped out after suffering huge losses. During the mid-1980s, financial institutions were so overaggressively lending on new construction that securitization could not easily find investors willing to match the terms these groups were willing to take. After the collapse of the property market, traditional sources of funds were no longer available.

The next development was that Congress set up the Resolution Trust Corporation (RTC) to clean up the savings and loan (S&L) mess. The RTC securitized the mortgages of the failed thrifts as a means of converting these assets into cash after unsuccessfully attempting to sell them off individually. The volume of deals done, and the RTC's willingness to enhance transactions with cash in order to obtain ratings, single-handedly created investor interest in highly rated commercial mortgage-backed securities (CMBS). The public's acceptance of these issues gave momentum to the securitization process for other commercial properties. This market is discussed further below.

The Agencies

GNMA is a wholly owned U.S. government corporation within the Department of Housing and Urban Development (HUD). It was founded in 1968. Its mandate includes maintaining a secondary market in government-guaranteed mortgages. GNMA guarantees the timely payment of principal and interest on securities issued by approved institutions and backed by certain guaranteed mortgages. The GNMA pass-through is called "fully modified" because it is fully guaranteed. The investor receives interest plus scheduled principal payments even if the borrowers have not made their payments.

To issue GNMA securities, an approved issuer applies for a commitment from GNMA for a guarantee. The issuer originates or acquires mortgage loans and assembles them into a pool of mortgages. The GNMA I program lets issuers create securities backed by pools of single-family, multifamily, and manufactured housing loans. The issuer is responsible for marketing the securities and servicing the underlying mortgages.

GNMA II supplements, rather than replaces, GNMA I. GNMA II securities are issued by private lenders and backed by pools of Federal Housing Administration, Veterans Administration, or Farm Housing Administration insured or guaranteed residential mortgages. The securities are guaranteed by GNMA. GNMA II offers geographically dispersed multiple-issuer pools, as well as custom pools, and provides for a mix of interest rates among mortgages within a pool. GNMA I pools tend to be more homogeneous. The GNMA II program permits issuers to issue securities backed by pools of 30-year, single-family level payment, adjustable rate, graduated payment, growing equity, and buydown loans, and manufactured housing loans.

Another major player in the pass-through market is the Federal Home Loan Mortgage Corporation (FHLMC), which is owned by the Federal Home

Loan Banks. Its mandate is to increase liquidity and available credit for the conventional mortgage market by establishing and maintaining a secondary market for conventional mortgages.

FHLMC pass-throughs differ from GNMA pass-throughs in several ways. First, they are not backed by the full faith and credit of the U.S. government. However, FHLMC is treated by the market as being practically equivalent to GNMA. Second, many FHLMC pools use "seasoned" mortgages that have been outstanding for some time. Thus, the underlying mortgage maturities may vary over a wide range whereas GNMA's tend to be more homogeneous.

FHLMC issues participation certificates (PCs) that are created under two programs: (1) Cash Program and (2) Guarantor/Swap Program. In the Cash Program, FHLMC buys mortgages from originators and then sells PCs reflecting ownership of the mortgages. In the Guarantor/Swap Program, FHLMC allows originators to swap pooled mortgages for PCs in those pools. In 1990, FHLMC introduced its Gold PC. This has stronger guarantees and is expected to be the only type of PC issued in the future.

The Federal National Mortgage Association (FNMA) is a federally chartered, privately owned corporation. It was established in 1938 to expand the liquidity of the mortgage market. In 1968, FNMA was rechartered as a privately held corporation authorized to buy and sell conventional FHA-insured and VA-guaranteed loans. FNMA obligations are not backed by the full faith and credit of the U.S. government, but do have U.S. agency status in the credit markets.

Pass-Throughs

Essentially, a pass-through certificate represents an ownership interest in the underlying assets and thus in the resulting cash flow. The seller records a profit (or loss) on the sale of the underlying assets to investors through the pass-through security. A pass-through allows the transaction to go off the issuer's balance sheet. Principal and interest collected on the assets are "passed through" to the security holders; the seller acts primarily as a servicer.

In the normal U.S. pass-through structure, the assets are sold to a "grantor trust," which is a pass-through entity that does not pay tax. Instead, the trust's tax liabilities flow through to the holders of the pass-through certificates. Legal title to the receivables is held by a trustee, but the trust must be passive and merely hold the trust property to protect and conserve it. The trustee should not have substantial managerial discretion over the trust assets, or the power to improve the investors' return by reinvesting the proceeds. Thus, pass-through payments should match the incoming payments on the assets.

By contrast, under the CMO structure (discussed later), the assets are typically held by a special-purpose vehicle that issues debt collateralized by the assets. Investors in the bond no longer are direct owners of the underlying assets; they have simply invested in a bond backed by some assets. Therefore, the issuing entity can manipulate the cash flows without tax consequences—hence the use of the structure for CMOs, which manipulate the incoming cash flows into separate payment streams. This structure is sometimes described as a pay-through structure.

Many different types of pass-through securities have been developed, but certain basic characteristics are common. Each pool has a coupon or pass-through rate, an issue date, a maturity date, and payment delay.

The pass-through rate is the rate paid to investors. It often differs from the various interest rates on the underlying mortgages. The difference between the mortgage rates and the pass-through rate that is paid to investors is called the servicing fee. This represents the servicing institution's fee for "servicing" loans by sending notices to home owners, collecting payments, and funding late payments. For example, a GNMA pool might have underlying mortgages with 9 percent interest rates, and pay a pass-through rate of 8.5 percent. From the total servicing fee of 0.5 percent, GNMA would receive 0.06 percent, and the servicer would keep 0.44 percent for its services. The weighted average coupon is calculated as a weighted average of the underlying mortgage interest rates as of the issue date, using the balance of each mortgage as the weighting factor.

The pool issue date refers to the date of issue of the pass-through security, not to the date of issuance of the underlying mortgages. GNMA pools consist of mortgages up to 1 year old. FNMA and FHLMC pools may contain "seasoned" mortgages, which have been outstanding for several years. The pool maturity date is the date of the latest maturing underlying mortgage in the pool.

In GNMA pools, most underlying mortgages have maturity dates in a relatively narrow range. This will not necessarily be true in FNMA and FHLMC pools. Thus, the pool maturity date can be misleading: 95 percent of the mortgages may mature in 15 years, and 5 percent in 30 years, but the maturity date would be 30 years. So, FNMA and FHLMC give, as extra information on the maturities of their pools, the weighted average maturity. This is calculated as a weighted average of the remaining term of the underlying mortgages, as of the issue date, using the balance of each mortgage as the weighting factor.

FNMA started issuing pass-throughs in 1981, almost a decade after GNMA and the FHLMC. By the end of the decade, it had become the largest guarantor of mortgage-backed securities with over $430 billion outstanding. FNMA mostly buys fixed rate mortgages that have been outstanding 1 or more years. The original maturities within an individual pool range either from 8 to 15 years or from 20 to 30 years.

Several private issuers have also issued pass-through securities. In 1977, the Bank of America issued its first pass-through security, for $150 million. Many other major banks have their own similar arrangements. These issues are often referred to as "private label" issues. Generally, they involve "nonconforming mortgages"—underlying mortgages that do not meet the criteria applied by the major agencies. Often, these mortgages (called "jumbo" mortgages) are larger than the agencies are prepared to guarantee.

Prepayment Experience and Payment Delay

One factor affecting the value of payment flows to an investor in mortgage-backed securities is the payment delay. For example, the payment delay is 14 days for GNMA-I and 19 days for GNMA-II. With FHLMC PCs, the payment delay is 44 days for the original program and 14 days for the Freddie Mac Gold program introduced in the spring of 1990. These varying payment delays reduce the present value of the payment stream to the investor.

Another, much more crucial, factor is prepayments. If no prepayments take place, the cash flow from a pass-through is rather predictable. But the risk of prepayments means that the true maturity of the pass-through security is uncertain. It is tempting to assume that a prepayment is desirable from the point of view of the security holder. But this is not the case. Most of the mortgages underlying the pass-through bear a fixed rate. A common cause of prepayment is refinancing by the borrower. This will not generally take place unless interest rates are low enough to make it worthwhile. But this is just when rates are lower than the pass-through yield. Therefore, prepayment (at par) is undesirable. In fact, prepayment means that mortgage-backed securities have negative convexity (see Chapter 3).

Several ways around this problem have been found, notably the CMO (see below). Also, many efforts have been made to find a way of predicting prepayments. If there is a large pool, the prepayments that do occur tend to become statistically more predictable. This is referred to as the prepayment rate of the pool, which can be compared to the norm.

In the early days of the market, the best known prepayment model was the Federal Housing Administration (FHA) experience. The FHA provides a national system for mortgage insurance. In the process, it has built up a wealth of information on the mortgages it insures, including data on prepayments. Each year, the Actuarial Division of HUD performs a statistical analysis of the FHA data going back to 1957. The results of this analysis became the basis for the FHA-experience model.

The problems with this are that the FHA data apply to mortgages originated over all sorts of interest rate periods, and most FHA mortgages are assumable. The FHA model therefore has been largely superseded by the constant prepayment rate (CPR) or by the Public Securities Association (PSA) model.

The CPR model has the virtue of great simplicity. We simply assume a constant fraction of the remaining principal in the pool is prepaid each month for the remaining term of the mortgage. The PSA model is slightly more subtle. In essence, the major dealers in mortgage-backed securities have agreed among themselves a prepayment benchmark. The PSA prepayment rate curve starts at 0.2 percent per year in the first month that pool of mortgages is outstanding, and increases by 0.2 percent each month until month 30, after which it remains at 6 percent per year for all succeeding months.

To put this problem in perspective, the experience of 1986 shows vividly how prepayments can damage an investor in mortgage-backed securities.

During the first half of 1986, as interest rates fell and borrowers hurried to refinance, the Salomon Brothers Mortgage Bond Index showed a return of 5 percent compared with 9.05 percent for the Broad Investment-Grade Bond Index. A similar phenomenon was seen during the 1991–1993 cycle of falling interest rates, although with some differences. The fall in interest rates was less dramatic, but the jump in prepayments was much higher, largely due to heightened borrower awareness of the value of the prepayment option.

All these complications make yield measurement in the pass-through securities market complex. The yields that are quoted for pass-through securities fall into two general categories: cash flow yield and option-adjusted-spread yields.

The cash flow yield is an attempt to make the underlying cash flow of the security as realistic as possible. This means accounting for all known factors, such as the age of the underlying mortgages, as well as projecting reasonable estimates for future prepayments. The cash flow yield is still very crude, because it ignores the value of the call option built into the bond—the borrower has the ability to prepay.

In the option-adjusted-spread approach, we try to model the cash flows of the bond, using some prepayment model and multiple scenarios of how interest rates will move. (This is often done by Monte Carlo simulation.) We then calculate (1) the present value of each set of cash flows generated by each path, and (2) the average present value of all these results. The option-adjusted spread over the Treasury bond is the spread that makes the average present value of all the paths equal to the price of the bond today.

The starting point in the process is the generation of a random simulation of the future course of interest rates (Figure 10.1). These paths are then used to generate a series of interest rate path-dependent mortgage prepayment rates. Built into this process is an assumption, or a set of assumptions, regarding the

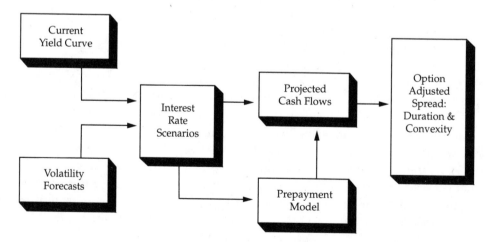

Figure 10.1 Option-adjusted spread modeling.

future volatility of interest rates. Estimates of volatility and of the degree of correlation between long-term and short-term interest rates are crucial to an option-based model. And, of course, they are subject to all the uncertainties and difficulties implicit in making a forecast about rate movements. Finally, a cash flow diagram is established that will then be used to create a series of present values. (The diagram displays a lattice of cash flows generated by running the model over a series of paths.) One can then use the OAS model to work out the basis points differential, expressed as a spread, to the entire Treasury yield curve.

MORTGAGE-BACKED BONDS

The development of the pass-through market led to the creation of the mortgage-backed bond market, in 1970, with a $130 million issue for Zenith Mortgage Company. (Mortgage bonds have existed in Germany and Denmark for well over 100 years; see below.) Mortgage-backed bonds are intermediate or long-term debt instruments that are collateralized by a pool of mortgage loans. The key difference between a mortgage bond and a collateralized mortgage obligation (CMO) is that the CMO is issued by a trust created by the institution selling the mortgages, and the sale of the mortgages to the CMO gets the mortgages off the issuer's balance sheet. With a mortgage-backed bond, the mortgages remain on the balance sheet. It is simply a tool to finance the mortgage holdings.

The current market value of the pledged mortgage loan must exceed the par value of the bond. If the mortgages have market values below the book value (as was often the case for thrifts issuing mortgage-backed bonds in the high-interest-rate environment of the early 1980s), the overcollateralization has had to be 150 percent or 200 percent of the book value of the loans.

Many mortgage bond indenture agreements have provisions for "value maintenance." The issuer must pledge extra mortgage collateral if interest rates rise and, as a result, the market value of mortgages initially pledged falls to unacceptable levels. Mortgage-backed bonds have also been collateralized with FHLMC PCs or FNMA-guaranteed mortgage-backed securities.

Unlike pass-throughs, the cash flow needed to service the mortgage-backed bond is not closely related to cash flow for the collateral. Therefore, the investor must evaluate the financial soundness of the issuing institution before deciding whether to buy mortgage bonds. The mortgage bond is a direct obligation of the issuer, who is responsible for timely repayment. In contrast, in the pass-through and the CMO (see below), investors depend on the collateral, not the issuer. For a mortgage-backed bond, the trustee holds collateral sufficient to pay off the bond. If the issuer fails to pay on time, or the collateral falls below agreed levels, the trustee must liquidate the collateral and repay the bondholders. The volume of mortgage bonds—as distinct from pass-throughs or CMOs—has never been that large. However, the technique is still used occasionally.

Issuers of mortgage bonds developed four general ways of integrating prepayment flows into the structure of financings:

1. By using prepayments, along with regular mortgage interest and principal payments, to fund scheduled debt service.

2. By financing new mortgages with funds accumulated through prepayments.

3. By randomly calling individual bonds proportionally across all maturities whenever prepayments accumulate (termed "strip calls").

4. By designating super-sinker maturities.

Super-Sinkers

In addition to the normal mortgage bonds, a number of U.S. state mortgage agencies have issued tax-exempt mortgage revenue bonds. Among these are a particular class of bond known as a "super-sinker." A super-sinker bond usually has a long stated maturity, but a much shorter, albeit unknown, actual life.

Essentially, the super-sinker is a specific maturity of a mortgage revenue bond issue. All funds from early mortgage payments are used to retire bonds of this maturity. This helps to overcome one of the problems of securitized mortgages—namely, uncertainty regarding prepayment. The investor knows prepayments will be applied to a particular tranche of the issue which will mature faster than the others. An example might be a $100 million, 20-year issue, maturing in the year 2016. Its repayment schedule might be as shown in Table 10.2.

In this structure, the 2015 maturity of $14 million might be the designated super-sinker maturity. All prepayments would be applied to it. Suppose mortgage prepayments are not made for 18 months after the time of the issue (which is reasonable if these are fresh mortgages), and thereafter are made at an annual rate of 5 percent of the outstanding pool of mortgages. The average

Table 10.2 Maturity Schedule for Super-Sinker Bond ($M)

1996	-	2003	1	2010	1
1997	-	2004	1	2011	1
1998	-	2005	1	2012	1
1999	1	2006	1	2013	11
2000	1	2007	1	2014	11
2001	1	2008	1	2015	14
2002	1	2009	1	2016	50

life of the super-sinker would then be around 4 years or so, rather than its apparent 19 years.

The advantage to the investor is generally that the yield on the super-sinker equates to a substantially longer maturity than its expected average life. This yield advantage occurs because super-sinkers do not fit neatly into traditional investment categories, which makes it more difficult for many institutional investors to buy super-sinkers. In addition, investors are rewarded very well for the risk of not knowing precisely how soon the bonds will be retired.

Adding super-sinker maturities to these mortgage revenue bond issues has been attractive for several reasons. First, when all payments are targeted at one specific maturity, cash flow uncertainty is reduced—at least for the early years of the bonds' lives—for all other maturities of the issue. Second, the super-sinker maturity itself could prove to be an attractive vehicle for investors, particularly those who expect mortgage interest rates to fall, over time, while activity in the housing market increases (they would be repaid more quickly), and who can tolerate some cash flow uncertainty.

COLLATERALIZED MORTGAGE OBLIGATIONS

The next step in mortgage securitization essentially followed the thinking that had led to the super-sinker. The result was the collateralized mortgage obligation, first developed in 1983 for the FHLMC. Its first version was the so-called "sequential-pay CMO"; later, many complex variations were developed. (See Table 10.3.) In every case, the object was to reduce the payment uncertainty that was associated with the pass-through structure. Each successive innovation

Table 10.3   Increasing Complexity of CMO Market

Year	Number of Deals	Average Number of Tranches
1983	8	6.6
1984	18	7.9
1985	59	7.4
1986	89	10.7
1987	94	10.9
1988	156	11.5
1989	236	11.1
1990	280	13.6
1991	440	16.1
1992	504	19.2
1993	441	24.0

Source: Adapted from F. J. Fabozzi et al., *Collateralized Mortgage Obligations: Structures and Analysis,* 2nd ed. (Buckingham, PA: F. J. Fabozzi Associates, 1994).

was aimed at defining more tightly the maturity of individual cash flows. Securities firms wanted to transform these securities from the messy unpredictability of the pass-through into something a conventional bond buyer would feel comfortable with.

DEVELOPMENT OF THE CMO MARKET

Table 10.4 shows the rapid growth of the CMO market, as measured by issuance by the main agencies. It also shows the effects of the events of 1994. In that year, a number of specialized mortgage-backed bonds (see below) became highly volatile during the bond market collapse of February/March. Next, those bonds became very illiquid, so that investors could not get out of their positions. This led to the collapse of the $600 million Granite Fund, which had invested heavily in these types of instruments on a leveraged basis and found that it was impossible to liquidate positions when it became necessary to do so. Other investment funds, such as the PaineWebber Short-Term US Government Income Fund, also experienced problems. This supposedly gilt-edged fund had to write down its value by 1.6 percent in one week, owing to its holdings of some of these specialized mortgage-backed securities. Other firms—Piper Capital Management, Hyperion Capital Management, Alliance Capital—experienced similar losses. All of these events led to a sharp contraction in investor demand for the instruments, which began recovering only in 1996.

On a related point, the question of reliability of pricing, it is enlightening to read, in an article in the trade press (J. Jozefek, "Red Flags Alert Mortgage Investors to Downside," *Bloomberg Magazine,* March 1995), that the range of prices quoted on January 24, 1995, for a Class Z Support Bond 1992–134, issued by FNMA, showed the following price indications: CS First Boston, 46–21; Bear

Table 10.4 Issuance of Agency CMOs

	1987–1996 (Second Quarter) ($ billions)			
	GNMA	FNMA	FHMLC	Total
1987	—	0.9	—	0.9
1988	—	11.2	13.0	24.2
1989	—	37.6	39.8	77.3
1990	—	60.9	40.5	101.4
1991	—	101.8	72.0	173.8
1992	—	154.8	131.3	286.1
1993	—	168.0	143.3	311.3
1994	3.1	56.3	73.1	132.6
1995	1.9	8.2	15.4	25.4
1996:Q2	3.2	7.2	10.6	20.9

Source of Data: GNMA, FNMA, FHLMC.

Stearns, 50–30; Asset-Backed Securities Corp., 71–12; and Merrill Lynch, 98–10. (The primary differences arose from different assumptions about pre-payment speeds.) With such a wide range of prices (one quote is actually dou-ble one of the others), investors may feel that the market is not fully reliable. All of these factors were clearly enhanced by the illiquidity of the market dur-ing the crisis, and investors became much more cautious about the market as a result.

CMO STRUCTURES

REMICs

An entity that issues a mortgage-backed security simply acts as a conduit in passing interest through to security holders. Thus, it wants to make sure that any legal structure created to distribute those payments is not taxable. The vehicle used by pass-through issuers is the grantor trust. Unfortunately, under U.S. tax rules, a grantor trust could issue only one class of bond. A CMO issues multiple classes. The problem was solved in 1986 when Congress created the Real Estate Mortgage Investment Conduit (REMIC). These trusts can issue multiple classes of securities without tax problems. It should be stressed that not all CMOs are REMICs.

The REMIC structure must be collateralized by a static pool of loans. These loans are pooled by property type, loan size, and common underwriting stan-dards. Once the portfolio reaches a particular size, the mortgage pool is securi-tized through a REMIC. The mortgage pools are placed into tranches reflecting the risk of the prevailing mortgages. A mortgage must be assignable and should be in a first-lien position. Any participants are likely to make it difficult to offer for sale a REMIC vehicle, and may be perceived negatively by the rating agencies.

From time to time, it becomes profitable to take a CMO and reconstitute the original cash flows. This is sometimes known as a Re-REMIC, or a REMIC on a REMIC. This became quite noticeable in 1994, when the volatile interest rate environment meant reconstituted CMOs became almost as big a business as CMOs for a time. REMICs on REMICs, in June 1994, rose to almost 20 per-cent of the underlying business, which had collapsed following the rise in rates in February 1994.

Sequential-Pay CMOs

The idea behind the CMO is to repackage the underlying mortgage pool to re-duce cash flow uncertainty. As an example, consider a $300 million pool of mortgages. A typical sequential-pay CMO would take this $300 million pool and split it three ways. There would be three bond issues of $100 million each.

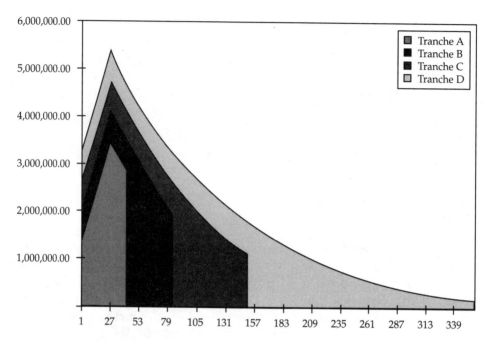

Figure 10.2 Sequential-pay CMO cash flows at 165 PSA.

The first would be the "fast pay" (often referred to by market participants as the A bonds). All principal repayments, up to the first $100 million, would be applied to this tranche. The second tranche (or B bonds) would be the "medium pay"; the second $100 million would be applied to this tranche. The third $100 million would be applied to the "slow pay" tranche (the C bonds). Figure 10.2 shows a 4-tranche example, illustrating the size of cash flow occurring in each month.

A variation adds another class of bond, the Z bond, or accrual bond. The Z bond combines features of zero-coupon bonds and mortgage pass-throughs. It receives no coupon payments until all earlier classes have been paid off. The cash flow from the remaining collateral is then paid to the Z bondholders. While the earlier classes are being paid down, the interest earned by the Z bonds is added to the principal balance. So, during the accrual period, the cash that would be used to pay interest on the Z bonds is used to speed the paydown of the shorter-maturity classes. Figure 10.3 shows the cash flows. Under this structure, the dates when tranches A, B, and C are paid off are, respectively, at months 36, 69, and 117 (compared with 42, 93, and 161 in the previous structure). The Z tranche allows for a much faster repayment of the other tranches, compared with Figure 10.2.

Figures 10.2 and 10.3 were calculated on the basis of 165 PSA, that is, 1.65 times the normal PSA model speeds. A comparison of the patterns at speeds of

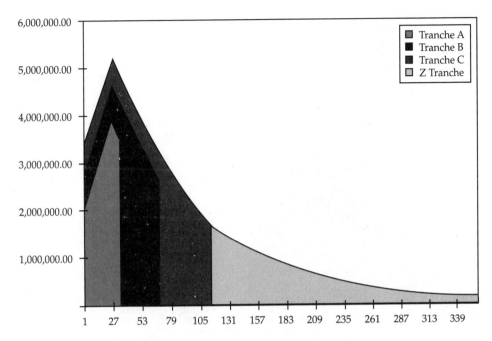

Figure 10.3 Sequential-pay CMO cash flows.

100 and 300 PSA is shown in Figure 10.4. Other refinements have been introduced to this structure, in the form of PAC, TAC, and VADM bonds, and various kinds of Z bonds, discussed below.

Floating Rate and Inverse Floating Rate Classes

By issuing floating rate CMOs (FRCMOs), the market can be broadened. Banks, for example, often prefer to buy floating rate investments because they typically fund themselves at floating rates.

The first FRCMO issues were brought to market in September 1986 by Shearson Lehman and by Centext Acceptance Corporation. The issues were for $150 million and $120 million, respectively, with floating rate tranches of $43 million and $37 million, respectively. The FRCMO was immediately successful for two basic reasons: (1) it inherited the existing fixed-rate CMO market, and (2) it was integrated into the Eurodollar FRN market.

A key feature of the FRCMO market is the use of the cap (see Chapter 7), or alternatively of an inverse floater, to control aggregate interest costs. This is because the CMO uses a separate legal entity for holding the pool of underlying mortgage loans to meet its interest payments. This legal independence gives the bondholder important protection against entanglement in the potential bankruptcy of the CMO's sponsor, which may be a weaker credit. But because

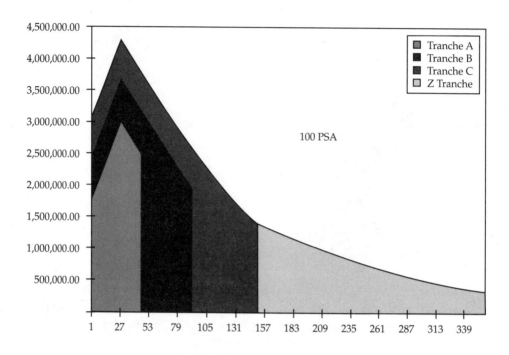

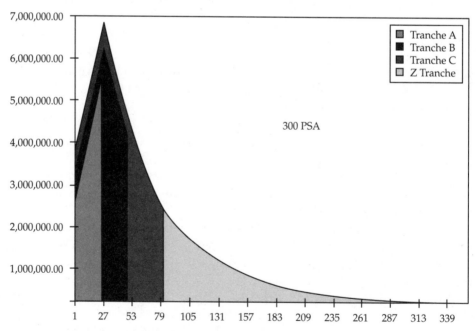

Figure 10.4 Comparison of CMO cash flows at 100PSA and 300PSA.

it is independent, the CMO pool's resources are inherently limited. Therefore, it cannot afford an unhedged exposure to floating rates, because its underlying income is from the fixed rate mortgages.

To handle this problem, FRCMOs often include reverse floater tranches (see Chapter 12). These tranches have interest rates changing in the direction opposite to the LIBOR index. An example can illustrate how this would work. Suppose we have a tranche of $62.5 million and we wish to split it into a floater and an inverse floater.[1] The relative size of the two tranches will depend on investor demand. Suppose we find that investors want $50 million of the floater. The balance of $12.5 million is allocated to the inverse floater. Suppose the coupon rate on the floater is set at 6-month LIBOR + 50 basis points. The coupon on the inverse floater will take the following form:

$$K - L \times 6\text{-month LIBOR}$$

where K is the maximum coupon rate for the inverse floater, and L is the leverage factor for the inverse floater. The size of the leverage factor will depend on the relative size of the two tranches. Here, we have the floater at $50 million and the inverse floater at $12.5 million, so the leverage is 4 to 1.

If we define

IT = inverse tranche amount,

FT = floater tranche amount, and

TT = total tranche size,

then TT = FT + IT, and we can write L = FT/IT = 4. The next critical factor in the equation is the floor (F) that we will set on the inverse floater. Let us set F = 0, which would be normal. Finally, we must consider the interest available to our structure from the underlying collateral. Let us suppose the underlying collateral pays 6.25 percent. We designate this R. We can now carve up the cash flows.

The first step is to find the maximum possible rate (the cap) on the floater. This is done from the formula:

$$\text{Floater cap (FC)} = \frac{R - F * \left(\dfrac{IT}{TT} \right)}{\dfrac{FT}{TT}}$$

In our example, we have FC = (6.25 − 0*(12.5/62.5))/(50/62.5) = 6.25/(50/62.5) = 7.8125

---

[1] This example is drawn from F. J. Fabozzi et al., *Collateralized Mortgage Obligations*, 2nd ed. (Buckingham, PA: F. J. Fabozzi Associates, 1994).

The next step is to find the cap on the inverse floater, using the formula:

$$\text{Inverse cap (IC)} = (FC - FM)^*L + F$$

where FM is the floater margin (50 basis points, in our case). So we have:

$$IC = (7.8125 - .5)^*4 + 0 = 29.25.$$

So, we set up a $50 million floater paying 6-month LIBOR + 50 basis points, capped at 7.8125 percent, and a $12.5 million inverse floater paying 29.25 − 4 × LIBOR, with a minimum coupon of 0. This creates a set of cash flows that can be supported by the underlying collateral paying 6.25 percent. The outcome for the floater and the inverse, over a range of LIBOR scenarios, is detailed in Table 10.5.

The payments are calculated assuming LIBOR periods equal to a half-year. Suppose LIBOR is 6 percent; the floater pays a coupon of 6.5 percent on $50 million, worth $1,625,000. The inverse pays a coupon of 5.25 percent on $12.5 million, worth $328,125. The combined payment equates to $1,953,125, equivalent to 6.25 percent on $62.5 million.

There are other possible solutions to this situation. One could simply create an inverse floater tranche and buy a cap from the market. Some FRCMOs include accrual or zero-coupon tranches that do not pay interest until the retirement of all other tranches. The absence of payments on these tranches while the floating tranche is outstanding frees cash flows to support it in higher interest rate environments. However, the above is, in many ways, the neatest solution, because it simply carves up existing cash flows, entailing no economic costs in buying protection from the market.

Table 10.5   Floater + Inverse Floater Tranches

LIBOR	Floater Coupon		Inverse Coupon		Total	
1	$ 375,000	1.5%	$1,578,125	25.25%	$1,953,125	6.25%
2	625,000	2.5	1,328,125	21.25	1,953,125	6.25
3	875,000	3.5	1,078,125	17.25	1,953,125	6.25
4	1,125,000	4.5	828,125	13.25	1,953,125	6.25
5	1,375,000	5.5	578,125	9.25	1,953,125	6.25
6	1,625,000	6.5	328,125	5.25	1,953,125	6.25
7	1,875,000	7.5	78,125	1.25	1,953,125	6.25
8	1,953,125	7.8125	0	0	1,953,125	6.25
9	1,953,125	7.8125	0	0	1,953,125	6.25
10	1,953,125	7.8125	0	0	1,953,125	6.25
11	1,953,125	7.8125	0	0	1,953,125	6.25

Superfloaters and Inverse Superfloaters

A superfloater is a floating rate CMO whose coupon rate is a multiple of the reference rate. It is like a leveraged inverse floater of the kind we were just looking at. But the superfloater's coupon rises as LIBOR, or the reference rate, rises. The form is as follows, assuming that the reference rate is 1-month LIBOR:

$$C \times 1\text{-month LIBOR} - M$$

where C is the coupon leverage and M is a constant. For example, if C is 3 and M is 16.5 percent, then the formula for the coupon rate for the superfloater is: 3×1-month LIBOR $- 16.5$ percent. If 1-month LIBOR is 9 percent, then the coupon rate is 10.5 percent. As with the inverse, there must be a floor on the coupon rate to prevent it from becoming negative.

PAC Bonds

In March 1987, the MDC Mortgage Funding Corporation CMO included a class of bonds described as "planned amortization class" bonds or " PAC" bonds. Since then, this structure has been widely used. It provides greater certainty of the timing of principal repayments because PAC bonds have priority, over all other classes in the CMO issue, for receiving principal payments from the underlying collateral. The greater certainty of the cash flow for the PAC bonds comes at the expense of the non-PAC classes, called the support bonds or companion bonds.

It works like this. If the actual principal repayment is more than the scheduled amount, it is paid to the support bonds. So the support bonds accept greater prepayment risk. Conversely, if repayment slows down, then the PAC bonds have priority for any later principal repayments received. This protects them somewhat against the risk that their maturity will lengthen as interest rates rise.

Reverse PACs and Lockouts

The PAC structure provides good protection against unexpected changes in payment patterns. But it is not complete protection. In an effort to strengthen the protection, two other structures have been devised: (1) the reverse PAC, and (2) the lockout.

A way to achieve a greater degree of protection for some of the PAC bonds is to alter the principal payment rules for distributing principal once all the support bonds have been paid off. We can specify that, after all the support bonds have been paid off, all excess principal payments are made first to the longer-dated PAC bonds. Thus, the medium-maturity bonds are protected to a greater degree. Such a structure is called a reverse PAC structure.

The lockout structure achieves greater protection for the PAC bonds by the simple device of having more support bonds and fewer PAC bonds. This can produce a result where no payments of principal are made to the PAC bonds during several of the early years. The payments are "locked out" of the PAC.

TAC Bonds, VADM Bonds

Another variant often used is the TAC bond, known formally as the Targeted Amortization Class bond. This resembles the PAC bond in that both have a schedule of principal repayment. The difference between a PAC bond and a TAC bond is that the former is much better protected against "contraction risk" (excess prepayment) and "extension risk" (prepayments less than expected). The PAC bond is protected over a wide range of PSA prepayment rates, whereas the TAC is protected at one single PSA rate. This implies that the TAC is protected against contraction risk, but not against extension risk. For example, suppose we have a TAC bond that is expected to have an average life of 6.86 years at a prepayment rate of 165 PSA. Assuming that this bond accounts for three-quarters of the total value of a theoretical CMO, with a support bond accounting for the rest, this bond is protected against significant contraction risk for all prepayment speeds below about 300 PSA. It is not perfectly protected, but there is a reasonable cushion of protection.

Some institutional investors are interested in protection against extension risk but are willing to accept contraction risk. This is the opposite protection from that sought by the buyers of TAC bonds. In this case, we would construct a reverse TAC bond.

A final class of bonds for consideration is the Very Accurately Determined Maturity (VADM) bonds, sometimes referred to as AD bonds, or Stated Maturity Bonds (SMBs). Here, we use an accrual or Z bond. The interest accruing (i.e., not being paid out) on a Z bond is used to pay the interest on a VADM bond. This effectively provides protection against extension risk even if prepayments slow down, because the interest accruing on the Z bond will be sufficient to pay off the scheduled principal and interest on the VADM bond. The VADM bond is similar in character to a reverse TAC. For structures with similar collateral, however, a VADM bond offers greater protection against extension risk. Moreover, VADM bonds will not normally shorten significantly if prepayments speed up. Thus, they offer greater protection against contraction risk than a reverse TAC with the same underlying collateral.

Support/Companion Bonds and Jump/Sticky Zs

The support bonds are the bonds that provide prepayment protection for bond classes in a structure providing a schedule of principal repayments—TAC and

PAC bonds. As a result, they are exposed to the greatest level of prepayment risk and require much more careful analysis. Their values will be very sensitive to changes in prepayment patterns.

It is even possible to create support bonds with a schedule of principal repayments—that is, support bond TAC or PAC bonds. If a structure has a PAC bond with a support bond that itself has a PAC structure, the former is called a Level I PAC, and the latter, a Level II PAC. The latter has better prepayment protection than the support bonds without a schedule of principal repayments, but the protection is less than that for Level I PAC bonds.

Within a PAC structure, all bonds will be either PAC or support bonds. If the Z bond is a support bond, its accruals will be derived from the cash flows outside the PAC bonds and will therefore be quite unstable. Support Zs typically have relatively little call protection and so are priced to deep discounts. Investors with liabilities with no targeted maturity may be able to accept the extension risk implicit in this structure, but others would probably avoid them.

This applies even more to a class of support Z introduced in 1989, the Jump Z. In a Jump Z, the maturity sequence shifts in priority if a specific event happens. It could be a specific PSA speed (e.g., 250 PSA is reached) or interest rate level (e.g., Treasury yields fall to 7 percent). If the trigger is activated, the Jump Z becomes the first bond to receive repayments, jumping ahead of all others. Such a bond is very much a gamble on interest rate movements.

There have been a number of variations on the trigger structure; many provided that cumulative events were required to trigger a jump (e.g., a 3-month cumulative prepayment speed of 250 PSA). A sticky Jump Z is one that, having once activated its trigger, makes a permanent change; a nonsticky Jump Z is one that reverts back to its former position if conditions revert back to normal. These bonds are extremely risky (as investors discovered the hard way) and have fallen into disfavor.

POs & IOs

In 1986, the mortgage-backed securities market saw the first application of the coupon stripping technique used in the Treasury bond market (see Chapter 9). This was achieved by creating two classes where the principal from the underlying collateral repayments is paid to one class and all the interest is paid to the other class. These two classes are referred to as the principal-only (PO) class and the interest-only (IO) class.

A PO bond class is sold at a substantial discount from par. Therefore, PO bondholders want a decline in mortgage rates, so that prepayments accelerate. They bought the principal at a discount; they get it paid back at par. The faster that happens, the better their return. Conversely, if prepayments slow down, the bondholders will not get such good performance.

The performance of the IO is the mirror image. The IO bondholder wants prepayments to slow down. In that way, they keep earning interest. The longer the mortgages are outstanding, the better the return. So these classes behave counter to any normal bond. As interest rates rise, householders tend not to repay their mortgages, and more interest flows through to the IO. These bonds perform well as interest rates rise.

The IO and PO together will accumulate to 100 percent of the underlying. Figure 10.5 illustrates their relative performance for a FNMA 9 percent mortgage-backed security with a weighted average coupon of 9.75 percent and a weighted average maturity of 29 years, 4 months.

Many tax and accounting games have been played with these instruments. For example, there was a period when thrift institutions' accounting regulations did not recognize the IO bonds for what they were. They were treated as pure interest income and no principal. This is economically true, but the sum paid to acquire the IOs should be, for accounting purposes, the principal value of the investment. For a while, the thrifts were reporting an almost infinite return on their purchases of IOs!

On the other hand, provided they are analyzed correctly and accounted for properly, they do represent an interesting investment alternative—as do the POs.

CMO Residuals/Equity/IOette

In January 1986, the California Public Employees' Retirement System issued a CMO that let the issuer sell the CMO's residual cash flows, or equity. The need

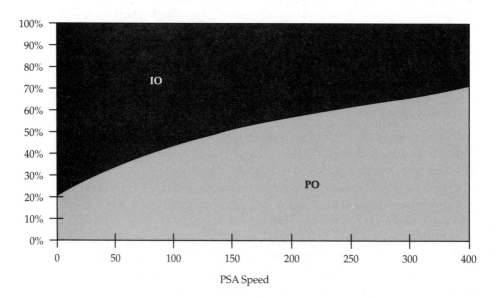

Figure 10.5   IO vs PO at differing PSA speeds.

for this arose from the U.S. generally accepted accounting principles (GAAP), which require the issuer to consolidate the CMO in its financial statements. To avoid this consolidation, the issuer must ensure that (1) it does not guarantee or redeem the debt tranches before maturity, and (2) it can receive only nominal amounts from the CMO issue. This latter condition can be satisfied if the CMO's equity is sold to third parties.

To an investor, the attraction of a CMO residual is its countercyclical nature. Returns rise as interest rates rise (it resembles the IO in this). This is because the main income for the equity holder is the spread between the CMO's rate cost and the yield on the underlying mortgages. The longer the CMO is outstanding, the more spread is earned. So, as rates rise and repayments fall, lengthening the CMO, the equity holder benefits. Conversely, as rates fall, the equity's value falls to zero.

In more recent deals, there have been two significant changes from the initial use of residuals. First, the coupon differential has been used to create a bond class called an IOette. This is not in itself a residual but is a normal interest-only bond receiving a nominal amount of principal. Before 1992, some principal had to be paid to this class because the tax law governing REMICs required that all regular interest bonds receive some principal; there could be no interest-only classes within the REMIC structure. This provision was changed in 1992.

The second change came about after the passage of the REMIC legislation. In the pre-REMIC structures, the sole residual class in the structure not only received the cash flows but also was responsible for any tax due. It is now typical for two residual classes to be included in a structure. One, denoted R, is a residual class that receives part of the coupon differential. The other residual class, typically denoted RL and often referred to as a de minimis residual, is responsible for the tax liability.

Other Structures: Extendomatics and Whole Loan CMOs

In some cases, the CMO structure has "front-loaded" principal repayments. This has the effect of shortening the bonds' weighted average life. However, once these repayments have been received, the principal cash flow falls off dramatically, and the weighted average life increases. Such structures are sometimes created in order to achieve an apparent lower initial weighted average life. Once the securities have been sold to the investor, the latter discovers that as soon as the front-loaded payments have been received, the remaining weighted average life actually increases. Such bonds are sometimes called "extendomatics."

A whole-loan CMO is based on mortgages that have not been modified by one of the agencies; in other words, the investor is not benefiting from the guarantee of a federal agency. Thus, there are questions of credit risk to consider. The normal technique is to undertake credit enhancement, sufficient to achieve a AAA rating. The two general types of such enhancement, external and internal, are discussed in Chapter 8.

OAS Modeling Considerations

Readers who have struggled this far through this chapter will realize that some mortgage-backed structures are quite complicated. In the brief discussion at the start of the chapter, mention was made of OAS modeling: the process of attempting to put a value on the options built into the CMO. The technology has become increasingly impressive and sophisticated. We need to remember, though, that all such models are built on sand, in the sense that they depend on forecasts of volatility and on forecasts of prepayment behavior, which themselves depend on forecasts about demographics, social patterns, and other imponderables. For example, there were two major refinancing cycles in 1986–1987 and 1991–1993. There were important differences between the cycles. In 1987, the bottom for mortgage rates at 9 percent was 75 basis points higher than in the second wave, which began in the summer of 1992. Second, 1987 brought an early increase in rates, whereas, in 1992, mortgage rates remained low for a much longer period of time.

The prepayment patterns experienced in 1986–1987 formed the basis of most assumptions applied to prepayment sensitivity in 1991–1992. But in 1992, refinancing started much earlier. The reason appears to lie in a major change in the mortgage financing process from the 1980s to the 1990s. In the earlier period, a large percentage of mortgages were held in the portfolios of savings and loan associations. They had little incentive to encourage refinancing. By the 1990s, mortgage originators were primarily mortgage bankers interested in new mortgages, and the economic incentive was shifting to the creation of servicing income. This shift caused the mortgage originators to become concerned primarily with keeping the mortgage portfolio in time. The best defense then became to encourage refinancing so that the mortgages could be kept on the books of the servicer and not refinanced elsewhere.

The difficulty in reliably handling this kind of structural shift makes the OAS model ultimately rest on shaky foundations. The technology is most impressive, and indeed very valuable, if used properly, but investors need to be cautious about total reliance on such models.

Who Buys CMOs?

CMOs are attractive to credit-sensitive investors. By virtue of their structure, most CMOs have been rated AAA. This is based not on the creditworthiness of the issuer, but on the collateral. The conservative structuring of CMO issues means that most are overcollateralized, most are backed by mortgages or mortgage pass-throughs guaranteed by FNMA, GNMA, or FHLMC, and most are issued by single-purpose finance subsidiaries. Their collateral is held in trust by a third-party bank, and, in most cases, all bond administration expenses are covered by a special reserve fund. This credit strength led to a rush to buy CMOs in the late 1980s, particularly after the leveraged takeover bid for R.J. Reynolds had demonstrated that even the largest corporations in the world were not exempt from "event risk."

The short average lives (generally, 2 to 3 years), high yields, and high credit quality of first-tranche bonds make them attractive alternatives to short-term Treasuries and agencies for liquidity investors—even though portfolio managers must be prepared to accept less certainty in the timing of the repayment of principal.

Middle and longer tranches have been attractive to institutional investors—insurance companies, commercial bank trust departments, pension funds, and investment advisers—who have traditionally met their intermediate maturity needs with corporate bonds. Many are international investors who are looking for high-quality securities but who cannot tolerate the monthly payment frequency and widely dispersed cash flows inherent in mortgage pass-throughs.

Insurance companies looking to match liabilities in the 5-year range (Guaranteed Investment Contracts and Single-Payment Deferred Annuities) might find the middle tranche an attractive alternative to high-grade corporates or private placements. The same institutions may find the longer tranche more attractive when they seek to match longer-term liabilities.

Z bonds are attractive to investors who normally would be buyers of zero-coupon Treasuries and who want to lock in yields for long periods. Pension funds and insurance companies have generally been the biggest investors in Z bonds. They have found the yield advantage attractive enough to outweigh the uncertainty of cash flows after the end of the Z bond's accrual period.

COMMERCIAL MORTGAGES

The process of mortgage securitization was originally confined to residential properties. A logical next step was the commercial mortgage market. In March 1984, Olympia and York, the Canadian real estate developer, arranged a $970 million private placement of a floating rate financing based on the mortgages on three seasoned Manhattan buildings (237 Park Avenue, 1290 Avenue of the Americas, and 2 Broadway). Table 10.6 lists some other early securitizations.

The first portfolio securitization for commercial mortgages was a U.S. domestic private placement for Penn Mutual late in 1984. In December 1984, the first public offering took place in the Euromarkets, a $1.3 billion transaction for Prudential. Subsequent offerings were made for New England Mutual and Connecticut Mutual. Each of these used the fixed payment format begun with

Table 10.6   Some Early Commercial Mortgage Securitizations

December 1984	Prudential	$1.3 billion	Secured on a portfolio of mortgages.
February 1985	New England Life Mortgage Funding Corp.	$298 million	Backed by mortgages on commercial property; prepayments reinvested.
June 1985	Middletown Trust	$208 million	Secured by an assignment of rentals from Aetna Casualty.
November 1985	Olympia & York	$200 million	Secured on 59 Maiden Lane, New York City.
	Fisher Brothers Financial Realty	$160 million	Secured by a mortgage on 605 Third Avenue.
January 1986	Mutual Benefit Overseas Corp.	$410 million	Secured by commercial mortgages and by Mutual Benefit Life Insurance Co.'s obligation to buy back or replace defaulted leases.

Prudential. For another insurance company, Massachusetts Mutual, a $700 million pass-through was structured in early 1985 to liquefy a portfolio of commercial mortgages by means of a domestic U.S. offering.

The key difference between the New England Life deal and previous mortgage-backed bonds, such as CMOs, lies in the treatment of prepayments. Instead of passing through the prepayments, these are reinvested by the issuer until the fixed payment date due on the bond. This is achieved by giving the issuer the right to substitute fresh mortgages for those that are redeemed, provided those substituted satisfy a cash flow test, which in turn ensures that the obligations on the bonds are met. If a mortgage is prepaid, the funds received are deposited by the issuer in a prepayment account with the trustee. They are either invested in eligible investments, or invested with the issuer's parent (in this case, New England Life), which undertakes to guarantee a return of 9 percent per annum compounded monthly. This structure is much more acceptable to the Euromarket, which is accustomed to fixed bullet maturities.

The 59 Maiden Lane deal by Olympia & York was backed by the building, the tenant leases, and a credit insurance policy from Aetna Casualty and Surety Company. This policy will supplement the cash flow from the leases to ensure that the cash available for servicing is at least 125 percent of the debt service obligation.

Around the same time, a similar issue for $160 million was brought to the Euromarket for Fisher Brothers Financial Realty Company, secured by a mortgage on property on 605 Third Avenue, New York (housing, among other tenants, John Wiley & Sons). In addition to the mortgage, the securities are backed by an irrevocable letter of credit provided by Union Bank of Switzerland (UBS), initial value $51.9 million, and a pledged bank account or eligible securities valued at US$10 million initially.

A significant development in commercial mortgage securitization was the Standard and Poor's AA rating on the American Express world headquarters building. For the first time, a building was given a rating of its own. In rating buildings, S&P creates a "worst case" scenario based on the cash flows generated by the lease, and then determines the credit required in the form of a letter of credit or surety.

One way of tackling the problem of securitizing individual buildings or groups of buildings has been the Real Estate Investment Trust (REIT). Examples include the financing for EQK Realty Investors 1 and EQK 2. EQK 1, in March 1985, was a real estate investment trust owning a warehouse/office complex in Indianapolis, an office development in Atlanta, and a regional shopping mall in Pennsylvania. EQK 2 is the second single property securitized and traded in the U.S. equity markets (after New York's Rockefeller Center), and the first of its kind using the limited partnership method. The financing consisted of $103 million of limited partnership units, a form of equity, and $44 million of zero-coupon debt securities.

As the market has developed, however, much of the commercial mortgage activity has been in either multifamily housing or retail, with the former the primary area of activity. One influential factor here was the role of the Resolution Trust Corporation (RTC), the body set up to sort out the mess the thrifts had made. Another was the emergence of "conduits." ARBOR National Commercial Mortgage Corporation (ANCMC), formerly Commercial Mortgage Corporation of America (CMC), founded in 1986, was the first commercial conduit and completed the first commercial securitization of newly originated loans in 1987. At that time, letters of credit were used as credit enhancements. The securities were comprised of multifamily and other types of commercial properties and were sold on a whole loan basis. Thus, an investor could invest in just one loan but have the benefit of a liquid security.

In 1991, CMC issued its first multifamily pool. This transaction involved 49 loans originated by CMC. Another key player in the evolution of conduits is Washington Mortgage, which started a conduit with Daiwa Securities America, Inc. The combination of huge spreads and falling rates in the 1992–1993 period led to a very crowded conduit field by late 1993, culminating in the arrival of the banks. In April 1994, Washington Mortgage announced the formation of a conduit with NationsBank to buy Washington's loans on a case-by-case basis.

Securitization of multifamily debt may be under private label or through government-sponsored agencies such as FNMA or FHLMC, or (in the past) Resolution Trust Corporation. The following example is an illustration of a multifamily CMO.

Resolution Trust Corporation, Multifamily Mortgage Pass-Through, Series 1992-M1

Issuer: Resolution Trust Corporation
Originator: Gibraltar Savings FA and Gibraltar Savings Bank FSB
Master Servicer: Midland Data Systems Inc.
Trustee: State Street Bank & Trust
Lead Manager: Kidder, Peabody & Co.

Class	Type	Initial or Mortgage or Fixed Amount (in millions)	Loan Coupon	Loan Index	Group	Rating
A-1	Senior	$ 36.5	4.6875	Miscellaneous	1	Aaa
A-2	Senior	71.9	7.61	Misc./Fixed	2;5	Aa1
A-3	Senior	28.3	8.00	6 months; 1 yr; 11th District COFI	3	Aa2
A-4	Senior	109.5	7.91	1 month; 11th District COFI	4	Aa2
B-1	Subordinate	24.3	6.0875	Misc.	1	Aa3
B2	Subordinate	20.1	7.73	Misc./fixed	2;5	A2

Loan Characteristics

	Group 1	Group 2	Group 3	Group 4	Group 5
Class	A-1; B-1	A-2; B-2	A-3	A-4	A-2; B-2
Index	96% Misc. 4% Fixed	68% Fixed 32% Misc.	11th District COFI	11th District COFI	Fixed
Principal amount (in millions)	$60.7	$71.9	$28.2	$109.5	$20.1
Number of loans	224	116	66	179	202
Avg. LTV	67%	71.3%	62.5%	75.5%	47%
Avg. CDSC	1.5	1.31	1.58	0.97	2.95
30+ day delinq.	0.86%	3.86%	0.77%	13.57%	0.01%
Avg. loan	$271,303	$619,794	$428,507	$611,936	$99,441
WAM	10.46	7.24	18.23	17.90	9.02
WAC	9.95%	9.55%	9.96%	9.15%	8.27%
Avg. margin	2.275%	2.83%	2.53%	2.389%	NA

Credit support				
	Class A-1	45%	Class A-4	37%
	Class A-2	37%	Class B-1	37%
	Class A-3	37%	Class B-2	30%

Notes:
COFI = Cost of funds index.
CDSC = combined debt service coverage (operating income/debt service).
LTV = loan-to-value.
WAM = weighted average maturity.
WAC = weighted average coupon.

Source of Data: Moody's Investor Services, "Structured Finance Research & Commentary," April 1992, p. 16.

The structure is a REMIC pass-through with (1) a reserve fund available to cover losses on all the certificate classes; (2) subordinated classes B-1 and B-2 to offset losses to class A-1 certificates; (3) subordinated class B-2 to offset losses to class A-2 certificates; and (4) cross-support payments bid (see Figure 10.6) from class B-2 to enhance classes A-1, B-1, A-3, and A-4. These are illustrated in Figure 10.6.

Class A-1 and class B-1 are primarily supported by loan group 1, which contains adjustable rate loans tied to seven indexes. The vast majority (65 percent) are 11th District Cost of Funds Index (COFI) loans. Loan group 1 also contains fixed rate loans (4.28 percent). Principal and interest from loan group 1 will be applied to pay class A-1 and class B-1 accrued interest, at a variable pass-through rate equal to the least of (1) LIBOR, plus a margin; (2) 11 percent for class A-1 and 12.25 percent for class B-1; or (3) the available funds cap. This is the excess available from loan group 1 payments after these have been applied to pay down the principal balance of classes A-1 and B-1. These payments

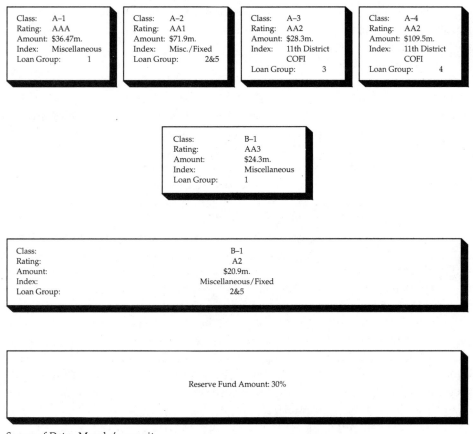

Source of Data: Moody's op. cit.

Figure 10.6   Credit support for RTC MF Series 1992-M1.

are made in an amount that will maintain the certificate principal balances equal to the principal balance of the loans in loan group 1.

Because the coupon on these two classes is tied to LIBOR, and the underlying loan group is paid interest according to a variety of indexes, these two classes have basis risk. To offset this, they also receive payments from excess cash available from all of the other loan groups after the other classes have been paid (1) interest, (2) scheduled principal, and (3) principal prepayments.

Class A-2 and class B-2 are supported by both loan group 2 and loan group 5. These loan groups contain fixed rate mortgage loans (68 percent) and adjustable rate mortgage loans tied to various indexes. Class A-2 is repaid before class B-2 is entitled to receive any principal repayments. Both classes can draw on the reserve fund for shortfalls and losses.

Class A-3 and class A-4 are supported, respectively, by loan groups 3 and 4, which contain COFI-based adjustable loans. Credit support for these classes is available from the reserve fund and from cross-support payments from class B-2. When the reserve fund is reduced to 10 percent of the aggregate loan balance, class B-2's scheduled principal payments are redirected to pay down the other classes on a pro rata basis. In addition, after the reserve fund falls to 3 percent of outstanding loans, class B-2's scheduled interest payments begin to absorb any realized losses.

Another protection for each of the classes is the availability of excess cash generated from loan groups 1, 3, and 4. On each distribution date, if there is enough cash to pay the related class of certificates its interest and principal, the excess is applied to other classes. The excess is applied sequentially to classes A-1, B-1, A-2, B-2 (unless subject to cross-support payments), A-3, and, finally, A-4. The excess cash from loan groups 2 and 5 will be used only to pay down class A-2, and then, provided no cross-support payments are in effect, class B-2. After class B-2 is reduced to zero, excess cash from these two loan groups can be used to pay classes A-1, B-1, A-3, and A-4 sequentially. These arrangements are summarized in Figure 10.7.

From the investor's angle, investments in multifamily mortgage-backed securities (MFMBSs) have both advantages and disadvantages over their residential single-family counterparts. The securities usually have a lockout period during which borrowers are not allowed to prepay (often, 5 years). This period is typically followed by another period during which prepayment is permitted with a penalty that declines over time. Other loans may not have a lockout period, but instead have a "yield maintenance" provision. Yield maintenance simply requires a borrower calling the loan to pay the lender an exercise price equal to the value of the loan if it were held to a specific date. So MFMBSs may yield sustained premium returns in a falling rate environment much longer than their single-family counterparts.

In March 1994, a new development occurred when Nomura Securities introduced its MegaDeal™ bonds. These were large issues of bonds backed by pools of commercial mortgages; their unique feature was that Nomura had

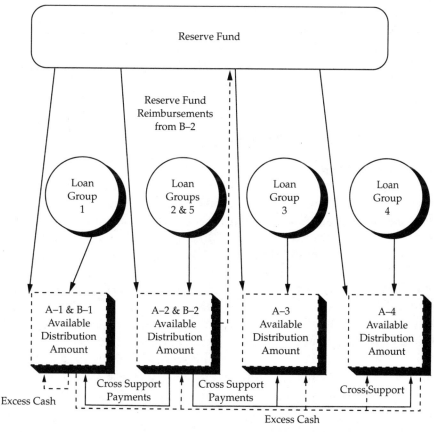

[1] To A–1 for interest
[2] To B–1 for interest
[3] To A–1 for principal, until retired, then to B–1 for principal, the Group 1 Priority Amount (principal from Loan Group 1 in an amount sufficient to keep the aggregate certificate balance of A–1 and B–1 equal to the principal balance on Loan Group 1
[4] To A–1 for principal, until retired, then to B–1 for principal, the Excess Cash from Loan Group 1.

[1] To A–2 for interest
[2] To B–2 for interest, unless Reserve Fund equals 3% of loan balance, then to Reserve Fund
[3] To A–2 for principal until A–2 is retired, then to B–2, unless Cross Support Payments are required, then to A–1, B–1, A–3 and A–4 pro rata
[4] To A–2 for principal from Excess Cash from Loan Groups 2 and 5 until A–2 is retired, then to B–2, unless Cross Support Payments are required, in which case Excess Cash goes to A–1, B–1, A–3 and A–4 sequentially until each such class is retired.
[5] If B–2 is retired, to A–1, B–1, A–3 and A–4 for principal from Excess Cash from Loan Groups 2 & 5, sequentially until each such class is retired.

[1] To A–3 for interest
[2] To A–3 for principal
[3] To A–1, B–1, A–2, B–2 (unless Cross Support Payments are required), A–3 and A–4, for principal, sequentially until each such Class is retired, from Excess Cash from Loan Group 3.

[1] To A–4 for interest
[2] To A–4 for principal
[3] To A–2, B–1, A–2, B–2 (unless Cross Support Payments are required), A–3 and A–4, for principal, sequentially until each such class is retired, from Excess Cash from Loan Group 4.

Note: Excess cash is generally used to pay down the classes sequentially, except for (1) Excess Cash from Loan Group 1, where it is applied to pay only Classes A–1 and B–1, and (ii) Excess Cash from Loan Groups 2 and 5, where it is first applied to Classes A–2 and B–2 and then to pay other classes sequentially.

Figure 10.7 Cross-supports for RTC MF series 1992-M1.

entered into the underlying mortgage transactions as principal, and therefore was able to achieve homogeneous underlying documentation. This provides much more standardization, making it easier for the investor to evaluate the bond. The first transaction was $410 million of fixed rate bonds backed by six loans backed by mortgages on 59 shopping center properties and 40 hotel properties.

Single-Family Mortgage-Revenue Bonds

Single-family mortgage-revenue bonds are tax-exempt debt instruments issued by U.S. state and local finance authorities to provide qualified first-time buyers with low-cost mortgages. These bonds have characteristics of both a municipal bond and a mortgage-backed security. Like the first, they have serially issued maturities and embedded options; like the second, they are subject to prepayments during periods of declining interest rates. However, they are less predictable than either a municipal or a mortgage-backed bond, because they are subject to many more redemption quirks. Redemption patterns are affected by unexpended proceeds in the early years, excess revenue, "cross-calls" (where an issuer has the right to redeem the higher-coupon debt of one bond series, using mortgage prepayments or excess reserve-fund earnings from another), and mortgage recycling (where an issuer uses principal repayments to fund new mortgages rather than to call bonds). All these factors make the maturity particularly hard to predict.

International Developments

Canada

The Canadian market for mortgage-backed bonds did not develop until the mid-1980s. In part, this was due to the existence of a strong national banking system, unlike the U.S. situation at the time. In December 1986, a government-sponsored National Housing Act (NHA) mortgage-backed securities program was launched. The Canada Mortgage and Housing Corporation (CMHC, a Crown Agency) guarantees the full and timely payment of the mortgage-backed security in exchange for an up-front fee. Homogeneous mortgages are pooled together in a fully assigned, registerable format with the supporting documentation placed with a custodian. Investors are then sold certificates representing undivided ownership interests in the pool. Following the initial success of the program, a new product line was introduced in the Fall of 1988. The scope of the program was expanded beyond single-family residential mortgages to include nonprepayable, multiunit, social housing, nonprofit mortgages. These mortgages result from government initiatives to provide subsidized housing for low-income Canadians. Typically, the government subsidies equal the operating deficits of the nonprofit corporations running the projects. These mortgages are usually amortized over 30 years and have initial terms of 5 years. They are also not permitted any prepayment privileges. The lack of practical or legal ability to make prepayments, coupled with the virtual impossibility of default, makes the resulting securities very attractive. The certainty of their cash flows makes them more attractive than even the most carefully structured CMO.

U.K. Mortgage-Backed Market

In 1987, HOMES (Home-Owner Mortgage Euro-Securities) was issued by the U.K.'s National Home Loans Corporation. It was AAA-rated by Standard and Poor's as the result of guarantee on the mortgage pool by Sun Alliance and London Insurance; interest payments were guaranteed by Financial Security Assurance of the United States.

In the following 7 years, nearly £16 billion in rated securities were issued. To start with, securitization was mostly used by the centralized, specialist mortgage lenders to originate business from a thin capital base. However, rising interest rates in the late 1980s made the centralized mortgage lenders less competitive against the more traditional mortgage lenders, who were able to tap their retail deposit bases at more competitive interest rates.

Despite some limited activity by two of the clearing banks—Barclays and National Westminster—both of whom made their debuts in the mortgage-backed market in 1993, the incentive to securitize remained limited for the major lenders. They generally retained healthy capital bases, and they had to deal with public concern about borrowers' agreements with "faceless investors."

The building societies (the U.K. equivalent of U.S. savings and loan institutions) have been even slower to securitize, because of legal, procedural, and regulatory issues. This market began with two residential mortgage-backed loans of £100 million for the Leeds Permanent Building Society and for the National & Provincial Building Society, respectively, and a £150 million commercial mortgage securitization for the Bristol & West Building Society. In 1995, Birmingham Midshires Building Society, through Pendeford Mortgage No.1 PLC, launched what was then the largest ever asset-backed securities issue in the Euromarkets. The transactions details are shown in Table 10.7.

A somewhat similar structure was used by U.K. Rents (No. 1) in October 1994. This was a special-purpose vehicle set up by six housing associations that collectively pledged future rental income to the vehicle. The special-purpose vehicle then issued a £36.6 million Eurobond with both interest and principal repaid from the rents. The structure was rated AAA and, accordingly, provided an attractive cost of funds. The same approach, but on a much larger scale, was used by National Westminster in March 1997. A special-purpose vehicle, called Orchardbrook, was set up to handle the transfer into the private sector of more than half the U.K. government's loans to British housing associations. More

Table 10.7 Pendeford Mortgages No. 1 PLC

Originator and Servicer of the Assets: Birmingham Midshires Mortgage Services Limited, based in Bracknell, Berkshire.

Originator's Ownership Structure: 100 percent owned by Western Trust and Savings Holdings Limited, itself 100 percent owned by Birmingham Midshires Building Society.

Tranches	Amounts	Ratings
A	£250,000,000	AAA/Aaa
A2	£200,000,000	AAA/Aaa
A3	£300,000,000	AAA/Aaa
A4	£195,000,000	AA/Aa2
A5	£30,000,000	AA/A2
B	£25,000,000	Unrated

Legal maturity: July 2037

Portfolio Details

Number of Mortgages: 15,911.

Average Mortgage Size: £60,952.

Regional concentrations: 50.94 percent London and Southeast, remainder in England, Wales, and N. Ireland.

Mortgage Product Types: Variable rate, fixed (all hedged), capped (all hedged), discounted (all hedged).

Loan-to-Value Ratios: 74 percent average on portfolio.

Repayment Types: Endowment, repayment, pension, interest only.

New Business: 47.7 percent of portfolio; 30 months old.

Seasoning: 35.4 percent of pool originated over 4 years ago.

---

than 38,000 loans to 1,000 housing associations were transferred and securitized by means of an issue of just under £1 billion. The average life of the bonds was estimated at 28.6 years, but a tranche of £115 million was created to absorb unexpected prepayments.

Shared Appreciation Mortgage. In 1997, the Bank of Scotland launched a new concept: the shared appreciation mortgage (SAM), fully refinanced by SBC Warburg in advance of a securitization in the first quarter of 1997.

The concept is simple: The homeowner pays zero or low interest; the bank, in return, gets participation in any increase in the value of the house when it is sold. In the case of a zero-interest SAM, as opposed to a low-interest SAM, the bank sees a return on the original loan of three times the increase in house values. So, if the Bank of Scotland lends a homeowner 25 percent of the value of a property, it will receive 75 percent of any increase in value when the home is sold, plus the original 25 percent loan. If the homeowner pays 5.75 percent interest, then the 3:1 ratio reduces to 1:1. A mortgagee might borrow 65 percent of the value of a property and pay 5.75 percent interest on that for life.

When the property is sold, the Bank of Scotland gets back its loan plus 65 percent of the increase in value. In short, the homeowner, as well as issuing debt, issues equity. This is the kind of risk that investors might well be happy with, but it is not a natural risk for a bank; hence the securitization. It is too early to tell whether the concept will work, but if borrowers are prepared to take up the mortgage, the securitization market for these mortgages could eventually become substantial in size.

U.K. Commercial Mortgages

Some commercial U.K. real estate transactions are worth mentioning. Another approach to mortgage-backed securities was seen in the 1985 sterling bulldog issue by Safeway Stores. This had a nominal amount of £100 million, but was issued on a deep discount basis with a stepped coupon. The stepped coupon concept mirrors what might happen on typical 5-year rent reviews. It starts with a yield that equates to current property yields and rises in line with today's best estimates of what property values might do, over a 25-year span. Thus, the initial 3 percent, at an issue price of 40, goes up after 5 years to 3¾ percent, then to 5 percent, then to 6½ percent, and then to 8¼ percent for the final 5 years. (The issue was called early when Safeway sold its U.K. stores.)

Another unusual issue came to market in January 1986, when London and Edinburgh Trust sponsored an issue of $50 million 8 percent bonds with profit participation, by International Mortgage Interests Ltd. (IMI). The funds were used by IMI to provide mortgages on commercial U.S. real estate. The terms of the loan provided for IMI to receive supplemental interest in the form of a share in the property's appreciation. This was paid to the bondholders until they earned 12 percent per annum. Thereafter, any further appreciation was split between IMI and the bondholders.

The first offering of shares in a City of London office building was made in June 1986. Billingsgate City Securities made a public offer of £52.5 million nominal of deep discount first-mortgage bonds to raise £35.4 million gross of expenses, and 25.79 million preferred ordinary shares. The offer securitized the Billingsgate Market building, formerly a fish market, which had been redeveloped into offices.

Property Income Certificates. A related development is the Property Income Certificates developed by Barclays Bank in the United Kingdom. Under traditional U.K. Stock Exchange rules, diversified quoted real estate investment trusts are not permitted. Barclays Bank wished to reduce its exposure to property markets following its involuntary acquisition of a large amount of property during the early 1990s. It therefore issued Property Income Certificates (PICs), which paid out to the investor the difference between the level of the

Investment Property Databank (IPD) Index at the date of purchase of the certificate and the level of the IPD index at the date of redemption. Thus, if the property market rose, Barclays would pay out more, but this would be offset by a parallel increase in the value of its property holdings. The first issue, PICs 1, included tranches of 2, 3, 4, or 5 years running from January 1, 1994. They paid a quarterly income return calculated as 88 percent of the return earned on the index. The second issue, PICs 2, was launched in July 1995. Several refinements were introduced: a U.K. Stock Exchange listing; income paid at par (rather than 88 percent of par); redemption only in years 3 and 4; and an exchange facility that allowed existing holders of the first issue to switch into the new issue.

France

Introduced in France by a December 1988 law that created the Fonds Commun de Créances (FCC), securitization did not, at first, meet with the success that was expected. This was mainly due to the restrictive nature of the law compared with the U.S. version. The law was gradually softened by a decree of March 1993, a decree of November 1993, and a law of December 1993, which introduced certain amendments. Specifically, the ability to buy new assets (to replace matured assets) gave much more flexibility to the structure.

An FCC is a vehicle that has no legal personality. Thus, it cannot be taxed, and it functions like the U.S. grantor trust or the U.K. unit trust. The original law placed a number of restrictions on what an FCC could do. For example, the debts purchased by an FCC must all be acquired at the same time. The issue of units is once-for-all: hence the FCC is "closed."

FCCs are now permitted to purchase receivables of less than 2 years' maturity. Only the securitization of receivables that are doubtful or are subject to litigation, together with bank overdrafts or cash facilities, remains forbidden. An FCC may be replenished with new receivables, although it is still forbidden to borrow or issue new securities. FCCs are permitted to contract Interest Rate Swaps (IRSs); it is now possible, by means of written notice to the debtor, for the seller to delegate the collection of receivables to another institution. (This condition must be stipulated in loan contracts signed after January 1, 1995.)

The effect of these changes was to start activity in a serious way in the French market. For example, in March 1994, the Comptoir des Entrepreneurs securitized a portfolio of FRF 9 billion of property loans to a special-purpose vehicle, Atlas Capital. Related activity in the asset-backed market also took off (see Chapter 11).

Danish CMO

Although, to listen to Salomon Brothers and the other U.S. investment banks, one would think they invented mortgage-backed securities, the Danish mortgage-backed bond market has been in existence for 200 years (and the German Pfandbrief market is of comparable age). For many years, the Danish mortgage market has operated on the basis that mortgages are pooled and the pool forms the security for debt issued with matching interest rate, maturity, and repayment characteristics. Essentially, this is an on-balance-sheet refinancing of the mortgage by the lender. Securitization of this form covers about half of the outstanding private-sector loans, which has resulted in the Danish bond market being traditionally much more important in terms of turnover than the economy's size would warrant.

However, U.S. techniques have still had something to offer these markets. The Danish mortgage-backed bond market saw its first CMO structure in July 1995, when Unibank brought a DKK2.5 billion kroner issue ($458 million equivalent). The underlying collateral was a mix of residential, commercial, and agricultural mortgages. The issue was structured in seven tranches with estimated average lives ranging from 1.68 years to 6.85 years.

Germany

The German market, like the Danish, has traditionally used on-balance-sheet refinancing of mortgages. The instrument used is the Pfandbrief. The inclusion of the Pfandbrief in this book is certainly not meant to suggest that the instrument, in and of itself, is new. What does justify its inclusion, however, is that, in recent years, the German banks have made significant efforts to widen the international appeal of the Pfandbrief market by bringing "jumbo" issues to the market, thereby increasing liquidity. Because, in aggregate, about 70 percent of today's Pfandbrief market is collateralized with loans to public entities, not with mortgages, it is discussed in the next chapter.

Australian Mortgage-Backed Securities

The majority of Australian mortgages have traditionally been floating rate, which naturally reduces prepayment risk. Securitization of mortgages was introduced into Australia in 1986 by the First Australian National Mortgage Acceptance Corporation (FANMAC). By the start of the 1990s, there were about a dozen issuers. The early FANMAC issues and the intermediate and long-dated issues made by the National Mortgage Market Corporation were pass-throughs, but later issues by FANMAC were CMOs. Despite various regulatory obstacles, the market grew quite rapidly in the early 1990s. At year-end 1995, estimated total outstandings were AUS$6 billion.

Reasonably typical would be an issue that made in October 1995 by PUMA Management Limited, Macquarie Bank's mortgage securitization vehicle. It issued AUS$600 million worth of principal and interest, fixed and floating rate bonds. The issue signaled the beginning of a new funding phase for PUMA, with the launch of a $2 billion multi-issue program. The program will allow fungible bonds to be issued from sub fund P-4, which will encourage greater market depth and liquidity in PUMA bonds.

The weighted average margin for the issue is 29.9 basis points over the 90-day bank bill swap rate (BBSW).

Recent PUMA bond issuances are as follows:

Fund	Outstandings (AUS$)	Issue Dates	Senior Ratings
Sub fund 1	116 million	June 1993	AA+/Aaa
Sub fund 2	42 million	March 1994	AA−/Aaa
Sub fund P-1	200 million	December 1994	AAA/Aaa
Sub fund P-2	300 million	February 1995	AAA/Aaa
Sub fund P-3	700 million	June 1995	AAA/Aaa
Sub fund P-4			
Series A	600 million	October 1995	AAA/Aaa
Series B	250 million	December 1995	AAA/aaa
Total	2.208 billion		

More recently, PUMA brought to market a total of U.S. $700 million of mortgage-backed bonds in the form of 2 tranches of certificates—class A1 and class A2 (respectively, average life of 2 and 5 years, with coupons of 8 and 13 basis points over LIBOR). These were issued in the international market for the first time in March 1997; previously, international issues had been discouraged by Australian withholding tax.

Chapter **11**

Asset-Backed Securities

From its beginnings as a minor outgrowth of the mortgage-backed securities (MBS) market, the asset-backed securities (ABS) market has become a substantial force, growing much faster than mortgage-backed issuance in 1994 to 1996. The MBS market in the United States suffered near-meltdown conditions during the first half of 1994. Investors learned once again that investing in complex securities where only a handful of major firms are market makers is a recipe for illiquidity in difficult markets. So they shifted to investing in asset-backed securities—complex securities with only a handful of firms as market makers.

As a result of this switch, Securities Data Company shows total issuance of asset-backed securities in the United States as $75 billion in 1994, $108 billion in 1995, and $87 billion in the first eight months of 1996, equivalent to an annualized rate of $130 billion. The international market (discussed further below) has also grown rapidly; according to Capital Data Bondware, issuance in 1996 was $102 billion compared with $38 billion in 1995.

In addition, the market has become far more diversified. A recent report by Moody's ("Securitization and its Effect on the Credit Strength of Financial Services Companies," November 1996) pointed out that, in 1985, the only classes of receivables being securitized were automobile loans, computer leases, and conforming first-lien mortgages. By 1996, the list was as shown in Table 11.1. The market shares of the key receivables are represented in Figure 11.1.

The first issuers in the asset-backed securities markets, after the mortgage issuers discussed in the previous chapter, were the large automobile companies, whose issue structures are described below. But as Figure 11.2 illustrates, much of the running in recent years has been made by trade receivables and revolving credits (credit card and consumer loan receivables). The growth seems set to continue, and indeed is expected to be encouraged by recent legislation in the United States to permit the creation of Financial Asset Securitization Investment Trusts (FASITs).

By 1996, the European market for asset-backed securities (detailed below, in the section titled "International Asset-Backed Securities Market") had begun to grow more rapidly, after a very slow acceptance of the idea during the 1980s and early 1990s. Of the asset-backed issues made in 1996, according to figures from Capital Data Bondware, 22 percent were in the European

Table 11.1 Types of Assets Securitized

Aircraft leases	Franchise loans
Automobile (prime) loans	Future receivables
Automobile (subprime) loans	Healthcare receivables
B & C class (lower credit grade)	Home equity
mortgage-backed securities	Insurance receivables
(B & C MBS)	Mutual fund receivables
Boat loans	Nonconforming first-lien mortgages
Computer leases	Small business loans
Conforming first-lien mortgages	Student loans
Consumer loans	Time share receivables
Credit cards	Trade receivables
Equipment leases	Viatical settlements (resold life
Equipment loans	insurance policies)

market (compared with 11 percent of the previous year's total). Table 11.2 lists some of the major securitizations in 1996.

The technique is also beginning to develop in Latin America, as Table 11.3 indicates.

Asian growth has been rather slower, but some transactions are discussed in the sections that follow. Asset-backed deals in Asia became more common in 1997. The Japanese asset-backed market finally began to develop when the Ministry of Finance introduced a package of 12 measures aimed at easing the securitization of property held as collateral for problem loans. Changes in the Australian tax arrangements allowed Macquarie's PUMA Management Ltd. to bring a $700 million mortgage-backed issue to the international markets (previous issues had been primarily domestic because of withholding tax problems). In March 1997, Sino Commercial Properties Funding Ltd. (a special purpose vehicle) issued $300 million of 6-year mortgage-backed bonds, backed by commercial mortgages. One factor behind the growth of asset-backed securitization has been the perception by investors that issuers, if of a sufficiently

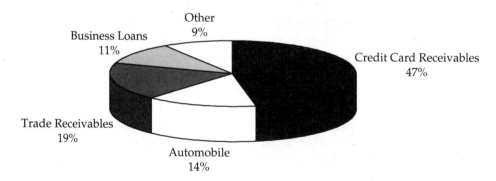

Figure 11.1 Asset-backed securities: market share.

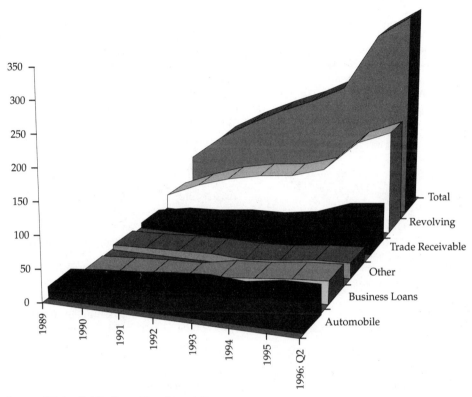

Source of Data: Public Securities Association.

Figure 11.2 Asset-backed securities: market growth, 1989–1996 (second quarter).

high standing, will be reluctant to allow a securitization they have created to fail. Some examples are listed in Table 11.4.

SECURITIES BACKED BY AUTOMOBILE LOANS

As Tables 11.2 and 11.3 indicate, the asset-backed securities market is now global, encompassing many different kinds of security. But the first market to develop, after the mortgage-backed market, was for securities backed by automobile loans. The first auto-receivable-backed security was a $10 million issue of CARS[SM] (Certificates for Automobile Receivables) for Marketing Assistance Corporation, in January 1985.

By October 1986, about $9 billion of such issues had come to the market. Most issues have been by captive finance subsidiaries of automobile companies, but banks and thrifts have also been involved. In December 1985, there

Table 11.2   European Securitizations 1996 ($ million equivalent)

Issuer	Amount	Month	Assets Securitized
Bullet Finance NV	1,228	January	Leases
AIG Finanzas II, Fondo de Titulizacion	23	February	Residential mortgages
Pendeford Mortgages No. 1	1,671	February	Residential mortgages
Volkswagen Car Lease No. 1	324	February	Auto loans
Road Management Consolidated	283	March	Shadow tolls
TAGS No. 1	686	March	Repackaging
Train Finance No. 1	391	March	Leases
Airplanes	4,048	March	Aircraft receivables
Atrium 1	239	April	Social housing loans
Orchid	355	May	Electricity tariff surcharges
ACRES (No. 2)	208	June	Commercial mortgages
ALPS 1996	353	January	Aircraft receivables
CARDS 2	411	June	Credit cards
Homeloans No. 2	416	June	Residential mortgages
Fondo de Titulización de la Moratoria Nuclear	1,656	January	Electricity tariff surcharges
Titriphar	771	June	Small business loans
FI Mortgage Securities	289	June	Small business loans
Cyber-Val 07-96	7,707	June	Corporate loan
Auto Funding No. 2	233	June	Auto loans
Prospect 3	381	June	Personal loans
Ulysses Securitisation (tap issue)	85	August	Residual mortgages
Fennica No. 2 PLC	221	September	Rental housing loans
City Mortgage Receivables	111	October	Residual mortgages
Homeloans No. 3	769	October	Residual mortgages
Annington Finance No. 1 PLC	1,549	October	Leases
Rolling Stock Finance 1	759	October	Leases
Rolling Stock Finance 2	176	October	Leases
ROSE Funding	3,144	October	Corporate loan
ROSE Funding	2,052	October	Corporate loan
City Mortgage Receivables 3	201	November	Residential mortgages
Volkswagen Car Lease No. 2	324	November	Auto loans
St. Goran Securities No. 1	176	November	Secured loan on multifamily housing loans
CARDS 3	411	November	Credit cards
Belenus Securities	184	November	Commercial mortgages
Auto Funding No. 1 (tap issue)	62	December	Auto loans
Leek Finance No. 1	1,363	December	Residential mortgages
Residential Mortgage Securities No. 1	110	December	Residential mortgages
SPLIT No. 1	527	December	Leasing contracts
Craegmoor Finance	137	December	Healthcare group assets

Source of Data: ING Barings.

Table 11.3   Latin American Securitizations 1996 ($ million equivalent)

Issuer	Amount	Month	Assets Securitized
Ceval Export Trust	150	February	Future export receivables
Grupo Bimbo	105	February	IFC enhanced notes
Acominas Overseas	200	March	Steel export receivables
Telephonos de Mexico	80	March	Phone fees
Cuervo	50	April	Future export receivables
Ocens-Triton	300	April	Oil tariffs
ISPAT Mexicana	300	May	Steel receivables
Nylamex	50	May	Export receivables
Cambuhy Export Trust	45	June	Orange juice receivables
Co Siderugia Nacional	300	June	Iron/Steel receivables
Perdigao Agro Industrial	100	June	Poultry receivables
Citmas Capital	21	July	Credit cards
Vitromatic	100	June	White goods
Philips Receivables Trust Series 1996-1	11.3	July	Export receivables
Acominas Overseas	71	August	Steel receivables
Rhodia Ster	55	August	Polyester film
TGN	215	August	IFC Trust—oil and gas
United Mexican States	6000	August	Oil revenues
Province of Mendoza	150	August	Oil royalties
BITAL	100	September	Remittance payments
Braspetro	90	September	Future oil revenue
Grupo Mexico	80	September	Mining receivables
Banco Mexicano (Remessase 96)	135	October	Remittance payments
Intel	28	October	Telephone receivables
Alcoa Brazil	400	November	Aluminum receivables
Banamex	115	November	Remittance payments
Banco del Istmo	55	November	Credit cards
Banco Hipotecario Nacional	93	November	Residential mortgages
Oil Trading Company	400	November	Forward oil sales
Rassini	75	November	Auto parts

Notes: Excludes U.S. credit card assets packaged in European currencies.
Many Latin American deals are privately placed, so complete data are hard to acquire.
Source of Data: ING Barings.

Table 11.4   Notable Instances of "Voluntary" Originator Support

Originator	Trust	Date	Action
Chrysler Financial Corporation	CFC-2 Grantor Trust	5/89	Increased letter of credit by 2 percent of invested amount.
Sears Roebuck & Co.	Sears Credit Account Trust 1990-C	11/91	Added higher-quality accounts.
Household Finance Corp.	Household Credit Card Trust 1990-1	2/93	Boosted "finance charge" collections by purchasing the Special Purpose Company (SPC's) residual interest in the cash collateral account (CCA) in installments; the nine installments were counted as "finance charge" collections.
Tandy Credit Corp.	Tandy Master Trust Series A	8/93	Increased credit protection for investors by 7 percent of invested amount, by increasing and purchasing additional Class B (subordinated) certificates and subordinating part of seller interest.
Household Bank N.A.	Household Private Label	11/95	Increased discount on new Credit Card Master Trust II and existing receivables.
Mercantile Bank of Illinois N.A.	Mercantile Credit Card Master Trust	2/96	Increased discount on new receivables; supplemented resources allocated to servicing of securitized receivables.
Chrysler Financial Corporation	Premier Auto Trust 1994-4, 1995-1	3/96	Waived rights to funds 1995-2, 1995-3, 1995-4, scheduled to be released from reserve fund to increase enhancement for investors.
First Union National Bank of Georgia	First Union Master Credit Card Trust	5/96	Removed lower-quality accounts.
Prudential Bank and Trust Co.	PB&T Master Credit Card Trust II	5/96	Began discounting new receivables.
FCC National Bank	First Chicago Master Trust II	7/96	Added higher-quality accounts.

Table 11.4 (Continued)

Originator	Trust	Date	Action
AT&T Universal Card Services Corp.	AT&T Universal Card Master Trust	8/96	Added higher-quality accounts.
Prudential Bank and Trust Co.	PB&T Master Credit Card Trust II	10/96	Added subordinated loan to increase enhancement.
Green Tree Financial Corp.	Green Tree SNIMC 1994-B, 1995-A	10/96	Transferred portion of servicing fees on underlying transactions to enhance cash flows to investors.
First Union National Bank of Georgia	First Union Master Credit Card Trust	11/96	Waived rights to portion of servicing fee to enhance cash flows to investors.

Source of Data: Moody's Investor Services, *Consumer Finance Industry Outlook,* February 1997.

was the first sizable issue ($524.7 million) by GMAC. On this issue, GMAC guaranteed 5 percent of the car loans against default, a proportion that was well above the company's normal loss rate of around 0.2 percent. In September 1986, the first Euro-issue was made: a $276 million Eurobond for GMAC.

In October 1986, GMAC followed this and other issues with its largest domestic issue to date: $4 billion. To make the issue more salable, several innovations were introduced. First, the issue was split into three tranches of notes with average lives of 1.05 years, 2.2 years, and 3.07 years, respectively. In addition, monthly loan payments were turned into quarterly interest and principal payments on the notes. Second, GMAC guaranteed investors that the notes would not be prematurely redeemed, as had happened in previous asset-backed issues when the underlying loans were paid off ahead of schedule.

Third, it set up Asset-Backed Securities Corporation as a wholly owned subsidiary to issue the notes and buy the loans from GMAC. This allowed investors who either would not normally have GMAC securities in their portfolio—or, at the other extreme, felt fully loaded—to buy a new name.

The other major manufacturers entered the market in due course. Ford entered the market last, in 1989, with two huge issues totaling $5 billion. Chrysler has been an active and regular issuer also. It currently has two separate entities, Premier and CARCO, handling retail and wholesale transactions, respectively.

There have been three classes of structure. The first is a "pass-through" format like the GNMA, FNMA, and FHLMC mortgage pass-through securities. Here, auto receivables are sold to a grantor trust. The trust then sells pass-through certificates. They represent undivided interests in the auto loan assets. The spread between the coupon on the certificates and the auto loan rates is used to pay servicing fees and other expenses. Generally, this has been the most common format.

The second type of format is the "pay-through," which resembles a CMO. An example is the Chrysler public CARS issue (CARCO 1986-1). For this issue, a specific fraction of all cash received (less servicing fees) is set aside first, to pay interest and then to repay principal. In general, pay-through CARS are backed by the cash flows, rather than by the par or market value, of the collateral.

The third kind of structure is the "fixed-payment" security. The simplest form uses incentive-rate loans, with low interest rates, as collateral. The issue is structured on an assumption of no prepayments, and a guaranteed investment contract with an insurance company (at a rate above the APRs of the loans) is used to ensure that the fixed debt service schedule can be maintained regardless of prepayments. This is an attractive feature. As we saw in the context of mortgage-backed securities, "negative convexity" can be a problem for pass-through and pay-through securities. Investors do not want to have principal repaid when rates are falling. However, experience shows that consumers rarely repay automobile loans ahead of schedule. For one thing, if they went to refinance the loan, they would now be borrowing against a car that is no longer new. For another, the loan is usually quite short in maturity, and the financial incentive to refinance is much less than for a mortgage. So refinancing is a minor issue for securities backed by automobile loans.

By way of example, let us look at the Ford Credit Auto Loan Master Trust Series 1992-1, an issue of $1 billion of securities backed by "dealer floor-plan loans"—essentially, loans to Ford dealers. The issue had the typical pass-through structure. It provided for a 54-month revolving period, during which time principal collections would be used to buy new receivables. After this revolving period, the certificates have an accumulation period, which began on July 31, 1996. It continued until the earlier of: payment in full of the outstanding certificates, or the January 1997 distribution date (the expected maturity date). Failure to make all payments due to investors on the expected maturity date is an amortization event. It results in payments being passed through to investors monthly until payment is made in full on the certificates or until the January 1999 distribution date.

The trust issued two classes of certificates: (1) investor certificates (90 percent) and (2) a seller certificate (10 percent). The seller certificate, which is subordinated to the investor certificates, is available to cover credit losses on the receivables. An incremental subordinated amount, which fluctuates in relation to the amount of ineligible receivables in the pool, provides additional credit protection.

The certificates pay interest semiannually at 6⅞ percent; the collateral bears a floating rate. To eliminate the interest rate mismatch, the trust entered into a swap with Ford Credit. Under the swap, the trust receives interest at the certificate rate from Ford Credit and pays the lesser of LIBOR or prime minus 1.5 percent. In addition, 1.48 percent of the total issue amount is set aside for a swap subordinated amount. This covers the potential difference between interest generated by the receivables and interest owed on the certificates. The structure is illustrated in Figure 11.3.

A huge variety of auto loan-backed securities have been issued, from the "jumbo" deals by GMAC and Ford, mentioned above, to the privately placed issues of securities backed by subprime assets. After the collapse of Mercury

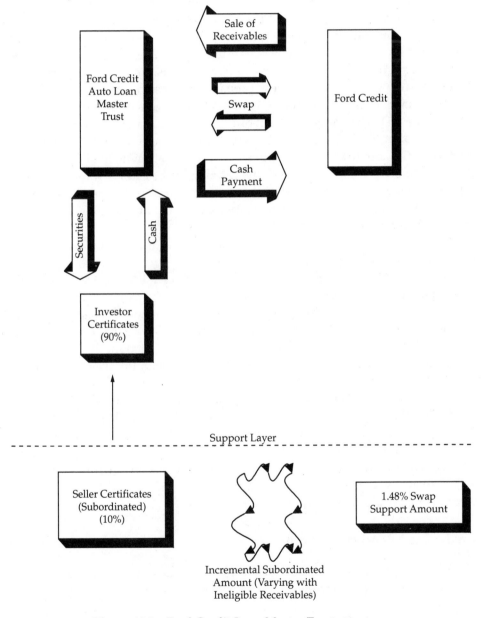

Figure 11.3 Ford Credit Loan Master Trust structure.

Finance, which specialized in this area, the growth of the latter market segment is expected to be limited. However, it continues to produce deals, as evidenced by the transaction, in February 1997, for ACC Automobile Receivables Trust 1997-A, which issued approximately $80 million of class A and B notes. The class A notes ($75.2 million) are guaranteed by Financial Security Assurance (FSA), a monoline insurer. The class B notes ($4.8 million) have protection available from a 1 percent class B reserve account.

The collateral securing the certificates consists of subprime automobile loans; approximately 45 percent of them are in California, Texas, and Florida. The ACC Automobile Receivables Trust 1997-A has a prefunded amount of $5 million, which may be used to buy subsequent receivables. The prefunding period ended on June 15, 1997. At that point, any funds remaining on deposit in the prefunding account were used to prepay the notes on a pro rata basis.

Financial Security Assurance (FSA) has three layers of protection against credit losses: (1) the 6.0 percent subordinated class B notes, (2) a 7 percent spread account, and (3) cross-collateralized excess interest from other outstanding ACC auto loan securitizations. Furthermore, payment of principal on the class B notes is subordinated to the funding of the class A spread account. (However, no amounts may be withdrawn from the 1997-A spread account to support other ACC auto loan securitizations until the outstanding balance on the class B notes has been reduced to zero.)

Credit protection to investors in the class B notes is provided by the 1 percent reserve account (which is only available to support the class B notes) and the excess cash flow in the deal. Cash flow is used first to pay expenses (servicer and trustee fees), class A interest and principal, amounts owing to FSA (premium and other reimbursements), and the funding of the class A spread account. Any excess will be used to pay interest and principal on the class B notes. Any amounts released from the class A spread account in excess of the required amount will also be used to "turbo, " or speed up, the repayment of the class B notes.

In the public market, a similar transaction was brought, in March 1997, for the $775 million issue by the Olympic Automobile Receivable Trust, 1997-A. These securities achieved AAA or Prime-1 ratings based primarily on the financial guaranty policies issued by FSA. "Classic" loans (i.e., those made to obligors with slightly blemished credit records) represent roughly 49 percent of the loans in the initial pool of approximately $579.6 million, reflecting Olympic's specialization in that market.

Credit Card Receivables Securities[1]

A logical extension of the loan receivables-backed security is the security backed by credit card receivables. Credit card-backed issues have much in

---

[1] This section draws on "Standard & Poor's Structured Finance Ratings Asset-Backed Securities: Credit Card Criteria," New York, 1997.

Table 11.5

Par Amount: $50 million

Collateral: 5.9 percent participation in a static pool of 1,350,000
  credit card accounts having a total balance of $848 million and a
  weighted average finance rate of 20.88 percent.

Coupon:	8.35 percent
Payment frequency:	Monthly, with a 14-day delay
First principal payment date:	October 15, 1987
Assumed monthly repayment rate:	9.4 percent
Projected weighted-average life:	2.2 years
Projected duration:	2.0 years
Projected maturity:	3.7 years

common with other asset-backed receivables. The unique feature is use of revolving consumer debt assets. The underlying security for the investor is, of
course, consumer loans via credit cards. The yields on these loans are lower
than the yields quoted on the credit card accounts because of convenience use
by consumers who repay before incurring a finance charge. Credit losses and
fraud losses further reduce the yields.

The market began, in March 1986, with a private placement of $50 million
for Bank One in Ohio. The certificates represented a pro rata participation in a
fixed pool of credit card accounts. The terms of the Bank One issue are summarized in Table 11.5.

As illustrated by Figure 11.4, credit card issuance has grown steadily and
has become a substantial portion of the asset-backed market.

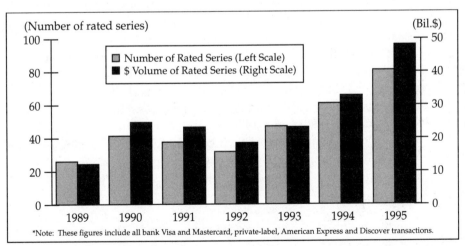

*Note: These figures include all bank Visa and Mastercard, private-label, American Express and Discover transactions.

Source: Standard & Poor's Structured Finance Ratings Asset-Backed Securities: Credit Card
Criteria, New York, 1997.

Figure 11.4 Publicly rated credit card receivable-backed securities.

The strength of the credit card securities structure was tested by Republic-Bank Delaware's $200 million issue of credit card-backed notes series A, brought to market in January 1987. This was the first transaction to experience a pay-out event, which occurred when RepublicBank became insolvent. In that instance, the FDIC made an immediate payment to investors upon receivership. The AAA rating was able to survive untainted, despite deterioration in the bank's credit situation, until the series was retired because the assets were properly isolated from the seller.

Bank of America's California Credit Card Trust Series 1987-A was the first transaction structured as a true sale of receivables. The revolving period lasted 18 months, and the transaction was amortized over the next 5 months. In 1988, Sears Credit Account Trust 1988-A was the first senior/subordinated series issued. This was also the first securitization of receivables from private-label accounts. Citibank's National Credit Card Trust 1988-1 was the first to provide investors with a bullet maturity. It did so with a 12-month accumulation period and a maturity guarantee that could be drawn on if the series did not accumulate enough principal in 12 months. This is a relatively unusual technique; although many of today's transactions have so-called "soft-bullet" maturities, maturity guarantees in term transactions are rare.

Structural innovations have included First Chicago's master trust, formed in 1988; the first rated subordinated class, in Citibank's National Credit Card series 1989-5 transaction; the first "socialized" master trust, formed in 1991 by Citibank; the first series with an unrated collateral interest, issued by Household Affinity Trust in 1993; and the first issue of fixed and floating rate A classes in the same series, in ADVANTA Credit Card Master Trust II's series 1995-F. Other innovations brought to the market have included series that incorporate controlled amortization or accumulation periods; series with variable-length accumulation periods; series with capped and uncapped floating certificate rates; and groups of series that share principal.

The greatest risk to a credit card issue is generally macroeconomic influences. The recession of 1990–1991 affected charge-off levels dramatically, and this in turn affected the level of excess spread, which is the first line of defense against losses (see Figure 11.5). As a result of these pressures, in 1991, Southeast Credit Card Trust 1990-A and 1990-B were paid down early because their net portfolio yield could not support their certificate rates, servicing fees, and charge-offs. This is known as a base-rate pay-out event, or "trigger."

Trust Structures

The first credit card transactions were issued from stand-alone trusts. Many of their important features were transferred to master trust structures as the market evolved. For example, eligibility criteria for accounts and receivables; representations and warranties of the seller; servicing and servicer requirements; cash flow allocations between the seller and investor interest; trust

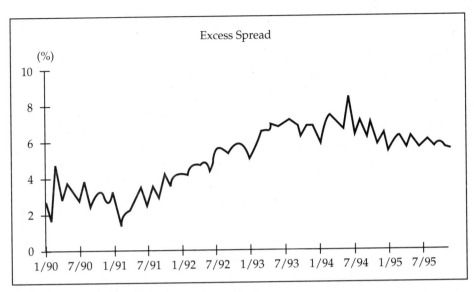

Source: Standard & Poor's, op cit.

Figure 11.5   Credit cards: excess spread earned over time.

pay-out events; and series termination method—all are used today in master trusts with little change. However, the advent of the master trust brought increased flexibility to issuers, and today only 20 series from stand-alone trusts are outstanding.

Master trusts allow the issuer to sell multiple series from the same trust, and each series shares the credit risk and cash flow of one large pool of credit card receivables. In effect, agreements exist among the investors in each of the series and provide the "firewalls" that preclude investors in one series from successfully seizing the support of another. There are two types of master trusts: (1) socialized and (2) nonsocialized.

In socialized master trusts, we allocate first by security groups and then by interests (seller/investor). First, the income is allocated to a group of securities. The split is based on the amount of that group's outstanding principal. The income is then split among the sellers' interests and investors' interests, based on size. The investor interests' shares of income are then reallocated to the investor interest of each series within the group. The split is based on the pro rata costs.

In nonsocialized master trusts, we split first between interests and then by security groups. The income is allocated to the total investor interest and seller's interest, based on the principal amount. We then split between security groups, paying no attention to each group's costs in the split. In a nonsocialized master trust, if a group of securities has high costs, tough luck. In the socialized trust, everybody in the group shares the pain.

A Typical Transaction from a Master Trust

The most common structure used for new issuance is a nonsocialized master trust that allows sharing of excess income among series in a group. Excess income arises only after each series pays its expenses in full. Excess income is shared pro rata according to need. Figure 11.6 shows a structure with three series outstanding and two methods of enhancement.

The investor interest for the trust shown (Series 1–3) totals $900 million, and the seller owns $100 million. Assuming a static amount of principal receivables,

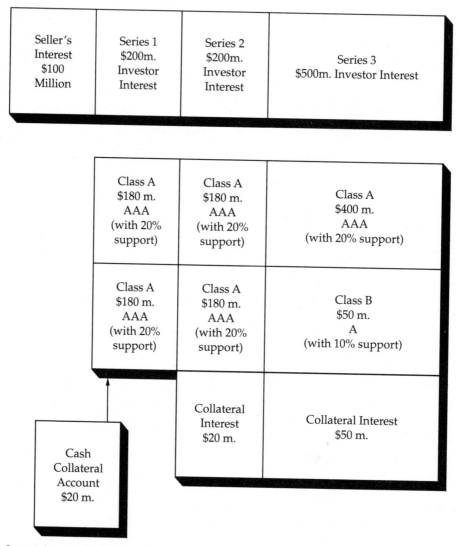

Source: Standard & Poor's, op cit.

Figure 11.6 Typical nonsocialized master trust.

as income is collected and charge-offs are realized, the investor interest would be allocated 90 percent of income collections and charge-offs. The seller in this example would be allocated 10 percent of those amounts. If we look at Series 3, we see that it totals 50 percent of the trust principal amount. It would then receive 50 percent of the income and would be allocated 50 percent of the default amounts. Each series in this structure type pays its own expenses—including the allocated charge-offs—from its allocated income. Only after it covers its own costs will it distribute excess finance charge collections (if any are available) to other series in the group. Those series share in the excess collections based on need.

Forms of enhancement backing credit card securitizations have evolved over the years from B classes and/or letters of credit to B classes and/or cash collateral accounts (CCAs), and most recently, to B classes and additional subordination known as collateral invested amounts (CIAs). CIAs, like CCAs, are the first line of defense (after excess spread). They support the class A and class B certificates in a senior/subordinated structure, but represent an interest in trust receivables versus a cash deposit. The CIA's interest in trust receivables entitles it to receive a pro rata allocation—along with the class A, class B, and seller's interest—of finance charge cash flows generated by the receivables.

Issuance in the market continues to develop many subtle variations. A recent transaction from a leading issuer, MBNA Master Credit Card Trust II, was an issue, in April 1997, of $1 billion in credit card-backed securities. The senior class A certificates were rated AAA, and an A2 rating was given to the class B certificates. The class C certificates were unrated.

The deal's protection included early amortization, trigger events, and credit enhancement levels that reflected potential risks from the uncapped floating rate payment obligations of the trust. It consists of three classes of interests with sequential payment claims to the cash flow from the underlying receivables. The class A certificates are $850 million, 85.0 percent of the total amount, and are supported by two subordinated classes: the class B certificates (7.5 percent of the total) and the class C interest (7.5 percent of the total). The class C interest serves as a first-loss credit protection for both class A and class B certificates.

The issue, which has a 15-year maturity and monthly interest payments, is slightly different from the typical MBNA structure. Here, the more normal collateral interest is replaced by an unrated class C. Together with the class A and class B certificates, the three classes are expected to pay down at the same time on the scheduled payment date, using funds accumulated in the principal funding account. This rules out the danger of writing down the collateral interest during the life of the deal for reasons other than loss protection. By contrast, required collateral interest in previous series may be reduced for non-loss-related reasons after satisfying certain rating agency conditions. The new structure, therefore, offers better credit protection for both class A and class B. They are supported by the entire class C principal until their full repayment to investors.

Trade Receivables[2]

Securities supported by trade receivables began to develop as a market in 1991. This segment was initially slow to develop but has now grown rather large. Credit enhancement has come in a variety of forms: overcollateralization (receivable reserve), subordinated classes, cash collateral accounts, letters of credit, and bond insurance. Overcollateralization generally has been the first line of defense for investors.

Several factors have driven growth in this market sector, including the increase in investors' acceptance of the asset type, which is seen as a logical extension of secured lending, and the need for corporate treasurers to widen their financing choices. The normal transaction structure is illustrated in Figure 11.7.

The high turnover of trade receivables makes this asset type very flexible. A single structure can provide for short-term commercial paper-like instruments as well as multiple series of multiclass term certificates. This gives a corporate treasurer the ability to access both short- and medium-term funding sources, depending on financing needs and general market conditions. As a result, the master trust has emerged as the structure most often chosen for issuance of trade receivable-backed securities. Another advantage of term trade receivable securitization relative to financing in the commercial paper market is the ability to obtain long-term committed financing. Most of the transactions so far have had 5-year revolving periods followed by expected amortization periods of 2 to 3 months. This is very attractive compared with commercial paper.

A factor specific to trade receivables is sometimes called "dilution risk." This refers to any noncash reduction to a receivable balance that is not attributable to default or write-off. Product returns, cash discounts, advertising allowances, volume rebates, good-customer programs, and standard pricing disputes are all examples of dilution.

To match the dynamics of rapidly revolving pools of trade receivables, some recent transactions have incorporated a dynamic credit support concept. This adjusts to payment delinquency and dilution performance during the last 12-month period.

Trade receivable securitizers have taken advantage of most of the structural technology developed for use in earlier credit card and dealer note transactions. Among the main questions are the revolving period, early amortization events, cash flow allocation provisions, and eligibility criteria.

Under normal circumstances, trade receivable pools usually liquidate in 2 to 3 months, assuming the pool is relatively constant and all collections are used to pay down debt. To extend the life of trade receivable-backed securities,

---

[2] This section draws on "Standard & Poor's Structured Finance Ratings Asset-Backed Securities: Trade Receivable Criteria," New York, 1997.

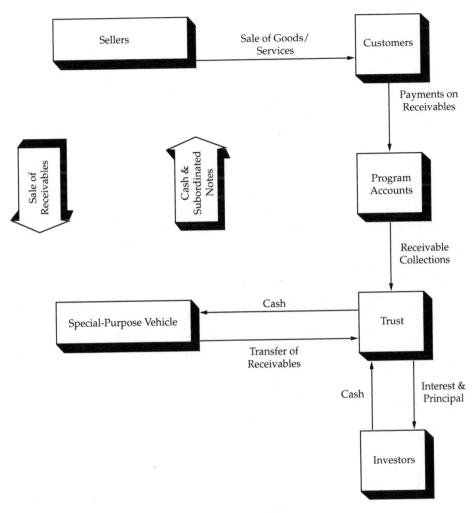

Figure 11.7 Typical trade receivables structure.

investors are paid interest only during the first stage. During this period, payments that would otherwise be used to amortize investor principal are paid to the seller to buy more trade receivables. Thus, revolving interest-only periods allow the issuer to set a maturity that matches the company's overall funding strategy as well as meet the investment targets of potential security holders.

The revolving period is followed by a principal amortization period during which investors receive monthly distribution of principal. As with earlier credit card-backed issues, principal can be paid out as received, distributed on a controlled basis, or paid into a principal accumulation account for payment in one lump sum. To protect investors against a deterioration in investment credit quality, early amortization events are usually included. These aim to raise credit quality by stopping the revolving interest-only period if things start to go wrong. A strong set of early amortization events will minimize the need for other credit enhancement levels. Although amortization events enhance credit quality, they can, of course, imply prepayment risk.

Trade receivable transactions are, from an amortization perspective, very similar to other asset types that use revolving structures. The typical transaction will have a long list of events that could cause early amortization. However, because of the typically dynamic nature of the credit support and the frequency with which the receivable pools turn over, an amortization event is needed that addresses the maintenance of the required levels of credit support. More specifically, each transaction should have an amortization event that would trigger if the net amount of eligible receivables for a specified period of time is less than the agreed levels. Along with this trigger, there needs to be a ban on any release of cash flow, for reinvestment purposes or otherwise, until there are enough eligible receivables to enhance a transaction to required levels.

To date, most trade receivable securitizations have used a borrowing base concept. The calculation of the borrowing base has varied, but most rated issues have calculated the borrowing base as eligible receivables minus reserves (see Figure 11.8). The rated instruments are then issued against the borrowing base. In this structure, investors are entitled to a share of collections that equals the investor amount as a percentage of the borrowing base. The approach aims to allocate collections to investors properly, and to ensure that agreed-on reserve levels are maintained.

A number of transactions have included variable funding certificates and principal funding accounts. Principal funding accounts protect investors against early amortization, if the borrowing base of receivables falls below required levels. To ensure that stipulated reserves are maintained, an amortization event occurs if the borrowing base plus cash held in a principal funding account falls below the investor amount. The principal funding account, therefore, provides a cushion against prepayment if the borrowing base falls (as might happen in a pool with very seasonal receivables, for example).

When a senior/subordinated structure is used, the subordinated class is not allowed to amortize if senior credit enhancement requirements are not satisfied. During a rapid amortization period, senior principal is paid down first. This is generally true for all revolving structures, but it is critical for trade receivable-backed issues. In most cases, more than half of the receivable pool would be expected to pay down in the first month of a liquidation scenario. If subordinated collections were released to the subordinated class (e.g., not used to cover monthly defaults and dilutions), credit enhancement would evaporate quickly and would not be available if needed in later months.

Conduit Structures

In a number of cases, banks have set up special "conduit" companies to invest in assets, financing themselves generally by access to the commercial paper

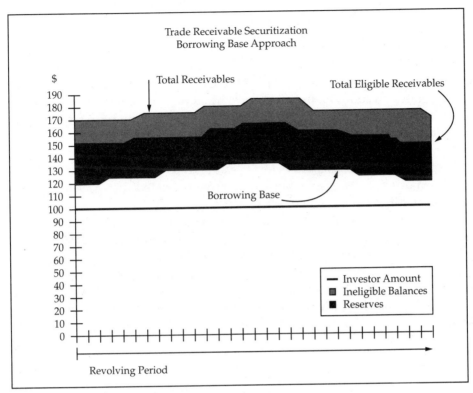

Figure 11.8 "Borrowing base" trade receivables structure.

Source: Adapted from: Standard & Poor's, op. cit.

market. (They may also tap the medium-term note market; compare the international equivalent discussed below in the section titled "Matched Loan Programs.") A typical example of such a structure might be the Variable Funding asset-backed commercial paper program sponsored by First Union. Variable Funding ("Variable" hereafter) is authorized to issue up to $2.519 billion in asset-backed commercial paper.

First Union provides most of the liquidity for Variable, but smaller portions come from Daiichi Kangyo Bank, Banco Santander, and Sumitomo Bank. At the time of writing, Variable has four equipment lease pools, diversified across industries and equipment types. Each lease pool also has pool-specific credit support and the benefit of equipment residual values. Beyond the four leasing deals, Variable has a $320 million deal backed by prime-quality auto loans, a $300 million deal backed by federally guaranteed student loans, and a $300 million deal backed by seven "B" pieces from different credit card master trusts. Variable's smaller deals include a $167 million container lease deal supported by a surety bond from MBIA, the monoline insurer; a $175 million insurance premium loan deal; and a $200 million deal backed by consumer installment loans for furniture and appliance purchases.

Securities Backed by Other Securities

A wide range of securities are themselves backed by other securities. In the international market (discussed below), many transactions consist of repackaged Eurobonds or perpetual FRNs, and a number of similar deals exist within the United States. In addition, there is a substantial flow of asset swap transactions in which investors are sold a bond coupled with a separate swap (see Chapter 5). Here, we discuss situations where the bond and the swap are bundled together into a new special-purpose vehicle, which then issues new securities. This approach simplifies matters for investors, who do not have to worry about credit exposure on the swap, but is of course restricted to repackagings of a size that justifies the issue of new securities.

As illustrated in Figure 11.9, there has been a wide variety of repackagings, many of which have been driven by tax or regulatory considerations. The prominence of Italian government bonds, for example, was initially due to (1) the deplorable inefficiency of the Italian authorities in repaying withholding tax claims, which made it attractive to hold bonds indirectly, and (2) tax arbitrage considerations whereby the ECU swap market benefited from cheaper swap rates off certain Italian ECU bonds.

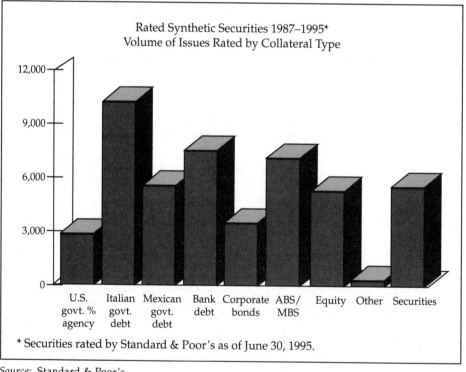

Source: Standard & Poor's.

Figure 11.9 Standard & Poor's rated synthetic securities, 1987–1995.

As Table 11.6 illustrates, the volume of synthetic securities has grown steadily over time.

It should be pointed out that, in one sense, Table 11.6 seriously underestimates the non-U.S. securities repackaging activity, because a very large number of Eurobond repackagings did not rely on ratings for issuance. In 1987 alone, $4 billion of repackaged Eurobonds were created.

Synthetic Structures: Swap-Dependent and Swap-Independent; Collateral-Dependent and Collateral-Independent.   For the rating agencies, analysis of swap-independent transactions differs from analysis of swap-dependent transactions. If the deal depends on the swap, it is assigned the weakest rating of the entities involved in the transaction. This includes the ratings of the swap counterparty and of the underlying collateral. But in a swap-independent transaction, the rating assigned to the collateral is the only rating that matters.

We can set up a synthetic security so that the swap counterparty has no impact on the bond's rating. In these structures, the swap converts the fixed rate cash flow on the underlying collateral to a floating rate, or vice versa. If the swap terminates, one of two events will occur. The trust, or the issuing vehicle, may come to an end. Investors receive the underlying collateral. Alternatively, the trust may continue, and investors receive unswapped cash flow from the underlying collateral. Generally, the "r" symbol is attached to the ratings of these transactions, to indicate that investors may be subject to market risk upon termination of the swap.

Suppose we had a fixed interest rate bond rated "AA+," issued by company X, paired with a swap agreement in which swap counterparty Y (rated "A+") pays a LIBOR-based floating rate of interest in exchange for the bond's

Table 11.6   Synthetic Securities Rated by Standard & Poor's, 1987–1995 (Second Quarter)

Year	Volume ($ million)	Number of Issues
1987	140	1
1988	162	2
1989	646	7
1990	1,228	7
1991	1,419	23
1992	3,066	19
1993	10,811	101
1994	18,982	123
1995*	11,197	188
Total	47,656,061	471

* As of June 30, 1995.

Source of Data: Standard & Poor's Global Synthetic Securities Criteria, New York, 1995.

fixed rate coupon. The deal is structured to be swap-independent. This security will be rated "AA+r" because the swap counterparty's rating is not a supporting rating. A swap-dependent rating approach to this synthetic would imply a rating of "A+."

Similarly, we can create a synthetic where the collateral is not a supporting rating. This strategy can achieve a rating that is higher than the collateral's. We use a swap that makes payments to the issuer regardless of whether the collateral pays. In essence, the swap *is* the collateral. If the swap is terminated, the swap counterparty must pay the issuer a termination payment that is equal to the principal and accrued interest of rated securities minus the proceeds from the sale of the underlying collateral. In other words, investors are paid full principal and interest up to the redemption date, even if the swap is terminated.

Grantor Trust Structures.   In the domestic U.S. markets, Merrill Lynch introduced Structured Enhanced Return Trusts (Steers) for the U.S. market in 1990. A grantor trust structure is used to house a bond purchased on the secondary market and a swap attached to the bond. The primary objective was to achieve standardized documentation and thus simplify the process of being granted a rating by the rating agencies. There should, in theory, be some liquidity benefit from this approach, in comparison with the traditional asset swap approach; the offsetting cost of creating the trust tends to limit the structure to larger deals. (By comparison, in international markets, rather than use the grantor trust structure, the conventional approach is a shell company in a tax-transparent jurisdiction such as the Cayman Islands.)

As Figure 11.9 indicates, another popular area for repackaging has been Mexico. By law, only qualified institutions can hold Mexican government debt through the central bank's clearing system. The effect of this law is that an investor wishing to purchase Mexican government debt has to arrange for a qualified institution to hold this collateral, or find an institution to establish a relationship on the investor's behalf. However, holding repackaged debt is simpler for the investor because the structure includes proper custodial arrangements.

Repackaged Mexican government debt also offers senior investors some protection from new peso devaluation. They do not have that protection when they hold the collateral alone. The repackagings are overcollateralized; the face amount of collateral securing the issue exceeds the face amount of rated securities. This excess collateralization is sold in the form of a subordinated security, typically unrated, which absorbs exchange rate fluctuations before payments on senior debt are affected.

Other Miscellaneous Asset-Backed Securities

In March 1985, the first computer lease-backed security was issued: $192 million for Sperry Lease Finance Corporation. A similar issue was made by Com-L

Corporation, a subsidiary of Comdisco, an Illinois computer leasing company. It issued $25 million in the form of a private placement of nonrecourse bonds, payable solely from the proceeds of its collateral. The collateral consists of security interests in the lease receivables, the leases, and an unperfected security in the leased equipment, backed by a letter of credit issued by Barclays Bank.

Equipment lease-backed securities have continued to develop, though remaining a small part of the market. The sector was estimated to account for 5 percent of the asset-backed market in 1996. It experienced rapid growth in 1995–1996, but the sector may have been temporarily damaged by the alleged fraud surrounding Bennett Funding Group in which BFG and related entities sold tens of millions of dollars in lease assignments that did not exist. BFG's core business was the financing of leases on small office equipment, primarily photocopiers, computers, and telephone equipment.

However, an offsetting event was the subsequent entry of AT&T into the sector. In October 1996, AT&T Capital announced that it had sold $3.057 billion of small-ticket lease-backed securities. Securities in connection with this transaction, the company's first public securitization, were issued by Capital Equipment Receivables Trust (CERTS) 1996-1.

CERTS 1996-1 consisted of $3.057 billion of lease-backed notes offered in class A and B notes. The senior class, class A in four sequential tranches, represented $2.9 billion in notes:

Class A-1 totaled $1.125 billion, had an approximate average life of .46 years, and was priced at 6-month LIBOR less 4 basis points.

Class A-2 totaled $695 billion, had an approximate average life of 1.25 years, and was priced at 29 basis points over the comparable Treasury note.

Class A-3 totaled $659 million, had an approximate average life of 2.05 years, and was priced at 31 basis points over the 2-year Treasury note.

Class A-4 totaled $400 million, had an approximate average life of 2.96 years, and was priced at 33 basis points over the current 3-year Treasury note.

The $179 million in subordinated class B notes had an approximate average life of 3.1 years and were priced at 49 basis points over the comparable Treasury note.

The transaction involved the securitization of a large and diverse pool of receivables related to primarily small-ticket equipment leases and loans originated by four wholly owned subsidiaries of AT&T Capital. This pool was composed of approximately 280,000 commercial leases and loans that had an average lease size of about $12,000, with significant geographical and customer diversification. AT&T Capital retained the servicing and customer relationships of the lease contracts.

A related development has been the sale of securities backed by the U.S. Small Business Administration (SBA). For example, First Wisconsin National Bank of Milwaukee assembled a package of SBA-guaranteed loans for sale to institutional investors in early 1986. The pool comprised six First Wisconsin loans, of which the SBA guaranteed a total of $1.05 million.

Another interesting application of securitization—securitization of loan losses—is, on the surface, unattractive. In January 1986, First City Bancorporation of Texas sold rights to future recoveries on charged-off loans to Signal Capital Corporation, a subsidiary of Allied-Signal Inc. Under the terms of the deal, Signal Capital provided $20 million for First City. In return, First City earmarked for Signal Capital the first $20 million (plus interest at 13 percent) it was able to recover from loans it charged off before 1986. In effect, the bank was securitizing the anticipated cash flow from recoveries on charged-off loans. The transaction was christened PARRS or Purchased Accelerated Recovery Rights. The bank's earnings benefited from the transaction because a sale of these rights allows the bank to reduce the amount of its loan loss provision for the quarter.

An interesting example of the use of asset-backed securities to monetize profits in illiquid derivatives positions was the shelf registration, in November 1993, of $500 million in medium-term-notes (MTNs) by GS Financial Products U.S. LP, one of the financial products subsidiaries of Goldman Sachs. This entity, based in the Cayman Islands, will back issues of MTNs under the facility by pools of in-the-money interest rate and currency swaps. This avoided Goldman's having to fund its subsidiary directly by allowing it to tap into the profits built into the subsidiary.

A number of asset-backed issues have been backed by medical bill receivables. For example, in November 1993, Medical Financial Management made a private placement of $50 million of 6-year floating-rate bonds backed by receivables from Medicaid, Medicare, and various third-party insurers such as Aetna, Travelers, and the Prudential. This market, however, was damaged by the $227 million default by Towers Financial in February 1993.

In November 1993, Case Corporation created a $460 million Case Equipment Loan Trust 1993-B. This trust was holding loans made to finance sales of agricultural equipment; other than the underlying security, the structure was a fairly standard asset-backed security.

One application of the asset-backed market has been the securitization of tax revenues in various ways. In June 1994, New York City raised $208 million in a AAA-rated bond offering backed by $1.5 billion in unpaid real estate taxes.

Finally, I cannot resist including in this catalog the first-ever securitization of royalties from rock music. In February 1997, $55 million of bonds were issued backed by royalties from David Bowie's music; apparently the bonds were rated single-A.

International Asset-Backed Securities Market

The international asset-backed securities market was very slow to grow, primarily because, unlike the U.S. position, the market lacked a similar range of large pools of homogeneous assets to be securitized.

Repackaged Securities.   The one exception to this statement is the market for securities backed by other securities, that is, repackaging. There is a large market for repackaged securities. Typically, these are bond issues that have not been very successful and are now trading at low prices in the secondary market. Investment banks will buy up the securities, usually restructuring them with a swap or series of swaps (e.g., converting fixed rate bonds into floating rate) and then reissuing them through a shell company in the Cayman Islands or some similar location. If the transaction is done on a smaller scale, the bond and the swap will be sold directly to a counterparty.

As mentioned earlier, the international markets for securities-backed securities have been active since the mid-1980s. Three early issues were BECS, MECS, and FLAGS, all of which were repackagings of U.K. government floating rate notes into fixed rate dollar bonds—"synthetic dollar gilt-edged." In the typical structure of such a deal, a shell company is set up. BECS had a Cayman Islands company called Bearer Eurodollar Collateralised Securities; MECS had Marketable Eurodollar Collateralised Securities; and FLAGS used FLAGS BV in The Netherlands. The first two were repackagings of the September 1985 $2.5 billion FRN issue, and FLAGS repackaged the $4 billion August 1986 issue.

A cross-currency repackaging took place in September 1986. A special-purpose company called Republic of Italy Euro Repackaged Assets Ltd. (Feraris) issued $204 million of FRNs yielding LIMEAN. The issue was backed by ECU100 million of Republic of Italy 9.6 percent ECU Treasury certificates 1985–1993 and ECU100 million of 9.75 percent Treasury certificates 1985–1993, together with a currency swap by Paribas.

Another version of these deals, in reverse, was the issue of TOPS, in January 1987. Trust Obligation Participating Securities Ltd. issued $200 million of FRNs backed by a charge on the Kingdom of Denmark's 7 percent 2-year bonds. The FRNs yielded a spread of $\frac{1}{16}$ percent over LIBOR. The underlying interest rate swap was written by Bankers Trust, which put the deal together. About 3 weeks later, TOPS2 was launched by the same house. It consisted of $100 million of FRNs, collateralized by a portfolio of Japanese bank-guaranteed ex-warrant bonds (i.e., bonds originally issued with equity warrants, from which the warrants were stripped for separate sale). The underlying pool of 64 bonds was guaranteed by 18 different Japanese banks. This was the first synthetic FRN backed by a pool of issues rather than one issue. It was quickly followed by literally dozens of repackagings over the years, by various houses.

Most opted for a specific name, which was then reused (e.g., Nomura's LIVES—Latest Investment Vehicle for Ex-warrant Swaps—was followed by LIVES II, LIVES III, and so on; later, it had Alisa I, II, III, IV, V, and VI).

Merrill Lynch followed up its Steers (see above) with Sires (Secured Individually Repackaged Exchangeable Securities), denominated in several currencies, for international investors. J.P. Morgan, in 1994, came up with a structure christened the Argo, which hedged the swap leg by buying puts.

Paribas Capital Markets launched in 1995 a series of Lasers (Liquid Asset Swap with Enhanced Return). The first U.S. dollar 1-year issue contained a repackaged Swiss franc private placement priced at 6-month LIBOR plus 25 basis points. It was rated A1 by Moody's, because, in the event of a failure of the Laser, holders receive the underlying coupon and principal payments.

Other repackagings into new synthetic securities continue to be done, and by no means always as the result of an underlying disaster. For example, a recent issue was the repackaging, in March 1995, of $100 million of European governments' debt into a 4-year FRN issued by a shell company called "Repackaged Sovereign Investments" carrying a coupon of LIBOR + 33. A fairly spectacular issue originated with ISIS Ltd. (created by J.P. Morgan): U.S.$630 million of 2-year FRNs paying 3-month LIBOR plus 12.5 basis points, accompanied by a simultaneous SFR250 million tranche. The issue was secured on a U.S.$800 million portfolio of multicurrency bonds issued by government, state, agency, and publicly owned issuers.

A recent transaction may illustrate the typical structure. This was an issue by Argentine Repackaged Bonds Ltd., a Cayman Islands company, which was launched by Morgan Stanley Bank AG. The company issued DEM150 million of fixed rate bonds in July 1996, maturing in 2005. The coupon is 10.5 percent until September 30, 1999, and thereafter, 13.75 percent. The underlying collateral is the Republic of Argentina floating rate Brady bond issued March 31, 1993, and maturing March 31, 2005, paying a coupon of 6-month LIBOR + .8125 percent. The structure is broadly described by Figure 11.10.

A very specific example of the repackaging technique was in the rescue of perpetual floating rate notes, which had collapsed in 1986–1987. An example of such a repackaging would be the issue of $271 million of Guaranteed Extendable Variable Rate Notes, due 2006–2007, called RSVP City Ltd., issued by a shell company incorporated in the Cayman Islands. The structure is illustrated in Figure 11.11.

What is happening here is that the investors buy a variable-rate note (of a standard type, discussed in Chapter 9) from the shell company. They then use the proceeds to buy perpetual FRNs, together with some zero-coupon bonds and a coupon bond (the secondary collateral). (The perpetuals are, of course, bought at a discount, and the discount allows the purchase of the other bonds; the long zero-coupon bond is a 40-year bond and so very low in cash price.)

The purpose of the secondary collateral is to make sure that investors are paid out in 16 years (the issue was done in 1990). The short zero-coupon bond

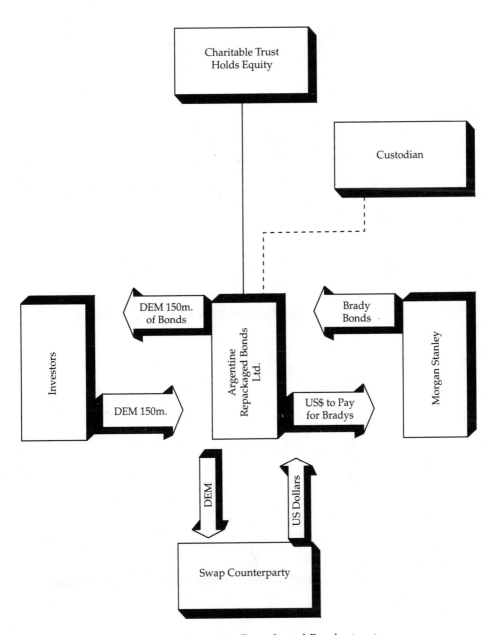

Figure 11.10 Argentine Repackaged Bonds structure.

matures in 16 years. By that stage, the other secondary collateral should have appreciated sufficiently in value that a refinancing of the transaction should be quite easy. In theory, FSA has the right to extend the FRNs to a 40-year life; however, if it does, it must hand over the proceeds of the short zero-coupon bond to investors. This gives FSA a strong incentive not to exercise the extension right. These factors, together with the quality of the underlying collateral

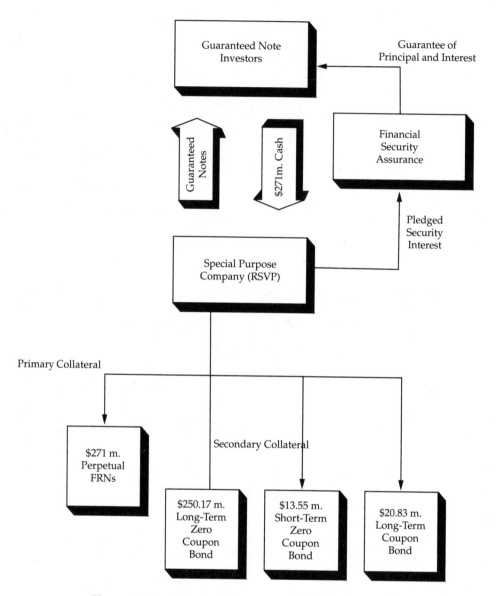

Figure 11.11 Repackaged perpetuals (RSVP City Ltd.).

(the FRNs were issued by banks of the standing of Midland Bank, Lloyds Bank, Hong Kong & Shanghai Bank, Bank of Ireland, and Canadian Imperial Bank of Commerce), led the rating agencies to apply a rating of AAA.

A related technique was applied in the French market; here, the concept was taken a step further, to the instantaneous repackaging of a newly issued perpetual. The issuer issued "titres à durée indéterminée" (TSDIs). Under French accounting rules, these qualified as akin to equity for balance sheet purposes. The next step was the creation of a special-purpose vehicle that commits to buy back the TSDIs after a period, typically 10 to 15 years, at the initial issue price. The obligation to repurchase is secured by charging, in favor of the investor, enough zero-coupon bonds to accumulate to a value matching the TSDIs at that date. Thus, the investor owns a bond that has a fixed redemption date, and the issuer is able to report perpetual debt. The structure is shown in Figure 11.12.

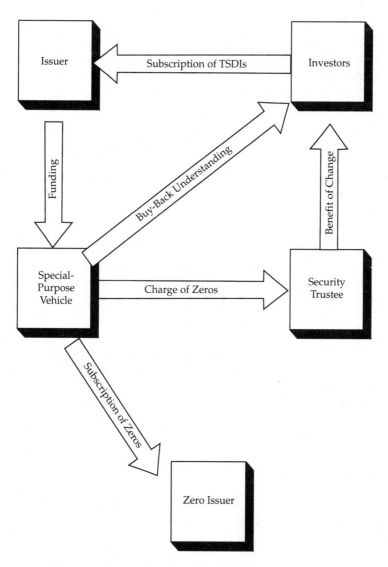

Figure 11.12 Instantaneously repackaged perpetual.

As usual when a structure is too good to be true, the tax authorities came charging in to change the rules, so the technique is no longer applicable in the French market. It might be used elsewhere, however, if the tax laws permit.

Collateralized Loan/Bond Obligations

Another application of the asset-backed securities market has been the securitization of "highly leveraged transactions" (HLTs; loans to highly leveraged borrowers) and "junk bonds." The first of the highly leveraged transactions was the securitization by Continental Bank of a pool of HLTs in the form of FRENDS Ltd. in 1987. (Generally, however, these have been less common than collateralized bond obligations (CBOs), which consist of bonds backed by sufficiently large pools of junk bonds that they are of investment grade.) In addition, the bonds were insured by a monoline insurer specializing in insuring financial obligations, such as Financial Security Assurance or Capital Markets Assurance Corporation. The net result was a AAA-rated security, at least for the top tranche. Subordinated tranches would also be issued; the most junior tranche would effectively represent equity in the underlying assets.

After a meltdown in 1991, caused by fears of credit problems in the United States, the market for CBOs began to emerge again in the mid-1990s; in this case, the assets backing the bonds were more diverse and included securities from emerging markets. For example, in January 1997, Australia and New Zealand Banking Group Ltd. issued $115 million in notes in emerging market debt through a special-purpose vehicle. The senior and junior notes, issued by First Emerging Markets CBO Ltd. and First Emerging Markets CBO Corp., will be invested in a wide range of high-yield emerging debt instruments starting with 29 assets in 25 countries. Investors can exit the closed-end product at net asset value after 3 years.

With these structures, as with highly specialized structured notes, the key issue is always liquidity. That, in turn, depends on investors' levels of confidence in the underlying assets. The 1991 crisis led to a collapse in liquidity for the CBO market because of fears of a collapse in the U.S. issuers' credit quality (even though, in many cases, the existence of the guarantee from the monoline insurer meant that the CBO credit quality was intact).

Credit Card Receivables

The credit card-backed market expanded first into Canada, with an issue by Eaton Credit Card Trust of $150 million in May 1992. The first European credit card-backed deal was brought by Crédit Lyonnais in 1994 with its Titricarte deal. This adopted the standard technology of the U.S. market, discussed earlier, using a senior/subordinated structure coupled with a guarantee from Union Bank of Switzerland. The details were:

Titricarte 12-94

Underlying Assets: Revolving credits/credit card receivables owned by Crédit Lyonnais in the amount of FRF 2,057,350,000.00.

Structure: Senior/Subordinated.

Reserve Fund: Equal to 1 percent of the initial amount of senior and subordinated securities.

UBS Guarantee: Amounting to 2 percent of the initial amount of senior and subordinated securities.

Launched: December 9, 1994.

Senior Securities: FRF 1,875,000,000.00.

Rating: Aaa by Moody's.

Average Life: 4 years.

Revolving Period: 2 years, during which investors receive a monthly coupon payment.

Amortization Period: 2 years. Principal is amortized in 24 equal parts.

Spread: 45 basis points over benchmark BTAN.

Subordinated Securities: FRF 141,200,000.00.

Rating: A3 (Moody's).

Average Life: 4.16 years.

Spread: 87.5 basis points over benchmark BTAN.

Lead Manager: Crédit Lyonnais (Senior Securities); UBS France S.A. (Subordinated Securities).

Custodian: Crédit Lyonnais.

Fund Manager: ABC Gestion.

Source of Data: Crédit Lyonnais.

The international market for credit card-backed securities has developed substantially over the past decade; a recent development has been the growth of "global" issues. A typical example is the issue by MBNA Master Credit Card Trust 1996-H, which totaled $1.02 billion with a coupon of 3-month LIBOR + 10 basis points. MBNA has also issued in the sterling market on several occasions. The first issue by its special-purpose vehicle, Chester Asset Receivables Dealings (CARDS), was launched in July 1995 and paid LIBOR + 22 basis points; CARDS No. 3, launched November 1996, paid 3-month LIBOR +10 basis points for a longer (7-year) maturity. The lower coupon and longer life reflected the increasing familiarity of the U.K. market with this type of paper.

Citibank launched the first credit card-backed issue by a foreign issuer in the German market, and a second Citibank issue in July 1996 was followed by an issue of DEM1.25 billion by Discover, paying a rate of 3-month LIBOR + 7 basis points. Similarly, in July 1996, Capital One Master Trust, a U.S. credit card company, brought a DEM1 billion issue of bonds backed by credit card receivables—the first such fixed-rate issue in the German market. Similar issues have been carried out in a number of markets; for example, Hong Kong Master Trust 1994-1 issued $200 million of securities backed by the credit card receivables of the Manhattan Card Company, a Hong Kong firm. Principal and interest payments denominated in Hong Kong dollars were swapped into U.S. dollars.

Consumer Loans

In France, consumer loans have played an important part in the securitization market. The underlying legislation was passed in December 1988, creating Fonds Commun de Créances. A substantial number of deals were done for Cetelem, a subsidiary of Compagnie Bancaire.

In the United Kingdom, in 1993, Barclays Bank issued—through its subsidiary, Gracechurch Personal Loan Finance—a floating-rate note of £280 million backed by unsecured loans of not more than £7,000 to Barclays' credit card customers. The issue was in two tranches: (1) £250 million of class A notes paying 22 basis points over LIBOR, and (2) subordinated class B notes, paying 85 basis points over LIBOR.

Trade Receivables

Most trade receivables securitization still takes place in the U.S. market via special-purpose vehicles, if necessary, for international issuers. In January 1994, the German tire manufacturer, Continental, announced a DEM100 million trade receivables program. The deal was structured as an off-balance-sheet sale of receivables to CXC, a securitization entity that sells commercial paper in the U.S. market. The deal was typical of a number of such securitizations. It allowed Continental to enter the U.S. commercial paper market without directly obtaining a rating. (The rating obtained for the commercial paper program applied to the vehicle.)

In the opposite direction, as it were, are U.S. issues that are brought to the market as global issues. Up to now, these have been rare in the trade receivables segment, but, in December 1996, an issue of $478 million was brought to market by Green Tree Receivables Master Trust. This was a global issue, though substantially placed in the United States. The bonds are backed by floor plan receivables from dealers selling Green Tree's products. The bonds paid a coupon of LIBOR + 8 basis points.

The Canadian market has seen a number of securitizations of trade receivables—for example, Case Canada Receivables (June 1995) and Ace Trust (Tenneco Credit Canada).

Leases—Aircraft, Rail, Automobile

In August 1994, GPA, the Irish aircraft leasing group, issued $782 million of pass-through certificates via the ALPS Pass-Through Trust 94-1. These certificates represented a fractional undivided interest in one of seven subclasses of notes issued by the trust, whose ratings varied from AA to BBB. These had different maturities; some were fixed rate and some were floating rate. They were secured by a security interest in substantially all of the special-purpose vehicle's assets: 27 aircraft, rights under the operating leases relating to the aircraft, and certain other assets. The aircraft collateral was sold by GPA to ALPS Pass-Through Trust 94-1, a special-purpose bankruptcy-remote company incorporated in Jersey, England. The trust issued securities (classes A, B, and C notes) to investors. In addition, the Jersey company issued a class E note, bought by GPA itself, and a class D note bought by General Electric Capital Corporation. The transaction is illustrated in Figure 11.13.

This was followed, in March 1996, by one of the largest international securitization issues, $4.05 billion for Airplanes Group, a special-purpose vehicle designed for the restructuring of the debts of GPA. The deal repackaged the cash flows from GPA's 229 aircraft under lease to 83 airlines. The global offering included five AA-rated senior classes worth about $2.9 billion, three subordinate tranches totaling around $1.2 billion, and a portion to be retained by GPA.

Another important set of deals was built around the U.K. privatization of British Rail. Three companies, known as Roscos (rail operating stock companies), were set up to own, maintain, and lease the trains. One, Angel, was bought by the GRS consortium, which includes Babcock & Brown and Nomura. The current leases with train operating companies (TOCs) run for between 7 and 10 years from April 1994, and are 80 percent guaranteed by the government. They are operating leases, split into a maintenance element and a capital element. In January 1996, Nomura raised £550 million toward a £700 million total acquisition price by securitizing the government-guaranteed part of the capital element of Angel's leases.

Aimed at asset swap investors, the securitization took the apparently unwieldy form of 98 zero-coupon bonds—one for each payment that Angel would receive from the TOCs. This structure took full advantage of the positive yield curve. It was hardly a liquid structure, but banks were attracted by the government-guaranteed bonds because they could take full advantage of the 20 percent risk weighting. Demand was strong. The yield was 15 basis points over LIBOR—a big saving on bank loans.

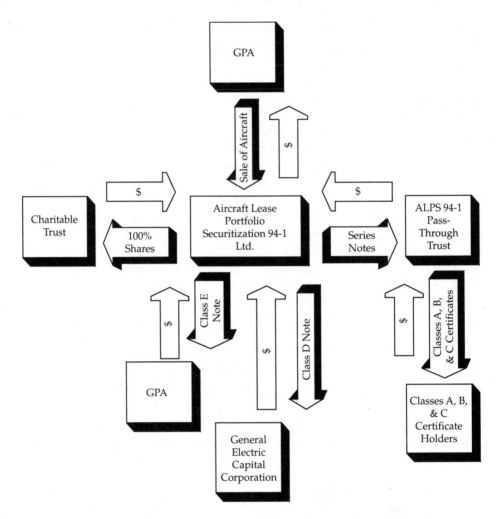

Figure 11.13   Structure of ALPS Pass-Through Trust 1994-1.

After this success, Nomura decided to attempt what had been unthinkable a few months earlier: the securitization of the 20 percent of the leases that did not carry a government guarantee. This involved getting shadow credit ratings for the TOCs. Two of the four bonds, together worth £130 million, had triple-A ratings, and came at less than 20 basis points over LIBOR. The other two were of £25 million each. One was triple-B, at about LIBOR plus 100 basis points. The final double-B tranche (effectively, a first-loss tranche because it was lower than the shadow credit ratings of the TOCs paying the leases) was 300 basis points over. In all, they saved Angel an extra £20 million.

A British bus company, Stagecoach, bought Porterbrook, the most aggressive of the Roscos, in August 1996, knowing that Angel's experience showed the securitization could be done. Of the £825 million Stagecoach paid for

Porterbrook, £520 million came in the form of a bridging loan from Union Bank of Switzerland (UBS), to be refunded with a securitization. Only £77 million was paid in cash; the rest came through a rights issue.

Whereas Nomura started with 80 percent of the receivables, UBS did 100 percent. It raised £545 million, and with a much simpler structure. There were five differing maturities ranging in price from 4 to 14 basis points over 1-month LIBOR. There are also two bonds for the other 20 percent of the receivables: a triple-A tranche at 16 basis points over and a triple-B tranche at 50 basis points over. What made the Stagecoach/Porterbrook transaction particularly interesting is that Stagecoach largely paid for the acquisition by securitizing Porterbrook's assets.

In February 1996, Volkswagen brought to market DEM500 million of auto lease-backed bonds, with credit protection provided by a 10 percent guarantee from Züricher Versicherungsgesellschaft. In November 1996, it brought a second issue of the same size, but, for the first time, a tranche of subordinated securities provided the credit enhancement. These issues represented something of a breakthrough because securitization has been somewhat frowned on traditionally in Germany; the advent of a blue-chip borrower like Volkswagen should accelerate developments.

An interesting deal was brought in 1996 for San Paolo Leasint, the second largest lease operator in Italy. The deal came to market via Paribas, whose local entity, ISIS Factor SpA, bought the portfolio and refinanced itself through SPLIT No.1, the special-purpose vehicle that issued Eurobonds secured on the lease portfolio.

Matched Loan Programs

An increasingly important part of the asset-backed market is the use of the market by banks that arrange loans and then securitize them. These so-called "matched loan" programs permit the banks to continue lending to the client, but allow them to remove the assets from their balance sheet. A classic example of this technique was the securitization by National Westminster Bank of $5 billion of corporate loans, in October 1996. The issue, for Repeat Offering Securitisation Entity Funding No. 1 Ltd. (ROSE Funding) securitized over 200 loans advanced by NatWest Markets to companies in 17 different countries.The transaction was divided into 11 tranches: 6 senior, 4 mezzanine, and 1 junior. The senior and subordinated tranches were further carved up into sterling and U.S.$-denominated portions. The most senior notes, class A1a, totaled $750 million of 5-year floating rate notes paying a coupon of LIBOR + 8 basis points. The £600 million issue of senior sterling notes, class A1b, had a similar 5-year maturity and paid a similar coupon of 3-month sterling LIBOR + 8 basis points.

The issue securitized around one-sixth of NatWest's large corporate loan book, freeing up credit lines for further lending. To preserve the bank's relationship with the companies that it lends to, the transaction was structured as a subparticipation and not a true sale. That imposes a ceiling of the bank's own rating on the transaction because, in the event of a bank default, the ROSE bondholders would become general NatWest creditors. It also means that NatWest continues its existing banking relationship and is obliged to continue to operate that relationship as if it had not entered into the subparticipation. No notification had to be given to the borrowers, and individual borrowers are unaware of whether their loan has been included. No information on individual borrowers will be passed to the trustee. An important factor in the transaction was that NatWest was able to make the rating agencies comfortable with its credit scoring system, so that the transaction could be analyzed on an actuarial basis without the need for the rating agencies to evaluate each individual loan. National Westminster has also used a U.S. vehicle, called Prime Assets Vehicle, to finance holdings of Australian securities using commercial paper.

Similarly, Citibank has used Alpha and Beta Finance to issue commercial paper to fund a managed portfolio of Eurobonds. These funds have often been called credit arbitrage vehicles. The companies are designed to maintain triple-A long-term debt ratings from Moody's and Standard & Poor's, and to produce returns to equity investors by locking in a credit spread between borrowings and investments in a range of instruments. These are mainly asset-backed debt, along with issues of financial institutions, governments, and a few corporates.

Citibank's most recent development in this area is Centauri Corporation, which signed $20 billion worth of debt programs in 1996. It will raise funds in four markets, issuing commercial paper and MTNs in the U.S. and European markets through four programs, each with a ceiling of $5 billion. Centauri, like its predecessors, relies for its triple-A rating: (1) on its layer of equity, which may rise to $1 billion; (2) on a hedging strategy designed to eliminate interest rate and currency risk; and (3) on funding markets, committed credit lines, and liquidity reserves to minimize refinancing risk. It will borrow short term and invest in a mix of longer-term debt. The maturity mismatch is expected to contribute a fair portion of earnings.

Centauri uses new methods of measuring portfolio configuration risk and allocating capital against risk. For example, Beta uses a weighted average of the credit quality of bonds in its investment portfolio to calculate a leverage ratio. An average quality of AA+ dictates that it can borrow no more than 7.5 times its equity capital. Centauri, by improving its portfolio risk measurement, can often leverage more and take larger positions than Alpha or Beta could in the same investments. By spreading investments over more issues, Centauri can increase its leverage.

Equity investors in Centauri are typically financial institutions seeking a floating-rate LIBOR-based return. Citicorp earns fees for managing the investment companies. It is not an investor itself; there are concerns that U.S. banking regulators might classify the fund as a Citicorp balance-sheet risk.

PFANDBRIEFE

As mentioned in the previous chapter, the Pfandbrief is hardly new and would not of itself qualify for inclusion in this book. Furthermore, until perhaps the mid-1990s, most international investors would have considered the Pfandbrief market obscure and illiquid. Although the market itself goes back 200 years, it has traditionally been a mainly domestic market. But recent developments have made the instrument more interesting internationally. In particular, German banks have been working hard to open the market up to international investors.

The structure is defined under German law, and the Pfandbrief issuers are restricted to about 50 German banks, primarily private mortgage banks, Landesbanken, or credit institutions under public law. There are two basic structures: (1) the Hypotheken-Pfandbrief and (2) the Offentliche Pfandbrief. The former is the traditional mortgage-backed bond, and the latter is an equivalent bond backed by loans to German state entities. The latter is, in fact, the more important instrument currently, because it is much easier to assemble a pool of large state loans to back a "jumbo" issue. Very few German mortgage banks have the capacity to issue jumbo Pfandbriefe on a continuous basis backed by home mortgages.

In May 1995, the first jumbo issue was brought to market by Frankfurter Hypothekenbank. An even more important development was the issue, in August 1995, of the first syndicated jumbo, for DEM3 billion, by Depfa. The market has continued to grow rapidly.

In April 1995, another interesting twist was introduced to the market. GEMS (German Mortgage Securities), a special-purpose vehicle based in Utrecht, The Netherlands, issued DEM380 million of 5-year notes and DEM142.6 million of 10-year notes to finance the acquisition of residential and commercial property loans from Rheinische Hypothekenbank. The purpose of the transaction was to allow the client to supplement the financing raised from Pfandbriefe. (German banks are allowed to raise a maximum of 60 percent of the value of the properties on which they extend mortgages from the Pfandbrief market.) GEMS was created to finance the difference between the amount raised from Pfandbriefe and the value of the underlying mortgages. The special-purpose vehicle bought subordinated portions of the loans.

The internationalization of the Pfandbrief market was illustrated, in August 1996, when Bayerische Vereinsbank's subsidiary in Prague issued the first mortgage Pfandbrief denominated in Czech koruna. The transaction was documented according to Czech law, but the differences between it and a German Pfandbrief were slight. The main difference was that 70 percent (rather than 60 percent) of the mortgages were eligible as pool collateral. The issue was small (Kc100 million, equivalent to DEM5.5 million), but illustrated the market potential.

Emerging Markets Asset-Backed

For the brave, perhaps, was the launch, in May 1996, by Union Bank of Switzerland of $500 million of medium-term notes backed by commercial bank debt of the former Yugoslavia, under the 1988 New Financing Agreement.

A simpler structure was used for an issue of high-yielding asset-backed debt in October 1996. This issue was made by Signum, a Turkish special-purpose vehicle that repackaged existing dollar debt into DEM-denominated bonds due in 1999. The novelty lay, to some extent, in the use of a Turkish entity for such a repackaging.

In September 1996, a securitization of Argentine Brady bonds was launched into the German retail market with an issue of DEM75 million by a special-purpose vehicle, Fidelio Trust No. 2. This followed the Argentine securitization discussed earlier, and various other similar securitizations of Brazilian bonds into DEM. At that time, German investors were attracted by the high yields available on these countries' paper.

In December 1996, an issue was made consisting of a securitization of Russian Ministry of Finance bonds. The DEM100 million issue by Russia Credit, a special-purpose vehicle based in the Cayman Islands, yielded 318 basis points over the German government bond at issue and was backed by $65.4 million of Series 3 Ministry of Finance bonds. These bonds trade in large size and are subject to complicated custody and clearing procedures, so, for international investors, the Russia Credit bonds were preferable.

A truly exotic asset-backed securitization was the DEM400 million issue by the NK Debt Corporation, a British Virgin Islands vehicle for holding defaulted bank loans to the North Korean foreign trade bank, Mooyokbank. NK Debt issued 13-year non-interest-bearing certificates of participation in the loans. The primary aim of the issue was to clean up the trading procedures in the underlying paper, which were particularly complex owing to a number of legal considerations—the NK Debt issue will clear through the standard international depositories. As one emerging markets trader commented, "The fast approaching implosion of North Korea is creating a certain opportunistic flow for hyper-exotic debt traders and investors" (International Financing Review 8, March 1997). Definitely an issue for the brave only.

Miscellaneous Receivables

In Australia, Macquarie Bank Limited has established a new securitization vehicle that will allow the bank to securitize a broad range of income-producing assets, starting with $160 million of equity loan receivables. The new structure, known as SECURE, is Australia's first generic securitization vehicle for which the issue of commercial paper will be directly linked to an underlying asset pool. Each issue will represent a new series; the first is announced as the SECURE GEI Series.

The first asset to be securitized will be $160 million worth of Geared Equities Investment (GEI) loans, written through Macquarie's Equities Lending business. The GEI allows investors to borrow 100 percent of funds to gear into the Australian share market without risking loss of capital. GEI loans are provided to investors to purchase a portfolio of blue-chip shares, and interest payments on the loans are made quarterly in arrears or annually in advance.

The GEI Series has been provisionally rated A-1 by Standard & Poor's, and the dealer panel is Bankers Trust Australia Limited, Commonwealth Bank, and Macquarie Bank. The GEI Series commercial paper will be issued at a discount to face value, with face value payable on maturity.

The proceeds from each series of debt instruments will be used to purchase a portfolio of assets that may include trade receivables, consumer loans, and other long- and short-term receivables. The assets that are purchased or originated with each respective series will be kept in distinct pools.

Rental Housing Loans. In November 1995, Housing Fund of Finland launched a securitization of rental housing loans, the first public securitization sponsored by a European government. The issue consisted of $350 million of senior asset-backed floating rate notes, supported by a $13.7 million tranche of mezzanine notes issued by Fennica No. 1, a special-purpose vehicle incorporated in Ireland for the purpose of the securitization. The assets backing the securitization are loans granted by the Housing Fund, a government agency, for the construction, renovation, or purchase of multifamily rental housing in Finland.

A similar deal for St. Göran Securities, a Swedish special-purpose vehicle, was the issue of SEK1.2 billion of asset-backed securities. The proceeds of the issue were used to purchase a loan from ABN Amro to Svenska Bostäder, a Swedish municipal housing company owned by the city of Stockholm.

In October 1996, an issue of £900 million was made by Annington Finance, a special-purpose vehicle created by Nomura International to finance the purchase of £1.66 billion worth of married quarters sold by the British Ministry of Defense. The bonds are secured on quarterly rental payments from the Ministry of Defense, guaranteed until 2001. The issue comprised a tranche of floating rate notes and two tranches of fixed rate bonds for 15 and 25 years, respectively.

Finance for Residential Social Housing PLC (FRESH) issued £885 million of bonds, in March 1997, to finance acquisition of a portfolio of loans to U.K. housing associations originated by The Housing Corporation (HC) and Housing for Wales, Tai Cymru (TC). The final maturity on the notes was 2058, and, of these series, 1 £727.9 million class A1, series 1 £115.9 million class A2, and series 2 £40.9 million class A are rated AAA. The series 1 £37.1 million class A3 are rated AA, and the series 1 £37.1 million class B and series 2 £3.1 million class B are rated BBB.

Credit enhancement for series 1 class A1, totaling 9 percent, is provided by subordination of the series 1 class A3 notes (4 percent of series 1), the series 1 class B notes (4 percent of series 1), and the fully fungible series 3 class C notes (1 percent of the total issue). Credit enhancement for series 1 class A2 is provided by subordination of the series 1 class A3 notes (4 percent), the series 1 class B notes (4 percent), and the fully fungible series 3 class C notes (1 percent). Credit enhancement for series 1 class A3 is provided by subordination of the series 1 class B notes (4 percent) and the fully fungible series 3 class C notes (1 percent). Credit enhancement for series 1 class B is provided by subordination of the series 3 class C notes.

Other.   In June 1996, the Spanish government launched an issue of ESP215 billion of international bonds backed by securitization of nuclear moratorium debts. These bonds are backed by 3.54 percent of electricity billings by four electrical utilities, which have been allocated to repay debt incurred as a result of the 1983 decision by the government to suspend the development of nuclear power plants. This issue, which was government-guaranteed, marked the first nonmortgage securitization in the Spanish market.

In the same month, Crédit Lyonnais brought to market a FRF5 billion securitization called Titriphar 06–96. The four-tranche offering of floating rate notes is backed by long-term loans granted by Crédit Lyonnais to pharmacists buying or modernizing their premises. The structure was enhanced by a cash deposit from Crédit Lyonnais, a letter of credit from Bayerische Vereinsbank, and an unconditional guarantee from Mortgage Bond Indemnity Assurance (MBIA).

In July 1996, the largest-ever issue of asset-backed floating rate securities was brought to market for Crédit Lyonnais. The issue was for FRF40 billion in the name of Cyber-Val 07–96, and it was backed by one-third of the loan made by Crédit Lyonnais to Établissement Public de Financement et Restructuration (EPFR), a vehicle set up in 1995 and guaranteed by the French state as part of the bank's restructuring package to manage the sell-down of bad assets from the bank.

The loan had been made at 85 percent of the overnight money market rate—well below Crédit Lyonnais' blended cost of funding—in exchange for government participation in the restructuring. For the purposes of securitization, this meant that the loan had to be carved into two separate tranches. An FRF40 billion class A loan with market coupon rates supported the Cyber-Val bonds, and a class B tranche, with rates adjusted downward, was needed to arrive at an overall rate equivalent to 85 percent of the TME rate. The class B loan effectively remained on the balance sheet of Crédit Lyonnais, but selling the class A tranche through the Cyber-Val vehicle allowed it to free up FRF40 billion of cash.

The bond consisted of four tranches priced in relation to PIBOR (Paris Inter-bank Offered Rate), ranging in maturity from 1 to 5 years. The 5-year tranche was twice the size of the others—FRF16 billion rather than FRF8 billion—but with half of that amount paid down early in year 4. Reception of the

Cyber-Val 07-96

Underlying Assets: Single loan made by Crédit Lyonnais to the Établissement Public de Financement et de Restructuration (EPFR) in the amount of FRF40 billion.

Structure: Five categories of units: class A1, class A2, class A3, class A4, and the Residual Unit.

The class A units shall be redeemed in sequence, in numerical order (A1, A2, A3, A4). The Residual Unit shall be redeemed at one time, upon the completion of the liquidation of the Fund through the distribution of any liquidation surplus.

Description of Issue:

Launched: July 11, 1996.

Class A1: FRF8,000,000,000.

Rating: AAA/Aaa (Standard & Poor's, Moody's).

Average Maturity: 1 year.

Face Interest Rate: 3-month PIBOR.

Class A2: FRF8,000,000,000.

Rating: AAA/Aaa (Standard & Poor's, Moody's).

Average Maturity: 2 years.

Face Interest Rate: 3-month PIBOR + 0.04 percent.

Class A3: FRF8,000,000,000.

Rating: AAA/Aaa (Standard & Poor's, Moody's).

Average Maturity: 3 years.

Face Interest Rate: 3-month PIBOR + 0.07 percent.

Class A4: FRF16,000,000,000.

Rating: AAA/Aaa (Standard & Poor's, Moody's).

Average Maturity: 4 years.

Face Interest Rate: 3-month PIBOR + 0.09 percent.

Lead Manager: Crédit Lyonnais.

Servicer: Crédit Lyonnais.

Custodian: Crédit Lyonnais.

Fund Manager: ABC Gestion.

Source of Data: Crédit Lyonnais.

bond was partly influenced by the treatment by regulatory authorities. The risk weightings assigned to the issue were: 0 percent by the French authorities, and 10 percent and 20 percent, respectively, by their U.K. and U.S. counterparts. Summary details of the transaction are shown in the box on page 365.

Increasingly, the Rule 144a market has seen the growth of more specialized and higher-yielding credits; for instance, in August 1997 Sasco, a Lehman vehicle, issued $355 million of Rule 144a debt backed by non-performing, subperforming, and performing commercial property debt in seven tranches. According to press reports, the issue was 25 percent placed in London, with the remainder largely being placed in the United States.

In August 1997, a high-yield issuer for the China market was made by the Guangzhou Shenzen Superhighway, a $600 million issuer for the owner of 50 percent of the toll road in southern China. The issue was made under Rule 144a and was partly guaranteed by Hopewell and its subsidiary, Delta, resulting in a BB rating.

In March 1997, another securitization for a high-risk country was brought to market: SBC Warburg brought to market $115 million of bonds for Garantasi Bankasi, the Turkish bank. They were backed by personal cheques and traveller's cheques cashed at its branches in Turkey. Because the cheques are cleared outside Turkey and the proceeds held in an offshore trust to repay bondholders principal and interest, the bonds paid only 2 percent over LIBOR for five years—significantly less than Turkish banks paid for normal funds.

An interesting recent asset-backed issue in the sterling market was by Welcome Break, the second largest operator of motorway restaurant franchises in the United Kingdom. The transaction, in August 1997, totaled £321 million in four tranches with fixed or floating rate coupons and maturities ranging from 10 to 20 years. The collateral consisted of the issuer's property portfolio, plus cash-flow from operations, resulting in a BBB rating. The funds were used to refinance a leveraged buy-out.

Finally, I cannot resist one last item. Benjamin Franklin once remarked that there are only two certainties: death and taxes. In a number of asset-backed structures, taxes have been used as a backing for bonds. In August 1996, the Italian municipal bond market (opened up by a new law, in early 1996) saw an issue from the small Sicilian town of Castelvetrano. The issue, for a total amount of $3.3 million, will be backed by revenues from the sale of four-person and ten-person tombs. Market comments suggested that redemption was a "dead certainty."

Chapter **12**

Structured Notes

The first edition of this book discussed a number of deals that had the effect of creating specific payoff structures, which were embedded into the underlying security issue, usually a Eurobond. This tend became particularly marked in 1985–1986, at the height of the Eurobond market boom caused by falling U.S. interest rates. Investors were searching desperately for instruments that would give more attractive payoffs than the low yields currently prevailing. The same pattern reemerged in 1992–1993, and in 1996–1997, for the same reason—low interest rates. Much of the activity this time around took place in the medium-term note market, which had, in the meantime, emerged as a flexible competitor for the domestic bond and Eurobond markets. This segment of the market came to be called the "structured note market."

These instruments are discussed here, although, because of their diversity and the overlap with other chapters, some instruments that might be expected here are in fact elsewhere in the book. Specifically, bonds whose structuring includes an equity component are discussed in Chapter 16 (and some, of course, in Chapter 15 on convertibles). Index-linked bonds, and some aspects of the medium-term note market, have been discussed in Chapter 9. Aspects of structured commercial paper programs have been discussed in Chapter 8.

As mentioned, these instruments are to some extent cyclically driven. In the bond market collapse of 1994, investors suddenly and painfully discovered that the liquidity in most of these instruments, particularly the more exotic varieties, was close to zero, and many investors lost large sums. Orange County in California, for example, lost over $1 billion in a class of structured notes called reverse FRNs. Their popularity faded considerably; however, by 1997 they had reemerged. In general, these are bull market instruments, although it should be pointed out that, in specific circumstances and for sophisticated investors, they can add value at almost any point in the cycle, if their risks are properly evaluated and understood.

We may define a structured note as a bond or note that has embedded in it contractual terms that result in an economic payoff to the investor. In this way, it differs from the classical bond market instruments of fixed or floating rate bonds. The payoff may be in the form of an adjustment to the coupon payable on the bond, or to its final redemption value. This definition is extremely wide and covers a multitude of sins; but this is because there has been an extraordinarily wide variety of instruments issued in this market.

Some readers may find helpful a classification used by Peng and Dattatreya.[1] They distinguish between "first-generation" and "second-generation" structured notes. In their view, first-generation structured notes have the following features:

1. The structure contains only one floating rate index.

2. The maturity of the floating rate index must coincide with the reset and payment frequency (e.g., 3-month LIBOR must be reset and paid quarterly).

3. The floating rate index must be of the same currency and country as the note denomination (e.g., if US$ 3-month LIBOR is the coupon, the note must be denominated in US$).

4. The structures may contain caps or floors but not exotic options.

By contrast, second-generation notes would contain one or more of the following features:

1. Mismatch between index maturity and reset frequency (e.g., an FRN paying a Constant Maturity Treasury rate whose coupons float on the 10-year Treasury rate, but are reset and are paid quarterly).

2. Multiple indexes. (Structures that pay off based on the sum of, or difference between, indexes).

3. Exotic option payoffs.

4. An index based on a foreign interest rate.

5. Unusual leverage (e.g., notes paying off in relation to LIBOR squared).

A very large number of possible variants could be developed. Given the very large volume of privately placed paper, which is not necessarily publicized, there is no possibility of being fully comprehensive in this book. What follows is an attempt to pick out some of the more prominent kinds of structured notes. This area is full of loose ends; it is, by definition, a sector in which securities are "mixed and matched."

In this context, the following tale by the then-editor of *International Financing Review,* a highly respected "journal of record" for the international securities markets, may be illuminating:

---

[1] S. Y. Peng & R. E. Dattatreya, *The Structured Note Market* (Chicago: Probus, 1995). A useful discussion of the issues in this area, from which I have lifted several examples.

The magazine had a tradition, come each April 1, of introducing an All Fool's day issue, an entirely invented financial transaction that would satirise the current marketplace fashions. One particular April we wrote up the ultimate bells and whistles Eurobond—a lampoon on the then craze for over-complex transactions with various gimmicks that few investors, let alone the lead manager, could really understand.

The fictional dual-currency dollar/yen bond in question was issued by a borrower IFR decided to call the Fugu Fish Co., of Osaka, Japan. It had equity warrants attached, puts and calls, of course, plus currency options, plus health "drop dead" clauses, protecting investors against the dangers of the Fugu fish, a poisonous species that kills a number of people in Japan each year if not properly prepared before cooking. The whole issue was obviously a send-up, underlining the craving of quants to design more and more complex bonds.

But imagine our amazement when, come Monday, we got calls from Japan, North America, and Europe asking us for more details, and who the lead manager was. They liked the bond and wanted a piece of the action. If we had found an issuer, I still think we could have got a bond away with most of the terms and conditions we invented out of thin air.

John Evans, *IFR* 1000th issue supplement, 1993.

On the other hand, it should be pointed out that structured notes have been issued on a regular basis by a number of highly reputable issuers. Indeed, one of the main supporters of the initial development of the market was the World Bank. During 1994, the World Bank launched a $5 billion global multi-currency note program aimed to achieve the following benefits:

- **Price transparency**—the seven sponsoring dealers agreed to publish regularly indicative bid prices for World Bank-structured bonds issued under the program, on dedicated screens distributed by major information vendors;

- **Secondary market liquidity**—by offering to exchange outstanding structured notes for new floating rate or structured notes, the World Bank aimed to be more supportive of the sponsoring dealers' secondary market activities;

- **Issuance, trading, and custody**—global documentation would allow for timely and streamlined issuance of structured notes in a wide range of markets and maturities, together with a choice of clearing systems and cross-market clearing and settlement.

In setting up these arrangements, the World Bank aimed to achieve up to 20 percent of its funding requirements through the issuance of structured notes. Thus, these instruments undoubtedly serve a valuable role as one of the issuer's possible sources of finance, and, if carefully used, can be of attractive benefit to investors, despite the collapse of 1994.

Incidentally, in response to the events of 1994, the rating agencies have moved to introduce, in some cases, a refinement to the basic ratings system. For example, Standard & Poor's has introduced an "r" subscript to denote instruments with high market risk. This was announced in September 1994, when the agency attached the subscript to 800 outstanding issues. These included IO and PO mortgage-backed securities (see Chapter 10); mortgage residuals; structured notes with interest payments linked to a swap; debt that converts to stock at the end of a defined period; debt whose principal is dependent on how an index performs; leveraged inverse floaters that do not move parallel to an index; obligations with interest rates linked to non-interest-related indexes.

In this context, the point should be made that traditional bond risk measures such as duration and convexity have very limited value in the evaluation of structured notes. As discussed in Chapter 3, key-rate duration may be of some help for some instruments, such as CMT-based floaters. In other cases, it may be necessary to estimate the duration using Monte Carlo or other simulation techniques to simulate the behavior of the note in different environments.

Understanding these instruments usually involves breaking them down into the component parts that have been used to build them. Given the variety of instruments covered in this chapter, space does not permit a full analysis of each instrument, but it may be helpful to consider a couple of issues to illustrate the processes involved. Let us look at a 6-year issue by Société Générale. The issue was for FRF300 million paying a coupon of (25% − 2 × PIBOR) plus, if PIBOR is below 8 percent, 2 × (8% − PIBOR), with a minimum coupon of 4 percent. We look first at the (25 percent − 2 × PIBOR) component. Here, in effect, by entering into a swap, the investor receives 12.5 percent and pays PIBOR on twice the face amount (i.e., FRF600 million). This position goes negative if PIBOR rises above 12.5 percent. And with the minimum coupon set at 4 percent, we have to sell to the investor a cap struck at 10.5 percent, again on double the amount. Futhermore, to provide the kicker if rates fall, the investor also buys a floor on PIBOR at 8 percent—again, on double the amount. The net result is represented in Figure 12.1.

It may be of interest to look at one of these bonds from the viewpoint of an issuer. Consider the issue by Hessische Landesbank, which paid 10 percent per annum for 1 year, and 19.5 percent—2 × LIBOR, with a minimum of zero, for years 2–10. We start by noting that the investor is in effect long of a 9.75 percent cap on twice the underlying, which gives the minimum coupon of zero. Let us suppose that, at the time of the issue, market conditions were as follows: 6-month LIBOR, 8.125 percent, 12-month LIBOR, 7.5625 percent, 10-year swap rate, 7.24 percent (annual bond basis), and a forward swap is available for Years 2 through 10 at 6.92 percent (semiannual, money market basis, versus 6-month

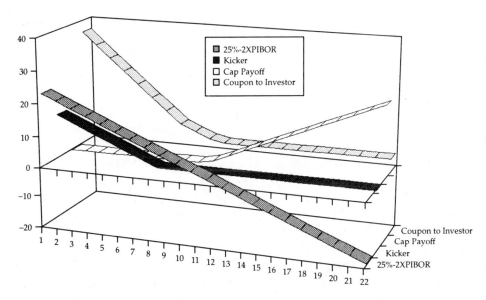

Figure 12.1 Société générale issue.

LIBOR, equivalent to 7.14 percent annual bond basis). A cap at 9.75 percent for Years 2 through 10 can be bought for a fee of 1.22 percent.

Consider first the payment at the end of Year 1. This is the fixed coupon payment of 10 percent. Because this is a bond coupon, it needs to be converted to a money market equivalent (actual/360) of 9.863 percent. We said that 12-month LIBOR was 7.5625, and so to equate this coupon with the later stream, we can rewrite it as LIBOR + 230 (9.863 − 7.5625). The present value today of 230 basis points a year from now is 214 basis points (230/1.075625). We can convert that into a stream over the 10-year life of the bond by using the PMT function of an HP calculator or a spreadsheet to translate this into an annual equivalent of 31 basis points.

Now we consider the remaining period. To convert 19.5 percent − 2 × LIBOR to a conventional LIBOR payment, we need to receive fixed and pay floating on an amount equal to 3 times the underlying. We then have a net cost to the borrower of:

$$19.5 - 2*LIBOR - 3*6.92 + 3*LIBOR$$

This equates to a total cost of LIBOR − 126, for Years 2 through 10. The present value of this stream of savings is 758 basis points. We spread this out again over the 10-year life, using the PMT function, and we arrive at a figure of 109 basis points per annum.

We now consider the caps. The cap price is 1.22 percent. We need it on twice the amount, so it equates to 2.44 percent. This is equivalent to 36 basis points per annum.

We now arrive at the total cost to the borrower as a spread against LIBOR:

	Basis Points
Amortized year 1 spread	+31
Amortized years 2 through 10	−109
Amortized cost of caps	+36
Net total	LIBOR − 42

Essentially, as always with these structured instruments, the structure has allowed the issuer to raise at well below LIBOR because investors did not break down and value properly the components of the issue (or, in some cases, were prepared to pay over the market price for the combined structure because of legal/regulatory/tax constraints preventing them from putting the package together for themselves).

We now look at the evolution of the structured note market, beginning with the first major wave of concepts developed in the 1985–1986 bull market.

EARLY VARIANTS

Currency-Based Notes

In this section, we discuss instruments that have a currency feature. These include dual-currency bonds, together with heaven and hell bonds and related features.

Dual-currency bonds are bonds for which the issue price is fixed in one currency, and the redemption value and coupon are fixed in another. (We looked at the swaps behind a dual in Chapter 5.) The first deals were in Swiss francs (CHF). Typically, a Swiss franc issue was launched on the public foreign market with an issue price set in Swiss francs, and a redemption value in dollars of a set amount per CHF5,000 bond.

We will look at an issue for First City Financial in 1985. The issue price for each CHF5,000 bond was par, and the redemption amount was fixed at $2,800. The bond had a 10-year maturity. The implied exchange rate between CHF5,000 and $2,800 is CHF1.79 to the dollar. That compares with the exchange rate at the date of issue of CHF2.45; so the initial US$ par value was $2,040.82.

Thus, at the exchange rates at the time of issue, a Swiss investor could buy just over $2,000 for CHF5,000. But by buying the dual-currency bond, the investor was guaranteed a redemption of $2,800, whatever the exchange rate. If at maturity the exchange rate is above CHF1.79, the investor will have earned more than the initial outlay of CHF5,000 when converting the principal back into Swiss currency. For example, if the exchange rate stayed the same, in 10 years' time, the investor would be able to convert back the $2,800 to give CHF6,860. If the dollar rises, the investor benefits even more.

If the dollar falls to the CHF1.79 level, the investor receives CHF5,000—the same amount as the initial investment. So the investor is protected against a dollar fall, down to the exchange rate implied by the set redemption amount. The investor takes the risk of a fall below that level, but gains from a rise.

The investor is protected further because the coupon received in Swiss francs is usually set at a higher level than it would be for a straightforward Swiss franc issue. By calculating the benefit of the extra coupon over the life of the issue, the investor can work out a break-even exchange rate at which level the investor would have done as well by buying an ordinary Swiss franc issue from the same borrower. If the dollar falls below that level, then the investor is worse off buying the dual-currency issue. As Table 12.1 and Figure 12.2 show, the investor in First City Financial's dual-currency issue would be better off as long as the Swiss franc remains above about 1.60 at maturity.

In the summer of 1984, the Swedish Export Credit agency, Svensk Export Kredit (SEK), created a reverse dual-currency bond with interest payable in dollars and principal in Japanese yen. Reverse duals have been issued on numerous occasions since then. A recent example is the 1995 issue by Export-Import Bank of Korea of ¥10 billion of 4.1 percent 10-year reverse dual bonds. Interest on the bonds was payable in Australian dollars at a fixed exchange rate of AUS$1 = ¥75.82. Reverse duals, where the currency risk is taken only on the interest, are generally preferred by many institutional investors, compared with the riskier duals where the currency risk is on the principal amount.

In 1985, yen/dollar dual-currency issues became very popular. The transaction appealed to Japanese investors' eagerness to enjoy high current yield at the price of exposure to possible long-term devaluation of the dollar against the yen. The issues offered high yen coupon rates and, in return, investors accepted the risk of a decline in principal value. This structure was attractive to Japanese investors, particularly insurance companies, which, under Provision

Table 12.1   Dual-Currency vs. US$ Straight and Swiss Francs Straight

Exchange Rate at Maturity	Dual-Currency Final Value	US$ Straight	CHF Straight
3.00	3,554.00	3,104.21	2,230.38
2.85	3,593.69	3,104.21	2,347.77
2.7	3,637.78	3,104.21	2,478.20
2.55	3,687.06	3,104.21	2,623.98
2.4	3,742.50	3,104.21	2,787.97
2.25	3,805.34	3,104.21	2,973.84
2.1	3,877.15	3,104.21	3,186.26
1.95	3,960.00	3,104.21	3,431.35
1.8	4,056.67	3,104.21	3,717.30
1.65	4,170.91	3,104.21	4,055.24
1.5	4,308.00	3,104.21	4,460.76
1.35	4,475.56	3,104.21	4,956.40

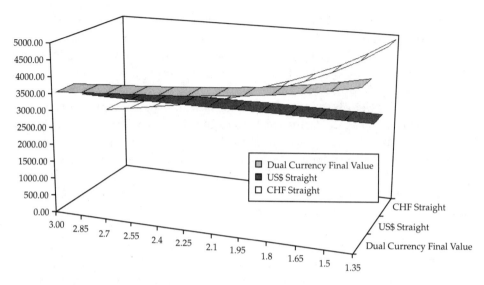

Figure 12.2 First City dual-currency vs. CHF straight.

80 of Japan's insurance law, were not allowed to pay dividends out of capital gains, but only out of coupon income. A security offering a high yield but with a risk of capital loss was relatively attractive to insurance companies in Japan.

We will take a dual-currency 5-year Japanese yen bond. It has a coupon of 4.25 percent and an implicit conversion rate of 102.95. The spot exchange rate is taken as 110. The bond is compared with a US$ straight yielding 4.5 percent and a Japanese yen straight yielding 3.125 percent. Table 12.2 and Figure 12.3 show the outcome graphically.

At the implicit conversion rate of about 106, the three bonds all have an approximately equal future value of about $1,247. If the yen is stronger than 106, the investor would be better off in a straight yen bond; if the yen is weaker

Table 12.2 Dual-Currency vs. US$ Straight and Yen Straight

Exchange Rate at Maturity	Dual-Currency	US$ Straight	Yen Straight
90%	1,286.33	1,246.18	1,469.23
100	1,260.74	1,246.18	1,322.31
110	1,239.81	1,246.18	1,202.10
120	1,222.36	1,246.18	1,101.92
130	1,207.60	1,246.18	1,017.16
140	1,194.94	1,246.18	944.51
150	1,183.98	1,246.18	881.54
160	1,174.38	1,246.18	826.44
170	1,165.92	1,246.18	777.83
180	1,158.39	1,246.18	734.62

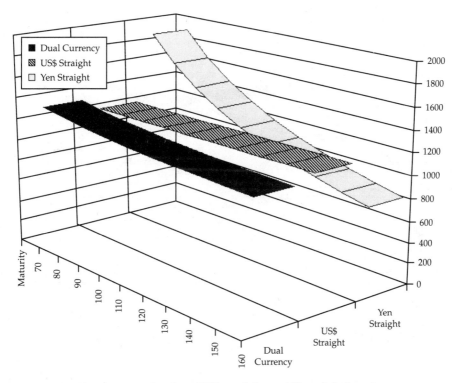

Figure 12.3 Dual vs. US$ straight and ¥ straight bonds.

than 106, the investor would be better off in the US$ straight. In general, the investor would have been better off in either the Japanese yen or the US$ straight bond.

In this case, the main attraction of the dual-currency bond is that it gives a hedge to the dollar-based investor who is not quite certain which way exchange rates will move. The investor gains some of the improvement in the yen if it strengthens beyond 106, at the price of giving up some of the strength of the dollar if the latter rises above 106. Figure 12.3 was constructed so that the lines depicting all three bonds met at around 106. The same viewpoint applies to the yen-based investor, as we can see from Figure 12.4.

The dual-currency structure continues to be popular, as indicated by the heavy sales made in Japan during 1996; a recent issue combined being a dual-currency with being asset-backed. This was the issue by America Ltd. of ¥50 billion of 4.85 percent dual-currency notes in February 1997, for redemption in November 1997. Notes of ¥500,000 are due for redemption at a price of US$4,044.98 (implicit conversion rate, ¥123.61). More recently, knock-out duals have been introduced (see below).

A further development was the "multicurrency" bond. An example would be the issue by Belgacom NV of ¥10 billion of 20-year bonds in December 1995. The terms of the issue provide that the annual rate of interest will

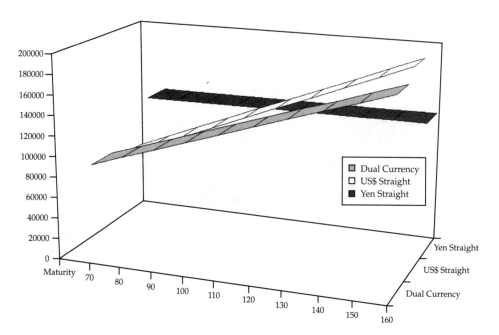

Figure 12.4 Dual-currency from the yen investor's viewpoint.

be set by the issuer 10 days prior to the payment date. It will be (presumably the lowest of) 5.86 percent in Australian dollars (based on a nominal amount of AUS$1,326,350); 5.31 percent payable in DEM (on a face amount of DEM1,411,100); or 6.61 percent payable in US$ on a face amount of $1 million. Here, the investor has sold the issuer a "rainbow" currency option (see Chapter 7).

A related variant was the two-tranche, dual-currency issue made by the Inter-American Development Bank (IADB), in May 1997. This was a 3-year issue totalling ¥14 billion. Tranche A paid a coupon in yen of 5.6 percent and redemption at $3,973 for ¥500,000. Tranche B paid a coupon in yen of 5.75 percent with redemption at £2,439.97 for ¥500,000. Here we have a multicurrency dual, but the effect is achieved by multiple tranches.

The so-called "heaven and hell" bond, a development of the dual-currency bond, was introduced, in November 1985, with an issue for IBM. In a dual-currency bond, the principal amount is fixed in terms of the implicit conversion rate. The interest flows depend on exchange rates over the bond's life. By contrast, the heaven and hell structure gives investors an upside and a downside risk on the principal amount. The two are mirror images.

The IBM issue was for $50 million of 10-year bonds, with a coupon of 10.75 percent, and a redemption amount at par if, at maturity, the yen/US$ rate is yen 169. If the rate is higher, redemption is over par. If the rate is lower, redemption is below par. The precise formula is that the redemption amount is equal to $100 \times (1 + (z - 169)/z)$, where $z =$ the spot rate at maturity. For

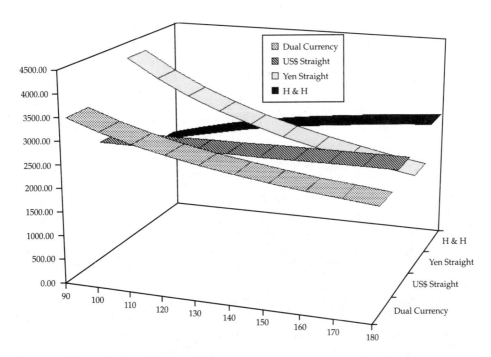

Figure 12.5 Heaven and hell vs. yen straight, US$ straight, and dual-currency bonds.

example, if the yen/$ rate stands at 170 at maturity, the repayment amount would be $100 \times (1 + (170 - 169)/170) = 100.59$. Figure 12.5 and Table 12.3 compare the dual, the heaven and hell, and straights in the two currencies:

A logical development was to create issues where there is a limitation on the currency effect. An example is the Kingdom of Denmark issue for 5 years, in April 1986. This was a ¥10 billion issue with a coupon of 5¾ percent, and an issue price of 101.25. Redemption of the issue was to be in yen, at par, if the yen

Table 12.3 **Dual-Currency vs. US$ Straight, Yen Straight, and Heaven and Hell Bonds**

Exchange Rate at Maturity	Dual-Currency	US$ Straight	Yen Straight	Heaven and Hell
90%	3,487.59	2,605.56	4,171.42	1,898.34
100	3,247.53	2,605.56	3,754.27	2,086.11
110	3,051.11	2,605.56	3,412.98	2,239.75
120	2,887.43	2,605.56	3,128.56	2,367.78
130	2,748.93	2,605.56	2,887.90	2,476.11
140	2,630.22	2,605.56	2,681.62	2,568.97
150	2,527.34	2,605.56	2,502.85	2,649.45
160	2,437.31	2,605.56	2,346.42	2,719.86
170	2,357.88	2,605.56	2,208.40	2,782.00
180	2,287.27	2,605.56	2,085.71	2,837.23

stands between ¥90.01 and ¥263.55 to the US$. If the yen is stronger than ¥90.01 to the US$, redemption is at a discount according to the following formula:

$$\frac{\text{Spot rate}}{90.005} \times 100.$$

If the yen is weaker than ¥263.55 to the US$, the formula is:

$$\frac{\text{Spot rate}}{263.55797} \times 100.$$

For example, if the yen stands at US$1 = ¥85, the redemption is at a discount price of 94.44 percent. If the yen is at ¥280 = US$1, redemption is at a premium price of 106.24 percent. The effect is to somewhat flatten the future value curve for values of the yen between ¥50 and ¥90.01, and to flatten it more after ¥263.5. Figure 12.6 shows how the instrument (christened the "minimax"), behaves, from the viewpoint of a yen-based investor.

The Kingdom of Denmark issue was issued the day before another issue, for Dansk Naturgas, which might be called a "reverse minimax." This issue was also for ¥10 billion for 5 years, maturing on April 22, 1991. Its issue price was 101.5, and its coupon was 7½ percent. The redemption was in yen according to the following formula, where S = spot exchange rate at redemption:

$$\text{Face value} \times \frac{S}{180.01} \times \frac{1 + \left(1.049 \times [S - 171.6018]\right)}{S}.$$

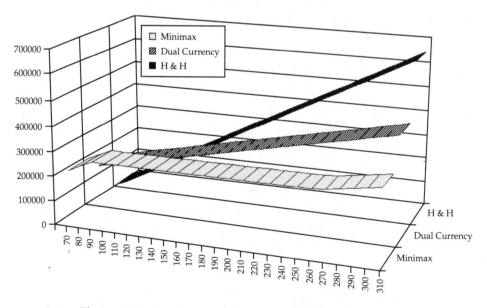

Figure 12.6 Dual-currency, heaven and hell, and minimax.

When S is on or between ¥263.55 and ¥90.01, S is exactly the same figure as the spot rate. When S is stronger than ¥90.01, the figure for S in the formula should be ¥90.005. When S is weaker than ¥263.55, S in the formula should be ¥263.55797.

The result of this peculiar construction can be seen in Figure 12.7. Between ¥50 per dollar and ¥90 per dollar, the final value of the bond falls sharply. From ¥90 to ¥263.55, it improves substantially. Thereafter, it weakens, until, at ¥500, its final value is almost the same as the minimax. As Figure 12.7 shows, the combined value of the two bonds—that is, a holding of 50 of each of the two bonds—compares almost identically with a holding of 100 bonds of a similar dual-currency, up to ¥263 per dollar. In effect, the characteristics of the dual-currency have been split between the two bonds. Over the total range of exchange rate values, the combined holding performs exactly the same as a dual-currency: Each individual bond performs in a mirror-image fashion. This peculiar construction appears to have been destined almost entirely for private Japanese portfolios. However, the combination of the two presents features of interest.

Another concept was the Eurofima issue, also issued in April 1986. The redemption for this issue is as follows. If the exchange rate at maturity is greater than ¥256.5 to the dollar (i.e., if the yen is weaker), redemption will be at 200 percent of face value. If the spot rate is less than ¥85.5 per dollar, the redemption value will be zero. In all other instances, the redemption amount will be calculated according to the following formula, where F equals the spot yen/US$ rate at maturity:

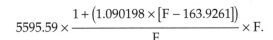

$$5595.59 \times \frac{1 + \left(1.090198 \times [F - 163.9261]\right)}{F} \times F.$$

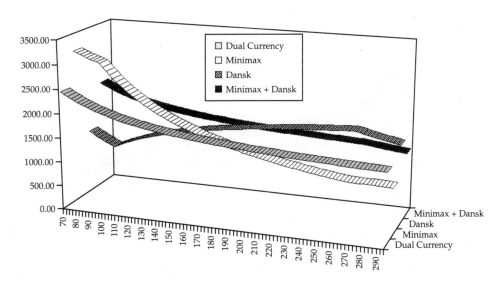

Figure 12.7 Minimax, Dansk, and dual-currency bonds.

Table 12.4 Dual-Currency, Eurofima, and Straight

Exchange Rate at Maturity	Dual-Currency	Eurofima	Straight
50%	27,453.64	23,178.50	37,542.75
75	20,251.75	15,452.33	25,028.50
100	16,650.80	13,285.16	18,771.37
125	14,490.23	12,967.30	15,017.10
150	13,049.85	12,755.40	12,514.25
175	12,021.01	12,604.04	10,726.50
200	11,249.38	12,490.52	9,385.69
225	10,649.22	12,402.23	8,342.83
250	10,169.09	12,331.60	7,508.55
275	9,776.26	11,487.00	6,825.95
300	9,448.90	10,529.75	6,257.12
325	9,171.91	9,719.77	5,775.81
350	8,934.48	9,025.50	5,363.25
375	8,728.71	8,423.80	5,005.70

As we can see from Table 12.4 and Figure 12.8, this issue provides greatest future value if the yen rises sharply. The effect of the strength of the yen on the compounded value of the future yen coupon streams offsets the fact that the total amount of the principal has to be written off at exchange rates below ¥85.5 per dollar. Correspondingly, if the dollar strengthens above ¥256.5, the future value of the bond declines. It outperforms the other two bonds, however, once the dollar rises above ¥175.

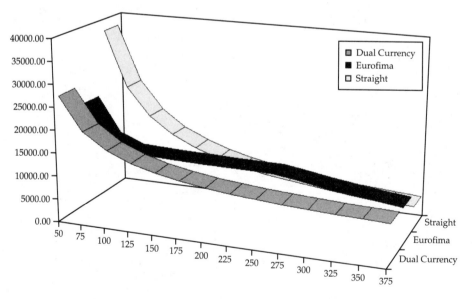

Figure 12.8 Dual-currency, Eurofima, and straight.

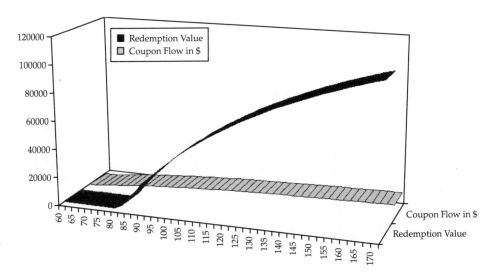

Figure 12.9   Duet bond.

In August 1986, the Kingdom of Denmark issued $100 million of "Duet" bonds, which extended the dual-currency effect to the coupon as well as the redemption value. The formula for the redemption value is:

$$\text{Redemption value} = 2D - \frac{Y}{E}$$

where D = US$100,000 (the base dollar value);
     Y = ¥16,300,000 (the base yen value);
     E = spot $/yen exchange rate at maturity.

Their coupon is found from:

$$\text{Coupon} = D \times 16.5\% - \frac{Y \times 6.5\%}{E}$$

where E = spot $/yen exchange rate on the coupon date.

Figure 12.9 shows that this bond is a heavy bet on the exchange rate, because both the coupon and the redemption value rise as the dollar strengthens.

BULL/BEAR BONDS

In June 1986, Swedish Export Kredit (SEK) issued the first so-called "bull and bear" bond. The issue was for ¥20 billion, with a coupon of 8 percent. The redemption price of the bonds is linked to the average of the Nikkei 225 stocks on the Tokyo exchange. The issue came in two tranches: a bull tranche and a bear tranche. The bull tranche had a "strike" level of ¥26,067; that is, if the Nikkei index at redemption, in July 1991, were at ¥26,067, redemption would be at 100 percent. The redemption price was reduced by 0.4425 percent for every 100 points the index fell below the strike level, and increased by a similar amount for any rise above it. There was a cap and a floor on the extent to which the investor could gain or lose. The maximum capital gain for the bull is at ¥28,461 for the Nikkei (at 110.59 percent), and the maximum loss is when the level of the Nikkei falls to ¥16,979 (the bond falls to 60 percent). Correspondingly, on the bear tranche, the strike level is set at ¥19,373, with the same floor and ceiling levels.

Figure 12.10 shows the results for various levels of the Nikkei. The bull bond and the bear bond offset each other, so that an investor who held equal amounts of both would always receive the same amount at redemption, no matter what the level of the Nikkei. However, the investor would always receive less than a comparable straight bond. This is the saving to the issuer, and the amount that the investor gives up in paying for the ability to have options on the Nikkei.

In fact, the bull bonds and bear bonds were sold to different groups of investors. The bear bonds could be sold to Japanese institutional investors who had huge paper profits on their Japanese stocks. They were loath to sell the shares because of their long term and the mutual relationship the investors had with some of the companies in which they held the shares. They feared that their hidden profits would be reduced significantly when share prices dropped. They could hedge their positions by investing in the bear bonds, because stock index futures were not yet available in Japan.

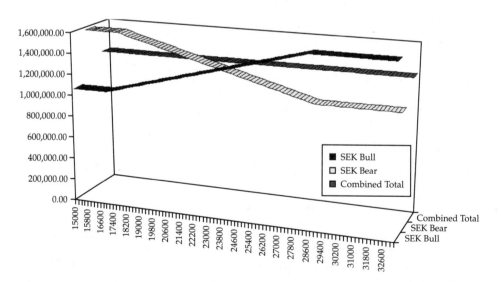

Figure 12.10 SEK bull/bear structure.

Correspondingly, the bull bonds would be placed with investors who were optimistic for the stock exchange but were attracted by a high current coupon. On the other hand, looked at overall, the terms are not overgenerous to the investor. Between ¥19,373 and ¥26,067, both bulls and bears lose out in that possible maximum losses for both bonds are 40 percent, while maximum gains are only 10.5 percent.

The bonds were designed to limit the exposure of the borrower. The redemption values balance each other out, so that whatever happens to the Tokyo stock market, the total repayment is always 85.3 percent of the principal amount. SEK was able to swap the proceeds of the bonds to gain funding at considerably less than LIBOR.

In October 1986, the Kingdom of Denmark used the same technique again to raise $120 million via the first bull/bear gold-linked Eurobond. The issue was for 7 years, in two tranches of $60 million each, maturing October 20, 1993. The coupon on both tranches was 3 percent, and the price of issue was 100⅛. The formula for the redemption amount of the bull tranche was par multiplied by 1.158 multiplied by (gold index at redemption divided by the current index). The bear tranche redemption formula was par multiplied by 2.78 minus 1.158 multiplied by (index at redemption divided by the initial index). In both cases, the initial index was the average of London and morning and afternoon fix on the day of issue ($426.50). The maximum redemption amount was set at 228 percent, and the minimum, at 50 percent. Working off the initial fixing, the bull redemption amount would drop to $50 if gold fell to $184. The redemption would be at par if the price was $369. The bear tranche redemption would be 100 percent if gold hit $656, or $50 if it reached $839.

It may be helpful to lay out the general method by which an index bond like this is put together. We have a starting index value, I (or $426.50), and a final value, V. We also have a ceiling, C (228), on the bond's value, and a floor, F (50). The first step is to find what one might call the average, A. The formula is:

$$A = \frac{C+F}{2}.$$

$$\text{In our example, } A = \frac{228+50}{2} = 139.$$

Now we set a multiplier. The multiplier is what we apply to the percentage rise in the index to get our bull bond value. If our multiplier is 2, then a 10 percent rise in the index implies a 20 percent rise in the bull bond. The multiplier (call it M) settles how sensitive our bonds are to the index. We then have:

$$\text{Price of bull bond} = \frac{M \times V}{I}.$$

$$\text{Price of bear bond} = A - \frac{M \times V}{I}.$$

The combined value is always A. The multiplier (1.158 here) also defines the minimum and maximum index values at which the ceiling and floor prices kick in:

$$\text{Index floor} = \frac{F}{M} \times \frac{I}{100} = \frac{50}{1.158} \times \frac{426.50}{100} = 184.15.$$

$$\text{Index ceiling} = \frac{C}{M} \times \frac{I}{100} = \frac{228}{1.158} \times \frac{426.50}{100} = 839.74.$$

The strike prices—i.e., the levels at which the bonds redeem at par—are easily found from the price equations above:

$$\text{Bull strike} = \frac{I}{M} = \frac{426.50}{1.158} = 368.31.$$

$$\text{Bear strike} = \frac{A-1}{100 \times M} \times I = \frac{139-1}{1.158 \times 100} \times 426.50 = 508.26.$$

A variant of the bull/bear technique was used by the Kingdom of Sweden. The bond was a 5-year bond, but the redemption value was fixed a year after issue. The initial index was 387.8 (the CAC index on the day of launching), and the final index was the average of the index for the three business days up to and including the fifth business day prior to October 30, 1987 (which, incidentally, put the fixing just after the October 1987 crash). The redemption value for the bull portion was defined as par multiplied by the final index divided by the initial index. The redemption value for the bear portion was defined as par multiplied by 2 less (par multiplied by final index divided by initial index). The maximum value was defined as par multiplied by 1.40 for each tranche, and the minimum value, as par multiplied by 0.60 for each tranche. The coupon on the bond was set at 3¾ percent for the first year, and 8 percent annually thereafter.

Effectively, therefore, the investor paid 4¼ percent for a 1-year option—call or put—on the French franc stock market index. The formula implied that a CAC index of 200, in October 1987, would give a redemption price of 60 percent for the bull tranche and a redemption price of 140 percent for the bear tranche. An index of 400 would lead to a redemption price of 103.15 percent for the bull tranche and a redemption price of 96.85 percent for the bear tranche. As with the other structures, in no case does the redemption price for the bull and bear bonds, added together, exceed 200 percent. The Kingdom of Sweden therefore sold a perfectly hedged option, charging 4¼ percent for 1 year for it, with no risk.

Although no longer as fashionable as it once was (after investors understood it), the structure still has applications. An interesting use was in the Italian lira Euro-medium-term note market in 1996. Investors were searching for ways around Italian withholding tax rules. (See the discussion of zero-coupon warrants in Chapter 15.) Issuing houses sold them pairs of bull and bear notes expressing an opposite view on the outlook for a particular currency or index. After a short period, the dealer bought back whichever note was then trading profitably, leaving the investor with a tax-exempt discounted note that had originally been issued at par. As the flow of issues grew to a flood, the Italian authorities inevitably stepped in, and the Banca d'Italia declined to give approval to any further issuance of linked bull–bear structures in the lira.

COUPON VARIANTS

FRN

Capped/Floored/Collared. The "capped" FRN was preceded by the "collared" FRN. This was an FRN paying a minimum and a maximum coupon. It was introduced in February 1985 with a $250 million issue for the Kingdom of Denmark. The first issue proved popular, and several others followed. But the then-narrow spread between minimum and maximum proved unpopular with investors, and the concept did not really become widespread, although, in June 1985, a collared FRN was introduced in the U.S. domestic market for Baltimore Gas & Electric. The difference from the Denmark deal was that the floating rate index was linked to 3-month Treasury bills. A number of similar collared U.S. domestic instruments were launched in the following months.

The collared FRN was quickly followed by the "capped" FRN, an FRN issued on the basis that the LIBOR payable will never rise above, say, 13 percent. Typically, such FRNs pay a better spread over LIBOR. In exchange for accepting a longer-term rate risk, the investor enhances the current yield. A further development came when issuers "stripped" the cap. The first reported stripped cap issue was for Banque Indosuez, in June 1985. The issue consisted of $200 million 12-year FRNs with a cap at 13 percent.

In this deal, Indosuez agreed to write a cap for a third party, which would match the cap on the FRN; i.e., Indosuez would agree to pay the third party if LIBOR rose above 13 percent, in our example. In exchange, the issuer would be paid an up-front fee. The value of this fee, spread over the life of the FRN, reduced the issuer's cost to below LIBOR, even though the FRN yielded a higher-than-normal spread over LIBOR.

The next step from the capped FRN was the introduction of the delayed cap. On these deals, the cap on the FRN is delayed, generally becoming effective only after 2 or 3 years. Thus, the investor owns a normal FRN until the cap takes effect. The first of these was the $100 million offering for Christiania Bank in Oslo, in September 1985.

After its application to FRNs, the stripped cap concept was quickly applied to the floating rate CD market. The first issue is believed to have been for Mitsubishi Bank, with a 5-year CD issue of $50 million capped at $12\frac{5}{8}$ percent. In

its various combinations—FRN and FRCD—the stripped cap market is estimated to have reached $5 billion within 3 months.

Capped, and collared, issues went out of fashion, largely because the secondary market had become rather illiquid. They then were issued in large
quantities to a new generation of investors in 1992–1993. An example was the
issue, in November 1992, of $150 million Euro-medium-term notes by the
World Bank in the form of a collared 10-year FRN paying 6-month LIBOR—
0.25 percent with a cap at 8.25 percent and a floor of 5 percent.

For low interest rate levels, the collared FRN will behave like a fixed rate
bond, because future rates are likely to be expected by the market to be below
the floor. The duration of the note then will be that of a fixed rate bond paying
the floor rate (in the World Bank example, about 8 years). As rates begin to
rise, a larger proportion of the forward rates will begin to fall within the collar
range, and the duration will start dropping toward that of an FRN; as rates rise
higher, the cap is triggered and the paper again starts to have the duration of a
fixed-rate bond. The duration of a collared paper, therefore, is normally a good
deal longer than that of a typical FRN. Even where we are within the range, the
bond is long of a floor option and short of a cap option; both positions lose
money when rates rise and make money when rates fall, adding to the duration
of the note. Figure 12.11 illustrates the fate of the collared FRN when interest
rates rose in the first quarter of 1994.

In the 1992–1993 cycle, caps and collars were applied not merely to FRNs
but also to structured commercial paper (see below) before falling out of favor

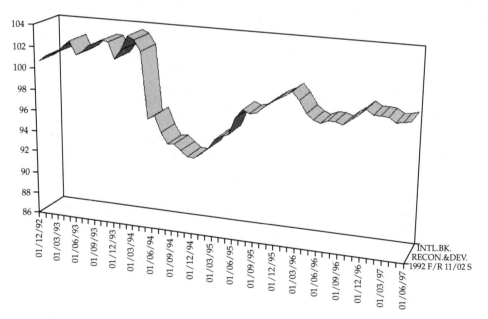

Figure 12.11   Performance of World Bank collared FRN.

again as the cost of their illiquidity was realized. Indeed, in June 1995, Lehman Brothers announced a tender offer for any or all securities from 57 issues of collared floating rate notes. Their value had collapsed following the rise in interest rates in early 1994. Many, having been issued at par, were then trading in the mid- to low 90s. But, at times, a substantial issue can still be done, given the right pricing.

Inverse/Reverse FRN.   An early variant of the FRN was the yield curve anticipation note (YCAN), which later became known as the "bull," "reverse," or "inverse" floater. The first issue was in February 1986, by the Student Loan Marketing Association ("Sallie Mae"). The issue was priced at 17.2 percent – LIBOR. Thus, as LIBOR fell, the coupon on the issue rose. The bull floater concept is attractive to investors when rates are falling, and it reverses the traditional appeal of FRNs as a safe haven for investors when rates rise.

The concept was followed quickly by other issuers, including Christiania Bank and Citicorp.With the strong emphasis on high coupons rather than capital gain, the concept quickly became very popular in the Japanese market. A large number of reverse floaters were issued in Japanese yen during the summer of 1986; for example, Kansallis Osake Pankki, the Finnish bank, did several issues. One was issued in late July, for ¥10 billion for 5 years, with coupon fixed as 14.7 percent – (1.5 × 6-month yen LIBOR). A second, in August, paid 15.125 percent – (1.6 × 6-month yen LIBOR).

Dozens of inverse floaters have been issued in a whole range of markets, including the U.S. municipal market (see the next section).

Inverse + FRN = Bond.   The combination of an inverse floater and a conventional FRN adds up to a classic fixed rate bond. The first issue to take advantage of this was the Hong Kong Mass Transit Railway Corporation's FIRST (Fixed Interest Rate Substitute Transaction), issued in 1986. It consisted of HK$600 million of a conventional FRN at HIBOR (Hong Kong Interbank Rate) + ⅛ percent, and an inverse floater paying 17 percent HIBOR. Combining the two produces a total fixed rate cost of 17.125 percent/2, or 8⁹⁄₁₆ percent.

In the domestic U.S. municipal bond market, this approach led to a product called RIBS/SAVRS. Residual Interest Bonds (RIBS) are issued in the primary market in tandem with Select Auction Variable Rate Securities (SAVRS). The interest rate on the SAVRS is reset every 35 days, or every 6 months, through a Dutch auction process (similar to the process used for auction rate preferred, discussed in Chapter 14). RIBS rates vary inversely with the SAVRS rate. RIBS investors can keep the RIBS linked to the SAVRS, in which case they have a synthetic fixed rate bond transaction like the FIRST described above. Alternatively, they can sell off one or the other. Variants of this approach have included structures in which three SAVRS-type securities were offered in tandem with one RIBS-type security; other variants have included custodial receipt or trust receipt structures that mimic the performance of RIBS and SAVRS.

A similar transaction was undertaken in 1993 by a Mexican company, Grupo Televisa. It issued simultaneously $100 million of FRNs with a floor and $100 million of reverse FRNs with a floor. The combination of one instrument paying 6-month LIBOR + 3.125 percent and another paying 12.25 percent – 6-month LIBOR creates a synthetic fixed rate instrument: The LIBOR is cancelled and the package pays (3.125 + 12.25)/2. Both issues traded up in the after-market, suggesting that, despite financial theory, the segmentation of a bond into a floater and an inverse floater did add value for the issuer (i.e., investors mispriced the combination).

Incidentally, realizing that an inverse floater can be paired with a matching floater to create a bond also provides one way of looking at the duration risk of an inverse floater. Consider an inverse 3-year floater with a face value of $50 that pays a 12 percent – 6-month LIBOR. Pairing this with a 6-month LIBOR floater of the same maturity with a face value of $50 will produce a $100 face value 6 percent bond. Suppose today the 6 percent bond is worth $103.34 and we are on a coupon date for both the floaters. The conventional floater will then reprice to par (assuming all is well with the credit), i.e., $50. It follows that the inverse must be worth $53.34.

Suppose that the modified duration of the 3-year $100 bond we have created by putting together the floaters is 2.81 years (see Chapter 3 for the duration concept). Because it is a coupon day for the floaters, the conventional floater has a duration risk of 6 months, i.e., 0.5 year. We want to find D, the duration of the inverse. We can do this by solving for it when we consider that the duration of the 6 percent bond must be a weighted average of the duration of the floaters, weighted by the price of the floaters:

$$2.81 = \frac{\$50 \times 0.5}{\$103.34} + \frac{\$53.34 \times D}{\$103.34},$$

and from this, we find that D = 4.98. This immediately points up the benefit—and the risk—of the inverse floater. The duration on the inverse is almost double that of the conventional bond. With this long duration, it will perform well if rates are falling—and the investor will be killed by rising rates. We can see that the damage is being done in two ways:

1. As rates rise, the present value of the future cash flows from the inverse falls, as with any bond.

2. The cash flows themselves fall because the coupon is 12 percent – LIBOR.

Deferred Coupon FRN.   Another coupon structure that has been used, particularly because of tax applications in certain areas, is the deferred-coupon FRN. This was adapted from the fixed rate deferred-coupon market discussed below;

a typical deal was the $100 million 5-year deal for Banque Nationale de Paris (BNP), in June 1986. The FRN pays no interest for 2 years. In Years 3, 4, and 5, the investor receives 450 basis points over LIBOR. A similar issue in September 1986 was for Christiania Bank, paying LIBOR – 6 percent for the first year; LIBOR flat in the third year; and LIBOR + 3 percent for the next 2 years. In this issue, the indenture provides that if the FRN coupon is negative, the negative amount is deemed a borrowing by the investor (at LIBOR + ⅛%) and is deducted from subsequent coupons.

This structure was then reversed, in August 1986, for a deal for National Australia Bank. Here, the coupon was accelerated. For the first 4 years, the coupon is LIBOR + 350; for the remaining 3 years, the coupon is nil.

In November 1986, a new variant came to market. The Nordic Investment Bank offered a ¥8.5 billion reverse FRN with a coupon (C) fixed as follows: $C = [9.125 - (L \times D)] \times 2$ where $L = 6$-month yen LIBOR and $D =$ number of days/360. The variant was that the same FRN also offered a dual-currency-type redemption.

In December 1986, Kansallis Osake Pankki Bank issued a "step-up" yen FRN which, in its first 2 years, paid $0.1 \times$ (6-month yen LIBOR + ⅛ percent) and in its last 3 years, 6-month yen LIBOR + 2.2%.

In September 1986, the reverse FRN was coupled with a fixed rate bond by Kawasaki Steel. The bond pays 14.89 percent – 2×6-month yen LIBOR for the first 5 years. In the second 5 years, it pays 8 percent. Such an issue is attractive for a borrower who sees a sustained rise in rates, and conversely for an investor.

A more conventional, but related, coupon structure is the step-up or step-down spread, sometimes known as the split spread. The spread over LIBOR is adjusted according to maturity, but not to the same extent as the deferred/accelerated coupon concept, in that a LIBOR-related coupon is always paid. The rationale for these deals is generally to sweeten a longer-than-normal issue. An example is the 30-year issue by Hill Samuel, the British merchant bank, in June 1986. More recently, as we have seen in Chapter 9, step-up coupons have been used to convince investors that notionally "perpetual" FRNs will in fact be called in 5 or 10 years' time.

Step-Up/Step-Down Fixed-Rate Bonds.   Like their counterparts in the floating rate note market, fixed rate bond market issuers have used step-up and step-down structures. Generally, these are designed to achieve a longer apparent than real maturity, although, in some cases, the reverse may be true. The change in coupon structure in the step-up is generally designed to give the issuer an incentive to call the bond early, while offering the investor compensation if this does not happen.

A recent example was the issue by Banco Sul America SA, the Brazilian specialist bank, of $40 million of step-up notes 1996–1999/04, whereby the coupon is 10.625 percent per annum until 1999 and 11.45 percent thereafter.

Another application of the technique, for a different reason, was an issue by Nordic Investment Bank of DKK400 million of 7-year, 9-month bonds (issued in January 1997 for payment March 1997, maturing December 2004). This issue paid a zero coupon until December 1999 and thereafter paid 10.25 percent until maturity. The deal was christened a "jump-up" bond. The rationale was to place the bonds with investors expecting to retire before the coupon kicks in (their tax rates would be lower) or with investors currently holding high-coupon bonds expected to mature by 1999.

Embedded Currency Options

Currency options embedded in bond issues are not new; one could consider the so-called "currency cocktail" bonds of the 1960s and 1970s as currency options. For example, the European Unit of Account (a private unit of account, not to be confused with the official EUA used later by the EEC) was introduced, in 1961, for a bond issue by the Portuguese company Sacor. The bond contract defined 17 reference currencies, which, in turn, had gold par values. The EUA's gold value would change only if (1) all reference currencies had changed in the same direction, and (2) at least two-thirds had changed in the same direction. It could be argued that Sacor had written a strictly limited currency option to its investors. In 1970, the private version of the European Currency Unit was introduced, setting up fixed exchange rates among the currencies of the member states (six, at that time) of the EEC. The investor could ask for repayment of principal in the strongest of the six currencies, so the concept was very attractive to investors but less so to borrowers.

In 1973, the European Composite Unit (EURCO) was introduced, in a loan to the European Investment Bank. In this issue, interest was payable in the currency chosen by the borrower, and principal was repayable in the currency chosen by the lender. Thus, the investor wrote a currency option on the interest, and the borrower wrote a currency option on the principal.

Simpler currency option issues were the sterling bonds issued in the 1960s with the option of repayment in deutsche marks. For example, in the Irish 1973–1988 7 percent £/DEM bonds, the investor could be paid in sterling, or in DEM at a rate of DEM7.5503 per £1 (compare the rate at maturity of the bond— around £1 = DEM 2.90).

In October 1985, in a $100 million issue for the Long-Term Credit Bank of Japan (LTCB), the concept of the Index Currency Option Note (ICON) was introduced. The LTCB paid 100 basis points over Treasury bonds for its 10-year issue; normally, it would have been expected to pay 35 to 45 basis points. In exchange, the investor received a reduced payment of the principal amount if the yen was stronger than 169 against the dollar at maturity in 10 years' time. Effectively, the investor sold the borrower a European-style 10-year yen/dollar call option with a strike price of 169.

The redemption formula is as follows:

$$\left(1 - \frac{\{169 - S\}}{S}\right) * F$$

where S = spot rate at maturity;
F = face value of note.

Here are some examples for a $1,000 note:

−Yen/Dollar Rate 1995	Redemption Amount
179	$1,000
169	1,000
159	937.11
149	865.77
84.5 ،	0

The U.S. domestic markets have seen several other currency option-linked issues. For example, Credit National, the large French bank, offered $150 million of floating rate notes convertible into European Currency Units (ECU), in November 1985, with an interest rate set at 35 basis points above the 91-day Treasury bill auction rate. On any interest payment date before the end of 1987, the notes could be converted at the holder's option into floating rate notes due in 1995, denominated in ECUs.

A further development, in March 1986, was the issue called Foreign Interest Payment Security (FIPS), by Pepsico Inc., in the Swiss market. The issue had two notable features: (1) the bond is perpetual—there is a put option for investors every 10 years; and (2) the coupon is payable annually in US$, to be reset every 10 years on the basis of the average yield on 10-year U.S. Treasuries less 50 basis points. The bond itself is denominated in Swiss francs (SFR).

The investor's put option is at par every 10 years if the value of the dollar is equal to or in excess of the reference exchange rate (SFR 1.8690 in 1996). If the value of the dollar is then below the reference rate, the put value is reduced. The Swiss franc amount received by the investor is 100 times the exchange rate then applicable, divided by the reference exchange rate. So a 10 percent fall below the reference rate would produce a 10 percent reduction in the value of the bond. This, in fact, is a one-way option written by the investor to the issuer, since the investor bears all the risk of the exchange rate falling but gains no benefit from its rising. In exchange, the investor receives an apparently high coupon, in the form of 10-year U.S. Treasuries less 50 basis points, payable in dollars. Critics of the bond argued that, in effect, it was a dollar bond, yielding a subdollar coupon. Two weeks later, the concept was followed by Adjustable

Long-Term Puttable Securities (ALPS), issued by Svensk Export Kredit (SEK). The issue was for SFR 200 million with a 25-year maturity and a put option for investors after 10, 15, and 20 years. Redemption is at par if the Swiss franc/U.S. dollar exchange rate is above 1.8870 per dollar. If it is below that rate, the redemption value is reduced by the same formula as applied to the Pepsico deal. The interest rate for the first 10 years was fixed at 7¼ percent, payable annually in U.S. dollars. Subsequent fixings will be for 5-year periods on the basis of the 5-year Treasury bond yield less 65 basis points.

The straight currency option bond continues to be seen regularly in a number of guises. A recent example was the issue, in March 1997, by Dresdner Bank, of DEM100 million of 4-year zero-coupon notes at a price of 87.40 percent. They are redeemable, at the option of the bondholder, at DEM1,000 or the DEM equivalent of US$570. The investor is buying an implicit 4-year call option at a strike price of DEM1.7544. If the dollar is at that level at redemption, the return will be 3.42 percent; if the dollar climbs to, say, DEM 2.00, the return is 6.87 percent.

Second Generation Instruments

Coupon Variants

Hybrid Fix/Float.   In a number of cases, bonds have been issued that consisted of a hybrid between fixed and floating rates.

The classic form consists of a fixed rate and either a straightforward FRN or an inverse FRN. For example, in January 1997, the Kingdom of Sweden issued, in the Spanish Matador market, ESP13 billion of 8-year notes bearing a 6.5 percent coupon for Years 1 through 4 and 13 percent –12-month LIBOR thereafter.

A converse structure was an issue, by Danone Finance, of Portuguese escudos: PTE7.5 billion of 7-year notes bearing a coupon of 6-month LISBOR (Lisbon Interbank Offered Rate) + 35 basis points for Years 1 through 3, and 7.3 percent annually thereafter. This issue is callable and so there is an embedded swaption struck at 7.3 percent.

Variants of the structure have included geared, capped, or collared structures. An ungeared but collared version was the issue by Deutsche Pfandbrief und Hypothekenbank AG of DEM150 million bonds, in January 1994, bearing a fixed rate of interest of 5½ percent until January 5, 1996. Thereafter, interest is paid at 6-month DEM LIBOR – ⅛ percent, subject to a minimum of 5 percent and a maximum of 7 percent.

A version operating in the opposite direction was the issue, by Daiwa Overseas Finance Ltd., of floating/fixed rate bonds, issued January 1994, in the amount of $50 million. This paid a coupon of 6-month US$ LIBOR + 0.45 percent until January 1997, when it converted to a fixed rate of 8 percent per annum. It had a call provision allowing the issue to be called in January 1997, and this was in fact done.

Another variant was the issue, in February 1994, of a fixed/FRN/fixed issue by Frankfurter Hypotheken Bank AG. This DEM100 million 10-year note paid 5.25 percent for Years 1 and 2, 6-month DEM LIBOR flat for Years 3 through 6, and 7 percent thereafter.

An interesting variant was the issue, by Crédit Lyonnais, of ¥10 billion of subordinated fixed/floating rate bonds, 1989–2004. These paid interest (7 percent per annum) from November 1989 to November 1999 annually in sterling at a fixed exchange rate of £1 = ¥225. Thereafter, interest will accrue at a rate equal to 1 percent above the yen long-term prime rate and will be payable in yen semiannually. This is, in fact, a dual-currency bond denominated in yen with interest payable in sterling at a fixed rate. The conversion to a floating rate note was unlikely to take place because a rate of 1 percent over long-term prime is not particularly attractive.

Some of these hybrid issues were combinations of a fixed rate with a reverse floater. Many of these issues were brought in deutsche marks at the time of German reunification, when market participants expected rising German rates, for a short period of time, to be followed by a decline. The Council of Europe Resettlement Fund, for example, brought to market DEM200 million of fixed/floating rates in August 1990. This issue paid a fixed coupon of 9½ percent until August 14, 1992, and thereafter paid 16 percent – LIBOR. In October 1993, the Kingdom of Denmark issued ESP15 billion of fixed/floating rate bonds. Interest, payable semiannually, was fixed at 10 percent until April 1994; thereafter, it was 15.5 percent – 6-month ESP LIBOR. The Spanish market saw a similar issue, in February 1997, when Deutsche Siedlungs und Landesrentenbank placed in the Matador Market a 10-year bond with a coupon of 6.67 percent for the first 5 years and 12.8 percent less ESP 12-month LIBOR with a minimum 4.0 percent floor.

A similar version, slightly more highly geared, was the issue by Crédit Local de France of fixed/reverse floating rate bonds, in December 1993, maturing in 2000. This consisted of FRF500 million, paying a fixed coupon, for the first year, of 7¼ percent. Thereafter, it pays 16.2 percent – 2 × FRF 6-month PIBOR.

Another type of hybrid involves partial index-linking. A supranational institution privately placed in the Euro-medium-term note market, in February 1997, a 5-year issue of ITL100 billion at an issue price of 101.5 and a redemption price of 100. It has three interest periods:

1. February 18, 1997, to March 18, 1998: zero coupon.
2. March 18, 1998, to March 18, 1999: a coupon calculated as (MIBF – MIBI)/MIBI, where MIBF is the monthly average of the closing value of the MIB-30 Italian equity index on the first business day of each month, April 1997–March 1999, and MIBI is the average of the index from March 3 to March 7, 1997.

3. March 18, 1999, to March 18, 2002: 9 percent, or, at the issuer's option, 6-month ITL LIBOR + 0.25 percent.

Superfloaters (Bear Floaters).   As discussed earlier, the inverse floater or bull floater is a floating rate note that performs well in bull markets when interest rates are falling. When rates are rising, investors might consider the opposite structure, the bear floater, which is sometimes called a superfloater.

A typical superfloater might have a coupon of 2 × LIBOR − 7 percent, with a coupon floor of zero. In this structure, unless LIBOR is above 7 percent, the initial coupon is going to be below current market levels, so investors have to make a yield sacrifice to buy the paper. Generally, this has meant that these instruments are not very popular except in times of panic over rising interest rates. This led to the adoption of the "deleveraged" approach, in which the structure becomes x percent + 0.5 × LIBOR, for example, or the deleveraged prime structure, discussed next.

Deleveraged Prime FRN.   Many U.S. investors who buy FRNs like to buy FRNs that have coupons linked to the U.S. prime rate, rather than to LIBOR, because prime is an "administered" rate; i.e., it is fixed by the banks rather than being a pure market rate, and is therefore believed to fall more slowly than LIBOR when rates are falling. During the 1990–1994 bull market rally in interest rates, as coupons fell, these investors searched for a more attractive alternative. The deleveraged prime note was developed in response. Let us consider a $25 million deleveraged prime note issued, in December 1993, by the Federal Home Loan Bank. The coupon was fixed as 0.5 × Prime + 0.80 percent. At the time, prime was 6 percent and overnight Fed funds were 3 percent. Thus, the deleveraged prime coupon of 3.8 percent on the initial fixing looked attractive; the downside was that, if rates rose, the investor participated in only half the rise. As a result, the duration of this note was not the same as that of an ordinary FRN; instead, it was about 1.4 years (midway between the duration of a 3-year fixed rate and a normal FRN on the fixing date). The effect is analogous to the SURF note (see below). As Figure 12.12 illustrates, the conventional prime-based floater outperforms the deleveraged prime FRN if prime rises above 6.7 percent.

CMT/CMS Floaters.   A class of second-generation structures in those whose index maturity does not match the reset frequency of the coupon. These include floating rate notes whose coupon is indexed to the constant maturity Treasury bond. The analysis of these instruments is discussed in part in Chapter 3. The typical objective of the investor in buying such instruments is to get a higher floating rate yield that can be got from LIBOR FRNs, while retaining the full upward potential in a rising interest rate environment. The CMT note will outperform a LIBOR FRN is an environment where the yield curve slopes upward more steeply, and, conversely, will suffer in an environment where the yield curve inverts.

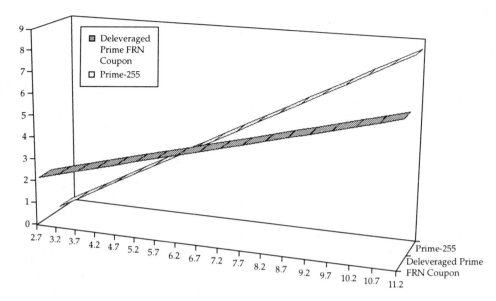

Figure 12.12 Deleveraged prime floater.

TEC-10 Floaters.   This type of French floating rate note closely resembles the CMT segment of the U.S. market. (TEC stands for Taux de l'Échéance Constante—Constant Maturity Rate.) In April 1996, the French Treasury issued FRF18 billion of floating rate Obligations Assimilable du Tresor (OATs). The coupon, payable quarterly, is a daily readjustment of the semiannual par yield of the OATs to a constant 10-year maturity. The TEC-10-based coupon is predetermined and is announced 5 days before the beginning of each quarter. By contrast, the previous floating rate index, the TME, was difficult to calculate and could vary during a coupon period.

The European Investment Bank launched the first collared TEC-10 bond, in November 1996. This was an issue of FRF1.5 billion of 10-year bonds with a coupon defined as the TEC-10 yield minus 142 basis points, with a minimum of 4.5 percent and a maximum of 7.5 percent.

SURF.   The Step-Up Recovery Floater (SURF) was a structure that took the CMT concept a step further. We have seen already, in the deleveraged prime FRN structure discussed earlier, a juicy coupon added on at the price of accepting only half of a later interest rate rise. The SURF applies this technique to the CMT FRN. (The step-up refers to the fact that, in the initial structure, there was a built-in floor that stepped up over time, but the name was used also for issues with a fixed floor.) As an example, in March 1993, the World Bank issued U.S.$100 million of floating rate notes maturing March 1998 and bearing a minimum coupon of 4.6 percent and a maximum of 25 percent. Within these ranges, the coupon paid was $0.5 \times$ U.S. 10-year CMT rate plus 1.45 percent. Figure 12.13 illustrates the performance of the note, showing

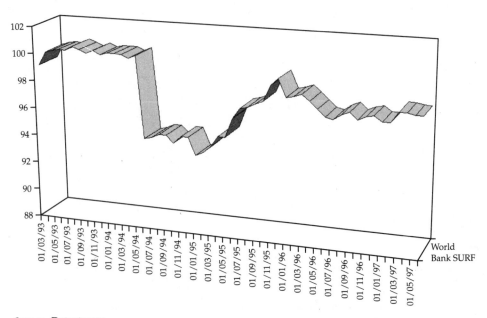

Source: Datastream

Figure 12.13   Performance of World Bank SURF.

exactly what happens when the yield curve flattens, as it did in the early part of 1994.

Leveraged Capped Floating Rate Paper.   The opposite of a deleveraged structure is a structure using a leveraged payoff. These structures have been used in FRNs and also in structured commercial paper. A typical transaction was an issue, in March 1993, by Walt Disney, of $75 million of commercial paper paying the lower of 1-month LIBOR + .07 percent or 18.82 percent − 4 × 1-month LIBOR, with a floor of 0 percent. These notes lose value rapidly, once LIBOR rises above 3.75 percent (the level that triggers a switch to the inverse coupon). If LIBOR rises by ½ percent above this level, the coupon is 18.82 − 4 × 4.25 = 1.82 percent. Figure 12.14 illustrates the result:

Spread-Linked Notes

CMT-LIBOR.   Another class of second-generation structure is the multi-index structure, which is priced in relation to the sum of or the difference between multiple indexes. The CMT-LIBOR differential note is a common variant. Recall from the discussion in Chapter 3 that the duration of these FRNs is, broadly speaking, similar to the duration of a comparable fixed rate bond, less the positive effects on duration of a rising CMT coupon. As with the SURF discussed earlier, the structure of these FRNs is such that they suffer in a period when short rates are rising relative to long rates.

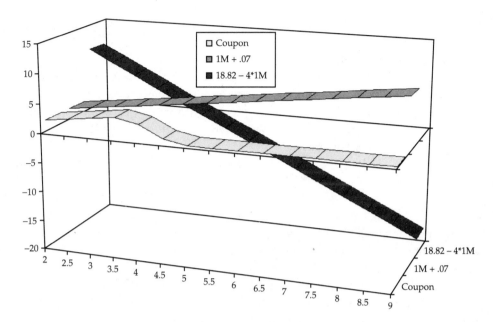

Figure 12.14   Leveraged capped note.

A variant of this structure was seen in January 1993, when SmithKline Beecham Corporation issued $45 million of 4-year notes with interest payable annually. The interest rate for the first year was 6.25 percent and was to be reset, with a maximum rate to be 6.25 percent and a minimum to be 0 percent. Under the formula, the interest rate will fall if the 10-year Treasury rate is within 150 basis points of the 3-month LIBOR rate. If the 3-month LIBOR rate exceeds the 10-year Treasury rate by more than 162.5 basis points, then the interest rate will fall to zero.

Prime-LIBOR.   In the 1993–1994 bull market, some investors turned to Prime-LIBOR Differential FRNs as an alternative way to pick up spread. An example would be the Federal Farm Credit Bank System issue of $150 million of 3-year FRNs, in July 1993. This paid a coupon of Prime – 3-month LIBOR + 1.95 percent. At the time of issue, the spread was high by historical standards. The primary risk faced by investors was that, in rising rate environments, LIBOR tends to move faster than prime (although the speed differential is less than in falling rate environments, where bankers try to hang on to their profits by being slow to cut prime).

Cross-Currency Interest Rate Spread-Linked.   In early 1994, Finance For Danish Industry placed a 6-month note whose redemption value was indexed to the spread between Spanish and German bonds. It paid a fixed coupon of 11 percent, and the redemption amount was 0.5 times geared to the spread between

10-year Spanish and German government bond yields, with a reference spread of 2.97 percent and subject to a minimum redemption of 87.5 percent and a maximum of 100 percent.

An issue by Crédit Local de France, in February 1997, offered investors the chance to bet, not on EMU convergence, but on EMU divergence. The issue was for ITL200 billion of 5-year notes paying 8 percent for the first 6 months, and, thereafter, 4.05 percent + 6-month Lira LIBOR – 6-month DEM LIBOR, with a minimum coupon of 8 percent.

Exotic Options

Range Notes (Corridor Notes, Fairway Bonds, Accrual Notes).   A very large number of bonds have been sold with a range feature embedded. A range note or corridor note allows investors to receive an enhanced return on days when the rate is within a range, at the risk of earning nothing when the rate is outside the range. The narrower the range and the more the range differs from the implied forward rates, the greater the potential return enhancement. The structure is also known as a "fairway bond;" by analogy with golf, we hope that rates stay within the fairway, rather than straying into the rough. Another term for the instruments is LIBOR Enhanced Accrual Notes (LEAN).

As discussed in Chapter 7, the classic range note involves the investor's earning a higher coupon in exchange for selling to the issuer a strip of digital options on the underlying instrument. For example, if the note pays off only on days when LIBOR remains between 5 percent and 6 percent, the investor is short two sets of digital options: one that pays off if LIBOR is above 6 percent, and one that pays off if LIBOR is below 5 percent. The number of options is equal to the number of business days in the period. The digital payoff is the amount of the coupon that would otherwise have been received. Pricing of these instruments requires careful attention to the structure of the payoff and the option strikes, but, in principle, is a simple combination of the digital options and a bond.

As an example, in early 1994, Exterior International Ltd placed privately a 6-month ITL50 billion lira corridor note, bearing a fixed coupon of 12 percent multiplied by the number of days that 3-month lira LIBOR remained within the range of from 7.25 percent to 8 percent. The accrual is zero outside that range. The coupon is paid quarterly in arrears. The theoretical duration of this note varies considerably. If interest rates fall below the bottom of the range, the duration is actually negative. (A rise in rates improves the prospect of climbing back up into the range.) When LIBOR is within the range, the duration is the same as for a normal FRN, except that, as LIBOR approaches the upper or lower barriers, the digital options the investor has sold increase in value and distort the normal duration effect. Above the upper barrier, the duration becomes very large, just as with the inverse FRN discussed earlier, and for the same reasons: the twin effects of rising rates on the present value of the bond's cash flow, but, more importantly, the disappearance of any coupon flows.

A variant is the digital-style cap. A classic example of this type of note was issued by the Royal Bank of Scotland PLC, in September 1994: £150 million of floating rate medium-term notes maturing September 1998. The coupon was fixed at 0.40 percent above 6-month sterling LIBOR. Interest does not accrue on days when 6-month LIBOR is above 15 percent.

Step-Up Range Notes. A variant of the standard range note is to apply a step-up structure. For example, in early 1994, Beta Finance Corporation issued a 2-year range floating rate note that bore a coupon of 3-month US$ LIBOR + 0.50 percent where the coupon accrued only if 3-month US$ LIBOR was above 4.0 percent and below the following cap levels: 5.60 percent (first period), 6.10 percent (second period), 6.60 percent (third period), and so on, until the eighth period, when the cap was 8.60 percent. The floor remained constant throughout. This not-uncommon structure is often of interest to investors when the forward rate curve is steepening.

An example was the issue, in July 1996, by Electricité de France, of PTE 5 billion of a 2-year "corridor accrual note." The coupon on this bond was 6-month LISBOR (Lisbon Interbank Offered Rate) plus 15 basis points, provided the 6-month LISBOR remained between 6.25 and 8.125 percent in the first year and between 6.25 and 8.375 percent in the second year. If LISBOR is outside that range, no coupon accrues.

A similar example was the issue, in February 1994, by Landesbank Hessen-Thüringen Girozentrale, of 1994–1997 floating rate notes in the amount of $100 million. This paid interest at 1 percent over 3-month US$ LIBOR, but interest accrued only on days when LIBOR fell within the following ranges: 3–4 percent until August 10, 1994; 3–4½ percent to February 10, 1995; 3–5½ percent to August 10, 1995; 3–6 percent to February 10, 1996; 3–6½ percent to August 10, 1996; 3–7 percent thereafter until maturity.

A cross-currency variant would be the European Bank for Reconstruction and Development's issue of HK$200 million of 1994–1999 corridor notes, in March 1994. Interest accrues at 8⅝ percent per annum on days when 6-month US$ LIBOR falls within the following ranges: 3½–4½ percent until September 15, 1994; 3½–5 percent to March 15, 1995; 3½–5½ percent to September 15, 1995; 3½–6 percent to March 15, 1996; 4–6¼ percent to September 15, 1996; 4–6½ percent to March 15, 1997; 4½–6¾ percent to September 1997; 4½–7 percent to March 1998; 4½–7¼ percent to September 1998; 4½–7½ percent to maturity.

A very similar issue, for a slightly shorter maturity and different initial floor structure, was made, in March 1994, for HK$200 million 6⅝ percent corridor notes 1994–1997, by the International Finance Corporation. These paid semiannual interest at 6⅝ percent on those days when LIBOR for 6-month US$ deposits fell within the following ranges: 3½–4½ percent from the issue date up to but excluding September 24, 1994; 3½–5 percent to March 24, 1995; 4–5½ percent to September 24, 1995; 4–6 percent to March 24, 1996; 4½–6¼ percent to September 24, 1996; 4½–6¾ percent to March 24, 1997.

Reset Range Note.   A variant is known as the resettable range note; the investor has the ability to change the range periodically. At issue date, the investor defines a constant width of the range, and the frequency with which it can be reset. For example, a floating rate note in U.S. dollars might pay (LIBOR + 60) × (percentage of time in range), with a resettable range of 100 basis points, with resets allowed quarterly. Here, we have an underlying set of digital options with a resettable strike.

Alternatively, the structure can be set up with preset levels for the reset. In March 1994, Pemex, the Mexican oil company, issued a $400 million 3-year MTN that was divided into two tranches. The first tranche of $200 million was a plain vanilla floating rate note, paying LIBOR + 85. The other tranche—described as a "resetting collar FRN"—paid 3-month LIBOR + 205, accrued daily, for each day in respect of which 3-month LIBOR was within a range of +50/−25 basis points from the last LIBOR fixing. The structure resembled a step-up range floater, but with the difference that the range was reset each time LIBOR was reset, rather than being fixed in advance. Like the range floater concept, the underlying hedging instruments were probably digital options, but, in this case, the strike levels on the digital options would have to reset every 3 months.

Yield Curve Range Notes.   A variant of the structure (also called a Yield Curve Accrual Note) is a combination of the CMT-LIBOR structure and the range note. A typical structure might be a 3-year note paying a 4.75 percent coupon in Year 1, and 7.125 percent in Years 2 and 3, provided that the 10-year CMT–6-month LIBOR spread is between 1.25 percent and 2.25 percent.

Binary Range Note.   A binary range note is another variant on the basic range note idea. Here, we have a structure where a 3-year note might be paying a coupon of 5.5 percent each day LIBOR is within the range, and 2 percent each day if it is outside. In other words, this is a fixed rate note with two coupons, one applicable inside the range and one outside.

Range Note with "Trigger" Option.   In early 1994, Exterior International Ltd. placed privately $7.4 million of synthetic peseta foreign exchange range notes. The fixed coupon was 12 percent multiplied by the fraction of the number of days that the ESP/DEM foreign exchange rate remained within the range of 79 to 84. Here, the underlying digital is not on the interest rate but on another instrument—in this example, the exchange cross-rate. Such structures are sometimes referred to as "triggers" and are also seen in the swap market.

At about the same time, the Council of Europe issued ITL20 billion of 1-year notes. These were an extension of the concept in that they paid a fixed coupon of 12 percent multiplied by the fraction of the number of days that the ITL/DEM exchange rate stayed within the range of 890 to 979 *and* the ITL/US$ rate remained below 1,575. The note provided for an additional payout of 5 percent, at maturity, if the ITL/DEM rate was below 900.

Knock-Out Options. In early 1994, Beta Finance Corporation issued $14.6 million of 4-month synthetic peseta notes linked to the ESP/DEM exchange rate. The bonds paid a fixed coupon of 10 percent. The redemption amount was set as (1) 101.68 percent if the ESP/DEM exchange rate remained within the range of 79.5 to 84 during the life of the note; (2) 100 percent if it stayed within 78 to 85; (3) and 97.64 percent if it traded outside 78 to 85 at any point in its life. In effect, the investor here is selling the issuer an option; the protection disappears if the exchange rate trades outside the range.

Knockout Dual-Currency. A related structure is the knockout dual-currency bond. We discussed dual-currency bonds earlier. During 1996, sales of dual-currency bonds grew rapidly in Japan because of low Japanese interest rates. An estimated 2 trillion of dual-currency bonds were sold between April and December 1996. But as the yen fell, in January 1997, savers demanded better protection against yen weakness. Borrowers responded by offering knockout dual-currency bonds, also called corridor dual-currency and range dual-currency bonds. These paid an attractive coupon, typically 5 percent, with redemption in yen under normal circumstances. But if the knockout levels were hit, they would be repaid in dollars. The levels were typically set at 10 percent away from the current market level. It is estimated that, in 1997, ¥50 billion of these bonds were sold in February, ¥100 billion in March, ¥150 billion in April, and ¥300 billion in May. Unfortunately, the yen then proceeded to jump sharply, knocking out many of the April and May contracts. The bonds then became repayable in dollars, when the dollar had just weakened sharply against the yen. A number of brokers took substantial losses because they had not yet sold the new issues; investors, of course, took even larger losses.

A similar structure, privately placed by a major AA-rated Japanese corporate name in February 1997, was a yen–sterling dual. The issue was for ¥3 billion with a 2-year maturity, bearing an interest rate of 4 percent payable semiannually. The coupons are payable in sterling at a fixed exchange rate of ¥100 million = £514,668.10. Redemption is calculated as follows:

1. If the ¥/£ exchange rate is always above £1 = ¥157, then the bond redeems at par.
2. If the ¥/£ rate ever falls below £1 = ¥157, then the redemption amount will be £15,440.043.

The net result is that if the exchange rate at maturity is ¥150, say, investors will receive the sterling equivalent of 77 percent of their initial principal.

Double Knockout. This structure was used, for example, in a private placement of an issue of £4.1 million, in February 1997, by a French bank. This was a 6-year zero coupon, but the redemption price is 100 percent + P1998 + P1999 + P2000 + P2001 + P2002 + P2003, where, e.g., P2000 is defined as 17 percent, provided the average of the FTSE *and* the S&P500, in the 5 days leading up to February 14, 2000, are above the levels for the same period in 1999. In essence, this is a digital cliquet with two knockout triggers.

One-Way Collared FRN (Ratchet FRN).   In January 1993, PepsiCo Inc. offered $50 million of medium-term notes to be issued March 15, 1993, with a maturity date of September 15, 1994. The initial interest rate was set at 3.6875 percent. Thereafter, it was reset monthly. The potential rise in rates was capped to a maximum of 31.25 basis points in a quarter. There was a floor of LIBOR plus 0.5 percent.

A number of similar issues were made, mainly by U.S. government agencies such as Federal Home Loan Bank System, which, in April 1994, issued $50 million of 3-year notes paying 3-month LIBOR + 0.655 percent. The rise in each quarter was capped at 25 basis points, and the floor for the FRN resets each quarter at the previous coupon; hence the alternative name of ratchet FRN sometimes given to these instruments (the coupon ratchets upward). This is essentially a combination of a ladder option structure for the floors (see Chapter 7), which the investor finances by selling the reset strike cap to the issuer.

Cash-Flow Variants

The index amortizing swap structure was discussed in Chapter 5. Its structured note equivalent has been widely used, particularly by U.S. federal agency issuers, for whom the financing structure was a convenient match to their liabilities. An example would be the issue, in March 1994, of $35 million 3-year notes by the Federal Home Loan Bank. These paid LIBOR + 1.40 percent for the first 9 months and then a flat 1 percent if the bonds are not called. The note was called if LIBOR averaged at or below 5 percent in the 10 days to December 7, 1994. Thus, the bond had the same extension risk as a mortgage: if interest rates rise, the bond remains outstanding. In this case, the risk is compounded by the fact that the interest rate drops to 1 percent.

Foreign Rate Index

Quanto Notes (Diff Notes).   These instruments are based on the diff swap structures discussed in Chapter 5. A typical example was the issue of $110 million of 3-year notes by SLMA ("Sallie Mae"), in August 1991. The coupon paid was a US$ coupon set at 4.6875 percent + (6-month DEM LIBOR − 6-month US$ LIBOR), with a coupon minimum of zero. In effect, the investor is entering into a diff swap to receive DEM LIBOR and pay US$ LIBOR. The risk components of the note (by analogy with the discussion in Chapter 3) are:

1. The discounting rate, which is the 3-year U.S. Treasury bond rate, with a duration of about 2.7.

2. DEM LIBOR, which can be converted into paying the fixed rate DEM swap, giving us a negative duration contribution (rising DEM rates pay off for us) of about –2.7.

3. US$ LIBOR, which can be converted to the 3-year swap rate (we receive fixed, so the duration is the same as owning a 3-year Treasury bond; i.e., 2.7).

The net overall duration is approximately 2.7 + 2.7 – 2.7 = 2.7.

Synthetic GKOs. Finally, an example of a note structured around a foreign rate index, but with a rather different objective—namely, to permit foreigners to access the Russian domestic market when they were restricted from doing so—is the synthetic GKO vehicle. Domestic investors could purchase, in the domestic market, GKO bonds yielding around 75 percent. International investment banks could only receive 20 percent. A number of structures—of varying degrees of reliability—were set up whereby vehicles purchased domestic GKO bonds and issued notes against them to foreigners paying coupons higher than the 20 percent available directly.

An example of this type of transaction was the issue, in August 1996, by ING Bank, of US$30 million of medium-term notes linked to the performance of Russian Ministry of Finance (MinFin) bonds. The principal is guaranteed by ING Bank, but the coupon payments were linked to the performance of MinFin Tranche 4 bonds.

Leveraged Securities

PERLS. Principal Exchange Rate Linked Securities (PERLS) consist of bonds denominated in U.S. dollars and paying interest in U.S. dollars. But the principal amount of the bond due at maturity depends on one or more exchange rates. Unlike a conventional bond, the redemption value of the PERLS is calculated as the equivalent of various amounts of foreign currencies—some positive, some negative. As an example, the SLMA 11.10 percent PERLS has a redemption value defined as follows. Each $1,000 face value bond is due to be redeemed for the sum of $1,000 + ITL 1,250,750 + ESP 105,000 – DEM 1,666 – ¥ 133,650.

Thus, the economic value of the bond is equivalent to owning a bond with a face value of $1,000, together with a lending in Italian lire and Spanish pesetas offset by a borrowing in deutsche marks and yen. An alternative description would be that we own a $1,000 bond and are "long" Italian lire and Spanish pesetas but "short" deutsche marks and yen. The relatively high coupon earned by the bond reflects this underlying position, because, at the time of issue, interest rates in Italian lire and Spanish pesetas were substantially above those prevailing in Japan and Germany.

The difference between a typical PERLS—the SLMA 11.1 percent—and a conventional bond whose coupon is chosen to match that of the PERLS (were such a bond to exist) is shown in Figures 12.15 and 12.16. Figure 12.15 shows the normal pattern of a conventional bond, with fixed coupons and a fixed redemption amount. By contrast, the PERLS pattern is as shown in Figure 12.16.

In principle, it would be possible for any investor to replicate the payoff pattern of such a bond. One would buy a conventional bond and enter into the borrowings and lendings mentioned above. The attraction to an individual or small corporate investor would be, first, that by buying the PERLS, the investor does not have to enter into the borrowings or forward foreign exchange deals. This avoids using up scarce credit lines. Second, the underlying borrowing and lending built into the bond is for a longer maturity than would often be available to such an investor, which is an attractive feature of the PERLS.

On the other hand, the advantages obtained by this structure are at the price of its risk: a leveraged foreign exchange position is inevitably risky. Although, at the time of writing, the SLMA bond had not matured, a similar 11.45 percent PERLS issued at a price of 100 by FNMA in 1991, matured in July 1996 at a redemption value of 47.4554.

Highly Leveraged Swap-Linked Structures. An example of a very highly leveraged swap-linked structure was the issue by BT Trustees (Jersey) Ltd. of a 6-month ITL20 billion bull note. This was a zero-coupon note whose redemption amount was 20 times geared to the 10-year lira swap rate at maturity, based on a reference rate of 9.45 percent and subject to a minimum redemption of 100 percent and a maximum redemption of 120 percent. If, however, the swap rate is below 8.45 percent at maturity, then the redemption amount will be equal to par.

A similar structure was used for an issue of DEM90 million of Euro commercial paper, with a 364-day maturity, by the Kingdom of Sweden in February 1994. This paid a fixed coupon of 5.3 percent, with redemption at the greater of

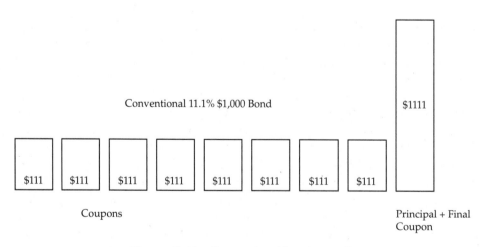

Figure 12.15 Conventional bond payoff.

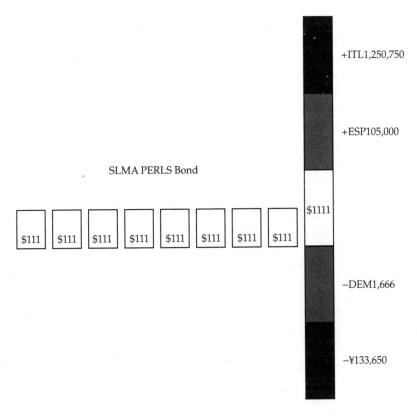

Figure 12.16 SLMA payoff.

DEM 0 and $100 + 15 \times (7.08 - \text{SWAP})$, where SWAP = the midmarket yield of the 3-year ESP swap rate on the redemption fixing date.

Because a number of these constructions came to grief at various times, it may be useful to break one down. Consider a 1-year Spanish peseta bond paying at maturity $100 + 6$ percent coupon $+ 10 \times (9.3$ percent $- 3$-year Spanish peseta swap rate), with a floor redemption value of 80 (i.e., maximum loss of principal of 20). Essentially, the investor is receiving a fixed forward rate of 9.3 percent but is exposed to a rise in the swap rate, subject to the floor protection. This protection is achieved by selling the investor a "payer" swaption whose strike is set at 9.3 percent + maximum loss/gearing (i.e., $9.3 + 20/10 = 11.3\%$). If swap rates rise above 11.3 percent, the investor notionally exercises the swaption to pay the swap rate and limit the loss.

Suppose we have the following market conditions: 1-year Spanish pesetas, 8.696 percent; today's 1-year forward price for a 3-year peseta swap, 9.55 percent. A payer swaption struck at 11.3 percent is priced in the market at 1.2 percent.

We start by calculating the sensitivity—basis point value—of the forward swap, which we do by calculating the present value at 9.55 percent of 1 basis point paid over 3 years. This comes to 2.51 basis points, or .0251. The next step is to find the implicit size of the swap underlying this transaction. We have a gearing of 10 times; to achieve this gearing effect today, such that a 1-basis-point change in the swap's value translates correctly into the bond price, we need a swap size of 10/.0251, which is 398.93. Thus, a 100-peseta note at this time is in fact driven by a swap notional of 398.93 pesetas.

The investor is committed to receive a forward swap rate of 9.3 percent. This is below today's forward swap rate of 9.55 percent, so the investor is sacrificing 25 basis points per annum. The value of this sacrifice in present value terms today is:

$$\frac{25 \text{ basis points} \times 2.51 \text{ basis point value} \times 398.93 \text{ notional}}{1.08696} = 2.30 \text{ percent.}$$

The cost of the swaption that is being sold to the investor is 1.2 percent on a notional swap principal of 398.93; i.e., it is 4.79 percent. The present value of the fixed component of the bond (redemption value of 100 + 6 percent coupon) is 106/1.08696 = 97.52.

If we add together all the parts, the combined package is worth 97.52 + 4.79 − 2.30 = 100.1. This represents the fair value of the package that is being offered to the investor.

Power Notes. A highly leveraged, very risky structure that has sometimes been done on a private placement basis is the power note. Here, the payoff is defined as, e.g., 25 percent − LIBOR squared. If LIBOR were, say, 3 percent, this would produce an attractive 16 percent return, but at the price of the coupon's being wiped out if LIBOR rises to 5 percent. The duration of a 2-year power note might be as high as 14, which is above what the duration would be for a typical 30-year bond. The degree of risk involved has meant that general investor appetite for this paper is very limited.

Structured Commercial Paper

Although, strictly speaking, commercial paper does not belong in this chapter (and is discussed separately in Chapter 8), it is convenient to point out here that, in a number of cases, the structures discussed in this chapter can equally well be applied to commercial paper. It is merely a matter of a shorter-maturity swap or option behind the structure.

For example, consider interest-differential commercial paper issued by the Treasury Corporation of Victoria in the amount of US$10 million with a 6-month maturity. The investor buying the paper believes that US$ rates will stay low, relative to French franc rates, over the next 3 months, and also for the remaining 3 months. The commercial paper might be structured as follows: The yield on the paper is fixed at FRF 3-month PIBOR less a fixed margin of

7.70 percent, the resulting yield payable in US$ (with a minimum of 0 percent). Supposing 3-month PIBOR is currently 11.64 percent. Then the investor receives 3.94 percent for the first 3 months. At the rollover date, the rate is fixed at the then-prevailing FRF 3-month PIBOR, less the fixed margin of 7.70 percent, again payable in US$. If the current U.S. commercial paper rate for 3 months were 3.19 percent, then the investor would gain a 0.75 percent incremental yield in exchange for the risk that US$ and FRF rates will converge over the second 3-month period.

The underlying hedge in this transaction would be similar to the hedge required for an interest diff swap (discussed in Chapter 5). Similar structures would be equally available in the structured note market for a longer maturity. The shorter maturity of the commercial paper market has helped to develop a very wide range of structures, given the relatively smaller hedging risk involved.

During 1993, a very large amount of money was invested in such structures, to the point where the SEC became concerned. In the United States, mutual funds are prohibited from calling themselves money market funds unless they comply with the risk-limiting provisions of rule 2a-7 under the Investment Company Act. However, structured commercial paper holdings that complied with the 2a-7 rules were bought by fund managers to give some extra zip to otherwise weak performance. Inevitably, when interest rates turned, in early 1994, investors suffered from losses in the value of certain adjustable rate notes held by some money market funds (managed by, among others, Paine Webber and Piper Jaffray). (The SEC had already begun to tighten its requirements—see Revisions to Rules Regulating Money Market Funds, Investment Company Act Release No. 19959, II.D.2.d.)

Chapter *13*

Credit Derivatives

In 1993, a new market began to emerge: the market for credit derivatives. The first of these were credit-linked notes, but other forms developed rapidly. To the extent that they provide a more systematic way of evaluating and transferring credit risk, credit derivatives offer several potential benefits to banks and financial institutions. First, they can now begin dynamically to manage their credit risk exposure to selected counterparties. They can, for example, reduce concentration of loans to a specific sector. Second, these adjustments can be made without some of the disadvantages of cash market transactions, such as transaction costs, unfavorable tax treatment, or the costly unwinding of associated market risk exposure (such as that on interest rates or foreign currency). Third, credit derivatives can be used to allow lenders or investors to achieve exposures not otherwise available to them; for example, a small U.S. regional bank may not easily be able to lend to a private German company. But by buying a credit derivative, it may be able to obtain that exposure, if it wishes.

In another common use of credit derivatives, the interest risk is split from the credit risk on a bond. An investor may hold a corporate bond that currently trades at a known spread over Treasuries. Fearing that it may weaken relative to Treasuries, the investor might buy a credit spread put on the bond. If the spread between the corporate bond yield and Treasuries widens, the credit spread put will pay off, insulating the investor from the associated loss. The option can be cash-settled, or might allow physical delivery: the holder would have the right to deliver an underlying bond to the counterparty at a predetermined price if the credit spread rises to a particular level.

A survey by the British Bankers' Association estimated the total size of the London market for credit derivatives in 1996 as approximately $20 billion notional amount. The Association found five institutions with a "book" of £1–5 billion notional amount. The estimate of the pattern of usage was that, among leading firms, credit default derivatives accounted for 22 percent of volume; credit spread derivatives, 30 percent; total return swaps, 23 percent; and credit-linked notes, 24 percent. Participants indicated that they expected the dominant future instruments to be credit default trades and credit spread trades.

ANALYTICAL FRAMEWORK[1]

Before plunging into a discussion of the instruments, some general observations may be useful. Credit risk is unlike market risk. It is much more difficult to quantify; much more depends on individual circumstances in each case. Furthermore, fewer data are available on which to base models or forecasts.

An interesting development in this regard is the introduction, in April 1997, of CreditMetrics™. This is a framework for quantifying credit risk in portfolios of traditional credit products (loans, letters of credit), fixed-income instruments, and market instruments subject to counterparty risk, such as swaps and forwards. The concept was launched by J.P. Morgan jointly with Bank of America, BZW,[2] Deutsche Morgan Grenfell, SBC,[2] and UBS,[2] together with a firm specializing in credit risk analytics, KMV Corporation. The approach has some resemblance to the approach taken in RiskMetrics™, but there are some key differences. RiskMetrics can use daily price observations from liquid markets; CreditMetrics must construct what it cannot directly observe: the volatility of value arising from credit quality changes. Whereas Risk-Metrics is primarily concerned with fitting distributions to observed data, CreditMetrics must focus on proposing models that explain the changes in credit instruments.

The basic technique employed is migration analysis—the study of changes in the credit quality of names over time. In essence, CreditMetrics looks to a specific horizon and builds a distribution of estimated credit outcomes. Each credit quality migration is weighted by its likelihood (transition matrix analysis). Each outcome has an estimate of change in value. Estimates of correlation are then applied to aggregate volatilities across the portfolio. Figure 13.1 illustrates the overall process.

The key feature of CreditMetrics is that, instead of focusing on individual credits, it takes a portfolio approach. This is a major benefit; it allows managers to consider questions related to risk concentration in a more sophisticated way than before. However, there are a number of problems to overcome. Whereas returns in equity and foreign exchange markets are reasonably well approximated by normal distributions, credit returns are highly skewed and have "fat tails"—a higher probability of extreme events.

The long downside tail of the distribution of credit returns is caused by defaults. The lending business consists of a good chance of earning a relatively small income from interest spread, coupled with a small chance of losing a lot of money. Across a large portfolio, there is likely to be a blend of these two forces, creating the skewed distribution shown in Figure 13.2.

---

[1] This section draws on: CreditMetrics Technical Document, J.P. Morgan, New York, April 1997.
[2] Barclays de Zoete Wedd, Swiss Bank Corporation and Union Bank of Switzerland.

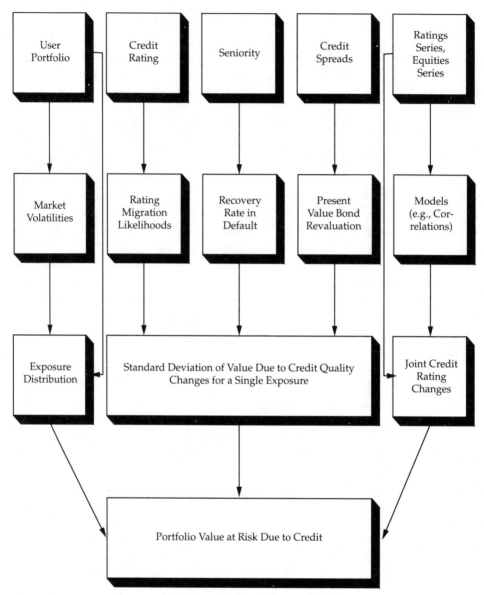

Top row boxes: User Portfolio | Credit Rating | Seniority | Credit Spreads | Ratings Series, Equities Series

Second row boxes: Market Volatilities | Rating Migration Likelihoods | Recovery Rate in Default | Present Value Bond Revaluation | Models (e.g., Correlations)

Third row boxes: Exposure Distribution | Standard Deviation of Value Due to Credit Quality Changes for a Single Exposure | Joint Credit Rating Changes

Bottom box: Portfolio Value at Risk Due to Credit

Source: CreditMetrics Technical Document, p. iv.

Figure 13.1   The CreditMetrics process.

A second, and far more difficult, problem is that of modeling correlations. For securities and foreign exchange, correlations can be directly estimated from liquid markets. For credit quality, the lack of data makes it difficult to estimate any type of correlation from history.

Let us start by considering a single BBB bond that matures in 5 years. We will consider risk over a 1-year horizon. We want to know the possible spread

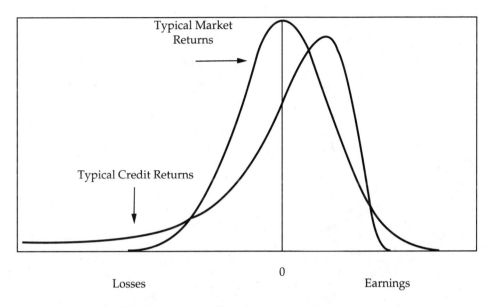

Figure 13.2 Credit returns vs. market returns.

of values for the bond at the end of 1 year. From historical data we can make the assumptions shown in Table 13.1.

In other words, there is a 86.93 percent chance that the rating will not change, a 5.95 percent chance it will improve to A, and so on. The next step is to calculate the value that the bond will have at the end of the year. This means calculating the present value of the cash flows remaining; this is done by using the forward interest rate curve applicable to that rating. Suppose the results are the values shown in Table 13.2.

The value distribution is shown in Figure 13.3. The vertical axis represents the probability, and the horizontal axis shows the value of the bond.

Table 13.1 Probability of Credit Rating Migrations in One Year for a BBB Bond

Year-End Rating	Probability (%)
AAA	0.02
AA	0.33
A	5.95
BBB	86.93
BB	5.30
B	1.17
CCC	0.12
Default	0.18

Source of Data: J.P. Morgan, quoting Standard & Poor's.

Table 13.2   Calculation of Year-End Values After Credit Rating Migration from BBB ($)

Rating	Coupon	Forward Value	Total Value
AAA	6.00%	$103.37	$109.37
AA	6.00	103.10	109.10
A	6.00	102.66	108.66
BBB	6.00	101.55	107.55
BB	6.00	96.02	102.02
B	6.00	92.10	98.10
CCC	6.00	77.64	83.64
Default	0	51.13	51.13

Distribution of Value of a BBB Par Bond in 1 Year:

Year-End Rating	Value	Probability
AAA	$109.37	0.02%
AA	109.19	0.33
A	108.66	5.95
BBB	107.55	86.93
BB	102.02	5.3
B	98.1	1.17
CCC	83.64	0.12
Default	51.13	0.18

Source of Data: J.P. Morgan.

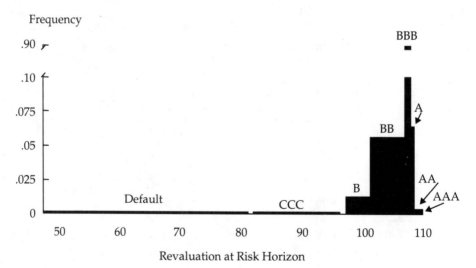

Source of Data: J.P. Morgan.

Figure 13.3   Bond value distribution at risk horizon.

The next step is to add another bond. Again, we can have eight possible outcomes. Then we can combine the two, resulting in 64 possible outcomes. We can find the portfolio's value at the risk horizon in each of the 64 states by simply adding together the values of the individual bonds. However, this approach is too simple, because the outcomes on the two bonds are not likely to be completely independent. Credit ratings are affected, at least in part, by macroeconomic factors that will have an impact on each bond. Therefore, we need to estimate the correlation between the migrations. For the moment, let us simply assume a correlation equal to 0.3. With this information, we can calculate the joint probability for each pair (for example, the probability that the BBB bond, and its A counterpart, stay unchanged; or the probability that one bond rises a grade and the other falls a grade). We will arrive at something like the pattern shown in Figure 13.4.

This process rapidly becomes very complex. Here we have 64 possible outcomes; with three bonds, the possible outcomes come to 512, and, in general, for a portfolio with N assets there are 8^N possible outcomes. Therefore, for larger portfolios, it is much more practical to use a simulation approach. Outcomes are sampled at random across all the possible joint rating states.

The concepts used so far have been applied using bonds, but the approach is general. It can include loans and other kinds of credit risk. Only the calculation of future values is different for the different instrument categories. The likelihood of being in each credit quality state is the same for all instruments, because it depends on the name of the counterparty, not the instrument.

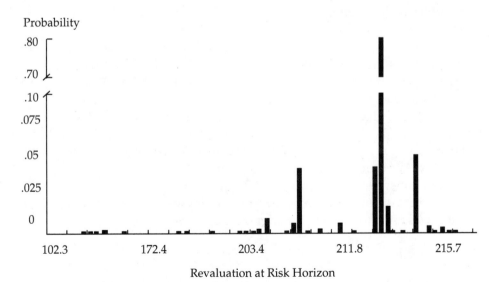

Source of Data: J.P. Morgan.

Figure 13.4 Distribution of value for a portfolio of two bonds.

The introduction of CreditMetrics, like that of RiskMetrics, represents a considerable step forward in developing a framework for credit analysis that will undoubtedly play an important role in further development of the credit risk market. The primary difficulty in credit risk derivatives has been the heterogeneous nature of the underlying assets. By starting the process of developing a coherent framework for analyzing credit portfolios, CreditMetrics has contributed to strengthening the analytical framework for credit derivatives. We turn now to the development of the market.

Credit-Linked Notes

The market started in 1992–1993, when firms such as Bankers Trust began selling notes whose redemption value depended on specified default events. Some of the notes were linked to several entities. The investor received a healthy spread over LIBOR—80 to 100 basis points—but if any of the entities underlying the note were to default, the investor took the coupon and principal losses. In effect, the notes passed Bankers Trust's risk on its lendings to the entities through the buyers of the notes.

The market developed substantially in the following years. In most cases, the pattern was similar. Typically, the instruments are issued by special-purpose vehicles. They combine the features of a standard fixed-income security with a credit option. Interest and principal are paid as normal, but the credit option allows the issuer to reduce interest payments if a key financial variable specified in the note's documentation deteriorates.

The technique is less popular than some of the others discussed here, but is still used quite regularly—for example, J.P. Morgan issued in September 1996 a $594 million 10-year note linked to Wal-Mart, the U.S. retailer. In the structure, a special-purpose vehicle was set up to issue the notes and enter into a total return swap with the bank. As will be seen below, one of the key issues in these structures is the definition of a "credit event." In this transaction, Morgan specified that the spread on the company's debt relative to LIBOR must weaken by at least 150 basis points before a credit event is declared. The bank has also set up a rigorous price discovery mechanism to help establish the recovery value of the debt if the company fails. Morgan would conduct a dealer poll of 5 leading market makers every 2 weeks for 3 months, to establish a market value for the company's debt after default.

In December, the same firm followed up with the placement of a $459.65 million structured note issued by a custom repackaged asset vehicle (CRAVE). The deal was for 10 years, with an average life of 6 years.

Default Swap

The most common credit risk derivative is the default swap. This is a contract in which one counterparty (the protection buyer) pays a periodic fee—typically expressed in a fixed amount of basis points on the notional amount. In return, the counterparty receives a variable payment contingent on the default of one or more third-party credits. This payment is designed to mirror the loss incurred by creditors of the reference credit, if it defaults. It is usually calculated as the fall in price of a reference security below par at some pre-designated interval after the reference credit has defaulted. Default swaps are now covered by standard documentation by the International Swap Dealers Association.

An example of a 5-year default swap might be as follows. XYZ Bank has lent extensively to the government of Japan and Japanese entities. It wishes to free up its credit lines to that country. Accordingly, it enters into a 5-year default swap using a Japanese government bond as the reference security. XYZ Bank pays a premium to the counterparty of, say, 8 basis points per annum. The counterparty makes a payment in exchange only if Japan defaults on its debts. In this case, the payment might be par less the final price of the Japanese government bond, multiplied by the notional principal amount of the swap. So if Japan defaults and the reference bond falls to 85 percent, XYZ Bank would collect the 85 percent by selling the bond, and the remaining 15 percent from its swap counterparty. This type of synthetic asset reallocation trade allows the hedging institutions to free credit lines in their loan or derivative portfolios, which then permits them to do new business.

Total Return Swap

A variant of this approach is the "total return swap." Conceptually, the total return loan swap is simple. One party pays the other the total return on a loan or group of loans, receiving in exchange another payment, which is usually LIBOR-based. The total return comprises the periodic interest payments on the underlying loan, plus other fee revenue such as commitment fees, plus or minus changes in the underlying value of the loan or group of loans. The exchange of payments generally occurs quarterly. At that time, the swap payer would pay the swap receiver the interest payments accrued and paid during the quarter, plus any fees accrued during the quarter. In return, the swap receiver would owe the swap payer LIBOR plus or minus a spread on the total amount. Finally, price settlements can be done at the end of the swap or more often. If there has been a rise in the value of the loan, the swap receiver would have a gain; conversely, the payer would gain if the value has fallen. The final price fixing usually provides prices to be set by an independent third party using actual market quotes.

The more frequent price settlement, evidently, has the merit of ensuring that the swap never builds up its own substantial potential credit risk. In the preceding default swap example, we have a 15 percent exposure to the swap counterparty by the close-out time.

Transfer Risk Note

An innovative "limited recourse debt issuance program" was set up by Rabobank of the Netherlands, in March 1997. These are medium-term notes that have embedded in them the country risk of a specific country. That is, payments of principal and interest may be restricted: (1) if the government of the specific country imposes any kind of exchange control that prevents transfer of the local currency; or (2) if there is a banking moratorium, or a nationalization or confiscation of foreign bank assets, or any war, revolution, insurrection, or other hostile act that interferes with exchanges or transfers of the local currency.

This interesting innovation allows the transfer of country risk to other investors. On the other hand, it is not yet clear how much investors will actually want to buy such a risk, and whether they will be prepared to do so at cheaper rates than the banks currently charge.

Other Structures

All of the existing technology from other markets can equally be applied to the credit derivatives market. Many of these specialist structures are likely to be highly illiquid. However, they may have merit in specific situations.

A credit derivative collar can be constructed to allow an investor to combine a low level of interest rate risk with a credit spread view. Consider a 5-year bond issued by ABC Inc., which currently trades at a spread of 250 basis points over Treasury bonds. The investor wishes to hold a short-maturity asset, but has a view that the spread on ABC will probably improve in the short term. We could construct a 2-year structured note issued by a AAA-rated firm and paying a coupon, say, of LIBOR + 0.25 percent. The principal redemption on the bond would be structured so as to be linked to the credit spread on ABC's bond. Specifically, the note could embed a 2-year zero-cost credit spread collar. Thus, in addition to the note, the investor in effect buys a spread call that profits if spreads tighten and is struck at the current spread level of 250 basis points. The investor finances the purchase by selling a spread put struck at 280 basis points. If the credit spread improves, the investor will benefit; if it weakens beyond 280 basis points, the principal value of the note will deteriorate.

In another structure, the investor would write a credit spread put if he or she were willing to acquire a given bond at a given spread that is not currently available. Suppose the investor considers that XYZ Inc.'s bond, trading at a spread of 215 basis points over the 10-year Treasury, is too expensive. The investor would be happy to own the paper at a spread of 250. One way of accomplishing this would be for the investor to sell a 1-year European-style credit spread put struck at 250 basis points in exchange for an up-front fee.

The investor here takes no interest rate risk, since he or she does not own the bond; it is a pure credit bet.

FUTURE DEVELOPMENTS

The area of credit derivatives is developing rapidly. The recent arrival of CreditMetrics should give further impetus to the analytical underpinning of the market. It seems likely that an assault will be made on the Basle Committee 8 percent capital ratio, which is presently applied to credit risk. This is becoming increasingly antiquated as a method of measuring credit exposure, although it was a great step forward, at the time, to persuade bankers that the good old days of simply ignoring capital requirements must come to an end. Going forward, it seems likely that we will see much further development in this area.

Chapter **14**

Preferred Stock

The process of innovation in the equity market has not, perhaps, been quite as wide ranging as that of the debt market. However, several innovations have been introduced in recent years. They include:

Floating rate preferred stock.

Convertible exchangeable preferred stock—convertible into equity, exchangeable into debt.

Mandatory convertible preferred stock.

Preferred stock issued by vehicles that invest in debt (MIPS, TOPRS).

Preference shares convertible into stock of another company.

Step-up/step-down preference shares.

Catastrophe preferred put structures.

One of the major developments has been the blurring of the line between debt and equity. One accountant has defined the difference between debt and equity as whether the issuer is obligated to expend resources to make the holder of the security whole. In theory, the issuer must do so only for debt issues.

But this definition does not cover the case of puttable equity (discussed in Chapter 17), or indeed of equity contract notes or commitment notes (discussed in Chapter 15). Perpetual debt (Chapter 9) has caused the same confusion. The issue is important not merely to investors trying to assess the shape of a company's balance sheet, but also to regulators—in the case of banks—and to the tax authorities. The latter are keen to cherish the distinction between interest payments, which can be deducted from tax, and dividend payments, which cannot. In a number of recent cases in the United States, preferred stock has been replaced by a two-tier structure involving preferred stock issued by a trust or other tax-transparent entity, which invests the proceeds in debt issued by the parent company (see TOPRS, MIPS, below), thus effectively creating tax-deductible preferred, at the price of creating an extra entity.

The blurring of the distinction between debt and equity has also been a constant problem for accountants, and in the past few years they have begun to address the issue. The FASB's Statement of Financial Accounting Standards No. 47 (SFAS 47) mandates footnote disclosures to include future obligations for 5 years subsequent to the balance sheet, in addition to a description of the redeemable preference-share terms. The international exposure draft E40 and the U.K.'s FRS4 (on "Capital Instruments," obligatory for all accounts from June 1994) have both addressed the question. FRS4 lays down that "Convertible debt should be reported . . . on the assumption that the debt will never be converted." This removes the cosmetic attraction (though not the tax attraction) of a convertible bond, making convertible preference shares relatively more attractive to issuers seeking to strengthen their balance sheet.

FRS4 distinguishes between equity and nonequity shares. The latter are defined as:

Shares possessing any of the following characteristics:

(a) any of the rights of the shares to receive payments (whether in respect of dividends, in respect of redemption or otherwise) are for a limited amount that is not calculated by reference to the company's assets or profits or the dividends on any class of equity share.

(b) any of their rights to participate in a surplus in a winding-up are limited to a specific amount. . . .

(c) the shares are redeemable. . . . "

Under the FRS, nonequity shares are treated virtually as debt, in that they are recorded on the balance sheet at the initial value of the net proceeds, and finance costs are accrued. For example, preference dividends must be accrued even if the company cannot pay a dividend by reason of its lack of distributable reserves.

CONVERTIBLE PREFERRED SHARES

Not a particularly new instrument in themselves, but used as the basis for other innovations discussed below, preferred shares that are convertible into equity can be attractive investment instruments in a number of situations. They are often used in start-up situations, or corporate reconstructions, where the investor wishes to have the extra protection given by the preferred status, but also to retain the possibility of benefiting from the rise in share value if the start-up or reconstruction goes well. But such shares have a more general application in corporate finance, being often used when a company wishes to strengthen its balance sheet with more equity without currently diluting existing equity shareholders.

A typical transaction, from the United States but with an international tranche, was the Delta Air Lines issue, in June 1992, of 20 million shares, each

Issuer: Delta Air Lines Inc.

Number of Shares: 20 million.

Type of Shares: Depositary shares.

Offer Price: US$50.

Par Value: US$1.

Total Amount Raised: US$1 billion.

Conversion Price: US$65.75.

Conversion Premium: 21.76 percent over the last reported sale price of common stock of US$54 on the NYSE on June 24 1992.

Dividend: US$3.50 per annum, payable quarterly.

Dividend Yield: 7 percent.

Call: Three years hard call, nonredeemable before July 1, 1995, and at no time for cash.

representing 1/1,000 of a share of series C convertible preferred stock at US$50 per share. The total size of the deal amounted to US$1 billion.

A more international issue—indeed, a true Euro-convertible preferred share issue—was the issue by Jardine Strategic Holdings, in March 1993. This took the form of a rights issue of 351,507 convertible cumulative preference shares. Each share was priced at US$1,020 and was offered for every 2,750 ordinary shares held and/or for each 8.53 existing preference shares held. The new preference shares offered a US$75 coupon and are convertible into ordinary shares at HK$24. An interesting technical feature was that the shares were

Issuer: Jardine Strategic Holdings.

Type of Issue: Rights issue of convertible cumulative preference shares.

Basis: One new convertible preference share for every 2,750 ordinary shares held, and one new convertible preference share for every 8.53 existing convertible preference shares.

Total Amount Raised: US$358.8 million.

Offer Price: US$1,020 per share.

Nominal Value: US$800.

Coupon: US$75 per annum.

Conversion Price: HK$24.

Exchange Rate: HK$7.74/US$1.00.

fungible, forming in due course a single series with the 250,000 existing convertible preference shares issued by Jardine Strategic at US$1,000 per share in May 1992. The higher price for the new issue reflected the subsequent fall in interest rates and illustrates the bondlike features of a fixed-dividend preference share. A variant of convertible preferred, the PERC, is covered in Chapter 16.

FLOATING RATE PREFERRED STOCK

Preferred stock whose dividend rate floats in line with prevailing interest rates has become a large sector of the preferred stock market. The concept was introduced in 1982. The idea was that, in the past, fixed rate preferred stock had proved unattractive to investors. A rise in interest rates meant they were looking at a loss in the value of the stock. Adjustable rates were viewed as ensuring that the stock traded close to par.

Rates on the stock were fixed by a formula in relation to Treasury bill rates. As rates rise, the rate on the stock is refixed on the next rate-setting date, when the stock price should trade back to par. The attraction to the issuer, on the other hand, is that, under U.S. tax law, adjustable rate preferred (ARP) stock can be placed with corporate investors who gain an 85 percent corporate tax exclusion on dividends from other corporations' stock. Thus, the issuer pays a lower rate.

Stock of this type proved very attractive to banks. When ARP stock was invented, bank stocks were depressed by fears over Latin-American debt and other problems. The fact that the paper had no maturity date—i.e., it was perpetual—meant that the bank regulators agreed the stock was primary capital. At the time, the banks were under pressure to obtain more permanent capital. The first issue was a $200 million issue for Chemical Bank, followed closely by a $250 million issue for Chase Manhattan. Thereafter, volume picked up slowly, until August 1984, when Money Market Preferred (MMP) stock issues began to be made. The popularity of MMPs meant ARPs became less common.

The major problem with an ARP, as compared with an MMP, lies in the mechanics of the interest-rate setting. A typical ARP pays dividends quarterly at a rate pegged to a formula, generally the highest of: the 3-month Treasury bill rate, or a 10-year or 20-year constant maturity Treasury bond rate. For example, a $45 million issue by United Virginia Bank Shares, in December 1985, was priced at 300 basis points below the appropriate formula rate. It also carried a "collar" that set 5.5 percent as the minimum, and 11.5 percent as the maximum interest rate the shares can pay. Earlier ARP issues were priced according to similar formulas.

The result was that, during periods when there was concern over the safety of the banking system, the ARP shares would fall to a sharp discount, rather than trading back to par each time the quarterly dividend was reset. The ARP did not protect the investor against a loss of principal if the credit quality of the issuer was seen to deteriorate. To overcome investor resistance, accordingly, during periods of pressure, the dividend might have to be set at quite a high rate if a new issue was to be successful.

For example, in June 1984 (immediately after the difficulties of Continental Illinois), Chase Manhatten issued a Series F ARP stock in partial payment for its acquisition of Lincoln First Banks. The initial proposed dividend was at a rate of 13.02 percent, but investor reaction was extremely poor, and the deal had to be repriced. The quarterly dividend was then set at $3.10 per quarter for the first four quarters on the $50 par value stock—an annual rate of 24.8 percent. The MMP helped to avoid this problem (see below).

Floating rate preferred stock fits two types of issuers particularly well: (1) companies that need equity and (2) companies that may or may not need equity but do need funding and do not pay taxes because they have net operating losses, tax credits, or some other advantage. The latter do not usually wish to issue debt, because they cannot deduct the interest payments. Still, issuers of floating rate preferred must be top-quality credits. The corporate investors who typically buy the shares insist on this because they must have liquidity and high quality in their short-term portfolios. This is more vital for preferred shares, because, as equity, they are junior to alternative investment options such as commercial paper and short-term municipal notes.

Thus, U.S. Steel, which has issued MMPs, achieved the quality criterion by arranging for a letter of credit from a triple-A bank, guaranteeing the investors that if U.S. Steel were unable to repay, the bank would do so.

Similarly, savings and loan institutions have found auction rate preferred stock attractive. In the first year after the concept was developed, they accounted for about 35 percent of total issues. Having amassed huge tax losses in earlier years, thrifts as a group were logical candidates for the MMP concept. But, for the same reason, their credit ratings were weak. The solution was to form special-purpose subsidiaries that were overcollateralized with, typically, government-agency mortgage paper that issued the preferred on behalf of the thrifts. In most cases, these "fireproof" subsidiaries, whose portfolios cannot interfered with by the parent, are rated triple-A.

The French firm of Rhone Poulenc arranged a similar issue. Because Rhone Poulenc is not a U.S. entity, it needed to form a U.S. financing subsidiary to issue the preferred stock, with the proceeds then being on-loan to the parent. Because the company had tax losses in the United States, it was happy to issue preferred stock rather than debt. Again, to guarantee the quality of the issue, the deal was supported by a letter of credit from a triple-A bank.

Floating rate preferred stock, whether it is auction rate or adjustable rate, has become an established capital-raising route, particularly for banks and thrifts, but also for industrial corporations. But there can be some problems. First, the strategic. Issuers find, by issuing more preferred stock, that their dividend payout strategies become less flexible. If interest rates rise, the rates on money market preferred will rise quite quickly. The typical reset period of 49 days compares perhaps with 6 months for a floating rate note issue. Second, the tactical. The auction of preferred stock is a public phenomenon. A failure at the auction could have embarrassing repercussions.

This happened to Ratners, a down-market British jewelry firm, whose then-chairman made the tactical error of describing the company's products as "crap." The resulting furor led the firm to suspend dividends on the preferred shares because auctions ceased to attract purchasers. Thus, firms tend to call the preferred before this happens. In February 1992, Tarmac, Britain's biggest construction company, announced plans to redeem U.S.$150 million in Auction Market Preferred Stock (AMPS). This followed news that Tarmac's credit rating might be under review by the rating agencies. Feeding through to the dividend paid by Tarmac on its AMPS, a downgrading to BBB would have pushed the level to around 175 percent of the commercial paper rate, making it expensive finance. In addition, Rank Organisation redeemed U.S.$200 million AMPS, following a downgrade of its rating by Standard & Poor's.

In February 1992, English China Clays (ECC) announced a £209 million cash call to redeem U.S.$350 million of U.S.$400 million of its outstanding auction market preferred stock; the company felt it had become an expensive alternative compared with some other sources of finance available to it. A number of U.S. firms have similarly paid down preferred—not all floating preferred—as discussed in the sections below on MIPS/TOPRS.

In April 1992, a U.S.$235 million AMPS issue for James Hardie (U.S.A), part of the Australian group James Hardie Industries, came to market. Issuance was through a new company, RCI Finance, by way of three tranches of 220 shares apiece, priced at U.S.$250,000 per share, and a fourth tranche consisting of 280 shares at the same price. The fourth tranche, or D series, was backed by a credit enhancement facility arranged by NatWest and Industrial Bank of Japan (IBJ), with the former as underwriter and the latter as issuer.

The issue was part of a complex refinancing package intended to reduce James Hardie (USA)'s debt. This was achieved through the purchase by RCI Finance of U.S.$70 million of preference shares in James Hardie (USA), the proceeds of which went toward reducing net debt.

Convertible Adjustable Preferred Stock

Convertible adjustable preferred stock (CAPS) was an attempt to overcome the problems presented by the ARP, which meant the investor could not be certain of the principal value of the preferred stock. The key features of the CAPS are that investors are entitled to convert the CAPS into common stock of the issuer during the period after the announcement of each dividend rate for the next period.

Conversion is based on the original issue price of the CAPS, with a maximum set on the number of shares of common stock to be received per share of CAPS. Therefore, an investor who is unhappy with the dividend payable on the CAPS can always convert into common stock. On the other side, CAPS allow the issuer to vary the dividend-setting formula from its initial level, providing flexibility to adjust the rate so the market price can remain sufficiently high to discourage a holder from converting, if the issuer prefers to do this rather than to allow conversion. The dividend can then be kept in line with market conditions, and the investor is always assured of conversion at par if need be.

An example would be the offering by Ohio Edison, in July 1984, of 1.8 million shares of CAPS at $25 per share. The initial dividend on the issue was 13.08 percent for the first quarter, then to be reset quarterly in line with the Treasury rate. The issue carried a collar: a minimum rate of 7.5 percent and a maximum rate of 15.5 percent. The preferred shares are convertible, at the end of each dividend period, into a minimum of 2.08 shares of Ohio Edison common, and a maximum of 6.15 shares. It has not been a particularly popular structure.

Money Market Preferred

Money Market Preferred (MMP) stocks were introduced in August 1984, in yet another attempt to overcome the problem with ARP stock—that the principal value could be uncertain. This mechanism has proved the most successful of the various methods chosen to achieve the objective. The rate on the stock is fixed by means of a Dutch auction.

The exact mechanics vary with the type of issue. Competing investment banks have produced similar products known as STARS (Short-Term Auction Rate Preferreds), DARTS (Dutch Auction Rate Term Securities), MAPS (Market Auction Rate Preferreds), and CAMPS (Cumulative Auction Market Preferred Stock). The usual mechanics are that every 49 days, investors bid at a certain rate for the stock. The lowest rate that fills a sufficient number of bids to cover all the shares outstanding becomes the rate the borrower will have to pay.

The reason for the 49-day interval between auctions is that this is the shortest period that is long enough legally to enable corporations to claim the 85 percent dividend tax exclusion. If the auction fails—if too few bids are submitted to cover all the shares outstanding—the dividend rate is fixed as a percentage of the composite commercial paper rate.

When the concept of MMP stock was introduced, there was some concern that the relative complexity of the concept might put off issuers and investors. But this concern proved to have been unwarranted, and the concept has been fairly readily accepted. During the first 12 months following the introduction of the concept, $2.6 billion of auction rate preferred were issued.

The concept has been expanded to apply to the FRN market. In September 1985, $200 million of Money Market Notes were issued by American Express Credit Corporation. The rate on these notes is set by auction every 35 days, a period designed to more closely parallel the 30-day period for commercial paper. Investors do not, of course, benefit from the 85 percent exclusion because the note is not equity.

The next step was taken by AIG, which, in December 1985, issued $150 mil-lion in the form of 1,500 shares, of $100,000 each, of exchangeable money market preferred. The stock is exchangeable into money market notes at the issuer's discretion. The rationale for the deal was that AIG needed more capital to sup-port the rapid growth of its insurance premium level, but, owing to tax-loss carry-forwards, the company was not a taxpayer. Given the rapid growth of the business, however, it expected to become a taxpayer and so needed the ability to convert the paper to debt.

SABRES

A related concept was used in an issue by Midwest Dakota Finance Corpora-tion, a subsidiary of MidWest Federal Savings Bank, in October 1988. The issue, for $75 million, took the form of Share-Adjusted Broker-Remarketed Equity Securities (SABRES[SM]). These are preferred shares that are remarketed by an investment bank appointed as agent for remarketing; essentially, investors ten-der their shares at each dividend date and repurchase them at a new dividend rate (or sell them to someone willing to accept a lower dividend). Under cer-tain circumstances, the shares are exchangeable for 10-year notes issued by the company.

International Variants

In 1993, the French company, Rhone Poulenc, issued $370 million worth of ARC-TSDI (Auction Rate Coupon—Titres Subordonnés à Durée Indéter-minée). This is a hybrid security which, if structured correctly under French law, counts as a form of equity for the issuer under "other capital funds." It is in fact perpetual junior subordinated debt, and the coupon payments are de-ductible for tax purposes. The equity categorization comes from the fact that the coupon can be suspended, the company is under no legal obligation to repay the principal, and investors have no put. The instrument pays a floating rate coupon at a fixed spread of 115 basis points over LIBOR for the first 10 years. After this period, the coupon is reset by an auction among the investors. The issuer has a call option throughout the life of the security. If investors are happy to keep holding the FRN after 10 years, they will continue to bid attrac-tive levels in the auction. If they want to encourage repayment of the principal, they will simply bid very high coupons. Then the issuer has the choice of pay-ing the very high rate or calling the issue.

Mandatory Convertible Preferred Shares

In 1992, when Sakura Bank [at that time, Mitsui Taiyo Kobe (MTK) Bank] wished to raise preference capital, it made a Euro-issue: ¥100 billion noncumulative guaranteed exchangeable preference shares. The securities were issued by Sakura Holdings, the Luxembourg subsidiary, and were guaranteed by MTK. The preference shares were mandatorily exchangeable into MTK shares on or before June 30, 1995, at 15 percent over the closing price of MTK shares at the time of issue.

The share price at maturity was subject to a minimum of 35 percent of the exercise price. This effectively put a cap on the number of shares that MTK would have to provide as investors will ultimately be repaid in equity rather than cash. The preference shares paid a dividend of 6¾ percent annually, somewhat larger than the interest MTK would have had to pay out for straight debt. MTK stock was yielding around 0.8 percent, giving the preference shares a huge income pick up. (See below for further discussion of this structure.)

In September 1993, Boise Cascade offered 7.5 million of "Automatically Convertible Equity Shares" (ACES). These are convertible preferred shares offering a yield of 7.5 percent. After four years, the stock automatically converts into Boise's common stock. Holders will receive one share of common for each ACES share if the common is at or below the ACES offering price of $21⅛; if the common is up by 25 percent or more, investors will get 0.8 shares for each ACES share. In between the conversion ratio will be between 0.8 and 1.0 so that holders essentially break even. These shares are, in one way, the preferred stock equivalent of the DECS product (see Chapter 15): Here the asset initially offered to investors is preferred stock, in the case of DECS the asset is initially a bond. In both cases, investors are switched into common stock later, on the basis that if the shares rise above a certain level they receive 0.8 shares for the initial asset, but if they fall below the initial issue level, shares are issued one-for-one in exchange for the initial asset. In August 1994, an $850 million ACES was brought to market for Arco (Atlantic Richfield), exchangeable into shares

---

Sakura Holdings SCA

Amount: Y100bn non-cumulative guaranteed exchangeable preference shares.

Mandatory Exchange Date: June 30, 1995.

Dividend: 6¾ percent semi-annually.

Issue Price: 100.

Guarantor: Mitsui Taiyo Kobe (MTK).

Call Option: None.

Exchange Premium: 15 percent.

Exchange Period: May 11, 1992, to June 23, 1995.

Listing: Luxembourg.

of its Liondell petrochemical subsidiary. The attraction of a 9 percent coupon on the exchangeables—compared with a 3 percent yield on Liondell's common stock—led to firm demand for the issue.

In September 1995, Morgan Stanley led a $2 billion convertible preferred issue for Mitsubishi Bank. Because the unsound Japanese banking practices of the 1980s made this a sector investors were cautious about, two novel features were added. Because the bank needed equity, but could not sell it in the current market conditions, the coupon on the bond was set very low, at 3 percent. Also, to protect investors from weakness in the Japanese stock market the conversion price would be reset each year to the current share price level, subject to a minimum level of 65 percent of the original level and subject to the provision that the conversion price would never increase. Finally, to ensure conversion, Mitsubishi was given the right to make conversions itself if investors choose not to do so: It can redeem 20 percent of the issue in exchange for its ADRs in each of the last five years of the issue's life.

The Mitsubishi issue was followed in 1996 by five other issues (Daiwa Bank, Fuji Bank, Sakura Bank, Sumitomo Bank, and Tokai Bank). Together with the 1992 Sakura issue, these collectively became known as "the Refixable Seven." The appalling performance of Japanese bank shares in early 1997, when some bank stocks lost nearly a third of their market value in one month, testing the refixing limits: the Fuji Bank and Daiwa Bank shares actually fell through the refix floor and now have no reset protection. The problem arose partly because most of the shares ended in the hands of hedge funds. As the issues came close to the reset floors, the rate of decline of the convertible price accelerated in relation to the share price. This forced the hedge fund arbitrageurs to sell even more shares, accelerating the downward spiral.

Offshore Convertible Preferred

One of the "disadvantages" of the convertible bond, from the issuer's viewpoint, is that it is classified as debt. Your balance sheet looks much nicer if the convertible is equity. In April 1988, a U.K. company called United Biscuits was making a significant acquisition, giving rise to goodwill of £190 million. The relevant U.K. accounting standard at that time permitted goodwill to be written off against reserves, rather than the United States requirement of amortization against income. But United Biscuits did not have a lot of reserves. So a Netherlands Antilles subsidiary was crated to issue preference shares at £5,000 per share. The nominal value of the shares was £1 and the difference was credited to "share premium reserve" allowing the Netherlands Antilles company to make the acquisition and write off the goodwill. There was also a tax angle in that the subsidiary could lend to the parent on a tax-deductible basis, and the following year the U.K. Inland Revenue cracked down on the use of tax havens for preference shares. This led to the development of the convertible capital bond structure (see Chapter 15).

Convertible Exchangeable Preferred Stock

Convertible exchangeable preferred stock (CEPS) was introduced with an issue by Martin Marietta in September 1982. The key features of this preferred stock are that it is convertible at the option of the holder into common stock of the issuer, and it is exchangeable at the option of the issuer for the issuer's convertible debentures. It is attractive to companies that are interested in issuing convertible debt but, for rating purposes, prefer equity, and do not expect to be paying taxes over the near term, but do expect a return to a tax-paying position during the life of the security.

CEPS allows an issuer to maximize its tax position by permitting exchange from preferred stock to convertible debt, the interest on which is tax-deductible, at the issuer's option, at any time after an initial waiting period. CEPS is also generally structured to make conversion to common stock likely: Final maturities are long, sinking fund payments do not typically begin until Year 10, and optional call provisions begin after 3 years, allowing the issuer to force conversion at a relatively early point in the life of the issue.

An example is the $100 million issue by Boise Cascade Corporation in January 1983. The preferred shares are convertible into common stock, at the option of the holder, at any time, at a price of $45.625 per share. They are exchangeable at the option of the company, on any dividend payment date beginning February 1985, for the company's 10 percent convertible subordinated debentures due 2013. Holders of the preferred stock will be entitled to receive $50 principal amount of the debentures in exchange for each share held by them.

An extension of the concept was the $17 million issue, in December 1986, by LSB Industries. The company had been a loss maker (hence the attractions of preferred) but expected to become profitable (hence its wish for exchangeability). However, because, for tax reasons, the issue was being made before the company could reestablish investor confidence, investors had to be given extra protection. If the company loses money in the 12 months after the issue, the price at which the preferred can be converted into common stock is reset.

MIPS

A recent innovation in the category of preferred stock is Monthly Income Preferred Stock (MIPS), introduced, in November 1993, in a deal for Texaco. The structure, in essence, consists of an issue of preferred stock in an offshore subsidiary of Texaco. The subsidiary then lends the funds back as a 100-year loan to Texaco, which is able to treat the interest payments on these funds as tax-deductible. But the interest payments received by the offshore subsidiary can be flowed through to the preferred holders free of withholding tax. The product is therefore quite close to achieving the Holy Grail in this segment of the market—tax-deductible equity. However, there are a few wrinkles.

The MIPS structure had been preceded by several quite similar deals, notably one for Banco Santander, in September 1991. Until the Texaco deal, it had not been thought possible to devise a structure that would work for U.S. issuers. The key to the Texaco deal was a law passed in the Turks and Caicos Islands, in 1993, which permitted the formation of limited life companies (LLCs). Under U.S. tax law, LLCs can be deemed partnerships, and the U.S. parent can funnel interest payments back to the subsidiary without incurring withholding tax (as of the time of writing). The MIPS structure includes monthly dividend payments, which were attractive to retail investors and also were convenient for the accrual accounting required for the partnership entity.

A critical question is whether this structure is debt or equity—not from the tax viewpoint, but from the viewpoint of the rating agencies assessing the balance sheet of the issuer. In one view, MIPS are simply repackaged 100-year debt that is deeply subordinated and has limited ability to defer interest payments. In another view, the economic advantages of tax-deductibility of the MIPS, when compared with conventional preferred, help to make them somewhat equitylike. The rating agencies clearly have assessed the structure as having some equitylike features, but appear to have been unwilling to treat it as fully equivalent to equity.

In March 1994, the MIPS structure was extended to convertible preferred stock by Parker & Parsley, an independent Texas oil company. Convertible preferred was sold by Parker & Parsley Capital LLC, a Turks and Caicos Islands limited life company, with the proceeds being on-loan to the parent. To enhance the equity credit given the product by the rating agencies, the deal provided that the preferred was noncallable for 3 years. Thereafter, the company could exchange the preferred for common stock if the shares were trading at more than 125 percent of the conversion price. A cash call is only permitted if it is funded with the proceeds of another equity offering. Finally, if the company's finances deteriorate, it will have the right to defer payments on its intercompany loan—and dividend payments on the MIPS as well—for up to 60 months (compared with 18 months in the original MIPS structure).

A variant on the MIPS structure was used by ConAgra, in May 1994. The dividend on the preferred was fixed at 95 percent of the highest of 30-year, 10-year, or 3-month Treasury securities. In a sense, this structure is a marriage of MIPS to ARPS (discussed above). "Trust MIPS" are a version of the MIPS issued by a grantor trust rather than a limited partnership or limited liability company. (See also TOPRS, below.)

In November 1994, Grand Metropolitan, a U.K. company, issued MIPS in the form of a $500 million perpetual fixed rate preferred issue. The transaction benefited Grand Metropolitan in several ways: the preferred was accounted for as a minority interest rather than debt, helping the balance sheet; but by combining the transaction with a series of intercompany loans, the dividend cost effectively became tax-deductible.

QIPS

A variant of the MIPS structure was introduced, in April 1995, for Cadbury Schweppes: Quarterly Income Preferred Securities (QIPS). The stock was sold by a Delaware limited partnership, which then made a perpetual loan to the U.K. company. The interest on the loan may be deferred. Although these features would cause U.S. tax problems, they were acceptable to the U.K. tax authorities.

TOPRS

Another variant on the MIPS structure is the Trust Originated Preferred Securities—essentially, MIPS issued by a trust rather than a limited partnership or a limited liability company.The trust structure allows simpler tax treatment for individual investors.

The TOPRS structure was used by RJR Nabisco, in August 1995, in a $1.2 billion offer to exchange TOPRS for the company's outstanding Series B preferred stock. The attraction to RJR Nabisco was the tax-deductibility of the TOPRS coupon, compared with the nondeductible dividend on the Series B. A number of other companies followed RJR's example, using either TOPRS/MIPS or their debt equivalents, QUICS/QUIDS (see Chapter 9). Table 14.1 shows some of the issues.

The TOPRS structure calls for a corporation to sell long-term junior subordinated debentures to a trust, which then issues the preferred. The corporation's interest payments on the debentures are tax-deductible. The investor, meanwhile, is left with a preferred security similar to the one being held, but with a higher dividend yield. The interest deductions for a corporation in the 35 percent bracket more than offset the higher coupon on the new preferred.

Table 14.1 Completed MIPS/TOPRS/ QUICS/QUIDS Exchanges for Preferred

Company	Size of Exchange Offer ($ millions)
AMR Corp.	1,100
Detroit Edison Co.	105
Equitable Cos.	408
McDonald's Corp.	500
PacifiCorp	125
RJR Nabisco	1,250
SunAmerica	137.5
UAL Corp.	582
Williams Cos.	90.75

Data as of September 1995.

Source of Data: Goldman, Sachs & Co.; Merrill, Lynch & Co.

In a more recent example, in November 1996, NationsBank, through NB Capital Trust I (NBCT), issued $600 million of 7.84 percent trust-originated preferred securities. NationsBank Corp. owns all of the common stock of NBCT, which exists for the sole purpose of issuing the preferred securities and investing the proceeds in junior subordinated debt of NationsBank. Interest payments on the subordinated debt, which are in turn passed through NBCT to the preferred security holders, will be serviced through existing liquidity and cash flow sources of the holding company. The structure is illustrated in Figure 14.1.

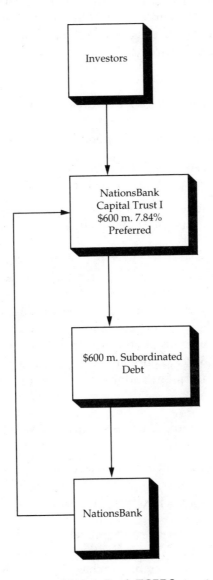

Figure 14.1 NationsBank TOPRS structure.

PEARLS

An issue by InterDigital Communications Corporation, in July 1993, of Preferred Event-triggered Adjustable Ratio Liquid Securities (PEARLS) consisted of $40 million of convertible exchangeable preferred stock. After 3 years, InterDigital had the option to replace the preferred with nearly identical convertible debt maturing in 2003. But 15 days after the company misses any quarterly preferred dividend payment, the conversion price will automatically drop to the common stock's price at the time of the offering. Thus, the conversion premium will drop from its 20 percent initial level to zero. In theory, therefore, the investor is compensated for the loss of the dividend by the opportunity to convert cheaply into the common stock. On the other hand, because the preferred dividend is likely to be passed only if the company is in dire straits, it is not clear how much this feature really offers.

Preferred Purchase Units

In 1992, Bankers Trust New York Corporation (BT) issued a hybrid unit consisting of:

1. A 3-year $100,000,000 debt obligation of a subsidiary.
2. A purchase contract requiring the debt holder to buy a BT cumulative preferred stock issue on March 1, 1995.

In addition to the 6.90 percent coupon on the debt, a holder will also receive, on an annual basis, 1.65 percent of the purchase price. This amount represents the difference between the expected yield on the preferred to be issued (8.55 percent) and the debt coupon. The prospectus labels this as a contract fee. The net effect is that the investors are in the same economic position as if they had bought the preferred today, but the payments are tax-deductible for BT for 3 years. (Compare the BT 1993 purchase units discussed in Chapter 15.)

Similarly, NBD Bancorp, Inc., offered 7½ percent Preferred Purchase Units consisting of:

1. A 7.40 percent subordinated debenture due May 10, 2023, in a principal amount of $25.
2. A related purchase contract paying a contract fee of $0.10 and requiring the purchase, on May 10, 2023, of 7.5 percent cumulative preferred stock of the issuer at a purchase price of $25.

The holders are entitled to receive an aggregate of 7.5 percent per year per unit in interest and contract fees. The debentures and the related purchase contracts are not separable and may be purchased and transferred only as units.

The debentures are unsecured and subordinated to all senior debt of the issuer. Once again, this is a delayed sale of preferred, and the investor is compensated during the waiting period.

Step-Up/Step-Down Preference Shares

As a parallel to the step-up floating rate note structure (see Chapter 9), there have also been issues of floating rate preference shares where the predetermined dividend will rise at a given future date; this would normally be coupled with a call provision and would be designed to give the investor comfort that the shares were not likely to prove perpetual. At the same time, the undated nature of the preference share gives the issuer equity on the balance sheet.

Such structures are often attractive to bank issuers seeking to raise capital under the Basle Committee rules. A recent example was the December 1996 issue by BPI Capital Finance, an offshoot of Banco Portugues de Investimento. This was an issue of $100 million of step-up, perpetual, noncumulative, floating rate preference shares, where the coupon steps up to 265 basis points over LIBOR (from 115 basis points) if the shares are not called after 5 years.

The converse (step-down) preference structure was used several times, raising, reportedly, $10 billion in the United States in 1996, until the U.S. cavalry, in the shape of the Internal Revenue Service, came thundering over the hill and spoiled the party with new regulations. A corporation would create a Real Estate Investment Trust (REIT) to which it would assign some property by way of creating a borrowing against the property. The company's interest payments to the REIT would be tax-deductible. The REIT would issue perpetual preferred to tax-exempt investors such as pension funds. It would pay very high dividends on the preferred in the early years, but the coupon then stepped down to nominal levels by year 11, and the value of the preferred would collapse as a result. In effect, the preferred holder is paid out by the artificially high early dividends, without technically being repaid because the preferred still exists.

SILVER DENOMINATED PREFERRED STOCK

In July 1994, Freeport-McMoran issued Silver Denominated Preferred Stock. The Silver Denominated Preferred Stock ranks pari passu with other preferred stocks of the issuer and is senior to its common stock but subordinate to its most deeply subordinated debt. The issue price of the Silver Denominated Preferred Stock was based on the spot price for 4 ounces of silver on the date of issue. The Silver Denominated Preferred Stock is to be outstanding for 5 years, after which it will be serially redeemed annually over 8 years. The redemption price is to be based on the dollar equivalent value, meaning the then-current spot price of a fixed number of ounces (4) of silver per share. Furthermore, the dividends are cumulative and payable quarterly, again based on the dollar equivalent value of a fixed number of ounces (4) per share. Thus, there is an annual dividend rate of 4.125 percent, but it will be a product of the current spot price of silver.

Catastrophe Preferred Equity Puts

An interesting example of the integration of equity preferred and the insurance business was seen, in October 1996, with the announcement by Aon Re, the reinsurance intermediary of Aon, that it had negotiated a catastrophe equity put program with RLI, a specialty property and casualty insurance company. The option allows RLI to issue up to $50 million of convertible preferred shares if a catastrophic loss occurs.

The 3-year put, developed by Aon Re and underwritten by Center Reinsurance, enables RLI to continue operating after a loss large enough to exhaust its $200 million reinsurance coverage. The puts give RLI protection for 1 year, renewable for up to 3 years every 12 months if a California earthquake does not occur. If RLI's surplus falls below a predetermined level at any time during the 3-year period, RLI's option is knocked out. If RLI exercises the option, Center Reinsurance has the option to buy a 25 percent unlimited quota share treaty (a type of reinsurance whereby Center can share in 25 percent of RLI's future premiums and losses).

A similar operation was carried out by Benfield Ellinger, a London reinsurance broker, in conjunction with AIG Combined Risk, to place a portfolio of catastrophe insurance bonds with a U.K. fund manager. The fund manager invests in an offshore special-purpose vehicle, which, in turn, sells a loss warranty reinsurance contract to a reinsurance company.

Chapter *15*

Convertibles and Warrants

We discussed, in Chapter 2, the basic characteristics of the convertible bond. In this chapter, we discuss some more recent variants. In addition, we discuss the warrant market, which has had an enormous number of developments in recent years.

RECENT DEVELOPMENTS

As we saw in Chapter 2, convertibles come in two main forms: (1) convertible bonds and (2) convertible preferreds. In the United States, convertible bonds are in fact convertible subordinated debentures. Elsewhere, they may be more senior. In most of the world's convertible markets, convertible bonds are more common than convertible preferreds. Among the world's major markets, convertible preferreds are most common in the United States and the United Kingdom.

By the start of 1997, the global convertible market had reached $400 billion outstanding, more than double the 1991 total. At the same time, however, rising equity markets resulted in substantial calls by issuers as a result of the so-called soft call provisions applied in many convertibles. These typically provide that the issuer can call the bond if the equity price is trading at 30 percent above the conversion price. In the United Kingdom alone, in 1996, 20 percent of the market was called away from bondholders. Thus, all the option elements of the convertible bond need to be considered, not just the conversion option.

Major issues in the international market for 1996 and early 1997 included INA ($2.1 billion), Fuji Bank (¥200 billion), Sakura Bank (¥150 billion); Tokai Bank and Sumitomo Bank (¥100 billion each); Kmart ($1 billion), News America Holdings/BSkyB ($1 billion), National Australia Bank ($1 billion), and Microsoft ($1 billion).

The German market performed strongly during 1996, with $3 billion in German convertible or exchangeable bonds issued for Volkswagen, Siemens, Bayer, and others. Most were issued by banks that were monetizing strategic holdings in these companies; various examples are discussed below.

MANDATORY CONVERTIBLES

An early development in the convertible market was the mandatory convertible bond. This is, in effect, a hybrid form of equity—a bond that must be converted into equity, and so (for balance sheet and regulatory purposes) can be treated as equity from the start of the issue. The bond was introduced, in 1982, in the form of equity commitment notes and equity contract notes, which collectively came to be called mandatory convertibles. They rapidly became very popular: in 1984, 40 percent of capital raised by the top 50 U.S. bank holding companies was attributable to the issuance of mandatory convertibles.

The first mandatory convertible took the form of a $100 million offering by Manufacturers Hanover, in April 1982. The 10-year fixed rate notes were accompanied by detachable stock purchase contracts. The owners of the contract were required to buy (at maturity on April 15, 1992) shares of ordinary shares equal to the principal amount of the notes. The price was the lower of $55.55 per share or the current market price, but not in any case lower than $40. Unlike the normal convertible, which gives the holder an option to exercise, these compel the holder to do so. Hence, this first version of the mandatory convertible was not particularly popular. Only Chase Manhattan issued a similar security. However, the concept was developed, in 1984, into the equity contract note. This note is exchangeable at maturity for primary equity securities having a market value equal to the principal amount of the notes. (Unlike the Manufacturers Hanover deal, the buyer of the notes does not take the risk of the stock price falling.) If the holder of the notes does not choose to receive equities at maturity, the issuer will undertake to sell the equity on behalf of the holder. If this sale cannot be made for any reason, the holder is required to accept equities.

After its successful use in the United States, the concept was applied in the Euro markets, in January 1986, with an issue by Thomson-Brandt International BV, guaranteed by Thomson SA. Thomson issued US$50 million of equity contract notes, at a coupon of 8 percent and an issue price of 100, with redemption in ordinary shares of Thomson-CSF. Redemption was at the holder's option any time after September 1986, at a rate of 6.194 shares per $1,000 principal amount of notes.

The attraction of the Thomson issue was that, although the structure has much of the appeal of a straightforward convertible, such as a lower coupon than on an ordinary fixed-income bond, because it is redeemable only in equities it could be shown as capital on the company's balance sheet. The issue was well received, against a background of good figures from Thomson, although the structure resembles that of the original Manufacturers Hanover deal in that the purchaser is taking the risk of a decline in the equity price. But it also had a put option. Upon exercising the put, the investor would receive shares at the share payment rate at any time on or after September 1, 1986. Therefore, a purchaser who felt that the equity was about to fall sharply could exercise the put, even though this might involve paying a premium for the shares; at least the premium would be less than if the equity subsequently fell more.

Another class of mandatory convertible is the equity commitment note. J. P. Morgan issued the first equity commitment note in April 1982. Unlike holders of equity contract notes, the equity commitment note holders are not obliged to purchase equity with the notes. Instead, Morgan is committed to redeem the notes with the proceeds of an equity issue at some future date. This structure proved very popular, and a large number of later equity commitment note issues led to the Federal Reserve's setting certain limits.

The Federal Reserve rules set a maximum 12-year maturity. Issuers must fund one-third of the equity in the first 4 years, another one-third in the second 4 years, and the final one-third by maturity. Equity contract notes were limited to 20 percent of primary capital before mandatory convertibles (any amount above this is treated as secondary capital). However, the rating agencies treat both equity contract and equity commitment notes as debt, and do not give any credit for improved capital ratios. From the point of view of the investor, there is also the question of dilution.

Variants of the mandatory convertible have been used in European privatizations, such as the Balladur bonds issued in 1991, which gave investors the preferential right to participate in French privatizations. The issue for Swedish Steel in 1992, which carried a zero coupon but came with a warrant entitling the holder to exchange bonds into equity, was another variation on the theme. A recent use of the technique in the Far East was the issue, in October 1994, by Hutchison Whampoa, of $250 million of mandatory bonds that convert into shares of Hutchison Delta Ports, a proposed spin-off of the company's coastal ports activities.

DECS

A variant of the mandatory convertible is the Debt Exchangeable for Common Stock (DECS) issued by American Express in October 1993. These were 3-year notes bearing a coupon of 6.25 percent. At maturity, they are redeemed in shares of First Data Corporation—or their cash equivalent. If the stock is at or below $36¾ (the price at which the stock was trading at the time of the DECS issue), then investors receive 1 share. If it is above $44⅞ they will receive 0.82 share. In between, the ratio is adjusted so that investors essentially break even. This DECS structure is to some extent the bond equivalent of ACES (see Chapter 4). In both cases, the investor, in essence, owns common stock with a cap on its price appreciation. In the DECS structure, the asset held is a bond, repayable in stock; in the PERC, the asset held is preferred, callable by the issuer and repayable in stock. The other key difference is that, whereas under the PERC structure the investors' possible appreciation is definitively capped, under the DECS structure the investor gives up only a fixed amount of appreciation (the first 20 to 25 percent). Once they have been given the shares at a ratio of, say, .80 per DECS, they get any subsequent appreciation. They have lost out by getting only .80 share instead of one-for-one, but if the shares rise more than enough to compensate for that, investors receive the extra increase. Under the PERCS structure, there is a fixed upper limit to the amount that investors can receive. Under the DECS structure, there is a "dead zone" between the issue price and the conversion price. Above that, investors get all the appreciation. In both structures, the investors get all the downside.

A variant of the DECS structure was introduced for MFS Communications Co. in May 1995. The issuer was able to pay quarterly dividends in the form of common stock rather than cash. This could be thought of as the preferred equivalent of a "pay-in-kind" bond (see Chapter 9).

In April 1995, J. P. Morgan issued a $75 million "synthetic DECS" called STEP (Securities Tied to Equity Performance). The rationale for this transaction was that Morgan had bought a large position in America Online from a client. This issue transferred the risk in the position to Morgan's clients.

An interesting mandatory convertible was launched, in May 1997, for Daimler-Benz. The issuing technique used was a preemptive rights offering of DEM1 billion in bonds plus a parallel book-built issue of between DEM600 million and DEM1 billion, subject to a 40 percent clawback.

At maturity, the notes automatically convert into common shares, but, as with DECS, the conversion ratio will vary, depending on the level of the share price. Investors receive full downside protection for the first 20 percent of any fall, because if the share price falls by 20 percent, they will receive 1.25 shares. If it rises by 16 percent, they will receive 0.86 share. Within the range −20 to +16, therefore, the investor is insulated from price movements.

STRYPES/SAILS

Variants of the DECS structure exist under numerous alternative forms. In July 1995, Merrill Lynch used Structured Yield Product Exchangeable for Stock (STRYPES), whereby Merrill issued notes mandatorily convertible, after 3 years, into 10 percent of MGIC Investment Corporation. The issue allowed Northwestern Mutual Life Insurance Co. to monetize half of its 20 percent holding in MGIC Investment Corporation. In a similar deal, Houghton Mifflin used Stock Appreciation Income Linked Securities (SAILS) to monetize its $119 million stake in Inso Corporation.

Another variant was developed for Browning-Ferris International (BFI), in June 1995. The investor received 3-year U.S. Treasury bonds, with a principal amount equal to the offering price, plus a purchase contract obligating the investor to purchase BFI stock in 3 years. Essentially, all of the proceeds of the offering were used to purchase the Treasury bonds; as a result, BFI received no proceeds for 3 years. At the maturity of the Treasuries, the proceeds were used to pay BFI for the stock. So BFI essentially sold stock for 3-year forward delivery. The number of shares issued will vary, as with all DECS-type structures. If, in 3 years, the stock is below the offering price, investors will get 1 share of common; if the stock is above the conversion price, they will receive just over 0.8 of a share. If in between, the fraction will be calculated so that investors essentially break even.

A variant, in March 1994, was the $500 million convertible bond for PT Indofood of Indonesia, in the form of a going public exchangeable bond, which was launched ahead of the company's expected $60 million flotation on the Indonesian stock exchange. The novel structure of the deal—in the name of Global Mark International—was designed to get around a domestic ceiling on IPO pricings in Indonesia, whereby shares cannot be floated at more than 15 times a company's earnings. The convertible bonds are exchangeable at a price of Rp7,692—a price/earnings ratio of 22 times earnings—thus allowing the company to demand a higher valuation for its shares than it would otherwise achieve in the local market. The bonds are mandatorily convertible into PT Indofood's stock on the earliest date permissible under Indonesian law after the IPO.

Despite the mandatory exchange, the 5-year bonds carried a complex structure involving a step-up coupon (3.50 percent until 1995, 5 percent until 1996, and 6 percent thereafter) and call and put options in the event of what is described in the prospectus as a "non-complying IPO." If the IPO failed to happen, investors had a put option in year 5 to yield 8.50 percent.

Partly Paid Converting Notes

In April 1997, an Australian property developer, Westfield Trust, issued AUS$250 million of 1-year-and-9-month partly paid converting notes. These notes were 25 percent paid (i.e., the initial cash raised was AUS$62.5 million) with the balance being payable in December 1998. At that date, the notes automatically convert into units of the Westfield Trust. The technique achieved a forward sale of equity by the trust, because the notes convert automatically.

CONVERTIBLE EXCHANGEABLE

In November 1993, Interpool Inc., a U.S. company, filed for an issue of $70 million of 25-year convertible exchangeable subordinated notes. These convertible bonds allow the issuer to substitute convertible preferred shares with an identical yield if it chooses. This gives the advantage that the finance is tax-deductible debt, but later can become equity, allowing the firm to gear up its balance sheet should it wish to borrow.

Convertible Capital Notes

A very similar technique was used by several U.K. companies under the guise of the convertible capital note. An example was the Reckitt & Colman issue of 1990. Here, an offshore special-purpose vehicle issued bonds that were initially redeemable in the form of exchangeable preference shares. This redemption helped them to be classified as debt for tax purposes, but, for accounting purposes, the shares were treated as equity because another layer was introduced. The preference shares carried a very low dividend rate, effectively forcing investors to convert into ordinary shares. Figure 15.1 illustrates the structure.

A slightly different structure—perpetual bonds convertible into preference shares—has also been used. In April 1993, Barclays Bank launched a US$300 million issue of convertible capital notes. The structure, the first of its kind, allows Barclays to issue perpetual debt, free of withholding tax in the United States, which can be converted into preferred stock. The deal was sold initially as fixed-rate debt with a yield of about 8 percent. It can be converted, at the bank's option, into preferred stock. Thus, the conversion option here is with the issuer rather than the investor.

However, the conversion option is unlikely to be exercised (unless Barclays' Tier Two capital is excessive in relation to its Tier One capital) because the loss

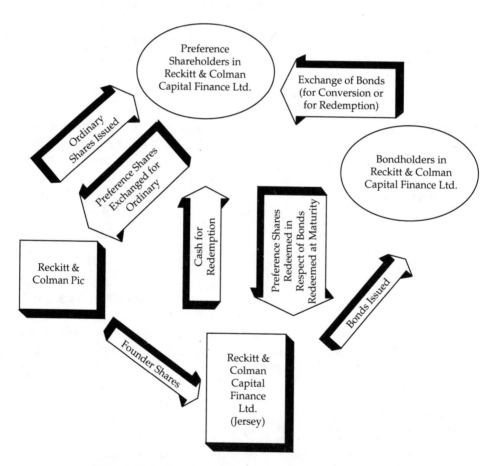

Figure 15.1 Reckitt convertible capital notes structure.

of tax deduction means that, once converted (assuming the fixed yield is 8.00 percent), the cost jumps to about 9.25 percent.

This deal was very similar to the Preferred Purchase Units issue by Bankers Trust (see below) and to the $500 million issue by National Westminster in November 1993. In both deals, the securities start as subordinated debt, but the issuer has the option to convert the securities to preference shares. Thus, with the Bankers Trust deal also, the security's coupon is tax-deductible but the security can be converted to equity for Basle Committee purposes.

One of the main difficulties in structuring these transactions was that, to comply with the U.S. 1940 Trust Indenture Act, issuers cannot remove the investors' right to sue the borrower directly if it is in default. On the other hand, the Bank of England allows investors to petition for the winding up of a bank only if it is in default. Barclays found a way to suit the Bank of England requirements by incorporating a clause stating that, if the bank does not pay interest, it is an event of default only if a dividend is paid immediately after that. The twist with the National Westminster deal is that there is a 3-year "lockout" period in which NatWest cannot convert the securities. For tax-exempt institutions, or those uncertain of their likely tax position in the next year or two, this was an attractive feature.

In the United Kingdom, British Land PLC used a somewhat similar structure. It issued, in March 1994, £150 million of irredeemable convertible bonds. The bonds can be exchanged into irredeemable convertible preference shares, which count as equity and will carry the same conversion price as the convertible bonds. The structure allows the company to exchange the convertible preference shares back into convertible bonds, provided that the convertible preference shares have been in existence for more than 6 months.

The bonds paid a semiannual coupon of 6 percent and were convertible into British Land shares at £5.10 per share (a 23 percent premium). The structure was complicated somewhat by the British requirement that new equity be offered first to existing shareholders, if the issue accounts for more than 5 percent of outstanding equity. The limit was raised to 10 percent in the case of equity raised for noncash consideration. Therefore, the structure was that a special-purpose vehicle in Jersey issued £150 million of convertible preference shares, the proceeds being used to buy the convertible bond. The issuer is allowed to convert the preference shares back into debt provided they have been shares for more than 6 months. The investor, whether holding preference shares or bonds, retains the right to convert the paper into British Land shares. Two call options were included to maximize the company's flexibility: (1) after 7 years, the issuer can redeem the bonds at par, provided the underlying share price averages more than £6.63 over a monthly period, and (2) after 14 years, there is an unconditional call if the issuer wishes.

In March 1997, National Australia Capital Securities issued $875 million of perpetual Exchange Capital Units (ExCaps), which consisted of a 7.875 percent perpetual bond together with a purchase contract entitling the bondholder to exchange the bonds for ordinary shares of the bank, at an initial exchange price of 1.635 shares per ExCap. (The exchange price is subject to certain antidilution adjustments.) The ExCaps are also exchangeable by the bank, at any time, into 7.875 percent noncumulative preference shares of the bank on a one-for-one basis. The preference shares themselves are convertible, at the holder's option, into ordinary shares—or at the option of the bank, after the fifth anniversary of the issue of the ExCaps, into the cash equivalent of such shares. This structure ensures that the bank can convert the paper from Basle Committee Tier 2 capital (subordinated perpetual) into Tier 1 capital (noncumulative preference or ordinary shares). In some respects, therefore, the structure resembles that for Interpool, referred to earlier.

PREFERRED PURCHASE UNITS

A technique rather similar to the Reckitt and Barclays deals discussed earlier was used in 1993 by Bankers Trust, which issued $150 million of "preferred purchase units" or convertible capital securities. These consisted of 40-year subordinated bonds that would yield 7.625 percent on issue and were callable after 5 years. The bondholders have the right to convert into perpetual preferred stock with the same yield. Bankers Trust, however, also has the option, on 60 days' notice, to cut the coupon on the debt by 1.5 percent at any time. This would probably "force" conversion by holders into the preferred. Thus, Bankers Trust was able to issue subordinated debt (Tier II capital for purposes of the Basle Committee capital requirements) on which the interest payments are fully tax-deductible. But at the same time, it has effectively guaranteed the availability of Tier I capital (perpetual preferred) on attractive terms. (Compare the Preferred Purchase Units discussed in Chapter 14.)

FIXED/FLOATING CONVERTIBLES

A structure seen in the FRN market—perpetuals with a coupon reset after 10 years to encourage the issuer to call the bond, so that it looks like a dated issue to the investor—has also been used in the convertible market. In 1993, BOT Cayman Finance Ltd., a subsidiary of Bank of Tokyo, issued ¥50 billion of perpetual subordinated convertible bonds. They pay interest at 4.25 percent until March 2003, and thereafter at 6-month Yen LIBOR + 1.8 percent, a rate sufficiently penal that it is very unlikely that the issuer would not call the bond. Thus, for regulatory purposes, Bank of Tokyo issued Tier 2 capital under the Basle Committee rules, but investors could tell themselves that they were buying a 10-year convertible bond. A similar structure was used in 1996 by the French financial institution, Crédit National, which issued FRF900 million of subordinated perpetual fixed/floating convertibles. The bonds pay 5.625 percent until 2003 and then LIBOR + 2.5 percent.

ZERO-COUPON CONVERTIBLES

The zero-coupon concept, discussed in Chapter 9, was taken a step further, in April 1985, by LYONS (Liquid Yield Options Notes), with an $840 million issue by Waste Management of zero-coupon convertibles. The notes had an effective yield of 9 percent over their 16-year life and an issue price of $250 per face value of $1,000. They were convertible into 4.3 shares of Waste Management common. The issue came shortly after an FASB ruling that zero-coupon convertibles should not be considered common stock equivalents unless their effective yields are less than two-thirds of yields on double-A-rated bonds at the time of pricing. Prior to the ruling, all zero-coupon convertibles were considered common stock equivalents.

In 1993, Roche, the Swiss pharmaceuticals company, issued $1.42 billion of LYONS. After Eurobond issues that had been equity-linked, the company recognized a need to expand the U.S. investor base for its equity before an eventual filing with the SEC. Because the company did not need equity, a convertible structure was preferred. The zero-coupon structure effectively means that the conversion premium increases over time: the effective conversion premium at maturity is 169 percent. Finally, the need to increase U.S. participation led to a specific new feature: the bond is convertible into ADRs, which cannot be canceled—i.e., exchanged for underlying shares—for 5 years.

In November 1994, Merrill Lynch introduced Exchangeable LYONS on Microsoft. The deal had a number of unusual features. The typical LYONS has a stated maturity of 15 or 20 years, is puttable at 5-year intervals, and is priced at a large discount to its par value. The Microsoft deal had a 4.6-year life, was priced near par, and was redeemable at a premium at maturity. This deal was also unusual because it was not done in conjunction with Microsoft. It was a third-party offering (essentially, a zero-coupon variant of the DECS discussed above).

The first French franc LYON was issued, in February 1997, by Clarins, the French cosmetic company. It issued FRF890 million of 15-year zero-coupon bonds, convertible into Clarins shares from the date of issue, and having put options, at 2002 and 2007, to yield 2.75 percent. The issue also included a call option at any time after 2002, the call to be priced to achieve a 2.75 percent yield.

CONVERSION PRICE ADJUSTMENT

In May 1994, Royce Value Trust issued a convertible security called ICONS (Investment Company Convertible Notes). It was a $60 million deal with a 10-year final maturity, convertible into Royce's common stock. The most novel feature of the deal is an annual adjustment in the conversion price. The conversion price can be adjusted downward to reflect the impact on the fund's net asset value of any distributions to holders of common stock. This is a straightforward adjustment reflecting Royce's legal structure as a trust. But there will also be a concurrent, preset upward adjustment each year—a percentage to be fixed when the deal is priced. This is designed "to compensate the fund's common stockholders for the preferential return payable to note holders." Another unusual feature is a provision that Royce must redeem the notes, or reset their terms, if they are trading for less than 95 percent of their par value after 5 years. At present, this seems unlikely (see Figure 15.2). The reset, which may include changes in the coupon, the rate at which the conversion pricing increases each year, or a one-time reduction in the conversion price, would be aimed at ensuring that the ICONS trade "as nearly as possible" to par value. In a sense, the investor is being sold a strike reset option (see Chapter 7), although, because the adjustment might come in the form of a changed coupon or changes in the conversion price, it might be more useful to look at it as a put at par.The ICONS will be unsecured obligations of the fund, but it will be required to maintain asset coverage of the ICONS—as well as any other senior debt—of 300 percent.

In July 1995, ThermoQuest Corp. (an indirect subsidiary of ThermoElectron Corp.) brought a 5-year convertible to market with a 5 percent coupon and a 10 percent conversion premium over the price at which the company's shares would be eventually issued in an IPO. For every year that the company fails to go public, the conversion premium steps down 2.5 percent and the bond coupon rises 0.50 percent, up to a maximum of 0.75 percent over the 5-year

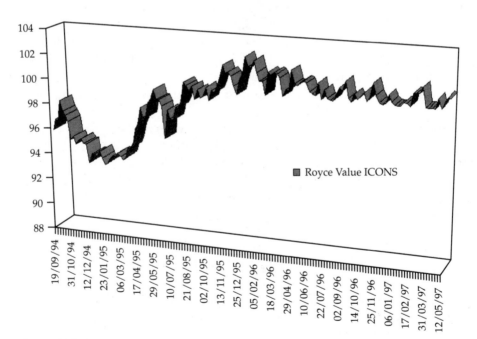

Source: Datastream.

Figure 15.2 Performance of Royce Value Trust ICONS.

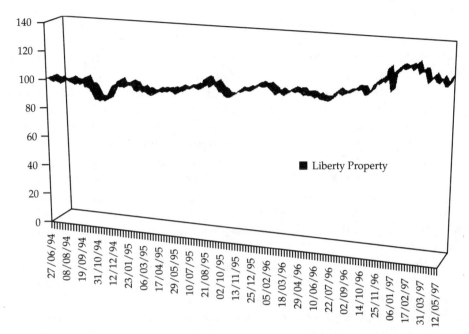

Source: Datastream.

Figure 15.3 Liberty Property Trust convertible.

Treasury yield. For investors, the main danger is that the company does very well but never does an IPO.

Interest Ratchet Feature

In June 1994, Kidder, Peabody and Company brought to market a $200 million convertible bond deal for Liberty Property Trust, a real estate investment trust. The convertible is a 7-year noncallable bond, priced to yield 8 percent, in line with the common stock of the trust, which was issued at the same time. The special feature of this convertible was a ratchet feature under which interest payments on the convertible will rise by the full amount of any increases in common stock dividend payments over the life of the bonds. It resembles, therefore, the ThermoQuest structure but without the conversion price adjustment. The bond seems to have performed well (see Figure 15.3). A similar feature was used by Goldman, Sachs in a $200 million convertible preferred deal for Property Trust of America, in November 1993.

PUTTABLE CONVERTIBLES

During the bull markets of 1987, a number of British firms (and others) issued Euro-convertibles with puts attached. An example was the £100 million 5¾ percent convertible puttable Eurobond, lead managed for Next PLC by Crédit

Suisse First Boston, which promoted the concept with enthusiasm. The bonds carried an unusually high conversion premium of 152 percent, but protected the investor with a put option. The investor could put the bonds back to Next in 1992 at 129, for a yield to maturity of 11.74 percent.

In the expectation that the puts would never be needed, Next did not provide in its accounts for the cost of the put option. Came the Crash of 1987, and, in the following year, rising interest rates in the United Kingdom. By December 1988, Next's shares were trading at 136 pence against a conversion price on the bonds of 430 pence. Investors seemed highly likely to take up the put option, and Next had to take a substantial charge against profits for the cost of the put. Saatchi & Saatchi had issued a similar bond. If investors had exercised the put, it would have had to find £210 million, which, at one point in 1990, exceeded the market value of the company. The company's finances had to be reconstructed.

Another retailer, Burton, had a similar problem but took a different route. The terms of the bond were revised to encourage investors to hold on for 5 additional years, thereby saving Burton from having to make a £40 million provision in its accounts. Another variant of this approach was the "rolling put." A typical example was the Slough Estates 6 percent 2003 convertible. Holders are entitled to sell bonds back to the company on a series of dates between 1993 and 1998, at prices that will always guarantee a yield to maturity of 9.45 percent from the issue date to the put date.

PUTTABLE AND REDEEMABLE CONVERTIBLE KNOCKOUT SECURITIES (PARCKS)

A variant of the mandatory redemption convertible was the issue by Bangkok Bank, in July 1996, of $350 million of PARCKS. These bonds are convertible into the underlying equity of the issuer. But they are also mandatorily redeemable at between 123.5 percent and 127.5 percent after 5 years, if the share price is less than the mandatory redemption level, and provided it has not traded above the knockout level (set at 7 percent above the mandatory redemption price, which, in turn, was set approximately 130 percent above the conversion price). That is, the bond is puttable back to the issuer if the share price performance is poor, provided the share price has not risen above the knockout level, in which case the put expires. This is an example of a knockout put being embedded into a convertible, as discussed in Chapter 7.

PRIVATIZATION EXCHANGEABLE NOTES (PENs)

As part of the Italian government's privatization process, INA issued a dual-currency issue called Privatization Exchangeable Notes. This issue was $2.35

billion of Republic of Italy-guaranteed bonds, in separate dollar and lira tranches, exchangeable into INA shares. It was the largest convertible bond ever issued in Europe and a vindication of the use of convertibles as a privatization method at a time of general investor fatigue, allowing the Italian government to reduce its 34 percent stake in the company to around 10 percent.

CREDIT-ENHANCED CONVERTIBLES

In early 1997, Indian Petrochemicals Corporation brought to market $150 million of Credit Enhanced Debt Indexed to Stock (CREDITS), a convertible bond whose principal value is guaranteed by a letter of credit from Bank of America. The deal produced funds for the borrower at 155 basis points below U.S. Treasuries. The success of the deal was such that one might expect to see similar transactions in the future.

SYNTHETIC CONVERTIBLES

A number of issues of "synthetic convertibles" have been made by companies that issue bonds that are redeemed in cash, but at a price linked to the company's shares. The first issue, by Lafarge Coppée in June 1991, was quickly imitated by other French companies such as Carréfour, Louis Vuitton, Moët Hennessy, and Pernot Ricard. Essentially, the investor is buying a straight bond together with a cash-settled call option on the issuing company's share price. The issuers achieved sub-PIBOR funding, without having to dilute the equity base by issuing shares at the time of redemption.

BONDS CONVERTIBLE INTO ANOTHER COMPANY'S SHARES

To back an issue, several companies have used their large holdings of equity of another company. For example, Inter North Inc., in 1983, offered $240 million in 25-year subordinated debentures exchangeable into Mobil stock; for many years, the company had held a block of 6 million common shares of Mobil, but now required the funds for further expansion.

There were several advantages to using the stock as underpinning for an issue, rather than selling directly. On the debt side, Inter North was able to borrow at 10.5 percent, two full percentage points below what it would have had to pay on a straight A-rated bond. On the equity side, Inter North's Mobil shares are exchangeable for $40; at the time of the offering, the price for Mobil shares was $29.50, which gave Inter North a 36 percent premium. And until the debentures are exchanged for the stocks, Inter North is entitled to the dividends, which help to cover the interest on the debentures.

If Inter North had sold its holdings directly, it would have received only $180 million; it would also have had to pay a large amount of capital gains tax. There are other tax advantages: the Mobil dividends fall under the 85 percent corporate exclusion rule, and interest payments on the debentures are deductible. From the point of view of the investor, the debenture was viewed as "a chance to get Mobil with a ten and a half percent yield."

In the United States, corporations were allowed to deduct interest expense from taxable income while receiving an 85 percent corporate dividend tax exclusion on the shares backing the bond, provided the shares were acquired before October 1984. Despite this allowance, only 15 such issues took place between 1980 and the Inter North issue in 1983. For one thing, few corporations had amassed enough stock to make such a deal worthwhile. Typically, the instrument has been used in situations where companies have failed in a takeover bid and hold a large block of stock.

For example, General Cinema Corporation (GCC) made a bid for Heublein, but was outbid by R.J. Reynolds. GCC's holding of 4 million shares in Heublein was automatically converted into more than 2.6 million shares of Reynolds common and more than 1 million shares of Reynolds preferred. The company therefore issued $100 million in exchangeable debentures. The exchange ratio was 15.936 shares of Reynolds common, at $62, for each $1,000 of principal amount of the debentures. The technique was also used by IBM to dispose of some of its Intel stock; in February 1985, it issued $300 million of bonds convertible into Intel shares at a substantial premium to the then prevailing price.

A parallel technique was used in 1986 by News Corporation. It offered 200,000 preference shares exchangeable into "B" ordinary shares of Reuters Holdings. The $200 million proceeds of the issue strengthened the equity base of News Corporation, and at the same time allowed it to dispose, at a high profit, of much of its holding in Reuters. The proceeds were almost three times the $68 million valuation of the group's 9.5 percent holding of Reuters' shares when the news agency went public in June 1984.

A very similar technique was used in 1993 by the Daily Mail & General Trust. It issued a 10-year £50 million bond convertible into Reuters shares. The bond carried a relatively low coupon (5.75 percent) and a conversion premium of 27 percent. Effectively, again, this was a deferred forward sale.

In September 1996, Dresdner Finance issued DEM500 million of bonds exchangeable into shares of Münchener Rückversicherung (Munich Re). The issue allowed the bank to finance its holding more cheaply than by issuing straight bonds. The bank was able to sell the shares through the convertible at a premium of about 15 percent, but the terms of the issue allowed a pay-out of the equivalent of the shares in cash, thus allowing the bank to hold on to the strategic stake.

Similarly, in October 1996, an issue was made by BGB Finance, a special financing vehicle for Bankgesellschaft Berlin, of DEM300 million of bonds convertible into bearer shares of Metro AG. As with a number of similar previous issuers, this structure allowed the issuer to dispose of a now-unwanted strategic stake in another company without disturbing the current market for the shares. Even more symbolic was the subsequent announcement, in January 1997, of the launch by Deutsche Bank of $1.3 billion of bonds convertible into shares in Daimler-Benz, as a first step to unwinding its 24 percent stake in that company. The bonds were zero-coupon bonds with a 20-year maturity.

A similar situation arises where a firm owns a large equity stake in a subsidiary that it has previously taken public. The value of its remaining block of stock has risen, and the parent would like to monetize its position but does not want to immediately recognize the built-in gain. This might be done through the sale of exchangeable subordinated debentures, using the subsidiary's stock. Thus, in 1994, McKesson Corporation, which owned a 57 percent interest in Armor All Products Corporation, sold exchangeable debentures due in 2004, where the debentures will be exchanged into stock of the subsidiary (Armor All). Thus, the issuer will be receiving cash up front, basically by monetizing its position in the subsidiary. However, the built-in gain in the stock of the subsidiary will not be triggered at the time of the receipt of the cash but will be deferred until the shares are delivered to the debenture holders in satisfaction of the exchange privilege (in this case, a 10-year deferral).

Another application of the technique occurred in March 1997, when the French pay-TV company Canal Plus, acquired a Dutch company, Nethold, which owned shares in an Italian company, Mediaset. Canal Plus wanted to offload the Mediaset stake, and chose to do so by issuing FRF2 billion of 5-year notes exchangeable into shares of Mediaset. Since there was some risk that the acquisition might not go through, the issue included a mandatory call if the issue had not gone through by August 1997.

Bonds Convertible, at Issuer's Option, into Third-Party Shares

A variant of this technique was introduced in 1991 with a number of issues, particularly in deutsche marks. In February 1991, Landeskreditbank Baden-Wuerttemberg (LKB) brought to market a 3-year, 3-month issue for DEM50 million. At maturity, LKB can repay either in cash or with 5 shares in the German chemical company, Bayer. The investors are effectively selling the issuer a put on Bayer for which, in this case, they received a coupon of 10 percent (1 percent over the then going market rate for a straight bond).

Other structures were redeemable partly in cash and partly in shares, lowering the number of shares to which the investor is exposed and, therefore, the downside risk. For example, in April 1991, a DEM50 million issue was brought to market for Landwirtschaftliche Rentenbank. Redemption of each DEM1,000 bond was either in cash or through delivery of two common shares of Commerzbank and DEM479 in cash. In these cases, the implicit strike price of the puts can be calculated by subtracting the cash amount deliverable if the put is exercised from the bond denomination. We then divide the result by the number of shares to be delivered. Hence, here, the implicit strike is $(1,000 - 479)/2 =$ DEM260.5.

A variant of this transaction, for the same issuer, featured an additional twist—a knockout option. If Commerzbank shares rose to DEM320, the bonds would redeem at par.

Bonds Convertible into a Company Yet to Exist

As an example of what can be accomplished with a respected issuer in an over-heated market, perhaps the neatest is the so-called "going public bonds" issued by Henderson Capital International. This Hong Kong company, well known and respected in that market, issued, in 1993, $460 million of bonds that will eventually be convertible into shares of Henderson China, a company that was to be spun off from the parent within the next 3 years. In other words, the company whose shares were to be acquired did not yet exist. The bonds carried a step-up coupon of 4 percent in the first year, 4.5 percent in the second year, and 5 percent in the third year. If the initial public offering of Henderson China was not completed within the 3 years, the bonds were to redeem at 107 percent of par, representing a yield to maturity of 6.66 percent. On completion of the IPO, bondholders are entitled to shares at a discount, which again increases with time. The discount is determined by dividing the principal amount by the IPO price divided by 105 percent in year 1, 106 percent in year 2, and 107 percent in year 3.

Insurance Risk Convertible

An unusual convertible transaction was the issue, in early 1997, by Winterthur Insurance, of a 3-year Swiss franc bond convertible into 5 Winterthur shares. The unusual feature was a proviso that payment of the 2.25 percent coupon is conditional on severe hail damage. If Winterthur has to make good on claims against a hailstorm that damages more than 6,000 vehicles in a single day, the coupon for that year is eliminated. (Compare the catastrophe insurance bonds discussed in Chapter 9.)

Nondetachable Warrants

An issue that tested the boundaries between the convertible and warrant markets was the DEM1.2 billion Notes with Equity Warrant Securities (NEWS), issued by Daimler-Benz in 1996. This consisted of a bond with nondetachable warrants attached. This structure circumvented tax problems and problems of German preemptive rights. The issue incorporated a DEM250 million increase option, enabling the issue of DEM750 million of shares that would not be subject to preemption. To exercise the warrant, investors have to tender the bond as well; alternatively, they can keep the bond and exercise the warrant for cash.

EQUITY WARRANTS

In one sense, warrants are nothing new to the market. As indicated in Chapter 2, they are one of the traditional, basic instruments. But equity warrants have become increasingly important in international markets, and they have begun to develop a wide range of different variants. In addition, although not particularly significant in the United States, the equity warrant market is important in several countries' domestic markets, as discussed in more detail in the next section.

The analysis of warrants has had, as it were, two faces: (1) the traditional one, touched on in Chapter 2, where the investor considers factors such as premium or gearing; and (2) the view that a warrant is a traded option and therefore the analytical approaches of Chapters 6 and 7 can be applied.

In this chapter, we will concentrate on outlining the structures and indicating the parallel to the option structure of Chapters 6 and 7. In general, unless otherwise indicated, the reader may assume that the warrant shares the risk characteristics of the underlying option.

An example of an equity warrant on an individual share might be the issue of $37.5 million floating rate notes by Hansol Paper Company of Korea, in May 1994. These notes had 15 warrants attached, each enabling holders to buy Won4,031,500 of nonvoting shares in Hansol Paper at Won36,900 per share, from June 14, 1994, to May 27, 1997.

A typical example of an American-style warrant on an equity index might be the 500 million Luxembourg francs 1991–1998 bond issued by Tractebel Invest International BV 4 percent notes with option certificates (equivalent to warrants, for all practical purposes) attached. These allowed the investor to acquire an amount in Belgian francs calculated as follows:

$$250,000 \times \frac{CV - 1,074.69}{1,074.69}$$

where CV = the closing value of the BEL 20 index 2 days after exercise. Certificates could be exercised from December 20, 1991, to December 5, 1995.

Another variant is an investment bank's issue of a warrant attached to a bond, into shares owned by a third party. An example is the issue, in February 1994, of CHF150 million 2 percent bonds 1994–2001 by Eurofima; each bond had 75 warrants attached, and 80 warrants enabled holders to buy one registered share of Sandoz at CHF4,160; the warrant, issued by UBS, was attached to the Eurofima bond. Warrants of this type are discussed further under "Covered Warrants" on page 454.

A further variant is where the warrant is into a group of shares. For example, the CHF100 million issue by Rabobank had 2¼ percent bonds together with warrants issued by Merrill Lynch Capital Markets AG (Schweiz). Each bond had 58 warrants attached, and 250 warrants enabled holders to buy one basket of registered shares consisting of 3 Zurich Versicherungs-Gesellschaft at CHF1,580 per share; 5 Winterthur Versicherungs-Gesellschaft at CHF820; and 5 Schweizerische Ruckversicherungs-Gesellschaft at CHF708. The life of the warrant was February 28, 1994, to January 23, 1997.

Market Structure

For practical purposes, the international warrant market may be said to have begun in 1982, when the Japanese Ministry of Finance authorized Japanese companies to issue Eurobonds with equity warrants attached. The volume of issuance grew rapidly, peaking in the late 1980s and then collapsing as the Japanese bubble burst. Some revival in the Japanese market has been seen in the 1990s, but it remains shrunken in comparison with the bubble era. The scale of the excesses and market manipulation of that period has provoked an extended market hangover. Other market segments have also developed, and since the pace of Japanese issuance slowed after 1989, they have become relatively more important.

At the level of national markets, issuance of warrants in the U.K. market has, with one or two exceptions, been confined to issuance by investment trusts (closed-end investment funds); France, Germany, and Switzerland, particularly the two latter countries, have relatively active markets, as does Australia. By contrast, in the United States, where warrants are quoted mainly on the American Stock Exchange (the NYSE refused to list them until 1970), the excesses of the warrant market in the 1920s and 1930s had led to some suspicion of the concept. Since 1970, issuance has increased, and a number of market-index warrants are listed on the various U.S. exchanges. However, without the tax advantages that made warrants so attractive in Germany and, to a lesser extent, in Switzerland, or the large issue flow from Japanese issuers, which underpinned the growth of the Euro-warrant market, the purely domestic U.S. warrant market is relatively small in proportion to the underlying equity market.

On the German stock exchange, equity warrants have accounted for up to 14 percent of turnover at the height of the early boom in the 1980s. Part of the reason for the growth of the warrant market was that it benefited from favorable tax treatment. This arose from the fact that, until recently, it was possible to structure warrant packages that were certain to generate a profit that was tax-free to individual investors. The German stock exchange admits covered (and also uncovered) warrants to the "free market," which is the relatively lightly regulated division of the stock exchange. Admission to the main market would require issuers to deliver prospectuses in respect of the underlying stock, which is normally too laborious for them to do.

The origins of the German market go back to 1986–1987, when the market for Japanese warrants began to grow. This was followed by a growth in the domestic German market, particularly for warrants on stocks included in the

DAX index, issued by securities firms that are able to hedge the transaction in the DAX options market. Typically, these "covered warrants" are smaller in size than "traditional" warrants issued by the companies themselves. In April 1994, a total of 64 traditional warrants were outstanding on 38 companies. The market capitalization of the warrants was DEM11.7 billion, of which almost DEM6 billion was accounted for by 8 warrants. By contrast, 268 covered warrants were outstanding on 23 companies, for an aggregate market capitalization of DEM7.7 billion. There were, in addition, about 240 index warrants (puts and calls) outstanding on the DAX or other German market indexes.

The retail investor's role is equally important in the second major European warrant market, the Swiss market. The role played by warrants, and particularly covered warrants, in the Swiss market, is very striking. For example, market statistics for January 1994 show that the total turnover on pure Roche warrants by various issuers amounted to CHF976 million, or 16 percent of trading in all Roche shares (Inhaber and Namen combined). In addition, there was trading in Pharma Vision warrants (and shares), which represent indirect trading in Roche, because Pharma was a substantial holder of Roche shares. In the case of EMS Chemie—a substantially smaller company—turnover in one covered warrant equated to just under 50 percent of the share's turnover. Adding in the second warrant listed on EMS brought the warrant turnover to 71 percent of the share turnover. The importance of the warrant market in Switzerland appears to be partly due to the fact that warrants, unlike shares, were not subject to the Swiss stamp duty; also, they have benefited from the relatively late development of SOFFEX, the Swiss options and futures exchange.

An interesting development in the French warrants market has been the commitment by the Stock Exchange in Paris to attract warrant trading back to the Exchange from the OTC market. Its chosen method has been to sign *contrâts d'animation* with securities firms. Each contract is an agreement between the Exchange and the securities firm under which the firm commits to post, continuously, on the CAC system, bids and offers for a minimum number of warrants for a maximum agreed spread. (The size of the spread varies according to the delta of the warrant.) In exchange for this commitment, the Exchange grants favorable terms of access (lower fees) to the CAC system, recognizes the securities firm as a "specialist" in the security, and gives special access to certain other facilities.

Similarly, the Australian Stock Exchange Automated Trading (SEAT) system has greatly contributed to the growth of the Australian market. In early 1997, the London Stock Exchange announced it was exploring the possibility of a similar approach.

Elsewhere in Europe, warrant markets are relatively limited, although Italy has a well-established market in monthly options traded on the Stock Exchange ("premi"), somewhat akin to the traditional options traded on the London market for many years. In the Netherlands, rivalry between the EOE and the Amsterdam exchange, together with the latter's insistence (until December 1992) that covered warrant issues be 100 percent backed by pledged securities, seem to have combined to hold back the market. Other warrant markets in Europe are relatively limited—aside from Luxembourg, where numerous warrants are, of course, listed alongside the Eurobonds to which they are attached. These, however, are almost exclusively traded outside the Exchange, on the OTC market. Though relatively limited in size, active warrant markets exist also in Hong Kong, Thailand, and various other Far Eastern countries.

EQUITY WARRANT DEVELOPMENTS

Covered Warrants

A covered warrant may be defined as a warrant issued by a third party on the shares of a company. Some of the earliest covered warrants were issued by Citicorp (Switzerland) on Mitsubishi Corporation and Casio Computers. These Swiss franc warrants, directed at the Swiss retail market, were a repackaging of U.S. dollar-denominated warrants issued by the companies concerned. Much of the early activity in the covered warrant market was of a similar nature— repackaging Japanese warrants into Swiss francs for the Swiss retail market. As such, covered warrants came generally to be viewed simply as an expensive means of buying exposure to Japanese companies.

However, as so often occurs, once the technique was invented, other uses were found for it. During 1986, there were twelve issues of "Stillhalteroptionen" in the Swiss market: issues of warrants backed by a pledge of shares in the underlying company. Here, the covered warrant is not a repackaging of other warrants. It is an issue, by a third party, of warrants on the company, on the basis that the commitment to deliver the underlying shares is guaranteed by the pledge of shares (they are "held still" to meet the obligation). In some cases, the percentage of shares pledged was significant; the issue for Merkur Holding (June 1987) involved the pledge of 20 percent of the company's outstanding shares.

The rationale for the covered warrant issue is normally a perceived market arbitrage opportunity. The issuing firm believes that investors will find a warrant attractive at a price that will cover the issuing firm's costs in assembling the issue. In these circumstances, the issuer is not a natural holder of the underlying shares, but will need either to buy shares to protect against its delivery commitment under the warrant issue, or to hedge the risk by means of some form of delta hedging. Original market practice when covered warrants were issued was to hedge the liability to deliver shares by either purchasing them outright or arranging for investors to pledge shares. A typical example of such a transaction was the issue of covered warrants on ASEA Brown Boveri in 1989. In this transaction, investors purchasing warrants were assured of the delivery of the underlying ABB shares by an arrangement whereby the issuer of the warrants approached investors who held shares in ABB, and obtained from them pledges of sufficient equity to ensure that if the covered warrant were exercised by holders of the warrant, sufficient equity would be available to meet the requirements of the issue.

Since 1986, the volume of covered warrant issuance, in both the Swiss markets and elsewhere, has been, in the aggregate, substantial. Most recent covered warrant issues, however, unlike the "Stillhalteroptiomen," are not backed by the pledge of underlying securities. Rather, they are delta-hedged. Many of the equity warrants discussed below are issued in this manner.

It should be pointed out that, in addition to a market arbitrage activity, another rationale for the issue of a covered warrant might be that a substantial holder of a block of shares may use the covered warrant as a means of earning premium, which reduces the funding cost of holding shares. An interesting example is the activity of BZ Bank in Zurich. BZ Bank has created investment companies (BK Vision, Pharma Vision 2000, Gas Vision) that hold substantial blocks of shares in selected companies. Thus, Pharma Vision 2000 holds 8.4 percent of Roche bearer shares, 2.2 percent of its dividend right certificates (Genussscheine), and CHF533 million of call warrants on Roche, as well as 10.7 percent of Ciba-Geigy bearer shares. BK Vision at one point held 17.6 percent of UBS registered shares and 2 percent of UBS bearer shares. Both companies have issued warrants on a number of occasions. In effect, BZ used warrants to finance its ongoing battle with UBS's management.

LEPO Warrants

Mention was made in Chapter 7 of Low Exercise Price Options (LEPOs). Similarly, there exist LEPO warrants. An example would be the series of 12.5 million warrants issued by Salomon Brothers in July 1996, expiry December 11, 1997, on a basket of Russian equities. By structuring the warrants with a very low exercise price, they are made closely equivalent to the underlying shares. But the attraction for international investors is that they never need concern themselves with the risks and intricacies of settlement in the domestic Russian market. The warrants can be traded and settled through Euroclear, Cedel, or DKV (the German settlement system), in DEM, CHF, US$ or even Portuguese escudos. The offering price was US$2 or its equivalent in any of the other currencies, and the strike price was US$3. Such warrants operate effectively as synthetic equity. They have also been used to circumvent restrictions on foreign holdings of equities. For example, in 1993, an issue was brought to market of low-exercise price warrants on Rolls-Royce, the U.K. aero engine manufacturer (not the car manufacturer) where foreigners' holdings of the equity had reached the maximum limit.

Recently, the technique was used in a slightly different structure. In April 1997, SBC Warburg issued so-called "bloc" warrants on Clariant registered shares. The strike price of the warrants was set at zero. These are, in other words, low-exercise-price options. They were priced with a cap level fixed 2 percent below the share price at the time of issue. They are cash-settled if the underlying at expiration closes higher or at the cap; they are settled by physical delivery of the shares if it is below the cap at expiry.

Index Warrants

A very large range of warrants linked to individual equity market indexes has been issued. Over the years, many hundreds of these have been issued in different markets. In a typical recent example, Citibank issued 1.5 million call warrants on the Nikkei index in March 1997, expiring in July 1997, with a strike level of 20,000. This type of warrant mainly attracts investors seeking to follow a leveraged "top-down" investment approach—one in which the investor decides, say, to "buy Italy." Another application is that these warrants can be useful in markets where the underlying settlement mechanics are difficult or uncertain, or the investor does not wish to take "jurisdiction risk." Hence, warrants on a number of "emerging markets" have been made by issuers out of a location, such as Luxembourg or London, with which investors feel comfortable. As an example, in May 1996, Bankers Trust issued "index return certificates" on the Hungarian, Czech, and Polish markets, based on the Investable Indices published by the International Finance Corporation.

Money Back Warrants

In December 1985, an issue for Emerson Electric Company introduced the "money back" warrant. The issuer raised US$100 million in 10-year host bonds maturing in 1995 with a $9\frac{5}{8}$ percent coupon and a call option from 1990. Attached to it were 100,000 warrants into noncallable bonds on the same terms. Exercise must be accompanied by surrender of the host bond during the first 5 years, and by cash payment for the back bond during the last 5 years. So far, the structure is a conventional "harmless" warrant, as discussed below.

The innovation was that the warrants, with an issue price of $25 each and a 10-year life, could be put back to the issuer at $15 between December 28, 1990, and December 26, 1995, and at $25 on the redemption date of the bonds, December 27, 1995. Thus, in return for a relatively expensive warrant, the investor has the security of the put back to the issuer, and potentially greater liquidity, because warrants that are out of the money should trade like zero coupons. From the issuer's point of view, there is a possibility of having to give the warrant proceeds back, but at a substantial discount unless the put is only on the redemption date. In the latter case, the issuer has had the use of the warrant funds for 10 years, interest-free.

A recent example of the technique, which is now quite commonly used in various guises, was the issue, in February 1997, by SBC Warburg of 50,000 Protected Equity Participation units (PEPs) on a customized basket of Swiss industrial stocks. Each CHF5,000 unit was priced at par and offered holders a guaranteed minimum redemption payout of 93 percent, with no cap on the upside. Here, the money back guarantee is not complete.

SWORDs

Starting in 1988, a number of U.S. biotechnology firms, including ALZA, Centocor, Immunex, and Genzyme began to make use of a financing arrangement known as Stock Warrant Off-balance-sheet Research and Development (SWORD). They set up a separate research and development organization whose financing was provided by a public offering of units. The units consist of one share of the new venture's common stock, which can be called for redemption by the parent, and a warrant to buy one share of the parent's common stock. Although the parent suffers dilution if the warrant is exercised, the warrants were designed to align the incentives of investors and managers, and to signal that the new venture has value because the current shareholders are willing to share the value of assets in place.

Endowment Warrants

A structure that has been particularly popular in Australia is the so-called "endowment warrant." The typical structure is a long-dated call warrant with a variable strike price and variable maturity, limited to about 10 years. Basically, investors pay an up-front premium (between 30 percent and 60 percent of the underlying share price). They receive the shares without further outlay if interest rates average current levels and required dividend growth rates are met. Rising interest rates and falling dividend rates work against the investor.

There are two possible outcomes: (1) the dividend growth has been sufficient to pay off the sum required to buy the shares; or (2) the "outstanding amount" is not paid off at maturity—dividends have not paid off the share price value. In the latter case, the investor can either put up sufficient funds to pay the remaining balance, or choose to receive a cash settlement equal to the share price minus the "outstanding amount" and transactions costs.

Much of the popularity of these endowment warrants stems from the leveraged nature of the warrants, which resemble a leveraged equity account where dividends received are used to pay off the outstanding "borrowings." Australian pension funds have found this feature attractive. Foreign investors have been a second source of demand. Certain issues of endowment warrants offer a way of receiving dividend tax credits that are not normally available to foreign investors. At least AUS$60 million of warrants of this type were sold in January and February 1997.

GDR + Warrant

In 1993, Hindalco Industries of India launched a $72 million Global Depositary Receipt (GDR) offering (see Chapter 17) with warrants attached. The issue consisted of 4,473,000 units of one GDR and half a warrant. Each unit was priced at $16.10. Full exercise of the warrants, therefore, on a one-for-two basis will raise an additional $36 million in GDRs. The warrants have a 2-year life and can be exchanged, at any time during this period, at the issue price.

A number of other "emerging markets" issues have been done using the GDR together with a warrant. This type of offering provides potentially attractive, leveraged exposure to the underlying equity.

EBOR

The issue, in 1993, of Cemex put warrants, dubbed Equity Buyback Obligation Rights by the arranger, J. P. Morgan, would have been unusual in any market, let alone an emerging market. The deal came to market following a request from the Mexican cement company, which was concerned about its falling share price. This is an unusual example of a company sponsoring a put warrant on its own shares. Morgan was, in effect, the guarantor to the at-the-money put warrants, which Cemex hoped would prevent further selling. The company earned the premium from the issue and supported the stock by agreeing to buy it back at the strike price, which it considered a low level. At the time, the stock was trading at historical highs in volatility terms, so the company earned a substantial premium.

EXOTIC EQUITY WARRANTS

Resettable Warrants

An issue by Merrill Lynch, in December 1993, of warrants on the American Stock Exchange index of 30 Hong Kong stocks included—for the first time in a public issue in the United States—a reset provision on the warrant strike level. The issue of 2 million call warrants provides that if the warrant is exercised after the first 60 days, then the calculation basis for the strike level of the warrant will be the lower of the initial issue price and the value on the 60-day anniversary. Thus, if the Hong Kong market were to tumble between the issue date and the 60-day anniversary, investors would not lose out. The underlying option is a reset strike option of the type discussed in Chapter 7.

In November 1996, the International Finance Corporation issued 1,250,000 S&P 500 Index Bear Market Warrants with a 3-month reset provision. Upon exercise, holders were entitled to receive the cash equivalent, if positive, of:

$$\$50 \times \frac{\text{Index strike price} - \text{Index spot price}}{\text{Index strike price}}.$$

The reset provision was: If the closing level of the index on February 20, 1997, was above 743.95, the strike price for the warrants would be reset to the higher value. The warrants were American-style (exercisable at any time).

Exercise was subject to certain limits: a minimum of 500 warrants at any one time, and a maximum of 250,000 by any one entity. Total exercise exceeding 1 million warrants on a single day would be subject to pro rata selection by the warrant agent.

A recent resettable warrant issue was also an asset-backed issue. Tulip International Ltd., a Cayman Islands special-purpose vehicle, issued ¥1.9995 billion of zero-coupon bonds with warrants attached. Each warrant is exercisable into 104 shares of Sanko Gosei Ltd. The warrant exercise price was ¥820, but it could be reset on April 24, 1998, and April 23, 1999, subject to a floor of 80 percent of the initial exercise price. The asset backing for the Tulip issue was a zero-coupon convertible bond issued by Sanko Gosei.

Outperformance Warrants

A number of warrants have been issued on the relative performance of two or more shares. (The underlying options are discussed in Chapter 7.) A typical example might be BZW's issue in August 1994. This was a play on the share price relationship between Cable and Wireless and its Hong Kong subsidiary, Hong Kong Telecom, in which it holds a 57 percent stake. The payout at expiry, in August 1995, was set at 50 pence plus the difference between one Cable and Wireless share and 2.95 Hong Kong Telecom shares (in sterling, converted at the prevailing exchange rate). Using a scaling factor of 2.95 reflects Cable and Wireless's holding in Hong Kong Telecom—for each of its own shares, Cable and Wireless owns 2.95 Hong Kong Telecom shares. The 50 pence is added to the payout so that the warrant is effectively deep in the money, and so moves closely with the "rump"—the value of Cable and Wireless without Hong Kong Telecom.

Another outperformance warrant was issued, in August 1994, by S. G. Warburg on the Swedish investment company Investor and its unlisted car and truck subsidiary, Saab Scania. This was a European-style warrant maturing December 21, 1995, and paying out the percentage performance of Investor minus the percentage performance of its listed core holdings.

A similar issue was the January 1997 issue by BZW of spread warrants on Reed and Elsevier shares. The issue was split into two tranches of 15 million units, one in guilders and one in sterling. For the latter, issued at 110.25 pence, the payout is (0.769 Reed – 1 Elsevier) + 250p; for the former, the payout is (0.769 Reed – 1 Elsevier) + NLG 6.28.

Range Warrants

As discussed in Chapter 7, options can be created to pay off if the underlying remains within a certain range—or, conversely, moves outside it.

Recent examples of this type of range structure include Bankers Trust's Expected to Accrue Return on Nominal (EARN) warrants. The payout of an

EARN warrant with a maturity of 1 year and a maximum payout of P is P*N/365 where N is the number of days that the underlying stays inside the barrier. The accrued amount is paid to the warrant holder at expiry. If the underlying stays inside the barrier throughout the life of the warrant, the investor earns P*365/365—the maximum. If the underlying stays within the barrier for, say, 183 days, then the payout is P*183/365 = P*0.5014.

As the spot price moves away from the middle of the range, value goes down rapidly because the probability of staying inside the band decreases. This means that the exposure to the underlying can be long or short, depending on the location of the spot. Similarly, the exposure of the warrant to volatility depends on the location of the spot relative to the bands. If the spot is within the range, value decreases with rising volatility because the chance of moving outside the range increases.

The transaction has been done in two variants: (1) single direction or (2) double direction (also called "dual accrual"). In the latter case, every day the underlying spot trades outside the range, a positive day is deducted. The payout for a 1-year warrant would then be P*max(0,N outside – N inside)*365.

Six series of these warrants were issued, in July 1996, on the US$/DEM exchange rate. These warrants were structured as dual accrual, whereby the payoff is based on the number of days the rate fixes within the range, less the number of days the rate is outside, multiplied by a DEM multiplier. For example, one series issued July 21, 1996, for expiry February 21, 1997, at a premium of DEM3.81 had a range of DEM1.45–1.55 and a multiplier of DEM0.046948357.

Merrill Lynch issued a similar series of dual-range warrants on Winterthur Insurance in July 1996. The accrual period was 116 days, and the final expiry was on December 20, 1996. The warrants pay CHF0.0877 for each day the stock trades within the range of CHF750 to CHF825 during the accrual period, less CHF0.0877 for each day the stock trades outside the range. Maximum payout was CHF10 per warrant, with the issue price being CHF3.30.

Another structure of this kind was Bankers Trust's so-called "sleepy warrant." Issued in July 1996 for expiry in February 1997, the Sleepy 85 series guaranteed a payout of DEM10 per warrant if the US$/DEM exchange rate remained between DEM1.4465–1.5515. It paid DEM4.25 (85 percent of the initial premium of DEM5.00) otherwise. BT launched similar US$/DEM warrants in May 1997, for maturity December 1997. There were three series; each paid out DEM10 if the currency remained within the range, as against the initial purchase price of DEM, so investors were offered the chance to double their money. Warrants with a range of 1.66–1.78 pay out DEM4.00 if the range is broken. Those with a range of 1.64–1.80 pay out DEM3.50, and those with a range of 1.63–1.82 pay out DEM2.50 if the range is broken.

A variant of this structure was the "onion" structure, consisting of a range within a range. In May 1996, Bankers Trust issued such warrants on the US$/DEM exchange rate. The issue price per warrant was DEM10. If the exchange rate trades within $1 = DEM1.43–1.61, Bankers Trust pays DEM10 at maturity of the warrant. If the exchange rate trades within a narrower range—$1 = DEM1.46–1.59—Bankers Trust pays DEM 20.

Similar warrants, where the investor benefits if the price stays within a certain range, are sometimes called corridor warrants. An example would be the issue by Société Générale of a corridor warrant on the FTSE index in July 1996. The warrants had an issue price of £165.60, with exercise determined by the number of days the FTSE trades outside a range of £3,500–4,000. If the index remained within the corridor for the whole period, until July 2, 1997, the investor payoff would be 52.8 percent.

A different variant is where the range structure is applied to several underlying assets. For example, in April 1996, Bankers Trust issued 1 million so-called "Quattro" range warrants on four asset classes: (1) the Bund 6 percent February 2006; (2) the US$/DEM cross rate; (3) the DAX equity index; and (4) the LIFFE 3-month deutsche mark December 1996 future. The issue price was DEM10. The ranges for each asset class were: (1) 94.50–99.00; (2) 1.4370–1.5800; (3) 2,350–2,700; and (4) 96.10–96.80, respectively. The payout was calculated as the number of ranges remaining unbroken during the life of the warrant, multiplied by DEM20, giving a maximum payout of DEM80.

In July 1996, Bankers Trust structured a series of 150,000 calls on four European stock indexes, where the payout was DEM20 for each index trading within a specified range until maturity on February 11, 1997. The indexes were (with the ranges in parentheses): DAX (2,450–2,675), FTSE (3,580–3,900), CAC-40 (1,955–2,200), and SMI (3,625–3,950). Issue price was DEM10 and the maximum payoff was DEM80 per warrant.

Figure 15.4 illustrates the behavior of some of the warrants issued by Bankers Trust and referred to in this chapter.

In January 1997, Crédit Lyonnais issued four sets of range warrants on the Swiss equity market (the SMI index), including a "range hot-dog" warrant. Under this structure, holders of the 100,000 warrants issued would be paid CHF1 for each day the SMI is within the bands. For the first 2 months, the bands were set at 3,900–4,100; for the next 2 months, at 3,850–4,150; and for the last 2 months, at 3,850–4,150. Each warrant cost CHF70.

Knockout Warrants

In April 1993, the Swiss drug company Roche issued a $1 billion Eurobond with knockout warrants. Each $10,000 7-year 2.75 percent bond was issued with 46 knockout call warrants on Roche Genussscheine (Swiss/German term for an equity participating in profits but nonvoting). Sixty warrants are required for exercise into one Genussschein. The warrants incorporated a floor conditional on the knockout level of CHF5,000 not being reached and an unconditional cap at CHF6,000. Like a conventional with-warrant structure, an attractive feature for the issuer was that the bond remains outstanding until

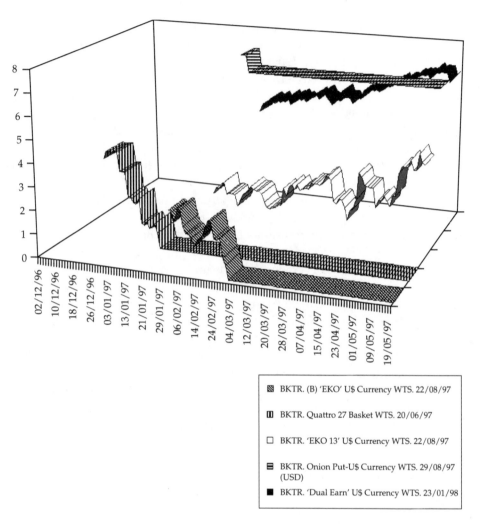

Figure 15.4 Some "exotic" warrants from Bankers Trust.

maturity, regardless of whether the investor chooses to exercise the warrants. This certainty enables the bond proceeds to be swapped, unlike the proceeds of a traditional convertible, where the issuer is uncertain how long investors will hold the bond before converting it to equity.

This issue was followed shortly thereafter by Benetton, the Italian clothing company, which issued an ITL200 billion Eurobond to which were attached call warrants on Benetton stock with an embedded knockout put. Terms are as follows: the warrant exercise price was ITL17,983 per share (a 4 percent discount from the share price at time of issue—the "base price" of ITL18,733). It was European-style, maturing on July 29, 1996. The put may be exercised at ITL21,543 (15 percent above the base price). The knockout level was at ITL24,353 (30 percent above the base price). Lastly, the performance of the warrant was capped at a maximum of ITL29,973 (60 percent above the base price). The warrants were listed in Luxembourg.

If, on the day after the issue, Benetton's share price collapsed and remained low until the maturity of the warrant, an investor buying the warrant was guaranteed a total return of 19.8 percent (we sell at 115 percent, having bought at 96 percent). But if the share price rises by 30 percent, the knockout comes into effect, and the put disappears. From that point on, the warrant would trade like any other call warrant, except that it had a built-in cap at the 60 percent level—and therefore would probably underperform once the shares got close to the cap level. The maximum total return is 66.67 percent (sell at 160 percent, having bought at 96 percent). The minimum is the total loss of the price paid today for the warrant, that is, −100 percent.

The investor faces the following possible returns:

	Percent
The share price rises by 30 percent, then collapses	−100
The share price never rises by more than 30 percent, and finishes below the put strike level	19.8
The share price rises by 30 percent, and then finishes between today's price and the cap level.	0 to 66.67
The share price rises by more than 60 percent	66.67

The attractions to the investor were: (1) there was no listed derivative instrument on Benetton stock, so the warrant did present an alternative; (2) the partial protection afforded by the knockout put did provide disaster insurance (provided the share price had not risen in the interim). The cost of the package to the investor is reduced by the knockout feature—the investor gets less protection, so the option is worth less—and by the fact that the investor is effectively selling back to the issuer a call option with a strike level 60 percent above the base price. One of the normal attractions of a warrant—gearing—is missing, because the purchase price of the warrant is approximately the same as the share price.

Digital Knockout Warrants

A version of the EARN warrants described earlier was introduced by Bankers Trust in February 1997: EARNS that knock out, or EKO warrants. The first two tranches expired in four months, with ranges of DEM1.63–1.85 and DEM1.60–1.78, respectively. The issue prices were DEM5 and DEM4.90, and the warrants paid DEM10 as long as the exchange rate stayed within the band until expiry.

In March 1997, Lehman Brothers issued 5 million European-style "X-Tra Chance" calls on the stocks of Deutsche Bank and Deutsche Telekom. These are cash-settled calls—holders will receive the payoff in DEM but, in addition, they will receive DEM10 if the stock price does not fall below the knockout level. The Deutsche Bank calls, for example, cost DEM7.25 with the strike set at DEM98 and the knockout level set at DEM88.

BOOSTs

In April 1994, Société Générale introduced instruments it christened Banking On Overall Stability (BOOSTs). Essentially, these were the warrant equivalents of range notes. The underlying asset must remain within a pre-fixed range. Every day that it does so, the investor earns one currency unit. Thus, if a 1-year BOOST remains within the set range throughout its life, the investor earns $365 (less the up-front cost of the product). If the asset falls outside of the range after 100 days, the investor earns $100 (again, less up-front costs). The initial product launch included six different series of BOOSTs over 1 and 2 years, at the DEM/FRF and US$/DEM exchange rates for OATs and Bunds.

   Although one of the first BOOSTS was knocked out before investors got a chance to break even, others were more successful. One offered investors $1,000 per day for each day sterling traded within the band, over and above the first 60 days (which effectively represented the break-even rate on the $60,000 premium). The structure was knocked out by mid-July 1994, by which time investors had made a 75 percent profit.

Quanto Warrants

Just as quanto options (discussed in Chapter 7) are available, so are quanto warrants available. An example would be the issue by Morgan Stanley of 85,000 Quanto Index Call Warrants on the Nikkei 225 index. The calls were European-style and denominated in DEM. The issue price was DEM159.3 per warrant with the issue date August 6, 1996, and expiry on June 27, 2000. The payout is the notional amount in DEM determined by the weekly average of the opening sessions in the Nikkei 225 during the first 13 weeks after initial trading, divided by the weekly average of the last 13 weeks before maturity—in other words, the percentage change in the Nikkei 225 over the period, payable in deutsche marks.

Chooser Warrants

As in the options markets (see Chapter 7), chooser structures are possible in the warrants. They have obvious applications in highly uncertain situations. For example, in 1994, Citibank launched a capped chooser warrant on the DAX index on September 26. The 10-million-warrant issue was aimed at retail influences that were uncertain about the effect of the forthcoming German election on the stock market. The strike price was fixed at-the-money at 2,106, which was the closing value of the DAX on Friday, October 14, the last working day before the elections. When the DAX fell to 2,091 the day after the elections, the warrants became put warrants. Holders of the European-style warrants were entitled to DEM0.015 per point difference between the DAX closing level and the strike price at maturity on October 17, 1995; the cap restricted the maximum payout to DEM6.33 per warrant.

Chooser warrants were also issued to give investors the possibility of property from any dramatic strengthening or weakening of the DEM after the election. On October 5, 1996, SBC Warburg issued 5 million European-style choosers on the US$/DEM exchange rate. They would become calls if the forward rate on October 17 exceeded the strike price, and puts if not. The forward rate was calculated from the formula:

$$T = S + \frac{(D - U) \times S \times t}{36,000 + (D \times t)}$$

where T = US$/DEM forward rate;
       D = 2-month DM LIBOR;
       U = 2-month US$ LIBOR;
       S = US$/DEM spot rate on October 17;
       t = lifetime (92 days).

The strike price was set at-the-money at DEM1.55, and the options were exercisable on January 17, 1995. Each warrant entitled the holder to buy or sell $100 from or to SBC Warburg on this date. The initial price was DEM4.80; the warrants became puts on October 17, when the spot rate fell to US$1/DEM1.5030. By October 27, the warrant price had risen to DEM6.55, giving a paper profit of 36 percent to those who bought at issue.

Look-Back Warrants

Look-back warrants have also been issued on a number of shares, including "emerging market" shares. For example, in October 1992, Bankers Trust issued a look-back call warrant, exercisable until October 28, 1993, at the lower of US$48.50 (Telmex NYSE close on October 28, 1992) and the lowest Telmex close during the following month.

Capped Warrants

Many warrants have been issued on the basis that there is a "cap" to the payout on the warrant. An example is the so-called Discount Purchase Options (DIPOs) issued by Citibank in July 1996. They were European-style warrants on the registered stock of SBC. If the price of the stock were above the cap level of CHF227.50 on the expiry date, July 22, 1997, warrant holders would receive the cap amount per warrant. Otherwise, they would receive the physical stock.

Basket Warrants

Numerous issues of "basket warrants" have been made, whereby the investor buys a warrant and becomes entitled to a group, or "basket" of underlying stocks. The economics of these deals are similar to the basket options discussed in Chapter 7.

A typical example would be the issue, by SBC Warburg, of 120 million call warrants relating to a basket of Italian industrial companies. The warrants were issued at an issue price of ITL222 per warrant. Each lot of 20 warrants could be exercised during the period from May 12, 1994, to August 31, 1995, and would entitle the holder to buy, at an exercise price of ITL24,549, a basket of shares made up as follows: Montedison, 5 shares; Olivetti, 2 shares; Fiat, 1 share; Pirelli, 1 share per basket.

The basket warrant technique also allows investment banks to create instruments that appeal to a particular type of investment view. An example is the "devaluation warrants" issued by UBS Phillips & Drew after sterling's departure from the ERM in the autumn of 1992. About 3 weeks after the crisis, UBS Phillips & Drew issued call warrants on a basket containing 14 different U.K. companies' shares: BTR (90 shares); ECC (12); TI (21); Guinness (90); Unilever (36); Thorn EMI (18); SmithKline Beecham (114); Allied Lyons (39); ICI (32); Courtaulds (18); British Airways (33); BAT (66); Lasmo (33); and HSBC (110).

The stocks were selected by UBS as those most likely to benefit from the devaluation of sterling. An average of 85 percent of the companies' earnings came from overseas, and they were all highly geared, standing to benefit from the fall in U.K. interest rates.

The implied volatility of the basket was above 25 percent, but the warrant was priced off a figure of 21 percent. However, the correlation to the FTSE 100 was relatively high, and the market-implied volatilities for FTSE options out to next year were around 17 percent at the time of issue. The terms of the issue were:

UBS Phillips & Drew Select Basket Warrants

Issuer: Union Bank of Switzerland, London.

Number of warrants: 1 million calls.

Exercise: 25 warrants control one basket of the select baskets (each containing 712 U.K. shares).

Exercise style: American.

Exercise period: November 11, 1992, until December 31, 1993.

Exercise price: £426.6.

Issue price: £414.20.

Premium: 13 percent.

Gearing: 10 times.

Listing: Luxembourg.

The basket approach can also be used to handle the cross-currency complications of an international sector; an example might be the issue by Banque Nationale de Paris, in May 1996, of warrants, maturing October 1997, on the international luxury goods sector: LVMH and Hermes, quoted in FRF in Paris; Gucci and Tiffany, quoted in US$ in New York; Bulgari, quoted in ITL in Milan; and Vendome, quoted in British pounds, in London. The issuer was BNP (Luxembourg), guaranteed by BNP Paris. Two series of 500,000 warrants were issued, the first in FRF hedged back into FRF, the second in US$ with hedging into US$. These were American-style warrants exercisable from May 1996 to maturity, and they were quoted on the Paris Bourse from the date of issue.

An exotic example of the genre was seen, in July 1996, when SBC Warburg brought to market Performance Linked to Equity Securities (PERLES) on a basket of five Peruvian American Depositary Receipts (ADRs) with a launch value of $1,008.75. Each PERLE referred to one basket, and holders will receive 100 percent of the spot price of the basket at expiry on July 19, 1999. The issue price for the PERLE was $1,013.80.

Sector Warrants

A specific subclass of basket warrants is warrants issued on stock market sectors. A large number of investment banks have issued warrants related to the performance of a specific market sector. For example, BNP, the French bank, issued, in 1994, a set of warrants that between them, covered the entire French stock market as represented by the SBF120 index—that is, a set of 12 warrants, subdivided into at-the-money, 10 percent out-of-the-money, and 20 percent out-of-the-money strikes. These were 2-year warrants, American-style, traded on the Paris Stock Exchange.

WARRANTS ON FIXED-INCOME INSTRUMENTS AND FOREIGN EXCHANGE

Warrants on fixed-income instruments have also developed rapidly in recent years. Broadly, we can classify them into the following major categories, reflecting in part the historical evolution of the market:

1. "Harmless" warrants, "wedding" warrants, and other variants of warrants allowing the investor to buy some other bond;

2. "Income warrants" and "floor warrants";

3. Currency and gold warrants;

4. Interest rate direction warrants (i.e., a play on the change in level of rates);

5. "Spread warrants"(i.e., a play on the change in relationship between one or more rates);

6. Other, exotic warrants.

Harmless Warrants

Harmless, or refunding, warrants were first introduced in 1985. The original concept was as follows. A $100 million bond would be issued, say, at 10 percent, for redemption in 5 years' time, and a call after 3 years. (This 10 percent bond is often referred to as the "front" bond or the "host" bond—it "hosts" the warrants.) A 3-year warrant was also issued, with expiry at the time of the first call on the 10 percent bond.

The warrant could be exercised into a new 5-year bond, say, at 9 percent. (This bond is often referred to as the "back" bond, or the "virgin" bond.) So, if rates fell 1 percent, the warrants would have value and would be exercised at expiry, but the proceeds of issuing the new 9 percent bond could be used to call the 10 percent bond. This concept had a potential problem. If the warrants were exercised before the call date, the issuer could be forced to increase the amount of debt outstanding. The idea depended heavily on investors' not exercising the warrants until the end of the warrants' lives. Experience shows that this tends to be the case, but in a longer-term warrant there can still be substantial early exercise. So there is still a risk from the issuer's viewpoint, particularly if the original issue had been swapped into floating-rate funds as the purpose of the exercise. To be left with unexpected fixed-rate debt was unattractive.

Some issuers solved this problem by agreeing with their swap counterparties that a contingent swap would take place—swaps would be written to match any warrants exercised.

Wedding Warrants

Another solution was introduced in October 1985: the "wedding warrant." The warrant is "wedded" to the host bond, in the sense that, until the call date on the host bond, the warrant can be exercised only by surrendering an equal amount of the host bond. That is, if I wanted to exercise $1 million of the back bond, I must surrender $1 million of the host bond with the warrant for the exercise to be effective. After the call date on the host bond, exercise of the warrant is for cash. An example of the concept was the issue by Gaz de France, in October 1985, of $100 million of 11 percent 10-year host bonds, callable at par in the last 5 years. They were accompanied by 100,000 10-year warrants into a 10-year noncallable back bond that had the same terms as the front bonds. In the first 5 years, the warrants can be exercised only by putting back for early redemption an equal face value of front bonds. During the last 5 years, the warrants are exercisable into back bonds in cash at 100.

The arguments in favor of this concept for the issuer are that it has control of its total liabilities. For the investor, it has been argued that although the warrant is not a normal cash warrant for the first 5 years, it still has value. The price at which the front bond trades in the market is influenced by its call feature. If rates fall sharply, the bonds will trade on yield to call rather than yield to maturity. Correspondingly, if yields begin to rise again, the bond's price will deteriorate more slowly than the market's—the "cushion bond" effect. Hence, the warrant allows the investor to switch between bonds of different volatilities, because the back bond will not be influenced by any call feature.

Against this, critics argued strongly that wedding warrants are liable to be highly illiquid during the period when exercise must be accompanied by front bonds, because of the likely illiquidity of the host bond issue. A number of warrant market makers refused to trade this type of warrant on these grounds, arguing that the investor might as well lock away the wedding warrants for the first 5 years and forget them.

Warrants into Another Bond

A number of issuers have issued bonds accompanied by warrants to purchase additional bonds, usually at a later date. For example, SNCF issued FRF6 billion of 7¾ percent bonds in March 1993, accompanied by a warrant allowing holders to purchase 8⅞ percent notes due August 11, 2023, issued by SNCF at 107.06 percent from May 10, 1993, to May 14, 1993. This allowed investors the possibility of gambling on a further sharp fall in interest rates at a time when rates were already falling sharply.

A similar technique was used by Autobahnen und Schnellstrassen-Finanzierungs-AG (guaranteed by the Republic of Austria). This entity issued, in April 1992, DEM 300 million of 8 percent Series A bonds 1992–2002, together with warrants allowing the holder to buy 8 percent Series B bonds at 101.25 on April 22, 1994; 100.75 on April 22, 1995; and at 100.5 in 1996. The same approach of allowing the investor the opportunity to buy more bonds is extended over 3 years.

A variant of this technique is to issue a bond accompanied by a warrant into a bond issued by another issuer. For example, Bank Nederlandse Gemeenten issued, in May 1993, notes with warrants attached. The warrants, issued by UBS, entitled holders to acquire either FRF2,000 of 8.5 percent OATs due 2003 at 107.5, or, at the issuer's discretion, an amount in FRF equal to FRF2,000 × V + A, where V = the closing price of the OAT on the day of exercise and A = accrued interest. In other words, UBS has the option to deliver the cash equivalent.

The logical next step was to issue the warrants directly, without bothering with an accompanying bond; for example, Deutsche Bank, in July 1986, issued

10,000 warrants exercisable into the Federal Republic of Germany 1986–1996 5¾ percent bonds during a 9-month exercise period. Similarly, Morgan Bank Nederland issued, in August 1986, 10,000 warrants (named Fixed Term Agreements of Short-Term Call Options on Netherlands Securities—FASCONS). They offered a 1-year exercise period and the holder could buy the 6¼ percent Dutch government bonds due August 1996.

Warrants Used to Create Synthetic Zeros

During early 1996, Italian investors were seeking methods to circumvent Italian capital gains tax rules. A flood of MTNs denominated in lira were issued featuring detachable warrants designed to minimize investors' exposure to coupon flows. Detachable warrants equal in value to the cash flow of a conventional zero were attached to the MTNs and immediately sold by the investor. This created an effective original issue discount, which was not taxable under Italian tax rules. Rapidly growing demand for the structure led the Banca d'Italia to announce, in June 1996, that it would no longer approve such structures issued in lira.

Cross-Currency Bond Warrants

Another warrant variant that should be mentioned is cross-currency warrants. An example is the Northern Telecom issue in October 1985, which consisted of US$50 million of 10 percent bonds coupled with 60,000 warrants at $15 apiece, allowing conversion into a 6-year ECU bond with a coupon of 8¾ percent. The idea was to allow investors who were cautious about the US$ the ability to switch into the ECU, a natural hedge. However, because the ECU coupon was perceived to be too low in relation to others available in the market, the issue did not trade well.

In an analogous issue, Standard Oil, in October 1986, issued CHF150 million of 7-year bonds with a coupon of 3⅛ percent, coupled with warrants to buy gold. Each bond of CHF5,000 carried one warrant entitling the holder to buy 3.3 fine troy ounces of gold at $565.20. The warrants had a four-year exercise period (November 1987–November 1991) and allowed monthly exercise.

Monetizing the Call Option

A number of issuers have used the warrant market to allow them to convert into cash today the value of the call option in an existing bond. An example is the issue by Dutch State Mines (DSM) in January 1986, of 150,000 warrants at $35 each. The warrants carried the right to buy, after 2 years, a 3-year 10¾ percent bond maturing in 1991. Not by coincidence, DSM had an outstanding issue of $150 million 11⅜ percent bonds, callable from March 1988 and maturing in 1991. In effect, by issuing the warrants, DSM cashed in today the value of the call option 2 years hence. If rates did not fall, it would effectively reduce its total borrowing cost by the $5.25 million warrant proceeds. But, in exchange, it committed itself to issue at $10\frac{3}{4}$ percent if rates fall to a point where warrant holders will exercise. It would be indifferent on that point only if the original borrowing had been swapped to final maturity rather than to the call date.

Warrants on Government Bonds

A very large number of warrants on government bonds have been issued in different markets. These offer attractive opportunities for speculating on the direction of interest rates. Given the underlying liquidity in the government bond markets, the hedging of these warrants is not too difficult.

In 1983, for example, a number of investment banks launched warrants allowing the investor to buy U.S. Government bonds at a set price. Salomon Brothers, for example, launched Warrants into Negotiable Government Securities (WINGS). Another example was the issue of Euro-Treasury Warrants by Merrill Lynch. Three hundred thousand warrants to buy $10\frac{3}{8}$ percent Treasury bonds, due 2012, at a price of $91\frac{3}{4}$ percent were issued in August 1983, at a price of $18.75 per warrant. The warrant exercise period ran for 6 months, from August 1983 to February 1984. After deducting the cost to Merrill of hedging its commitment to deliver Treasuries to warrant holders, the balance of the $5.625 million issue proceeds was used for general corporate purposes.

A typical European example would be the issue of 2 million call warrants by Société Générale, in January 1990. These were exercisable into the $8\frac{1}{8}$ percent OAT due May 25, 1999. Each call warrant entitled the holder to buy one OAT for a nominal FRF2,000 at a flat price of 90.91. The warrants, whose maturity was 2 years, were priced at FRF101.80.

The same issuer, in August 1992, through Société Générale Acceptance NV, issued an interesting variant: call warrants on the OAT $8\frac{1}{2}$ percent, due 2002. The warrant strike price was resettable after 1 month. The point was that, during that month, the referendum on the Maastricht Treaty was due; hence, investors were buying the ability to reset the strike after the result of the referendum was known.

Income Warrants

Income warrants were introduced in December 1985, in an issue for Banque Francaise du Commerce Exterieur (BFCE). They followed on the introduction of wedding warrants, referred to earlier. With a wedding warrant, the investor effectively was faced with holding the warrant for a long time before being able to exercise without buying the host bond as well. There were objections that the investor was tying up money in the wedding warrants, which were effectively worthless until the redemption date on the host bond. Income warrants provided an answer; they paid an income on the warrant.

Here, the borrower raised a total of $300 million: $270 million in 10-year and 3-month FRNs (due March 1996), coupled with 300,000 5-year income warrants at an issue price of $100 and carrying a coupon of 9.25 percent. Each warrant was exercisable into a 9.75 percent 10-year and 3-month noncallable bond, due March 1996, at a price of $900 per $1,000 nominal value. The warrants are exercisable on each interest date (i.e., 20 times in the 5 years). Note that the investor is given a strong incentive to exercise the warrants; the bond is priced at 90 percent instead of par. Hence, the relatively more expensive warrants and the need to pay coupons on the warrant.

The attraction to the issuer is this. If the warrants expire unexercised, they make a $30 million capital profit after 5 years. They also pay interest on only $270 million rather than $300 million. But if the warrants are exercised, they achieve cheap short-term funding via the FRN. For the investor, if the warrants are converted in year 5, the new bonds yield 12.56 percent. In this case, if all the warrants were exercised in year 5, the issuer would have a $30 million 5-year fixed-rate borrowing at a coupon of 9.75 percent. But, LIBOR would have to have averaged 8.5 percent in year 1 and 11 percent thereafter for the overall cost of this $30 million tranche to exceed the cost of a comparable 10-year fixed-rate bond (10.3 percent). Hence, even on this assumption, the income warrants approach was probably attractive to the issuer. From the investor's point of view, although the warrants were relatively high-priced and therefore offered less leverage, they could, for the first time, be match funded. The income warrant concept has proved popular and has been introduced elsewhere; for example, Rhone Poulenc, in March 1986, raised FRF600 million in the Euro-French market with an income warrants bond.

A logical development of the income warrants structure was to create put warrants rather than call warrants; this was done with a Bank of Nova Scotia issue, in May 1986. Coupled to the $150 million 5-year bond issue at 7⅞ percent were 120,000 warrants priced at $12 each, bearing interest at the same rate as the bond. They were used to sell the bond back to the borrower at a price of 98.375 percent on June 30, 1989.

Floor Certificates

In April 1993, the World Bank issued floating rate notes paying 6-month DEM LIBOR + ¼ percent, subject to a cap of 7.25 percent from the April 1995 coupon date. They bore no minimum but were accompanied by a separate issue of 20,000 certificates, each enabling holders to receive the difference between 7 percent and LIBOR, where LIBOR is below 7 percent. A similar issue was made by BMW at about the same time.

In May 1993, Britannia Building Society issued £100 million of 4-year floating rate notes paying a coupon of LIBOR + 15 basis points, together with Additional Detachable Income Rights, which entitled the holder to receive 5 percent

– 3-month LIBOR if 3-month LIBOR falls below 5 percent. In other words, these were also separate floor certificates.

Interest Rate Direction Plays

REX and Other Index Warrants.   A number of warrants have been issued on the basis that a warrant gives the investor a return linked to the performance of a specific bond index. A typical example would be the issue of REX warrants, in 1991, by Salomon Brothers. The REX index is based on the most liquid segments of the German bond market: 30 notional bonds with whole-number maturities of 1 to 10 years, and 3 coupon classes (6 percent, 7.5 percent, and 9 percent), each weighted with its respective market share. The Salomon Brothers issue was for 5 million put and call warrants. Each call warrant entitled the holder to receive from the issuer the difference by which the closing price of the REX index on the exercise day exceeded the exercise price. The issue price was DEM2.80 per call warrant; the exercise price was 96.00 (compared with a market level of 95.88).

CMT Yield Increase Warrants.   In January 1994, Merrill Lynch filed to issue 1 million Constant Maturity U.S. Treasury Yield Increase Warrants. These pay investors $400 times the increase, if any, in the yield on 5-year CMT bonds. Thus, if the CMT yield rises 1 basis point, investors receive $4 per warrant. Because the warrants paid off if rates rose, there was a danger in fixing them to a specific 5-year Treasury bond. All other things equal, such a bond's yield would decline over time as its maturity shortened; investors would "roll down the yield curve." Hence the decision to index the warrant to the CMT yield, which gets round this problem.

Yield Decrease Warrants.   In 1992, Paine Webber issued Long Bond Yield Decrease Warrants, representing a play on 30-year bond yields. The warrant entitled the holder to receive, upon exercise, an amount equal to $0.10 × (strike yield – spot yield × 100). At date of issue, the strike yield was 8.35 percent. Originally issued at $4¼, the spot yield would have to be 7.93 percent to break even. A spot yield of 7.50 percent would double the investor's money [$0.10 × (8.35 – 7.50) × 100]. A spot yield of 8.35 percent would return nothing to the investor. The high degree of volatility generated the nickname "Turbo Warrants."

Spread Warrants

In August 1992, Caisse des Depots et Consignations brought Bund/OAT yield spread puts and calls. The deutsche mark warrants, 1,000 calls and 1,000 puts, were on the differential between two benchmark Bund-OAT yields. The strike of both the calls and the puts was DEM2.950, with each basis point equal to DEM100. The warrants were priced with forward yield rates up to the date of expiry, which stood at close to 120 basis points at time of pricing, giving the warrants at-the-money strikes.

Likewise, in August 1992, Société Générale brought a French franc OAT call issue that offered investors the opportunity to reset the strike price at the money on September 28 if the market level were lower than the current strike price, or leave it unchanged if OATs rallied after the September 20 vote on the Maastricht Treaty. If the strike were not reset, the warrant would be fully fungible with tranche E of Société Générale's July issue of OAT warrants.

Warrants on Currencies

A huge range of warrants has been issued on currencies; given the liquidity of the underlying market, this area has been one of the most dynamic in all the international securities markets. Again, most of the activity has been in the international rather than the U.S. markets.

This area of the market began to develop relatively early, mainly because of the liquidity of the underlying markets, which made hedging relatively easy. In October 1983, Phibro-Salomon issued 100,000 call warrants on sterling, and 100,000 put warrants, exercisable at $1.52 and $1.46 respectively, with a 1-year exercise period. The same issuer later made issues of DEM and ECU warrants.

A typical recent example of such a warrant attached to a new bond issue is the issue, in Netherlands guilders, by ABN Amro of NLG500 million of 9⅛ percent subordinated bonds 1992–2002, which were accompanied by one warrant for each bond, enabling holders to buy NLG10,000 cash at the fixed exchange rate of US$1 = NLG 1.9378, exercisable on January 15, 2002, by cash payment or surrender of a bond. This was a European-style warrant.

Many firms, of course, issue currency warrants on their own, i.e., without an accompanying bond issue. The object of the exercise is to sell investors tradable currency option instruments that have a longer maturity than those available on the standard exchanges, or are precisely tailored to perceived investor demand. Banks active in the foreign exchange markets, such as Citibank, have issued hundreds of such warrants over the years. (A search on Datastream, in May 1997, showed Citibank listed as having 1,478 warrants outstanding, and Société Générale as having 743 warrants outstanding. In both cases, the largest single group was currency warrants.)

A variant was the development of a capped warrant that limited the payout on the warrant. A typical example might be the issue by the Council of Europe, in August 1992, of capped US$/DEM call and put warrants. Each of the 350,000 call warrants entitled the holder to receive from the issuer 1,000 times the difference by which the official US$ mid-price on the Frankfurt foreign exchange fixing on the exercise day exceeds the exercise price, subject to a cap of DEM400 per call warrant. The 3-year warrants were issued at a price of DEM111.40 per call warrant with an exercise price of DEM1.55; the put warrants, similarly capped, were issued with a strike price of DEM1.95 at a premium of DEM208 per warrant.

Power Warrants

Among the instruments that are definitely only for the brave, "power calls" have been issued on Russian dollar Vnesh debt (nonperforming loans incurred by the old Soviet Vnesheconombank) and Argentinian Brady bonds. As discussed in Chapter 7, the special feature of power calls is the payout—the *square* of the difference between the warrant's strike price and the price of the asset at expiry. These were issued, in August 1995, by ING Capital in London. The Russian issue was $100 million in two tranches; the Argentine issue was for the same amount in September 1995.

Emerging Markets Fixed-Income Warrants

As we have seen in Chapter 8, annual turnover in LDC debt grew from around $100 million 10 years ago to $2 trillion in 1993. One of the attractions of derivatives in this area has been the relative ease with which investors can access the market for emerging market debt through warrants, compared with the cash market. The smallest size purchase possible in the cash market is US$250,000, but the average trade is between US$1 million and $3 million, a deterrent to smaller institutions and high-net-worth individuals. The warrants also offer leveraged exposure and limited downside, making them ideal for first-timers to emerging market debt. Additionally, the use of derivatives allows the investor to access, relatively economically, pools of bonds that allow diversification.

A typical example would be an issue by Merrill Lynch, in May 1993, of calls on an LDC sovereign debt index: 400 call warrants were issued, with each warrant controlling US$250,000 face value of the underlying debt instruments. The warrants were cash-settled, using the average of the index bid price at 12:00 P.M. New York time for the last four Wednesdays prior to maturity. The index composition was: 23 percent Bulgaria, 17 percent Ecuador, 10 percent Panama, 18 percent Peru, and 27.4 percent Poland (percentages applied to the flat bid price of each country's debt).

BUNNY BONDS

In this section, we include an instrument that incorporates warrantlike features even though there actually is no separate tradable warrant. For this bond, the interest is payable in cash, or, at the investor's option, in further issues of the bond itself. The technique was first introduced in the U.S. domestic market in 1985, for an issue by ITT and, subsequently, an issue by Chrysler. (In some quarters, the bonds were nicknamed "bunny bonds" because they multiply like rabbits.) Later, it was introduced into the French domestic market under the acronym OSCAR (Obligation Speciale à Reinvestir).

From the investor's point of view, there is, effectively, ownership of a warrant to subscribe to further issues of the original bond; this option becomes increasingly valuable as rates fall. The option increases the positive convexity of the bond (see Chapter 3). Another way of looking at the instrument is to say that, as rates fall, it becomes a zero coupon, because it eliminates reinvestment risk. As rates rise, it becomes like a conventional bond. A variant of this approach is also, of course, used in the junk bond market ("pay-in-kind" bonds), but there the object is normally to allow the issuer to avoid handing over cash. Here, the investor has the option of taking bonds in payment.

Chapter **16**

Equity Derivatives

For practical purposes, equity derivatives may be said to have begun in 1973 with the introduction of equity options on the Chicago Board of Options Exchange (CBOE). Thereafter, most development concentrated on exchange-traded options until the arrival of equity index futures in the early 1980s. Then developments followed thick and fast. Americus Trust issued PRIMES and SCORES in 1987; long-term equity options called LEAPS were introduced by the CBOE in 1990. In 1992, Leland O'Brien Rubinstein introduced SuperUnits. Meantime, in the over-the-counter derivatives market, a whole range of highly customized derivatives evolved. In a related area, the Toronto Stock Exchange introduced the Toronto 35 Index Participation Units (TIPS) in 1990, and the American Stock Exchange introduced its S&P Depositary Receipts (SPDRs) in 1993. These are discussed in Chapter 17.

BREAKING EQUITY INTO COMPONENTS

PRIMES and SCORES

These securities were issued by Americus Trust in 1987. They had a life of 5 years and were dependent on a U.S. Internal Revenue Service tax ruling that was later reversed. Thus, in their original form, they seem unrepeatable, at least in the United States. The trusts were redeemable unit investment trusts. The units of each trust could be split by their owners into a Prescribed Right to Income and Maximum Equity (PRIME) and a Special Claim On Residual Equity (SCORE). Each trust was separate and distinct. Investors tendered shares of stock into each of the trusts and received a unit for each share tendered. Each trust had its own termination date and termination claim (strike price). In essence, the PRIME and SCORE were the income and the capital gain on an individual share. The PRIME was equivalent to a buy-write strategy. The PRIME investor received the dividend income on the share and all the appreciation of the share price up to the termination claim level (strike price). The PRIME investor owned the voting rights on the share also. By contrast, the SCORE investor owned all the appreciation of the share price above the termination claim level (strike price). In effect, the SCORE investor owned a call option on the share at that level. However, for legal purposes, the SCORE was a security, not a full option. Thus, PRIMES and SCORES could be bought on margin and could be included in, for example, individual retirement accounts (IRAs) and similar pension plan instruments.

PECS and SECS

The Canadian equivalents of PRIMES and SCORES, respectively, were christened Payment Enhancement Capital Securities (PECS) and Special Equity Claim Securities (SECS). Three Canadian securities firms formed, in 1994, a joint venture company, Structured Derivative Products Corporation, to take over the existing operations of a previous firm operated by only one broker-dealer. Although 11 issues had been made, representing just under C$300 million in issuance and based on shares in the six major Canadian banks, Thomson Corporation, and various other Canadian firms, volume had been held back by the perception that the market was controlled by only one firm.

SuperShares and SuperUnits.   In 1992, Leland O'Brien Rubinstein introduced two SuperUnits securities—redeemable for (1) shares in an S&P 500 index mutual fund and (2) shares in a mutual fund holding short-term U.S. Treasury securities—and four SuperShares. Of the SuperShares, one paid all dividends plus the value of the S&P 500 to a specified level; the second paid the value of the S&P 500 above the specified level (a call option); the third paid the value of any decline in the value of the S&P portfolio below the specified level (a put option); and the fourth paid the interest plus any residual value from the Treasury securities. The SuperUnits were listed on the American Stock Exchange, and the SuperShares were listed on the CBOE. However, at the end of the initial 3-year maturity, both were redeemed and the project was discontinued.

EQUITY INSTRUMENTS USING OPTIONS

Retail Guaranteed Equity Index Structures

A wide range of "guaranteed" stock market bonds has been issued into the retail market in the United Kingdom, France, and elsewhere. Similar structures have also been used by a number of insurance companies in the United States. Initially, most of these were fairly straightforward guarantees against a fall in the market. Generally, investors were given, in essence, a call option on the market (without dividends reinvested—a feature of key importance in helping the issuer pay for the call options).

A typical U.K. scheme was the Legal & General Guaranteed Equity Fund III, launched in 1989. The investor was guaranteed the better of:

1. 116 pence per 100 pence invested.
2. 100 pence increased by the whole rise in the FTSE 100 index from noon January 15, 1990, to noon January 15, 1993.

Subsequently, a number of refinements were made, particularly to protect investors against the risk that the market would rise initially and then, by the critical date, fall below the target level. This protection could be achieved either by "ladder" or "cliquet" options or by using Asian options covering the last few months (see Chapter 7).

A typical example of the first approach is the Guaranteed Stock Market Bond issued by Save & Prosper in the UK, in 1992. This was a 5-year investment that incorporated a "ladder" option. The basic structure was that, at maturity, the investor was guaranteed the better of:

1. 99 percent of the original investment, increased at the same rate of growth as that of the FTSE 100 index (without income reinvested).
2. 100 percent of the original investment.

The investor was offered a further protection option. If the investor chose this option, then the redemption value would be the better of:

1. 92 percent of the original investment, increased at the same rate of growth as that of the FTSE 100 index (without income reinvested). The investor's gains are secured whenever the index rises by a 10 percent "step" above its level at the start, up to a maximum of 50 percent. So the investor is assured that gains of 10 percent, 20 percent, 30 percent, 40 percent, and 50 percent on the index level can be locked in. This protects the investor against a sharp initial rise followed by a crash in the FTSE.
2. 100 percent of the original investment.

A typical example of the second approach was the issue, in 1992, of a "Triple Guarantee Bond" by Britannia Life Assurance. The investor is guaranteed, over a 5-year term, 110 percent of the growth in the FTSE 100 index, where the return is calculated on the average FTSE 100 level during the last 6 months of the investment term. Alternatively, the investor receives 100 percent of the initial investment. (The third guarantee of the "triple" is "100 percent peace of mind"!)

GROI

In the Swiss retail market, a substantial market has developed for equity-linked structures. The first of this type was the Guaranteed Return On Investment (GROI) introduced by Swiss Bank Corporation in January 1991. These were 1-year term investment instruments; the investor could choose among three combinations of security and risk. One choice was to have a guaranteed 7 percent return on the investment, possibly receiving a bonus of 2.03 percent if the Swiss Market Index (SMI) performed well. Alternatively, an investor willing to accept a 0 percent guaranteed return could receive 24.72 percent if the SMI performed well. There was also a middle option of 4 percent guaranteed return, where the potential bonus could take the total return up to 16 percent. The GROI is a straight combination of a bond plus a call option at different strike levels.

Competitive products were rapidly introduced: the Index Growth-Linked Unit (IGLU) from Union Bank of Switzerland, and the SMI deposit from Swiss Credit Bank. A variant was offered by Winterthur Insurance; its Windex life insurance policy, issued in December 1993, was a single-premium insurance bond offering a payoff linked to the SMI. Essentially, the embedded option was an Asian call option with a 10-year maturity. This was followed by other structures—an ECU issue (using an Asian quanto call), an Asian cliquet, and a ladder version—by the firm and its competitors. (See Chapter 7 for option structure details.)

LEAPS

Long-Term Equity AnticiPation Securities (LEAPS) are long-term American-style options on specific stocks and indexes. The first LEAPS, introduced in 1990 by the Chicago Board of Options Exchange, were soon followed by versions created by the American, Philadelphia, and Pacific Stock Exchanges. LEAPS offer maturities up to 3 years.

The standard or traditional option on an equity or index has a lifetime measured in months. The problem for the investor is that the right timing becomes very critical with such a short-life instrument. Furthermore, the time value (see Chapter 6) decays very quickly. The more time an option has until its expiration date, the more slowly the premium declines, and the more time is available for an investor's market opinion to be realized. This is one of the major attractions of the product to investors.

The underlying index for OEX LEAPS is the S&P 100 index divided by 10. SPX LEAPS are based on the S&P 500 index divided by 10. If OEX is at 600.00, representing an underlying value of $60,000 (600.00 × $100), OCX and OAX, the symbols for OEX LEAPS, would be based on a price of 60.00, representing an underlying value of $6,000 (60.00 × $100). Similarly, if SPX is at 620.00, the two SPX LEAPS, LSZ and LSW, would be based on a price of 62.00, and would represent an underlying value of $6,200 (62.00 × $100).

PERCS

The Preferred Equity Redemption Cumulative Stock (PERCS) is essentially a convertible preferred share which, when issued, is priced at the same level as the issuer's stock. In exchange for an enhanced dividend yield, the investor accepts a cap on the security's price appreciation over the next 3 years. At that time, the shares automatically convert back into common stock. The structure is essentially a "buy-write": the investor who buys the PERCS is buying the common stock and selling a call on the stock.

The market for PERCS began in 1988. Avon Products was faced with a situation where its stock price had fallen to $20 and the company needed to conserve cash and reduce the dividend. The solution was to offer shareholders a choice of continuing to hold the common stock, at a reduced dividend, or exchanging the common for a new issue of PERCS. The dividend rate on the PERCS was set at the existing common dividend level of $2.00, and the cap on the share's appreciation was set at $31.50. In fact, the PERCS was redeemed at a rate of 0.72 common share per PERCS share, because the common stock had reached $44.125.

The technique proved popular with investors. From 1991 (when the market really began to grow) to 1994, almost $14 billion of PERCS or related variants were issued. (Variants included: Mandatory Conversion Premium Dividend Preferred Stock—MCPDPS; Yield Enhancement Securities—YES; Targeted Growth Enhanced-Term Securities—TARGETS.)

A very successful use of PERCS, at least from the viewpoint of the issuer, was the issue by Texas Instruments, in 1991, of 11 million PERCS, raising roughly $300 million in capital. In the next 18 months, the environment for technology stocks improved dramatically. In the summer of 1993, the common stock of the company had risen so much that the company was able to buy back its PERCS through issuing only 6.23 million common shares. This was an example, it could be said, of "reverse dilution."

One use of PERCS was to complement a Limited Yield Option Notes (LYONS) issue. In 1992, Time Inc. monetized its stake in Hasbro Inc. by selling a 5-year zero-coupon LYONS with a conversion price of $54.41 per share. By August 1995, the Hasbro price was drifting in the low 30s, so the prospect of conversion by 1997 was remote. The dividend yield on the PERCS was set at 4 percent, compared with a yield of 1 percent on the common stock. The PERCS was priced at $31 (the then-current price of the common stock), and its appreciation was capped at $54.41—the LYONS conversion level. In effect, the PERCS allowed Time Warner to sell the Hasbro appreciation that had not already been sold by the LYONS.

In October 1994, the PERCS structure was used to solve a specific problem for Times Mirror. The company announced a very large dividend cut, in conjunction with the proposed merger of its cable television properties with Cox Cable Communications. By offering to exchange PERCS for some of its common stock, the company was able to pacify those shareholders for whom the dividend yield was particularly important. Because the securities would mandatorily convert back to common stock after 3 years, the deal would have no impact on the company's credit ratings.

A "synthetic" PERCS on America Online was issued by Goldman Sachs, in January 1995. This was an issue of $75 million of 3-year notes giving holders the lesser of America Online's share price at redemption, or 165 percent of the offer price. The issue was reportedly hedged by a transaction between Goldman Sachs and Apple Computer, which owned warrants on 1 million America Online shares. (Compare the "synthetic DECS" done by J.P. Morgan on America Online.)

TARGETS

A version of PERCS called TARGETS (Targeted Growth Enhanced Terms Securities) was used by Sun Oil Company, in July 1995, to smooth over the impact of a dividend cut. The company's stock had previously been regarded as a dividend stock, so shareholders were given the opportunity to tender their shares in exchange for the TARGETS, which paid the same level of dividend as the common stock had paid before the cut. However, the TARGETS' maximum price was capped at $40 per share (45 percent above the then-prevailing level of the common stock). (Compare Time Mirror's use of PERCS.)

Contingent Value Rights

A contingent value right (CVR) is, in essence, a cash-settled put on a company's shares, issued by the company itself. To date, its main use has been in mergers or takeovers. Suppose Company X is bidding for Company Y. Company X wants to pay for the acquisition using its shares, but shareholders in Y have doubts about how X's shares will perform after the merger. Suppose X's shares are trading now at $5.50 and it sets a trigger price of $5.80. X promises to pay the difference between the trigger price of $5.80 and the actual share price at the exercise date, say a year from now, subject to an upper limit. It will pay this difference to shareholders in Y, if they take X's shares during the bid.

The CVR is being used to protect investors who are receiving the company's shares in exchange for their shares in the target company. All too often, as investors know, the shares of the new and larger entity underperform after the takeover goes through (the "winner's curse"). The CVR is intended to protect them, at least in part, against this outcome.

The company issuing the CVRs may face a substantial liability if its shares do not reach the trigger price. Alternatively, if the shares perform well, the CVRs expire worthless. Inevitably, the promise to compensate for poor share-price growth—and, presumably, for poor earnings growth—is only credible if the issuer is a strong company. Otherwise, the CVR becomes a "double whammy": a poorly performing company is forced to pay out more to shareholders.

Dow Chemical issued the first CVRs, in December 1989, as a deferred installment payment in connection with its acquisition of a 67 percent interest in Marion Laboratories. Under the terms of the CVRs, Dow committed itself to pay the difference between $45.77 and the average trading price of Marion Merrell Dow's common stock over a 90-day trading period ending at the close of trading on September 18, 1991. If the stock traded below $30, holders would receive the difference between $30 and $45.77: $15.77. Thus, the CVRs are, in effect, put warrants on the share whose payout is capped if the share falls below $30.

The CVRs helped accomplish several objectives. They helped Dow avoid paying a large premium for goodwill. In a complicated series of steps, Dow purchased nearly 39 percent of Marion in a tender offer and acquired control of 51 percent of the company via a voting proxy. It then transferred to Marion shareholders stock of Merrell Dow, its pharmaceutical subsidiary, and the CVRs. In return, Marion issued to Dow enough shares to lift Dow's ownership to 67 percent. Because both Marion and Merrell Dow were controlled by Dow at the time, the need to book goodwill on the accounts of Marion was eliminated. Had Dow sought to acquire Marion outright, at $38 per share, or $5.9 billion, it would have paid a huge premium—$3.79 per share—over the book value of Marion's assets.

The CVRs helped with another problem: reducing the up-front cash requirement for the merger. All Marion shareholders received the CVRs, which provided them with some price protection and thus sweetened the deal. It turned out that Dow did have to pay up on the CVRs.

Another firm that used CVRs was Rhone-Poulenc, in its deal with Rorer. Shareholders selling their Rorer shares to Rhone-Poulenc were paid in three forms. They received cash totaling $1.7 billion, shares in Rhone-Poulenc-Rorer (RPR, the new unit formed following the merger of the French group's pharmaceuticals business with Rorer), and CVRs. If, at the end of 3 years, the RPR share price did not exceed $98, Rhone-Poulenc had to pay CVR holders the difference between the share price and $98, to an upper limit of $46 per CVR. If the RPR share price was below $52 on August 1, 1993, Rhone-Poulenc would have to pay the CVR holders $1 billion (in FRF over 5 billion).

By the end of 1991, the price of the CVR had fallen by four-fifths of its value. Its close at under $1 reflected the good performance of the group. Rhone-Poulenc took the opportunity to buy all the CVRs it had been offered. During the first year after issue, the group gathered in 20.7 million CVRs, half the total number issued.

In 1994, Viacom gained an edge in the bidding war for Paramount Communications by giving subscribers to its tender offer some protection against a downturn in the price of Viacom B shares. The shares were the main currency in the deal, which also included a cash component, equity warrants, and class A shares. Paramount's shareholders were offered a CVR as part of the package of cash and securities. This set two floors for Viacom's share price: (1) a year after the merger, and (2) a year later. If the share price dips below the relevant floor, the CVR will kick in and its value will begin to increase. Viacom sweetened its offer several times, reworking the terms attached to the CVR. In June 1996, Viacom announced that payment to holders of CVRs issued in connection with the merger was set at $1.44375 per CVR in cash, or a total of approximately $83 million. The CVRs were thereby extinguished.

In July 1995, when CVRs were introduced in Canada for Algoma Steel, they were a solution to the problem of a poor reception for Algoma's recapitalization plan. CVRs were introduced as a way of getting the holders of $262 million of Algoma Finance preferred shares to go along with the further restructuring of Algoma. Algoma wanted to redeem the preferreds. In the final package that emerged, the preferred holders would receive, in exchange for one $25 par value preferred share, $18.188 in cash, 0.6875 of a common share, and 0.6875 of an attached CVR.

A recent use of the CVR was to help the merger of AXA and UAP, two French insurance companies. The CVRs helped to protect UAP shareholders. For every 10 shares they held, UAP investors received 4 new AXA shares plus 4 CVRs. If AXA shares fall below FRF392.50 in June 1999, they will receive up to FRF 80 in cash per CVR.

"Standby Equity Facility" via Options.   An interesting issue was made in October 1994, by an Australian entity, General Property Trust (GPT). This is a listed property unit trust. It raised AUS$500 million; the deal offered to shareholders was that they could buy an option at a price of AUS$1.35. This would give them the right to buy AUS$15 worth of units in the trust at a guaranteed 15 percent discount to the market price at the time of exercise of the option. In fact, the AUS$1.35 option is divided into three separate calls, and the investor has the right to exercise one of them on each of three scheduled dates in 1996–1998. In effect, GPT has a standby line of equity; it knows that it can probably raise equity from its investors at each of the call dates. If, however, GPT wishes to borrow from rather than sell units to investors, the facility also includes a separate AUS$300 million commercial paper facility. Furthermore, the issuer has the right to buy back the options from investors at a fixed price.

For investors, the attraction is that they can accrue new units at a favorable price if market conditions are encouraging. On the other hand, if the market is difficult, exercising the option will risk serious dilution. In that event, the issuer might well pay cash for unitholders' options rather than seriously dilute its earnings per unit.

Debt Instruments Linked to Equity

Share Indexes

A wide range of issuers have launched debt that is linked to equity markets. One of the first was Guinness Finance. Its first Eurobond issue, in July 1986, was a $100 million issue of Stock Performance Exchange Linked (SPEL) bonds with a redemption amount linked to the New York Stock Exchange (NYSE) Composite Index. The SPEL bonds were linked to the index via the formula:

$$\text{Variable index amount} = \$10,000 \times \frac{X - 166}{166}.$$

The investor was guaranteed redemption at par as a minimum. In addition, there would be a further premium if the index rose above 166. At the launch of the issue, the index stood at 134, a 20 percent discount to the strike price. Suppose at redemption the index rises to, say, 300; then the holder of a $10,000 bond would receive $18,072.29. The coupon on the 3-year issue was set at 3 percent, or ½ percent below the calculated average annual dividend yield of shares on the NYSE.

Investors thus have an equity surrogate. They receive about the same yield as they would get from the underlying shares, but with protection against capital loss because the bonds redeem at a minimum of par. This issue was only a bull tranche, rather than the bull/bear structure discussed in Chapter 12, so Guinness was left with an exposure to the redemption amount, depending on the NYSE index. It eliminated this exposure through a swap in which it agreed to pay 7.55 percent semiannually in return for receiving 3 percent together with the variable redemption amount, whatever that turned out to be. (An early example of an equity swap; see Chapter 5.) The bonds were placed primarily among retail investors in the Far East and, to some extent, in Europe.

Subsequently, the technique has been applied in a wide range of markets. In the U.S. domestic market, the technique was applied by Salomons with $100 million of SPINs (Standard & Poor's Indexed Notes) with a 2 percent coupon and an increased redemption amount in the event of a rise in the S&P 500 index over the 4-year term. However, the ready availability of index hedging instruments in the United States (and the tax points discussed below) reduced the attractiveness of the issue.

In January 1991, the Republic of Austria brought to market $100 million of equity-linked debt called Stock Index Growth Notes (SIGNs). These were bonds with approximately a 5.5-year maturity, paying no interest before maturity. If the value of the S&P 500 is below 336.69 at maturity, the investor gets back the principal. If the value is above that level, the investor receives $100 plus $100 multiplied by the percentage appreciation in the S&P 500 above 336.69.

This issue triggered a major tax problem in the United States. Under existing interpretations, the investor would pay no tax on the equity appreciation until it was received at maturity. In the month following the issue, the Internal Revenue Service brought out "contingent payment debt instruments" tax regulations, which required such securities to be split ("bifurcated") into a straight zero-coupon bond and an option on the S&P 500. Investors would have to accrue the interest on the bond portion.

These regulations were withdrawn, in December 1992, and replaced with new regulations which themselves were withdrawn, in January 1993, to allow the incoming Clinton Administration to review them. Thus, for a long period of time, investors were uncertain of the tax treatment of the instruments.

Despite this uncertainty, United Technologies, on August 29, 1991, issued $75 million of Pharmaceutical Exchange Notes (PENs), a structure with some unique features. The zero-coupon PENs were issued at par, and matured in 6 years at the greater of par or the principal amount times a fraction composed of the S&P Pharmaceutical Index immediately prior to maturity, divided by 121.24. The denominator represents a 12½ percent markup vis-à-vis the index at issue date.

The company may not prepay the note. A holder may, after March 6, 1992, put the note to the company on any business day, but only if the Pharmaceutical Index equals or exceeds 121.24. If the index stays below 121.24, the holders cannot redeem, and United Technologies has borrowed at no interest expense.

In August 1996, the Chicago Board of Options Exchange (CBOE) began trading Smith Barney Holdings, Inc. S&P 500 Equity Linked Notes due August 13, 2001. The notes are denominated in units of $15 principal amount, and they allow holders to participate in the upside of the S&P 500 Index. The securities are quoted in round lots of 100. The offering size was 2.67 million units. At maturity, the unit holders will be entitled to receive, with respect to each unit, the principal amount (i.e., $15) plus a "Supplemental Redemption Amount" based on the percentage increase, if any, in the S&P 500 Composite Stock Price Index over the Starting Index Value of 664.16. In no event will the Supplemental Redemption Amount be less than zero. The notes do not provide for periodic interest payments, nor will they be redeemable or callable by Smith Barney prior to maturity.

Outside the United States, the international market in equity-linked bonds has developed rapidly during the 1990s. A wide range of issues has appeared, in different currencies linked to different markets. (Some of these are discussed in Chapter 12.) A recent example is the Matador Market bond issued by the European Investment Bank, in February 1997. The coupon was 4 percent and, at maturity in 2000, it will return 92.28 percent of face value plus a maturity premium based on the average IBEX35 close between March 7 and March 20, 1997, and the last working day of each month from March 31, 1997, to September 29, 1997.

DAX Participations

A concept very similar to the TIPS (discussed in Chapter 17) was brought to the German market in 1990 in the form of DAX Participations issued by Dresdner Bank. They were issued via Amsterdam in the form of bearer securities "creating a payment claim in the amount of the DAX as it may be from time to time." One advantage was that they could be traded by German investors without incurring the German stock exchange turnover tax then in force. The certificates had a 5-year life. No interest or dividends were payable. (The DAX index, unlike the S&P 500 or the FTSE 100, is a total-return index including dividends paid, so this was perfectly reasonable.)

OPALS

A somewhat different approach to creating debt with equity characteristics was the Optimized Portfolios As Listed Securities (OPALS) product introduced by Morgan Stanley in 1993. OPALS consisted of bonds that were listed on the Luxembourg Stock Exchange and were designed to track the performance of a given country's equity index. They were backed by a basket of shares that had been optimized to deliver a return matching that of the index selected (subject to some tracking error). During their life, OPALS pay income semiannually, comprised of dividends on the shares in the basket, proceeds from the sale of rights accruing to those shares, and income from lending such shares. At maturity, the investor receives the basket of shares. In essence, OPALS were the SPDR or WEBS product (see Chapter 17), dressed up in bond form.

Individual Shares

A number of bonds have been issued on the basis that they will pay out a return linked to the performance of the share price of the issuer. An example is the Performance Bonds issued by ABB International Finance NV, in July 1993, in respect of another group company, Brown Boveri. The issue consisted of CHF100 million of 5-year bonds to pay a coupon amount defined as "one-half of the percentage increase in the Stock Exchange price quotation for BBC Brown Boveri Ltd., Baden, Switzerland, bearer shares during the period in respect of which the coupon amount advised, subject to a maximum 12 percent and a minimum of 0 percent." In fact, this bond benefits from a cliquet option structure (see Chapter 7).

Another variant was a deposit arrangement directed at the retail market in Spain at the time of the Telefonica de España privatization. This took place in February 1997, and it resulted in heavy retail demand, which was unsatisfied. Caja de Madrid announced an 18-month deposit guaranteeing return of principal together with 70 percent of any rise in the share during the life of the deposit.

Embedded Stock Options

ELKS. In July 1993, Salomon Brothers issued $60 million of Equity-Linked Securities (ELKS) on behalf of Digital Equipment Corporation (DEC). These bonds, issued by Salomon, were paying 6.75 percent. At maturity, investors will receive the lesser of 135 percent of the issue price or Digital's average closing price over the 10 previous trading days. These securities are, in a sense, "synthetic PERCS"—that is, PERCS-like securities issued by a third party. (DEC was not involved in the issue at all; the bonds are purely Salomon obligations.) Thus, like PERCS, they offer investors a high current coupon in exchange for a cap on the price performance of the share. In this case, if DEC were to double, over the life of the deal, investors would receive only a 35 percent appreciation.

CHIPS. In February 1994, Bear Stearns and Company brought an issue of CHIPS (Common-Linked Higher Income Participation Securities). These are debt obligations of Bear Stearns with a 3-year maturity and a coupon of 5.5 percent. At maturity, investors will receive the lesser of the stock price of Merck & Company at that time or 130 percent of the issue price—$47.6125 per CHIPS. The deal is essentially a clone of the ELKS structure.

In April 1994, a similar deal was brought on CUC International. At maturity, investors will receive the lesser of the stock price of CUC International at that time and a cap, set at 50 percent above the offering price. In exchange for the cap, investors receive an annual coupon fixed at 5.5 percent. The underlying common stock pays no dividend.

PERQS. A similar structure, entitled Performance Equity-Linked Redemption Quarterly-Pay Securities (PERQS), was introduced, in July 1994, for International Game Technology Corporation. The structure was used again for Telmex, the Mexican telephone company, in September 1994. Here, the 3-year bonds issued by Morgan Stanley were linked to the value of the American Depository Shares (ADSs) issued by Telmex. At redemption, the investor receives the lesser of the ADS price at the time, or the maximum appreciation of 33 percent. In essence, the investor has sold a call option at 33 percent above the current market level.

In February 1996, Morgan Stanley issued $168 million of 6 percent PERQS linked to the ADSs of Telecomunicacõçes Brasileiras S.A. (Telebrás). The PERQS mature February 16, 1999. They pay quarterly interest—in this case, at an annual percentage rate of 6 percent of the $56 offering price, or $3.36 per year. At maturity, holders of PERQS will receive the lesser of $79.80 (142.5 percent of the $56 issue price) or the average closing price of Telebrás ADSs for the 10 trading days ending 2 business days prior to maturity.

The product was introduced into the United Kingdom in 1995, with a £50 million 3-year offering linked to the performance of shares in SmithKline Beecham, the pharmaceuticals company. Another issue, in March 1996, was made of 9 million PERQS on Guinness ordinary shares at a price of 459 pence per share.

YEELDS. Yield Enhanced Equity Linked Debt Securities (YEELDS) are the Lehman Brothers equivalent of ELKS. They have been issued on, among others,

Oracle ($64 million yielding 7.25 percent, capped at 155 percent of the stock price at time of issue); Amgen ($64 million yielding 6.5 percent, capped at 140 percent); and Micron Technology ($30 million yielding 9.13 percent, capped at 150 percent).

Other Option-Based Structures

A huge range of other option-based structures has been brought to international markets. Most have been issued without the tiresome habit of the American investment banks, which create a stupid acronym and then trademark it in a sad attempt to convince investors that the investment bank concerned has done something original. Many of these structures (discussed in Chapters 12 and 15) involve currencies and interest rates, or warrants. Here, we give some examples of debt linked to options on individual equities.

In May 1994, Société Générale introduced an issue of notes with a covered call on Telmex stock. In effect, the investor owned an at-the-money call option on Telmex ADRs at a strike of $61.75. The investor was short an out-of-the-money call at a strike of $74.10. The premium earned from selling the higher-strike call pays part of the cost of the lower-priced call.

The formal structure is that, if Telmex is below $61.75, the investor takes exposure to Telmex. For example, if Telmex falls 10 percent, then the investor loses 10 percent. If it is trading at $61.75, then the return is 0 percent. Between $61.75 and $74.10, the payoff formula is:

$$100 * \frac{1 + 2 * \left(\text{Telmex share price} - \$61.75\right)}{61.75}.$$

In other words, within this range, the investor gets a leveraged payout of $2 \times$ the increase in the share price. Above that level, the appreciation is capped at 140. Furthermore, the note has embedded in it a call option for the issuer. Société Générale can call the issue after 6 months. The investor has, in effect, sold Société Générale a call option, and the premium from the option helped to pay for the $2 \times$ gearing.

Embedded Basket Options

CUBS. A typical example of a bond with an embedded basket option was the issue of Customized Upside Basket Securities (CUBS) by Bear Stearns, in August 1995. These were 3-year debt obligations of Bear Stearns. Investors receive no interest but they receive 90 percent of the average monthly gains in the value of a basket of 23 underlying shares, from industries where takeovers can be expected.

SUNS. The first Stock Upside Note Securities (SUNS), issued in April 1994, is a 6-year Lehman Brothers note for $35 million, with a $25 par amount.

Investors receive an annual coupon equal to 100 percent of the average price increase of 24 global telecommunications stocks, equally weighted in the portfolio, minus 5 percent.

The second issue, linked to regional bank stocks, was for a much shorter maturity (2 years). The payout, instead of being annual, was a single payment at maturity.

MITTS.   In 1993, Merrill Lynch issued $110 million of Market Index Target-Term Securities (MITTS). These were 5-year bonds that paid no interest. However, investors at maturity would receive the greater of 90 percent of par value, or par value plus 100 percent of the average price increase in the stocks of 22 global telecommunications companies. The MITTS were sold mainly to retail accounts, who compared them typically with mutual funds specializing in telecommunications stocks. MITTS paid no dividends, but they did offer a downside guarantee and did not charge the front-end or annual management fees typical of mutual funds. The first of Merrill's MITTS, in July 1992, was a 5-year bond guaranteeing return of the investor's principal at worst, and, at best, 115 percent of any gains in the S&P index.

In August 1996, the Chicago Board of Options Exchange began trading a new issue by Merrill Lynch: Technology Market Index Target-Term Securities (MITTS), due August 15, 2001. The Technology MITTS are denominated in units of $10 principal amount and are quoted and traded like other equity securities, generally in round lots of 100. The offering size consisted of 2.5 million units. At maturity, unit holders will be entitled to receive the principal amount (i.e., $10) plus a "Supplemental Redemption Amount" based on the percentage increase, if any, in the CBOE Technology Index over the Benchmark Index Value of 189.48. The Supplemental Redemption Amount will not be less than zero nor more than $10 per $10 principal amount of securities. The securities are not redeemable or callable by the company prior to maturity.

SMARTs.   Apparent concern by taxable investors (as contrasted with tax-advantaged IRAs and Keogh accounts) over tax treatment of original issue discount income and possible mark-to-market requirements in the MITTs product prompted Merrill Lynch to launch 7-year Stock Market Annual Reset Term (SMARTs) Notes. SMART Notes feature a coupon that will be reset and paid each year and is equal to 70 percent of the change in the S&P 500 from the first business day of the year to the seventh business day before year-end.

With an expected floor and ceiling of between 3 percent and 10½ percent, the annual reset was expected to keep the mark-to-market rules at bay because the issuer viewed the instrument as six separate unlisted options. Terms for all subsequent years cannot be determined by the end of the first year, so no market value can be derived. However, the economic reality is that this is a cliquet structure (see Chapter 7), and, although the structure may have been recharacterized for tax purposes, it was not unhedgeable.

Contracts for Differences

The term "contracts for differences" is applied in many derivative contexts, but there is a specific market in the United Kingdom for contracts for differences in the equity market.

The origins of the market lie in the fact that U.K. regulations regarding the borrowing of equities to take short positions were once rather restrictive. Contracts for differences were evolved as an alternative means to the same end. Typically, investors will pay the counterparty an initial margin of perhaps 5 percent of the value of the shares they wish to sell short. They then receive interest—on an amount equal to the market value of the shares plus the 5 percent initial margin—usually at a rate around LIBOR – 2 percent. The contracts are marked to market regularly (usually weekly), and variation in the margin is charged as the value of the contract moves up or down. The contracts have no expiration date, and termination is entirely at the discretion of the investor. One advantage of this structure is that it allows short traders to avoid liability to stamp duty, which is generally charged on stock purchased to cover short positions. The mirror position, a long contract for differences, can of course be taken, though this action is less common. Indeed, one such contract aroused considerable controversy. In 1995, Trafalgar House entered a long contract for differences with Swiss Bank Corporation during its bid for Northern Electric. Many criticized the transaction as an attempt to circumvent takeover rules, and the rules were later changed to prevent the use of OTC derivatives to circumvent the existing regulatory framework.

Share Ratios

In 1994, the Australian Stock Exchange introduced trading in share ratios. These instruments reflect the relationship of a share to the aggregate market. For example, suppose that ANZ shares are currently trading at AUS$4 per share, and the Sydney All Ordinaries index is trading at 2050. The share ratio is defined as the ratio of the share price to the index, multiplied by 1,000. So, in our example, the ratio would be $400/2050 \times 1,000 = 195.1$.

Perhaps the volume of trading in share ratios has not been overwhelming because it is a derivative-type product being traded on a traditional stock exchange. However, the attraction of the product is that it allows fund managers to make relative performance trades. Furthermore, an arbitrage trade of this kind can be done without requiring large amounts of capital. This product might work more successfully on an exchange that is integrated, having both derivatives and equities—such as the Deutsche Termin Börse (DTB) or the Swiss exchange.

Specialist Derivatives-Based Issue Structures

Some equity derivative structures, developed to help with a specific problem, use relatively traditional derivative instruments in a broader financial structure. One example is the use of protective puts in the context of a privatization issue.

The technique was first used in the French government's offering of shares in Rhone-Poulenc. Under the rules of the French privatization program, 10 percent of the available shares had to be set aside for employees. In the run-up to the sale, however, the French government began to worry that the employee allocation would not be fully taken up. A deal was arranged under which Crédit Commercial de France (CCF) agreed to lend Rhone-Poulenc employees enough money to subscribe to 9 extra shares for each share bought outright, thereby leveraging their investment 10 times. Protection was arranged by Bankers Trust through a series of equity options and swaps that put a floor into the stock price for the employees.

The structure ensured that the employees would be able to repay the loan, while guaranteeing them a minimum return and leaving their upside uncapped. The employees will, however, forgo one-third of any increase in the share price. No specific interest charge was set on the bank financing. Instead, employees' loan repayments are indexed to the value of Rhone-Poulenc shares when the deal matures after 5 years. A large number of Rhone-Poulenc employees took advantage of the financing available to them; the 10 percent employee allocation was, in fact, oversubscribed. The technique was used again in the privatization of Elf-Aquitaine.

It was also used in Germany for the Deutsche Telekom issue, in 1996. Two techniques were applied: first, a so-called "financed purchase program" consisting of a special trust. The trust borrowed four times the initial stake of DEM300 allotted to each employee. The resulting total of DEM1,500 is invested in Deutsche Telekom shares until December 31, 2001. At that date, the trust will be wound up and the full upside return will be passed to the employees, giving them a fivefold leverage on their stake. To protect the stake, the trust buys a 5-year put option. The underlying tax advantages, together with a subsidy from Deutsche Telekom, combined to create an attractive deal.

Chapter *17*

Special Types of Equity

In this chapter, we discuss different equity structures that have been developed in recent years. These are not derivatives; they are different types of equity, or methods of issuing or trading equity.

PUTTABLE EQUITY

The development of puttable equity was spurred by problems in the initial public offering (IPO) market. A number of new issues had run into difficulties. So, in November 1984, in an issue brought out for Arley Merchandise Corporation, a $600 million offering of common shares was accompanied by rights for investors to put their stock back to the company at the original price after 2 years—but not necessarily for cash. Cash settlements would be made with small shareholders, but block holders choosing to return their Arley common would be paid the equivalent value in senior subordinated notes paying 128 percent of the 10-year Treasury bond rate.

But the Securities and Exchange Commission (SEC) decided that the proceeds of the issue were redeemable equity, in the grey zone between debt and equity, and thus not entitled to be placed on the company's books as equity until the puts had expired. Therefore, the next issue of this type, for Gearhart Industries, an issue of $85 million common stock, was redeemable by the issuer in cash, debt, or common stock.

The SEC agreed that the deal gave Gearhart more control over how the puts would be made good, and that the issue was bona fide equity. Still, the issuer needs to be confident that its stock price will rise. Otherwise, the potential cost is that the company may be forced to issue large extra amounts of stock.

In the case of Gearhart, each "unit" sold by the company consisted of 5 shares of common and 5 "rights" to sell those shares back to Gearhart for a guaranteed price of at least $14.68 per share ($73.40 per unit) 1 year from the date of issue. The guaranteed price then rises each year, for 4 more years, by about 10 percent annually. If the company's stock price dips below $14.68 when the puts become available, shareholders can exercise the puts by requesting extra common stock to top their units back up to $73.40. Suppose the company's stock has fallen to, say, $3 per share. Then the company could conceivably end up paying out 4 extra shares for each share outstanding. Thus, the issuer must be confident that the price will remain firm. Because of this and the regulatory issues, use of this technique has been rather rare. (A related technique, contingent value rights, is discussed in Chapter 16.)

Money Back Issue

An interesting variant of the puttable approach was used, in March 1995, by Repsol, the Spanish oil group. It faced a situation where it had to sell a substantial block of shares previously owned by a state entity. The Spanish market had performed very poorly over the preceding 15 months. The approach taken was to offer a guarantee that if the share price fell below the offer price in the 12 months following the sale, Repsol would compensate investors for the difference, in cash, for losses up to 10 percent. Effectively, the issuer sells the investor a capped put option.

Non-Voting Shares

This type of equity is hardly new, but there are interesting international variants. A typical transaction was the issue, in October 1986, by Allianz, the German insurance company, of 3.2 million profit participation certificates to raise around DM700 million. Of these, 1.9 million were for international issue. The choice of profit participation certificates, carrying no voting rights, was controversial. But, in exchange, the investor is guaranteed a minimum yield of 5 percent, with a put after 15 years, and is ranked ahead of ordinary shareholders. The annual dividend is 20 percent above the dividend paid on ordinary shares, as compensation for the absence of tax credits on dividends. (Allianz's payments are tax-deductible. Once again, the line between equity and debt is blurred.)

Swiss corporations, in particular, have been prolific issuers of nonvoting stock. In the first 6 months of 1986, there were 57 issues of bearer participation certificates (BPCs) carrying no voting rights. These issues represented 42 percent of the total Swiss market volume of equity issues in that period. Companies from other countries, such as France, Germany, Sweden, and Italy, have also made use of this instrument. French nonvoting shares, called *certificats d'investissement* (CIs), have been widely used. Some Scandinavian banks have used Primary Capital Certificates, which are listed on the stock exchanges but carry no voting rights. If international pressure for companies to have "good corporate governance" continues to increase, it seems likely that nonvoting shares will be increasingly discouraged.

Shares Linked to the Performance of Key Subsidiaries (Targeted Stock)

Some of the techniques discussed in this chapter have been used by companies that might justifiably be regarded as not quite blue chip. But the next technique has been adopted by a company that could scarcely be classified as less than blue chip: General Motors (GM). In its acquisition of Electronic Data Systems (EDS)

Corporation, GM issued class E shares whose dividends and price are linked to the performance of EDS, even though they represent ownership of GM. The stockholder then has the security of owning GM stock, but anticipates the performance of the higher-flying EDS. The issue was made in October 1984.

Moreover, the initial class E shareholders—many of them EDS employees—also received a contingent promissory note. This amounts to a type of put option that effectively guarantees them a 16 percent compounded annual return if they hold their shares for between 5 and 7 years. After some initial doubts, the class E shares seem to have performed well: the stock doubled between the issue in October 1984 and the issue in June, 1985. The success of the class E share concept meant that, when GM came to buy Hughes Aircraft Corporation, GM issued class H shares. Owners of class H shares will not have the same rights as holders of GM common stock. Each class H share will have half a vote on GM corporate matters, and class H liquidation rights are half of those held by common stock shareholders. In exchange, the value of the shares is partly tied to the performance of the Hughes business.

Recently, the technique has been used by the telecommunications company, US West, which divided its stock in two, in November 1995. US West Media follows the cable TV and cellular businesses; US West Communications tracks the basic telephone company. In March 1997, Viacom announced plans for shares targeted to the performance of its Blockbuster Video subsidiary.

International Equities: Multicurrency Equity and Stapled Stock

Most countries do not allow companies incorporated locally to denominate their capital in other currencies. Exceptions include Singapore and Luxembourg, which permit capital—at least of local subsidiaries of foreign companies—to be in ECU (European Currency Units). During 1986, the United Kingdom gave permission to several U.S. banks to switch the capital of their U.K. subsidiaries from sterling to dollars. Permission was also given to Scandinavian Bank to switch its capital from sterling into a basket of four currencies, including sterling.

The rationale for the Scandinavian Bank group was that its balance sheet was largely in nonsterling loans, and the requirement to keep capital in sterling meant that, as sterling fell, the shareholders had to put up fresh capital to maintain existing levels of business. Scandinavian Bank's new capital structure consisted of 50 percent dollars, 20 percent sterling, and 15 percent each for deutsche marks and Swiss francs. There were four classes of shares, one for each currency. One share from each class has been combined into a "capital currency unit." The constituent shares could only be bought or sold together; no share can be transferred unless an equal number of shares of the other classes is transferred at the same time. Accounts were published, and dividends were declared, in sterling. Reserves were allocated to each currency class in proportion to the sterling value of the shareholders' capital contributions. Further issues of shares were conditional on shareholders' accepting shares in all classes, so that each class contains the same number.

This was an example of "stapled stock"—a technique used sometimes by companies with cross-border shareholding structures. The best known example (but perhaps the worst example of share performance) is Eurotunnel, the company that owns the tunnel between France and England. Its shares consist of a U.K. unit and a French unit stapled together. Another example of the technique—albeit short-lived—was the stapled stock issued, in June 1995, when NYNEX CableComms successfully completed a dual listing on the London Stock Exchange and on NASDAQ, raising £383 million. NYNEX offered shares in its U.K. subsidiary by means of an issue of 270 million units, each of which included one ordinary share of NYNEX CableComms Group PLC, a U.K. company, and one common share of NYNEX CableComms Group Inc., a U.S. company. The former accounted for 90 percent of the stated value of each unit. The U.K. and U.S. shares could not be traded separately. The separation between the two sets of underlying assets avoided a tax problem for NYNEX. In October 1996, the company was merged into a joint deal with Cable & Wireless and Bell Cablemedia, and the units disappeared.

Grantor Trust Structures

A type of "synthetic equity" was developed by Salomon Brothers for its subsidiary, Phibro Energy, an oil trader and refiner. Salomon underwrote a public offering of units in a grantor trust at a price of $4.65 per unit. Funds invested in the grantor trust were used to acquire a forward contract to buy one-quarter of a barrel of crude oil per unit from Phibro for delivery in September 1995. This created a contract right, on the part of the grantor trust, to acquire oil from Phibro at a fixed price on a future date.

After the grantor trust acquired the oil in September 1995, the Trustee would sell the delivered oil at auction; if the price offered in the auction process was less than the then-current futures contract price, Phibro would buy back the oil at the futures contract price (which, in effect, would be similar to a cash settlement of the contract). The grantor trust would then deliver the cash to the unit holders in a single payment, on November 1, 1995. The units were publicly traded and listed on the American Stock Exchange.

UPREIT

The concept of an Umbrella Partnership Real Estate Investment Trust (UPREIT) essentially was devised in the United States to allow large real estate owners to defer taxes on the transfer of properties and mortgage interests, and to enable them to circumvent IRS rules requiring broad ownership of real estate investment trusts. A typical transaction was undertaken, in June 1994, by Starwood Capital Group in connection with Hotel Investors Trust. The trust contributed its assets to the deal and became the general partner. Starwood contributed cash and mortgage note interests, becoming a limited partner.

Index Participation Units

TIPS. It could be argued that index participation units are derivatives, but I have included them here on the view that they constitute an index fund. Toronto 35 Index Participation Units (TIPS) were introduced by the Toronto Stock Exchange in March 1990. Each unit represents an interest in a trust that holds baskets of the stocks in the Toronto 35 Index. Thus, they are backed by the underlying stocks, and the shares are redeemable for the underlying stocks at any time. They resemble the SPDRs and WEBS discussed below; their major advantage is that they allow investors to track a broad market without incurring the costs associated with similar products. Index mutual funds may not have complete freedom of trading and can impose management fees. Index futures, which do not include dividends of the underlying shares, are subject to margin requirement, marking to market, and continual rollover. Index options require constant rebalancing to track the movements of the underlying index because the hedge ratio changes constantly as the level of the index changes.

The specifications are as follows. Each unit represents approximately ⅒ of the value of the Toronto 35 Index level. For example, if the Toronto 35 Index is 185, the unit would be priced at about $18.50. Dividends received by the trust are distributed to unit holders quarterly, in April, July, October, and December. Investors holding the prescribed minimum number of units may redeem their units for the underlying basket of stocks at any time. Investors holding less than the minimum may redeem their units for cash at any time.

Spiders (SPDRs)

In 1993, the American Stock Exchange created S&P Depositary Receipts by setting up a unit investment trust "to provide investors with the opportunity to purchase units of beneficial interest in the trust representing proportionate undivided interests in the portfolio of securities held by the trust consisting of substantially all of the common stocks, in substantially the same weighting, as the component common stocks of the Standard & Poor's 500 Composite Stock Price Index." In other words, it created an index fund that was listed on the stock exchange. The benefit to investors is clear: They can now directly access the S&P 500, rather than having to invest in a mutual fund and pay its fees, or trade in S&P 500 futures. Because the units in the fund are themselves quoted on the stock exchange, they can be treated by investors as any other share (e.g., traded on margin). The experiment seems to have been successful, with several hundred million dollars' worth of underlying shares outstanding.

Country Baskets

In March 1996, a series of stock issues were made, representing individual country markets. The first were issued by Deutsche Morgan Grenfell and consisted of a set of 9 country-specific index stocks (stocks representing an

FT/S&P securities index for the country in question). Essentially, they are open-ended funds holding index portfolios of shares from the countries in question. Redemption of the shares is restricted to large blocks (typically 100,000 shares). The index stocks are listed on the New York Stock Exchange. This issue was followed shortly by World Equity Benchmark Shares (WEBS), issued by BZW and Morgan Stanley, which aimed to track the Morgan Stanley Capital International country indexes. They are listed on the American Stock Exchange, and, in a sense, represent the international equivalent of the latter's Spiders (SPDRs), discussed above, though here the construct is sponsored by individual investment banks rather than by the exchange itself.

Depositary Receipts

The concept of a depositary receipt is not new. It was developed in the form of the American Depositary Receipt (ADR) in the 1930s. But the instrument qualifies for inclusion here because the international market in Global Depositary Receipts (GDRs) has recently become of sufficient importance to deserve a mention. According to the Bank of New York, during 1996, approximately 11 billion depositary receipts, with a value equivalent to $345 billion, were traded in the United States, an increase of 26 percent from the $278 billion traded in 1995. In addition, an estimated 1.5 billion depositary receipts, worth $20 to $25 billion, were traded in European or OTC markets. Growth in the dollar value of trading since 1990 has been estimated at 22 percent per annum. By year-end 1996, there were more than 1,600 programs outstanding, from 63 countries.

Historically, American Depositary Receipts (ADRs) were the first type of depositary receipt to evolve. They were introduced in 1927 in response to a law passed in Britain, prohibiting British companies from registering shares overseas without a British-based transfer agent. United Kingdom shares were not allowed physically to leave the United Kingdom. To accommodate U.S. investor demand, a U.S. instrument was created: the American Depositary Receipt.

The three types of ADR are called Level I, Level II, and Level III. (Privately placed ADRs, sometimes called restricted ADRs or RADRs, also exist.) A sponsored Level I ADR program offers the easiest and least expensive means for a company to provide for issuance of its shares in ADR form in the United States. The issuer has a certain amount of control over the ADRs issued under a sponsored Level I program, because a depositary agreement is executed between the issuer and a selected depositary bank. Level I ADRs can, however, be traded only over-the-counter. They cannot be listed on a national exchange in the United States.

A sponsored Level II ADR must comply with the SEC's full registration and reporting requirements. Registration allows the issuer to list its ADRs on one of the major national stock exchanges. Sponsored Level II programs are generally used by non-U.S. companies to give U.S. investors access to their stock in the United States.

Sponsored Level III ADRs are similar to Level II ADRs in that the issuer initiates the program, deals with a depositary bank, lists on one of the major

U.S. exchanges, and files registration statements with the SEC. The major difference is that a Level III program allows the issuer to raise capital through a public offering of ADRs in the United States.

Rule 144(a) ADRs, or restricted ADRs (RADRs) are simply privately placed depositary receipts that are issued and traded in accordance with Rule 144(a) (see Chapter 9).

In June 1990, the National Association of Securities Dealers (NASD) established, for RADRs, a closed electronic trading system called PORTAL (Private Offerings, Resales and Trading through Automated Linkages). This system is designed to provide a market for privately traded securities (e.g., RADRs), and access to it is available to investors and to market makers.

The attraction of both the ADR and the GDR is that they allow the investor to be shielded from the complexities of dealing with local market settlement structures. However, as will be touched on below, the question of linkage with the domestic market can cause problems, as illustrated in the case of Gazprom, the Russian gas company, which launched ADRs, in October 1996, and sold 1.15 percent of its equity to international investors. The shares were offered at four times the price of domestically traded shares. The investment banks managing the issue argued that international investors were paying a premium for liquidity, security, and more favorable tax treatment. At the time, Gazprom promised to ensure that there would be no leakage of cheap domestic shares into the international offering. But, in February 1997, an attempt was made by Regent Pacific Group to create an offshore vehicle that would invest onshore. Eventually, as always, the matter will doubtless be resolved by the market. However, the affair illustrates some of the potential problems.

GLOBAL DEPOSITARY RECEIPTS (GDRs)/ EUROPEAN DEPOSITARY RECEIPTS (EDRs)

In the past few years, the depositary receipt concept has developed considerably. Issuers in a variety of countries have realized that there are advantages in making their stock available in a form convenient not only to U.S. investors but also, or alternatively, to investors in the Euromarkets or elsewhere. This has prompted the development of European Depositary Receipts (EDRs) and Global Depositary Receipts (GDRs).

The EDR accesses the Euromarkets but not the U.S. market. It settles and trades through the Euromarket clearing systems, Euroclear and Cedel, and may be listed on a European Stock Exchange, normally in London or in Luxembourg.

A GDR will access two or more markets, usually the Euromarkets (like an EDR) and the United States (like an ADR). GDRs are often launched for capital-raising purposes, so the U.S. element is generally either a Rule 144(a) ADR or a Level III ADR, depending on whether the issuer aims to tap the private placement or the public U.S. markets.

EDRs and GDRs are generally denominated in U.S. dollars, but may be denominated in any currency. They represent the underlying shares in exactly the same way as ADRs, and they make it possible for foreign investors to trade in the issuing company's stock without the problems associated with custody and settlement in foreign markets.

In 1996, GDRs accounted for around one-fourth of total depositary receipt issuance in the first 9 months, with a further two-thirds in the form of ADRs and the remainder in either Rule 144(a) issues or EDRs. Since the London Stock Exchange amended its rules regarding the listing of GDRs, 52 companies (by December 1996) had listed GDRs on the exchange, including RAO Gazprom, the large Russian gas company, 13 Korean companies, and 13 Indian companies.

The number of GDR programs has expanded rapidly during the 1990s; GDRs now account for a rising proportion of the total number of programs and are of growing importance to emerging markets issuers. However, some investors maintain that the differences between ADRs and GDRs are mainly semantic. Both are receipts issued against an underlying stock held in a depositary bank and, in that respect, the only difference is where they settle.

The choice of whether to issue an ADR or a GDR sometimes can be based simply on geographical convenience or force of habit. Latin American companies, with their traditional orientation toward the United States as a source of foreign capital, tend to look to the ADR market. In the case of Chile, this predilection is enforced by central bank requirements for any overseas equity issuance to be on the New York Stock Exchange. GDRs by Latin American companies, therefore, have been a rarity: Celesc in Brazil and Uruguay's Banco Commercial are the exceptions to the rule.

Advocates of the GDR believe it has a number of advantages. Primarily, it offers a wider investor base than an ADR, which trades only in the United States. By issuing under Rule 144(a), a GDR can be sold to U.S. investors as well as to the core of European investors.

When GDRs are structured with a Rule 144(a) offering for the United States and a Regulation S offering for non-U.S. investors, there are two possible options for the structure.

1. Under a unitary structure, a single class of DRs is offered both to QIBs in the United States and to offshore purchasers outside the issuer's domestic market, in accordance with Regulation S. All DRs are governed by one Deposit Agreement and all are subject to deposit, withdrawal, and resale restrictions.

2. Under a bifurcated structure, Rule 144(a) ADRs are offered to QIBs in the United States, and Regulation S Depositary Receipts (DRs) are offered to offshore investors outside the issuer's domestic market. The two classes of DRs are offered using two separate DR facilities and two separate Deposit Agreements. The Regulation S DRs are not restricted securities and can therefore be deposited into a "side-by-side" Level I DR program, and they are not normally subject to restrictions on deposits, withdrawals, or transfers. However, they may be subject to temporary resale restrictions in the United States.

The second advantage of the GDR is that it is cheaper than an ADR, which requires a New York Stock Exchange or NASDAQ listing. The simplicity of the DR is, however, achieved at a price: the premium between many DRs and the underlying stock. Market distortions also create pricing anomalies, which can lead, for example, to some Korean GDRs trading at huge premiums. Korea Mobile Telecom was trading at close to a 100 percent premium in October 1996. Hyundai was trading at 60 percent, and Samsung, between 35 percent and 40 percent.

In a totally free market, arbitrageurs would be able to take advantage of price disparities and could soon eliminate discrepancies between the GDR price and the underlying price. The relationship between the two should reflect the exchange rate and nothing else, a situation that has virtually been achieved for Mexican ADRs.

However, regulations often frustrate arbitrageurs. In Korea, foreign ownership restrictions affect the relationship between GDRs and domestic shares. In India, it is possible to buy the GDR in London or Luxembourg and cancel it back into India; but, once canceled, the GDR cannot be reissued. In other words, the arbitrage works in only one direction. Over time, as in Mexico, these restrictions will presumably disappear, but the investor in these instruments should be aware of the background influences.

BUYING AND SELLING DRs

An investor who wishes to purchase shares in a foreign company can either buy the foreign shares in the local market, through a broker in that country, or, providing the foreign company in question has a DR program, request his or her broker to buy DRs. The broker may purchase existing DRs, or, if none is available, may arrange for a depositary bank to issue new ones.

The process for issuing new DRs is that the investor's broker contacts a broker in the issuing company's home market and acquires shares in that company. These shares are then deposited with the depositary bank's local custodian. Upon confirmation that the custodian has received the shares, the depositary issues the requisite number of DRs to the investor via the broker.

In some exceptional cases, DR programs may not provide for issuance of new DRs (e.g., Indian GDR programs) because of local regulations.

DRs can be sold in DR form, in which case they trade and settle like other U.S. or Euro securities. They can also, however, be canceled: The broker, acting on behalf of the owner of the DRs, will request the depositary bank to cancel the DRs and release the underlying shares to a domestic broker in the issuing company's home market. The domestic broker will then sell the shares locally, and the proceeds will be remitted to the investor who canceled those DRs.

The ADR route has also been used for the issuance of debt securities, notably French OAT bonds in 1988. The experiment does not seem to have taken off, and ADRs remain primarily equity instruments.

Bibliography

Chapter 1   Financial Innovation

Bank for International Settlements. *Recent Innovations in International Banking*. Basle, 1986.
I. Cooper. Innovations: New Market Instruments. *Oxford Review of Economic Policy*, 1986.
Financial Innovation issue. *Continental Bank Journal of Applied Corporate Finance*. Winter 1992.
C. P. Kindleberger. *A Financial History of Western Europe*. G. Allen & Unwin, London, 1984.

Chapter 2   Basic Instruments

Z. Bodie, A. Kane, & A. J. Marcus. *Investments*. Irwin, Homewood, IL, 1989.
J. C. Francis. Investments, 4th ed. McGraw-Hill International, New York, 1986.

Chapter 3   Some Analytical Tools

P. J. Brown. *Formulae for Yield and Other Calculations*. ISMA, London, UK, 1992.
B. Manson. *The Practitioner's Guide to Interest Rate Risk Management*. Graham & Trotman, London, UK, 1992.
S. Y. Peng & R. E. Dattatreya. *The Structured Note Market*. Probus, Chicago, IL, 1995.
B. Tuckman. *Fixed Income Securities*. John Wiley & Sons, New York, 1995.

Chapter 4   Forwards and Futures

F. R. Edwards & C. W. Ma. *Futures & Options*. McGraw-Hill International, New York, 1992.
J. C. Hull. *Options, Futures and Other Derivatives*. Prentice-Hall International, Upper Saddle River, NJ, 1997.
J. K. Walmsley. *Guide to Foreign Exchange & Money Markets*. John Wiley & Sons, New York, 1992.

Chapter 5   Swaps

S. Das. *Swaps & Financial Derivatives*. IFR Publishing, London, UK, 1994.
B. Manson, op. cit.
J. F. Marshall & K. R.Kapner. *Understanding Swaps*. John Wiley & Sons, New York, 1993.

Chapter 6   Option Basics

N. A. Chriss. *Black-Scholes and Beyond*. Irwin, Chicago, IL, 1997.
D. F. de Rosa. *Options on Foreign Exchange*. Probus, Chicago, IL, 1992.
G. Gemmill. *Options Pricing: An International Perspective*. McGraw-Hill International (UK), London, UK, 1993.
*R. Jarrow, & S. Turnbull. *Derivative Securities*. South-Western College Publishing, Cincinnati, OH, 1996.
R. G. Tompkins. *Options Analysis*. Probus, Chicago, IL, 1994.
P. Wilmott, J. Dewynne, & S. Howison. *Option Pricing: Mathematical Models & Computation*. Oxford Financial Press, Oxford, UK, 1993.

Chapter 7   Option Instruments

Most of the books listed under Chapter 6 also have material relevant to this chapter.
*S. Das. *Exotic Options*. IFR Publishing, London, UK, 1996.

---

*Somewhat mathematical.

* I. Nelken. (Ed.) *The Handbook of Exotic Options.* Irwin, Chicago, IL, 1996.

† R. Rebonato. *Interest-Rate Option Models.* John Wiley & Sons, Chichester, UK, 1996.

N. Taleb. *Dynamic Hedging: Managing Vanilla and Exotic Options.* John Wiley & Sons, New York, 1997.

Chapter 8 Securitization

F. G. Fisher. Eurosecurities and Their Related Derivatives. *Euromoney.* London, UK, 1997.

H. Morrissey (Ed.). *International Securitisation.* IFR Publishing Ltd., London, UK, 1992.

Z. Shaw (Ed.). *International Securitisation.* Macmillan, London, UK, 1991.

Chapter 9 New Types of Bonds

F. J. Fabozzi (Ed.). *Handbook of Fixed Income Securities.* Probus, Chicago, IL, 1994.

F. G. Fisher, op.cit.

P. Phillips. *The Merrill Lynch Guide to the Gilt-Edged and Sterling Bond Markets.* The Book Guild. Lewes, Sussex, UK, 1996.

Chapter 10 Mortgage-Backed Securities

W. W. Bartlett. *The Valuation of Mortgage-Backed Securities.* Irwin, Chicago, IL, 1994.

A. S. Davidson, T. S. Y. Ho, & Y. C. Lim. *Collateralized Mortgage Obligations.* Probus, Chicago, IL, 1994.

F. J. Fabozzi, C. Ramsey, & F. R. Ramirez. *Collateralized Mortgage Obligations: Structures & Analysis.* F. J. Fabozzi & Associates. Buckingham, PA, 1994.

Chapter 11 Asset-Backed Securities

F. J. Fisher, op. cit.

H. Morrissey, op. cit.

Z. Shaw, op. cit.

Chapter 12 Structured Notes

G. Gray & P. Cusatis. *Municipal Derivative Securities.* Irwin, Chicago, IL, 1995.

Peng & Dattatreya, op. cit.

Chapter 13 Credit Derivatives

British Bankers' Association. *Credit Derivatives: Key Issues.* London, UK, 1997.

J. P. Morgan. *CreditMetrics Technical Document.* New York, 1997 (available at www.jpmorgan.com).

Chapter 14 Preferred Stock

R. McCormick & H. Creamer (Eds.). *Hybrid Corporate Securities: International Legal Aspects.* Sweet & Maxwell, London, UK, 1987.

Chapter 15 Convertibles and Warrants

K. Connolly & G. Philips. *Japanese Warrant Markets.* Macmillan, London, UK, 1992.

J. C. Francis, W. W. Toy, & J. G. Whittaker. *The Handbook of Equity Derivatives.* Irwin, Chicago, IL, 1995.

Chapter 16 Equity Derivatives

J. C. Francis, W. W. Toy, & J. G. Whittaker, op. cit.

---

* Somewhat mathematical.

† Highly mathematical.

Index

Notes: Initials or first names in parentheses, e.g., Penney, (J.C.) indicate a company rather than a person. Firms, people, or countries mentioned only once have *generally* been omitted. Financial instruments are shown in bold. The first or main reference for each instrument is in bold.